3. The Competitor Environ
      A. Describe your main competitors and their products, plans, experience, know-how, financial, human and capital resources, suppliers, and strategy. (Do they enjoy any favor or disfavor with the customer? If so, why? What marketing channels do competitors use? What are your competitors' strengths and weaknesses?)
   4. The Company Environ
      A. Describe your product, experience, know-how, financial, human and capital resources, suppliers, etc. (Do you enjoy any favor or disfavor with the customer? If so, why? What are your strengths and weaknesses?)

III. The Target Market
   1. Describe your target market segment in detail using demographics, psychographics, geographics, life style, or whatever segmentation is appropriate. (Why is this your target market and not some other segment?)

IV. Problems and Opportunities
   1. State or restate each opportunity and indicate why it is in fact an opportunity. State or restate every problem and indicate what you intend to do about each problem.

V. Marketing Objectives and Goals
   1. Precisely state marketing objectives in terms of sales volume, market share, return on investment, or other objectives for your marketing plan.

VI. Marketing Strategy
   1. Consider alternatives for overall strategy. Further describe your strategy as to whether you are using product differentiation, market segmentation, or positioning, etc., and how you are employing these strategies. Note what your main competitors are likely to do when you implement this strategy and what you will do to take advantage of the opportunities created and avoid the threats.

VII. Marketing Tactics
   1. State how you will implement the marketing strategie(s) chosen in terms of product, price, promotion, distribution, and other tactical or environmental variables.

VIII. Control and Implementation
   1. Calculate break-even and accomplish a break-even chart for your project. Compute sales projections on a monthly basis for a three-year period. Compute cash flows on a monthly basis for a three-year period. Indicate start-up costs and monthly budget for this period.

IX. Summary
   1. Summarize advantages, costs, and profits, and clearly state the differential advantage that your plan for this product or service offers over the competition and why the plan will succeed.

X. Appendices
   1. Include all supporting information that you consider relevant.

The Practice of Marketing Management

ANALYSIS, PLANNING, AND IMPLEMENTATION

Second Edition

The Practice of Marketing Management

ANALYSIS, PLANNING, AND IMPLEMENTATION

Second Edition

William A. Cohen

Department of Marketing
California State University at Los Angeles

Macmillan Publishing Company
New York
Collier Macmillan Canada
Toronto
Maxwell Macmillan International
New York   Oxford   Singapore   Sydney

Editors: **Michele Rhoades, David Boelio**
Production Supervisor: **J. Edward Neve**
Production Manager: **Sandra Moore**
Text Designer: **Eileen Burke**
Cover Designer: **Eileen Burke**
Cover Photograph: **Marjory Dressler**

This book was set in 9½/11 New Aster Roman by Waldman Graphics, Inc., printed by Halliday, and bound by Halliday.
The cover was printed by Lehigh Press, Inc.

Macmillan Publishing Company
866 Third Avenue, New York, New York 10022
Collier Macmillan Canada, Inc.

Library of Congress Cataloging in Publication Data
Cohen, William A.,
    The practice of marketing management : analysis, planning, and implementation / William A. Cohen.—2nd ed.
        p.   cm.
    ISBN 0-02-323171-8
    1. Marketing—Management.   I. Title.
HF5415.13.C635   1991
658.8'02—dc20   90-34233
                                                                     CIP

Printing: 2 3 4 5 6 7 8   Year: 1 2 3 4 5 6 7 8 9 0

This book is dedicated to my wife Nurit
. . . my partner and my inspiration

Preface

There are many good textbooks on marketing management. Perhaps partially because of this fact, colleagues, fellow authors, and my own as well as competitive publishers asked one question when I wrote the first edition of this book. "What niche are you targeting?" The assumption was that it was no longer possible to write a generalist marketing management textbook for future marketing managers. Rather the write had to choose among an emphasis on the traditional tactical approach of product, price, promotion, and distribution; an emphasis on planning; an emphasis on strategy; an emphasis on implementation; or an emphasis on something else. This is not to say that some very excellent books hadn't appeared in each of these specialty areas. But what I was trying to do was entirely different, and I answered accordingly. This was that I wasn't writing for a niche at all, but rather for a clearly defined segment of students of marketing: those who must not only understand the theory, but must apply it in the marketplace. The success of that edition proved that concept, and I am proud to continue the process.

The Practice of Marketing Management was written to be used by marketing professors in educating marketing students to this purpose. While I consider it evolutionary rather than revolutionary, I have departed from standard practice in textbook writing to achieve this design. First, it is structured around the marketing plan. The marketing plan is that single tool that leads the marketing manager to accomplish marketing objectives. To develop it requires analysis, planning, and workable strategies and tactics. And lest it become simply one more report merely demonstrating the theory of marketing, it must be implemented. The layout and content of this book can lead to a professionally prepared marketing plan, whether accomplished by upper-division undergraduate students or by those completing their MBAs. I know this not only because I have taught both groups using the methodology contained in this textbook, but because students have in some cases entrepreneurially used the plans they developed or sold their plans outright to someone else who did.

For some years I was particularly proud of the fact that one of my students sold his marketing plan, completed in my course, for $5,000. Then in the summer of 1985 I made a presentation that included sample plans to an audience of both academics and practitioners at the University of Missouri at Kansas City. Several practitioners who were in the business of preparing such plans professionally stated most emphatically that they were undervalued. They appraised samples that I had with me as being worth $25,000 each. Yet these had been accomplished not by MBAs, but by undergraduate students. To amplify what I have said, a fully developed marketing plan doesn't have to be a product of the marketing management course taught—but it can be.

My second major deviation in preparing this text was in the style of writing. I was determined to use the very latest scientific research from the marketing journals that act as a conduit in making available the developments in our profession. But I did not want to make the error emphasized by David Ogilvy in his book *Ogilvy on Advertising*. Ogilvy quoted from an article from one of our most prestigious scientific journals. Then he stated that he could not even understand it. If a foremost practitioner cannot understand such an article, how can we expect a marketing student to do so? The truth is, we cannot. It is the job, even more the duty, of the textbook author to include the latest scientific developments in the field, but to make certain that they can be understood by the student who is required to read and master them. To accomplish this task, I have relied on my experience as the author of books for practitioners. I have included what I consider to be the latest and most relevant scientific research on marketing. But I have written about it in the most interesting way that I could. Tests that I and several of my colleagues have conducted in using material written in this style have led us to the conclusion that not only does the style not detract from the content, but that it motivates both toward a more through reading and understanding of the material.

The third major deviation for a generalist marketing management text is the inclusion of cases for classroom discussion and student analysis. Accordingly, you will find not only 22 full-length cases, but more than 60 vignettes, all of which illustrate important points about marketing.

As I indicated earlier, *The Practice of Marketing Management* is about applying theory to practice. A such, I have tried to not stop at explaining the theory, but to go on and show how it can be applied. I am extremely proud of the manuscript's reception by reviewers of both editions. In this vein, such as one by a well-known author of a textbook on marketing strategy said about one chapter, "one of the most thorough strategic marketing management chapters that I've ever read."

But in the final analysis, it is for you, as marketing students, and educators, to determine whether this text fulfills its purpose. Its success I share with many—not only my editors at Macmillan, Bill Oldsey, Ron Stefanski, David Shaffer, and for this second edition, Michele Rhoades, but also my many reviewers and evaluators whom I have thanked by name elsewhere. Any of the book's faults are mine alone.

The Second Edition ─────────────────────────

This second edition had been extensively updated from the first. For example, there are more than two hundred new footnotes. Six full length cases are entirely new and older cases have been updated. More than twenty new vignette cases have been added. With economic instability due to upheavals in world politics a distinct possibility, a new chapter on marketing under differing economic conditions has been included. Each chapter is now followed by an ethical question for general class discussion. The material in the appendix has been greatly expanded. Sample student marketing plans, and forms that will assist students in marketing plan preparation have been added to the appendix. Considering the high cost of reproduction as well as that of textbooks, I believe this will make the book more valuable for the student's future career while it reduces the uses of scarce reproduction resources for the professor.

Instructor's Manual:

The accompanying *Instructor's Manual* is divided into five parts. Section I lists alternative syllabi for various semester length courses. Section II gives chapter overviews, lecture outlines, discussion questions, and additional reading lists for each chapter. Simulation or experiential exercises for each chapter are also included. Section III contains student examples of marketing plans. Section IV covers the teaching objectives, issues, and epilogues for each of the twenty-two cases found in the text. Finally, Section V contains fifty-five transparency masters for classroom use.

Test Bank:

The Test Bank, written by Thomas K. Pritchett of Georgia College, includes 2,200 multiple-choice and true/false exam questions. These have been completely rewritten for the new edition.

Computerized Test Bank:

A computerized version of the test bank is available for IBM microcomputers.

Spreadsheet Exercises for Marketing:

A set of Lotus 1-2-3 templates, prepared by Dennis A. Pitta, is available to help students address several questions per marketing management concept. The questions will help familiarize the student with topics that appear in the text.

 The *Instructor's Manual, Test Banks,* and software are available through your local Macmillan sales representative.

Acknowledgments ─────────────────────────

The responsibility for THE PRACTICE OF MARKETING MANAGEMENT is mine alone. But it is with great pleasure that I acknowledge and thank my reviewers. Whether they evaluated the entire manuscript, or only portions of it, their contributions were many and significant and greatly enhanced the final product.

Second Edition Reviewers:

Danny R. Arnold, *Mississippi State University*
Roger J. Calantone, *University of Kentucky*
Homer Dalbey, *San Francisco State University*
Salvatore Divita, *George Washington University*
Brien Ellis, *University of Kentucky*
Alfred G. Hawkins, *Rockhurst College*
Valerie Kijewski, *University of Lowell*
Ruth Krieger, *Oklahoma State University*
Bill P. Pierce, *Morehead State University*
Mary Beth Pinto, *University of Maine*
Paul Prabhaker, *DePaul University*
Thomas K. Pritchett, *Georgia College*

First Edition Reviewers:

Kerri Acheson, *Northwestern University*
Cynthia L. Bascom, *Ohio University*
Joseph A. Bellizzi, *Kansas State University*
Harold W. Berkman, *University of Miami*
Louis E. Boone, *University of South Alabama*
Alan Brokaw, *Michigan Technological University*
Herbert E. Brown, *Wright State University*
John Burnett, *Texas A and M University*
Richard Buskirk, *University of Southern California*
Lawrence B. Chonko, *Baylor University*
John C. Crawford, *North Texas State University*
Edward W. Cundiff, *Emory University*
William P. Dommermuth, *University of Missouri—St. Louis*
Joel R. Evans, *Hofstra University*
O. C. Ferrell, *Texas A and M University*
Ashok K. Gupta, *Ohio University*
Subhash C. Jain, *The University of Connecticut*
George Kress, *Colorado State University*
David L. Kurtz, *Seattle University*
Marilyn L. Liebrenz-Himes, *The George Washington University*
Lynn J. Loudenback, *Iowa State University*
James R. Lumpkin, *Baylor University*
Ken W. McCleary, *Central Michigan University*
Jim McCullough, *Washington State University*
Gary F. McKinnon, *Brigham Young University*
William Nickels, *University of Maryland*
William M. Pride, *Texas A and M University*
George E. Prough, *The University of Akron*
Marshall E. Reddick, *California State University Los Angeles*
Jaqdish N. Sheth, *University of Southern California*
Bruce L. Stern, *Portland State University*
Gerald L. Waddle, *Clemson University*
William G. Zikmund, *Oklahoma State University*

William A. Cohen

Author Biography

Dr. William A. Cohen is professor of marketing and former chairman of the Marketing Department at California State University, Los Angeles. His 21 books and more than 100 professional papers have been published in 7 languages. He is series editor of the JOHN WILEY SERIES ON BUSINESS STRATEGY. He is also a member of five business journal advisory boards and former associate editor of the *Journal of Direct Marketing Research*.

Dr. Cohen has held a number of senior corporate management positions, including Manager of Research and Development at Sierra Engineering Company, Manager of Advanced Technology Marketing at McDonnell-Douglas Astronautics Company, Director of Research at Advanced Materials Technology, and President of Global Associates. He is currently on several boards of directors and governmental commissions.

He is the recipient of numerous awards, including Outstanding Professor Award 1982–1983; the Freedoms Foundation at Valley Forge Honor Medal for Excellence in Economic Education; an award for excellence in research for a first-of-its-kind research project for the joint staff of the Joint Chiefs of Staff; a national award from

(Photo: Brian G. Ewing)

the U.S. Small Business Administration, and many others. His biography is in many directories, including *Who's Who In America*.

Dr. Cohen has a B.S. in Engineering from the United States Military Academy, an MBA from the University of Chicago, and an M.A., and Ph.D. from Claremont Graduate School. He is also a graduate of the prestigious Industrial College of the Armed Forces, National Defense University, Washington, D.C.

Brief Contents

PART THREE
Organizing and Planning Strategic Marketing Activities

PART FOUR
Strategy Alternatives

PART FIVE
Organizing and Planning Tactical Marketing Activities

Contents

PART TWO
Marketing Situational Analysis

PART ONE

The Marketing Manager: Tasks and Responsibilities

This section is the foundation for understanding the sections of the text that follow, and is therefore crucial for mastering the tasks and responsibilities of the marketing manager. Chapter 1, The Role and Functions of the Marketing Manager, introduces the concept of marketing in the context of the activities of the marketing manager. You will learn what a marketing manager does and what he (or she) is responsible for and how the activities of the marketing manager contribute to the success of the firm. This is followed in Chapter 2, Strategic Marketing Management, by the introduction to one of the major activities of the marketing manager: the development of strategy. You will learn how strategic marketing management is integrated with marketing strategy and marketing tactics, and you will learn practical techniques for applying these important skills. Finally, in Chapter 3, The Marketing Plan and Planning Process, you will be given procedures that will allow you to develop a marketing plan for any product, project, or service that you choose. I consider this one of the most valuable chapters in the book, for my own students have used this information to write plans that have won competitions for planning, that were sold for thousands of dollars, and that benefited those who implemented them by helping their projects succeed.

The Role and Functions of the Marketing Manager

1

CHAPTER OBJECTIVES

- Understand the basic concepts of marketing.

- Understand the functions and responsibilities of the marketing manager.

- Understand the importance of the marketing manager's responsibilities to the success of the firm.

The Power of Marketing Management

Boom to Bust in Three Years

In a single year, Adam Osborne built his computer company from $0 to $150 million in sales and over a thousand employees. He did this by developing a computer that, while heavy and cumbersome looking, sold for a price that was profitable to the company but was less than half the price of its competitors' offerings. Yet, only two years after this major success, the company was in such serious financial difficulties that it had to cease production, even though technologically, its products were improving and a new product had been introduced. What had gone wrong in the two-year interim? Many analysts say that Osborne's difficulties boiled down to one major

factor. IBM had entered the marketplace, and IBM compatibility of software became a major factor in the purchase decision for many consumers. Osborne's software was not IBM-compatible.

The Queen of the Social Circuit Returns

Until 1986, Wendy Moss was considered the queen of the Texas social circuit. She had built a million-dollar business. Her sales came from two market segments. The first was in helping debutantes make their entrance; the second, helping oil men celebrate their success. Then oil prices fell. When the Texas economy took a dive, Ms. Moss's sales were cut in

2

half. Oil successes were few and far between. But Ms. Moss knew her marketing. Through marketing, Wendy became queen of the social circuit. Recognizing that the corporate events market was booming and that company incentive parties were becoming like social and society affairs, Ms. Moss restructured her business. "Instead of sending champagne to every deb in Texas, I hired sales reps to go beyond the state's borders and woo corporate CEOs," she explained. In order to come up with money for her new sales force, media package, and advertising, she drastically cut expenses and reinvested some of her own money. She also insisted on up-front fees from her new corporate customers. But in the end it was all worth it. After only six months, she landed major accounts including Pepsi Cola International, RJR Nabisco, and others. Sales climbed to $1.5 million.[1]

Right Guard's Deodorant No Longer Smells

Gillette's Right Guard deodorant once held a huge 25 per cent share of the deodorant market. This was in the mid-1960s. By the mid-1980s the share had dropped to only 8 per cent. For two years major departments of the company, including marketing research, marketing, research and development (R&D), manufacturing, sales, and finance, as well as the product's ad agency, Young & Rubicam, Incorporated, met monthly to coordinate plans for rejuvenating this product. Operations opened with a $28.2 million ad campaign, the most expensive in the company's 82-year-old history, and brand new packaging for the Right Guard product. Did it work? Sales ran 14 per cent higher for the product than even Gillette planned![2]

These stories, both successes and failures, are due to **marketing management**. Recent articles, not only in business magazines such as *Business Week,* but also in *Time, Newsweek,* and *U.S. News & World Report,* have all emphasized the power of marketing for businesses of all types serving both the consumer and the industrial buyer. As an article in *U.S. News & World Report* headlined, "Marketing Is the Name of the Game for the Eighties."[3] Indeed it would be hard to find a more interesting or powerful business discipline—interesting because it involves human decision making on both the marketing and purchasing ends, and powerful because, more than any other functional area, it determines the success or failure of the enterprise or endeavor.

_____ Marketing and the Marketing Concept

The Marketing Mystique

Some time ago I received a telephone call from the president of a small company that had lost a huge share of its market to competitors over the previous year and a half. When questioned as to the specific nature of this company's problems, the president said, "I don't know what's wrong, but I know that marketing can cure it."

What Is Marketing, Anyway?

After years of conceptual as well as technical development, many practitioners still confuse sales and marketing and use the two terms synonymously. Even many very knowledgeable marketing practitioners and theoreticians in academia disagree as to exactly what marketing is. In fact, an old adage that might be applied to marketing definitions says that if four marketers got together, there would be five definitions of the discipline they were practicing.

The American Marketing Association (AMA) once defined **marketing** as "The performance of business activities that direct the flow of goods and services from producer to consumer or user." But this definition, formulated in 1946 and published in 1960, should be noted as only the starting point rather than the final word.[4]

Only five years later, in 1965, the marketing staff of the Ohio State University suggested that marketing be defined as "The process in a society by which the demand structure for economic goods and services is anticipated or enlarged and satisfied through the conception, promotion, exchange, and physical distribution of goods and services."[5] In other words, it was suggested that marketing was more than a process of simply directing the flow of goods, and by implication, marketers had vastly increased responsibilities.

A few years later it was suggested that the concept of marketing be broadened to include nonbusiness organizations[6] and that the marketing definition had some societal dimensions.[7]

Today the majority of marketing educators believe that the scope of marketing should be broadened to include nonbusiness organizations and that marketing goes beyond goods and services to include many activities in which the ultimate result is not a market transaction. An example of such a nonmarket transaction might be the promotion of a political candidate or an antismoking campaign.[8]

Taking note of the developments since the AMA had last defined marketing, in early 1985 the AMA's board of directors redefined marketing as "the process of planning and executing the conception, pricing, promotion, and distribution of ideas, goods, and services to create exchanges that satisfy individual and organizational objectives."[9]

Surveys of marketing educators, managers, scholar-experts, and students have confirmed that this definition best represents the discipline of marketing at this time.[10] This means that as currently viewed by the largest marketing organization, marketing is a system of activities that facilitates the dissemination and acceptance or adoption of not only products and services, but also ideas. Furthermore, this system of activities is used by any organization, business or nonbusiness, to satisfy or attain its objectives.

This definition is most important because it clearly delineates marketing's close involvement with devising and implementing plans to accomplish goals or objectives. In other words, strategy.

Marketing systems can either be closed or open. This is illustrated in Figure 1-1. In the upper part of the figure, the originator promotes using **advertising**, **sales promotions**, **face-to-face selling**, and **publicity** to the available **distribution channels**, as well as to the **target market** selected, which in this case consists of consumers. The originator receives marketing intelligence from both the target market and the distribution channels. Both receive money in exchange for the product. This can be contrasted with the open marketing system, shown in the lower part of the figure, in which the originator submits an idea that goes through a distribution channel to the target market. Once again promotional activities take place, including advertising, sales promotion, face-to-face selling, and publicity. And marketing intelligence is also received from the target market and the distribution channel that returns to the originator. However, in this case, the target market is a group of citizens, and the originator is attempting to get the citizens to take some required action, perhaps vote a candidate into office or pass

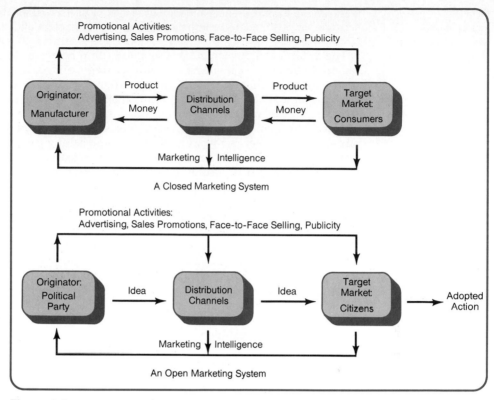

Figure 1-1

Suggested by an illustration "Basic Marketing System," *Marketing Management*, 3rd ed. Douglas J. Dalrymple and Leonard J. Parsons (New York: John Wiley & Sons, 1983), p. 2.

some legislation. As a result, money is not returned to the distribution channel or the originator, and an economic transaction has not taken place. Note that both systems are marketing systems by our definition in that a system of activities has facilitated the dissemination and acceptance or adoption of either a product or service or an idea.

Can Marketing Eliminate Selling?—The Marketing Concept

Earlier we noted that **selling** and marketing are not the same. Professor Theodore Levitt of Harvard describes the difference as follows:

Selling focuses on the need of the seller; marketing on the needs of the buyer. Selling is preoccupied with the seller's need to convert his product into cash; marketing with the idea of satisfying the needs of the customer by means of the product and the whole cluster of things associated with creating, delivering and finally consuming it.[11]

Professor Peter F. Drucker of Claremont Graduate School goes even further. He says:

selling and marketing are antithetical rather than synonymous or even complementary. There will always, one can assume, be a need for some selling, but the aim of marketing is to make selling superfluous. The aim of marketing is to know and understand the customer so well the product or service fits him and sells itself.[12]

The difference between marketing and selling brings us once more to noting marketing's close involvement with **strategy**, and with **tactics**. As we will see in the next chapter, if it is strategy that we will use to accomplish our business objectives, it is tactics that must be employed to implement our strategy. Viewed in this light, marketing is strategy; selling is but one of many tactics to implement whatever marketing strategy is to be employed. Were our strategy perfect, we would still need some selling (tactics) to implement it. But even more important to understand, no matter how good our selling, if our strategy is bad, wrong, or inappropriate, it cannot make up for our strategy deficiencies. In fact, a tactical success in selling may even be wrong.

Consider American automobile companies in the early 1970s. Their positioning strategy was dependent on products emphasizing comfort and power as opposed to fuel economy and, later, quality. When the oil crisis struck, some American companies tried to make up for an inappropriate strategy with selling. It didn't work. But what if it had? Good selling might have helped to buy time for devising and implementing a new and effective strategy. But it could not overcome the basic problem of the wrong strategy. Furthermore, conceivably great success in selling might have masked the very real need to adjust strategy until the company benefiting from the tactical success was in even more difficulties due to delay in changing its strategy.

This brings us back to Peter Drucker's position, which says essentially that if we get our marketing (strategy) right, we can reach our objectives with a lot less work in selling (tactics).

Company Business Orientation

Many business historians have noted an interesting phenomenon in the development of the basic orientation of businesses since the concept of the business was born. First, there was an emphasis on production, then on the product, next on selling the product, and only then to an emphasis on marketing. But the process didn't stop there. Many businesses today have a **societal orientation**. Maximum opportunities for societal as well as company benefit are obviously in the last two orientations. Less obvious is the fact that a number of businesses are not only behind their competitors, but they are lagging from a century to several centuries behind in the orientation of their businesses. Thus, the marketing manager or anyone with marketing responsibilities must pay close attention to how his or her business is oriented.[13]

Production Orientation

Consider Gutenberg's invention of movable type for printing. Use of the Gutenberg press made books much cheaper and more available than before. Consumers who in the past could not afford book ownership could now do so. In fact, the demand for books still far exceeded the supply, even after Gutenberg's invention. As a result, organizations manufacturing books did not need to give marketing much emphasis. They could sell all the books they could produce. Production orientations persist today. A company with this orientation believes that people will buy its products if the products are priced cheaply enough. Marketing for such a company is seen as a production problem, and as a result, other opportunities are missed.

Product Orientation

Other companies still maintain a **product orientation**. They believe, as did Emerson, that if you build a better mousetrap, the world will beat a path to your door. Unfortunately this isn't always true. The Wright brothers built their first working airplane in 1903. Yet it was four long years before the U.S. army made its initial purchase from them. Think of this for a moment. Here was an invention that enabled us to realize man's dream of flying. It had the potential for revolutionizing virtually every aspect of civilization. Yet it took the U.S. government four years before contracting to obtain even a single unit to test. This is not necessarily an indictment of government; rather it is a partial description of a market characteristic.

Every so often, since about 1950, an automatic lawn mower appears in the marketplace. This lawn mower, controlled electrically through radio, has built-in safety features so that it will not run over trees, shrubbery, children, or errant pets. It is fully automatic. Yet, although its technical performance is proven again and again, every time this product is introduced, it fails.

A California engineer resigned his position with a major aerospace company and with his own and borrowed money invested in a unique automobile engine that could be regulated for high performance or economy by the vehicle driver. After several years and $200,000 of expenditures, he was able to perfect and patent his device—only to discover that he had no customers.

Finally, as if to refute or confirm Emerson, mail-order marketer Joe Sugarman, president of JS and A Sales, actually built a better mousetrap, priced it at $2,400, and advertised it in a large space advertisement in *The Wall Street Journal*. It was his only ad that failed to attract a single buyer.

Sales Orientation

A company with a **sales orientation** takes a product as a given and the market as a given and tries to sell the product to the consumer or the industrial buyer. Such a company has a philosophy that a good salesperson can sell anything to anyone. It is true that there are those who are superior salespeople who can maximize the chances of selling once a product has been produced. However, from a marketing perspective, this is the more difficult way to create a sale because this task is far easier if a target market exists that wants a particular product you have developed specifically for it. In Drucker's words, "the product or service fits him and sells itself."

Marketing Orientation

The previous business orientations stretch back over the centuries, but the **marketing orientation** has become popular only within the last thirty years. A company having a marketing business orientation focuses on the customer. Its philosophy is: "It is not what you want to sell but what your customer

Table 1-1 Does Your Organization Have a Marketing Orientation?

1. Are you easy to do business with?
   - Easy to contact?
   - Fast to provide information?
   - Easy to order from?
   - Make reasonable promises?
2. Do you keep your promises?
   - On product performance?
   - Delivery?
   - Installation?
   - Training?
   - Service?
3. Do you meet the standards you set?
   - Specifics?
   - General tone?
   - Do you even still know the standards?
4. Are you responsive?
   - Do you listen?
   - Do you follow up?
   - Do you ask "why not" rather than "why?"
   - Do you treat customers as individual companies and individual people?
5. Does your organization work together?
   - Do you share the blame?
   - Do you share information?
   - Do you make joint decisions?
   - Do you provide satisfaction to your members?

Source: Adapted from Benson P. Shapiro, "What the Hell is 'Market Oriented,'" *Harvard Business Review*, vol. 66, no. 6 (November–December 1988), p. 125.

wants to buy." Accordingly, a company with a marketing orientation seeks to find a need and to fill it.[14]

There is no question but that this works when done properly. Stephen Pistner took over as chief executive of Montgomery Ward and Company in 1981, the year after it lost $163 million. Investigating his market, he found what the customers wanted and what they did not. Adopting a philosophy of "quality and availability of products that customers want, when they want them," Pistner dropped tailored men's suits and carpeting and picked up the types of products his target market wanted. The results weren't long in coming. Montgomery Ward earned $40 million in profits, its first in four years.[15]

If you want to bring the marketing orientation out of the theoretical, look at Table 1-1. It is a self-examination checklist developed by Harvard Professor Benson P. Shapiro. A marketing manager giving him- or herself this test would no longer be in doubt.[16]

Societal Orientation

A societal business orientation is the most recent to be articulated by marketers. Such an orientation recognizes that a firm has additional responsibilities involving consumerism, the struggle of the poor for subsistence, the marketing of social and cultural services, the day-to-day function of the economy, and the use and pollution of society's resources.[17] Furthermore, and interestingly, research has shown that Machiavellian behavior in marketing—that is, aggressive manipulative exploiting and devious moves to achieve objectives—is basically unrelated to success.[18]

In recognition of societal responsibilities, many companies have modified their approach to include a societal emphasis. For example, R. Gordon McGovern, president of Campbell Soup Company, stated the goal for Campbell as, "To be positioned with consumers as somebody who is looking after their well-being."[19]

The clear implication here is that firms with a societal orientation do not seek profit as their primary purpose. Instead, profits are viewed as a business requirement. Again according to Harvard's Theodore Levitt,

Without profits, business stops. Like food for the body, profit for the business must be defined as the excess of what comes in over what goes out. In business it's called positive cash flow. It has to be positive, because the process of sustaining life is a process of destroying life. To sustain life, a business must produce goods and services that people in sufficient numbers will want to buy at adequate prices. Since production wears out the machinery that produces and the people who run and manage the machines, to keep the business going there's got to be enough left over to replace what's being worn out. That "enough" is profit, no matter what the accountants, the IRS, or the Gosplan calls it. That is why profit is a requisite, not a purpose, of business."[20]

Instead of profit as the purpose of business, Levitt proposes that the purpose of a business is to create and keep a customer.

Each of these business orientations is shown in Figure 1-2. Opportunities for marketing payoff for any organization are found in a combination of the marketing and societal emphases.

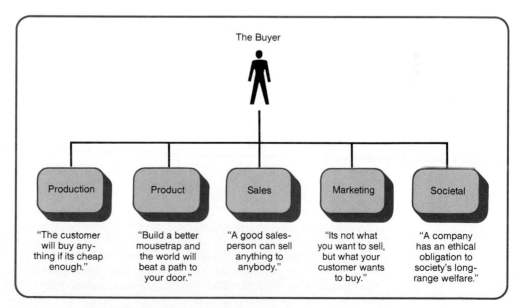

Figure 1-2 The Different Company Orientations

Elements of the Marketing Concept

Implementation of the **marketing concept** in the 1990s requires attention to three basic elements of the marketing concept. These are

1. *Consumer orientation.* This means that the focus is on the customer and satisfying his or her needs, rather than on the product or service.
2. *An organization to implement a consumer orientation.* This element notes that an organization with a customer emphasis is necessary. In a firm with a sales orientation, or in the old days when sales was the major business emphasis, rather than marketing, a true marketing manager may not have existed. There may have been a sales executive and perhaps a separate marketing research manager whose primary function was to see how well the product was selling. But an organization intending to implement the marketing concept requires a marketing organization, as opposed to one whose function is sales. The marketing manager's functions are far broader and will be explained later.
3. *Long-range consumer and societal welfare.* Because the broadening of the definition of marketing to include organizations and individuals served outside of business and even beyond the exchange process, the marketing concept must include the obligation to work not only for the short-term welfare of the buyer, but the long-range needs of the consumer and society as a whole. This includes groups such as customers, employees, suppliers, the host community, and the general public.[21]

Fortunately, as indicated previously, some evidence exists that indicates that a marketer need not be unethical to succeed. But even if this were not so and if we recognize that there is a "dark side of the marketing force," then the marketing concept says that this dark side of marketing must not be employed.

Furthermore, research indicates that Fortune 500 executives believe that, as their firms and industry face increased competitive intensity in the mid-1990s, they will place increased emphasis on these philosophies. They believe that by doing this, it will help to increase the performance of their organizations then.[22]

Marketing Management and Its Function _____

What Is Marketing Management?

Having reviewed current definitions and concepts of marketing, we are ready to have a close look at marketing management. One definition of marketing management is, "The analysis and planning leading to selection of one or more market targets—the design of an integrated marketing strategy to reach selected market targets—and implementation and control plan strategy to achieve corporate marketing objectives."[23] Once again we see marketing's and, hence, marketing management's close involvement with strategy.

The American Marketing Association defines marketing management this way:

> The process of setting marketing goals for an organization (considering internal resources and market opportunities), the planning and execution of activities to meet these goals, and measuring progress toward their achievement.[24]

Basically marketing management is simply the management of marketing activities. This is true because the activities of a marketing manager have changed and will continue to change in their specifics as technology and the scope and functions of the marketing discipline continue to develop. Thus, a marketing manager may have responsibilities for planning and implementing the traditional "four Ps" of product, price, promotion, and place, as conceptualized by Professor E. Jerome McCarthy of Michigan State University, or responsibilities for decision making in determining the strategic marketing direction of an organization.

Failure to execute marketing management responsibilities properly can cause catastrophes in any organization. An article in *Business Week* discussed the fact that a significant number of those companies judged excellent in Peters and Waterman's best-selling book, *In Search of Excellence,* since found themselves in severe difficulties in the marketplace. According to *Business Week,* the reason many of these excellent companies stumbled, after being judged excellent, was due to fundamental changes in the market and those companies' inability to adapt—a failure of marketing management to adapt—to environmental changes.[25]

A specific example cited was Levi Strauss & Company. Levi Strauss, more than 134 years old, built its reputation on two principles: quality and a happy family corporate culture. Without question, Levi's made quality jeans. As the industry grew 15 per cent annually almost every year for the next twenty years, every pair of jeans that Levi produced could be sold. But the market shifted. Levi's failed to detect the shift toward more fashionable apparel. As a result, Levi's sales slipped 6 per cent and earnings fell by 72 per cent, despite maintenance of a high-quality product. Allen L. Stein, director of corporate finance at Montgomery Securities and a Levi director, said, "Levi's needs to become more a marketing company and less of a production company."[26] The failure, however, was one of marketing management. A major environmental variable—consumer demand—changed. But Levi's continued doing the same thing it had done previously.

The Basic Functions of the Marketing Manager

Marketing management can be characterized by five basic functions. These are planning, organizing, coordinating, controlling, and appraising. Their mastery is the key to top performance as a marketing manager in any organization. Note that all these functions are interrelated in Figure 1-3.

The Planning Function. The **planning function** is usually the first step in attainment of any marketing objective because a plan acts as a roadmap in directing you and your company from where you are at the time the plan is initiated until you reach your goals or objectives. Although most marketing executives recognize the need for planning, in practice some avoid serious

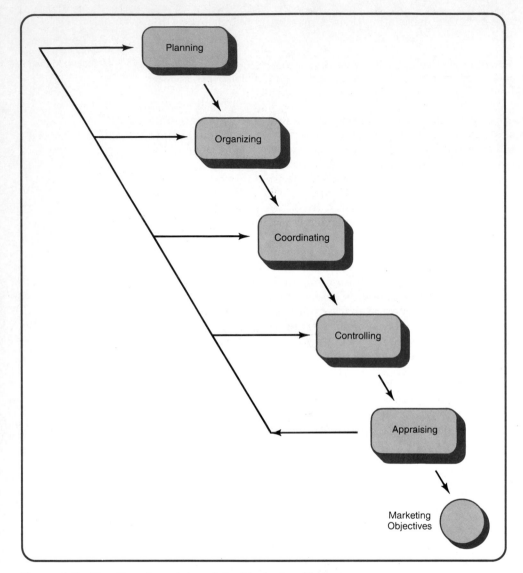

Figure 1-3 The Five Functions of the Marketing Manager

planning due to the pressures of time and activities of the moment. They express sentiments such as "I don't have time to plan" or "I do all my planning in my head." These are reminiscent of remarks made by Union General John Pope during the Civil War who said, "My headquarters are in the saddle." General Robert E. Lee, who defeated Pope at Manassas, said, "His headquarters are where his hindquarters should be."

The Organizing Function. The **organizing function** is one of the most important for completing marketing objectives successfully. Getting things done "somehow" won't work. The organizing function establishes efficient relationships among people, resources, and functions. And this organizing

12

must be accomplished within the context of the overall business environment.

The Coordinating Function. As marketing researcher Thomas V. Bonoma stated it, "The marketing job by its nature is one of influencing others inside and outside the corporation."[27] The implication here is that any marketer must, by the very nature of his or her organization, interface with others and interact with them, and influence these others to accomplish the task at hand.[28]

One major responsibility of the marketing manager is **new product development**. New product development at its very early stages requires not just interfacing with other marketing functions, but also business functions within the company, including engineering, production, and finance. As many responsible for new product development have learned to their dismay, excluding just one of these other business functional areas can lead to disaster, even though the product developed may satisfy the demands of the market in a technical sense. One company lost thousands of dollars and suffered significant time delays in introducing a new product simply because production representatives were excluded early in the product's technical development. As a result, although a workable prototype was produced that fully satisfied the needs of the intended customer, the product could not be produced in quantity at a cost that would allow a competitive price. Before the product could be introduced, it had to be completely reengineered at considerable expense and loss of time.

Accordingly, the function of coordination involves the orchestration of all other areas that in some fashion interface with the marketer and his or her activities.

One study explored the interactions of ninety-five marketers with manufacturing, R&D, and accounting personnel and fifty-six nonmarketing personnel from these business units with marketers. The study showed that influence by marketing personnel on other business units, and the personnel of these other business units on marketing, was directly related to coordination between them.[29]

Twenty-five product managers were surveyed during the course of an advertising decision study. Some results were quite surprising. Not only were coordination and interface among different marketing groups considered important, but interface among seven groups in the marketing system was considered absolutely essential for success. These groups were:

1. Buying public.
2. Distributors.
3. Sales force.
4. Advertising agency.
5. Product development.
6. Marketing research.
7. Other marketing and corporate personnel.[30]

The Controlling Function. The controlling function involves keeping on the planned track to reach the objectives that are set while maintaining the productivity, efficiency, and effectiveness of the individuals and organizations involved in the task. Thus, it is not enough simply to reach marketing objectives successfully but to reach them while complying with performance, time, and cost parameters.

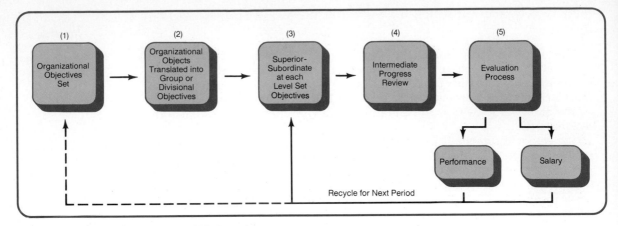

Figure 1-4 The Generalized MBO Process

Source: Michael J. Etzel and John M. Ivanevich, "Management by Objectives in Marketing: Philosophy, Process, and Problems," *Journal of Marketing*, (vol. 38, no. 4, October 1974), p. 50.

The Appraising Function. Appraising involves assessing both performance and progress to reach goals. Thus, it goes hand in hand with the controlling function mentioned previously. Control is not possible without assessing progress on both an individual and an organizational basis. This function enables that assessment. For example, review Figure 1-4, which is a generalized **management-by-objectives** process applied to marketing.[31] The process begins with organizational objectives being set and proceeds to these objectives being translated into group or divisional objectives. In box 3 a superior and subordinate at each level set objectives that are in keeping with the objectives of the organization to which they belong. Appraisal is accomplished in boxes 4 and 5, Intermediate Progress Reviews and Evaluation Process.

The latter is a final meeting, during which performance of the entire period is evaluated. The result of the process leads to two separate activities: (1) an evaluation of the objectives achieved and the relation of these objectives to a reward system, such as salary or promotional considerations, and (2) an evaluation of performance intended to aid the subordinate in self-development and set the stage for the next period. These, in turn, lead to another cycle for the next period, with the superior and subordinate in each level setting objectives that are in harmony with the organizational objectives set for this next period.

The Tasks and Responsibilities of Marketing Managers

Functions of the marketing manager define general areas of marketing practice. But what are the specifics? What are marketing managers responsible for and exactly what do they do?

In Figure 1-5, the total **marketing environment**, you will note there are

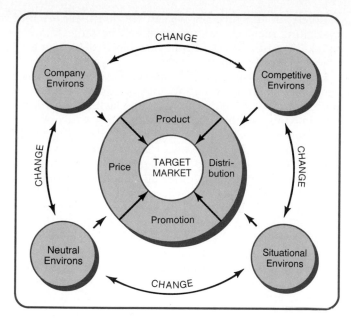

Figure 1-5   The Total Marketing Environment

four environs affecting the marketplace: (1) company, (2) competitor, (3) neutral, and (4) situational. **Company environs** include know-how, experience, financial resources, human resources, capital equipment, suppliers, and marketing intermediaries. **Competitor environs** include these same subareas. The **neutral environs** are organizations or groups that are usually neutral regarding you, relative to your competitors. They may help you or any or all of your competitors under different circumstances. They include financial environs, government environs, media environs, and special-interest environs. **Situational environs** include politics, law and regulations, economic and business conditions, the state of technology, demand, social and cultural factors, and demographics.

The objective in the total marketing environment is to satisfy the target market with products, services, or ideas. To learn about the environs, we gather and analyze as much relevant information as we can about the marketing situation. This is known as **marketing intelligence**. Through marketing intelligence, marketing managers can react to the environmental changes in the following ways:

1. By continuously monitoring consumer incomes, expenditures, lifestyles, and market segments for clues to market and product variations
2. By building flexibility into marketing programs and by planning for radically different alternatives to cope with a rapidly changing environment
3. By coordinating operations more closely with purchasing, R&D, production, and finance, so that investments in products, inventory levels, promotion, price, and so on can be affected on short notice
4. By maintaining the closest liaison with relevant governmental bodies that may be expected to play more active roles in peacetime and directing and supervising economic activities[32]

Referring to Figure 1-5, we can see that there are four major variables the marketing manager can use to affect the target market. This is the familiar **marketing mix**, or "strategic variables," of product, price, promotion, and place or distribution.

Product decisions involve various actions that can be taken regarding the product, including initiating introduction, withdrawing from the marketplace, modifying the product in some fashion, positioning the product in the mind of the consumer, or branding the product. **Pricing decisions** involve what margins to be set, pricing versus the competition—either to meet the competition or pricing below or above—pricing variation due to discount or geographic location, and pricing margins. **Promotion** has been subdivided into advertising, sales promotion, face-to-face selling, and publicity. At all levels it involves the mix of these activities—the budget and how it is set, the media that are chosen, and the message that the originator is trying to communicate. Finally, **distribution** or **place decisions** involve the channels to be used—whether distribution is to be intensive or selective or exclusive—and the degree of channel ownership.

One can also work with the **environs** themselves. For example, a firm could establish and maintain variable images in the minds of those making up the environment or environ through corporate advertising campaigns. A company could engage in private legal battle with a competitor on antitrust, deceptive advertising, or other grounds. Or a company could initiate efforts to influence or elect representatives to create a more favorable business environment or limit competition through direct lobbying or advertising or corporate constituency programs.[33,34] From these examples, you can see that a marketing manager can work with environs as well as with the four Ps of the marketing mix to accomplish marketing objectives. However, it is usually easier to develop strategies based on manipulation of the marketing mix rather than the environs, but we'll look at this closer in Chapter 5.

One final cautionary note in the use of both the **strategic variables** and in attempting to influence environs: **timing** is critical. Timing is critical because environs are constantly changing. Therefore it is not simply a matter of working with the strategic variables or environs in accomplishing objectives set, but also of working when these actions or marketing activities take place.

From this discussion it is clear that the tasks and responsibilities of the marketing manager and marketing executive include overall strategy development, marketing intelligence, product decisions, pricing decisions, promotion decisions, and distribution decisions, as well as decisions having to do with the various environs of the marketplace. It is not easy. As Silicon Valley marketing guru Regis McKenna says, "This approach to marketing demands a revolution in how businesspeople act—and even more important, in how they think. These changes are critical to success, but they can come only gradually, as managers and organizations adapt to the new rules of marketing. . . ."[35]

Summary

In this chapter we have seen the importance of marketing management for all types of organizations. And while the precise definition of marketing is still changing and may differ according to different groups or individuals, its proven power is agreed to by all. In this book we will use a broad definition and define marketing as a system of activities that facilitates the dissemination and acceptance or adoption of products, services, or ideas. The successful practice of marketing management involves mastery of five basic functions: planning, organizing, controlling, coordinating, and appraising. Specific marketing tasks and responsibilities of marketing managers may include top strategy development, marketing intelligence, product decisions, pricing decisions, promotion decisions, distribution decisions, and decisions affecting the marketing environs. This makes marketing management one of the most complex jobs in business, and an essential one. As pointed out in an article in *Newsweek*, "Corporate leaders nationwide are discovering that their most powerful competitive weapon is marketing."[36]

Questions

1. Do you think marketing can eliminate or at least drastically reduce selling? Why or why not?
2. Name a local or national firm that has each of the following business orientations: production, product, sales, marketing, societal. Explain your answer.
3. Many business practitioners feel that the main objective of a company should be to make a long-term profit. If this is assumed so, can you find any business justification for societal orientation for a company?
4. Are there any marketing situations where planning would not be desirable? Explain your answer.
5. You can develop a successful marketing strategy based on manipulating the "strategic variables," or marketing mix. Name a company and use the strategic variables to demonstrate why the company was successful or unsuccessful due to the marketing mix it adopted.
6. You can develop a successful marketing strategy based on manipulating one or more of the environs of the marketplace. Name a company that developed a strategy based on manipulating one or more environs and explain why this company was successful or unsuccessful.
7. Timing has been noted as an important variable in strategy development. Illustrate an example of a success or failure in marketing due to timing.
8. How would the marketing manager of a company selling breakfast food go about achieving each of the following objectives: maximizing sales, maximizing unit packages sold, maximizing profits, maximizing buyer satisfaction, maximizing buyer or societal benefit?
9. Are the environs of equal importance? Why or why not? Are the strategic variables of equal importance? Why or why not?
10. How might an environmental change cause an unexpected success or failure of a product, service, or idea? Be specific.

Ethical Question

Marketing is concerned with satisfying a customer's needs. In fact, this is part of the marketing concept. How does ethics fit in with the marketing concept?

Endnotes

1. C. G. Brower, "From Debutantes to the Fortune 500," *Success,* vol. 34, no. 6 (July–August 1987), p. 29.
2. "Marketing—A New Priority," *Business Week* (November 21, 1983), p. 96.
3. Gail Bronson, "Marketing Is the Name of the

Game for the Eighties," *U.S. News & World Report* (March 12, 1984).

4. Committee on Terms, *Marketing Definitions: A Glossary of Marketing Terms* (Chicago: AMA, 1960).

5. Marketing Staff of the Ohio State University, "Statement of Marketing Philosophy," *Journal of Marketing*, vol. 29 (January 1965), pp. 43–44.

6. Philip Kotler and Sidney J. Levy, "Broadening the Concept of Marketing," *Journal of Marketing*, vol. 33 (January 1969), p. 15.

7. William Lazer, "Marketing's Changing Social Relationships," *Journal of Marketing*, vol. 33 (January 1969), p. 9.

8. William G. Nichols, "Conceptual Conflicts in Marketing," *Journal of Economics and Business*, vol. 26 (Winter 1974), p. 142.

9. ————, "AMA Board Approves New Marketing Definition," *Marketing News*, vol. 19 (March 1, 1985), p. 1.

10. O. C. Ferrell and George H. Lucas, Jr., "An Evaluation of Progress in the Development of a Definition of Marketing," *Journal of the Academy of Marketing Science*, vol. 15, no. 3 (Fall 1987), p. 12.

11. Theodore Levitt, "Marketing Myopia," *Harvard Business Review* (July–August 1960).

12. Peter F. Drucker, *Management Tasks, Responsibilities, Practices* (New York: Harper & Row, 1974), p. 64.

13. At least one researcher does not agree with this framework. Noting that the antecedents of modern marketing go back to the time of Columbus, Ronald A. Fullerton recommends a different developmental structure, encompassing three eras: origins, institutional development, and refinement and formalization. See Ronald A. Fullerton, "How Modern Is Modern Marketing?" *Journal of Marketing*, vol. 52, no. 1 (January 1988), pp. 108–123.

14. Jack Harms, "Are You a Marketing-Oriented Company?" *Small Business Reports* (March 1990), pp. 20–24.

15. Bronson, "Marketing Is the Name of the Game," op. cit.

16. Benson P. Shapiro, "What the Hell is 'Market Oriented'?" *Harvard Business Review*, vol. 66, no. 6 (November–December 1988), p. 125.

17. Robert J. Lavidge, "The Growing Responsibilities of Marketing," *Journal of Marketing*, vol. 34, no. 1 (January 1970), pp. 25–28.

18. Shelby D. Hunt and Lawrence B. Chonko, "Mar-

keting and Machiavellianism," *Journal of Marketing*, vol. 48, no. 3 (Summer 1984), p. 40.

19. "Marketing: New Priority," *Business Week* (November 21, 1983), p. 103.

20. Theodore Levitt, *The Marketing Imagination* (New York: Free Press, 1983), p. 6.

21. Robert F. Lusch and Gene R. Laczniak, "The Evolving Marketing Concept, Competitive Intensity and Organizational Performance," *Journal of the Academy of Marketing Science*, vol. 15, no. 3 (Fall 1987), p. 1.

22. Ibid., p. 11.

23. David W. Cravens, "Marketing Management in an Era of Shortages," *Business Horizons* (February 1974).

24. Peter D. Bennett, *Dictionary of Marketing Terms* (Chicago: AMA, 1988), p. 116.

25. "Who's Excellent Now?" *Business Week* (November 5, 1984), p. 78.

26. Ibid., p. 79.

27. Thomas V. Bonoma, "Making Your Marketing Strategy Work," *Harvard Business Review*, vol. 62, no. 2 (March–April 1984), p. 75.

28. Robert W. Ruekert and Orville C. Walker, Jr., "Marketing's Interaction with other Functional Units: A Conceptual Framework and Empirical Evidence," *Journal of Marketing* vol. 51, no. 1 (January 1987), p. 1.

29. Ibid., p. 10.

30. David J. Luck, "Interfaces of a Product Manager," *Journal of Marketing* (October 1969), pp. 33–34.

31. Michael J. Etzel and John M. Ivancevich, "Management by Objectives in Marketing: Philosophy, Process, and Problems," *Journal of Marketing* (October 1974).

32. David Carson, "Gotterdammering for Marketing?," *Journal of Marketing*, vol. 42, no. 3 (July 1978), p. 17.

33. Carl P. Zeithaml and Valarie A. Zeithaml, "Environmental Management: Revising the Marketing Perspective," *Journal of Marketing*, vol. 48, no. 2 (Spring 1984), p. 50.

34. Dennis E. Garrett, "The Effectiveness of Marketing Policy Boycotts: Environmental Opposition to Marketing," *Journal of Marketing*, vol. 51, no. 2 (April 1987), p. 55.

35. Regis McKenna, *Harvard Business Review*, vol. 66, no. 5 (September–October, 1988), p. 95.

36. "To Market, to Market," *Newsweek* (January 9, 1984).

Strategic Marketing Management

2

CHAPTER OBJECTIVES

- Understand the concept of strategic marketing management and where it fits in overall marketing and strategy development.
- Know the alternative approaches to managing marketing strategically.
- Be able to accomplish strategic marketing planning.

Strategic Marketing Management: The Key to Victory in the Marketplace

Rubbermaid Bounces Out of Sight

Rubbermaid, Inc., was founded in 1920 as the Wooster Rubber Company. In those days the company produced toy balloons. Today it produces a half-million house specialty and commercial products of all sizes, shapes, and colors in injected molded plastic resin. The quantum leap began in 1980, when Stanley Gault took over as chairman. Sales were $341 million per year, although earnings had dipped to only $21 million. According to Gault, the company was facing "severe pressure and challenges of the 80s." Gault reviewed every operation to determine its

strengths and weaknesses. In 1981 he began a number of strategic moves. They included discontinuing Rubbermaid's in-home party plan company; selling its domestic car mat and automative accessories business; acquiring Carlan, Inc., maker of Con-Tack self-adhesive decorative coverings, and other companies making plastic quality molded products; scrapping its applied products business; selling its losing industrial business in Holland; establishing a new international division based on several new foreign acquisitions; installing a product management system; and expanding and enlarging its manufacturing capacity. Did these strategic moves have any

19

impact? You'd better believe it. Since 1981 Rubbermaid has expanded from seven to twenty-five operating sites. By 1987 net sales had climbed to $1 billion and earnings to $84.5 million. The expectation is for continued growth at approximately 15 per cent per year.[1]

What if the Avon Lady Calls and No One Is at Home?[2]

Only a few years ago, Avon stocks stood at $140 a share. But recently each share sold for only $20. Avon's sales force was the smallest since 1980; its operating margin fell from 21.7 to 11.4 per cent. Why these major problems for a company that was traditionally not only very strong, but a force to be reckoned with in the marketplace? Avon's problems had a great deal to do with the change of a major marketing environ: the influx of women into the work force and the fact that in the United States of the 1990s more than 50 per cent of the women are working.

As a result of this major behavioral shift in Avon's customers, President Hicks B. Waldron went hard to work on strategic marketing and redefined the company's goals to establish a long-term strategic plan. He said, "The approach will cause people to view their responsibilities and their businesses differently." For the short term, Avon attempted to solve its problems by exploiting direct-mail and telephone sales. But for the long term, a strategic question loomed. Was Avon's traditional channel of direct selling through door-to-door sales still viable, considering this significant change in the marketplace: the fact that the majority of women are no longer in the home and that this trend may continue? Only Waldron's strategic marketing management could save the company. ●

The Concept of Strategic Marketing Management

The concept of **strategic marketing management** has evolved through interaction among marketing management, strategy, and planning. We will define the term to mean managing a business unit to anticipate and respond to changes that affect the marketplace so that decisions are made today that allow the business unit to be ready for tomorrow in such a fashion as to avoid the threats and take advantage of the opportunities.[3]

The Characteristics of Strategic Marketing Management

The characteristics of strategic marketing management include

- Looking beyond immediate issues.
- Specific decisions and actions.
- Top management level of involvement.
- Holistic perspective.
- Flexibility.
- Proactiveness.[4]

Looking Beyond Immediate Issues. Looking beyond immediate issues implies concerns with issues other than those that we are immediately involved with today. Therefore, "firefighting" or tactical or day-to-day operational issues are not a part of strategic marketing management.

Specific Decisions and Actions. Strategic marketing management is not philosophizing about the future, management, marketing, or strategy, but is rather specific actions that must be taken to attain objectives and goals through avoiding the threats and taking advantage of the opportunities.

Top Management Level of Involvement. Strategic marketing management tends to be done by the top levels of management of the organization or business unit, as opposed to the strategy and tactics that are implemented by lower-level units and thus lower levels of management.

Holistic Perspective. As pointed out in the previous chapter, all elements of the marketing situation are interrelated, including those strategic variables that can be controlled and the environs that may or may not be controlled. It is important that an overall approach be taken, not only to ensure not excluding an element that may turn out to be critically important, but to avoid optimization of any element so that even though it is successful, the overall strategy of the parent business unit is unsuccessful. For example, one company producing safety products for the federal government invested millions of dollars in R&D for new products. Unfortunately, the company did not pay close enough attention to controlling the quality of its current products—one reason was that too many resources were allocated to R&D. As a result, before these technologically advanced products could reach the marketplace, the company lost its customers and the new products were never introduced.

Flexibility. The environment in which marketing is practiced is always changing. If that weren't in itself a difficult problem, there is always a great deal of uncertainty not only as to the direction of these changes but as to when changes will occur. Strategic marketing management encourages flexible thinking. That is, not only is a marketing strategy developed to reach specific goals and objectives, but contingency planning is accomplished for alternate strategies and, in some cases, even for alternate goals and objectives.

Proactiveness. Proactiveness means designing the future. Designing for the future does not mean making decisions in the future, for as Peter Drucker points out, decisions can only be made in the present. Rather, we should build our own future as we desire it. If we do not like the future that we see for ourselves, due to the changing environment into which our business unit is heading, it is up to us as marketing managers to make the changes necessary so that the future we end up with is more to our benefit.

For example, what is a company like McDonald's doing competing with the Kellogg Company and Kraft General Foods? Simple. Although McDonald's has had a 15 per cent growth over the last ten years and controls 20 per cent of the $56 billion fast food business, the industry sales growth is stalling out. It's now only 7 per cent. And McDonald's share is only a tiny portion of the $400 billion American food market. So CEO Michael R. Quinlan made the decision to go all out to win the increasing number of working consumers who don't feel like cooking after working a full day. That's operating proactively. It means that McDonald's is investing a bundle in opening new restaurants, in more drive-through capability, and in new products. Says CEO Quinlan: "We're putting the pedal to the medal."[5]

It should be clear by now that strategic marketing management attempts to answer some very basic questions, including defining what businesses we are in and what businesses we should be in.[6] To do this involves an anticipatory analysis of our present product market entries, likely environmental changes, and actions to result in potential or possible reallocation of resources among our present efforts.

Strategy and Where Strategic Marketing Management Fits In

Strategy involves how we go about reaching the objectives or goals set for our organizational or business unit. At the very top is grand strategy. Grand strategy is equivalent to strategic marketing management and is set at the top, corporate level of the organization. One level down from grand strategy is marketing strategy. Marketing strategy involves a lower level of the organization and is set in support of grand strategy objectives. A typical marketing strategy might involve segmentation, whereby the overall market is divided into segments with like characteristics and the organization resources are concentrated and allocated to marketing in these segments. Or a marketing strategy of product differentiation could be adopted in which the product is differentiated from those of competitors. Traditionally, the four Ps of marketing—product, price, promotion, and place—have been known as the strategic variables because we can control and manipulate them to achieve our marketing objectives. However, this manipulation is tactical, not strategic and is used to accomplish a marketing strategy: market segmentation, product differentiation, or some other marketing strategy, as mentioned previously.

This concept is illustrated in the marketing strategy pyramid, Figure 2-1.

Figure 2-1   The Marketing Strategy Pyramid

Type of Maneuvering	Controlled by	Decisions Made About	Example
Strategic marketing management	Corporate management	Groups of businesses, groups of products	Allocation of company resources among product groups to maintain a portfolio positioned for maximum growth
Marketing strategy	Marketing organization management	Market segments to serve, product differential characteristics, product positioning	Allocation of marketing resources to achieve a competitive advantage through emphasis of a product's differences
Marketing tactics	Marketing subunit management	Product, price, promotion, distribution environs	Allocation of marketing resources to achieve a tactical competitive advantage in emphasis of a product's differences through a superior sales force

Figure 2-2   Marketing Strategy Matrix

Note that at the very top of the apex is strategic marketing management, which is accomplished by corporate management. At the intermediate level is marketing strategy, normally accomplished by marketing organization management. At the lowest level is **marketing tactics**, which are accomplished by marketing subunit management.

Note also that the strategic marketing management level of the pyramid overlaps with the marketing strategy level, and that this level in turn overlaps the marketing tactics level. The overlap occurs because occasionally strategic marketing management encroaches on the marketing strategy level and vice versa. The marketing strategy level sometimes operates in the marketing tactics level, and the reverse is also true.[7]

To understand the concept further, let's take a look at the **marketing strategy matrix** in Figure 2-2. Down the vertical axis, you will see strategic marketing management, marketing strategy, and marketing tactics. Along the horizontal axis, you find who performs the controlling function, what decisions are made about each strategy, and an example of each.

Clearly, strategic marketing management has a high degree of overlap with overall business strategy. And in fact, it can be viewed as an integral part of and perspective for business strategies in any company. The difference, as pointed out by Yoram Wind and Thomas S. Robertson, is that strategic marketing management serves as a boundary function between the firm and its customers, competitors, and other stakeholders. Thus, it is turned outward toward the environment and the marketing environs of the situation. It is positioned uniquely to assess the needs of all classes of buyers, as well to infer a potential for gaining a differential advantage over the competition and fulfilling the overall objectives set for the firm.[8]

It would be difficult to overestimate the importance of strategic marketing management. In fact, many researchers as well as practitioners feel that in considering the relative importance of tactics, strategy, and strategic marketing management, the latter is far more important. Robert E. Wood, who was chief executive officer of Sears, Roebuck and Company during its years of greatest growth and also a retired army general, stated, "Business is like war in one respect—if its grand strategy is correct, any number of tactical errors can be made, and yet the enterprise proves successful."[9] Harvard Business School Professor Michael Porter spoke about another significant aspect when he said: "Corporate strategy is what makes the corporate whole add up to more than the sum of its business unit parts."[10]

Let's look at McDonald's recent strategy decisions to see how these different levels of strategy fit. At the strategic marketing management level, McDonald's noted that the growth rate of its traditional fast food burger business was declining, despite population increase. At the same time, the total food consumed in the United States represented an opportunity. McDonald's decided to make a major move into a new area: a more conventional restaurant service. It established a corporate marketing objective involving such a service. At the marketing strategy level, McDonald's decided to follow a market segmentation strategy to reach this corporate marketing objective. McDonald's was focusing on the working consumer, who has less time or inclination either to (1) go to a fancier conventional restaurant or (2) fix his or her own meals. Note how this decision put McDonald's into competition not only with traditional restaurants, but also with microwave and ready-made food packagers. Now we'll look at the tactical level. McDonald's decisions regarding food offered (product), restaurant location, and drive-through capability (place), meal pricing (price), and promotion (advertising, sales promotion, etc.) should all be aimed at influencing the working consumer in order to be successful in the marketing strategy selected. Ask yourself this question: Are the tactics the same that would be followed in McDonald's traditional business?

Incorporated in strategic marketing management are goals and the concept of vision. It is partly from strategic marketing management that the corporate marketing leader refines his or her goals and develops his or her vision. It is through strategic marketing management that he or she articulates these goals and vision of the company's future and begins to inspire and motivate executives and workers throughout the organization. As a pharmaceutical executive explained: "One rule of thumb that I've learned is to know, to the bottom of my soul, what it is I am trying to accomplish, so I can take advantage of opportunities when they come along."[11]

Structured Approaches to Strategic Marketing Management

How Is Strategic Marketing Management Accomplished?

As pointed out in Chapter 1, it is unwise to attempt to practice any sort of approach to strategy in your head. You will ignore too many areas and not give critical issues sufficient attention. Fortunately marketing experts have developed a structured approach to accomplishing this. It is known as **strategic planning** and is one of the functional responsibilities of the practicing marketing manager. The use of a structured approach for strategic planning is growing. Two primary factors encourage this acceptance and growth.[12]

1. A structured approach for strategic marketing management provides a conceptual framework for systematically mapping an organization's focus to attain a differential advantage.
2. Analytical techniques are available, and many have been developed to assist the marketing manager with this process.

The Questions Strategic Marketing Management Attempts to Answer

Strategic marketing management attempts to answer the following questions:

1. Should funds be committed to a proposed new market entry?
2. When should funds be committed?
3. How large should the commitment of funds be?
4. Should expenditure of funds for plant and equipment or marketing to support existing product lines be expanded, continued at previous levels, or diminished?
5. At what time should a decision be made to withdraw and cease the expenditure of resources for an unprofitable product or business unit or area?[13]

The Process of Strategic Marketing Management

The process of strategic marketing management can be categorized by six distinct stages: (1) **situation assessment**, (2) **goal development**, (3) **constraint identification**, (4) **strategy selection**, (5) **implementation**, and (6) **control**.[14] The situation assessment has to do with answering the question: What is our current situation? Goal development: What do we want our future situation to be? Constraint identification: What constraints might inhibit us? Selection of strategies: What actions should we take to achieve our goals? Implementation: How do we carry out these actions? Control: How do we keep on track to reach our goals when things don't go as planned?

This process, along with the main information sources to each of the process procedures, is shown in Figure 2-3. The main information source for a situation assessment is customers. For goal development—what we want our future situation to be—the main source is our potential customers. For constraint identification, we obtain information mainly from our competitors, the government, and other constraining environs in the marketplace. In strategy selection, we use all environs of the marketplace to supply us with the information we need to proceed.

The implementation is the payoff for everything that has gone before. No matter how well you succeeded in doing the previous steps, if you don't implement successfully, it was all for naught. For many years some marketers thought that everything ended with the selection of strategy. Today we know better. Books, and even whole courses of marketing instruction, have been devoted to this step. In this book the last chapter focuses entirely on implementation.

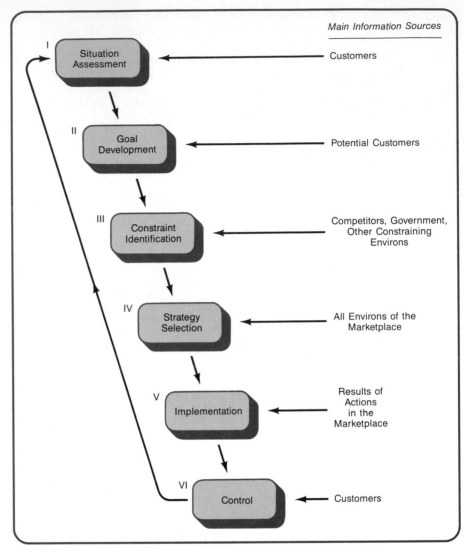

Main Information Sources

I — Situation Assessment	← Customers
II — Goal Development	← Potential Customers
III — Constraint Identification	← Competitors, Government, Other Constraining Environs
IV — Strategy Selection	← All Environs of the Marketplace
V — Implementation	← Results of Actions in the Marketplace
VI — Control	← Customers

**Figure 2-3 The Strategic Marketing Management Process
and Sources of Information**

Control is really a part of implementation. But it is also the connection
back to the first step, situation assessment. When you implement, everything
that can go wrong, will go wrong. To have control and make midcourse
corrections to reach your objectives, you once again assess your situation.

The Boston Consulting Group's Four-Celled
Share/Growth Matrix

Once the most widely used and one of the earliest implemented structured
approaches to strategic marketing management was the **four-celled share/
growth matrix**. It is a product portfolio analysis developed by Bruce Hen-

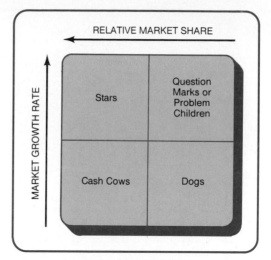

**Figure 2-4 Boston Consulting
Group's Four-Celled Share/Growth
Matrix**

derson of the **Boston Consulting Group** (BCG) back in 1960 and used first
by the Norton Company. This matrix, which is still important as the basis of
all structured methodologies, is shown in Figure 2-4.

Along the horizontal axis is **relative market share**. Relative market share
means market share measured by the ratio of the company's share of the
market to the share of its largest competitor. Along the vertical axis is **market
growth rate** measured in constant dollars, relative to **gross national product** (GNP) growth. Note that both the horizontal and the vertical axes increase toward the uppermost left corner of the matrix.

Strategic business units (SBUs)—that is, groups of businesses or groupings of products with some commonality in how they perform—are plotted
in each of the four quadrants, depending on relative market share and market
growth rate. SBUs are of like businesses or products that perform similarly
in the marketplace. Where each SBU falls implies different facts about an
SBU and different strategies. Those in the upper left quadrant are known as
"**stars**," the upper right quadrant as "**question marks**" or "**problem children**," the lower left quadrant as "**cash cows**," and the lower right quadrant
as "**dogs**." The objective of this approach to strategic marketing management
is to develop the best mix of products to maximize long-term earnings of the
firm and to allocate resources properly among these products to achieve these
ends.[15] Some typical strategies are summarized in Figure 2-5.

Stars: High Growth, High Relative Market Share. SBUs that fall in
the star quadrant are growing rapidly, but they also require continual expenditures to maintain their growth and expansion. Earning characteristics
of these SBUs can vary from the very low to high. However, because of the
requirement for capital to finance growth, cash flow is usually negative. An
appropriate strategy for a star is to continue to increase market share by
reinvesting earnings back into the SBU, even though this further limits short-
term profits.

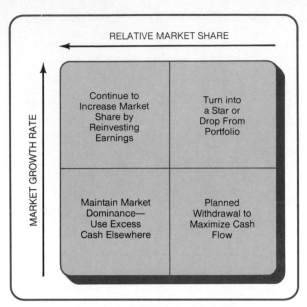

Figure 2-5 Boston Consulting Group's Four-Celled Share/Growth Matrix Typical Strategies

Cash Cows: Low Growth with High Relative Market Share. The cash cow SBUs tend to have high earning characteristics as well as a positive cash flow. They generally generate more cash than is required to maintain the market share held by the firm. The basic strategy implied here is to maintain market dominance until such time as additional investment becomes marginal.

Excess cash is not invested in this SBU but is used elsewhere for other SBUs—for example, to finance a star.

Question Marks or Problem Children: High Market Growth and Low Relative Market Share. These SBUs, like stars, tend to result in negative cash flow and require heavy initial expenditures and high R&D costs. In fact, the combination of rapid growth and poor profit margins results in a tremendous demand for cash, while earning characteristics are negative to low. Strategy here depends on the chances of dominating this segment. If the chances of dominating are good, the usual strategy is to go after and fight for this market share. If the chances are not so good, the company should consider withdrawing from this SBU or product grouping and allocating resources elsewhere.

Dogs: Low Market Growth Rate and Low Relative Market Share. Strangely, dogs have a positive cash flow and their earning characteristics may vary from high to low, but markets here are not growing. They are mature. There is little new business to win. Competitors who are dominating will fight to maintain their share because your dog is someone else's cash cow. Basic strategy recommended here is to plan a withdrawal in such a fashion as to maximize cash flow while doing it, although it is also possible to redefine the business to dominate a smaller or specialized segment of the market.

The theoretical basis for BCG's four-celled product portfolio matrix was that the greater your share of the market, the more units of a product you produce and therefore the farther along you are on your "**experience curve**" and the lower your cost of production. The experience curve idea grew out of the learning-curve concept first documented in the aerospace industry during World War II. It was found that as greater quantities of a product were manufactured (in this case an airplane), the cost of each unit decreased as workers learned better how to make the product and their productivity increased. This cost decrease could be represented by a predictable curve. BCG extended this assumption to include material as well as labor costs and called the new curve the experience curve.

Another obvious assumption was that the two most significant variables were earnings represented by current market share and the potential for growth represented by the growth rate of the market segment in which your business competes.

The Need for a Balanced Portfolio

It is extremely important when practicing strategic marketing management using a BCG matrix to strive for a **balanced portfolio** of products. That is, cash cows are positioned with stars to provide for maximum growth and for yielding high cash returns in the future as the stars become mature. At the same time, question marks or problem children are either supported or dropped, and dogs are managed or dropped in the most profitable fashion possible. It is clear that unbalanced portfolios are very dangerous.[16] For example:

1. Too many losers can result in inadequate cash flow, inadequate profits, and inadequate growth, or
2. Too many question marks can result in inadequate cash flow and inadequate profits, or
3. Too many profit producers may mean both an inadequate growth and an excessive cash flow, or
4. Too many developing winners may make excessive demands on finances, management, or other resources of the company and result in instability of both growth and profits.

Problems, Limitations, and Pitfalls with BCG's Product Portfolio Matrix

Although it is still used by many firms, the BCG matrix has limitations that must be thoroughly understood by the marketing manager. These include the fact that cost reductions through the experience curve aren't automatic but that an effort must be made to achieve this reduction. Furthermore, the fact is that situations exist where profit margins are not related to market share or when the experience curve does not yield a cost advantage. Also, there is no direct input for consideration of risk, government regulations, the firm's resources, or other important factors. And, considerable profits may be possible with a very small share of the market dominated by a specific firm.[17,18]

In fact, most firms cannot achieve market share preeminence, if for no other reason than the market leader usually competes with far greater resources. A victor in a head-to-head confrontation for market share by two nearly equal competitors can be truly Pyrrhic. The "winner" may wish that the battle had never been fought.[19] Finally, there is evidence that rate of return on equity building, rather than market share building, is the most profitable way to exploit cost advantages.[20]

The GE/McKinsey/Multifactor Portfolio Matrix

Partially because of limitations indicated for the BCG's product portfolio matrix, a nine-celled multifactor portfolio matrix was designed by General Electric working with McKinsey and Company to overcome some of the limitations of considering only market share and market growth in accomplishing strategic marketing management.

Note that the **GE/McKinsey multifactor matrix**, as shown in Figure 2-6, considers two broad categories. Across the horizontal axis is **industrial attractiveness** and along the vertical axis, **business strength**. Both, as with the BCG matrix, increase toward the upper left corner of the matrix. The general categories of industry attractiveness and business strength permit additional factors to be considered in positioning SBUs or product groupings in the matrix. For example, GE originally considered **size**, **market growth**, **pricing**, **market diversity**, and **competitive structure** as the major factors

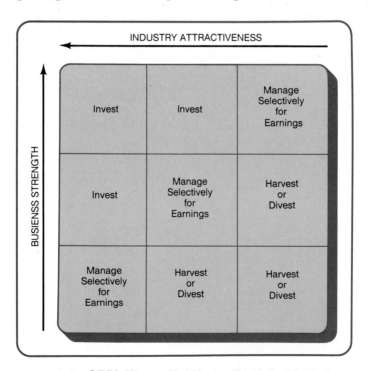

Figure 2-6 GE/McKinsey Multifactor Portfolio Matrix

to describe industry attractiveness and size, growth, share, position, profitability, margins, technology position, strength/weaknesses, image, pollution, and people as the major factors for business strength. However, a company can use different factors in either the business strength or industrial attractiveness category, depending on the situation. Note also that there are nine cells rather than four. Once again, SBUs falling in different cells imply different strategic actions. For example, in Figure 2-6, SBUs or product groupings falling in the upper left three cells define those that should be invested in for growth; those falling in the lower right three cells of the matrix are harvested or divested. This leaves three cells, starting from the upper right corner down to the lower left corner of the matrix. The general instructions for these three cells are to manage those SBUs selectively for earnings.

Procedures for Locating SBUs or Product Groupings on the GE/McKinsey Multifactor Portfolio Matrix

To locate SBUs in the matrix, it is first necessary to determine the values for both business strength and industrial attractiveness for each SBU. In both cases, relative importance weightings are used. Let's look at **business strength** first.

Calculating the Business Strength Criteria

Following is a list of factors that might be considered:

- Current market share
- SBU growth rate
- Sales effectiveness
- Proprietary nature of product
- Price competitiveness
- Advertising promotional effectiveness
- Facilities location or newness
- Productivity
- Experience curve effects
- Value added
- Raw materials cost
- Image
- Product quality
- R&D/technology advantages
- Engineering know-how
- Personnel resources
- Product synergies
- Profitability
- Return on investment
- Distribution

Other business-strength criteria might be added to this list, depending on the situation. Let's assume for our example that only the following four business-strength criteria are considered important: image, product synergy, productivity, and price competitiveness.

Business Strength Criteria	Relative Importance Weighting
Image	0.40
Productivity	0.30
Product synergy	0.15
Price competitiveness	0.15
	1.00

**Figure 2-7 Relative Importance Weightings
of Business Strength Criteria**

We must now establish the relative importance weightings for each of these four business-strength criteria. This is a subjective process in which we weigh the pros and cons and consider how important each of these factors is relative to the others. Let us assume that we do this and come up with weightings as shown in Figure 2-7. Note that image is most important with a relative weighting of 0.40, productivity is next in importance with a relative weighting of 0.30, and product synergies and price competitiveness each have a relative importance weighting of 0.15. Note that the total of all importance weightings must equal 1.00.

We must now rate each business-strength criterion for the particular SBU we are analyzing. To do this we will assign points depending on the strength of a business-strength criterion for that particular SBU. If the rating of the SBU in a particular criteria factor is judged very weak, we will assign 0 points. If it is weak, we will assign 3 points. If it is only fair, we will assign 4.5 points; strong, 7 points; and very strong, 9 points. Let us assume that we make this analysis for a specific SBU and that image is assigned 7 points, productivity is given 7 points, product synergies are given 3 points, and price competitiveness is given 4.5 points. To compute the total weight or rank for each business strength criteria, each weighting must be multiplied times a point value assigned, as shown in Figure 2-8. Note that the total weighted rank for business-strength criteria for this SBU is 6.825. In the same fashion, we must now calculate total weighted rank for industry attractiveness criteria for this SBU.

Business Strength Criteria	Relative Importance Weighting		Point Rating (points)		Weighted Rank
Image	0.40	×	9	=	3.6
Productivity	0.30	×	7	=	2.1
Product synergy	0.15	×	3	=	0.45
Price competitiveness	0.15	×	4.5	=	0.675
			Total weighted rank =		6.825

Figure 2-8 Computation of Weighted Rank for Business Strength

Calculating the Industrial Attractiveness Criteria

Once again we consider all relevant industry attractiveness criteria. Such a listing might include size of **market segment**, growth of market segment, market pricing, customer's financial condition, extent of demand, vulnerability to inflation, vulnerability to depression, need for the product, government regulation, raw materials availability, energy impact, ease of entry, life-cycle position of products, competitive structure, product liability, political considerations, and distribution structure.

Let's again assume that only four factors are relevant: size of market, growth of market, ease of entry, and favorable life-cycle position. Again we must determine the relative importance by assigning weights of relative importance. In this case we will assume that an analysis shows that the size of the market is most important, and we assign a weight of 0.30; growth of market is of equal importance at 0.30; ease of entry is of slightly less importance at 0.25; and favorable life-cycle position is at 0.15. Note again that these values must all equal unity, or 1.00. These criteria and their importance weightings are summarized in Figure 2.9.

Again we must assign point values, depending upon the attractiveness of the criteria for the SBU being analyzed. We will assign points as follows: for very unattractive industry attractiveness, 0 points; unattractive, 3 points; fair, 4.5 points; attractive, 7 points; and very attractive, 9 points.

Using this point system, we will assume that we have analyzed the SBU or product grouping and assign points as follows: size of market for this SBU, very attractive, 9 points; growth of the market, fair, 4.5 points; ease of entry, very attractive, 9 points; and favorable life-cycle position, very unattractive, or 0 points. The point assignment is multiplied times the relative importance weighting to find the weighted ranks. The ranks are added and found to equal 6.3 for industry attractiveness, as shown in Figure 2-10.

We now plot the two values for total weighted rank for business-strength criteria and industry-attractiveness criteria on the matrix in Figure 2-11 at coordinates business strength = 6.825 and industry attractiveness = 6.3. Note that the SBU falls in the uppermost left cell, a cell that suggests we should invest in this SBU as a strategic move. We now take all the other SBUs that we intend to analyze for our company, and, keeping the relative importance weightings that we have already assigned, we assign appropriate point values to plot them in this matrix as well. After we have accomplished this, guidance as to the strategic efforts necessary for every SBU is clearly

Industry Attractiveness Criteria	Relative Importance Weighting
Size of market	0.30
Growth of market	0.30
Ease of entry	0.25
Favorable life-cycle position	0.15
	1.00

Figure 2-9   Relative Importance Weightings of Industrial Attractiveness Criteria

Industry Attractiveness Criteria	Relative Importance Weighting		Point Rating (points)		Weighted Rank
Size of market	0.30	×	9	=	2.7
Growth of market	0.30	×	4.5	=	1.35
Ease of entry	0.25	×	9	=	2.25
Favorable life-cycle position	0.15	×	0	=	0
			Total weighted rank	=	6.30

Figure 2-10   Computation of Weighted Rank for Industry Attractiveness

and graphically shown in the matrix. This has been accomplished for SBUs 2 through 6, as indicated in Figure 2-11. Note that the size of the circle can be used to represent the size of the market.

The Directional Policy Matrix

The **directional policy matrix** is yet another refinement of the matrix system of strategic marketing management. The directional policy matrix, as shown

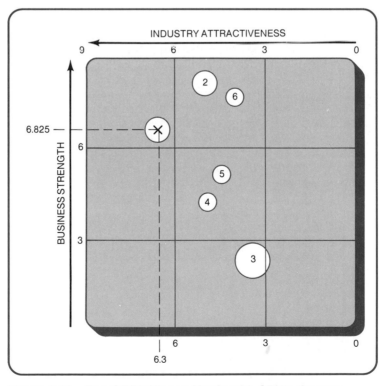

Figure 2-11   The GE/McKinsey Matrix with SBU's Plotted

in Figure 2-12, also has nine cells. Along the horizontal axis are business sector prospects, and along the vertical axis are the company's competitive capabilities. However, note that, unlike the two previous matrices discussed, business sector prospects increase from unattractive to attractive from left to right, and company competitive capabilities increase from weak to strong from top to bottom. Thus, unlike the other two matrices, values increase toward the lower right-hand corner of the matrix. Again, location of an SBU in any cell of the matrix implies different strategic actions. However, zones covered by various actions are not precisely defined by the cell division, and it has been noted that experience has shown that the zones are of irregular shape; they do not have hard-and-fast boundaries but shade into one another and in some cases overlap. Descriptors for strategies for each zone follow:

- Leader—allocate major resources to the SBU.
- Try harder—okay for the short term but may be vulnerable over a longer period of time.
- Double or quit—collect major SBUs for the future from this zone.
- Growth—allocate sufficient resources to grow with the market.
- Custodial—maximize cash generation without further commitment of resources.
- Cash generator—a cash generator with little further need for finance or expansion.

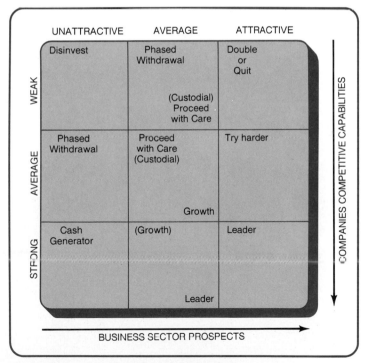

Figure 2-12 The Directional Policy Matrix

Source: Adapted from S. J. Q. Robinson, R. E. Hichens, and D. P. Wade, "The Directional Policy Matrix—Tool for Strategic Planning," *Long Range Planning Journal*, vol. 2 (June 1978), p. 12.

- Phased withdrawal—put resources to better use as company withdraws from this business.
- Divest—get rid of assets as rapidly as possible and redeploy.[21]

Financial Models for Strategic Marketing Management

The previous models have been shown to have various weaknesses, but none more obvious than that they are not directly linked to corporate financial goals and that the strategic recommendations implicit in the location in the matrix are not specific enough. To alleviate these problems, structures based on corporate financial goals have been developed. An example is the Sheth-Frazier margin return model.[22] This model is based on the fact that the two most common financial goals for all for-profit corporations are net profit margin and return on investment. Therefore, using these corporate goals, a matrix is constructed as in Figure 2-13.

Across the horizontal axis of the matrix is **targeted return**; on the vertical axis, **targeted margin**. Both increase toward the upper left quadrant of the four-cell matrix. In each cell are found two alternate objectives, and for each objective two different strategies that can be used to attain the objective indicated. For example, SBUs falling in quadrant 1 are offered either a **market entrenchment objective** or a **market expansion objective**. Furthermore, for **market extension**, two specific marketing strategies are noted: (1) a **share protection strategy** and (2) a **repositioning strategy**. Users are advised that a firm should seek objectives and follow strategies for the quadrant in which it is located. However, in cases where the firm is in danger of

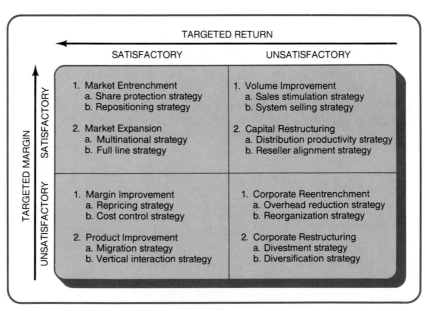

Figure 2-13 The Sheth-Frazier Margin-Return Model

Source: Adapted from Jagdish N. Sheth and Gary Frazier, "A Margin-Return Model for Strategic Marketing Planning," *Journal of Marketing*, vol. 47 (Spring 1983), p. 102.

moving into a less desirable position in the matrix, a preempting strategy is advised.

Technology Portfolio

One of the more innovative structured means of strategic planning is based on the impact of technological change. A Technology Portfolio serves as a model for technological resource allocation and as an aid in choosing an optimal set of technologies from a set of feasible alternatives.

Figure 2-14 is one formulation of the Technology Portfolio. It has eight cells. The upper half represents premarket conditions and the lower half postmarket; the vertical axis is a time dimension. From top to bottom, this represents the life cycle of a product: research, development, high growth, and low growth. The horizontal axis represents the relative technological strength of the firm in the premarket phase and the relative market share in the postmarket stage.

Each circle in the matrix represents a technology, and the size of the circle reflects the relative resource flow associated with that technology. The circles in the postmarket phase are partially shaded. The shaded portion represents a cash user, and the unshaded portion a cash generator. For that reason, in the premarket phase all of the circle is shaded.

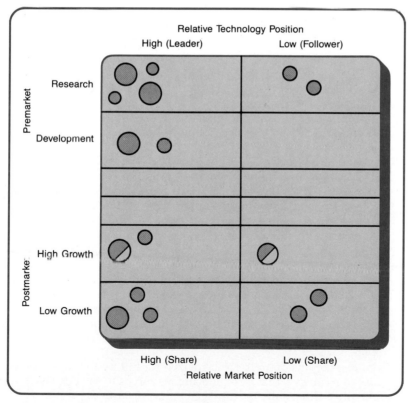

Figure 2-14 The Technology Portfolio

Source: Adapted from Noel Capron and Rashi Glazer, "Marketing and Technology: A Strategic Coalignment," *Journal of Marketing*, vol. 51, no. 3 (July 1987), pp. 10–11.

The matrix is a representation of how a firm's resources are distributed among its mix of technologies and where they stand relative to development, exploitation, and competitive strength. Heavy concentrations of large circles in any part of the matrix imply a negative flow of resources, which may be impossible to sustain regardless of opportunity. For most firms, a balanced portfolio in terms of circle distribution and size (as in Figure 2-14) is desirable.[23]

Limitations and Cautionary Notes for the Structural Methods of Strategic Marketing Management

Marketing manager practitioners of strategic marketing management should be aware that there are limitations and cautionary notes that should be observed when using the structural methods discussed previously. Here are some of the more important ones to consider:

1. Weightings of factors are subjective and highly judgmental.[24] Both the choice as to which factors would be applicable for use in any given situation, as well as the relative importance of each, are selected in a subjective fashion by the strategies and, therefore, depend highly on a manager's experience and talents for making these judgments.

2. Different SBUs may actually require different relative-importance weightings. Once the importance weightings are selected in the nine-celled methodologies, it is assumed that these factors, as well as the relative importances, are the same; subsequently, all SBUs are analyzed according to these same factors. In reality, different SBUs may not require the same factors, or they may not be of the same relative importance. For example, with one SBU, competitive structure may be absolutely critical. In another product grouping from the same firm, competitive structure may not be so important at all. Yet both must be assumed to have the same relative importance for this criterion in this type of analysis.

3. Cell performance is not precise. As pointed out with the directional policy matrix, there are many overlappings, and the simple definition of the cell and its assumed square shape may not be correct at all. Yet, for all but the directional policy matrix, this shape is assumed to be square and location within that cell to imply a certain strategy.

4. Assumptions in forming the SBU may not be valid.[25] To develop a workable number of SBUs or product groupings in a company with many different businesses or products, it is necessary to make assumptions to treat these products or businesses alike, to form a single product grouping, or SBU. However, such assumptions may not always be valid, and this can result in inaccuracies regarding implied strategies that may be used.

Financial models may also be criticized for failure to focus on the ultimate purpose of strategy—that is, to allocate resources to the decisive point where a competitive differential advantage can be sustained.

A major problem with strategic planning and strategic marketing management in the past has been a disconnection between those who did the planning and the line managers who were required to implement the plan. Many companies, especially larger ones, tended to form planning organizations, whose sole responsibility was to plan. Ownership of the plans was rarely shared by the marketers, whose responsibility it was to implement them. This might have been predicted. Studies have proved that shared organizational values can play a crucial role when it comes to implementing strategies.[26]

Japanese who became involved in U. S. operations were at times amazed: "I don't understand American management. The strategic planning department has developed a strategy that is a very thick book. No one has read it. No one seems to care. How can the company succeed without everyone working toward the same goals? Our president has not yet captured the minds of the managers. In Japan, we try hard to have everyone, on every level, discuss, understand, contribute, and be committed to a strategy."[27]

Some companies "solved" the problem by ceasing to do strategic planning. More thoughtful executives integrated the CEO and line managers directly in the planning process.[28] In this way the planning departments became facilitators for developing a plan to which implementors had agreed.

Researchers discovered that strategic planning and strategy formulation aren't sterile processes that can be carried out in isolation. They involve communication factors, political factors, and personal factors.[29] However, if done right, strategic planning can lead to self-reflective learning instead of a self-perpetuating bureaucratic system that produces "a thick book no one reads."[30]

Implementation Issues

Even after these limitations have been accepted in the analysis itself, there are limitations due to implementation that must be considered. As pointed out by one researcher, greater attention should be given, to the following types of implementation problems.

1. Balancing short-run, program-related measures with longer-term performance criteria.
2. Achieving synergy between different elements of the marketing mix.
3. Developing appropriate criteria for assessing performance within market segments.
4. Developing appropriate criteria for allocating resources among market segments.
5. Implementing product market decisions within the broader framework of business-level considerations of strategic marketing management.[31]

Notwithstanding the limitations, structured methods of strategic marketing management should not be summarily dismissed by the marketing manager. First, the corporation in which the marketing manager is employed may be using certain methods that, while not ideal, are those to which top management are accustomed. Corporate policy may require their use. Therefore, the practicing marketing manager must understand their use and development to present an analysis to his or her superiors, whether he or she relies primarily on these methods for making judgments for strategy or not. As noted by strategist Michael Porter, "The question is not whether a company has a strategy or not. Every company has one. It exists whether it's explicit or is something that just happened."[32]

Second, various combinations of the different structured methods can be chosen to minimize their disadvantages—for example, a combination of financial as well as portfolio methods. Finally, as Robin Wensley notes, an assessment can be made independent of the cell classification, and the structured method of the cells be used merely to help in supplying information to develop strategy.[33]

Regardless of the limitations, structured methods for strategic marketing management are far better than simply a gut feeling with no support or selecting certain strategic objectives or certain strategies at the top management level of a company simply because there was a full moon the night before or because various decision makers were feeling well or poorly at the time a strategy was articulated.

Summary

In this chapter we've looked at the concept of strategic marketing management—that is, managing a business unit to anticipate and respond to changes that affect the marketplace such that decisions made today allow the unit to be ready for tomorrow, to avoid the threats, and to take advantage of the opportunities. The characteristics of strategic marketing management also were discussed, including looking beyond the immediate issues; designing for the future; and developing specific decisions and actions, top management level of involvement, holistic perspectives, flexibility, and proactiveness. We have seen how strategic marketing management fits with marketing strategy and tactics. We have looked at the various methods of developing strategies at the corporate level, including the Boston Consulting Group and GE/McKinsey matrices, the directional policy matrix, financial methods such as the Sheth/Frazier margin return model, and even a technological portfolio. Finally, we have seen that, while there are limitations both conceptually and in implementation, structured methods are not only useful, but knowledge of them for strategic marketing management may be essential for corporate success in marketing.

Questions

1. Robert E. Wood, former CEO of Sears, Roebuck, stated that strategy is more important than tactics. Why should this be so? Give specific examples.

2. Why does a middle-management marketing manager have to know anything about top-management issues such as strategic marketing management? What advantages do you see for educating middle management about strategic marketing management processes and procedures? Are there any disadvantages?

3. What examples can you recall of major marketing campaigns that failed, even though tactically the marketing operations of the firm in the campaigns may have been successful?

4. Can strategy ever be developed or selected without assessing the situation, without selecting goals or objectives, without identifying constraints? Explain your answers.

5. Your company has four product groupings. One falls squarely in the middle of each one of the four cells of the BCG product portfolio matrix. Explain

the situation for each product, as well as the strategy implications.

6. You are vice-president of a small company that has exactly ten different products. Should you group them into product groupings or position each separately in one of the portfolio matrix structures? On what criteria will you base your decision?

7. You decide to use both the BCG four-celled matrix and the GE/McKinsey multifactor matrix to check your strategy implications. One of your product groupings falls in the cell designating it a "star" in the BCG matrix, but in the extreme lower-right-hand corner cell indicating "divest" in the GE/McKinsey matrix. Is this possible without an error on your part? What does this mean?

8. Financial models of strategic marketing management have been criticized for their failure to focus on a differential competitive advantage. Is this a valid criticism? Why can we not simply allocate our resources based on relative potential return on investment, for example?

9. Discuss each of the limitations of the structured methods of strategic marketing management and explain how you would minimize each limitation.

10. Inasmuch as conditions are changing daily and all strategy selection is based first on an assessment of the environment, how frequently should you make this reassessment and how frequently should strategy be changed?

Ethical Question

You are vice-president of marketing. You receive two analyses that you requested from your staff regarding product areas to pursue for the future. One analysis that you have never used before shows that a "pet" SBU of yours should be dropped. The type of analysis that you usually use says to continue with this SBU. Your boss, the president of the company, makes the final decision based on your recommendations and the analyses you show him. In the past, you have only used the single analysis that shows your company should continue with this SBU. Should you show the analysis that indicated you should drop this product to your boss?

Endnotes

1. James Braham, "The Billion-Dollar Dustpan," *Industry Week*, vol. 237, no. 3 (August 1, 1988), pp. 46–47.

2. "Avon Tries a New Formula to Restore Its Glow," *Business Week* (July 2, 1984), p. 46.

3. Derek F. Abell, "Strategic Windows," *Journal of Marketing*, vol. 42 (July 1978), p. 21.

4. Ian H. Wilson, William R. George, and Paul J. Solomon, "Strategic Planning for Marketers," *Journal of Marketing*, vol. 41 (April 1977), p. 12.

5. Brian Bremner and Gail DeGeorge, "The Burger Wars Were Just a Warm-up for McDonald's," *Business Week* (May 8, 1989), p. 67.

6. Harper W. Boyd, Jr., and Jean-Claude Larreche, "The Foundations of Marketing Strategy," in G. Zaltman and T. Bonoma, eds., *Review of Marketing* (Chicago: AMA, 1978), pp. 41–72.

7. The fact of the commingling of the borders between different strategy levels was suggested by a handout for a course on Joint and Combined Warfare taught at the Industrial College of the Armed Forces, National Defense University, Washington, D.C., by Col. James A. Velezis, U.S. Army, in 1988.

8. Yoram Wind and Thomas S. Robertson, "Marketing Strategy: New Directions for Theory and Research," *Journal of Marketing*, vol. 47 (Spring 1983), p. 12.

9. Robert E. Wood, quoted in A. D. Chandler, Jr., *Strategy and Structure* (Cambridge, Mass.: MIT Press, 1962), p. 235.

10. Michael E. Porter, "From Competitive Advantage to Corporate Strategy." *Harvard Business Review*, vol. 65. (May–June 1987), p. 43.

11. Daniel J. Isenberg, "The Tactics of Strategic Opportunism," *Harvard Business Review*, vol. 65, no. 2 (March–April 1987), p. 93.

12. Ronald L. Zallocco, Donald W. Scotton, and David A. Jeresko, "Strategic Market Planning in the Commercial Airline Industry." *Journal of the Academy of Marketing Science*, vol. 11 (Fall 1983), p. 404.

13. Abell, op. cit., pp. 21–22.

14. William R. King and David I. Cleland, "Environ-

mental Information Systems for Strategic Marketing Planning," *Journal of Marketing*, vol. 38 (October 1974), p. 36.

15. P. Rajan Varadarajan, "Product Portfolio Analysis and Market Share Objectives: An Exposition of Certain Underlying Relationships," *Journal of the Academy of Marketing Science*, vol. 18, no. 1 (Winter 1990), p. 17.

16. George S. Day, "Diagnosing the Product Portfolio," *Journal of Marketing*, vol. 41 (April 1977), p. 29.

17. Ibid., pp. 35–36.

18. Carolyn Y. Woo and Arnold C. Cooper, "The Surprising Case for Low Market Share," *Harvard Business Review*, vol. 60 (November–December 1982), p. 107.

19. William L. Shanklin, "Market Share Is Not Destiny," *Journal of Consumer Marketing*, vol. 5, no. 4 (Fall 1988), pp. 8–9.

20. William W. Alberts, "The Experience Curve Doctrine Reconsidered," *Journal of Marketing*, vol. 53, no. 3 (July 1989), pp. 36–47.

21. S. J. Q. Robinson, R. E. Hichens, and D. P. Wade, "The Directional Policy Matrix—Tool for Strategic Planning," *Long Range Planning Journal*, vol. 11 (June 1978), pp. 8–15.

22. Jagdish N. Sheth and Gary L. Frazier, "A Margin-Return Model for Strategic Marketing Planning," *Journal of Marketing*, vol. 47 (Spring 1983), p. 102.

23. Noel Capron and Rashi Glazer, "Marketing and Technology: A Strategic Coalignment," *Journal of Marketing*, vol. 51, no. 3 (July 1987), pp. 10–11.

24. Robin Wensley, "Strategic Marketing: Betas, Boxes or Basics," *Journal of Marketing*, vol. 45 (Summer 1981), p. 179.

25. Ravi Singh Achrol and David L. Appel, "New Developments in Corporate Strategy Planning," in Patrick E. Murphy et al., eds., *1983 AMA Educators' Proceedings* (Chicago: AMA, 1983), p. 306.

26. Gordon J. Badovik and Sharon E. Beatty, "Shared Organizational Values: Measurement and Impact Upon Strategic Marketing Implementation," *Journal of the Academy of Marketing Science*, vol. 15, no. 1 (Spring 1987), p. 25.

27. Thomas Gross and John L. Neuman, "New CEOs Steer by Yielding the Wheel," *Marketing News*, vol. 23, no. 11 (May 22, 1989), p. 19.

28. Thomas Gross and John L. Neuman, "Winning CEOs Participate Rather Than Preempt," *Marketing News*, vol. 23, no. 12 (June 5, 1989), p. 15.

29. Stephen J. S. Holden, "The Nature of Strategy Formulation," in Paul Bloom et. al., eds. *1989 AMA Educators' Proceedings: Enhancing Knowledge Development in Marketing* (Chicago: AMA, 1989), p. 118.

30. R. T. Lenz, "Managing the Evolution of the Strategic Planning Process," *Business Horizons*, vol. 30, no. 1 (January–February 1987), pp. 34–39.

31. Robert E. Spekman, "Insights on Implementation: A Conceptual Framework for Better Understanding the Strategic Marketing Planning Process," in Patrick E. Murphy et al., eds., *1983 AMA Educators' Proceedings* (Chicago: AMA, 1983), p. 314.

32. Don Wallace, "Strategy," *Success*, vol. 36, no. 5 (June 1989), p. 32.

33. Wensley, op. cit., p. 181.

3

The Marketing Plan and Planning Process

CHAPTER OBJECTIVES

- Understand the importance of the marketing plan to the organization using marketing.
- Know the benefits and uses of the marketing plan for the marketing manager.
- Know the contents and structure of the marketing plan.
- Be able to develop a marketing plan.

Scuttling the Marketing Plan That Makes Pip a Success

Pip Printing was the undisputed market leader in the fast printing industry. A powerhouse marketing plan allowed its 1,169 franchise stores to rack up $250 million in sales a year. Not any more. President Tom Marotto is dropping the successful plan to implement a new marketing plan. Why? Although the market leader, Pip owns just 5 per cent of the market. There are some 24,000 competitors and price cutting for printing is rampant. So Marotto is introducing a new plan to target a higher-level customer. At the high end are commercial printers that print annual reports and other four-color reports. At the low end are the duplicators. According to Marotto, "The customer was lumping us in the low end. He didn't know that most of our shops had the ability to do two-color work—things like flyers, invoices, training manuals. In fact, there are only about 20 per cent of printing jobs that we can't do." Pip's new marketing plan would reposition it as the world's largest business printer. It includes allocating sophisticated and more expensive equipment for its franchisees, as well as training and advertising during prime time, not to mention new store layouts. It's not certain whether Pip will succeed or not. But it's certain that, as in the past, it can only be successful with a well thought through and executed marketing plan.[1]

Clorox Cleans Up with a Plan

Not too long ago, the Clorox Company hit $1 billion in sales, but profits were only $34.6 million. A year later half the company's revenue disappeared with the sale of a major division. Six years later Clorox once again hit $1 billion in sales, but this time profits were doubled. What made the difference? Analysts noted considerable internal growth through new product development, especially in household grocery products. As evidence of this, an estimated $20 million was spent on R&D alone, resulting in many new products, including Tilex mildew remover; bottled versions of its Hidden Valley Ranch dry salad dressing mixes; Fresh Step, a cat litter with microencapsulated deodorant fragrance released when the cat steps into the box; and a liquid bleach with a fragrance. But all this R&D activity was orchestrated; it resulted from the coordinated efforts due, as one analyst noted, to a "game plan."[2]

We call such game plans "marketing plans." A marketing plan can make the difference, and not just for big business. Graduate student Leon Ashjian, at California State University Los Angeles, developed a marketing plan for a business directory for the Los Angeles area listing only businesses owned by Armenians. He followed the identical concepts found in this chapter. Before he could implement the plan, he was offered $5,000 for it by another entrepreneur. University of Southern California student Robert Schwartz was written up in *Entrepreneur* magazine while still an undergraduate. He started a million-dollar chain of pizza restaurants. The basis of his success was also a marketing plan, and the concepts are explained in this chapter.[3]

Marketing Planning ———————————

Why Marketing Planning Is Necessary

Marketing planning is needed because top management time and talent, as well as money and other company resources, are always in short supply. A marketing plan saves this time and these important resources by making it unnecessary for many hours, days, or weeks to be wasted on daily short-range, firefighting-type decisions. But firms that fail to develop and use marketing plans lose far more. It is much more difficult for them to take advantage of opportunities compatible with the firm's resources. As a result, changing environments lead to missed opportunities and frequently threats build to crises that cannot be avoided or overcome other than by wasteful "firefighting." Sometimes they cannot be overcome at all.

Less tangible benefits of marketing planning that are also important include

1. Systematic futuristic thinking by management.
2. Better coordination of company efforts.
3. Development of performance standards for control.
4. Sharpening of objectives and policies.
5. Better preparedness for sudden new developments.
6. A more vivid sense by the participating executives of their interacting responsibilities.[4,5]

Objectives of the Marketing Plan

The marketing plan itself has certain objectives that will be achieved if the plan is prepared properly. All marketing plans should accomplish the following:

44

1. *Act as a roadmap.* A marketing plan should act as a roadmap and tell management how to get from the point of initiation of the plan to reach the plan's objectives and goals. Like a roadmap, the plan must describe the environment in which the company will find itself along the way. A roadmap might describe terrain and the class and types of roads, as well as times, distances, and emergency stops for gasoline, food, car repairs, or lodging. A marketing plan will describe the varying environs of the marketplace, including the company and its competitors; neutral environs with which the company must contend, including the government, media, and special-interest and financial institutions; and the situational environs, including politics, laws and regulations, economic and business conditions, state of technology, demand, social and cultural factors, and demographics.

2. *Assist in management control and monitoring the implementation of strategy.* Every time an airplane flies outside the local area from where it is based, a pilot is required to prepare and file a flight plan with federal aviation authorities. A flight plan lists the distances, fuel, and the time between important points along the flight path, as well as emergency airfields, identifiers of different navigational aids, radio call signs, weather forecasts, and so forth. This information permits a continuing monitoring of changing environmental conditions during the flight. Thus, if headwinds are greater than anticipated, a glance at the flight plan can be used to tell the pilot whether sufficient fuel exists to arrive at the destination planned or whether the flight must be cut short and a landing made at an alternate destination. Similarly, if some other environmental change occurs or an emergency occurs during the flight, use of the flight plan will immediately indicate the pilot's available options, and a decision can be made more easily and rapidly. In the same fashion, a marketing plan assists a marketing manager in management control and allows better decisions to be made and to be made much more quickly than would otherwise be the case.

3. *Inform new participants in the plan of their role and function.* Marketing plans describe the use of resources, and while these resources may be things or money, they are primarily human resources and have to do with people. In most cases, all individuals involved in the marketing plan should be familiar with the plan in its entirety. In other situations, because of the nature of the plan and security, individuals should only have access to the portions of the plan that apply to their activities and what they are required to do. But in all cases, individuals being assigned to activities involving the plan must be brought up to date on what it is that they are responsible for, what actions they will be required to take, and how what they do will fit in with everyone else's actions. The marketing plan permits informing all these participants about what the objectives of the marketing plan are and exactly how they will be accomplished.

4. *To obtain resources for implementation.* The implementation of any marketing strategy requires a firm to allocate resources to its accomplishment. As noted earlier, these resources may be dollars, executive time, or allocation of materials and capital equipment. In any case, resources are not unlimited, and this is true regardless of whether you are working in a small, one-person company or a major corporation. Therefore, resources are not automatically allocated, and whether you are an entre-

preneur trying to get resources from a lending institution or are part of a marketing team trying to get resources for implementing your marketing plan from top management, those who have the authority to allocate the resources must be convinced that you are going to allocate them in the most effective and efficient manner. A marketing plan is the sales vehicle that will assist you in persuading those individuals having authority over allocation of resources of your planned efficient and effective use of them.

5. *To stimulate thinking and make better use of resources.* Strategy in marketing depends on utilizing and building on your strengths and making your weaknesses irrelevant. In this way you can attain a sustained differential advantage at the decisive point in your campaign. That leads to success. As you develop a marketing plan, thinking is stimulated; as the plan unfolds, it is changed and modified as new ideas are generated. As a result, the strategy and the tactics necessary to reach the objectives and goals of the marketing plan are continually improved as the plan develops.

6. *Assignment of responsibilities, tasks, and timing.* Any marketing plan is only as good as those who must implement it. Therefore, it is absolutely crucial that the responsibilities of everyone be indicated and that tasks be thoroughly understood by all individuals who have roles to play in implementation. Furthermore, these actions must be scheduled so that the overall plan is executed in a coordinated fashion to maximize the impact of the strategy, while taking full recognition of the environs of the marketplace. There is an old adage that "if everyone is responsible for accomplishing any task, then no one is responsible." In other words, there is great likelihood that the task will not be accomplished or at least not be accomplished with the proper timing and coordination. The marketing plan assures that every task has an assigned individual who is responsible, and the timing and scheduling are coordinated to maximize the effectiveness of what is done.

7. *Awareness of problems, opportunities, and threats.* The very construction of a marketing plan requires an investigation into the environs in such a fashion that problems, opportunities, and threats are precisely identified. So the more you plan as the plan develops, the more you understand the nature of the problems, opportunities, and threats and what can be done about them. In no case should you ignore problems, opportunities, or threats; rather, construct the marketing plan and, if necessary, modify it during its development to take advantage of the opportunities, solve the problems, and, if possible, avoid or overcome the threats.[6]

All Marketing Managers Must Master Marketing Planning

Knowledge of marketing plans is not an option for marketing managers. It is a requirement. Every marketing manager must not only understand and have a working knowledge of marketing plans, he or she must be able to develop and implement them. Studies by many researchers have shown that coordinating plans and strategies is the hallmark of excellence in the multinational company[7] and that the development of an annual marketing plan is perhaps the single most important activity for a marketing or product manager.[8] Furthermore, the marketing plan cannot be delegated to someone else. The responsibility for the marketing plan belongs to whoever is in charge of the marketing activities concerned.[9] Theodore Levitt of the Harvard Business School states that because product-line planning is so important to a company's future, a CEO has a particular responsibility to expect that the marketing department will inform him or her with both data and advice.[10] This process is made possible through the vehicle of the marketing plan.

Criticisms of Marketing Planning

Notwithstanding the fact of the advantages and the critical essentiality of marketing plans, there have been criticisms of formal marketing planning. A marketing manager should understand these criticisms and their validity for his or her particular situation and company so as to eliminate them or minimize their effect.

1. A formal plan put together once a year can be quickly overtaken by events. This means that plans must be reviewed not only periodically but also as the environs of the marketplace change. As marketing consultant Lloyd H. Bakan of Marina del Rey reports: "Marketing programs and practices can become so set in concrete that they do not adequately respond to the changing marketplace. Methods that have always 'worked' in the past don't always continue to do so. A stagnant growth pattern over time is an indication that all is not well."[11]

2. Elements of the plan may be kept secret from those who are affected by it with no reason. For example, if resources are allocated to one department, this means that they must by necessity be lessened in another. To the maximum extent possible, all individuals affected by a marketing plan should be integrated into the planning process. They should be informed early about the implications of the planning and about the reasons why different elements of the plan and resources have been allocated. To pull off one of the great marketing turnarounds, Harley-Davidson, the motorcycle company, made some major changes in the way it did its planning. Emphasizing the process of employee involvement, which affected all operations at Harley, CEO Richard Teerlink said, "It's the process by which you run the business."

3. There is a gulf between the designers of the plan who are staff and the line managers who have to implement it. As noted earlier, the individual in charge of a marketing operation—that is, a line manager—is the one responsible for the marketing plan. The line marketing manager must ensure that planning done by staff is integrated with the input of all line managers who are affected by the plan. The plan should not be a product only of the staff, but rather a product of both line and staff working together, with the final responsibility belonging to the line marketing manager who heads the project.

4. A plan should not merely be a descriptive document but a scheme of actions and decisions that are carried out to achieve precise objectives.

5. Essential marketing information may be lacking to make decisions about the future. Considering the time available for construction of the plan, market research and marketing information systems should be utilized to their fullest for obtaining information. But when all else fails,

logical assumptions should be made and stated clearly. Then, if necessary, the plan can be altered and modified if the basic assumptions prove inaccurate.

6. Implementation must be properly controlled by management throughout the life of the plan. If implementation is not controlled by management, the plan is worthless. In fact, it can have a negative impact on a company's marketing activities or operations because some parts of the plan will be followed and objectives achieved, and others not. Marketing plans can always be modified as required as the environs change, but a plan must be closely monitored and controlled throughout its implementation to be successful.[13,14]

Marketing Plans: Costs and Benefits

There are costs associated with marketing plans and planning. These include the time that must be devoted to planning, as well as money in the form of planners' salaries. But, as you can see very dramatically in Figure 3-1, the benefits far outweigh the costs.

Types of Marketing Plans

Marketing plans tend to fall into two general categories: (1) strategic plans, as discussed in the previous chapter, which tend to be done by the company's

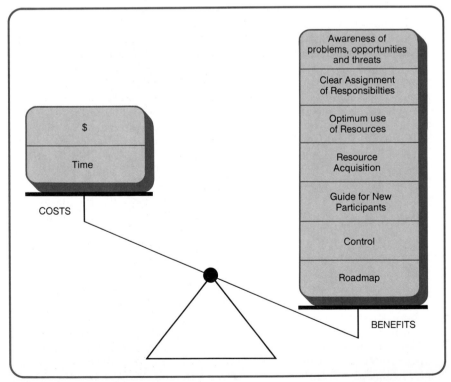

Figure 3-1   The Benefits Outweigh the Costs of Marketing Planning

top management, and (2) operational plans, which tend to be done by marketing organizations. **Operational plans** are further divided into two different types: (1) the **new product plan** and (2) the **annual plan**.

The New Product Plan

The new product plan is for a product, product line, or service that has not yet been introduced by the firm. Many companies require the development of a complete new product plan even before the product has been developed. In such a way alternate candidates for development can be compared at an early stage and a decision made as to which are more suitable for full development. The marketing plan for a new product or new service will generally have more unknowns than that of an annual plan because actual feedback from the marketplace is not yet available in most cases. However, frequently, logical assumptions can be made from similar products or services that the company has marketed, or products or services marketed by other companies from which information may be available. A marketing plan for a new product or new service may also include product development. Other companies will separate development from marketing and the marketing plan will include only those elements having to do with actual sales of the product.

Annual Marketing Plans

Annual marketing plans are for products, product lines, or services that are already established as a part of a company's product line. Periodic planning requires a look into the future in a formalized fashion. The advantages were mentioned previously: identifying opportunities, problems, and threats that otherwise might be missed in the day-to-day handling of crises associated with an ongoing product line or service. Here again, because the plan is for the future, there will be various unknowns, unknowns for which information must be forecast or in some cases assumed. Generally, annual planning is for a one-year period only, although some companies plan for several years at a time and then revise their plans annually.

The Contents and Structure
of the Marketing Plan

There are many different structures that may be used to format a marketing plan. One such structure is shown in Figure 3-2. Although structures tend to vary somewhat, depending upon the situation, the industry, and other factors, certain items are common to most. These include an executive summary, table of contents, a situational analysis, designation of marketing objectives, marketing strategies, marketing tactics, schedules of budgets, financial data, and evaluation and control methodology. Let's look at each in turn.

Executive Summary (Overview of entire plan, including a description of the product or service, the differential advantage, the required investment, and anticipated sales and profits).

Table of Contents

I. Introduction. (What is the product and why will you be successful with it at this time?)

II. Situation Analysis
   1. The Situational Environ
      A. Demand and demand trends. (What is the forecast demand for the product? Is it growing or declining? Who is the decision maker, the purchase agent? How, when, where, what, and why do they buy?)
      B. Social and cultural factors.
      C. Demographics.
      D. Economic and business conditions for this product at this time in the geographical area selected.
      E. State of technology for this class of product. Is it high-tech state of the art? Are newer products succeeding older ones frequently (very short life cycle)? In short, how is technology affecting this product or service?
      F. Politics. Is politics (current or otherwise) in any way affecting the situation for marketing this product?
      G. Laws and regulations. (What laws or regulations are applicable here?)
   2. The Neutral Environ
      A. Financial environs. (How does the availability or nonavailability of funds affect the situation?)
      B. Government environs. (Will legislative action or anything else currently going on in state, federal, or local government be likely to affect marketing of this product or service?)
      C. Media environs. (What's happening in the media? Does current publicity favor or disfavor this project?)
      D. Special interest environs. (Aside from direct competitors, are any influential groups likely to affect your plans?)
   3. The Competitor Environ
      A. Describe your main competitors and their products, plans, experience, know-how, financial, human and capital resources, suppliers, and strategy. (Do they enjoy any favor or disfavor with the customer? If so, why? What marketing channels do competitors use? What are your competitors' strengths and weaknesses?)
   4. The Company Environ
      A. Describe your product, experience, know-how, financial, human and capital resources, suppliers, etc. (Do you enjoy any favor or disfavor with the customer? If so, why? What are your strengths and weaknesses?)

Figure 3-2　Marketing Plan Outline

III. The Target Market
1. Describe your target market segment in detail using demographics, psychographics, geographics, life style, or whatever segmentation is appropriate. (Why is this your target market and not some other segment?)
IV. Problems and Opportunities
1. State or restate each opportunity and indicate why it is in fact an opportunity. State or restate every problem and indicate what you intend to do about each problem.
V. Marketing Objectives and Goals
1. Precisely state marketing objectives in terms of sales volume, market share, return on investment, or other objectives for your marketing plan.
VI. Marketing Strategy
1. Consider alternatives for overall strategy. Further describe your strategy as to whether you are using product differentiation, market segmentation, or positioning, etc., and how you are employing these strategies. Note what your main competitors are likely to do when you implement this strategy and what you will do to take advantage of the opportunities created and avoid the threats.
VII. Marketing Tactics
1. State how you will implement the marketing strategy(ies) chosen in terms of product, price, promotion, distribution, and other tactical or environmental variables.
VIII. Control and Implementation
1. Calculate break-even and accomplish a break-even chart for your project. Compute sales projections on a monthly basis for a three-year period. Compute cash flows on a monthly basis for a three-year period. Indicate start-up costs and monthly budget for this period.
IX. Summary
1. Summarize advantages, costs, and profits, and clearly state the differential advantage that your plan for this product or service offers over the competition and why the plan will succeed.
X. Appendices
1. Include all supporting information that you consider relevant.

Figure 3-2 **(Continued)**

The Executive Summary. The executive summary is an overall view of the marketing project and its potential, including what you want to do, how much money and what other resources are needed for the project, and specific financial measurements, such as return on investment, that might be anticipated. The executive summary is extremely important and should not be overlooked. As its name implies, executive summary is an overview or summary or abstract of the entire plan intended for a top management executive audience. As the top management executives review your marketing plan, they will frequently skip around to parts of the plan that are of more interest to them. In fact, few marketing plans will be read word for word in their entirety by top executives in a company. Rather, certain sections will be read in detail and other sections only scanned. However, almost every executive will read the executive summary.

It is therefore important that in this summary you capture the essence of your plan in a few short, terse paragraphs. Describe the thrust of what the plan purports to do, the objectives and goals that are its intent, and a bird's-eye view of the strategy that will be used to accomplish the objectives and goals. This summary shouldn't exceed two or three pages at the maximum. After reading your executive summary for a few minutes, the reader should understand what it is you want to do, how much it will cost, and what the likely chances of success are. Most important, he or she will understand the competitive differential advantage inherent in your marketing plan that will cause it to succeed.

A cautionary note here: Although the executive summary comes first, it is written last. This is because it must capture all of the essential points in your plan and emphasize how you approach the project. If you write your executive summary first and don't go back to rework it after you complete your plan, not only are you likely to miss something, your summary may miss the emphasis it should have.

Table of Contents. You may wonder about the discussion of something so mundane and simplistic as a table of contents in a discussion as important and sometimes as complicated as that of marketing planning. Yet, the table of contents is extremely important as a part of the marketing plan. As noted previously, most top-level executives will not read the entire plan in detail except for the executive summary and certain areas that may be of particular interest to them.

For example, in top management, the vice-president of finance will be very interested in the financial part of your marketing plan. He or she will want to know what different elements of the plan will cost to implement and when the monies will be needed. A vice-president of engineering or of R&D will probably be more interested in the technical aspects and performance characteristics of the products that are required. These executives may even skip items that you as a marketing manager think are crucial, such as distribution channels, sales promotion, and advertising. Therefore, it is not sufficient that every subject area critical to the project be covered in your plan.

In addition, because of other readers who may be interested in your plan or may be required to take some actions as a part of it, you must make it as easy as possible to find any topic of interest quickly. The table of contents is used for this purpose. If you do not use a table of contents, other executives and individuals involved in the implementation of your marketing plan will probably make some attempt at locating the information they want. But, if they cannot find it, they may assume that it is not there. This is not only a question of wasted time, but of a negative impact on those whose support in adoption or implementation may be crucial to success. Therefore, including a table of contents is mandatory.

Situational Analysis and Target Market. The situational analysis is a detailed description of the environment or the company and the product, product line, or service at the time the plan will be initiated and implemented. It should include a detailed discussion of the environs of the marketplace, including your company, your competition, neutral environs, and situational environs; and it must have market characteristics, including the segments of the overall market in which you are interested, growth trends, specific customer identification, buyer attitudes and habits, geographical location of the market segments, industry pricing, size of the various market segments in dollars and units, technological trends, distribution factors and issues and other factors the marketer may feel important in the situation.

Many marketing plans draw all this together in a summary of problems, opportunities, and threats. However, it is insufficient simply to state the problem or the opportunity or threat. You must also state alternative courses of action for overcoming the problems, taking advantage of the opportunities, and avoiding the threats.

Marketing Objectives and Goals. Objectives and goals must be clearly spelled out and identified. A marketing objective might be to become the leading supplier of a certain product. Underneath this objective, certain goals are established. One goal might be attainment of 30 per cent market share within the next three years. Goals could pertain to volume of sales, return on investment, or measurable aims. Remember that you can't get "there" until you know where "there" is. Thus, the importance of objectives and goals. Also, be careful that objectives or goals are not mutually exclusive. For example, attaining a certain market share may require sacrifice of some profit.

Marketing Strategies. Strategies are the actions that you must take to reach your goals and objectives. We will discuss them in more detail in forthcoming chapters in this book. A marketing strategy may mean **mass marketing**—that is, trying to sell the same product to everyone; a strategy of **market segmentation**, where you attempt to sell your product and concentrate your resources only on certain segments of the marketplace; a strategy of **product differentiation**, where your product is differentiated from those of your competitors; a strategy of **positioning**, where your product is positioned in the minds of its potential buyers relative to other products offered; a strategy of **internationalization**, where your product is differentiated depending upon the country in which it is marketed; or one of **globalization**, where the same product is marketed identically in the same manner in every single country. In any case, strategies must be specified and described in detail along with the differential advantages that adoption will make possible.

Marketing Tactics. As described in the previous chapter, tactics describe how you carry out your strategy. Thus, a strategy of product differentiation may require differentiation by product tactics in which the packaging is changed; pricing tactics where the price is altered or modified; promotion tactics where a previously ignored difference is emphasized and promoted; or distribution tactics where a faster means of getting the product to the consumer or buyer is used to differentiate your product from that of your competitors.

Schedules and Budgets. It is important to recognize that every single marketing action costs resources. Of primary interest are the financial resources required and when they may be needed. As a result, a schedule is prepared as in Figure 3-3. Each task is listed in addition to when the task begins and when the task ends and what it costs. This is done on a monthly basis. In this way, not only are resources required to implement your plan known, but once the marketing plan is implemented, the schedule can be used to monitor the plan and make changes as required to keep within planned budget and on time.

Task	Weeks after Project Initiation											Total
	1	2	3	4	5	6	7	8	9	10	11	
Initial Production	$5,000	$5,000	$5,000	$5,000	$5,000	$5,000	$10,000	$10,000	$10,000	$10,000	$10,000	$80,000
Distribution and Storage		$5,000	$7.500	$10,000	$10,000	$10,000						$42,100
Advertising					$5,000	$5,000	$7,500	$10,000	$10,000	$10,000	$10,000	$57,500
Special Sales Promotion							$3,000	$3,000	$3,000	$3,000		$12,000
Special Publicity								$5,000	$5,000			$10,000
Planned Product Modification										$2,000	$2,000	$4,000
Monthly totals	$4,000	$10,000	$12,500	$15,000	$20,000	$10,000	$20,500	$28,000	$28,000	$25,000	$200,000	$206,000

Total for project

Figure 3-3   Marketing Plan Schedule

Financial Data and Control. As noted earlier, because the implementation of any marketing plan requires the use of financial resources, finances and financial data are closely integrated with marketing planning and are a requirement of it. Because resources are never unlimited, an ideal strategy may not be possible—a company may not have the necessary resources. Rather, a more realistic but less ideal strategy may be needed that is within the financial resources available to the company. In this section on financial data, **sales estimates** on a monthly basis through the life of the plan should be given along with **cash flow requirements** based on the sales or revenue coming in less the cost of implementation of monies going out. Certain calculations and ratios are also important, including a **break-even analysis**; an estimate of **inventory turnover**; measures of **profitability**, including **asset earning power** determined by the ratio of earnings before interest and taxes to total assets; **net profit on sales ratio**, which measures the difference between what you take in and what you spend in the process of doing business; **investment turnover ratio**, which is the annual net sales to total assets; and any other financial ratios or data felt to be important to the execution of the plan.

For example, you may want to calculate the point at which a cash flow turns profitable. This is not necessarily the same as the breakeven point in your breakeven analysis, as a result of the investment in receivables and inventory that a growth oriented company can make. This could be of some interest to potential investors and other outsiders.[15]

Simply initiating the plan and hoping for the best are insufficient to ensure success. As a matter of fact, due to a changing environment, such a procedure is almost certain to result in failure. Therefore, it is important to specify a means of evaluation and control even before the plan is implemented and as a part of the plan itself. For example, what will be done if sales are not at the level anticipated or forecast? Will the plan be dropped? Will the plan be modified? How will it be modified? What if certain parts are profitable and others not? Or certain geographical areas are profitable and others not? What will you do about new competitors entering the market or a change in an old competitor's strategy? How will these facts alter the plan and, indeed, how will these results be known and their effects be determined? Failing to anticipate an evaluation and control means is like pointing an automobile at a destination, closing your eyes, pushing the gas pedal, and crossing your fingers. The chances of arriving safely at your destination, even if it is only a short distance, are slim. Feedback is needed to measure the changes in the environment as you proceed. Then, action must be taken to allow for these changes and keep your vehicle on course to your destination. In the same fashion, changes in the environs must be anticipated. Means of measuring these changes as well as variances in anticipated results and means of measuring these variances must be developed and specified in the marketing plan.

If you need to develop a marketing plan as a part of this course, or at any time in the future after you graduate, use the material in the appendix of this book to help you. You will find a complete set of forms, as well as sample marketing plans. These forms have been used by students to win numerous awards for marketing planning. One student sold a plan he developed in the course for $5,000. Several went into the business of preparing marketing plans and many implemented their own plans successfully.

_____ Information Input for Marketing Plans

A marketing plan cannot be developed in a vacuum. Naturally it requires input from various other divisions, departments, and functions within a company. However, and more important, it requires considerable information coming externally from the company. These evolve into two basic methods, primary sources and secondary sources. Primary sources are those you obtain firsthand. An example might be marketing research in which you go out and survey your potential customers to find out what type of product they like or whether certain features of a product are desired and at what price. Secondary sources are where you obtain similar information, but secondhand, from someone who has already done the marketing research. In developing information for a marketing plan, both primary and secondary sources will be used, depending upon the time available, the money available, and other elements of the situation. Use of **primary sources** may be constrained due to the time and money that you have for the task and may dictate the use of secondary sources. On the other hand, certain types of research can actually be done faster through primary contact. This is especially true where the number of contacts that must be made are few, known, and easy to reach, and the information can be obtained through a short, nonstructured verbal interview.

Secondary Sources of Information for the Marketing Plan

Secondary sources of information for the marketing plan have a variety of origins. One study investigated sources of marketing information used for marketing planning by three different company subsidiary nationalities: American, European, and Japanese. The sources of information for marketing planning included **distributors**, the **sales force**, the management of other **subsidiaries**, the **marketing research department**, **historical data**, **trade sources**, **commercial suppliers**, **official sources**, and the **home office**. This study showed that the sales force was an important source of information for all three nationalities of subsidiary firms and that historical data were important for American and European firms but not nearly as much for Japanese firms. Note the relative importances of different sources for these subsidiaries, expressed in the proportion of firms using them, as shown in Figure 3-4.[16]

Another study of 107 firms and the sources of new ideas for their **products** indicated a heavy emphasis of idea sources from internal sources other than R&D and analysis of competitor's products. This is shown in Figure 3-5.[17]

The marketing manager should also be alert to other sources of secondary information, including such federal sources as the *Statistical Abstract of the United States*, published annually by the Bureau of Census; productivity measures for selected industries, published by the Department of Labor; *U.S. Exports* published by the Department of Commerce; other publications by U.S. government agencies, such as the Small Business Administration; statistics and other information available from local chambers of commerce; studies done by trade associations, such as the Direct Marketing Association, the American Marketing Association, and the American Management Association; studies done by various trade journals and magazines, such as *Sales and Marketing Management's* annual survey of buyers indexes for both consumer and industrial buyers; and research studies that have been syndicated and made available to other firms that seek to purchase them, such as *Findex*.

Sources of Information	Proportion of Firms Using Souce			
	American	European	Japanese	Total
Distributors	43%	38%	33%	40%
Sales Force	75%	71%	83%	74%
Management of other Subsidiaries	39%	54%	50%	47%
Marketing Research Department	57%	71%	0%	57%
Historical Data	75%	79%	33%	72%
Trade Sources	29%	29%	50%	31%
Commercial Supplliers	36%	8%	33%	24%
Official Sources	39%	58%	50%	48%
Home Office	14%	38%	17%	24%
Number of Firms	28	24	6	58

Figure 3-4   Relative Importance of Various Sources of Secondary Source Marketing Research for Marketing Planning (Expressed by Proportion of Firms Using the Source)

Source: Adapted from James M. Hulbert, William K. Brandt, and Raimar Richers, "Marketing Planning in the Multinational Subsidiary: Practices and Problems," *Journal of Marketing*, vol. 44 (Summer 1980), p. 10.

Source of Information	Percentage of Firms Using Source
Customer Oriented Sources— Complaints or Suggestions from Users	10.3%
Formal Research of Users and Their Needs	11.2%
Noncustomer Oriented Sources— Research and Development	16.8%
Internal Sources Other Than Research and Development	33.6%
Analysis of Competitors Products	29.9%
Analysis of Relevant Published Information	8.4%
Suggestions of Suppliers	11.2%

Note: 21.5% of the firms used multiple sources for the identical new product

Figure 3-5   Information Sources for New Product Ideas (107 Firms)

Source: Adapted from Leigh Lawton and A. Parasuraman, "The Impact of the Marketing Concept on New Product Planning," *Journal of Marketing*, vol. 44 (Winter 1980), p. 23.

To locate associations, see the Gale Research Company's *Encyclopedia of Associations.* For locating magazines, try one of the Ayer directories or the Standard Rate and Data Service publication dealing with business and consumer magazines.

For additional help in obtaining information on secondary sources, both *Business Services and Information* (John Wiley & Sons) and *Information Sourcebook for Marketers and Strategic Planners* (Chilton Book Company) are good.

Full utilization of primary and secondary sources, marketing research, and marketing information systems available in the company will result in more complete information for marketing plans and better marketing plans that require fewer changes once implemented due to incorrect earlier assumptions.

The Planning Process

The Plan for Planning

The marketing plan requires bringing together a great deal of complicated information and involves many individuals, both within and without the firm. As a result, you will find it worthwhile and a timesaver to develop a plan for planning. Naturally, such a plan may be designed in different ways and may be further tailored to fit the needs and characteristics of a particular firm including its culture, its people, its product, and its normal policies and procedures. But despite consideration of so many variables, all such plans for planning should endeavor to be both simple and systematic.[18]

Figure 3-6 is a flow model for a marketing planning procedure. Note that it starts with the assignment of responsibility for marketing planning and then moves to setting objectives, analyzing the situation, forecasting the environment, developing marketing programs, issuing a management review

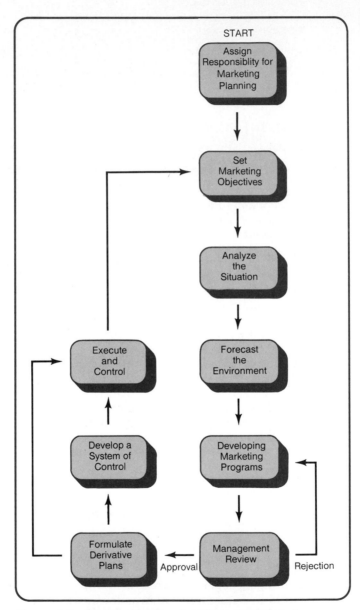

Figure 3-6   Model of a Plan for Marketing Planning

Source: Adapted from Leon Winer, "Are You Really Planning Your Marketing?", *Journal of Marketing*, vol. 29 (January 1965), p. 2.

with approval or rejection, formulating derivative plans, developing a system of control at the time of execution, and then returning control and feedback to the marketing objectives.[19] Figure 3-7 is an alternative model. With this process it is assumed that the assignment for marketing planning responsibility has already been made. It then proceeds to establish marketing objectives, assess the opportunities and state assumptions, generate strategies,

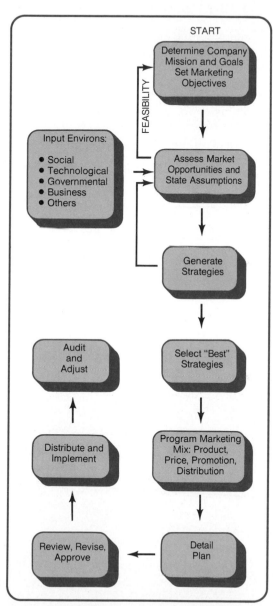

**Figure 3-7   Alternative Model for Developing
a Marketing Plan**

Source: Adapted from Mark E. Stern, *Marketing Planning: A
Systems Approach* (New York: McGraw-Hill, 1966), p. 13.

select the best strategy, proceed to a marketing mix, and then go on to product communications and distributions programs. It integrates the programs and coordinates them, choosing the plan, reviewing it, revising and approving it, distributing and implementing it, and then auditing and adjusting it, which corresponds to control in the first model.[20]

Desirable Planning Characteristics

Certain planning characteristics significantly aid an organization's effectiveness. Figure 3-8 shows these desirable planning characteristics and their frequency of observation in six different firms, A through F. The relative effectiveness of each firm, as measured by the following objective and subjective criteria, is also indicated: recent trend of increasing sales and market share, recent history of successfully introducing new products, rate of profitability, and reputation of the organization's marketing expertise.[21] Note how the firms with the desirable planning characteristics listed tend to be more effective.

Planning Characteristic/ Effectiveness	Firm A	Firm B	Firm C	Firm D	Firm E	Firm F
Effectiveness	Highest	Highest	#2	#3	Lowest	Lowest
1. Planning Direction from Senior Management	Yes, Much	Yes, Much	Little or None	Little or None	Some	Little or None
2. Senior Management Participation in Plan Development	Frequent	At Key Periods	Primarily At End of Plan Development	Primarily At End of Plan Development	Little or None	Some
3. Use of Staff, Other Line Managers	Extensive	Extensive	Some	Some	Little	Little
4. Planner Communcations with Staff, Senior Management	Very Good	Very Good	Good	Fair-Poor	Fair	Fair-Poor
5. External Sources Used in Planning	Heavy	Few or None	Heavy	Few or None	Some	Few or None
6. Use the Pratice of Plan Draft, Review and and Revise	Yes, Much	Yes, Much	Yes, Much	Yes	Some	Yes
7. Training Orientation	Very Much	Very Much	Very Much	Little	None	None
8. Incentive Plan	Yes	Yes	Yes	Limited	None	Yes

Figure 3-8 Desirable Planning Characteristics and Effectiveness of Six Firms

Source: Adapted from Stanley F. Stasch and Patricia Lanktree, "Can Your Marketing Planning Procedures Be Improved?," *Journal of Marketing*, vol. 44 (Summer 1980), pp. 81, 86.

Who Does Planning?

Many different "stakeholder groups," all of which have a stake in the plan, even though they are outside the marketing organization, may be intimately involved in the planning process, including top corporate management, the corporate planning staff, other corporate staff groups, business unit top management, business unit planning staff, other business unit staff, and other business unit line management.[22] But there are only four basic alternatives for preparing the marketing plan:

1. Functional marketing executives prepare the plan.
2. A special planning staff group prepares the plan.
3. Everyone who has a part to play in the project, including outside organizations, participates.
4. The responsible brand product or project manager prepares the plan him- or herself.[23]

While any of these approaches may work in a particular company or situation, it is again important to recognize that the overall responsibility must belong to the responsible marketing manager. He or she is the brand product or project manager who ultimately has the line responsibility for implementing the project. As Michael E. Naylor, General Motors' general director of corporate strategic planning, said, "Planning is the responsibility of every line manager. The role of the planner is to be a catalyst for change—not to do the planning for each business unit."[24]

Alternative Planning Approaches

Aside from the responsibility for the physical preparation of the marketing plan and for the absolute necessity of top management and/or upper management of the marketing organization's involvement in it, there are various approaches that can be taken in any planning process. These are **top-down planning**, **bottom-up planning**, or a combination of **top-down/bottom-up**.

Top-Down Planning

Top-down planning, as the name indicates, is planning accomplished at the top of an organization. The objectives, the analysis of the situation, the marketing strategies and tactics, implementation and control, and virtually all other main elements of the marketing plan are designated by the top management of the marketing organization. Lower-level organizations and functional organizations such as sales, advertising, and marketing research prepare derivative plans or simply implement what has been directed by top management planners.

Bottom-Up Planning

Bottom-up planning works the other way. Lower-level organizations, either together or individually, prepare the marketing plan in detail, including all the elements indicated previously. It is then reviewed and approved or rejected by top management.

Top-Down/Bottom-Up

The top-down/bottom-up combination denotes planning that may be initiated at either end of the organization. Two different approaches may be used to achieve this combination. In one instance a plan is initiated at either end of the organization and then is sent to the opposite organizational level for extensive modification and reworking. It is then returned to where it was initiated for additional work. Depending on the situation, additional cycles may follow. In its final form, the plan is approved by top management. Alternatively, top management representatives are integrated temporarily into a lower-level organization to achieve a top-down/bottom-up combination simultaneously. Again, the final product is approved at the top rung.

Each alternative approach has advantages and disadvantages. Top-down planning is usually quicker because lower-level organizations need focus only on implementation of what top management desires. On the other hand, the top-down approach to planning frequently excludes important inputs from lower-level organizations.

Bottom-up planning also has advantages and disadvantages. It requires initiation by front line marketers. Therefore, those who must ultimately implement the plan regard it as being more their own rather than dictated by someone far removed from the situation. On the other hand, the bottom-up plan may reflect the prejudices and needs of the lower-level organization preparing it. Also, there is a greater danger with bottom-up planning that the marketing plan will not reflect the corporate perspective of top management. Finally, if the plan is not approved, much frustration is felt by the planner and the line manager responsible for the planning at the lower-level of the organization.

But even a combination of top-down/bottom-up does not have all the advantages with none of the disadvantages. Simultaneous participation of top management and lower-level managers may still inhibit the input from lower-level managers. Recycling from one end to the other of the organization for extensive modification creates frustration over the changes made by the other end of the organization and over the amount of time it takes to do it.

Selecting a Planning Approach

The selection of a particular planning approach that is top-down, bottom-up, or a combination of the two is very much situational. It depends on the organizational structure, the management style of the line managers and staff managers involved, and on the internal environment and culture of the company. It also depends on the company's external environment and the pressures of the marketplace, especially the competition and demand for the product or the service and the objectives that the organization has for developing the marketing plan.

After the Planning Is Over _____

In a very real sense, the planning is never over until the plan is executed and all objectives and goals are achieved. It is an ongoing process that changes with the environment. Even when a new plan is prepared, feedback from the old plan is utilized. Review, revision, and updating are extremely important and are necessary throughout the implementation process. Incorrect preliminary basic assumptions may not only result in incorrect objectives and strategies or tactics, but also in inappropriate criteria for performance evaluation, especially if a number of events occurred that were unanticipated during the planning period.[25] Various elements that must be constantly monitored and evaluated include the effectiveness of the plan, the efficiency of the plan, the adequacy of the resources, and the appropriateness of the goals and objectives.[26] To make these measurements, a system of control must establish the necessary standards, measure the activities and results, compare the measurements to the standards, and report variances between the measurements and the standards. Only in this way can the plan be kept on course and decisions be made as to whether to continue with the marketing plan as envisioned originally and, if so, how.[27]

Implementation

Effective implementation of the marketing plan is heavily dependent on all managers within the company involved in it. It requires not only that they understand what the marketing plan is supposed to do, but that they believe it is a valuable management process. Furthermore, it is important that managers expect the time frame of the plan to be specific and complete and become involved in controlling the plan's evaluation, implementation and review to ensure adherence or knowledgeable modification.[28]

Effective Planning

Common Ingredients to Good Plans

Researchers have found certain ingredients common to all good, workable, and successful marketing plans. These include the following:

1. A definition of objectives and goals with quantification, wherever possible.
2. A subordinate relationship of the objectives and goals to those of the next higher management level.
3. A recognition and acceptance of basic environmental assumptions and premises.
4. A statement of relevant objective facts and forecast.
5. A presentation of alternative courses of action.
6. A statement of required resources, costs, anticipated risks, and rewards.
7. A schedule for the selected course of planned action, setting the pace and stating when, by whom, and where.
8. A method of follow-through to ensure performance and execution on schedule in the manner desired.
9. A review and analysis of results against goals for future planning.
10. Continuity, attainability, simplicity, systemization, and flexibility.[29]

Cautionary Notes for Effective Planning

Certain pitfalls should be avoided to make your marketing plan effective. This is especially true when you are dealing with a great deal of quantitative data. Some good hints of what to avoid follow:

1. Don't blindly rely on mathematical or statistical calculations. Use your judgment, as well.
2. Don't assume that past trends can be extrapolated into the future forever.
3. If drawing conclusions from statistical data, make certain that the sample size is sufficiently large to make the statistical inference meaningful.
4. Don't establish objectives or goals simply on the basis of current or past rates of growth unless there are factors and good reason for you to believe that these rates will continue.[30]

One study demonstrated an additional problem. Executives perceive the existence and significance of a variety of "behavioral planning problems that must be considered. These include:

- Planning recalcitrance: resistance and noncooperation by executives in planning
- Fear of uncertainty in planning: a lack of comfort in planning activities
- Political interests in planning: resource bargaining, padding of requirements, and avoidance of consensus
- Planning avoidance: compliance rather than commitment to planning.[31]

Making Your Marketing Plans More Effective

Researchers have found that certain actions will make your plans more effective if you follow them than if you do not. Some of these factors have been mentioned earlier. However, to draw them all together, you should consider the following:

1. Senior managers should participate in all stages of planning, especially the early stages.
2. Product managers and others who have the ultimate responsibility for the marketing plans should be kept informed and continually guided by top management and top-management staff planners.
3. Individuals ultimately responsible for the marketing plan should be required to get the best inputs from all feasible sources, both internal and external.
4. Line managers responsible for planning should be encouraged to suggest new planning ideas at the beginning of the planning period, before the plan is fixed.
5. Line managers responsible for planning should communicate both horizontally to other organizations as well as up the organization to senior top management.
6. Planning procedures should include methods whereby marketing plan

development is channeled in directions desired by top management. These may include guidance documents and presentations.

7. Marketing plans must be joined with the overall business strategy of the corporation, as developed in Chapter 2; otherwise they may contradict it, which will result in "suboptimization." That is, although the marketing plan in itself is excellent and may succeed, this "success" may harm the overall corporate strategy.

8. Marketing plans must reflect the fact of a product's life cycle and not make an assumption of arithmetical increase in sales growth.[32,33,34]

Summary

Marketing plans will always be subject to risks, and the process and the product are as much an art as a science, with judgment and experience being crucial.[35] Yet mastering marketing planning is essential for any marketing manager in today's highly competitive environment. In this chapter we've seen why formal planning is absolutely essential, as well as what a marketing plan will do for you as a marketing manager. We've also seen that while there are criticisms of formal marketing planning, these criticisms can be overcome. There are two general categories of marketing plans: the strategic plan discussed in the previous chapter, and operational plans. The latter include those for new products, product lines, or service plans, or the annual plan. We have looked at a typical marketing plan structure and investigated various sources, both primary and secondary, to provide informational input to the marketing plan.

We have also looked at several marketing plan processes and at successful marketing plan characteristics. The question of who does planning has been explored, especially as to the ultimate responsibility being the line manager responsible for implementation of the plan and the critical involvement of top management. Several alternative planning approaches have been explored, including top-down planning, bottom-up planning, and a combination of top-down/bottom-up. We have seen that the choice of an approach is dependent on the organization, management style, internal environment, external environment, and the main objectives of the plan. We have also seen that the plan is constantly reworked over its lifetime through constant review, revision, and updating.

Henry W. Haimsohn, CEO of PACE Membership Warehouse, Inc., built a billion-dollar business in only four years selling merchandise at a discount to businesses and consumers. He says that planning, even strategic planning, must be reviewed every day. "In a marketplace that is always changing, it is always possible—and always necessary—to shape your company to do better."[36]

Finally, we have looked at common ingredients to good plans, cautionary notes for effective planning, and how to make marketing plans more effective. This chapter on marketing plans is one of the most important in this book. The marketing plan brings together all aspects of marketing management, and when implemented results in the successful marketing of the product or service. The remainder of this book discusses elements that are used to help prepare or are part of the marketing plan.

Questions

1. You are a marketing manager in a small company. Your immediate supervisor, the vice-president of marketing, thinks that formal marketing planning is a waste of time. How would you answer this criticism?
2. Why is it necessary to write down a marketing plan? Why can't you have a marketing plan in your head?
3. Because the environs of the marketplace are constantly changing, a marketing plan, to one extent or another, is always out of date. How would you ensure that the marketing plan you develop is kept up to date once you begin implementation?
4. How would a new product or service plan differ from an annual product plan in the setting of objectives? In the situational analysis? In determining strategies? In determining tactics? In determining budgets? In determining timing? In determining methods of implementation and control?
5. You have been given the responsibility for developing a marketing plan for a new product: eyeglasses cast in one piece of plastic so that the lenses are an integral part of the frame. Where would you get information for the situational analysis for this new product, including potential markets and their size, methods of distribution, pricing,

competition, demand for the product, and so forth?
6. Which model of the marketing planning procedure, the one in Figure 3-6 or in Figure 3-7, is more appropriate for a small company? A company engaged in marketing to the federal government? A large company with many divisions?
7. Based on your personal preference alone, which alternative planning approach do you prefer as a marketing manager? Top-down planning, bottom-up planning, or a top-down/bottom-up combination? Why?
8. Describe some methods that you would use as a marketing manager to find out whether your goals are being met in the most efficient manner possible.
9. You have been told to develop a marketing plan by yourself for a new banking service in which subscribers can move monies around their various accounts or make certain types of purchases using their personal computer. Describe the steps that you would follow in developing this plan.
10. This chapter has dealt primarily with the benefits and the essentiality of marketing plans. Criticisms have been discussed only as obstacles that should be overcome. Are there any other costs to the firm for developing a marketing plan?

Ethical Question

The vice-president of marketing tells you to develop a new marketing plan. "I don't want you using one word from that old plan," he says. You begin working on the new marketing plan in accordance with his instructions. However, it occurs to you that many concepts in the old plan are salvageable. Furthermore, the situational analysis only needs to be updated to be ready to go. Using the basics of the old plan will save your company a considerable amount of money. And, of course, you'll be able to complete the project a lot sooner. You realize that its stupid not to use what you can from the old plan. However, the vice-president of marketing has a reputation for "saying what he means and meaning what he says." After some thought you decide to do it his way and to start from scratch. Is this an ethical decision? Would it be more ethical to do the new plan the way you believe it should be done, and just not tell him? Is this a decision that has anything to do with ethics at all?

Endnotes

1. Paul B. Brown, "What Business Are You In?", *Inc.*, vol. 11, no. 5 (May 1989), pp. 125–126.
2. "Clorox: An R&D Game Plan Is Brightening Its Profit Picture," *Business Week* (April 23, 1984), p. 113.
3. "Entrepreneurship on Campus: A Panel Discussion on the Teaching of Entrepreneurship," *Entrepreneur* (November 1984), p. 49.
4. Mark E. Stern, *Marketing Planning: A Systems Approach* (New York: McGraw-Hill, 1966), p. 1.

5. Darryl J. Ellis and Peter P. Pekar, Jr., *Planning for Nonplanners* (New York: AMACOM, 1980), p. 23.

6. William A. Cohen, *Developing a Winning Marketing Plan* (New York: Wiley, 1987), pp. 2–6.

7. James M. Hulbert, William K. Brandt, and Raimar Richers, "Marketing Planning in the Multinational Subsidiary: Practices and Problems," *Journal of Marketing*, vol. 44 (Summer 1980), p. 7.

8. Stanley F. Stasch and Patricia Lanktree, "Can Your Marketing Planning Procedures Be Improved?" *Journal of Marketing*, vol. 44 (Summer 1980), p. 79.

9. William M. Luther, *The Marketing Plan* (New York: AMACOM, 1980), p. 51.

10. Theodore Leavitt, *Marketing for Business Growth* (New York: McGraw-Hill, 1974), p. 15.

11. Lloyd H. Bakan, "Is Your Marketing Plan Tired?" *Drake Business Review*, vol. 3, no. 1 (1988), p. 40.

12. Peter C. Reid, "Harley Beat Back the Japanese," *Fortune*, vol. 120, no. 7 (September 25, 1989), p. 162.

13. John N. Stengrevics, "Corporate Planning Needn't Be An Executive Straight Jacket," *Wall Street Journal* 26 September 1983.

14. Alvin A. Achenbaum, "Marketing Plans Still Getting Short Shrift," *Marketing News* (July 9, 1982), p. 6.

15. Richard D. Haddrill and Joseph J. Cegala, "Does Your Business Plan Make a Profitable Statement?" *Ernst & Whinney Ideas* (Spring–Summer 1988), p. 10.

16. Hulbert, Brandt, and Richers, op. cit., p. 10.

17. Leigh Lawton and A. Parasuraman, "The Impact of the Marketing Concept on New Product Planning," *Journal of Marketing*, vol. 44 (Winter 1980), p. 23.

18. John M. Brion, *Corporate Marketing Planning* (New York: Wiley, 1967), pp. 206–207.

19. Leon Winer, "Are You Really Planning Your Marketing?" *Journal of Marketing*, vol. 29 (January 1965), p. 2.

20. Stern, op. cit., p. 13.

21. Stasch and Lanktree, op. cit., p. 86.

22. William R. King, "Evaluating the Effectiveness of Your Planning," *Managerial Planning*, vol. 33 (September–October 1984), p. 5.

23. Winer, op. cit., p. 7.

24. "The New Breed of Strategic Planner," *Business Week* (September 17, 1984), p. 62.

25. James M. Hulbert and Norman E. Toy, "A Strategic Framework for Marketing Control," *Journal of Marketing*, vol. 41 (April 1977), p. 12.

26. King, op. cit.

27. Winer, op. cit., p. 8.

28. Achenbaum, op. cit.

29. Brion, op. cit., pp. 204–205.

30. Stern, op. cit., p. 5.

31. Nigel F. Piercy and Neil A. Morgan, "Behavioral Planning Problems Versus Planning Techniques in Predicting Marketing Plan Credibility and Utilization," in Paul Bool et al., eds. *AMA Educators' Proceedings: Enhancing Knowledge Development in Marketing* (Chicago: AMA, 1989), p. 318.

32. Stasch and Lanktree, op. cit., pp. 88–89.

33. Daniel T. Carroll, "How to Make Marketing Plans More Effective," *Management Review*, vol. 68 (October 1979), pp. 60–61.

34. Malcolm H. B. McDonald, "Ten Barriers to Marketing Planning," *Journal of Services Marketing*, vol. 4, no. 2 (Spring 1990), p. 5.

35. Philip Kotler, "Corporate Models: Better Marketing Plans," *Harvard Business Review*, vol. 48 (July–August 1970), p. 149.

36. Henry W. Haimsohn, "The External Game," *Success*, vol. 34, no. 9 (November 1987), p. 16.

Adolph Coors Brewing Company

One of the largest, oldest, and most interesting brewers in the United States was the Adolph Coors Brewing Company. It faced a perplexing set of circumstances, opportunities, and problems as an organization and was part of an industry that showed great structural change, extensive modifications of traditional consumer behavior, and public relations problems.

The U.S. Beer Industry

After the prohibition era, about 750 brewing companies went into business in the United States. Of course, many failed quickly, and the number of firms kept going down. However, the industry underwent a massive shakeout and restructuring between the late 1960s and the mid-1980s. About 60 brewing companies disappeared, some by closing down and some by merging with stronger organizations. Among the approximately 43 remaining, a few were in difficulty, a few faced significant problems, and some others faced problem-laden opportunities. Two thirds of the 43 were extremely small and insignificant in the industry. The top 5 firms sold about 87 per cent of the beer made in the United States.

For a long time fourth in size behind Anheuser-Busch, Inc., Joseph Schlitz Brewing Company, and Pabst Brewing Company, Coors fell to number 5 as the seventh-ranked Miller Brewing Company of Milwaukee surged into second place in the late 1970s. Formerly independent, Miller had been acquired by Philip Morris, Inc., the tobacco-based firm, in 1970 and had been given needed fixed investment, working capital, and marketing expertise for growth. Coors fell to sixth in 1981 as G. Heileman Brewing Company expanded.

In late 1981 the number 4 producer, G. Heileman Brewing Company, attempted to take over number 3 Schlitz, which was in difficulty with declining sales and profits. The Schlitz brand was in severe difficulty for several reasons, perhaps the most important of which was an ill-considered change in the recipe or brewing formula. A second reason was the greater sophistication of marketing at arch-rival Miller. Schlitz agreed to the proposed takeover. However, the Antitrust Division of the U.S. Justice Department was displeased with the additional ownership concentration that the deal would bring to the brewing industry and with the potential for significantly reduced competition. When the Justice Department announced that it would file suit to block the acquisition, it was canceled. This government action surprised many people because, in a much larger and more important merger about two months earlier, Du Pont had acquired Conoco. The reason for the different government posture was that, without the Du Pont action, Conoco, an important oil, natural gas, and coal producer, would have been taken over by Seagram, a Canadian corporation. In mid-1982 seventh-ranked Stroh Brewing Company took over the ailing Schlitz. Thus, the rank order became the following for the next few years: Anheuser-Busch, Miller, Stroh-Schlitz, Heileman, Pabst, Coors.

Heileman, of La Crosse, Wisconsin, was one of the fastest-growing companies in the country, but Schlitz would have been Heileman's first nationally distributed

From Thomas Greer, *Cases in Marketing,* 4th ed. (New York: Macmillan, 1987)

brand. In an unusual strategy, Heileman operated a network of regional brewers offering over thirty brands. Among its better-known brands were Carling Black Label and National Bohemian along the East Coast, Rainier in the Northwest, and Blatz and Old Style in the Middle West and parts of the East. Colt 45, Blitz, Mickey's Malt Liquor, and Weinhard were also popular brands belonging to Heileman. Heileman's fundamental strategy was to revitalize the acquired regional brands, gradually bring in some of its other regional brews, and then promote heavily.

There were only a few other important brewing organizations. An independent regional firm that was growing was Pittsburgh Brewing Company, which made Iron City brand. Genessee Brewing Company, Christian Schmidt Brewing Company, Hudepohl Brewing Company, and Joseph Huber Brewing Company were other noteworthy regional corporations. With a capacity of 500,000 barrels per year in its Monroe, Wisconsin, plant, Huber made Augsburger brand beer, a Bavarian-style favorite in the Middle West.

A number of tiny local breweries had started up and were referred to in the trade as "boutique breweries" or microbrewers or both. By common consent, the term was confined to those making only 10,000 barrels or less per year. Interestingly, Coors had spillage of almost 70,000 barrels per year. The number of small brewers was variable, but it averaged about 28. Prominent examples were Sierra Nevada of Chico, California; Anchor Brewery of San Francisco; and Independent Ale of Seattle, the three that got the movement going in the 1970s. Other examples were Kessler of Helena, Montana; Samuel Adams (Boston Beer) of Boston; Reinheitsgebot (approximate translation: legal code of purity) of Plano, Texas; New Amsterdam of New York City; William S. Newman Brewing Company of Albany, New York; White Tail of Fordyce, Arkansas; Chesapeake Bay of Virginia Beach, Virginia; Hibernia Dunkel Weizen Fest of Eau Claire, Wisconsin; Snake River of Caldwell, Idaho; Boulder Brewing of Longmont, Colorado; and Grant's Imperial Stout of Yakima, Washington. White Tail added 10 per cent rice to give crispness, and Imperial was the strongest beer offered in North America. Chesapeake Bay called its Munich-style lager Chesbay Amber and distributed it in the eastern parts of Pennsylvania, Maryland, Virginia, and North Carolina. All boutique beers were high-priced, usually above prestige imports, and all taken together held less than half of 1 per cent of the U.S. market. A few, such as Anchor, were outgrowing their placement in this category. Anchor Brewing, owned by Fritz Maytag, heir to the Maytag home appliance fortune, made about 30,000 barrels of Anchor Steam annually and distributed it in 30 states. Whether this operation was just fun and a hobby or a serious enterprise remained to be seen.

Many beer drinkers preferred to consume regional beers for various reasons, such as perceived unique taste, desire to enjoy local color, a wish to support local business and thus local jobs, or avoidance of beers that were thought to be mass-appeal, mass-produced goods. In the case of the boutique beers there was also a strong prestige factor for most brands. However, it was well understood in the industry and had been demonstrated experimentally countless times that most beer consumers could not recognize their favorite brands in blindfold tests that compared several brands. The majority of taste differences among popular U.S. brands were imaginary or too slight for the average beer consumer to detect.

The demand for beer in the United States rose rather rapidly in the 1950s, 1960s, and 1970s, but the growth rate slowed down markedly in the early 1980s. Despite an increasing population, in 1984 there was a small decrease, the first in over three decades. This was followed by another small decrease in 1985. The 1985 demand was almost exactly the same as the 1981 demand. The demand

Exhibit 1   U.S. Beer Sales by Segment and Year in Percentages

Segment	1981	1982	1983	1984	1985
Domestic					
Superpremium-priced	7.0%	7.0%	6.3%	5.0%	4.1%
Premium-priced	51.5	48.5	47.0	45.0	43.8
Popular-priced	21.4	20.1	21.3	23.0	24.3
Light	13.8	17.7	18.5	19.9	20.5
Malt liquor	3.4	3.5	3.5	3.2	3.0
Imports	2.9	3.2	3.4	3.9	4.3

for light beer was still growing but not enough to offset the decrease in demand for regular beer. See Exhibit 1. Most of the industry was pessimistic and believed that there would be very little growth in the future.

There was significant production overcapacity in the industry. Most large and medium-size firms built in the late 1960s and 1970s as though the high-growth trend line of the industry would go on indefinitely. This was despite the clear demographic evidence that the age distribution of the U.S. population would no longer be as encouraging for this industry after the early 1980s. In late 1984, Miller Brewing decided to write down part of the value of a new $450 million brewery in Trenton, Ohio, because some of it was not needed then and would not be needed in the future. The amount was $140 million after income tax effects. In 1985, Stroh abandoned its Detroit headquarters brewery, the oldest and least efficient facility in that company, because of lack of need. Although there was clearly overcapacity in the industry, there might still be some construction of new breweries. This was primarily because some of the unused capacity was poorly located in relation to the geographical demand patterns. Beer was bulky, heavy, and costly to transport long distances. A secondary reason was that a few plants were underautomated and required too much expensive labor.

There were several reasons for the lack of growth in the brewing industry, among them the decrease in the number of people in the traditionally heaviest per capita beer-consumption stage of the life cycle. This stage was from the drinking age to age thirty-four, especially from the drinking age to age twenty-four. The U.S. population was much older on average than a generation earlier. The older that people became, the less beer they consumed. Second, the minimum drinking age was being raised in almost every state to twenty-one under extreme pressure from the federal government and the threat of cancellation of federally provided subsidies and matching funds for many programs if the states did not do so. There certainly were violations of the age requirement, but retailers, restauranteurs, and bar owners were anxious not to lose valuable licenses and had become rather careful. Third, there was greater concern about physical fitness and being "in shape." Fourth, there was a ground swell of public concern about misuse of alcoholic beverages, including the weak products such as beer. The Mothers Against Drunk Driving (MADD) organization was influential and effective. A broad coalition of groups ranging from the Consumer Federation of America to the National Parents and Teachers Association was pushing hard for a legal ban on television and radio advertising of all alcoholic beverages similar to that imposed on cigarettes in 1969. According to William K. Coors, chairperson of the board of Coors Brewing, "The image of the alcohol beverage industry is the greatest challenge facing brewers today." He went on to argue that sanctions against advertising have little influence on the alcohol abuser. "This is an individual behavior problem, the solution to which is to teach people how to accommodate the pressure and stress of everyday life without the crutch of alcohol." He added that sanctions would reduce the consumption of alcohol by responsible users. Coors was a leader in "Drink safely" messages placed on point-of-purchase displays and packages. The large U.S. and Canadian brewers established and funded the Alcohol Beverage Medical Research Foundation at Johns Hopkins University School of Medicine in Baltimore.

Anheuser-Busch launched an interesting product in May 1984 in response to criticism of the industry. Called L.A. for low alcohol, it was the first such beer from a major company. This product was difficult to place with accounts. Sports facilities looked promising, for managers of stadiums and arenas were anxious to prevent and control rowdyism. Tiger Stadium in Detroit decided to offer only low-alcohol beers. Following that breakthrough, several other sports complexes added L.A. to their assortment. Michael Roarty, marketing vice president of Anheuser-Busch, noted that there was a problem getting people to try L.A. However, when Anheuser-Busch could get people to try it, the repeat sale rate was almost twice what this company normally experienced with a new product.

The brewing industry's promotion targeted to college-age people proved to be especially upsetting to critics and some executives in the industry itself. This part of the industry's promotional efforts was criticized for poor taste as well as possibly raising the risk of abuse. Included were advertising, personal selling, and sales promotion practices such as chug-a-lug contests and wet T-shirt competitions. These practices raised the ire of William Coors. He said that he personally thought they were "outrageous" and that everyone else in the company agreed with him. He doubted that the members of the industry would cooperate to change them.

Peter Coors delivered a major speech to the National Beer Wholesalers Association annual convention, in which he talked about both the abuse and tastefulness issues. Coors dared wholesalers

to be even more responsive to societal concerns about the proper use of alcoholic beverages. . . . It is our challenge for all three tiers of the industry to promote beer properly and with good taste and common design to enhance the credibility of the product and its quality. . . . Ideally, we need to be so good at what we do that we are never placed in the position of having to run around putting out fires. If we are sensitive to our many publics and listen to what they are telling us, we can take action that will never let the fires get started in the first place. We're fully aware of the intense competitive environment in which we operate, but the industry can unite in common purposes.[1]

Pabst Brewing was an old, established company with headquarters in Milwaukee, but it had been suffering from sluggish sales and profits and high managerial turnover for a decade. An offer by Pabst to buy Schlitz for a larger sum of money than Heileman proposed was rejected by the Schlitz board of directors. Much of the business public and the brewing industry saw this rejection as a slap in the face for Pabst and a commentary on how Pabst's future was perceived. Pabst itself was clearly vulnerable to a takeover, dissolution, or splitting up. Its marginal performance grew worse, but in 1983 it acquired Olympia Brewing Company in Tumwater, Washington, which held about 3 per cent of the U.S. market. Olympia had viable subsidiaries, Hamm's in Minneapolis and Lone Star in San Antonio.

[1]*Beverage World,* December 1985, p. 53.

Exhibit 2 Largest Brewing Companies in U.S. and Their Share of U.S. Market

Company	1980	1982	1984	1985
Anheuser-Busch	28.2%	32.4%	35.0%	37.0%
Miller	20.9	21.5	20.5	20.5
Stroh	13.9	12.6	13.1	12.9
G. Heileman	7.5	7.9	9.2	8.9
Coors	7.8	6.5	7.2	8.0

In 1983, G. Heileman Brewing Company was poised to make a friendly takeover of Pabst to save it from two aggressive, unfriendly bidders, Paul Kalmanovitz and Irwin Jacobs. Kalmanovitz owned Falstaff Brewing Comany, Pearl Brewing Company, and General Brewing Company. The Antitrust Division of the U.S. Justice Department agreed at the end of 1984 to a complex arrangement by which Heileman was to acquire within a reasonable time period about two-thirds of Pabst. However, Heileman was required to give up the Tumwater brewery and the Olympia, Hamm's, and Olde English 800 Malt Liquor brands to S & P of Vancouver, Washington, the Kalmanovitz holding company.

Thus, by 1986 the rank order of the largest U.S. brewing companies was the following: Anheuser-Busch, Miller, Heileman, Stroh-Schlitz, and Coors. See Exhibit 2. A secure hold on sixth place for the next few years had not been established. It could be Pabst, or it could be the several companies controlled by the Kalmanovitz family if one added their sales together.

Coors was eager to improve its sales and profits and move up in the industry rankings. For the company to climb to fourth or third place and lock in that rank without marketing nationwide would be a noteworthy accomplishment, but, of course, it planned to be in all states fairly soon. Nevertheless, its coverage of many markets was quite thin, and it had little more than a token presence in a number of states. Some concerned people thought it was more realistic to approach this objective another way, that is, seek an extraordinary penetration of selected geographical markets and high brand loyalty among a hard core of consumers.

Beer Imports

Imported beers amounted to 7.8 million barrels, or 4.3 per cent of the American market, in 1985. The dollar amount was $1.54 billion. This category did not include beers made in the United States under license from foreign brewing concerns, such as Lowenbrau. Imported beer competed with domestic premium and super-premium beers. Imports' share of the market was rising. In 1971 the figure was only 0.6 per cent, but it rose to 2.9 per cent in 1981, 3.2 per cent in 1982, 3.4 per cent in 1983, and 3.9 per cent in 1984. The bulk of market analysts believed that the import segment would total about 10 per cent by 1991.

Heineken from Holland was the leading foreign-made beer. Imported since 1933 by Van Munching & Company of New York, it held about 34 per cent of the import market in 1985, compared to about 40 per cent in 1981. Molson from Canada with 13 per cent was second. Other highly important ones were Beck's from West

Germany with 10 per cent, Moosehead from Canada with 7 per cent, Labatt from Canada with 4 per cent, and St. Pauli Girl from West Germany with 4 per cent. An Irish import, Guinness-Harp; a Dutch import, Amstel Light; and five Mexican imports, Corona Extra, Dos Equis, Carta Blanca, Tecate, and Bohemia all did well but much less than the brands mentioned earlier. Moosehead had had a meteoric rise in the United States that was doubly impressive in view of the fact that the other Canadian brands suffered a small decrease in the United States. Moosehead was a small company and did not even have nationwide distribution in Canada. It was imported by All Brands Importers, Inc., of New York City, a subsidiary of Heublein, Inc., the large distiller, which was itself a subsidiary of R. J. Reynolds Industries, Inc., the tobacco-based conglomerate. The importer had taken the initiative and done all the planning. Grizzly was a new import from Canada but was made by Heineken in Canada. Exotic brews were now being imported from such places as Ivory Coast, Congo, Thailand, Venezuela, and the People's Republic of China. In total, there were about 250 foreign brands imported. G. Heileman Brewing Company became the U.S. distributor of Hacker-Pschorr beers from Munich, West Germany, in 1985, and Anheuser-Busch became the U.S. importer-distributor of highly regarded Carlsberg and Carlsberg Elephant beers from Denmark in 1986.

Americans bought imported beer for three major reasons: prestige, variety, and flavor. Beer was often perceived as a blue-collar beverage. Accordingly, many people, certainly not the majority, in the middle and upper classes found it psychologically necessary to separate themselves from the blue-collar consumers by choice of brands. The same thinking or emotional process sometimes applied to domestic higher-priced beers. Nearly all imports have a heavier, stronger, and more distinctive flavor than American beers. Most foreign tourists in the United States and a small percentage of Americans were contemptuous of U.S. beers, regarding them as caramel-colored carbonated water. American commentators and writers on food and beverages almost all agreed that American beers were bland by prevailing world standards and were rather similar to each other. In addition, there was some speculation but no evidence that some ethnic groups in the United States might begin to look favorably on beers from foreign cultures with which they partially identified.

Curiously enough, the physical characteristics of the vast majority of beers produced in the United States and Canada made them harder, not easier, to produce than the beers from other countries. This refers to knowledge of chemistry, extreme precision in the blending, perfect consistency, and meticulous quality control. Finn Knudsen, director of brewing research and development for Coors Brewing, stated that it took greater skill to make North American lighter-flavored beers consistently than to make European beers. He had twenty-four years of brewing experience, including ten in Europe. As a general principle, the lighter a beer is in flavor, color, and calories, the more difficult is the manufacturing process. Carelessness and inconsistency could not be masked. Yet almost no North American consumers had any inkling of this principle.

The Coors Company

For many years, Coors was the only large brewer in the United States that was not national in scope. Based in Golden, Colorado, a suburb of Denver, this organization distributed its output in only sixteen states, all of them in the West or the western edge of the Middle West, at the beginning of the 1980s. At that time

Exhibit 3   Adolph Coors Company Statements of Income and Retained Earnings

	For the years ended		
	December 29, 1985	December 30, 1984	December 25, 1983
	(In thousands)		
Sales	$1,424,533	$1,262,903	$1,242,182
Less—federal and state beer excise taxes	143,411	130,260	131,776
	1,281,122	1,132,643	1,110,406
Costs and expenses:			
Cost of goods sold	864,193	804,793	720,152
Marketing, general and administrative	307,320	258,557	221,402
Research and project development	19,401	18,420	14,532
	1,190,914	1,081,770	956,086
Operating income	90,208	50,873	154,320
Other (income) expense:			
Interest income	(12,081)	(12,033)	(11,320)
Interest expense	1,714	1,407	1,796
Miscellaneous—net	4,159	4,068	7,983
	(6,208)	(6,558)	(1,541)
Income before income taxes	96,416	57,431	155,861
Income taxes	43,000	12,700	66,600
Net income	$ 53,416	$ 44,731	$ 89,261
Net income per share of common stock	$1.52	$1.28	$2.55

it covered all the West except Oregon and Alaska. In the early 1980s it gradually added one to three states each year. Then in 1983, Coors added Florida, Georgia, North Carolina, South Carolina, Alabama, Virginia, eastern Tennessee, the District of Columbia, Hawaii, and Alaska. In 1984 the company added Kentucky, West Virginia, Ohio, Maryland, and Oregon. Although it was a logical part of Coors's early market territory, Oregon was not available until it repealed its law barring the sale of packaged unpasteurized beer. Illinois and the six New England states were added in 1985 and Michigan in 1986. As of that time, Coors did not distribute in Pennsylvania, New Jersey, New York, Delaware, and Indiana but had plans to add those states in the future. Despite this rather orderly spread, the distribution was quite thin in many of the states added in the 1980s. The Coors company had always had a distinctly western image among both business people and consumers.

The company had beer sales of $1,077,880 in 1985, compared to $937,876,000 in 1984, $947,445,000 in 1983, and $765,909,000 in 1982. See Exhibit 3. The company's share of the U.S. market for beer was 8.0 per cent in 1985, 7.2 per cent in 1984, 6.5 per cent in 1982, 7.4 per cent in 1981, 7.8 per cent in 1980, and 8.0 per cent in 1977. In 1985 the company sold 14,738,000 barrels of beer.

Canada had looked attractive to Coors for several years for its first international expansion. Consumer awareness of Coors was already high in western Canada. Yet it was perplexing to think seriously about distributing in that country when there were still a few states in the United States without Coors products and many states in the United States with only scattered availability of Coors products. Distribution in Quebec would require French-speaking salespersons and French language advertising. Montreal-based Molson Companies, Ltd., and Coors held

Company	Percentage
Anheuser-Busch	91%
Miller	85
Stroh	99
G. Heileman	62
Coors	96
Total U.S. beer industry	81

extensive talks in 1985 about three possibilities: distribution of imported Coors products in Canada by Molson, licensing Molson to make Coors products, and a joint venture in Canada. The Coors executives commented, "We have a product that is difficult to replicate and we want to protect the Coors mystique." Nevertheless, an agreement was reached with Molson for that company to make Coors products in Canada. They became available in Canada, except for the Maritime Provinces, by the end of 1985. For the first time not all Coors products were being made in the same plant and using the fabled "Pure Rocky Mountain Spring Water." A few independent financial analysts suggested a merger between the Coors and Molson corporations.

Coors Company operated only one brewery, but this facility in Golden was the largest brewing plant in the United States. For several years the company had had tentative plans to enlarge the facility, but there had not been a need so far. See Exhibit 4. No finished product was stored at the plant. Golden was reasonably centrally located for the company's geographical distribution area until the middle 1970s. Yet even by the early 1970s, in terms of the population density of the markets served, the plant could not be considered logistically well located. This was primarily because of the importance of the California demand for the product. Among the secondary reasons for marketing area geographical expansion, mainly eastward and southeastward, was making logistics more rational. In particular, the cultivation of Texas, the nation's second most important beer market, was desirable for logistical balance. Another interesting point was that the average shipping distance for a unit of beer had been rising rapidly for several years, going up 20 per cent between 1982 and 1984 alone, as the company pushed farther afield. Intensive cultivation of the upper East Coast would push this figure up drastically. Three-fourths of Coors output was sent by rail, and one-fourth, by truck.

This organization took an option in 1979 to buy a large parcel of rural land in the Shenandoah Valley near Elkton, Rockingham County, Virginia, in case it should actually expand nationwide and might need additional production capacity, storage space, or packaging operations on the East Coast or a combination of these. The tract consisted of 2,245 acres. At first there were aggressive, noisy demonstrations by temperance groups, but they stopped. In 1985 the company announced that it would build a $70 million plant on this tract to package Coors beers in cans, bottles, and kegs. Considering the number of brands of beers, the types of container, sizes of containers, and variations by state on legal requirements for labeling, the plant would need to work with 238 different containers. Beer would arrive by refrigerated rail tank car from Golden. Employing 250 and

Exhibit 5   Recent Balance Sheets of Adolph Coors Company

Assets	December 29, 1985	December 30, 1984
	(In thousands)	
Current assets:		
Cash, including short-term interest bearing investments of $125,927,000 in 1985 and $70,562,000 in 1984	$ 166,131	$ 87,603
Accounts and notes receivable	90,698	75,050
Refundable income taxes		14,400
Inventories:		
Finished	14,927	12,009
In process	26,738	22,387
Raw materials	70,296	67,000
Packaging materials	30,989	28,226
	142,950	129,622
Prepaid expenses and other assets	51,567	52,332
Accumulated income tax prepayments	3,238	6,322
Total current assets	454,584	365,329
Properties, at cost, less accumulated depreciation, depletion and amortization of $621,968,000 in 1985 and $549,026,000 in 1984	827,928	835,254
Excess of cost over net assets of businesses acquired, less accumulated amortization	3,513	3,754
Other assets	10,682	10,806
	$1,296,707	$1,215,143

involving no borrowing, this facility was to open in 1987. Annual packaging capacity was 2.4 million barrels.

Whether a brewery would be built on the tract remained undecided, but the economic evidence was favorable on balance. Moreover, Peter Coors stated that the company had found an exceptional source of pure spring water there that matched the quality of Golden's pure Rocky Mountain spring water. If built, the brewery would be put up in phases as eastern demand warranted. If built in the early and middle 1990s, the cost of such a brewery would probably be about $550 to $600 million for an annual capacity of ten million barrels.

The Coors company was partially integrated up-channel in that it produced its own bottles and cans. In fact, it owned and operated the nation's largest aluminum can factory. Moreover, the company supplied itself with natural gas and coal from its own fields and mines and grew all its own barley. The company was slightly integrated down-channel in that it owned its own beer wholesale distribution firms in Tustin (California), Spokane, Omaha, Denver, and Boise. These distribution investments furnished profit as well as what management termed "better insight in working with the company's independent distributor network."

The Coors company was in excellent financial health. See Exhibit 5. It did not have any significant debt, short- or long-term. In fact, the management was philosophically opposed to borrowing money and financed its expansion and other needs through its stream of profits.

Liabilities and Shareholders' Equity	December 29, 1985	December 30, 1984
	(In thousands)	
Current liabilities:		
Accounts payable	$ 69,953	$ 66,463
Accrued salaries and vacations	38,725	31,155
Taxes, other than income taxes	26,105	24,650
Federal and state income taxes	5,127	4,846
Accrued expenses and other liabilities	43,392	45,309
Total current liabilities	183,302	172,423
Accumulated deferred income taxes	165,462	136,409
Other long-term liabilities	11,482	15,366
Shareholders' equity		
Capital stock:		
Class A common stock, $1 par value, authorized and issued 1,260,000 shares	1,260	1,260
Class B common stock, non-voting, no par value, authorized and issued 46,200,000 shares	11,000	11,000
	12,260	12,260
Paid-in capital	7,330	2,011
Retained earnings	942,506	903,129
	962,096	917,400
Less: Treasury stock, at cost, Class B shares, 12,062,276 in 1985 and 12,448,376 in 1984	25,635	26,455
Total shareholders' equity	936,461	890,945
Commitments and contingencies		
	$1,296,707	$1,215,143

The U.S. beer industry exhibited a seasonal pattern in demand. Sales rose in the warm weather and fell in the cool weather. Coors Brewing experienced the same pattern as the industry. The third quarter, July–September, at Coors typically accounted for about 34 per cent of sales, whereas the first quarter, January–March, accounted for only about 19 per cent. The second quarter and fourth quarter accounted for about 25 per cent and 22 per cent, respectively.

Established in 1873, Adolph Coors Company was now managed by the founder's grandsons, William K. and Joseph Coors, and Joseph's sons, Jeffrey and Peter Coors. William Coors was chairperson of the board of directors. Joseph Coors had been vice chairperson of the board and president until June 1985, when he yielded the presidency to Jeffrey Coors. The latter had been serving as divisional president of operations and technical affairs. At the same time, Peter Coors, who had been serving as divisional president for marketing, sales, and administration, was appointed president of the newly carved-out brewing division. The company's attempt at diversification of the business and the ages of William and Joseph Coors, both in their late sixties, made it advisable to make some changes. Jeffrey Coors was age forty and Peter Coors age thirty-nine. Early in their careers, both sons had been what were essentially unspecialized vice presidents. There were several other vice presidents. Peter Coors, who held a master's degree in business administration, was the only member of the family who had done graduate study in management. The family owned 86 per cent of the corporate stock, and the remaining 14 per cent of the shares of stock carried no voting rights. The Coors family was close-knit, inward-looking, and conservative. This philosophical stance and personality characteristic had been reinforced by a family tragedy in 1960, when Joseph Coors's other son, Adolph III, was kidnapped and murdered.

The company was rethinking its philosophies of marketing and general management. Some officials, including Peter Coors, described the corporation as arrogant about itself and its output. Ideas that did not originate within the family were not even considered. The firm was frequently referred to by outsiders, investment counselors, and workers as "baronial" and "feudal" and a "nineteenth-century industrial dynasty." Yet more potential changes were coming in the form of the younger Coors men and a new marketing officer. A new senior vice president for marketing, Robert A. Rechholtz, then age forty-two, arrived in 1982 from Schlitz, where he had held the same title.

However, allegations of rigid inflexibility were a little exaggerated. It was worth noting that Coors was the first brewer to adopt aluminum cans, now widely used in the industry. Management admitted, on the other hand, that its improved Press-Tab II, a can that was environmentally appealing to the company's largely western market because it had no pop-top, was a mistake because the average consumer found it impossible to open.

Top management's old-fashioned views, provincialism, and egotism had been temporarily reinforced by a fad occurrence on college campuses during the mid-1970s. Coors beer was the "in" beer among millions of educated young adults, people who were likely to enjoy good incomes and community positions in the future. This voguish product was carried long distances outside the normal trade territory by students. An informal distribution network arose among enthusiasts, and few college parties were complete without Coors. The bubble burst by 1977.

Labor relations in recent years had been stormy and harmful to Coors. In 1977, Local 366 of the Brewery Workers Union struck the company's plant, and it was quickly joined in a boycott by several other groups that were strongly opposed to the Coors family's conservative political stands. The effect of the boycott was particularly noteworthy in California, the company's largest market. Greatly increased advertising by Miller and Anheuser-Busch simultaneously affected Coors in California, so it was not known how much effect the unions and their political sympathizers had had on the sales. Coors's share of the important California market dropped from 40 per cent to 20 per cent. By the early 1980s, this figure had risen to only a little over 20 per cent and essentially stabilized thereafter. Opponents of Coors claimed all the credit. To the consternation of the labor movement, about two-thirds of Coors employees returned to work soon after the strike began. Not only did the strike fail, but the workers even petitioned the U.S. Department of Labor to hold an election on the fate of the local union. In accordance with normal legal machinery, such an election was held under government supervision, and the workers overwhelmingly rejected Local 366 as their bargaining agent. Thus, the Carter administration decertified the local union. However, embarrassed and infuriated national union leaders, some local union leaders in other states, plus some radical-left political groups kept the boycott alive. The Coors company became the object of great pressure and vilification, which still existed. The Coors fad on college campuses might have lasted longer if it had not been for the boycott call. Many students in particular embraced the boycott even though the Coors workers had overwhelmingly voted out their union. Many students were also extremely angry that the members of the Coors family made generous donations to conservative political groups.

Relations between Coors and minorities received much adverse publicity in the early and mid-1980s. A tiny number of people alleged ethnic discrimination. However, two large, respected national civil rights groups, one predominantly black and one predominantly Hispanic, conducted their own inquiries and concluded the allegations were without merit. A national television news program of investigative journalists made an inquiry and concluded the same. The television program questioned the true motivations of the complainants in this matter. Clearly, Coors was no community leader in ethnic relations, but it was not engaged in discrimination.

On the other hand, the company clearly made a major public relations blunder in 1984. William Coors, not known as an articulate, smooth public speaker who could build goodwill for the organization, nevertheless addressed a meeting of minority business owners in Denver. He aggressively criticized the political and economic leadership of the new black African republics, including their educational and technical preparation. He organized and phrased the speech so poorly that it was misinterpreted as a criticism of the black race and received international publicity. Despite Coors's explanations, clarifications, and apologies for the lack of clarity, significant public relations harm had been done and would linger.

The Coors organization had always been production-oriented rather than marketing-oriented. It had concentrated on perfect uniformity and turned out only one beer until 1978. It was a medium- to premium-priced product made in an unusual process that avoided pasteurization because the family was convinced that heat caused deterioration. The lack of pasteurization meant that extra care was used in handling and storing Coors goods. The company used refrigerated rail cars and trucks and had a corporate policy in effect in the channel of distribution to avoid offering Coors products to the public if they were more than sixty days old. In 1978 the company belatedly introduced a second product, Coors Light. Some family members, especially Jeffrey Coors, admitted to being furious that chemists in the organization had been secretly conducting some experimental work leading to the development of a light beer for the company. Management had previously told them not to do so.

The primary competitor in the reduced calorie category was Miller Lite, a successful brand that came out in 1975 and started the entire category of products. Miller Lite came out in response to consumer consciousness about feelings of fullness and the high calorie count in beers. However, the new Coors Light had 105 calories per 12-ounce serving versus 96 for Miller Lite. Coors's regular beer had 145 calories versus 150 for Miller High Life. See Exhibit 6.

Whether Coors Light was going to succeed was extremely questionable for several years. Michelob Light and Natural Light, both made by Anheuser-Busch, were number 2 and number 3 in the reduced-calorie category. At least fifteen other brands of light beer were launched in the industry. Yet Miller Lite, the innovator, was still hanging on to 57 per cent of the light market in 1981 and, in fact, had surpassed its owner's flagship brand, Miller High Life. In 1982, Anheuser-Busch introduced Budweiser Light nationally after an eleven-month period of meticulous test marketing and supported it with heavy advertising. Regular Budweiser was the number 1 selling brand in the country, and its name carried great commercial value for the light version. Bud Light outperformed Natural Light quickly, and it became questionable whether the latter should be retained. By 1982, Coors Light was judged a modest success. By 1984 it was a major success, second in

Exhibit 6   Calories per 12-ounce Serving, Selected Brands of Beer

Brand	Number of Calories
Michelob	168
Budweiser	156
Miller High Life	150
Schlitz	148
Stroh	148
Coors	145
Pabst	140
Budweiser (low alcohol)	137
Pearl	136
Michelob Light	134
Heidelberg	133
Stroh Light	115
Budweiser Light	108
Coors Light	105
Miller Lite	96
Schlitz Light	96
Heidelberg Light	96
Pabst Extra Light	70
Pearl Light	68

the reduced-calorie category and tenth in the industry. It moved to eighth place in the industry in 1985 with 3.1 per cent of the industry's sales. However, Bud Light was only an insignificant distance behind, with 3.0 per cent of the industry's sales, third place in the light category, and ninth in the industry. Bud Light was growing much faster than Coors Light.

Coors, the flagship brand of the Coors Company, suffered a declining share of the market for several consecutive years. Even temporary rises in Coors sales did not obscure the long-run trend line downward. Production of Coors brand dropped from 12.1 million barrels in 1977 to 8.7 million barrels in 1985. The company was finding it difficult to position this brand in the industry. See Exhibit 7.

After appropriate test marketing in the early 1980s, Coors Brewing added a premium Irish beer called George Killian's. It was under license from a French brewer, Société Brasserie Pelforth. However, Coors Brewing decided later to call it Killian's Irish Red. Offered in only twenty-four states, it was growing in sales and popularity. Geographical expansion for it had not been decided.

A test market was conducted in early 1984 for a proposed new product called Golden Lager. It was to appeal to consumers who wanted a little heavier taste and was aimed directly at Budweiser. Taste tests with blindfolded consumers showed that Coors brand was as full-bodied as Budweiser, but consumers had a strong nonrational perception that the Coors brand was lighter than Budweiser. Golden Lager was provided in the advertising with the theme "a rich, full-bodied beer that could remind you of Budweiser." It failed badly. The constant comparisons to Budweiser were later considered a mistake. Moreover, the executives suspected that many people falsely perceived Golden Lager as a superpremium-priced beer.

Brand	Company	Percent of U.S. Market
Budweiser	Anheuser-Busch	24.8%
Miller Lite	Miller	10.1
Miller High Life	Miller	7.0
Coors	Coors	4.8
Old Milwaukee	Stroh	4.1
Michelob	Anheuser-Busch	3.3
Busch and Busch Bavarian	Anheuser-Busch	3.3
Coors Light	Coors	3.1
Bud Light	Anheuser-Busch	3.0
Pabst	Pabst	2.7
Stroh	Stroh	2.7
Old Style	G. Heileman	2.7
Schaefer	Stroh	2.2

Therefore, a test market for a new premium beer, Coors Extra Gold, was begun in early 1985 in selected regions of California, Florida, Texas, Idaho, and Nevada. This product was positioned to appeal to consumers who desired a more full-bodied beer. It had a distinctly darker color. The advertising was placed in the hands of Tatham-Laird & Kudner of Chicago. This brand was presented as "the beer with a taste you can see." It was characterized as "bolder, golder, broad shouldered beer, the way beer oughta be." Advertisements featured power, muscles, sports prowess, and whimsical violence. There was a little humor, but the appeal was strongly to those who longed to be seen as extremely masculine.

The company began a test market of Colorado Chiller in late 1985. It was to compete in the wine cooler segment of the beverage industry, but it was not wine-based. Instead, like White Mountain Cooler from Stroh, it was based on malt and citrus. Anheuser-Busch had failed with a similar type of product quite a few years earlier.

The Coors organization had had in test market for five years a superpremium beer named Herman Joseph's 1868 to honor the founder of the company and the year he arrived in the United States as a young stowaway. If the tests were successful, it was planned to roll out the new product, introducing it in several cycles of a few states each until it was distributed everywhere the company offered Coors and Coors Light. The test area was expanded to include parts of Florida, Georgia, and Virginia, but the data were distinctly mixed. The length of the test market was one of the longest ever recorded on any type of product in the United States. The emotional involvement with the name of the founder made it difficult to perform an evaluation in a completely rational manner.

A joint venture was formed in August 1985 by Coors Brewing, Molson Companies, Ltd., of Montreal, and Kaltenberg Castle Brewery of Neuschwanstein, West Germany. They created Masters Brewing Company "to investigate new products that might be marketable here in the U.S." A new beer that had been under development since mid-1984 was on the market by the end of 1985 in four selected metropolitan areas, Miami, Boston, Columbus, and Washington, D.C. The product, made in the Coors plant, was named Masters Beer, and the launch was not considered a test market. Geographical expansion was to follow. Advertising for the new beer heavily emphasized the ages and experience of the three members of the joint venture. One of Canada's big three brewing firms, Molson was founded in 1786, and the venerable Kaltenberg Castle company was founded in 1260. There was some consideration of constructing brewery capacity for this product on the tract of land Coors owned near Elkton, in Rockingham County, Virginia.

Molson and Coors began their joint planning for Masters Beer in early 1982. The Bavarian firm was brought into the venture in September 1984 because the fundamental concept for the product and the joint company required a German presence. A German participant could provide technical knowledge and advice. Just as important, if not more so, was the consumer perception that Germany was the home of beer and the place where the finest beer in the world was made. As part of the $2.5 million spent on research and development by Molson and Coors for the joint venture, there was research on American consumer behavior. It showed clearly that the Americans who were studied perceived European-made beers as of finer quality than American beers and perceived Germany as the finest source of beer in Europe.

The Masters Brewing Company was a prominent part of an emerging industry reaction to imports and the additional segmentation of consumers. This reaction dealt with "specialty beers," that is, those outside the United States and Canadian tradition but not foreign-made. It was especially important in view of a nongrowing demand for beer. There was the feeling or suspicion among some industry executives that, if some consumers were going to drink less beer at any given time, then those people might want the product to be "more advancing" or have "more bite" or both. Jeffrey Coors stated that if there were a trend toward specialty beers, Coors Brewing wanted to lead that trend. This posture was unlike the corporate tradition of Coors. G. Heileman countered quickly, opening a Milwaukee facility costing $6 million in 1986 to make European-style beer. Russell Cleary, president of G. Heileman, stated that his new product was "goof-proof to make."

Until recent years, Coors Brewing spent little on advertising. At the beginning of the 1970s, it budgeted $3 million to $4 million annually, but this figure grew rapidly. By the early 1980s, despite dramatic increases in its advertising expenditures, Coors Brewing was still underspending its major national competitors if advertising were expressed as a ratio to barrels of beer produced. The discrepancy ranged from about 10 per cent to 50 per cent, depending on which firm one compared against. The company continued to push the advertising budget upward.

By 1984, Coors Brewing's advertising reached $138,750,000, which was 14.8 per cent of its beer sales, and in 1985 the corresponding figures were $165,050,000 and 15.3 per cent. See Exhibit 8. If advertising were expressed as

Exhibit 8   Advertising Expenditures of Coors Brewing by Year, 1980–1985

1985	$165,050,000
1984	138,750,000
1983	118,742,000
1982	88,103,000
1981	85,817,000
1980	66,752,000

spending per barrel, Coors Brewing apparently had become the largest spender in the industry, whereas it had been one of the smallest spenders fifteen years earlier. It was ordinarily to be expected that advertising per unit of product would have to rise in a period when extensive new geographical territories were being entered. Whether this per centage leadership in the industry would continue was very much a topic for internal discussion. The Coors brand beer, the company's flagship product, was the fifth-largest dollar spender for advertising in the industry, behind the number 1 spender, Budweiser; number 2, Miller High Life; number 3, Michelob; and number 4, Stroh's. The second five spenders were, in order, L.A., Meister Brau, Lowenbrau, Old Milwaukee, and Heineken. Both Budweiser and Miller High Life outspent Coors brand by about three to one. Coors augmented print and electronic media with sponsorship of concerts and some sporting events, such as rodeos, motor sports, and the Coors International Bicycle Classic.

In the last few years, Coors brand advertising had been using a theme, "Coors is the One." The expression "the difference worth tasting" was repetitively used. Actor Mark Harmon was featured in many of the messages built around this theme. The objectives were twofold: to gain consumer awareness of Coors and to position the brand as "a distinctive superlative product—the desired choice among premium beers." Killian's Irish Red employed the tag line "Killian's Red, Instead" quite effectively, and Coors Light used the "Silver Bullet" theme.

Until recent years, Coors Brewing relied on a conservative, inhouse advertising department to a greater extent than most other brewers. The company retained a large national advertising agency under contract for at least media relations but would not delegate much decision-making authority to the agency. For the light beer, Peter Coors was able in 1978 to switch the advertising to a large international agency based in New York. By the mid-1980s, each Coors product was in the hands of a large advertising agency.

The Coors company was making some effort to diversify. The largest attempt was Roberts Rice Mill in Weiner, Arkansas. Others included Coors Energy Company, which owned or had interests in 355 oil or gas wells or both and held oil and gas leases on 466,000 acres of land, and Coors BioTech Products Company in Johnstown, Colorado. Using the Coors knowledge of fermentation chemistry, this plant produced refined starch, fructose syrup, and animal nutrition supplements. Coors owned grain elevators in seven western and southern cities and paper converting plants in Boulder, Colorado, and Lawrenceburg, Tennessee. Suncoa Foods, Inc., of Greeley, Colorado, manufactured snack foods. In 1984, Suncoa test marketed the CocoMo candy bar made with brewer's yeast by a patented process. The product provided chocolate flavor without caffeine or other potentially objectionable ingredients. Coors owned an aluminum recycling plant that produced aluminum foil. It was not yet profitable. Coors Porcelain Company was another subsidiary, and it itself had some related subsidiaries, including Royal Worcester Industrial Ceramics, Ltd., in Wales, which was bought in 1984. Other ceramics locations were in Norman, Oklahoma; Hillsboro, Oregon; Lakewood, Grand Junction, and Denver, Colorado; El Cajon, California; Benton, Arkansas; Glenrothes, Scotland; and Rio Claro, Brazil. The nonbeer subsidiaries provided $197,767,000 of the company's $1,132,643 sales revenue in 1984, compared to $203,242,000 in 1985. Taken as a whole, the subsidiaries were marginally profitable in most years but lost money in 1984. However, the porcelain subsidiaries earned acceptable profits in most years.

Advise the Coors organization.

Mermax Toy Company, Inc.

Thomas Smith, vice-president of marketing for Mermax Toy Company, sat at his desk contemplating the memorandum he had just received from William Jones, president of Mermax. The memorandum, as well as the request outlined therein, came as no surprise to Smith, as it was merely a follow-up to the conference held the previous day among the top executives of Mermax. Various problems that Mermax was presently experiencing has been examined and analyzed by the group during their meeting. Among those problems were such issues as: (1) decreasing sales; (2) a loss in market share; (3) declining profits; and (4) excess inventory—consisting, mainly, of several "fad" items that had been overproduced. The executives were particularly concerned because, until recently, the company had experienced steady growth since its inception. However, that pattern of growth had been interrupted by what seemed, in hindsight, to be several ill-advised decisions.

The executives had decided that a long range plan for the next decade should be completed. They agreed that the plan should outline steps designed to turn the company around. The executives felt that at least some of their bad decisions had been the result of a lack of long-range planning. Smith's particular role in the planning process involved his taking a hard look at the results of several marketing research studies recently completed by his staff. He had been instructed to utilize the results of these studies to develop a revised, overall marketing strategy for the company. The company's existing marketing plan was sketchy, at best, and had not been updated in recent years to reflect the type of strategies needed to compete successfully in a dynamic, ever-changing industry such as the toy industry. Specifically, the memorandum stated that Smith should overhaul the marketing strategy for the company's present product line; propose alternatives for the elimination of excess inventory items; investigate the possibility of new target markets; propose new products to reach those target markets; outline procedures for the production and timely introduction of those products; and develop procedures to create a sales force.

Smith, who had only been with the company for two months, knew that his performance on this task was crucial to his future with the company. His predecessor had been asked to resign as a result of the predicament in which the company found itself. The previous vice-president of marketing had failed to utilize marketing studies routinely performed by the marketing staff. He preferred instead to make "seat of the pants" decisions based upon his "feel" for the market. This method had proven successful for him in several instances, and, consequently, his fellow executives had come to rely on his judgment quite heavily. However, several poor decisions he had made regarding the production of "fad" items, as well as his increasing emphasis upon the marketing of such items, had caused the company to sustain some very heavy losses in the past.

Background on the Company

Mermax Toy Company was started in 1953 by William P. Jones, father of the present company president. During its first decade and a half, the company was

This case was developed by Charles M. Futrell for Mermax Toy Company. The company name has been changed.

a closely held corporation; all of its stock was held by members of the Jones family. In the late 1960s, the corporation went public in an effort to raise additional capital for expansion. During the first fifteen years of operation, Mermax manufactured toys and games for children in the five- to fourteen-year-old age bracket. Their product line consisted of "staple" items—cars, trucks, trains, dolls and traditional games. They manufactured high-quality toys—a major objective of the company from its inception. The company's distribution channel was a manufacturer's agent, Glass and Associates, that sold directly to retailers—primarily exclusive toy stores and better department stores in large cities throughout the nation. Jones and Bob Glass, head of Glass and Associates, had been friends since high school. Glass handled noncompeting lines of toys and had excellent relations with major department stores and toy stores in the fifteen largest cities in the United States.

As disposable income grew, the top executives of the corporation decided they must expand their product line if they were going to maintain their market share. The expansion monies were used to introduce a greater variety of staple products, as well as several "fad" items. The fad items proved successful for a few years, encouraging the company to venture even further into this area. As a result, more and more emphasis was placed upon the introduction of fad products. Such items have a short life cycle and are risky to manufacture. Most of the fad items introduced by the company had failed in the marketplace. This resulted in the profit loss with which the company was now faced.

The Toy Industry

The toy industry is a highly competitive industry in the United States. As an industry, it has enjoyed steady growth since the early 1950s. In 1969 total industry sales were about $2.2 billion. By 1972 industry sales reached the $2.7 billion mark, an increase of 12.8 per cent over the previous year's $2.4 billion in sales. By 1989 annual sales were an estimated $6.0 billion. Toy sales are highly sensitive to consumer spending patterns, i.e., they depend heavily upon disposable income. The product lines of toy companies are generally characterized as broad and constantly changing, and a company's success is largely dependent upon its ability to develop new products that respond to changing shifts in tastes and preferences. Furthermore, the toy industry has historically been considered highly seasonal in nature; it has been heavily dependent upon Christmas for the bulk of its sales. With the advent of television, promotion became a major component in the marketing mix, as companies came to rely more and more heavily on television commercials to promote their products.

Over the years, costs rose as a result of several variables: (1) increasing costs of raw materials; (2) increasing costs of labor; and (3) increased emphasis upon toy/product safety. Toy companies also began to receive criticism from various consumer groups for deceptive packaging and advertising. Furthermore, the industry was faced with a declining birth rate, as well as shifting preferences, primarily in the ten- to fourteen-year-old age group. Moreover, distribution patterns were changing as discount stores entered the retail scene throughout the country. In order to combat the seasonal nature of their business, as well as the declining birth rate situation, many toy companies began to diversify. They entered related areas such as motion pictures, pet products, amusement parks, sporting goods, swimming pools, and beach products.

Mermax Marketing Studies

Thomas Smith was well aware of the various shifts and movements in the industry as a whole. With hindsight he identified quite readily numerous opportunities that had been missed by Mermax. He believed that some of the strategies that had been implemented by various successful toy companies were worthy of consideration by Mermax. However, he was also aware that if Mermax was to regain and/or increase its market share, he must also anticipate future trends upon which Mermax could capitalize. For such projections, he turned to the recently completed marketing studies that had been done by the Mermax marketing staff. In these studies he noted a rising demand for: (1) preschool products; (2) toys that were educational in nature; (3) unisex toys; (4) games; (5) crafts; and (6) sporting goods. He noted also that there was a growing demand among adults for the last three product areas mentioned. Furthermore, one of his studies indicated an increasing demand in overseas markets. These markets had proven successful for some companies in the marketing of fad items whose life cycle had peaked in the United States. Yet, Smith felt he needed to be cautious. An article in *Standard & Poor's Industry Survey* reported that electronics had increased sales for the entire toy industry, but several of the large toy makers were experiencing profit losses.

With these variables in mind, he proceeded to sketch out the first draft of his new marketing proposal for Mermax Toy Company. Included in this plan would be a strategic marketing management analysis using a GE/McKinsey nine-cell multifactor matrix with classification of product groupings into appropriate cells and recommendations as to which product groups to proceed with, based on this analysis, including a list of relevant industry attractiveness and business strength criteria.

QUESTION

1. Discuss and/or develop a strategic marketing program for Mermax, including the analysis noted above.

The Southwestern Company

History

The Southwestern Company was founded in Nashville, Tennessee, in 1855. The first college students began selling books door to door in 1868, and the company has had a student program continuously since then. Today, students from more than 500 colleges and universities across the country participate in the program.

This case was developed and written by Daniel W. Moore, vice-president of marketing, The Southwestern Company.

Southwestern is a publisher of home reference, religious, and children's books. These books are sold at wholesale prices to independent contractors (virtually all of whom are college students), who sell the books at retail to individual consumers in their homes during the summer months each year.

Students travel to Nashville at their own expense at the beginning of the summer for an intensive week of training in selling, business management, and attitude. This week of training, known as Sales School, is designed to teach people who have never sold anything before how to be successful in door-to-door sales. It includes all the elements of effective personal selling, but in addition teaches the rudiments of business management and record keeping, since each dealer is responsible for his or her own merchandise and money.

Students then travel to another part of the country generally quite removed from where they attend college. In Sales School, they are taught how to locate a place to stay in a private home, and students live and work in the same community for the entire summer. First-year dealers usually work alone, although experienced dealers (called Student Managers) frequently are accompanied by first-year dealers for further training as they make their calls.

Dealers understand that their profits depend entirely on how much they sell and that perseverence and long hours are prerequisites for financial success. A sales meeting held each Sunday afternoon provides positive feedback, further guidance in sales technique, competition, and esprit de corps.

Each dealer may pay cash with each order or (as virtually all do) may submit a Letter of Credit signed by two financially secure individuals who agree to be responsible for up to $500 each, in the event of a default in payment by the dealer. This opens a merchandise account in the name of the dealer.

As sales are made, deposits are collected by the dealer. From these deposits, dealers pay their expenses and remit the balance to their accounts at the company. At the end of the summer, dealers order books for delivery to their customers, collect the balances due upon delivery, and then return to Nashville to wrap up their summers. The amount charged to their accounts is subtracted from the amount remitted, and a check for the credit balance is issued.

Experienced dealers who return for additional summers have the opportunity to recruit other dealers and receive dealer discounts from the company based on the sales of those dealers. This provides additional profits for dealers and encourages them to return each year and continue building a sales organization, as these discounts encompass anyone within their organization or the organizations built by those they initially recruited.

Products

Southwestern publishes a line of home reference, children's and specialty books, all of which are available only through student dealers. While Southwestern owns the copyrights on virtually all books sold, both editorial and printing work are contracted out.

Dealers sell in one of two distinct product divisions, each having an array of four or five titles. While this is not a large number, the books are written with broad appeal, so that almost every family will find something of interest in a dealer's sample case.

Editorial investment is an important priority for the company, since keeping products current and exciting is a significant part of keeping dealers enthused about what they are selling. The company's marketing department conducts regular surveys both of dealers and ultimate consumers that form the basis for product revisions or new product creation.

Southwestern books are moderately priced; the average retail sale is about $75. Dealer profit averages about 40 per cent of suggested retail, or approximately $30. A dealer averaging two sales a day during a 66-day summer would therefore have gross profit of just under $4,000. Expenses vary depending upon the spending habits of the individual. Average expenses are about $1,500 for the summer.

Ownership

Southwestern was privately held by executives from its origin until 1969, when it was acquired by the Times-Mirror Company of Los Angeles. In 1982, a group of employees bought back the company in a leveraged buyout, and the company is once again privately held by those who manage it.

Organization

Southwestern employs more than 150 people full time in both sales management and administrative positions.

Sales Organization

In addition to several thousand first-year and experienced independent dealers, the company has several levels of employee managers. District sales managers, sales directors, vice-presidents, and the president all sold books for several summers as college students.

Administrative Organization

Accounting, data processing, operations, secretarial services, traffic, and marketing all exist as separate support functions for the sales organization. In some cases, individuals heading these departments sold books as students, but the majority have different backgrounds.

The company is highly sales driven, which in the direct-selling industry also translates into *recruiting* driven. Support staff is therefore oriented toward the importance of supporting the sales managers as they travel campuses throughout the school year recruiting dealers. In the summer, of course, attention is directed exclusively toward the sales effort.

Results

Average dealer profit recently was $2,006.68 *per month,* ranging from an average of $1,482 per month for first-year dealers, to an average of $3,614 per month for fourth-year dealers (figures based upon dealers working more than 20 days). Although not all dealers finish the summer, about 70 per cent do.

Abbreviated financial statements appear on the last page of this summary.

Diversifications

Southwestern management has from time to time developed other businesses to leverage on existing strengths in the areas of sales training, motivation, and ability to sell effectively on a cold-call basis.

Student Buying Service

The intention was to provide large-scale buying power for student dealers through wholesale buying. However, the base of dealers was simply not large enough to secure adequate discounts; the diversity of items wanted created ordering and fulfillment problems; and the advent of the mass merchandisers at approximately the same time eliminated the competitive price advantage. The venture was therefore short-lived. Among the lessons learned was the importance of thinking carefully through the *implementation* issues for a good idea before getting into it, as well as listing the potential gains.

Fund-raising

Many students who had graduated from college were not willing to make career commitments, because of desires to travel, continue recruiting, go eventually to graduate school, and other reasons. This left them with "free time" in the fall of the year, before recruiting season began. A program was started in which these dealers called on elementary and high school groups, setting up fund-raising programs through selling Southwestern products in their communities. This program expanded to become the School and Club Division, and eventually a separate company, Great American Opportunities, which is now in some 35 states and with a full-time sales force of more than 150 people.

Direct Sales of Home Devotional Program

In an effort to retain still more of the highly trained student dealers who would otherwise go with other companies, Southwestern started a full-time division selling religious products on an appointment/referral basis as opposed to door to door. The product had an average price of more than $500, compared to about $70 in the student business. Many of the new recruits had evangelical backgrounds, which gave them conviction in the product line, but also limited their available selling time because of extensive church and family commitments. In addition, a competitive home devotional product sold through direct sales hit the market at about the same time which offered just as much but at a lower price.

This operation was discontinued after approximately four years. Among the lessons learned was the importance of recruiting a sales force with both sufficient time to make the number of presentations necessary for success *and* proclivity toward the product. Since sales of this magnitude usually require both spouses to be present, selling in the evenings was very important, yet it was the sellers' evening hours which were occupied by other events.

Career Placement

As a service to students, a full-time placement counselor was hired to help set up career job interviews with interested companies wanting to hire students with this kind of sales experience. After a short time, the decision was made to charge companies a fee for this service, in recognition of the value employers placed on dealers' background. This operation has grown steadily so that now four full-time counselors work with more than 100 companies in placement activities, and the division has a positive net contribution to Southwestern from its operations. It is a licensed placement agency and has expanded into executive-level searches as well as placement of people without Southwestern background. Continued growth is planned for the future.

Direct Response

Beginning initially with attempts to sell additional product to dealers' customers, the direct response operation split off to become a completely separate company in 1984. Concentrating on selling collectibles and annual book programs, this company is showing rapid sales growth.

Athletes' Division

Southwestern hired the former head football coach of a major Southeastern Conference university to build a new division oriented toward college athletes. This new division involves direct sales during the summer, but these athletes stay in their home areas and sell to people in their personal "networks"—people they know and people to whom they are referred. The product line involves health and safety-oriented products, including fire extinguishers and water purification systems.

Market Outlook

The company's most recent strategic plan highlighted the following threats and opportunities during the next five to ten years.

Threats

1. Increased general affluence of the population means parents have more resources to finance their children's college education—less need for students to make large amounts of money in the summer may dampen recruiting.
2. Shrinking numbers of teen-agers and college-age students reduces the available recruiting pool and bids up wages of competing summer opportunities, putting pressure on Southwestern's comparative financial advantage.
3. Increasing percentage of working women means fewer people home during the day. More than 60 per cent of mothers are projected to be working outside the home by 1990.
4. Stricter regulation of door-to-door sales in many localities hampers placement of dealers.
5. Alternative buying methods (retail, direct mail, TV advertising) make book purchases from other sources easier for the consumer.
6. "Life-style"–oriented value structure reduces the number of students interested in becoming district sales managers despite its excellent financial potential, because of the heavy travel and long hours involved in such a career.

Opportunities

1. Cuts in federal financial aid and disproportionate increases in tuition and school expenses put pressure on students to find summer work with potentially higher profits.
2. College students are generally "probusiness" in their attitudes. The most recent UCLA/Department of Education study found that 25 per cent of in-

coming freshmen are planning on majoring in and finding careers in business, the highest percentage in several decades. This enhances Southwestern's appeal.

3. "Mommy boom" means large growth in the population of preschoolers and primary-age children during next ten years. This is Southwestern's main target market for its educational and reading books. This segment is prepared to invest in educational materials for children.
4. Growth in suburban and small-town populations increases available prospects for books in the company's traditional selling areas.
5. Continued payback of obligations frees up capital for investment in both current and new ventures.
6. Highly trained dealers are much in demand by other companies anxious to hire recent college graduates with a proven track record of success at an early age.

APPENDICES

Appendix A. Abbreviated Income Statement (Disguised and Modified)

Years Ending December 31, 1990 and December 31, 1989 ($000)

	1990	1991
Total revenues	$25,400	$24,600
Cost of sales	6,200	6,200
Selling expenses	8,800	8,200
General and administrative expenses	2,800	2,200
Depreciation and interest	4,700	5,800
Total expenses	22,500	22,400
Pre-tax income	$ 2,900	$ 2,300

Appendix B. Recent Recruiting Results

After three years of declining numbers of student dealers, Southwestern reversed this downtrend in 1986, increasing in the numbers of both first-year and experienced dealers.

Appendix C. Excerpts from "Criteria for Starting a New Profit Center," Internal Paper, The Southwestern Company

I. Fundamental Criteria for New Ventures
A. New profit centers should only be started when the eventual returns from their development have a positive net present value, and ideally equal or exceed those that could be achieved if the same resources were devoted to existing businesses. Target return on sales before taxes is 12 per cent.
 1. What can the new business do that a new product or an enhancement of the current business could not do?

2. How does the new venture fit into the company's overall business philosophy?

3. Is it truly a sound business move, or is it a knee-jerk reaction to competition, a place to put disaffected managers, or jumping onto a trend-wagon without proper thought?

B. How would profits generated by the new venture be additional profits, not simply profits cannibalized from portions of the existing business?

C. Cost calculations for developing the new business should include the following, hard-to-quantify costs:

1. The cost to the current business of management time diverted into the new business.

2. The dollar impact of retaliation by other firms already in the business, including potential price-cutting which could lower the margins that may have attracted us in the first place.

3. The "costs of learning" involved in developing procedures and personnel which will operate the new business most effectively.

D. Do we currently possess the management skills required for the new business, and if not, how much are we willing to invest to acquire those skills?

E. What is the synergy with our existing businesses we plan to create?

F. What is our distinct comparative advantage whch leads us to believe we are well-suited to the business?

II. Positioning the New Venture

A. What *need* will the new business address?

1. Whom are we targeting as customers?

2. What is the potential of this market segment?

3. Who is already addressing this market?

   a. What are their resources, weaknesses, and strategies?

   b. How do they currently address the market need?

4. How will our new business specifically address this need?

   a. What are the comparative advantages *to the customer* of our approach?

   b. How will we communicate these advantages to potential customers?

   c. Why hasn't this idea been tried before? Will it be easy for others to copy our advantage? How long will that take?

Appendix D. Statement of Mission and Purpose

To excel within our industries in product and service quality, building for the future as we fulfill our commitments to our customers, our employees, and our investors.

Question

1. How should The Southwestern Company diversify into other businesses without jeopardizing the success of the core business? What other businesses should the company consider? Why? How should it go about getting started in those businesses?

PART TWO

Marketing Situational Analysis

Every marketing manager is faced with a constantly changing environment. If you can dominate this environment, you are well on your way to success as a marketing manager. The first key to dominating your environment is to understand its makeup. You will learn the latest techniques to accomplish this in Chapter 4, Marketing Research and the Marketing Information System. Not only are alternative methods explained, but patterns observed in successful companies are revealed. Then in Chapter 5, Environmental Scanning, Situational Analysis, and Problem Solving, you will be given a methodology useful for solving complicated marketing problems and making the hard decisions necessary to take advantage of the opportunities and to avoid the threats inherent in any business situation. Many students have used this technique in other than marketing courses with highly gratifying results. Chapter 6, Competitive Analysis, will show you methods for analyzing this most dangerous of environmental forces at loose in your environment—dangerous because it is an intelligent force that can act against your company's interests. It possesses great capacity for causing your strategy to fail. Chapter 7, Buyer Behavior, gives you a powerful weapon for marketing to consumers and organizations. Finally, Chapter 8, Forecasting, offers techniques that will permit you to predict results before implementation.

Marketing Research and the Marketing Information System

CHAPTER OBJECTIVES

- Understand the concepts of marketing research and the marketing information system.

- Know the importance of marketing research and of the marketing information system to the marketing manager.

- Know how to use marketing research and the marketing information system in reaching marketing objectives and for preparing a marketing plan.

Increasing Sales by 28 Per Cent from Established Customers

Most retail stores get approximately 75 per cent of their volume from only 25 per cent of their customers. Therefore, there is a tremendous potential for expansion among the 75 per cent of repeat shopping customers who only contribute 25 per cent of total sales. To go after this 25 per cent, Marvin J. Rothenberg developed a specialized marketing information system called "The Customer Intensification System" (CIS). This system enables the marketing manager to determine customer classifications and locations with the most opportunity, isolate the classifications at each location that are underperforming, identify the

specific competitive stores at which customers purchase similar merchandise, reveal customer classifications for which compatibility is most important, plan sales events to give more emphasis to certain classifications and locations, determine whether the inventory by price line for those classifications is in accord with customer demand, find price-line inconsistencies across classifications, set inventory levels by price zone, supply buyers with guidelines for assortment planning and markdown depth, and make advertising more productive. If this sounds pretty impressive, the results are even more so.

As a result of this capability, CIS has been credited with producing a 28 per cent sales increase in one merchandise group for a company, for adding

172,000 more transactions in a single department within two months for another company, and for increasing gross margin by $2.7 million during the spring season for yet another company.[1]

The Ultimate Competitive Advantage

George Moody is president of Security Pacific Corporation. Security Pacific is the fifth largest bank holding company in the United States. When President Moody enters his office, he may decide that he would like to review the profitability of all of his 1,000-plus retail branches and maybe check the status of Third World loans. How would he do this? If you think he would press a bunch of buttons and have executives come out of the woodwork to make the reports, you would be wrong. Moody, using simple oral commands, calls up all the data he wants, to whatever detail he requires, using a desktop computer. If he wants to strategize and see what would happen with different inputs, closing twenty or thirty of his least profitable branches or stretching out some country's loans for two or three or more years, he can do all of these things as he sits, projecting the results onto a big screen. Nor does he need to wait for memos to be dictated, typed, and proofread. He simply taps out the orders and they go off via electronic mail. When will this wonderful scientific gadgetry actually be in place at Security Pacific so that George Moody can do these things? It already is. Moody is one of those rare top executives who has converted his operation into the age of MIS with his own desktop computer. Security Pacific is an acknowledged leader in MIS and, as George Moody sees it, a PC on the CEO's desk is the ultimate competitive advantage.[2]

How the Army Uses MIS to Win Recruits

To maintain manpower strength, the Army has to make 780,000 sales a year. While many of these sales are soldiers who reenlist or sign up for extended service in the army, almost 140,000 involve contracts with new recruits from civilian life. After some tough times, the army has routinely reached its sales quota in the last few years with the help of the Program Analysis and Evaluation Directorate of the U.S. Army Recruiting Command.

This unusual marketing research agency must monitor all the environmental variables, the environs of the marketplace—especially direct competition from civilian businesses and universities—and other alternatives that new recruits might otherwise seek. Because the army uses increasingly complex and sophisticated weapon systems, it must aim its efforts at recruits who have the intelligence necessary to operate them.

Like any good MIS organization, the Program Analysis and Evaluation Directorate analyzes its market and spots variables that can improve performance. One of its analyses showed that the over-twenty-one age group consistently scores higher in mental aptitude tests than do the younger recruits. The army accordingly changed its advertising to appeal to that segment of the population. Another analysis noted youth's attitudes toward recruiting incentives. Incentives such as enlistment bonuses were changed accordingly. Said one army recruiter, "Advertising positioning is something we're getting more involved in. If you can find out what issues the individual with the propensity to join the military is interested in, you can emphasize those issues in recruitment ads."[3]

MIS: The Marketing Revolution: What and Why

MIS, the **marketing information system**, is in fact revolutionizing marketing. Researchers have found sales increases arising from MIS to be from 10 per cent to more than 30 per cent; return on investment in some cases exceeds 100 per cent.[4] Yet, misused, MIS provides as much danger as it does potential. One marketing executive forgot to include a price discount plan for one key component. The net result, despite the good MIS system, was an $8 million error.[5] But despite problems and blunders, few argue against the MIS revolution or its tremendous potential.

The chairman of a Hollywood entertainment company recently acquired a rather unique MIS system. It allows him to track the minute-by-minute status of every important deal his executives are pursuing. He can instantly view who is involved in each deal, all pertinent communications, and all actions needed to close the deal—he even gets the margin notes of comments by his top subordinates who have access to the system.[6] In fact, the whole world has "gone Hollywood," and MIS is beginning to get top billing in many firms.

In 1984 the FMC Corporation, the Chicago-based producer of machinery and chemicals, promoted perhaps the first general of corporate communications. A young executive, Dan W. Irwin, was given the title of director of information, reporting directly to the president of FMC, with a charter "to effectively apply information technologies to increasing the returns of the corporation."[7] A survey of executives conducted by *Industry Week* also supplied indicators of an explosion. As indicated in Figure 4-1, this survey showed that roughly two-thirds of the executives surveyed used a computer or word processor for business purposes, and an incredible 47 per cent indicated that this use was frequent. Forty-five per cent of the executives stated that they had a computer terminal, word processor, or electronic work station in their office, and of those that did not, 29 per cent stated that it was very likely, or somewhat likely that they would have one within the next six months.[8]

How often, if ever, do you use a computer or word processor for business purposes?

Frequently	47%
Occasionally	14
Rarely	6
Never	32

Do you have a computer terminal, word processor, or electronic workstation in your office?

Yes	45%
No	55

If you do not have one now, how likely is it that you will have one in the next six months?

Very likely	12%
Somewhat likely	17
Not too likely	19
Not at all likely	52

Source: Perry Pascarella, "Computer Arrives in Executive Suite," *Industry Week*, August 6, 1984, p. 15.

Figure 4-1 Usage of Computers and Word Processors by Executives

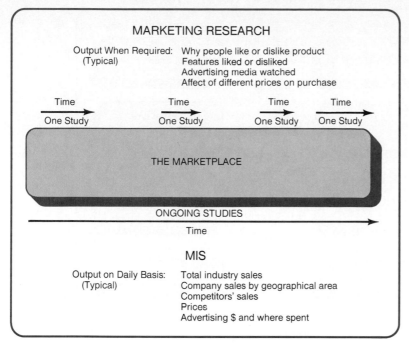

MARKETING RESEARCH

Output When Required: Why people like or dislike product
(Typical)   Features liked or disliked
                                      Advertising media watched
                                      Affect of different prices on purchase

Time →   Time →   Time →   Time →
One Study   One Study   One Study   One Study

THE MARKETPLACE

ONGOING STUDIES →
Time

MIS

Output on Daily Basis: Total industry sales
(Typical)   Company sales by geographical area
                                      Competitors' sales
                                      Prices
                                      Advertising $ and where spent

Figure 4-2   MIS and Marketing Research

The enormous growth in the popularity and stature of data as a marketing tool is due in large part to the proliferation of personal computers.[9] Marketers have greater and easier access to data and can analyze and apply the results of their analysis more easily than ever before.

MIS and Marketing Research

MIS grew out of marketing research, but the two are not the same. Marketing research tends to be research of a particular facet of marketing over a discrete time period. Accordingly, it is a snapshot of one or more aspects of the marketplace for a fixed time period. This can be seen in Figure 4-2.

MIS differs from marketing research in the following ways:

1. MIS is a continuous study of the market factors important to the enterprise, not only intermittent studies.
2. MIS utilizes many more data sources, both external and internal, than does marketing research.
3. MIS receives, analyzes, and distills a far greater volume of information inputs than does market research.

You can see the contrasts between MIS and marketing research in Figure 4-3. As a result, in many firms, instead of MIS being considered a subset of market research, the Market Research Department is considered to be one part of MIS. In firms with an MIS system, marketing research tends to concentrate more on specific individual projects or in areas in which inputs to

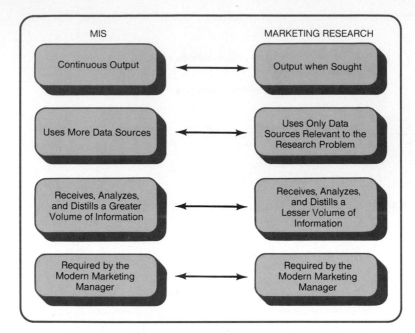

Figure 4-3   MIS vs. Marketing Research

the MIS have not yet been established or to concentrate resources on a specific area of sudden or immediate interest to the marketing manager or the firm. In firms without an MIS, market research attempts to fill the gap by routinely monitoring sales and customers without an overall system.

What Exactly Is MIS?

The American Marketing Association defines MIS as a set of procedures and methods for the regular, planned collection, analysis, and presentation of information for use in making marketing decisions.[10]

Basic inputs into marketing information systems are shown in Figure 4-4. These include inquiry handling of market research, competitive tracking, sales force management, sales forecasting, telemarketing, sample quotation tracking, and call report generation.[11]

What Can MIS Do for You?

The benefits of MIS for any marketing manager are many. Here are just a few:

1. *More timely information and reports.* Information eventually goes stale in any business situation. In a fast-moving marketing situation, it goes stale rapidly. Therefore, more timely reports within time constraints imposed by the situation mean better performance.
2. *More flexible and selective retrieval of data.* Marketing managers can ask specific questions to provide selective retrieval of information, thus

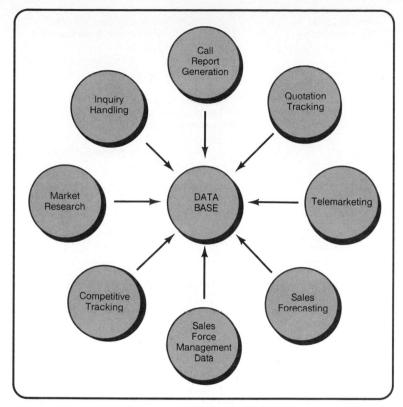

Figure 4-4   Areas of Data Input into the MIS

Source: Adapted from John B. Kennedy, "Start with a Data Base," *Sales and Marketing Management* (December 3, 1984), p. 68.

obtaining only the information they want when they want it. For those areas of interest they can ask deeper and supplemental questions to help pinpoint and obtain additional information.

3. *Instantaneous spotting of problems, opportunities, and trends.* Because of the availability of so many additional sources of information, these problems, opportunities, and trends can be rapidly confirmed or denied by other sources, beyond simply perceiving what is happening.

4. *Use of a multitude of different informational sources with rapid integration.*

5. *Easy or even automatic translation of market demands into production requirements.*

6. *Testing of alternative strategies or plans using simulation models with the capability of varying one or more inputs to achieve different results.* Thus, the marketing manager can much more easily ask the question: What would happen if?

7. *The capability of making and taking immediate decisions based on sales reports and market reaction to any action taken by the marketing manager.*

8. *Preventing information suppression by anyone within the firm.* Thus, difficult decisions, such as when a product or product line should be withdrawn, can be more accurately made.

Collecting data	Gather more data and retrieve it faster
Organizing data	Data input in any order and organized later
Retrieving customer data	Can be done faster, easier, and with fewer personnel
Educating	Determine your own format for presenting for training
Processing	Do or redo any calculations far faster than the human mind
Persuading	Customized reports for customers
Planning	Projections easy and quick; planning time cut
Communicating	Personalized communications, simple charting and graphing
Traveling	Plan sales calls efficiently; adjust unproductive scheduling

Source: Adapted from Norman Wiener, "PCs and Marketers Forge a Productive Alliance," *Sales and Marketing Management* (February 6, 1984), p. 37.

Figure 4-5 How Integration and Use of Personal Computers as a Part of MIS Can Help Sales Managers

9. *Permitting the emergence of politically unmentionable or unpopular so-lutions to a particular marketing problem.*
10. *A more accurate basis for relating marketing inputs to marketing results, thus allowing for a better basis for marketing planning.*[12–18]

As MIS has grown more sophisticated, personal computers have entered the picture and been integrated into the MIS system. Personal computer benefits specific to sales managers are shown in Figure 4-5. Figure 4-6 shows computer usage in management activities of both main frames and personal computers.

To summarize the benefits, MIS will increase the ability of the marketing manager to assess the market and sales potential, to improve strategies and the marketing mix, to reduce costs, and to improve return on assets.[19]

Activity	Avg. % of Time on This Activity	Managers Using Mainframes	Managers Using PCs	Managers Using Both
Promotional Strategy Development	18.5%	17%	80%	19%
Forecasting Sales	10.5%	46%	87%	47%
Making Pricing Decisions	10.8%	42%	71%	30%
Selling Activities	23.1%	24%	68%	29%
Product Development	15.8%	10%	61%	24%
Sales Force Management	21.1%	36%	45%	23%
Product Distribution	11.3%	32%	26%	22%
Managing Inventory	10.7%	41%	25%	18%
Quality Control	10.0%	9%	22%	7%

Source: Adapted from John T. Mentzer, Camille P. Schuster, and David C. Roberts, "Microcompter Versus Mainframe Usage by Marketing Professionals," *Journal of the Academy of Marketing Science*, vol. 15, no. 2 (Summer 1987), p. 6.

Figure 4-6 Managerial Activities: Importance and Use of Computers (Based on 346 Marketing Executives)

Organizing for MIS

It should be clear from the foregoing that the implementation of an MIS in a company may not be easy and that four major issues must be considered. These include (1) top management support, (2) involvement of line marketing managers in the system development, (3) composition of the system development team, and (4) provision for convenient system use by marketing managers. Let's look at each of these in turn.

Top Management Support

Top management support is absolutely required not only because of the expense of the system, but because of the allocation of resources—mainly human—necessary for the system's implementation and for its efficient and effective use once installed. Few of the problems mentioned in previous paragraphs can be overcome by the users themselves without the support of top management. In addition, top management involvement can minimize friction between user and designers and ensure that the requirements of the system from the users are both accurate and satisfied by the design.

Involvement of Line Marketing Managers in System Development

Without user support—that is, line marketing managers—the design is almost certain to be faulty and may have little support by the user once it is installed. The result of eliminating line manager involvement during the design and implementation process has resulted in million-dollar "white elephants" in certain companies. In such companies, the MIS installed resulted in more harm than good.

Composition of the System Development Team

It is essential that the system development team include representatives of those who develop the models, those who accomplish marketing research, and those who operate the computer systems. Eliminating any one of these three components can result in a lopsided system with less than full operational efficiency.

Provision for Convenient Use by Marketing Managers

An MIS should be designed not as a corporate edifice, but to be used. If it is not used by marketing managers, its design, development, and implementation are a sheer waste. Therefore, it is extremely important that the system be designed so that it can be conveniently used. This means everything from location of terminals or subcomponents to user friendliness and anticipating the necessary software. Along these lines, all aspects of the marketing manager/user must be considered, including their physical location, level of education and sophistication, and the type of usage.[20]

The Organization and Location of MIS Within Companies

Several other major decisions must be addressed when implementing a new MIS in a firm. These include the following: Should there be one central MIS or should there be a multiple number of independent divisional systems? Should MIS be directed and controlled by the marketing department or should it be controlled by someone else—perhaps by one separate subdivision of a companywide management information or data processing system? The answers to these questions in large part have to do with the culture of the individual company—whether it is centralized or decentralized, whether its divisions are some mixture of central and decentralized organizations. The advantages of centralized MIS include minimalization of duplication of personal space and equipment, better usage of full-time employment of a few highly paid and competent specialists, and facilitation of companywide decision making. In many cases these advantages are negated, however, if information problems or usage tend to be regional, product oriented, or customer oriented and are radically different between these different subunits.

The issue of the reporting of MIS to marketing or nonmarketing managers is also an important one. Considerations include whether the informational activities are primarily in support of marketing or some other functional area, whether to maintain freedom from the influence of those whom the work affects—that is, whether the MIS organization should be independent—and how best to assure the maximum efficiency of operations and the cooperation and support of both operators and users and their managers.[21]

Today MIS has grown to such importance within firms that the success of other marketing management functions and decision-making responsibilities—including planning, strategy, tactics, and day-to-day operational efficiency—depends, to a great degree, on this intelligence function. To evaluate any MIS, consider the questions in Figure 4-7.[22]

The Need for Marketing Research

Despite the increasing importance of MIS, the need for marketing research has not diminished.

In 1987, the American Marketing Association adopted a new definition of marketing research.

Marketing research is the function which links the consumer, customer, and public to the marketer through information—information used to identify and define marketing opportunities and problems; generate, refine, and evaluate marketing actions; monitor marketing performance; and improve understanding of marketing as a process. Marketing research specifies the information required to address these issues; designs the method for collecting information; manages and implements the data collection process; analyzes the results; and communicates the findings and their implications.[23]

Note that marketing research is that part of the MIS that seeks to answer questions concerning marketing problems not ordinarily provided through MIS inputs or an analysis of the information available in the system. Thus,

Nature of the Information Provided

1. Can I compare operating costs across company organizations to permit valid conclusions about relative product costs, margins, and sales volumes?
2. Are my subordinates satisfied with their information resources?
3. Do my competitors have better marketing information systems than I do?

Business, Marketing, and MIS Planning

4. Is there an approved long-range MIS plan?
5. Does my MIS support my business and marketing planning effectively?
6. Is MIS planning, operations, etc., reviewed at a high organizational level?
7. Am I involved in MIS planning as a marketing manager?
8. Am I kept up to date on the latest MIS technology and applications?

Organization of MIS

9. Do I know how MIS is organized?
10. Do I have the authority and responsibility to get the marketing information I need from the MIS?
11. Does MIS keep me informed about cost, time, and performance alternatives?

Costs

12. Do I know how much I am spending on using MIS?
13. Do I have any idea as to whether these costs are excessive, too low, or about right?
14. Do I know how resources are allocated within MIS?
15. Do I agree with the current allocation of expenditures within MIS?

Source: Adapted from Martin D. J. Buss,"Managing International Information Systems," *Harvard Business Review,* vol. 60, (September–October 1982), p. 158.

Figure 4-7   Questions to Help You Evaluate Your Company's MIS

a special study to determine why consumers buy or do not buy a certain product is marketing research. Other examples of marketing research include determining the best name for a new product, service, or brand; whether one product tastes better, or is perceived to taste better than another; and buyer preferences for various advertising themes; and potential buyer interests and opinions. Although the automatic monitoring features of the MIS and the capability of extracting and analyzing information without initiating a special study have greatly increased the marketing manager's ability to make better decisions on a day-to-day basis, without marketing research an understanding of the marketing situation is severely restricted and may lack essential data for decision making that will lead to success.

Exploratory Research

Exploratory research tends to be done when it is apparent that there is a problem but not what that problem is. A new product recently introduced may be failing in the marketplace. Why is it failing? A product or service that has been successful for years suddenly begins losing market share. Why is this happening? A company is successful and does not know why, but wishes to exploit its success. Exploratory research is launched to define the problem in more detail, to explore it. Exploratory research generally involves lengthy and in-depth interviews with a relatively small number of people.

An example of a type of exploratory research that has enjoyed popular use by market researchers over recent years is the focus group. The focus group consists of a panel of individuals, perhaps six to ten, considered to be representative of the target audience. This panel is interviewed in depth concerning the issue being investigated. The results of these interviews are analyzed and the conclusions drawn are assumed to be indicative of the results that would be attained if a far larger group were consulted. The conclusions may be used as is to guide marketing decision making, or they may be used to develop questions for specific research.

Specific Research

Specific research, as opposed to exploratory research, is undertaken once the problem is clear. It involves the researching of specific questions to obtain specific answers. For example, once the problem has been uncovered as to why the new product introduced is failing in the marketplace, specific research can be undertaken to decide what to do about it, to discover the various alternatives and determine which are more likely to succeed. In the same fashion, once problems have been defined regarding why an established product or service is losing market share or a company that wishes to increase and exploit its market further can define the general reason for its success, alternative ways to handle these problems or opportunities can be researched to find which are best.

While exploratory research tends to dig deep into a general area of inquiry, specific research tends to be broad, with a large number of individuals questioned. Because of the very fact of larger numbers, the length of the interview—whether face to-face, on the telephone, or through the mail—tends to be much shorter. And because we already know what we want, the questions can be quite specific with the minimum amount of latitude left to the participants supplying in-depth answers.

Primary Research

Primary research involves the collection of primary data by the marketing researcher or agents of the marketing researcher directly from respondents. Because these data must be collected firsthand, the process tends to be more costly and may be more time consuming than the collection of secondary research data. However, the use of primary data is sometimes mandatory when secondary data are unavailable. Primary data are usually much more relevant to what is being researched.

Secondary Research

Secondary research depends on secondary data or data obtained from sources other than directly from respondents. In other words, the research has already been accomplished. Most researchers usually begin by examining published secondary research sources to see what data already exist—what data have been collected for some other problem or some other purpose. In some cases, the problem has already been researched in its entirety, and the data are timely and directly relevant and applicable to the problem at hand. In such a case, use of secondary research data could save the time and money of putting together and conducting a primary research project.

The Roles of the Marketing and Research Managers

Interaction of the Marketing Manager and Marketing Research Manager

Research regarding the roles and the interactions of marketing managers and **marketing research managers** has implications for marketing executives using and developing marketing research. These include the following:

- The effectiveness and efficiency of marketing decisions are largely contingent upon how well the marketing researcher participates in the managerial process.
- How well the marketing researcher performs his or her role depends in part upon the satisfaction he or she derives from the job, as well as the minimization of friction with other marketing managers.[24]

Figure 4-8 shows 17 different satisfaction items that were presented to 85 marketing research directors. From this, we might conclude that, at least for the firms researched, marketing research directors are reasonably well satisfied with their role in providing marketing research and participate in the managerial process to a considerable degree.[25]

The Requirements for Line Manager Involvement

There is no question that the **line manager** must be closely involved in the research project and process from their inception.[26] This means, first, that rather than simply request certain information, the marketing manager must take the time to give the marketing researcher or director a thorough understanding of why the research is being done and the time constraints and cost constraints that may be applicable. The line manager must request research and methodology alternatives. It is crucial that the marketing researcher take responsibility for maintaining contact with the marketing manager once the project has been initiated and maintain this contact on a continuing basis, including updating the marketing manager on problems, alternative solutions, and recommendations. The marketing researcher gives the user, or marketing manager, an understanding of the logic of the experimental design and the statistical analysis used and actively involves him or her in them and in the interpretation of results. This is especially important because many studies have shown that managers tend to discount research results not in agreement with their prior beliefs.[27] This bias can only be minimized by active involvement. And only in this way will both the effectiveness and the efficiency of the research be maximized.[28]

Satisfaction Item	Very Well Satisfied	Fairly Well Satisfied	Fairly Dissatisfied	Very Dissatisfied
1. The extent of pursuit of objective research	56%	40%	3%	0%
2. Support from superiors	48	45	7	0
3. Freedom to follow up to check management usage	44	47	9	0
4. Participation in definition of problems studied	41	47	9	2
5. Amount of contact with marketing executives	48	35	16	1
6. Acceptance of research results by management	28	62	10	0
7. Receptance of honest opinions by marketing executives	35	46	18	1
8. Open-mindedness to marketing research findings	24	58	17	1
9. Management's attitude toward the value of research	22	59	17	2
10. Marketing research director's role in strategy formulation	23	51	21	5
11. Time deadlines on marketing research activities	14	68	14	5
12. Position of marketing research department in corporate organization structure	30	38	23	9
13. Procedure for using marketing research services	20	51	26	3
14. Budget for running department	18	56	17	8
15. Extent to which capabilities of department are used	15	60	21	5
16. Time available for professional self-improvement	13	38	43	6
17. Overall job satisfaction	38	57	5	0

Source: Adapted from James R. Krum, "B for Marketing Research Departments," *Journal of Marketing*, vol. 42 (October 1978), p. 9.

Figure 4-8   **Marketing Research Director Satisfaction**

Integrating Marketing Research in Planning Requirements

Just as a close interface between the marketing researcher and marketing manager must be maintained, marketing research should also be integrated into the planning activities of the firm. For example, in the strategic plan, a marketing research subplan is desirable. Such a marketing research plan would require the marketing researcher to identify the critical strategic planning issues and assumptions to be addressed in the marketing research plan; to set priorities of critical issues and applications; to develop a preliminary proposal for the plan with project descriptions, resource requirements, and timing estimates; to determine priorities by ranking the issues and assumptions; to integrate the priority list of tactical research and ongoing projects into the marketing research plan; and to submit the completed marketing research plan for budget approval.[29]

Marketing Research Is Not Always the Answer

Despite the many benefits that marketing research has to offer, it is not the correct action in all cases. A marketing manager must always keep in mind that research costs money, resources, and time. And other things may happen in the marketplace during the time the research is being carried out. For example, while a company delays a decision to acquire marketing research, a competitor may enter and capture a major share of the market. Therefore, the cost of marketing research must always be weighed against the benefits. While the marketing manager should never be afraid to do research if it is needed, he or she shouldn't always assume that doing marketing research is the answer to every problem and every uncertainty. A lack of complete information is in the nature of marketing.

Five Myths About Marketing Research

Alan R. Andreasen, at the University of California at Los Angeles, has pointed out that there are five myths about marketing research that can muddy the thinking of the marketing manager and could cause him or her to make decisions for or against research at the wrong time. These are shown in Figure 4-9.[30]

The most important variables regarding the use of marketing research have been found to be the interaction between the market researcher and marketing manager, the political acceptability of research results, the purpose of the research, and the presentation and technical quality of the research.[31]

Therefore, it is very important that, to be effective, marketing research strategies must correspond to the nature and level of management decisions in the organization. That is, marketing research must be tailored by type to the organization using it.

What Type of Research?

In an earlier chapter we discussed the levels of marketing actions needed to reach objectives as being strategic marketing management, strategy, and tactics. One might usefully divide the stages of the marketing management process in marketing to be analysis, planning, execution, and control. These stages can be used with the levels of marketing actions to construct a matrix for different types of marketing research that may be required to develop research strategy that corresponds to the nature and level of management decision making in marketing. This is shown in Figure 4-10.

Note that here types of marketing research are categorized as **policy research**, **evaluation research**, **strategy research**, **action research**, and **operational research**. Each different type of marketing research requires different information and thus different methods to obtain it. For example, policy research may require methods that focus on predicting future condi-

- *The big decision myth.* This is the myth that you should only use marketing research for major decisions and not for day-to-day operational decision making. Remember, it's not the size of the decision that is important, but the cost perspective. If benefits exceed costs, the decision should probably be for research, even if the decision does not require one in which major financial resources of the company or sales are involved.
- *The survey myopia myth.* This myth implies that only sophisticated survey research is marketing research. This, of course, is not always the case. Any reliable information that improves marketing decisions can be considered marketing research. Secondary research can be extremely important in marketing decision making; so can test marketing and focus groups.
- *The big bucks myth.* Marketing research is so expensive that it can only be used by larger firms that have the money to afford it. Not so. Again, there are so many different types of research that can be accomplished, even to simple observation of buyer behavior or a few telephone calls or secondary research, that an all-inclusive statement that research always costs a lot of money is just plain wrong.
- *Need for a sophisticated researcher.* Is research so complex that it requires a Ph.D to do it right, an elaborate design, extensive computer use, and sophisticated analysis? Sometimes there is a need for great sophistication in research, but many times simply preference for one ad over another, measured by response rates, is all that is required. Senior-level high school statistical techniques may be more than adequate.
- *Most research is not read.* The myth persists that a very high proportion of marketing research is irrelevant to the problem or simply confirms what is already known. While poor research probably isn't very useful or read, good research is rarely rejected and may be extremely helpful.

Figure 4-9 Marketing Research Myths

Stages of the Marketing Management Process	Levels of Marketing Activity		
	Strategic Marketing Management	Strategy	Tactics
Analysis	Policy Research	Strategy Research	Operational Research
Planning			
Execution	Evaluation Research	Action Research	
Control			

Figure 4-10 Matching Research to Levels of Marketing Activity and Stages of the Marketing Management Process

Source: Adapted from J. R. Brent Ritchie, "Roles of Research in the Management Process," *MSU Business Topics* (Summer 1976).

tions and their implications for the organization or methods for establishing priorities and trade-offs among alternative policies. Evaluation research may involve methods for evaluating historical performance. Strategy research may require survey research methods or secondary research means. Action research may require methods for identifying problems and opportunities in the organization from performance measures. Operational research may demand various techniques designed to develop, as well as test, relationships and their optimization between inputs and outputs of a given operational procedure.[32]

Designing the Research Project

Steps in Conducting Research

Once the decision has been made to do marketing research, the process can be stated in easy (and sometimes not so easy) steps. Step 1 is to define the unknown in terms of one or more objectives. Who buys such and such a product? How often do they buy it? Where do they buy it from? You see, if you don't define what you are looking for in pretty precise terms, it is easy to get lost in a forest of information. No wonder experts claim that this is the most important step![33] Step 2 is to decide on the method of research you will use. We'll look at the available methodologies shortly. Step 3 is to collect the data. In step 4 you analyze the data to answer your objectives. Step 5 is easy. You use the data. These five steps in marketing research are shown in Figure 4-11.

Determining the Methodology of Research Used

Major methodologies used for gathering research are analysis of trade journals, trade associations, and other external secondary data; and analysis of internal company records, personal interviews, telephone surveys, mail surveys, focus-group interviews of six to ten people in an informal setting, consumer panels that provide information on a continuing basis, and store audits.

   Figure 4-12 shows the relative use of different methodologies for gathering research by the size of the circle. You should also know that the larger a company is, the more likely it is to make use of secondary research data, as well as the three basic survey methods: (1) personal interviews, (2) mail surveys, and (3) telephone surveys.[34]

> Step 1: Define the unknown in precise objectives.
> Step 2: Decide what research methodology to use.
> Step 3: Collect the data.
> Step 4: Analyze the data and answer your objectives.
> Step 5: Use the data.

Figure 4-11 Five Easy (and Sometimes Not So Easy) Steps in Conducting Marketing Research

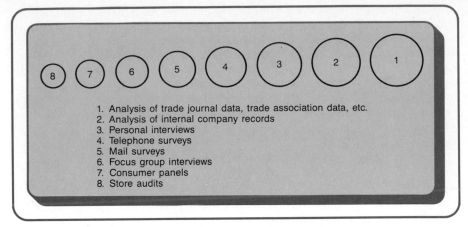

Figure 4-12   Relative Use of Different Research Methodologies

Personal Interview Surveys. The **personal interview survey** is one of the most frequently used methods in marketing research. This is primarily due to its flexibility. Of the three most popular methods—mail surveys, telephone surveys, and personal interview surveys—it is personal interview surveys that collect the best feedback from voice, facial expressions, and body actions. Many different aids can be used in the survey, including pictures, problems, diagrams, and advertising copy. In addition, the selection of respondents can be far more careful. A marketing research study of brand preference for beer eliminated individuals who were intoxicated at the time of the testing. Accurate eliminations due to intoxication would have been more difficult or impossible with the use of an interview method that was not face-to-face.

Furthermore, because of the rapport that can be built up in a face-to-face situation, and the reluctance of many potential respondents to reject a face-to-face request, the number of refused responses is much less when compared to other survey methods.

However, face-to-face interviews do have drawbacks. The primary disadvantage is the cost. The personal interview survey is the most expensive method. Even though cost can be minimized by keeping the researcher at one location or by using a limited number of respondents for exploratory research, you can expect to pay more for research done by this method than any other.

Mail Surveys. With the **mail survey** method, a single questionnaire is prepared, duplicated, and sent to a list of potential respondents. The method requires minimal time for gathering the research, and for this reason it is potentially very economical. In exchange for the costs of printing the questionnaire, mailing it, and providing return postage, a completed interview is accomplished. Despite this major advantage, there are drawbacks for mail surveys. First and primary is probably the response rate. The response rate from the general public is generally very low, sometimes less than 15 per cent, although much higher response rates can be achieved by using special techniques and surveying specialized groups.

To get the maximum response rate, make it as easy as possible for the respondent to respond. This means a relatively short, easy-to-answer questionnaire, as well as the use of a self-addressed, stamped envelope so that the respondent only needs to put the answered questionnaire in the envelope to return it. It was once thought that personalization, such as hand-addressed envelopes, would add to the response rate. However, it has been found that computer labels can be used without a significant loss.[36]

Other factors that increase the response to mail surveys include the length of the interview, subject matter, use of mail and/or phone reminders, and the use of incentives. Reminders can have a tremendous effect, in some cases doubling or tripling mail survey response rates.[37] Incentives can be given after you receive the completed questionnaire or can be included right in the envelope along with it. The prepaid incentive has been found to be extremely effective and to yield higher response rates in mail surveys than incentives paid upon completion.[38]

A typical incentive is money. A very successful survey from one researcher included a questionnaire that was accompanied by an uncirculated one dollar bill. In the cover letter, the one-dollar bill was described as a small gift in appreciation for the time spent in filling out the survey. The one-dollar bill was extremely effective in increasing respondents' results because of its psychological impact. On the one hand, it is very difficult, if not impossible, to throw the "gift" away. On the other, it is equally difficult to pocket the money without a feeling of guilt if the survey is not completed.

However, if you are going to include something of value to increase response, you may need to advertise this fact on the outside envelope. A textbook publisher wanted to use this technique to increase response in a survey of professors. A one-dollar bill was included in every envelope. The envelope was also marked with the publisher's logo. Unfortunately, the publisher had been using a similar envelope for its advertising literature. The marketing researcher won no kudos when it was discovered that most of the envelopes had been thrown away unopened with their one-dollar bills. The results may also say something about this company's advertising material.

Telephone Surveys. Telephone surveys combine some of the advantages and disadvantages of both mail and personal interview surveys. As does the mail survey, telephone surveys avoid interview travel expenses, and they are useful for research over wide geographical areas. They are more flexible than mail surveys because, based on verbal feedback, interviewers can ask more detailed questions or encourage respondents to answer questions when respondents hesitate. However, it is more difficult to obtain the same rapport that is possible through face-to-face, personal interview surveys, because the researcher loses the advantage of what he or she can see. Additional problems with telephone interviews are that respondents must be limited to those with telephones and with listed numbers and that there is a nonresponse bias due to busy signals, no answers, and refusals—and more commonly than with personal interview surveys. To maintain high response rates, a common technique is to make repetitive calls while constantly monitoring the results or to cycle each attempt at contact through a schedule of calls to improve the contact rate. However, it is also important to eliminate or reduce the bias when using these techniques by controlling the sample and considering a number of factors, including the number of call attempts, time zones, the timing of calling efforts based on previous call results, quota groups, controlled replica sampling, and the length of the survey field period. Control of these variables has been computerized in a system that determines the optimal sequence of dialing for sample pieces in telephone research projects. This system ensures that all call-back attempts are made at times specified by respondents, adjusts for time zone differences, ensures that the specified number of calling attempts are made, rotates calling times so nonproductive sample pieces have the best chance of being contacted on the next attempt, rotates call attempts among various days, uses replica sampling procedures, and structures calling attempts so that all previously dialed sample pieces are attempted before any new sample is issued on any given interviewing shift.[39]

Minimizing Erroneous Responses

For a variety of reasons, the responses obtained from respondents are sometimes inaccurate: respondents may lie; they may really not know but will attempt to answer anyway; they may give definite replies even though they are undecided, indifferent, or neutral; they may answer truthfully but conditions may change from the time the research is taken until it is used; and they may be sincere and truthful but the recording instrument may be defective.

These inaccuracies in responses can be minimized by including a battery of questions in the questionnaire that can be used to assess the consistency of each respondent's answers. Several years ago a survey was conducted indicating that 30 per cent of viewers with cable TV would be eager to pay an additional $5.00, or even more, per month for a cultural programming service. Rather than act on these extremely favorable results, an additional survey was done with consistency-type questions to discover the value the respondent placed on culture compared to other activities, such as sports and so forth, frequency of attendance at cultural events, attitude about the importance of cultural events, and attitudes toward interpersonal behavior (such as respondents who might answer what the surveyer would apparently like to hear). The result was that only about 8 per cent of the original total sample were really interested in paying the additional amount for a cultural program.[40]

High Technology Yields Unique Marketing Research Techniques

Twenty-five years ago a device was invented to measure pupil size and the direction of a subject's eyes. Marketing researchers soon realized that this could yield important results when reading advertising copy, and marketing research was initiated shortly thereafter. Researchers soon concluded that nonverbal messages conveyed by the eyes in pictorial advertisements may be an important aspect of what is communicated to a viewer.[41]

More recently, an on-site computer has been utilized as a self-interviewer to yield research data instantly and continuously. With this device, instructions are provided and the respondents complete the questionnaire on personal computers by themselves under the supervision of a guide who may handle several respondents simultaneously. Benefits of such a device include speed, accuracy, portability, visual prescreening of respondents, and lack of interviewer bias. The future may enable combinations by interviewers along with color pictures of products integrated with a questionnaire text or, perhaps, direct transmission of data to clients using minicomputers to move the data processing to remote site locations. This would enable interviewing people in their own homes using their personal computer or videotext terminals.[42] Additional benefits would include overcoming the shortage of interviewers and eliminating missed or muddled questions and skip patterns, because the computer helps to guide the respondent during the answering process.[43]

The Future of Marketing Research

George Gallup, Jr., president of the well-known public opinion research firm known as The Gallup Poll, surveyed a number of senior marketing information executives.[44] How did they see the future? They predicted:

- Greater use of survey research.[45]
- Less reliance on the paper processing of questionnaires and more direct access into computers.
- Better targeting of respondents through the use of psychographics.
- More emphasis on explaining behavior.
- Wider dissemination of survey data.
- More emphasis on tracking as opposed to "snapshots."
- An extension of market research into product categories other than mass market products.
- Research geared toward the total marketing picture, not just parts of it.
- Growth in international research.
- New professional descriptions of the roles of survey researchers and a decline of the "generalists" in the field.
- An increase in computer modeling, "intelligent" computers for interactive surveys, and widespread use of scanners in surveys.

Summary

In this chapter we have had a glimpse at both the present and the future of MIS. We learned that the terms *MIS* and *marketing research* are not identical and that the definition of MIS has to do with a continual flow of information as a baseline for marketing decision making built on the interaction of people, equipment, methods, and controls. Next we looked at the needs for MIS and saw that they have to do with the complexity of modern business coupled with rapidly advancing technology leading to much shorter product life cycles. Noting that no revolutionary concept such as MIS is implemented without some problems and adjustments, we looked at some of the organizational factors with which the marketing manager must contend. We turned to that most critical subcomponent of MIS, marketing research. We saw that different variables impact on the use of marketing research, the most important of which are the interaction between the market researcher and marketing manager, political acceptability of the research results, the purpose of the research, and the research's technical quality. It became clear that the type of research done depends very much on available resources, time, and people. This led us to the design of the research project and a discussion of the steps needed in competent research. Focusing on the three major methods of conducting surveys, we examined the advantages and disadvantages of personal interviews, mail surveys, and telephone surveys.

Recognizing that traditional survey methods will one day be displaced by newer techniques, we glimpsed nontraditional techniques, including devices that measure pupil size and follow eye direction and angle and on-site techniques using computers. Finally we considered the future of marketing research.

Questions

1. How does MIS differ from marketing research? Should marketing research be subordinated to MIS or MIS to marketing research?
2. What needs of the marketing manager are met by adoption of an MIS?
3. If a firm or a marketing department of a firm adopts an MIS, what benefits can be expected to accrue?
4. What are the major components of an MIS and what function do they perform?
5. What are the major problems associated with operational usage of an MIS and how may they be best handled?
6. An MIS is going to be adopted by a firm that has never had one before. How should the firm go about organizing for adopting an MIS and with what cautionary concerns should those implementing the MIS operate?
7. Describe the process or steps necessary for conducting a marketing research project.
8. State the three main survey methods as well as the advantages and disadvantages of each.
9. What methods might be used to increase response on personal surveys? Mail surveys? Telephone surveys?
10. What are some of the variables that may affect response rates in different methods of surveying?

Ethical Question

You work for a marketing research firm. You are given an assignment that requires you to obtain competitive information. You see no way of doing this, and so you ask your supervisor. He says, "It's easy. Just call up the company and tell them you are a student doing a report. They'll give you the information every time." Is this ethical? Would you do it? Comments on this?

Endnotes

1. Arthur I. Stern, "Computer Marketing Analysis System Slices Promotional Budget 25% Without Slicing Sales," *Marketing News* (September 14, 1984), p. 13.
2. Steven W. Quickel, "Management Joins the Computer Age," *Business Month*, vol. 133, no. 5, (May 1989), p. 42.
3. ————, "Today's Army Relying on Marketing

Research to Attain Recruitment Goals," *Marketing News* (July 6, 1984), p. 1.

4. Rowland T. Moriarty and Gordon S. Swartz, "Automation to Boost Sales and Marketing," *Harvard Business Review*, vol. 67, no. 1 (January–February 1989), p. 100.

5. ————, "How Personal Computers Can Trip Up Executives," *Business Week*, September 24, 1984, p. 94.

6. Michael R. Gauthier, "Executives Go High Tech," *Business Month*, vol. 134, no. 1 (July 1989), p. 45.

7. ————, "An Information Guru in FMC's Executive Suite," *Business Week* (October 8, 1984), p. 124.

8. Perry Pascarella, "Computer Arrives in Executive Suite," *Industry Week*, August 6, 1984, p. 15.

9. Richard Kern, "The 1990 Census: The Good, the Bad, and the Underaccount," *Sales and Marketing Management*, vol. 141, no. 8 (July 1989), p. 49.

10. Peter D. Bennett, *Dictionary of Marketing Terms* (Chicago: AMA, 1988), p. 116.

11. John B. Kennedy, "Start with a Data Base," *Sales and Marketing Management* (December 3, 1984), p. 68.

12. Conrad Berenson, "Marketing Information System," *Journal of Marketing*, vol. 33 (October 1969), p. 21.

13. Donald F. Cox and Robert E. Good, "How to Build a Marketing Information System," *Harvard Business Review*, vol. 45 (May–June 1967), p. 146.

14. Norman Wiener, "PCs and Marketers Forge a Productive Alliance," *Sales and Marketing Management* (February 6, 1984), p. 37.

15. Ibid., p. 38.

16. John B. Kennedy, "Start with a Data Base," *Sales and Marketing Management*, (December 3, 1984), p. 68.

17. Philip Kotler, "The Future of the Computer in Marketing," *Journal of Marketing*, vol. 34 (January 1970), pp. 12–13.

18. David B. Montgomery and Charles B. Weinberg, "Modeling Marketing Phenomena: A Managerial Perspective," *Journal of Contemporary Business* (Autumn 1973), pp. 20–21.

19. G. David Hughes, "Computerized Sales Management," *Harvard Business Review*, vol. 61 (March–April 1983), pp. 104–108.

20. David B. Montgomery, "Developing a Balanced Marketing Information System" (Cambridge, Mass.: Marketing Science Institute, 1970).

21. Kenneth P. Uhl, "Marketing Information Systems," in Robert Ferber, ed., *Handbook of Marketing Research* (New York: McGraw-Hill, 1974).

22. Martin D. J. Buss, "Managing International Information Systems," *Harvard Business Review*, vol. 60 (September–October 1982), p. 158.

23. Peter D. Bennett, *Dictionary of Marketing Terms* (Chicago: AMA, 1988), p. 117.

24. Robert J. Small and Larry J. Rosenberg, "The Marketing Researcher as a Decision Maker: Myth or Reality?" *Journal of Marketing* (January 1975), pp. 2–7.

25. James R. Krum, "B for Marketing Research Department," *Journal of Marketing*, vol. 42 (October 1978), p. 9.

26. Rohit Deshpande, "The Organizational Context of Market Research Use," *Journal of Marketing*, vol. 46 (Fall 1982), p. 99.

27. Hanjoon Lee, Frank Acito, and Ralph L. Day, "Evaluation and Use of Marketing Research by Decision Makers: A Behavioral Simulation," *Journal of Marketing Research*, vol. 24 (May 1987) pp. 193–194.

28. Russell L. Ackoff and James R. Emshoff, "Advertising Research at Anheuser-Busch, Inc. (1963–68)," *Sloan Management Review* (Winter 1975), pp. 1–15.

29. Richard F. Tomasino, "Integrate Market Research with Strategic Plan to Get Budget Okay," *Marketing News* (January 4, 1985), p. 8.

30. Alan R. Andreasen, "Cost-Conscious Marketing Research," *Harvard Business Review* (July–August 1983).

31. Rohit Deshpande and Gerald Zaltman, "A Comparison of Factors Affecting Researcher and Manager Perceptions of Market Research Use," *Journal of Marketing Research*, vol. 22 (February 1984), p. 33.

32. J. R. Brent Ritchie, "Roles of Research in the Management Process," *MSU Business Topics* (Summer 1976), pp. 13–23.

33. Randall G. Chapman, "Problem-Definition in Marketing Research Studies," *Journal of Consumer Marketing*, vol. 6, no. 2 (Spring 1989), p. 51.

34. Barnett A. Greenberg, Jac L. Goldstucker, and Danny N. Bellenger, "What Techniques Are Used by Marketing Researchers in Business?" *Journal of Marketing*, vol. 41 (April 1977), p. 65.

35. Pamela Rogers, "One-on-Ones Don't Get the Credit They Deserve," *Marketing News*, vol. 23, no. 1 (January 2, 1989), p. 9.

36. Linda L. Nieder and Paul K. Sugrue, "Addressing Procedures as a Mail Survey Response Inducement Technique," *Journal of the Academy of Marketing Science*," vol. 11 (Fall 1983), p. 459.

37. Marvin A. Jolson, "How to Double or Triple Mail-Survey Response Rates," *Journal of Marketing*, vol. 41 (October 1977), pp. 78–81.

38. Louis I. Weiss, Debra Friedman, and Carlisle L. Shoemaker, "Prepaid Incentives Yield Higher Response Rates to Mail Surveys," *Marketing News* (January 4, 1984), p. 30.

39. Marjorie A. Michetti and Gregg Kennedy, "On-Line Sample Control: Cost Efficient Way to Raise Response Rates in Phone Surveys," *Marketing News* (January 4, 1985), p. 34.

40. Robert S. Duboff, "Produce More Accurate Projections with Consistency Filtering Technique," *Marketing News* (January 6, 1984), p. 16.

41. Albert S. King, "Pupil Size, Eye Direction, and Message Appeal: Some Preliminary Findings," *Journal of Marketing*, vol. 36 (July 1972), p. 57.

42. Bernie Whalen, "On-Site Computer Interviewing Yields Research Data Instantly," *Marketing News* (November 9, 1984), p. 17.

43. Joseph E. Rafael, "Self-Administered CRT Interviews," *Marketing News* (November 9, 1984), p. 16.

44. George Gallup, Jr., "Survey Research: Current Problems and Future Opportunities," *Journal of Consumer Marketing*, vol. 5, no. 1 (Spring 1988), p. 28.

45. Survey research is being used increasingly in legal cases. See Fred W. Morgan, "Judicial Standards for Survey Research: An Update and Guidelines," *Journal of Marketing*, vol. 54, no. 1 (January 1990).

5

Environmental Scanning, Situational Analysis, and Problem Solving

CHAPTER OBJECTIVES

⬤ Understand the concept of the marketing environment and the environs of the marketplace.

⬤ Know how the situational analysis fits into the structure of the marketing plan.

⬤ Understand how, and under what conditions, the marketing environs can be manipulated.

⬤ Be able to analyze marketing problems to reach solutions and make decisions using the analysis methodology presented.

OSHA Upsets the Corporate Environment

OSHA is a government agency whose letters stand for Occupational Safety and Health Administration. OSHA has always had an important impact on the environment in which firms do marketing. Not too long ago, OSHA made its presence felt as never before. In a single action, the maximum permissible work place exposure levels of nearly four hundred hazardous and toxic substances were substantially lowered. This environmental factor is still in the throes of change. OSHA plans to establish rules for the medical surveillance of employees and for monitoring all chemical exposures in the work place. This means a company will need a new management approach to ensure that OSHA maximum exposure level requirements are met. According to Dr. Richard F. Boggs, vice-president of the consulting firm of Organizational Resources Counselors, "It will no longer be acceptable for companies to say they are meeting an OSHA standard. Companies will have to more explicitly evaluate chemical exposure problems in the work place and start doing what's right for worker protection instead of what's necessary to meet a standard."[1]

Will Hamburgers Become a Gourmet Food?

Important changes are brewing in the fast-food market. One chain of hamburger restaurants has started serving baked potatoes; some new restaurant chains are offering so-called "upscale chicken"; and Fuddruckers, Inc., a Texas-based restaurant chain, is now selling hamburgers as gourmet food, even going so far as grinding raw meat and baking buns in front of the customer to prove that both are fresh. What has caused this amazing change in the way that fast-food restauranteurs are attempting to service their public? It is simply a significant shift in public taste. People in the United States now in their mid-thirties are the first generation to grow up on fast food and are America's fastest-growing age group. Studies show that those individuals, as with other age groups, want to eat out more often and are accustomed to and enjoy the convenience of fast food. However, they are looking for more varied, more nutritious, and higher-quality food. This change in the marketplace has sparked an explosion of new developments in fast food, and fast-food marketers are rushing to capitalize on this new demand.

Burger King, a division of the Pillsbury Company and the number two hamburger chain, immediately stressed a claimed higher quality for its burgers. This must have been the right thrust, as sales increased significantly. Jeff Campbell, president of Burger King, said, "We see consumers continuing to be more quality oriented."[2]

Counterfeiting Goods Is Now Worse Than Counterfeiting Money

In 1984 President Reagan signed a new Trademark Counterfeiting Act. What caused this act was not an upsurge of counterfeit currency. In recent years some errant marketers have taken to imitating or closely imitating various types of well-known products, brands, and trademarks. The new act provides stiff criminal and civil remedies against those who engage in this illegal marketing, whether the product is blue jeans, drugs, a look-alike watch, or some other product. Now it is a federal crime to traffic intentionally or attempt to traffic in such goods or services, and the penalties are tough. Individuals can receive criminal penalties of a $250,000 fine or five years imprisonment or both for a first offense and a $1 million fine or fifteen years imprisonment or both for subsequent offenses. Corporations can face a maximum $1 million fine for a first offense and a $5 million fine for subsequent offenses. Other severe penalties, including goods seizure, may also be imposed. What was once considered by some marketers to be a relatively harmless, if somewhat unethical, method of satisfying the consumer demand for certain types of goods at prices much lower than those prevalent in the market will now bring such severe penalties that marketers are well advised to avoid such counterfeiting at all costs.[3] ●

What do OSHA rules, the change in fast-food demand, and the law against counterfeit goods have in common? They are all part of the marketing environment: the environs of the marketplace. All marketers must contend with these environs, over which they usually have very little control. If these environs are analyzed correctly and the right strategy is used to avoid the threats and take advantage of the opportunities, the result is success in the marketplace. If the marketing manager fails to do this, he or she will eventually fail.

What Makes Up the Environment? The Environs of the Marketplace _____

An environ is an uncontrollable force in the marketplace. Unlike the traditional four Ps of product, price, promotion, and place, over which the marketing manager has control, the marketing manager usually has little control over the environs. There are four classes of environs: company environs, competitor environs, neutral environs, and situational environs. Let's look at each in turn.

Company Environs

Company environs include know-how of a certain industry or target market or way of doing business, experience, financial resources, human resources, capital equipment, suppliers, and marketing intermediaries such as agents and field representatives who may be available. All share in common the fact that they are part of the marketing manager's environment and that, at any specific point in time, he or she may have little control over them. Of course, the environmental situation can change. A company can obtain necessary know-how or experience and an influx of money can change its financial situation.

Competitor Environs

Competitor environs are the mirror image of our own company environs. They also include know-how, experience, financial resources, human resources, capital equipment, suppliers, and marketing intermediaries. Competitor environs are the most dangerous to our interests of all the environs because the competition is not only intelligent, but will actively operate against our own interests and attempt to overcome our strategy. You can see this in Figure 5-1. This environ is so important we will examine it in detail in the next chapter.

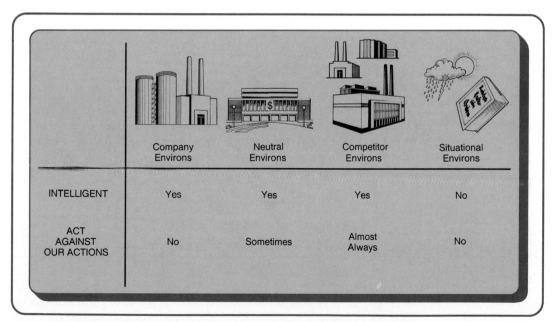

	Company Environs	Neutral Environs	Competitor Environs	Situational Environs
INTELLIGENT	Yes	Yes	Yes	No
ACT AGAINST OUR ACTIONS	No	Sometimes	Almost Always	No

Figure 5-1   **Why the Competition Environs Are the Most Dangerous**

Neutral Organizational Environs

The neutral organizational environs consist of institutions or organizations that are neither friendly nor allied with our own organization or an adversary, such as a competitor. Neutral agencies and organizations include media that may promote for or against our company's interests and special-interest environs such as consumers' groups or labor organizations that have their own interests in mind and that we must take note of in planning our marketing campaigns.

Situational Environs

Situational environs consist of those environs that are peculiar to the particular marketing situation in which we find ourselves. They have nothing to do with our own organization, with a competitive organization, or with a neutral organization. Rather they are a part of the situation itself. Situational environs include politics, the existing distribution channel or distribution structure, current economic and business conditions, the state of technology, demand for a product or service, and social, cultural, or other factors, such as demographics, that affect that demand. They also include social responsibility, which can be defined as generally accepted relationships, obligations, and duties that relate to the corporate impact on the welfare of society.[4]

Look at these situational environs. Note that their source isn't a single organization—friendly, competitive, or neutral. How would you respond to each?

- Well-publicized cases of product tampering
- The effect on well-known trademarks of hostile corporate takeovers
- The effect of chapter 11 bankruptcy proceedings
- New electronic purchasing channels
- Foreign introduction into the United States of has-been traditionally American machinery products (such as farm equipment)
- Public demand for pollution control
- Petroleum embargo by foreign suppliers[5]

Figure 5-2 shows how the marketing environment is structured with the four basic environs. It also shows how the four affect the four basic controllable variables as we attempt to influence the buyer with our marketing efforts—whether the buyer is a consumer, an organizational representative, a voter, or someone else.

Environmental Scanning and Situational Analysis _____

If you've been to an airport recently, you've seen the results of effective environmental scanning in action. Marketers are now thinking of airports as markets as much as terminals for the departure and arrival of aircraft.

What happened? Marketers did their job by continually monitoring pur-

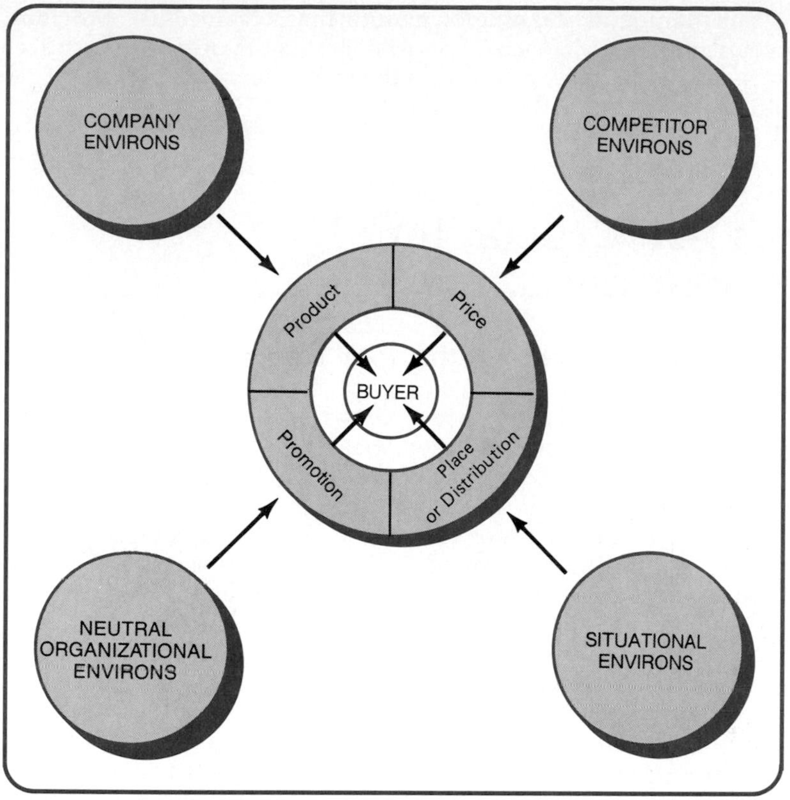

Figure 5-2 The Environs of the Marketplace

chases and conducting marketing research in the terminals. Over time, changes in the environmental situation were spotted. There was an increasing number of passengers and others who either accompanied or went to meet them. All demonstrated an increasing propensity to purchase at the airport. Look at O'Hare International in Chicago. Experts calculate that with 60 million passengers departing this single airport every year, the total market potential is 120 million. The doubling is due to "meeters and greeters," and those who accompany departing passengers.

According to Susan Luzar, senior associate at Thompson Consultants International in Los Angeles, "Often passengers wait two hours in the airport before their flight leaves. So we gear the concessions to attract passengers and, of course, the well-wishers who accompany them . . . meeters and greeters also have a lot of time to kill, while the passenger checks in or gets his luggage."

Airports formerly planned the terminal only to accommodate the airlines. Patricia Corcoran, director of the Center for Professional Programs at Embry-Riddle Aeronautical University says, "Now everything is becoming organized."

Environmental scanning hasn't stopped. Marketers are learning what consumers want and where to locate retail outlets for maximum convenience and airport profitability.[6]

Environmental scanning or monitoring is defined as "Activities aimed at keeping track of changes in external factors that are likely to affect the markets and demand for a firm's products and services."[7] Analyzing the output of these activities is the situational analysis.

Why Environs Are Crucial for Successful Marketing

The Dynamic Nature of the Total Marketing Environment

As pointed out previously, the environs of the marketplace are never fixed. Today, there is a tremendous emphasis and demand for health and fitness products in the United States. It was not always so. It may not be so in the future. Today the politics are of *glasnost* on the international scene. This was not always so. This may not be so in the future. Our company or a competitor may be strong in one particular facet of our business today and weak tomorrow. Economic and business conditions, social and cultural factors, and the way people think about and demand certain types of products and services are continually changing, and sometimes very rapidly. The computer, once the domain of only major corporations and governments, now is not only available to everyone, but has in turn created new needs among consumers for new types of equipment, new capabilities, and even new jobs that we expect personal computers to accomplish in our lives. It was the great management philosopher Peter F. Drucker who first pointed out that any business, no matter how successful, that continued to operate as it had in the past was doomed to failure at some time in the future. This failure, of course, is due to the fact that the environs are continually changing and what causes success in one set of environmental conditions causes failure in another.

Increasingly Rapid Change of Environs

Environs in the marketplace are changing at a particularly frantic pace today, with the explosion of technology and various "revolutions," be they consumer, social, cultural, political, or competitor. These major shifts in the environs are causing rapid and dramatic changes in our society and in the way we live, think, and do business. As Ronna Klingenberg, program director of the Trend Analysis Program conducted by the American Council of Life Insurance, has said, "Rapid technological advances and shifting social values are transforming our society so radically that even standard organizational methods of making decisions may no longer work."[8]

Demographic changes are a part of this environ acceleration. The number of households in the United States increased by 12.7 million between 1981 and 1990, a 15.4 percent gain. But married-couple households increased only 6 per cent during those years, resulting in a continuing decline in the share of households headed by married couples. Households that contain only one person increased at twice the rate for all households—30 per cent versus 15 per cent. Unmarried households constituted only 3 per cent of all households

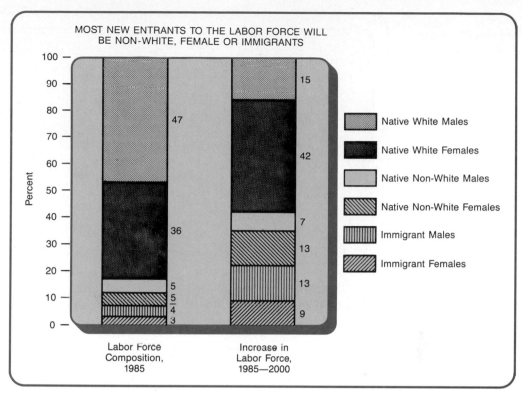

Figure 5-3 Most New Entrants to the Labor Force Will Be Non-white, Female, or Immigrants

Source: Adapted from William B. Johnston and Arnold E. Packer, *Workforce 2000* (Indianapolis: The Hudson Institute, 1987), p. 95.

and 5 per cent of all households in 1990, even though they dramatically increased over the past seven years.[9]

According to the Hudson Institute, a "think tank" in Indiana, there will be a tremendous change in the ethnic and racial composition of the U.S. workforce by the year 2000. White males, once thought of as the mainstay of the U.S. economy, will only be 15 per cent of the total number of new entrants.[10] You can see the entrants in the labor force in the year 2000 compared with the 1985 work force in Figure 5-3. This same work force will be aging. There will be an increase of workers between the ages of thirty-five and fifty-four by more than 25 million. That's about equal to the total increase in the work force. You can see the rate of aging from 1970 to 2000 in Figure 5-4.[11] Obviously these changes will have a tremendous impact on the situational environ that marketers face.

Some "Truths" Are No Longer True (and Some Never Were)

It is interesting to note that some so-called "truths" are no longer true. In fact, it is a great mistake to consider that anything that has been true in the past will continue to be true in the future. This goes against the very thing we know to be true: that the environs are continually changing. Let's look at some of these so-called truths, summarized in Figure 5-5.

123

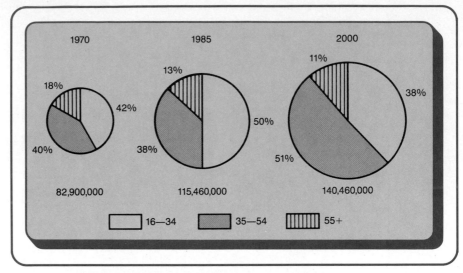

Figure 5-4 How the Workforce Is Aging

Source: Adapted from William B. Johnston and Arnold E. Packer, *Workforce 2000* (Indianapolis: The Hudson Institute, 1987), p. 81.

We are in the midst of a baby boom. Well, we were, but that is no longer true. The average number of children born to a woman of child-bearing age is only half what it was during the 1950s, and it is near record lows. By 1990 a baby bust is expected.

The family is dead. Not so. Over 90 per cent of all Americans marry. Well, if this is so, does the typical American family consist of four people? The actual figure is closer to three. The typical American family now has 3.25 people in it, which is down from 3.58 in 1970. If there is any "typical American family" at all, it is anticipated that by 1990 its size will be exactly 3.0.

With life expectancy rising all the time, the myth says that we are a nation of elders. True, Americans age eighty-five and older will grow 52 per cent between 1980 and 1990, but due to the previous baby boom, today one-third of all Americans are between twenty and thirty-five. We are not forecast to be a nation of old folks until well into the next century.

It is stated by politicians, educators, and both women and men that half of all women are currently in the labor force. This is a half-truth: 52 per cent are currently in the labor force. However, with men, 65 per cent of those who work are working all year, full time. But with women, the figure is only

1. We are in the midst of a baby boom.
2. The family is dead.
3. A typical family consists of four people.
4. We are a nation of elders.
5. More than half the labor force consists of women.

Source: Bryant Robey, "Five Myths," *American Demographics* (December 1983), pp. 2, 4.

Figure 5-5 Five "Truths" About America That Are Not True

1. Establishing a list of legal safeguards and teaching them to employees.
2. Making all employees aware of their potential culpability via a product modification, unsafe packaging, absence of warnings to users, etc.
3. Making certain that all products in stock are safe products.
4. Checking all "doubts" with legal counsel.
5. Maintaining as much sales and marketing insurance as is affordable.
6. Making certain that legal counsel is competent in dealing with potential marketing problems.
7. Reviewing risk management policies to ensure that products needing disclaimers and warnings about misuse and abuse are identified.
8. Instructing salespeople to investigate applications of products that could lead to potential risks.
9. Sponsoring seminars for customers on the use of hazardous equipment.
10. Establishing a system of management review for all price quotations not based on listed prices.
11. Scrutinizing purchase orders for "hold harmless" agreements that protect the user from liability due to misuse of a product sold them.

Source: "Selling and the Law," *Industrial Distribution* (October 1981), p. 40.

Figure 5-6 Some Actions That Marketing Managers Are Taking in Response to Changes in Situational Environs Having to Do with Potential Legal Problems

45 per cent. Furthermore, 33 per cent of working women only work part time, while 22 per cent work full time but do not work all year round.

These data show that you should be aware of the myths in the marketplace, that the environs you thought to be true may not actually be so.[12]

Radical Changes in the Environs

Let the Seller Beware. Once upon a time there was a saying, "Let the buyer beware." Today, environs have shifted, and it may be that the seller should beware. Product liability suits are statistically decided in favor of the plaintiff, and the number of million-dollar settlements is not insignificant.[13] Marketers are reacting to this change in situational environs by taking some of the actions listed in Figure 5-6.[14]

Nor is product liability today necessarily within the scope of what an individual marketing manager may consider fair or even reasonable. For example, the author is familiar with a product liability case in which the design of a handgun was called into question. An individual had purchased this handgun, a revolver, and had left it cocked in its holster—a clear misuse of the product. The individual stumbled while wearing it, and the gun discharged and shot him in the foot. He sued the handgun company because of the accident, claiming that a design deficiency allowed it to discharge, even though few handgun owners would dream of having one cocked while holstered. Yet the gun manufacturer was held liable, even though the handgun design was over a hundred years old.

One expert had predicted this: "It is reasonable to assume that sometime in the future, liability will be imposed upon the producer's or marketer's product without regard as to whether or not there was a defect in the product."[15] Clearly, this has already come to pass, and the marketing manager must adjust his or her strategy accordingly.

Marketing Law: Another Radical Change in the Environs. In 1967 the Supreme Court handed down a decision in the case against Arnold Schwinn and Company, a manufacturer of bicycles. The Court found that many previously common restrictions imposed not only by Schwinn but by other manufacturers on their distributors were illegal, regardless of motive. As a result of this decision 25 years ago, a manufacturer today can now rarely prevent its customers' independent distributors from selling to any purchaser in any location.[16]

Importance to Planning Action

The importance of environs to planning, and especially **strategic planning**, was pointed out in an earlier chapter. The environs play a major role in determining an organization's future; thus, effective strategic planning must include an assessment of the environs and then the development of strategies to take advantage of them to the maximum degree possible. In this way, the marketing manager takes advantage of the opportunities and avoids the threats.

You Can Change the Environs or Your Environment

In traditional approaches to marketing management, the "strategic" variables were known as the **controllable variables**—that is, those of product, price, promotion, and place—as opposed to the **uncontrollable** or **situational variables**, those forces we call the environs of the marketplace. In general it was felt that the uncontrollable variables could not be controlled without great expense or difficulty, and the marketing manager was well advised to attempt to manipulate only the strategic variables. However, it is now recognized that the environs can be manipulated and that the marketing manager can exercise a certain amount of control over the environment in which he or she operates.

Research by Carl and Valarie Zeithaml resulted in extensive possibilities for **environmental management strategies**. For example, resources can be allocated toward manipulating the political environ to influence elected representatives or to lobby. Legal environs might be altered through private antitrust suits brought against competitors. Other environmental management strategy examples are illustrated in Figure 5-7.[17] Thus, the marketing manager must remember that, as a result of his or her environmental scanning and situational analysis, he or she has the capability of achieving the company's or organization's objectives through manipulating not only the strategic variables, but also the environs.

The Relative Importance of Different Environs at Different Times

At different times different environs have different relative importances. Some environs, because of their great importance, require immediate action on the part of the marketing manager. Others, because of their lesser importance at a particular time or in a particular situation, can be ignored, or

Strategy	Example
Competitive aggression	Comparative advertising
Competitive pacification	Helping competitors find raw materials
Public relations	Corporate advertising campaigns
Voluntary action	Energy conservation programs
Dependence development	Providing vital information to regulators
Legal action	Private antitrust suits against competitors
Political action	Direct lobbying
Smoothing	Lower weekend rates for telephoning
Demarketing	Shorter hours of operation by gasoline service stations
Implicit cooperation	Price leadership
Contracting	Contractual vertical and horizontal marketing systems
Co-optation	Consumer representatives on boards of directors
Coalition	Industry association
Domain selection	Selection of markets with best chances of success
Diversification	Vertical integration
Merger and acquisition	Gaining possession of an ongoing enterprise with a desired product line rather than developing the product line "in-house"

Source: Adapted from Carl P. Zeithaml and Valarie A. Zeithaml, "Environmental Management: Revising the Marketing Perspective," *Journal of Marketing*, vol. 48 (Spring 1984), pp. 50–51.

Figure 5-7 Examples of Environmental Management Strategies

action at least can be postponed. An example might be the environ of **consumer protection**. **Consumerism** has grown steadily stronger over the last twenty or thirty years, interacting and partially causing increasing responsibility on the part of the marketer and manufacturer of product or service liability. Additional remedies for consumer protection exist and are increasingly utilized.

Professor Dorothy Cohen of Hofstra University, in a study of consumerism and marketing management, devised a paradigm of prevention, restitution, and punishment, as illustrated in Figure 5-8. The prevention column illustrates ways in which consumer problems can be avoided before they affect your ability to obtain your objectives through whatever strategy you have instituted. Thus prevention might have been used by Nestlé to avoid its prob-

Prevention	Restitution	Punishment
Codes of conduct	Affirmative disclosure	Fines and incarceration
Disclosure of information	Corrective advertising	Loss of profits
Disclosure of requirements	Refunds	Class action suits
Substantiation of claims	Limitations on contracts	
	Arbitration	

Source: Adapted from Dorothy Cohen, "Remedies for Consumer Protection: Prevention, Restitution, or Punishment," *Journal of Marketing*, vol. 39 (October 1975), p. 25.

Figure 5-8 Consumerism and Marketing Prevention, Restitution, and Punishment

lems with boycott and loss of money and goodwill. The restitution column indicates possible actions the company might take after a problem has become evident. Finally, the punishment column should be considered to be what a marketing manager could face should action be initiated by a plaintiff.[18]

The Intelligent Environ That Works Against Us

Competition is the intelligent adversarial environ that, in pursuing its objectives, may impede our ability to achieve our marketing objectives. In fact, in the planning of any strategy or marketing action, we must always remember that the competitor will not remain static or fixed but will take some action in response to our action. Frequently, the reaction of a competitor may occur in three stages: (1) blindness, (2) an attempt to destroy, and (3) direct confrontation with overcompensation.

In the blindness stage, the competitor typically hopes that nothing will change and that everything will continue to work as it did previously. In other words, you will be ignored. However, if your plans continue successfully, your competition will not fail to note it.

In phase 2, an attempt to destroy, frustration may actually lead to an attempt to destroy, if not you, then your strategy. Two common countertactics of your competition in this stage are to cut off your source of supply or to attempt to secure legislation that would prevent your mode of operation.

Should this fail, a competitor may progress to phase 3, direct confrontation and overcompensation. Basically, your competitor attempts to take you head on. If you have cut prices, your competitor will cut prices; if you have increased promotion, your competitor will increase promotion. This last stage is a stage of desperation and, as with any direct strategy, can succeed only if the competition has superior resources to your own.[19] Of course, a more astute competitor will skip the blindness stage and employ a more effective indirect strategy. But whether your competition is clever or not in reacting to your moves, recognize that your competitor will intelligently move to thwart your strategy and further his or her own.

Environs Cause Marketing Problems, Opportunities, and Threats _____

The existence of the various environs and their interactions and changes causes problems, opportunities, and threats to any marketing campaign. Therefore, as already noted, a marketing manager must continually scan his or her environment and analyze the resulting problems, opportunities, or threats. This is done through MIS and marketing research, as explained in the previous chapter. However, information must be analyzed to be useful. This analysis must be accomplished in a clear, logical manner and include all relevant factors of the environs. It must consider all alternative solutions or courses of action; present your analysis, conclusions, and recommendations in a concise manner; and persuade those in authority in your organization to follow your recommendations.

Analyzing Problems, Opportunities and Threats

To accomplish the foregoing objectives, the **staff-study method** and **analysis structure** has been used by business firms, law firms, and military organizations. Its use permits attaining all the objectives just listed in the shortest period of time and with the greatest chances of reaching recommendations that will be successful in the marketplace.

The basic outline of this structure follows:

1. Define the central issue.
2. List the relevant factors.
3. List alternative courses of action, with their advantages and disadvantages.
4. Analyze the relative merits of each alternative.
5. Draw conclusions.
6. Make recommendations.

Let's look at each of these elements of the problem, opportunity, and threat analysis structure in turn.

Defining the Central Issue

Defining the central issue is probably the most important of the whole analysis and problem-solving methodology. Of course, when we speak of the central issue, we may be talking about a problem, threat, or an opportunity. In almost every marketing situation you will be confronted with many different problems, opportunities, or threats. Some will be important, some less so. Some will be of primary interest, some of secondary interest. Those of lesser importance and of secondary interest confuse the main issue. What at first appears to be a central issue may not be so at all, or what first appears to be a major issue may simply be a symptom of a problem. Many such problem-solving situations in marketing involve measurements in terms of money—profits may be down, sales may be down, marketing costs may be up or rising. Yet very frequently these particular issues with descriptions in terms of profit, sales, or cost are simply symptoms of a more central and deeper issue. To define the central issue, you must ask yourself why profits are down, why sales are down, or why costs are up. The answer will help you to define and analyze the real central issue. Even though you spend a considerable amount of time in wording the central issue as clearly and as succinctly as you possibly can, you may modify it as you proceed. This is because you may acquire new insights on facts as you work through the analysis.

Take care to limit the number of solutions through wording. For example, the question of whether to develop a certain specific new product or not as a central issue limits the solutions to either develop or not to develop. The development of yet a second product might be the proper solution to the real central issue you are facing in this particular marketing situation.

Central issues worded as "What should be done about . . ." usually lack specifics. These specifics are particularly important when the analysis is presented to a second party.

Another cautionary note is to avoid incorporating your planned solution into the central issue. Focusing on the solution in the wording of the central issue may cause you to miss yet a better solution as one of the alternatives or, if retained, may prejudice your case when attempting to present your analysis to higher-level managers. You will have revealed the solution before building a proper case to support it.

List the Relevant Factors

Relevant factors are concerned with the environs you face in this particular situation. There are two important aspects of this element of the analysis structure. First, note the word *relevant*. This means that even though there may be considerable information regarding every single environ, not all is truly relevant in every situation. Therefore, do not list every single factor involved. Each factor must be relative to the central issue as you have defined it. If you attempt to list every single factor, you will waste time, confuse yourself, and ultimately confuse those to whom you are presenting your analysis.

Also consider the word *factor*. Factor is not the equivalent of the word *fact*. In addition to the facts you know, you must also include in your analysis assumptions, calculations, and estimates. Not only must you list these other types of factors, but it is important to differentiate and label the facts, estimates, and assumptions in your list.

List Alternative Solutions or Courses of Action with Their Advantages and Disadvantages

The third element in the analysis and problem-solving structure is to define every reasonable alternative solution or course of action and write it down. Every single course of action will have advantages and disadvantages. It is important not to leave out any. You will rarely find an alternative that has all advantages and no disadvantages. Usually you will have an obvious solution, and there is no need to proceed through the analysis process. However, it is possible to have advantages that are so weak that the solution is not a viable one, even though it does not have disadvantages. Even then, a closer examination is required. As Alfred P. Sloan, president of General Motors, is reported to have said, "Gentlemen, I take it we are all in complete agreement on the decision here. Then, I propose we postpone further discussion of this matter until our next meeting to give ourselves time to develop disagreement and perhaps gain some understanding of what the decision is all about."[20]

It is also important never to fail to list whatever it is you are doing presently as an alternative course of action, even if you are currently losing money or it is an otherwise poor solution. This is because other solutions or courses of action may be a lot worse, and doing what you are doing now may actually be the best. You can only know this for certain by analyzing what you are currently doing as an alternative.

After you have listed each alternative course of action or solution, make certain that each solves the central issue as you have stated it. If you have introduced a solution that does not solve the central issue you have stated, but you know that this solution should be considered, it generally means that the central issue must be reworked and redefined. For example, let's assume that the central issue as you defined it is how to capture a certain share in the market for a certain product. Maybe this product should never have been introduced in the first place, but the way the problem has been defined eliminates the solution of withdrawing it. So after you have listed your alternatives, compare each alternative with the central issue and redefine the central issue if necessary.

Analyze and Discuss the Relative Merits of Each Alternative

Be brief when you write your analysis. It is best, for example, to discuss the central issue in a single brief statement and, if there is more than one central issue, to use the method of analysis to analyze each issue separately. List the relevant factors and alternative courses of action in the same fashion. However, in the discussion and analysis section write as much as necessary to do a complete analysis of each advantage and disadvantage. Explain the relative importance of each in consideration of the relevant factors you have listed. Naturally, as you proceed, redefine the central issue, add additional alternatives, or list additional relevant factors as you think of them. When you complete this section of the analysis, go over it and rework it as necessary to present your thinking in a logical manner. At the very end, the conclusions you reach must be identical to those anyone reading your analysis would make. If others might conclude something different, something is wrong with your analysis or its wording, and you should go over this section once again.

Conclusions

State your conclusions separately. They are the result of your analysis and discussion. Do not explain or discuss them further. Return to brevity by stating each conclusion separately in a single sentence, if possible. All explanations and discussion should be contained in the previous section. This will make your conclusions stand out, will assist you in eliminating those that are faulty, and will encourage you to return to the analysis if insufficient support exists for a conclusion you have made tentatively. Never introduce additional information after your discussion and analysis. All conclusions should be the result of your discussion and analysis and not, for example, be simply a relevant factor restated.

Recommendations

The final element in this structure of analyzing the problems, opportunities, and threats of your environment is your recommendations. Recommendations follow from your conclusions. They are, again, brief, one-sentence statements listed sequentially, in the imperative form. This differentiates them from conclusions. For example, a conclusion might be "Market research should be accomplished." A recommendation from this conclusion would be, "Initiate market research." Or a conclusion might be, "An additional salesperson should be hired." The recommendation resulting from this conclusion would be, "Hire an additional salesperson." These changes in form are important, for they demonstrate exactly what you say should be accomplished to solve the central issue that you have defined.

Let's consider the change in the OSHA environ mentioned at the beginning of this chapter. Can this analysis methodology help a company faced by the new OSHA demands?

According to the article, OSHA has made it tougher to meet the standards for toxicity in the factory by lowering the maximum permissible amounts for four hundred substances. Furthermore, OSHA plans to establish rules for medical surveyance and other chemical exposure. In other words, even if your company meets the new toxicity standards, we may still run afoul of OSHA if our employees get sick.[21]

Now we need to develop the central problem It isn't only the new requirements for the four hundred substances. In fact, it may not be just OSHA. There is increased interest in health and well-being in general, beyond the workplace. To a significant degree, OSHA is simply responding to consumer demand!

We might select the following as our central problem.

Central Problem

"How should the ABC Company respond to increased demand for worker protection from chemicals and toxic substances in the workplace?"

Now let's look at our relevant factors.

Relevant Factors

Facts

- OSHA has lowered the maximum exposure levels of nearly four hundred toxic substances.
- OSHA plans to establish rules for the medical surveillance of employees and for monitoring chemical exposure.
- Future OSHA requirements and plans have not yet been fixed.

Assumptions

- OSHA is responding to increased interest in health and demands for safer conditions in the workplace.
- Requirements are likely to become more stringent in the future rather than less so.

There is also a growing ethical element here. Whereas once the risk of toxic chemical exposure was considered one of the hazards of working, today employer responsibility for employee safety is a matter of ethics, as well as law. This trend will continue.

Increased protection varies directly with increased costs. That is, the more protection the company provides to its workers, the more it will cost. A greatly expanded program to implement safer environmental conditions for workers will not bankrupt the company, but it will reduce profitability and may necessitate increasing prices over the short term.

All that is required at the present time is that the company (as in the past) meet OSHA standards.

Now we are in a position to proceed with developing alternative solutions or courses of action for the central problem. Here are a few alternatives. Can you think of others?

Alternative Solutions and Courses of Action

1. Continue to meet OSHA standards, as in the past.
   Advantages
   A. Least cost in the short run.
   B. New management approach not needed.
   Disadvantages
   A. Will only prolong the inevitable because OSHA plans on going further, and we have assumed that future requirements will be more difficult to meet.
   B. May cost more to change in the future.
   C. May also cost the company more in the future if workers become sick due to marginal conditions that aren't corrected now.
   D. Poor ethical stance: we are accepting the possibility that unknown current exposures may have a negative impact on worker health.
   E. Will not solve problem of safer working conditions over long term.
2. Meet new OSHA standards and also establish a new program that will anticipate OSHA plans for rules for medical surveillance of employees and of chemical exposures.
   Advantagegs
   A. Probable reduced cost for making required changes after OSHA plans implemented.
   B. Less probability of successful employee suits due to unknown current exposure dangers.
   C. Potentially fewer sick workers in the future could lower costs of production.
   Disadvantages
   A. Added cost will probably impact negatively on profits or product pricing, at least over the short run.
   B. Because the problem is not OSHA, but interest in better health and the demand for safer working conditions, the long-range problem may still not be solved.
3. Implement an aggressive program of our own to improve significantly environmental safety for our workers above and beyond the OSHA requirements.
   Advantages
   A. Has greatest probability of solving the central problem over the long term.
   B. Fewer sick employees in the future should lower costs over the long run due to increased productivity.
   C. This should be promotable; may have positive affects on worker morale, our relationship with the union, our image, and in terms of general good will.

D. We should have no problem meeting OSHA standards.

Disadvantages

A. High cost

B. Will require an entirely different management approach and significant company change.

Now is the time to analyze our alternatives and the relative importance of the advantages and disadvantages we have listed for each.

Analysis/Discussion

This environ is still changing, but the trend in demand for employee safety is growing, not declining. Therefore, sooner or later we are not only going to have to meet the new OSHA standards, but we will have to make concern for our employees' safety a major element in our policy. That is, the ethical aspect of our responsibility for our employees safety cannot be avoided, either now or in the future.

The question then is how far we should go at the present time. Should we meet the new OSHA requirements as they exist today, meet them as we know they will exist in the future, or go all out to make employee safety a major concern of the company?

The cost of the alternative to be adopted is extremely important. High cost could cause a decline in profitability and might require us to increase our prices, making our products less competitive. Even employee well-being may be negatively affected in the form of layoffs, wage increase restrictions, or other employee benefit limitations. However, it is important to remember that these risks are over the short run only. Over the long run, providing maximum protection to our employees may actually lower costs as a result of a decline in employee illness, potential lawsuits, and unplanned expenses in meeting OSHA requirements. There may also be a concomitant rise in employee morale, company goodwill, and productivity.

Cost is clearly the driver in this situation. No one would deny the desirability of maximizing employee safety. However, few would want to do this at the cost of serious consequences to the company and its employees. Until we know more about cost trade-offs in quantitative terms, it would be counterproductive to maximize employee safety. It could actually hurt employees as well as the company. However, it would be equally counterproductive only to meet current OSHA requirements because we know they are changing, and we know what they are going to become.

Now we are ready to draw conclusions as a result of our analysis.

Conclusions

1. We should access the financial impact of implementing an aggressive program of our own to improve significantly environmental safety for our workers above and beyond OSHA requirements.
2. We should meet new OSHA standards and also establish a program that will anticipate OSHA plans for rules for the medical surveillance of employees and chemical exposure.
3. If the financial risk is acceptable, we should implement a full-blown

program to improve significantly the environmental safety of our employees above and beyond OSHA requirements.

Remember, the recommendations are simply the conclusions made imperative.

Recommendations

1. Assess the financial impact of a full, comprehensive program of employee environmental safety.
2. Establish a program now that meets current OSHA requirements, as well as those planned.
3. If financial risk is acceptable, initiate a comprehensive program for maximum employee protection.

Summary

In this chapter we have seen what makes up the environs of the marketplace and the environment in which every marketing manager must operate to fulfill his or her duties and responsibilities. These environs include the company environs, with subsets of know-how, experience, financial resources, human resources, capital equipment, suppliers, and marketing intermediaries; the competitor environs, with the same subsets; the neutral environs with financial environs, government environs, media environs, and special-interest environs; and situational environs, with politics, law and regulations, distribution structure, economics and business conditions, state of technology, demand, social and cultural factors, and demographics.

We have seen that an environmental scanning and situational analysis are absolutely crucial for successful marketing and that the environs are different in every marketing situation and are continually and sometimes rapidly changing. It was demonstrated that demographics are changing rapidly and that some demographic "truths" are no longer true. Furthermore, it was shown that consumerism, law, and other environs have a tremendous effect on the success or failure of a marketing campaign, independent of the strategy that has been decided upon in terms of the strategic variables. Clearly, the environs are crucial to successful planning and action. But while it is necessary to scan the environment to know, understand, and allow for the situation we are facing, it is also important to remember that we can affect and change the environment under certain situations. We have listed examples of environmental strategies. Two important concepts conclude this portion of the chapter: the relative importance of different environments is different at different times and the competitor environ is not only intelligent but will actively maneuver against the strategy you intend. Thus, any marketing action you undertake will provoke reaction from your competition.

We have concluded that the environs cause problems, opportunities, and threats, and that these must be analyzed in a clear, logical manner to demonstrate logical reasoning; include all relevant factors; consider all alternative solutions and courses of action; persuade others who may be in decision-making positions in your organization; and present your analysis, conclusions, and recommendations clearly and succinctly. To accomplish this, the staff-study method was explained in detail and an example given.

While there may be no substitute for experience,[22] proper environmental scanning, analysis of the marketing situation, and your ability to solve marketing problems and plan marketing strategy in the face of the environs of the marketplace differentiate the master marketing manager from others who simply hold the title marketer or marketing manager.

Questions

1. How can corporations anticipate environ changes such as with OSHA?

2. Give an example of a company environ, competitor environ, neutral environ, and situational environ and state how the specific environ cited might affect strategy that you as a marketing manager would plan.

3. The definition of environmental scanning has to do with the analysis of the environs, including their interactions and relationships. Give examples of how different environs of the marketplace interact.

4. It is said that environs are always changing and that if a company fails to adapt to these changes, it will eventually fail, even though it is presently successful. Discuss the environments for the railroad industry over the last hundred years. What changes occurred in them that affected marketing strategies and objectives? Similarly analyze the environs and the changes that have occurred over time for Sears, Roebuck and Company. For the banking industry.

5. Important demographic changes are discussed in this chapter and are illustrated in Figures 5-3 and 5-4. How might these changes affect a company selling toothpaste? A company selling vitamins? A company constructing homes?

6. Discussion in this chapter implies that product liability is becoming increasingly important. How will the forecast changes in product liabilities and marketing law affect marketing management decisions? In other words, what might the marketing manager do to take advantage of the opportunities and avoid the threats?

7. Traditionally the marketing manager has manipulated the four Ps of marketing and taken the environment as a given. But, as demonstrated, the environs can be manipulated. Give an example of how an environ can be manipulated as an alternative to manipulating the product variable, the price variable, the promotional variable, and the distribution variable.

8. The text states that at different times there is a relative difference in the importance of different environs. In recent years consumerism has become very important. Do you think this importance will continue? How should the marketing manager respond to either an increase or a decrease in importance?

9. The competitor has been defined as the intelligent environ that will be provoked to strong action by our strategy if we are successful. Because you know ahead of time that the competitive environment will change in reaction to our strategy, how might you prepare for these changes?

10. In which section of the method of marketing analysis discussed in this chapter might you expect to find statements pertaining to the environs of the marketplace?

Ethical Question

A company is facing increased demand by the union for "complete employee safety" in the workplace. The company calculates that to do exactly what is demanded will result in increased prices and probably in the loss of market share. This in turn will cause layoffs and in theory could cause the company to fail. The union disagrees with company calculations and continues to insist on its demands. Under these circumstances, is it ethical for company management to go along with the demands?

1. Michael A. Verespej, "The OSHA 400 Ignite Industry's Ire," *Industry Week*, vol. 238, no. 5 (March 6, 1989), pp. 64–65.
2. Sue Shellenbarger, "Fast Food Chains Improve Menus to Tap Big Change in Public Taste," *Wall Street Journal* 27 October 1983, p. 29.
3. William N. Borchard, "Law Gets Tough on Counterfeit Goods," *Advertising Age* (January 7, 1985), p. 26.
4. Donald P. Robin and R. Eric Reidenbach, "Social Responsibility, Ethics, and Marketing Strategy: Closing the Gap Between Concept and Application," *Journal of Marketing*, vol. 51 (January 1987), p. 45.
5. Ted Karger, "Marketplace Scenario Research," *Journal of Consumer Marketing*, vol. 5, no. 2 (Spring 1988), pp. 17–18.
6. Kathleen Vyn, "Airports Sold On Marketing to Build Concession Profits," *Marketing News*, vol. 23, no. 12 (June 5, 1989), pp. 2, 16.
7. Peter D. Bennett, *Dictionary of Marketing Terms* (Chicago: AMA, 1988), p. 68.
8. Ronna Klingenberg, "Decision-Making and the Forces of Change," *Management Review*, vol. 68 (December 1979), p. 13.
9. Paul C. Glick, "How American Families Are Changing," *American Demographics* (January 1984), pp. 21–25.
10. William B. Johnston and Arnold E. Packer, *Workforce 2000* (Indianapolis: Hudson Institute, 1987), p. 95.
11. Ibid., p. 81.
12. Bryant Robey, "Five Myths," *American Demographics* (December 1983), pp. 2, 4.
13. "Selling and the Law," *Industrial Distribution* (October 1981), pp. 38–42.
14. Ibid., p. 40.
15. Conrad Berenson, "The Product Liability Revolution," *Business Horizons* (October 1972), p. 80.
16. S. Powell Bridges, "The Schwinn Case: A Landmark Decision," *Business Horizons*, vol. 11 (August 1968), pp. 77–85.
17. Carl P. Zeithaml and Valarie A. Zeithaml, "Environmental Management: Revising the Marketing Perspective," *Journal of Marketing*, vol. 48 (Spring 1984), pp. 50–51.
18. Dorothy Cohen, "Remedies for Consumer Protection: Prevention, Restitution, or Punishment," *Journal of Marketing*, vol. 39 (October 1975), pp. 24–31.
19. Alfred Gross, "Adapting to Competitive Change," *MSU Business Topics* (Winter 1970), pp. 68–72.
20. Peter F. Drucker, *Management: Tasks, Responsibilities, Practices* (New York: Harper & Row, 1973), p. 472.
21. Verespej, op. cit.
22. Steven W. Perkins, and Ram C. Rao, "The Role of Experience in Information Use and Decision Making by Marketing Managers, *Journal of Marketing Research*, vol. 27, no. 1 (February 1990), p. 8.

Competitive Analysis

6

CHAPTER OBJECTIVES

- Understand the importance of the competitor environ in developing marketing strategy and preparing marketing plans.
- Understand the theory and basic principles of competition.
- Know the importance of a competitive advantage.
- Know how to analyze competitors.

The Computer Wars

More than twenty years ago, giant IBM looked at its existing lineup of computers and saw confusion and disorganization. Each IBM model was an individual product with its own language and its own software; none was compatible with the other. Thus, every time a model became obsolete and a customer thought about buying a new one, he or she might just as well go to a competitor as stick with IBM. This factor dominated all product considerations. IBM's solution, still revolutionary, was to make all IBM computers obsolete and make new models compatible with one another. Thus, in 1964, IBM introduced the Series 360, the first of a family of computers that shared basic compatibility under a single standard.

But the competitive environ did not lie dormant for long. Add-on devices with greatly increased memories and other capabilities that were compatible with IBM computers were designed by IBM competitors. Thus, IBM customers could hold on to the old models longer before buying a new system.

Again, IBM responded to the competition. Prices on peripheral and memory add-ons dropped sharply in the IBM line, while mainframe computers were marked up. In this way those companies manufacturing IBM add-ons were devastated.

Then Gene M. Amdahl of the Amdahl Corporation devised a new strategy intended to place IBM on the horns of a dilemma. Noting that IBM 370 Series' pricing was by performance and not production cost, and that the power of the largest machine was limited not by technological capabilities but by the IBM pricing structure, Amdahl reasoned that a bigger machine would have to be priced so high by IBM that its potential market would be too small to be profitable. Cleverly, Amdahl introduced a totally IBM-compatible machine, larger than IBM's largest unit but no more expensive. IBM was trapped. To respond, IBM would have to reprice its entire line of computers. While IBM did nothing, Amdahl's share of the large-system market doubled in a single year, and the company issued an annual report showing a 30 per cent pretax profit. Finally, IBM reacted. Biting the bullet, IBM announced a computer system 40 per cent more powerful than Amdahl's and 30 per cent cheaper. IBM's old performance-pricing structure was dropped. Amdahl was defeated, and Gene Amdahl himself left the company.

Recognizing the potential for similar competition in the future, IBM invested more than $1 billion for the most advanced computer technology possible. Faced with the extreme difficulty of defeating IBM head on, companies began to succeed by going where IBM was not and finding niches of computer types where the market was of a size that it did not make it worthwhile for IBM to compete. For some time, such a market was the personal computer area. A start-up company, Apple, entered the fray and captured and held two thirds of the market. Then, in 1981, IBM introduced its PC and immediately seized 34 per cent of the entire personal computer market and another 60 to 70 per cent of the corporate segment for the same computer. Weaker companies servicing the personal computer market, perhaps as many as 150, fell as a result of IBM's competitive action.[1]

But the computer wars were far from over. Apple Computer, Inc., launched the Lisa to compete with IBM, but the Lisa was a closed system that could not communicate with other computers and it did not fare well. Apple bounced back with the Macintosh. Before this, an updated version of the basic Apple, the IIc, helped to defeat IBM's PC Jr. It was withdrawn from the market. Though a technological powerhouse, the Macintosh started out as a disaster. Apple expected to sell 80,000 to 100,000 Macs a month. They were selling 20,000. On the brink of disaster, Apple CEO John Sculley shifted the strategic focus of the company. "We would have to shift from being a home/education company to one that served education."[2]

Meanwhile one of Apple's leading generals and founder, Steve Jobs, jumped ship and started his own company, Next, Inc., which also went after the education market. At an unveiling in October 1988, he said, "We've built the best computer in the world."[3]

Did you think IBM was sitting on its hands? Not on your life. IBM came out with the PS/2 series, using newer chips and a brand new high-capability operating system. Apple fought back by increasing the capabilities of the MAC. The industry leaders continue to innovate with technology and strategy, even as the environment changes. Amazing reductions in the price of computing power require that the demand rise at least 20 per cent a year just to keep the industry from shrinking, according to one source.[4] The computer wars go on!

Big Mac Fries Competition

McDonald's is hardly a small competitor. The dominant company in the fast-food business, it operates 10,577 restaurants in 50 countries. It controls 20 per cent of the $56 billion fast-food business. The competition in the past has been tough. Now it's getting frenzied. The target markets are working parents who have little time to cook their own meals. Everyone is after them, not only Burger King and Wendy's, number two and number three in the fast-food category, but also some of the nation's most sophisticated food marketers. These include the Kellogg Company, Kraft, General Foods, and Campbell, who are competing with microwaveable products.

McDonald's is fighting back by adding restaurants at an increasing pace, increasing the capacity for drive-through at restaurants, and increasing new product development. And well it might. The heavy hitter in the future may well be the American household and the companies that service it directly via the microwave oven. The market for microwaveable food is currently $3 billion a year, and microwaveable sandwiches alone ring up annual sales of $150 million. That may not seem like very much compared with the business the fast-food restaurants do. However, with 40 per cent annual growth this segment is a major threat to McDonalds. A thorough analysis of all the competition and proactive strategy will be necessary not only to be successful and to maintain position, but to survive in the coming years. As Michael R. Quinlan, CEO of McDonald's Corporation, says, "We're putting the pedal to the metal."[5] And he means now. ●

139

The Most Dangerous Environ

Competition is the most dangerous of the environs. First, competition is an intelligent entity, as opposed to, say, the business cycle, the weather, or environs in the marketplace, which may be intelligent in its area but acting in an unintelligent way in responding to our company or our company's actions. Competition is also dangerous because it is reactive to our planned strategy and tactics. Second, as already demonstrated, one competitive action inevitably leads to another. Finally, in a market that has leveled off and is no longer growing, expansion in sales or even survival has to be at the expense of the competition, and vice versa. Is it any wonder that famed business strategist Bruce Henderson maintains that "all strategy depends on competition."[6]

His words are echoed by those of practitioners. According to Norman Heller, president and CEO of Pepsi Wines and Spirits International, identifying competitive edges is the first step toward developing fresh approaches to marketing new products. Heller says, "To be successful in new product marketing, you must first know what is going on out there and the advantages your company's business system gives you over the competition in new product introductions."[7]

Basic Principles of Competition

The Universal Laws and Systems of Relationships of Competition

After thirty years of developing business strategies for thousands of firms and noting competition in nature, Bruce Henderson concluded that the basic principles of competition are as universal as the laws of chemistry and physics. Henderson sees fixed principles of competition that can be described as a system that includes twenty-one characteristics as shown in Exhibit 6-1. A close reading of these principles will do much to help any marketing manager understand this environ.[8]

Exhibit 6-1 Bruce Henderson's Universal Laws and Systems of Relationships of Competition

1. To survive, a competitor must have a unique advantage over other competitors.
2. The more similar competitors are to each other, the more severe their competition.
3. Different coexisting competitors must have a distinct advantage over each other. The characteristics that enable these distinct advantages emanate from the environment, which gives them their relative value.
4. Coexisting competitors must be in equilibrium. This equilibrium can exist only if any change produces forces that tend to restore the conditions prior to a disturbance.
5. There must be a point or series of points where the advantage shifts from

Exhibit 6-1 **(Continued)**

141

Competitive Analysis

one competitor to the other. Those points in which there is no relative advantage to any competitor define a competitive segment boundary.

6. There are as many significant variables or combinations of variables in the competitive environment as there are competitive survivors. These variables or combinations of variables enable a competitive advantage.

7. If multiple competitors coexist, then any given pair of competitors must differ from any other possible pair by a different combination of characteristics or factors.

8. Because each and every pair of competitors act as a constraint on one another, the equilibrium point between them constitutes a segment boundary.

9. Should a given competitor have multiple coexisting competitors, then each such competitor defines a sector of the competitive segment boundary. At such point where one sector ends and another begins, all three are equal and have no advantage over one another.

10. Any given competitor may have a large number of competitors, each of which defines a sector of the competitive sector and acts as a constraint. However, each sector of the competitive segment is defined by only one competitor.

11. For a competitor to fail to maintain a competitive segment and monopolize the advantage within it is failure to have an advantage over any competitor.

12. Any change in the environment changes the factor weighting of the environmental characteristics and therefore shifts the boundaries. Competitors who can adapt best or quickest gain an advantage from this change.

13. A critical environmental constraint for all competitors is their interface with other competitors. Thus, any change in the environment requires an adaptation of some sort or another.

14. The richer and more varied the environment, the greater number of potential competitors and the smaller the potential advantage of any one relative to the others. Thus, competition between them will be correspondingly more severe.

15. The total competitive environment can be seen as a web of interfacing competitors, all of which are uniquely advantaged and all of which are constrained by their competition while they are in a dynamic equilibrium with those with whom they interface.

16. Within this interfacing web is a competition for resources.

17. All the competitors on this interconnecting web are dependent on one another to some degree or the other no matter how strong, as each is dependent upon or competing for resources. Thus, while the strongest competitor is not prey to the others, its supply line is the most fragile. The most severe and critical competition is between adjacent elements of parallel-vertical resource chains that can also use the resources of a parallel chain.

18. Specialization of function is a prerequisite for effectiveness. Differentiation is a requirement for survival. Independence is unavoidable.

19. The control of the relationships within the competitive web and its elements is, like biology, based on the Darwinian fitness factor, which is defined as the ratio of the numbers of the species in one generation compared to the numbers of the preceding generation. The fitness factor below "1" will lead to extinction, whereas above "1" it will grow to infinity if compounded indefinitely.

Exhibit 6-1 (Continued)

20. As a corollary of the previous, a significant competitor has had a fitness factor above "1" above the entity; however, it is inevitable at some point in time that eventually the fitness factor will decrease to no more than 1.00.

21. Common evolution means a common gene pool in which natural selection within that pool affects the characteristics of each subsequent generation of that pool. Specialization of function that results in mutually exclusive selection of characteristics to the point that the gene pool is not shared by the alternative specialization is effectively the emergence of two separate identities with independent Darwinian fitness factors.

The Concept of the Competitive Advantage

Note that Henderson's very first observation states that a competitor must have a unique advantage over other competitors to survive. To assess competitive advantage in any business requires answering three difficult questions:

1. What is the basis of the present advantages that we have?
2. How valuable are these advantages and what is their relative value?
3. Can these advantages be sustained?[9]

The value of this **competitive advantage** in the marketplace eventually involves value to the customer. Thus, differences cannot be profitably exploited unless they can be converted into benefits. Furthermore, these benefits must be perceived by a sizable customer group, be such that are valued by the customer, and be something for which the customer is willing to pay and cannot readily obtain elsewhere.[10]

Sources of the Competitive Advantage

Sources of the competitive advantage can be categorized by skills or by resources. Skills include unique capabilities of personnel in your company that distinguish them from your competition. Resources include capital, equipment, materials, buildings, and other tangible items. But they may also include image, breadth of the salesforce, and distribution coverage. Superior skills and resources together represent the capability to do more, better, or faster than competitors.[11] These capabilities might include

- Specialized knowledge of the market and its needs.
- A customer service orientation.
- Design expertise.
- Applications experience.
- Trade relationships.
- Ability to utilize relevant technologies.
- Systems design capability.
- Ability to respond rapidly and in a flexible manner.

Superior resources as a differential competitive advantage might include the following:

- Coverage of distribution.
- Availability or access to capital.
- Business contacts.
- Low-cost manufacturing and distribution systems.
- Production capability or capacity.
- Raw material ownership or knowledge or access to sources.
- Long-term supply contracts.[12]

Basic Forces Governing Competition

There are five basic forces governing competition, as shown in Figure 6-1: the threat of new entrants, the bargaining power of customers, the bargaining power of suppliers, the threat of substitute products or services, and finally, the industry itself, in which current competitors are in continual motion attempting to achieve a new position. In this flurry of competitive activity, the marketing manager's job is to consider these forces and to locate a po-

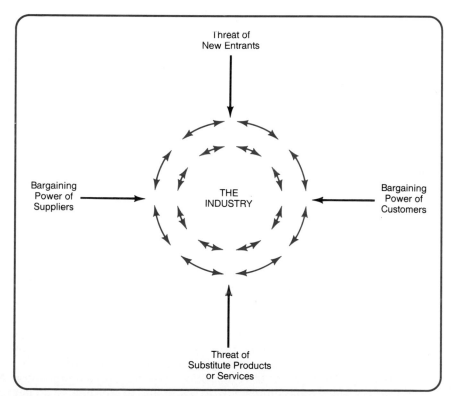

Figure 6-1 Five Basic Forces Governing Competition

Source: Adapted from Michael E. Porter, "How Competitive Forces Shape Strategy," *Harvard Business Review*, vol. 47 (March/April 1979).

sition in the industry where his or her company can best defend itself and, if possible, take advantage of these forces for the success of his or her endeavors.[13]

Reaction to Competitive Forces

As pointed out in an earlier chapter, reaction to competitive forces tends to have four stages. In the first stage, when a competitive force changes in the environment, a successful businessperson tends to hope that the force will not affect his or her operations and that all will continue as in the past. Therefore, no action is taken. However, if the competitive force continues to grow to the point where profits, sales, or some other success measurement is affected, the businessperson, in the second stage, will overreact and attempt to destroy the competitor force causing the change. The two classic methods are to cut off the competitor's source of supply or to foster restrictive legislation to outlaw the competitor's mode of operation.

In the third stage, direct confrontation and overcompensation, the businessperson attempts to counter by fighting the competition on his or her own ground—be this pricing, quality, warranties, or whatever factors the competitor touts or has as his or her differential advantage. Except for a company with almost unlimited resources, this head-on confrontation strategy almost invariably fails. All else being equal, it eventually leads to the fourth stage, adjustment and adaptation, in which the businessperson attempts to adjust and adapt to the major changes in the environment. He or she thinks through a more effective strategy, such as those in the examples at the beginning of this chapter.[14]

Why Competition May Be Good for Us

Although competition is the most dangerous of the environs, it may actually be good for us in the long, if not the short, term. Competition may make it easier for a company to differentiate its product. The fact that computers generally cost several hundred dollars when first introduced into the consumer market made it easier for the little Sinclair computer, selling for less than $100, to be sold in large quantities. Because of its many higher-priced competitors, it was clearly differentiated from them.

Competitors help to develop a new market or a new technology through their advertising, promotion, and other market activities. This stimulates the growth of such a market and makes the buyer more aware that the product or service exists. Considering again the computer example, if only one company produced computers, it itself would have had to expand resources to develop and make the public aware of the capabilities of computers, as well as establish the credibility of the new tool for its potential users in the marketplace. The fact that many competitors existed at the time of the computer's introduction took some of the burden off of any single company.

Perhaps the greatest benefit of competition, however, is as a motivator. A competitor motivates your company to do better and to continue to do better to survive. Without question, many companies, if not industries, have disappeared partly due to lack of strong competition. These companies were destroyed by their own complacency, doing business as usual, and failing to adapt to changes in the marketing environs. So-called substitute industries or indirect competition were able to take advantage of their inaction in the face of change to throw out the old. They had real live, direct competitors in their markets to "keep them honest."[15,16]

The Concept of Competitive Analysis

The Objectives of Competitive Analysis

The first step in living with the competitive environ is competitive analysis. There are three basic objectives for competitive analysis:

1. **Competitive analysis** permits you to understand your differential competitive advantage, as well as the comparative advantages, if any, of your competition.
2. Competitive analysis allows you to understand thoroughly and anticipate your competitor's strategies both in the present and in the future.
3. Competitive analysis is the key criterion of your strategy selection because of the horrendous potential that the competition presents as a marketing environ.[17]

Important Questions That Must Be Answered to Accomplish a Competitive Analysis

Certain questions are key and represent the heart of making an accurate assessment of the competition. These questions include

- Who is the competition now and who will be the competition in the future?
- Who are the key competitors in the marketing situation for which the competitive analysis is being accomplished?
- What are the competitor's strategies, objectives, and goals?
- How important are specific markets to each competitor, and are these specific markets important enough that they will continue to invest resources to win?
- What unique strengths do each of the competitors have?
- What weaknesses does each competitor have that makes it vulnerable?
- What changes are likely in the future strategies of the competitors?
- What are the implications of competitor strategies on the market, on the industry, and on your own company and current strategy?[18]

The Kinds of Information You Need About Your Competitors

Various surveys have been accomplished regarding the expert opinion of practicing managers and what they feel it is essential to know about their competition to accomplish an effective competitive analysis. One study showed the importance in twelve different areas, ranking from most important to least important: pricing, expansion plans, competitive plans, promotional strategy, cost data, sales statistics, R&D, product styling, manufacturing processes, patent infringements, financing, and executive compensation. Pricing was considered most important with the retail or wholesale trade in manufacturing industrial goods and in companies with under a thousand employees. This information, its rank, and percentage of all respondents considering it important, as well as the industries most interested in the companies, are shown in Figure 6-2.[19] Another summary of competitive analysis

Kind of Information	Rank	Per Cent of All Respondents	Industries Most Interested (by Per Cent of Respondents)		Companies Most Interested (by Per Cent of Respondents)	
Pricing	1	79%	Retail or wholesale trade Manufacturing industrial goods Manufacturing consumer goods	91 88 82	Under 1,000 employees	80%
Expansion plans	2	54	Retail or wholesale trade Education, social services Transportation, public utility	70 62 61	10,000 or more employees	64
Competitive plans	3	52	Transportation, public utility Advertising, media, publishing Banking, investment, insurance	75 70 61	20,000 or more employees	62
Promotional strategy	4	49	Advertising, media, publishing Retail or wholesale trade Transportation, public utility	79 69 61	1–49 employees 10,000 or more employees	54 52
Cost data	5	47	Defense or space industry Construction, mining, oil Manufacturing industrial goods	59 56 54	20,000 or more employees	53
Sales statistics	6	46	Retail or wholesale trade Advertising, media, publishing Manufacturing industrial goods	63 61 56	10,000 or more employees	55
R&D	7	41	Defense or space industry Manufacturing consumer goods Manufacturing industrial goods	72 52 52	500 or more employees	48
Product styling	8	31	Manufacturing consumer goods Advertising, media, publishing	53 52	10,000 or more employees	34
Manufacturing processes	9	30	Manufacturing consumer goods Manufacturing industrial goods Government	54 45 44	10,000 or more employees	40
Patents and infringements	10	22	Manufacturing industrial goods Manufacturing consumer goods	38 30	20,000 or more employees	34
Financing	11	20	Construction, mining, oil Transportation, public utility	34 30	20,000 or more employees	26
Executive compensation	12	20	Education, social services Banking, investment, insurance	39 38	Under 250 employees	23

Source: Adapted from Jerry L. Wall, "What the Competition Is Doing: Your Need to Know," *Harvard Business Review* (November–December 1974).

Figure 6-2 **Information Managers Want About Competitors**

Engineering	Production	Marketing	Finance	Management
Technical resources	*Physical resources*	*Sales force*	*Long term*	*Key people*
Concepts	Capacity	Skills	Debt/equity ratio	Objectives and priorities
Patents and copyrights	Plant	Size	Cost of debt	Values
Technological sophistication	Size	Type	*Short term*	Reward systems
Technical integration	Location	Location	Line of credit	*Decision making*
Human resources	Age	*Distribution network*	Type of debt	Location
Key people and skills	Equipment	*Research*	Cost of debt	Type
Use of external technical groups	Automation	Skills	*Liquidity*	Speed
Funding	Maintenance	Type	*Cash flow*	*Planning*
Total	Flexibility	*Service and sales policies*	Days of receivables	Type
Percentage of sales	*Processes*	*Advertising*	Inventory turnover	Emphasis
Consistency over time	Uniqueness	Skills	Accounting practices	Time span
Internally generated	Flexibility	Type	*Human resources*	*Staffing*
Government-supplied	Degree of integration	*Human resources*	Key people and skills	Longevity and turnover
	Human resources	Key people and skills	Turnover	Experience
	Key people and skills	Turnover	*Systems*	Replacement policies
	Work force	*Funding*	Budgeting	*Organization*
	Skills mix	Total	Forecasting	Centralization
	Unions	Consistency over time	Controlling	Functions
	Turnover	Percentage of sales		Use of staff
		Reward systems		

Source: Adapted from William E. Rothschild, "Competitor Analysis: The Missing Link in Strategy," *Management Review* (July 1979).

Figure 6-3 Summary of Competitive Analysis

information is shown in Figure 6-3. Note that the information important to accomplish a competitive analysis is not limited to marketing alone. It also has to do with finance, management, production, and engineering.[20]

Methods of Competitive Analysis

The Components of Competitive Analysis

Certain elements are key to the analysis of any competitor. Typical components of a competitive analysis are shown in Figure 6-4. They comprise, on one hand, what drives or motivates the competitor and, on the other, what the competitor is currently doing and what he or she has the capability of doing in the future. The components involve future goals, current strategy, assumptions, and capability, all of which affect and result in a competitor's response profile. From this profile we will know whether the competitor is satisfied with his or her current position in the marketplace, what moves in strategy the competitor is likely to take, where the competitor is vulnerable, and what actions or strategies on our part will provoke the greatest and most effective retaliation by the competitor.[21]

The Collection of Data

One model for the collection of data for a competitor intelligence system and its functions is shown in Figure 6-5. Note that it comprises field data and published data. This compares roughly with secondary and primary research, as discussed in an earlier chapter. From the figure you can see that in both

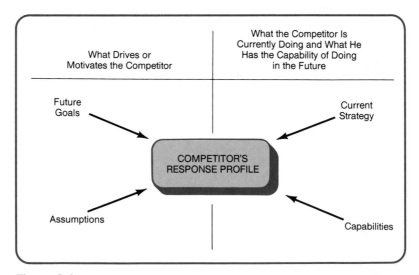

Figure 6-4

Source: Adapted from Michael E. Porter, *Competitive Strategy* (New York: The Free Press, 1980), p. 49.

cases the data are collected, compiled, cataloged, digested, communicated to
the strategist, and finally used in a competitive analysis for strategy formulation.[22]

There are unusually wide and varied sources of the data necessary for
competitive analyses. Three basic sources of data can be categorized as what
competitors say about themselves, what others say about them, and finally

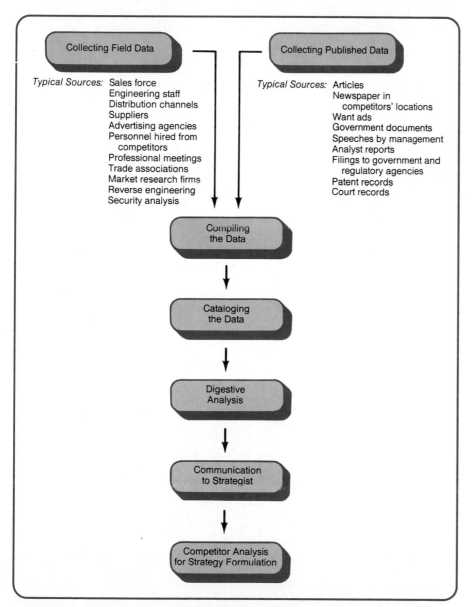

**Figure 6-5   The Collection of Data for a Competitive Intelligence System
and Its Functions**

Source: Adapted from Michael E. Porter, *Competitive Strategy* (New York: The Free Press, 1980), p. 73.

what individuals in your firm have observed while monitoring competitor activities. Competitors talk about themselves in advertisements, promotional materials, speeches by their executives, in personal changes they make and report in the press, and even in ads for employment opportunities. They also talk about themselves in information provided to the government by regulation and to investors in the various types of documentation required by the Security Exchange Commission.

Individuals outside of the competitor's organization also write, speak, and analyze the competitor. Such information is published in books, magazine articles, newspaper articles, the trade press, and other studies made of the industry.

Finally, a great deal of data are available from your own **field representatives**, who deal with the ultimate purchasers and know their feelings about the competition's products, service, strengths, weaknesses, and other assorted information.

Other sources of competitive information may include local government offices, including the county clerk, recorder, register of deeds, property appraiser, tax assessor, building department, consumer protection agency, health department, planning department; local media; chambers of commerce and boards of trade; trade shows; universities; other local companies who have contracts with the company that is being analyzed; banks; state governmental offices, including air pollution, banking, commerce, and economic development; and federal governmental offices, including consumer protection, corporate, environment, food and drugs, franchise, insurance, labor and industrial relations, occupational and professional licensing, occupational safety and health, purchasing, securities, uniform commercial code, and water pollution. Other federal government sources include the Security and Exchange Commission, the Internal Revenue Service, information obtained under the Freedom of Information Act, information obtained in Congress regarding lawsuits, and antitrust from agencies. Information also can be obtained from federal, state, and local courts. Additional sources are trade and professional associations, labor unions, stockbrokers, credit reporting, bond rating services, and most recently business data bases.[23,24,25]

Business Segment Analysis

Because many companies may be involved in a number of different businesses, especially large companies, to analyze our company along with a competitor, it is first necessary to segment our business into subsegments and to analyze them against our competitors' similar segments. In a similar fashion one could analyze a product line or a product instead of a business segment. In every case the key competitors are selected and, drawing on the data we have collected, important aspects are documented. Included are its positioning of the business, product line, or product and its commitment to its success; the importance to it of the segment being analyzed (and this can be determined by the percentage of total company salaries involved or the percentage of total company earnings); its apparent current marketing strategy; its current financial strategy regarding resource allocation; and its current investment strategy. Such an analysis is shown in Figure 6-6.[26]

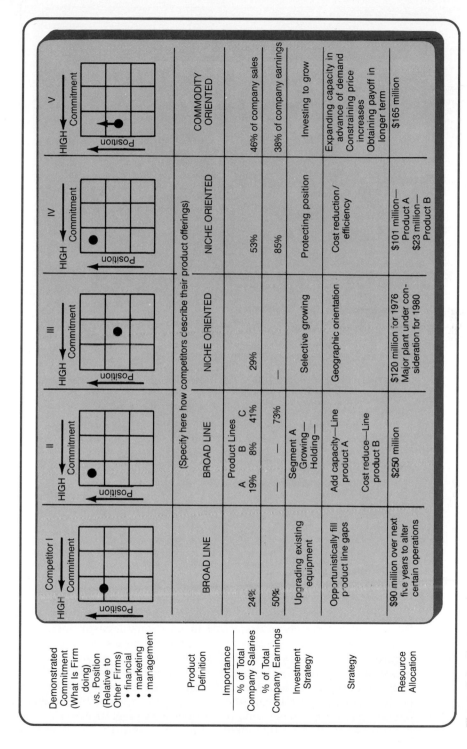

	Competitor I	II	III	IV	V
Demonstrated Commitment (What Is Firm doing) vs. Position (Relative to Other Firms) • financial • marketing • management	HIGH Commitment / Position	HIGH Commitment / Position	HIGH Commitment / Position	HIGH Commitment / Position	HIGH Commitment / Position
Product Definition	BROAD LINE	BROAD LINE	NICHE ORIENTED	NICHE ORIENTED	COMMODITY ORIENTED
		(Specify here how competitors describe their product offerings)			
Importance					
% of Total Company Salaries	24%	Product Lines A 19% B 8% C 41%	29%	53%	46% of company sales
% of Total Company Earnings	50%	73%	—	85%	38% of company earnings
Investment Strategy	Upgrading existing equipment	Segment A Growing— Holding—	Selective growing	Protecting position	Investing to grow
Strategy	Opportunistically fill product line gaps	Add capacity—Line product A; Cost reduce—Line product B	Geographic orientation	Cost reduction/ efficiency	Expanding capacity in advance of demand; Constraining price increases; Obtaining payoff in longer term
Resource Allocation	$90 million over next five years to alter certain operations	$250 million	$120 million for 1976 Major plant under consideration for 1980	$101 million— Product A $23 million— Product B	$165 million

Figure 6-6 Business Segment Analysis

Source: Adapted from William E. Rothschild, "Competitor Analysis: The Missing Link in Strategy," *Management Review* (July 1979).

Events	Vulnerability of the Competitor to the Event	Degree to which the Event will Provoke Retaliation by the Competitor	Effectiveness of the Competitor's Retaliation to the Event
Feasible Strategic Moves by our Firm List all alternatives such as: Fill out the line Increase product quality and service Reduce price and compete on costs			
Feasible Environmental Changes List all changes such as: Major increase in raw material costs Downturn in sales Increase in cost consciousness of buyers			

Figure 6-7   Competitor's Response Profile Matrix

Source: Adapted from Michael E. Porter, *Competitive Strategy* (New York: The Free Press, 1980), p. 69.

Competitor's Response Profile

An essential step in our competitive analysis is to assess the competitor's defensive capability in each case. Michael Porter, a well-known strategist and professor at the Harvard Business School, recommends developing a special analysis matrix. Feasible alternative strategies of our firm as well as possible environmental changes are listed on the vertical axis and are considered against the competitor's vulnerability to the event, the degree to which the event will provoke the competitor's retaliation, and the effectiveness of that retaliation to the event on the horizontal axis. Such a matrix is illustrated in Figure 6-7.[27,28]

Financial Analyses

Marketing strategists sometimes forget that any strategy must be tied to allocation of resources and that resources allocation—be it machinery, land, or human—ultimately is described in monetary measurements. Therefore, many companies also employ a form of financial analysis such as shown in Figure 6-8, which was developed by DuPont. This is known as the DuPont **profitability matrix**. In this matrix operating asset turnover is plotted against operating margin. A series of different **return-on-asset** (**ROA**) percentages is also plotted, derived from the following formula: ROA percentage equals operating margin and per cent, times operating asset turnover. Different competitors are plotted on this identical matrix. What they may indicate is that

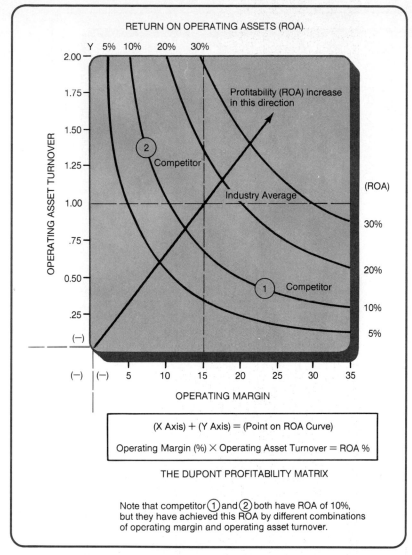

RETURN ON OPERATING ASSETS (ROA).

Profitability (ROA) increase in this direction

Industry Average

(ROA)

Competitor

THE DUPONT PROFITABILITY MATRIX

(X Axis) + (Y Axis) = (Point on ROA Curve)

Operating Margin (%) × Operating Asset Turnover = ROA %

Note that competitor ① and ② both have ROA of 10%, but they have achieved this ROA by different combinations of operating margin and operating asset turnover.

Figure 6-8   The DuPont Profitability Matrix

Source: Adapted from William L. Sarmon, Mark A. Kurland, and Robert Spitainic, *Business Competitive Intelligence* (New York: John Wiley & Sons, Inc., 1984), p. 105.

while different competitors have the identical profitability, as defined by ROA, and a position on the line of equal ROA percentages, they arrived at these positions using different strategies—some with a low operating margin and high turnover, and others with the opposite. This information can be plotted over time to show changes in strategies and competitors' comparative positioning. The DuPont matrix is useful because it shows underlying relationships between strategic variables and financial performance.[29]

Company A | Company B

	U.S. Army	U.S. Navy	U.S. Air Force	U.S. Marine Corps
PRODUCTS	Ground-Air; Short Range Ground-Air; Medium Range Ground-Air/Space; Long Range Ground-Ground; Short-Medium Range	Sea-Ground; Long Range Air-Ground; Short Range Air-Air Sea-Sea; Short-Medium Range	Ground-Ground; Long Range Air-Ground; Long Range Space-Ground; Long Range Air-Ground; Intermediate Range Air-Ground; Short Range Air-Air Space-Space	Air-Ground; Short Range Air-Air Ground-Air; Short Range Ground-Air; Medium Range Ground-Ground; Short-Medium Range
SERVICES	Consulting Feasibility Studies Trade-off Studies Applied Research Pure Research Development Testing	Consulting Flexibility Studies Trade-off Studies Applied Research Pure Research Development Testing	Consulting Feasibility Studies Trade-off Studies Applied Research Pure Research Development Testing	Consulting Feasibility Studies Trade-off Studies Applied Research Development Testing
COMPONENTS	Warhead Guidance Air Frame/Space Frame Propulsion Defense Launch	Warhead Guidance Air Frame Propulsion Defense Launch	Warhead Guidance Air Frame/Space Frame Propulsion Defense Launch	Warhead Guidance Air Frame Propulsion Defense Launch
PARTS	Electrical Mechanical Hydraulic Fuels Armor Explosive	Electrical Mechanical Hydraulic Fuels Armor Explosive	Electrical Mechanical Hydraulic Fuels Armor Explosive	Electrical Mechanical Hydraulic Fuels Armor Explosive

Figure 6-9 Competitive Arena Map

Source: Adapted from William A. Cohen, *Winning on the Marketing Front* (New York, John Wiley & Sons, 1986).

Many marketing strategy experts have noticed the similarities between marketing and business strategy and military strategy. However, it was probably William E. Rothschild of GE who first suggested some sort of mapping to investigate your position versus that of your competitors and, further, what the competition is trying to do over time. For example, in Figure 6-9 an entire industry has been mapped. This is called a **competitive arena map**. With a competitive arena map, you first define your business in terms of the need you intend to fill. For example, it might be an educational need, a transportation need, a computer need, a food need, and so forth. Next, you develop a map of the business arena that you serve. The vertical axis is used to document the products and services that fill your arena. Along the horizontal axis various types of customers in your arena are designated. As an example in the figure, the horizontal axis may be categorized by land, sea, air, and space customers, or by Army, Navy, Air Force, NASA, or Department of Energy customers for government marketers. The competitive arena map encompasses the entire industry.[30]

After this map is completed, a **segmentation matrix business battle map** is constructed. Here we get down to the real nitty-gritty for specific products and services. First, we must select those products and services we are going to analyze, along with those of our competitors and determine how they can

PRODUCT SEGMENTATION	Children/Teens	Age 19–34	Age 36 +
Plain Toothpaste	Colgate—Palmolive Proctor & Gamble	Colgate—Palmolive Proctor & Gamble	Colgate—Palmolive Proctor & Gamble
Toothpaste with Fluoride	Colgate—Palmolive Proctor & Gamble	Colgate—Palmolive Proctor & Gamble	Colgate—Palmolive Proctor & Gamble
Gel	Colgate—Palmolive Proctor & Gamble Lever Bros.	Colgate—Palmolive Proctor & Gamble Lever Bros.	Colgate—Palmolive Proctor & Gamble Lever Bros.
Striped	Beecham, Inc.	Beecham, Inc.	
Smoker's Toothpaste		Topol	Topol
Pump Packaging	Oral-B	Colgate—Palmolive Proctor & Gamble	Colgate—Palmolive Proctor & Gamble

CUSTOMER SEGMENTATION

Figure 6-10   Segmentation Matrix Business Battlemap for Toothpaste

Source: Adapted from William A. Cohen, *Winning on the Marketing Front* (New York: John Wiley & Sons, 1986).

best be described. A convenient description depends on the situation and what we think is most important. It may be by pricing, size, quality, complexity, function, or positioning. This description goes on the vertical axis. The horizontal axis is used to segment the customers into groups, but the segmentation is more precise than with the competitive arena map. Typically the segmentation is by geographics, demographics, psychographics, or lifestyle. Such a segmentation matrix battle map is shown in Figure 6-10.[31]

Perhaps the ultimate in business or marketing battle maps is as shown in Figure 6-11, where a third dimension has been added to make the map more useful in planning, for analyzing the strategies of the competition, and for analyzing both the threats and the opportunities in every situation. In this figure the dimension that has been added is **total market potential**. Total market potential is calculated by multiplying the number of potential cus-

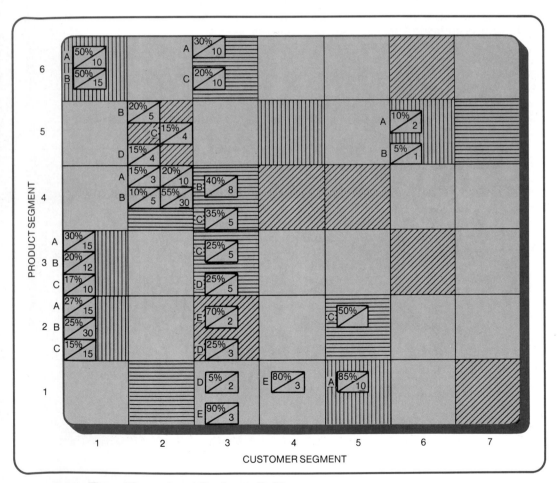

Figure 6-11 Three Dimensional Business Battlemap

Notes: 1. Only companies A, B, C, D, and E plotted. 2. Smaller, unplotted companies may have remaining market shares.
3. Sales estimated in millions of dollars.
Source: Adapted from William A. Cohen, *Winning on the Marketing Front* (New York: John Wiley & Sons, 1986).

tomers in the segment by the average price of the product sold. Thus, if a certain segment has a potential of two million customers and the average product price is $2.00, the segment would encompass a total market potential of $4 million.

Each segment is indicated by a different code, color, or other distinguishing feature. In the figure, a segment of less than $5 million in potential sales is left blank. Potential sales of $5 to $10 million are indicated by a series of 45-degree lines, $11 to $20 million by a series of horizontal lines, and $21 to $30 million by vertical lines. A small rectangle outlining the area indicates the competitor's or your own activity in a particular segment. The rectangle is divided by a line going from the lower left corner to the upper right. The upper division of this division shows a percentage. This percentage is the market share of that segment of the company outlined by the rectangle. The figure in the lower right part of the rectangle separated by the diagonal is a quantitative representation of the assets committed to doing business in this segment. With overlays, even additional information can be shown on these marketing battle maps.[32]

Summary

In this chapter we have seen that the competition is the most dangerous of the marketing environs because it is intelligent and can react to affect your strategy and tactics adversely. In nongrowth markets your growth and even your survival must be at the expense of a competitor. The basic principles of competition involve universal laws and relationships; thus, studying and understanding these laws and systems of relationships will help you understand how to analyze the competition in any marketing situation and how best to compete. Winning out over your competition is based on the concept of a unique competitive differential advantage. This is something you have to do better than your competition. Determining this competitive differential advantage involves answering three difficult questions: (1) What is the basis of your present advantages? (2) How valuable are these advantages? and (3) Can they be sustained?

Next, we looked at some potential sources of competitive differential advantages and noted how these sources led to forces that govern all competition and reaction to those forces. We also found that competition may actually be useful and accomplish some good. Thus, even the competition might be incorporated into your overall marketing strategy.

Having established a basis, we turned to the construction of a competitive analysis structure. In sequence, we established the objectives of competitive analysis and looked at important questions that must be answered. We also examined the types of information it is important to know to accomplish the analysis. The method selected for accomplishing the analysis was derived from the various components that make up the structure—future goals, current strategy, assumptions, and capabilities. Combined, these result in a competitor's response profile. The development of these elements was based on extensive data collection and a number of data collection sources. Sources of information were listed. Using these data, a business segment analysis was accomplished. Having noted the positioning of the products, services, or businesses of competitors, as well as our own, we utilized the competitor response profile to predict likely outcomes of alternative strategies that we might implement, as well as changes in the environs. We also saw that a financial analysis such as the DuPont matrix could be very important, especially when plotted over time to discover not only whether companies were profitable, but how they arrived at their profitability. Using some of the latest graphic concepts, we discussed mapping a marketing battlefield, including a competitive arena map and segmentation matrix, as well as the possibility of three-dimensional mapping to include all important aspects of the competitive situation.

The analysis of the competition is always important, and in situations of scarcity or where markets are no longer growing or are actually shrinking, competitive analysis is critical to success in the marketplace. Therefore, the notions of competition, competitive action and reaction, and the other concepts in this chapter will be used later in developing marketing strategies and tactics.

Questions

1. It has been stated that the competition is the most dangerous of the environs of the marketplace. Is this always so in every marketing situation? When would this not be so?
2. Bruce Henderson has stated that all strategy depends on competition. How can you reconcile this with the marketing concept, specifically as satisfaction of customer needs being the primary focus of marketing?
3. Certain forces govern competition. Among these are assumptions and capabilities. In analyzing a competitor, should you consider what a competitor is capable of doing or what he or she is likely to do?
4. In this chapter it has been stated that competition may actually be good for your company or your business, and several examples of this were listed. Can you think of other examples when competition may be good for your company or your strategies?
5. Of what advantage is it to understand your competitor's past strategies?

6. Do you, your customers, your competitors, and other outside agencies always view differential competitive advantages as being identical in value?
7. Can a competitor ever be totally invulnerable? Justify your answer.
8. Why do managers in different industries feel that different types of information are more important for assessing a competitor?
9. This chapter primarily discusses secondary sources of information for competitive analysis. What are some primary methods of collecting competitive information? Are these methods ethical?
10. Construct a business battle map and plot your own company and your major competitors. What can the information on the map tell you about your situation relative to that of your competition?

Ethical Question

In the book *No Contest* (Boston: Houghton Mifflin, 1986), Alfie Kohn argues that competition is inherently destructive and that society would be better off without it. For example, without competition, the cost of competitive analysis would be eliminated. Do you agree or disagree with Kohn's position? If you disagree, how do you justify competition? If you agree, how do you reconcile competition with ethical behavior?

1. Myron Magnet, "How to Compete with IBM," *Fortune* (February 6, 1984).
2. John Sculley, with John Byrne, *Odyssey* (New York: Harper and Row, 1987), pp. 270, 273.
3. Katherine M. Hafner and Richard Brandt, "Steve Jobs: Can He Do It Again?" *Business Week* (October 24, 1988), p. 74.
4. Geoff Lewis, "Is the Computer Business Maturing?" *Business Week* (March 6, 1989), p. 68.
5. Brian Bremner and Gail DeGeorge, "The Burger Wars Were Just a Warm-Up for McDonald's," *Business Week* (May 8, 1989), p. 67.
6. Bruce D. Henderson, *Henderson on Corporate Strategy* (New York: New American Library, 1979), p. 108.
7. "Spotting Competitive Edges Begets New Product Success," *Marketing News* (December 21, 1984), p. 4.
8. Bruce D. Henderson, "The Anatomy of Competition," *Journal of Marketing*, vol. 47 (Spring 1983), p. 8.
9. George S. Day, *Strategic Market Planning* (St. Paul: West, 1984), p. 26.
10. Ibid., p. 29.
11. George S. Day and Robin Wensley, "Assessing Advantage: A Framework for Diagnosing Competitive Superiority," *Journal of Marketing*, vol. 52, no. 2 (April 1988), pp. 2, 3.
12. Day, op. cit., pp. 30–31.
13. Michael E. Porter, "How Competitive Forces Shape Strategy," *Harvard Business Review*, vol. 47 (March–April 1979), pp. 137–145.
14. Alfred Gross, "Adapting to Competitive Change," *MSU Business Topics* (Winter 1970).
15. Michael E. Porter, "A Good Competitor Is Not Always a Dead Competitor," *Wall Street Journal*, 1 April 1985.
16. Michael E. Porter, *Competitive Advantage* (New York: The Free Press, 1985), p. 202.
17. Peter R. Sawers, "How to Apply Competitive Analysis to Strategic Planning," *Marketing News* (March 18, 1983), p. 11.
18. William E. Rothschild, "Competitor Analysis: The Missing Link in Strategy," *Management Review* (July 1979).
19. Jerry L. Wall, "What the Competition Is Doing: Your Need to Know," *Harvard Business Review* (November–December 1974).
20. Rothschild, op. cit.
21. Porter, *Competitive Strategy*, (New York: The Free Press, 1980) p. 49.
22. Ibid., p. 73.
23. Rothschild, op. cit.
24. Ibid.
25. Washington Researchers, *How to Find Information About Companies*, 2nd ed. (Washington, D.C.: Washington Researchers, 1981).
26. Rothschild, op. cit.
27. Porter, *Competitive Strategy*, op. cit. p. 49.
28. Ibid., p. 69.
29. William L. Sammon, Mark A. Kurland, and Robert Spitalnic, *Business Competitor Intelligence* (New York: Wiley, 1984), pp. 105–110.
30. William E. Rothschild, *How to Gain and Maintain the Competitive Advantage* (New York: McGraw-Hill, 1984), pp. 12–25.
31. Ibid.
32. William A. Cohen, *Winning on the Marketing Front* (New York: Wiley, 1986).

Buyer Behavior

7

CHAPTER OBJECTIVES

● Understand the basic concepts of buyer behavior and be able to apply them to actual marketing situations.

● Know the difference between the two categories of buyer behavior: consumer and organizational.

● Know the problems and opportunities inherent in buyer behavior and how to proceed, given their existence.

What Is the Sport of "Yuppies"?

Young upscale professionals and young upwardly mobile adults, the so-called Yuppies and Yumpies, have a certain sport of their own, and marketers attempting to satisfy their needs by identifying their particular segment of the market by the behavior of its participants are making a lot of money. This sport is not tennis, golf, or even the traditional baseball, football, or basketball. What is the Yuppie sport? You've heard of it. It's one of the martial arts and it's called karate. The California-based Professional Karate Association, or PKA, has really taken off. Treco, the first PKA major sponsor on television, sells power-stretch exercise equipment and other karate peripherals. It advertises on PKA's "Best Kicks" program. Not too long ago Treco logged nearly 590 phone calls from four 30-second, direct-response spots that were advertised along with a "Best Kicks" show that was in its tenth to fifteenth repeat. As a result, Treco made a high six-figure deal with PKA. Recently PKA executives have been talking with Anheuser-Busch and Adolph Coors. PKA is also talking about major networks now, offering a planned package of several title matches. Success has resulted not because PKA has attempted to market karate to everyone, but rather because it has identified a specific demographic market segment that exhibits certain buyer behavior patterns.[1]

160

Football Coaches Play Marketing to Increase Game Attendance

Because increased attendance at football games usually means more revenue for sports programs and other activities in education, 33 college and high school football coaches were not at all averse to participating in a survey to rank 13 factors relevant to attracting fans to their games. These football coaches came from a dozen states, mostly in the Midwest, and were at the time attending the annual University of Arkansas Coaches Clinic. Each coach was asked to rate 13 factors on a scale of 1 to 7, with 7 being very important and 1 being unimportant. The coaches were also permitted to list any other factors they considered to be important. Here are the results of that survey, from the most important to the least important, along with their ranking.

Winning, 6.8
Convenient parking, 5.5
Right information to promote games, 5.37
Right personnel to sell the team, 5.25
Right time to play games, 5.25
Right place to play games, 5.11
Right amount of money to finance games, 5.05
Concessions, 4.9
Additional services for the games, 4.84
Right ticket price, 4.5
Band, 4.08
Booster club, 3.78
Cheerleaders, 3.67
Pom-pom girls, 3.61

It remains to be seen whether the coaches' perception of buyer behavior for increasing ticket sales is accurate or not. Clearly, if the correct factors were identified, they could be used by good marketing managers to increase greatly sales and attendance.[2]

Those Cheapskate Millionaires

How do you spot the hidden millionaire? Does this well-heeled consumer drive a Rolls Royce or a Birdcage Maserati? Does he or she wear a Rolex and sport expensive diamonds? Not according to marketing professor Thomas J. Stanley, author of the book *Marketing to the Affluent.* According to Stanley, most millionnaires wear Timex or Seiko. As a consequence, marketing executives frequently make the mistake of targeting those with only the trappings of wealth, rather than the actual superaffluent. Stanley defines this group with these demographics: households earning $100,000 or more a year, or with a net worth of $1,000,000. Who are these consumers? Most are business owners, and about 20 per cent are retired. Currently there is one millionaire for every 100 households, and the group is growing. Their average income is $120,000 per year. If you want to sell to this group, you'd better understand buyer behavior. According to Stanley most millionnaires are a frugal bunch and tend not to live in the fanciest neighborhoods. They are generally not well known, and many of those that are business owners don't even incorporate. They tend to work harder and longer hours, so if you're going to call them on the telephone, you'd better call their offices before 8 A.M. They are often the first in the office and the last to go home.[3]

What Buyer Behavior Is and Why It Is Important

The study of buyer behavior brings an understanding of how individuals or organizations behave in the purchase situation. It is really psychology applied to marketing, specifically to the buy decision. It is important because if the buying behavior of a segment of the market is understood, it presents an opportunity for the marketing manager to fulfill the needs of potential customers in a unique way: not only physically but psychologically. There is another side of the coin: if the marketing manager fails to fulfill the psychological needs of his or her potential customers, he or she will probably fail, even though the product or service satisfies physical needs.

This has been conceptualized as the **consumer behavior** goals that marketing managers seek to achieve. They include increasing product adoption and repeat usage, satisfying consumers at a profit, protecting and educating consumers, satisfying consumers at an acceptable and nominal cost to them, and educating a social response.[4]

Consumer behavior can also help us in implementing strategy and tactical goals. One study of psychographic segmentation, or grouping people by the way they behave, indicated that psychographic segmentation solutions developed for a market in one geographic location were generalizable to markets in others.[5] Thus, consumer behavior concerns both strategy and tactics.

Let's look at some examples of what we're talking about here. We spoke about the PKA marketing primarily to **Yuppies** because this segment of the market has proven to be the one most interested in the sport. If, instead, the PKA had gone by gut feeling, it might have attempted to market karate to the same one as other spectator sports—such as baseball, basketball, or football—or the other combative spectator sports—such as boxing or wrestling. Yet the buyer behavior of these segments of the market is not the same. They are different groups with different physical and psychological needs. Therefore, the segments interested in those other sports behave differently. Failure to consider differences in behavior can result in failure in the marketplace.

Look at these other examples. Why have sushi (raw fish with rice) bars enjoyed great success in California, but much less success in other parts of the country? Perhaps it is because larger segments of California's population are from the Orient and already know and enjoy the product. How about the failure of baby foods in countries where the mother is expected to prepare fresh baby foods on her own? Or the failure of instant foods some years ago in this country when the wife was expected to prepare all foods herself—when not preparing foods on her own meant being a "bad wife"? Why are these products more successful today? This is the age of equality and the working woman. And, by the way, do you like the odor of cigars? An odorless cigar was invented some years ago. But men who smoked cigars wouldn't buy them. It was found that these smokers equated the odor with a macho image.

The Categories of Buyer Behavior

There are two basic categories of buyer behavior. So far we've talked mainly about the consumer. But there is also an organizational category of buyer behavior that is equally, if not more, important. You can consider how important if you look at the U.S. government. Some years ago, the U.S. Air Force had severe problems with aircraft safety due to the potential entanglement with its then standard pilot's knee board and the flight controls. An independent inventor found the solution, obtained a patent, sold several thousand of his invention to individual pilots, and gave many more away for Air Force tests. Yet, he lost the contract to manufacture thousands of his invention at the time it was adopted simply because he did not understand buyer behavior in the U.S. government—which is similar to other organizational buyer behavior but different from individual consumer behavior.

It is important to understand not only the motivations and background of the behavior of the individual consumer, but also that of the organizational buyer, whose motivations may be at least as complicated and difficult to comprehend. Neither may behave in what we could consider a "logical" fashion.

Understanding both groups can be of great value because of the potential of what Professor John A. Quelch of Harvard calls **dual marketing**—that is, marketing to both individual and organizational consumers. Benefits include serving a broader range of consumers, smoother production scheduling, the capability of shifting resources, more profitable use of production capacity, and the opportunity to sell excess inventory.[6]

—————— The Consumer Buyer-Behavior Process

Generalizations About the Consumer Buying Process

Certain generalizations can be made based upon purchase-influence studies regarding the consumer buying process. These include factors having to do with **family decision making**, internal factors that influence the consumer, and external factors that influence the consumer. Let's look at each general category in turn.

Household Decision-Making Factors

Basically there are three factors that we must consider:[7]

1. Involvement of the husband versus the wife varies widely, depending upon product category.
2. Influence within each product category varies by decision stages. That is, there is less joint effort during the information search stage than in other decision stages of the process.
3. For each type of consumer decision, family member influence varies considerably among families. This can be seen in Figure 7-1.[8]

Product	Dominant Decision Maker	Typical Decision
Women's casual clothing	Wife	Price, style
Vacations	Syncratic (both)	Whether to go, where
Men's casual clothing	Husband	Type, style, price
Life insurance	Husband	Company, coverage
Homeowners'/renters' insurance	Husband	Company, coverage
Household appliances	Wife	Style, brand, price

Source: Adapted from Robert M. Cozenza, "Family Decision Making: Decision Dominance Structure Analysis—An Extension," *Journal of the Academy of Marketing Science*, vol. 13 (Winter 1985), p. 99.

Figure 7-1   Dominant Family Purchase: Decision Makers, Depending on Product

Internal Factors That Influence the Consumer

Internal factors that influence the consumer in the buying process include stages of **information processing** and consumer characteristics and behavior. A psychologist might divide human information processing into various stages. One such division of process includes successive steps of exposure, perception, comprehension, agreement, retention, retrieval, decision making, and action. Depending upon the stage, influence and behavior will vary. Consumer characteristics of behavior might include information such as age, sex, occupation, ethnic group, life-style, and psychographics, which includes ways of thinking.[9]

External Factors Influencing Purchase Decision

External factors influencing the **purchase decision** by the consumer include promotion, contact with others, direct experience with the product, and perceived price-value relationships.[10]

The Consumer Buying Process

The **consumer buying process** is shown in Figure 7-2. Note that the inputs are both marketing and psychological. Both work together on the consumer's psyche to result in purchase decision outputs, including what products and brands are selected, where and from whom they are bought, and how frequently and in what amount.

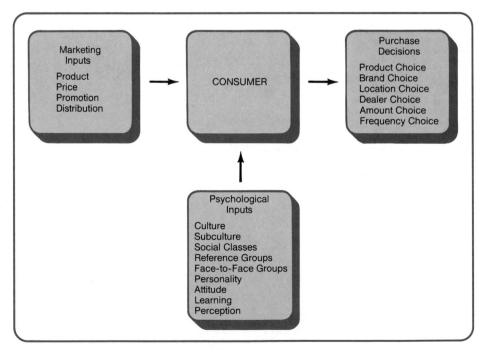

Figure 7-2 The Consumer Buying Process

It is possible to categorize consumer buying behavior and process as two distinct models, one simple, the other complex. The simple model is known as habitual brand choice. This purchase decision model works after the complex model has already resulted in a purchase decision and generally involves low-involvement products. The simple model simply means that one continues to purchase the brand or product or go to the dealer or store used in the past, providing that the consumer was satisfied with it. Do you eat candy? Do you stop to think of the type of candy bar and go through some sort of complicated decision-making process every time you buy one? Usually not. Or how about your choice of toothpaste, soap, shampoo, or any other product or service that is purchased frequently, is inexpensive, and for which you have had favorable or at least acceptable experiences in the past? Thus, through habitual brand choice, you make decisions without much thought and without wasting much time; at the same time you lower your risk of satisfaction due to a favorable experience, or at least an acceptable experience, with the product in the past.

The Problem-Solving (Complex) Model

In the purchase of an unfamiliar product or one that is more expensive, a more complex decision-making process may occur. This includes (1) recognition of the problem or felt need based on the interaction between two components: desired state and the actual state,[11] (2) the search for alternative solutions to the desire, (3) the evaluation of alternatives, (4) the purchase decision, and (5) postpurchase feelings and evaluation. Note the similarity of this decision-making process with the problem-solving, or staff-study, outline recommended to you in Chapter 5. The only new element is that of postpurchase feelings and evaluation. Technically this is known as **cognitive dissonance**.[12]

Cognitive dissonance is the tension caused by uncertainty about the rightness of a purchase decision. This may lead the consumer to search for additional information to confirm that the decision was the right one in the first place. Thus, the buyer may continue to shop and look at competitive products even after the product has been purchased. Postpurchase feelings and phenomena are important to marketing managers because they may influence future purchase or nonpurchase.[13] Of equal, if not greater importance, they may directly impact on word-of-mouth influence on other potential buyers.

Major Factors Influencing Consumer-Buyer Behavior

Motivational Theory and Maslow's Hierarchy of Needs

In 1943 Abraham H. Maslow, at the University of Chicago, published his theory of human motivation.[14] Basically Maslow's theory was that human beings were motivated by a **hierarchy of needs**, beginning with physiological needs and progressing successively to safety needs; love; esteem, or self-respect; and self-actualization. Also at a high level, but not quite fitting in with the previous needs, were two other classes: aesthetic needs and the need to know and understand. While there might be some overlap between each type of need, according to Maslow, as one need becomes satisfied, we seek to satisfy the next, and so on. The way that these needs are seen as motivators can be understood if we start with a physiological need, such as breathing. If you suddenly begin to choke and can no longer breathe, your interest in marketing management, your course work, your career, or any of the other higher needs would immediately disappear. Your immediate need would be to breathe and nothing else. But once you regain the ability to breathe, you might be interested in safety and security. For example, would it really be possible to concentrate on this page if you didn't know where your next meal was coming from? Or could you concentrate on this chapter if you were reading it in an airplane that was in imminent danger of crashing? These fall under the classification of safety and security needs; once satisfied, you would again move up the chain. The importance of Maslow's needs in marketing can be demonstrated by a practical example.

Stop reading the text at this point and refer to Figure 7-3, an advertisement called "The Lazy Man's Way to Riches." Read the ad and then return to the text.

The advertisement you just read was written by marketer Joe Karbo. The ad was written in about two hours in 1973. It appeared in three major newspapers, running one-third of a page as a test. The first time it appeared it brought in $50,000 in sales. Of some interest is the fact that the product, a 156-page booklet, "The Lazy Man's Way to Riches," did not exist at the time the ad was written. The ad appeared as a "dry test." The author and entrepreneur, Joe Karbo, who wrote the ad and ultimately "The Lazy Man's Way to Riches," wrote letters to his first customers offering them their money back or the option to wait for the booklet's appearance, which was in accordance with existing FTC regulations at that time. The version of the ad you have read was not the first. It contains testimonials received after the product had been furnished. The ad ran steadily in various forms for about ten years. It is still run in some versions today, although the author himself died several years ago.

This advertisement sold over one million copies of "The Lazy Man's Way to Riches" worldwide, in thirteen different languages. Considering it a powerful advertising tool would therefore be an understatement. When it first appeared, it brought in fourteen times the cost of the advertisement in sales, although break-even was something like 1.25 times the cost of the advertisement.

The question to ask yourself is this: Which need in Maslow's hierarchy of needs did Karbo address in writing this advertisement? If you go through the advertisement line by line, you will see that Karbo used every single one, an incredible example of the applied use of a theoretical concept. Even knowing and understanding was included as an element of the ad. Do you know what the product is other than the fact that it is in printed form? To know you must order the product.

The Lazy Man's Way to Riches

'Most People Are Too Busy Earning a Living to Make Any Money'

I used to work hard. The 18-hour days. The 7-day weeks.

But I didn't start making big money until I did less—a *lot* less.

For example, this ad took about 2 hours to write. With a little luck, it should earn me 50, maybe a hundred thousand dollars.

What's more, I'm going to ask you to send me 10 dollars for something that'll cost me no more than 50 cents. And I'll try to make it so irresistible that you'd be a darned fool not to do it.

After all, why should you care if I make $9.50 profit if I can show you how to make a *lot* more?

What if I'm so sure that you *will* make money my Lazy Man's Way that I'll make you a most unusual guarantee?

And here it is: I won't even cash your check or money order for 31 days *after* I've sent you my material.

That'll give you plenty of time to get it, look it over, try it out.

If you don't agree that it's worth at *least a hundred times* what you invested, send it back. Your *uncashed* check or money order will be put in the return mail.

The only reason I won't send it to you and bill you or send it C.O.D. is because both these methods involve more time and money.

And I'm already going to give you the biggest bargain of your life.

Because I'm going to tell you what it took me 11 years to perfect: How to make money the Lazy Man's Way.

O.K.—now I have to brag a little. I don't mind it. And it's necessary—to prove that sending me the 10 dollars . . . which I'll keep "in escrow" until you're satisfied . . . is the smartest thing you ever did.

I live in a home that's worth $250,000. I know it is, because I turned down an offer for that much. My mortgage is less than half that, and the only reason I haven't paid it off is because my Tax Accountant says I'd be an idiot.

My "office," about a mile and a half from my home, is right on the beach. My view is so breathtaking that most people comment that they don't see how I get any work done. But I do enough. About 6 hours a day, 8 or 9 months a year.

The rest of the time we spend at our mountain "cabin." I paid $30,000 for it—cash.

I have 2 boats and a Cadillac. All paid for.

We have stocks, bonds, investments, cash in the bank. But the most important thing I have is priceless: time with my family.

And I'll show you just how I did it—the Lazy Man's Way—a secret that I've shared with just a few friends 'til now.

It doesn't require "education." I'm a high school graduate.

It doesn't require "capital." When I started out, I was so deep in debt that a lawyer friend advised bankruptcy as the only way out. He was wrong. We paid off our debts and, outside of the mortgage, don't owe a cent to any man.

It doesn't require "luck." I've had more than my share, but I'm not promising you that you'll make as much money as I have. And you may do better; I personally know one man who used these principles, worked hard, and made 11 million dollars in 8 years. But money isn't everything.

It doesn't require "talent." Just enough brains to know what to look for. And I'll tell you that.

It doesn't require "youth." One woman I worked with is over 70. She's travelled the world over, making all the money she needs, doing only what I taught her.

It doesn't require "experience." A widow in Chicago has been averaging $25,000 a year for the past 5 years, using my methods.

What *does* it require? Belief. Enough to take a chance. Enough to absorb what I'll send you. Enough to put the principles into action. If you do just that—nothing more, nothing less the results will be hard to believe. Remember—I guarantee it.

You don't have to give up your job. But you may soon be making so much money that you'll be able to. Once again—I guarantee it.

The wisest man I ever knew told me something I never forgot: "Most people are too busy earning a living to make any money."

Don't take as long as I did to find out he was right.

Here are some comments from other people. I'm sure that, like you, they didn't believe me either. Guess they figured that, since I wasn't going to deposit their check for 31 days, they had nothing to lose.

They were right. *And here's what they gained:*

$260,000 in eleven months

"Two years ago, I mailed you ten dollars in sheer desperation for a better life . . . One year ago, just out of the blue sky, a man called and offered me a partnership . . . I grossed over $260,000 cash business in eleven months. You are a God sent miracle to me."

B. F., Pascagoula, Miss.

Made $16,901.92 first time out

"The third day I applied myself totally to what you had shown me. I made $16,901.92. That's great results for my first time out."

J. J. M., Watertown, N.Y.

'I'm a half-millionaire'

"Thanks to your method, I'm a half-millionaire . . . would you believe last year at this time I was a slave working for peanuts?"

G. C., Toronto, Canada

$7,000 in five days

"Last Monday I used what I learned on page 83 to make $7,000. It took me all week to do it, but that's not bad for five day's work."

M. D., Topeka, Kansas

Can't believe success

"I can't believe how successful I have become . . . Three months ago, I was a telephone order taker for a fastener company in Chicago, Illinois. I was driving a beat-up 1959 Rambler and had about $600 in my savings account. Today, I am the outside salesman for the same fastener company . . . I am driving a company car . . . I am sitting in my own office and have about $3,000 in my savings account."

G. M., Des Plaines, Ill.

I know you're skeptical. After all, what I'm saying is probably contrary to what you've heard from your friends, your family, your teachers and maybe everyone else you know. I can only ask you one question.

How many of them are millionaires?

So it's up to you:

A month from today, you can be nothing more than 30 days older — or you can be on your way to getting rich. You decide.

"*. . . I didn't have a job and I was worse than broke. I owed more than $50,000 and my only assets were my wife and 8 children. We were renting an old house in a decaying neighborhood, driving a 5-year old car that was falling apart, and had maybe a couple of hundred dollars in the bank.*

Within one month, after using the principles of the Lazy Man's Way to Riches, things started to change — to put it mildly.

- *We worked out a plan we could afford to pay off our debts — and stopped our creditors from hounding us.*
- *We were driving a brand-new Thunderbird that a car dealer had given to us!*
- *Our bank account had multiplied tenfold!*
- *All within the first 30 days!*

And today . . .

- *I live in a home that's worth over $250,000.*
- *I own my "office". It's about a mile and a half from my home and is right on the beach.*
- *I own a lakefront "cabin" in Washington. (That's where we spend the whole summer — loafing, fishing, swimming and sailing.)*
- *I own two oceanfront condominiums. One is on a sunny beach in Mexico and one is snuggled right on the best beach of the best island in Hawaii.*
- *I have two boats and a Cadillac. All paid for.*
- *I have a net worth of over a Million Dollars. But I still don't have a job . . .*"

Sworn Statement:

"On the basis of my professional relationship as his accountant, I certify that Mr. Karbo's net worth is more than one million dollars."

Stuart A. Cogan

Bank Reference:
Home Bank
17010 Magnolia Avenue
Fountain Valley, California 92708

Joe Karbo
17105 South Pacific, Dept. 88-R
Sunset Beach, California 90742

Joe, you may be full of beans, but what have I got to lose? Send me the Lazy Man's Way to Riches. *But don't deposit my check or money order for 31 days after it's in the mail.*

If I return your material — for *any* reason — within that time, return my *uncashed* check or money order to me. On that basis, here's my ten dollars.

Name _____

Address _____

City _____

State _____ Zip _____

© 1978 Joe Karbo

Figure 7-3 Joe Karbo's Advertisement

The Social-Psychological Model of Influence on Consumer Behavior

Modern social scientists have theorized that several different levels and segments of society influence the consumer purchase decision. These include (1) culture, (2) subcultures, (3) social classes, (4) reference groups, and (5) face-to-face groups.[15]

Culture and Subculture

Culture involves aspects of people that are more psychological than simply biological, physiological, or organic. An ethnic group, for example, has a certain culture. A religion or nationality also may have a certain culture. When a culture can be further divided into segments, these are known as subcultures. For example, one might speak about an American culture. But American culture also contains subcultures of religious and ethnic groups and even geographical locations. One can speak about a Japanese culture in which women have traditionally been subservient to men. Yet Japanese women dominate consumer markets today in Japan, and their influence will probably grow as women enter the job market. In fact, one study showed that 28 per cent of young working Japanese women are able to afford fur coats and 50 per cent are able to own a dressing table, stereo, and color TV. Furthermore, inasmuch as Japanese women have always controlled their family finances and husbands have always turned over their paychecks to their wives, women control about 80 per cent of all household budgets.[16]

The situation of Japanese women isn't the only one that is changing. Take a look at Figure 7-4. Women are holding a growing share of managerial and professional jobs. In thirteen years the percentage of women lawyers tripled and the percentage of executives and women administrators almost doubled.[17] Not shown in Figure 7-4 are some recent data released by the American Banking Association. It says that women make up 47 per cent of officials and managers in the top banks. That's up from 33 per cent in 1978.[18]

These increases aren't limited to the civilian sector. Women cadets were first admitted to the U.S. Naval, Military, and Air Force academies in 1976. Today there are increasing numbers of women who hold general or flag rank in all of the services, including the Marines.

In both the case of the culture of the country and the subculture of women in Japan and America, you can see how the marketer can take advantage of the fact that these two subcultures of women may behave in certain ways because of their earning power and of their being in the work force. Certainly the high numbers of working women is one reason that in-home marketing methods, typified by such mediums as direct mail and mail order in magazines and on television, have grown and are still growing in the United States and Japan.

In a similar fashion, a marketing manager must recognize the extreme difficulty, if not the impossibility, of selling certain types or classes of products to certain groups. It would be unlikely that a marketer could succeed in selling pork products to religious Jews or Moslems. It is also very difficult for marketers to succeed in selling certain other types of foods to various groups due to their culture or subculture. Soybean milk has not succeeded in the United States as a product except among Chinese groups accustomed

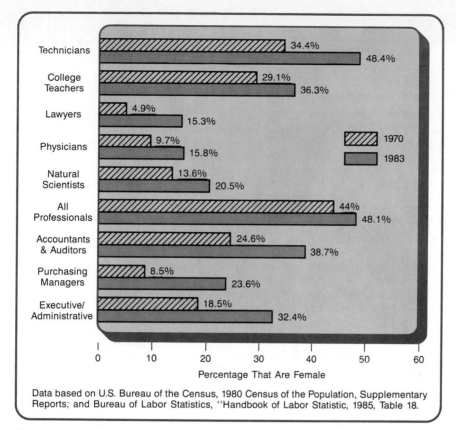

Data based on U.S. Bureau of the Census, 1980 Census of the Population, Supplementary Reports; and Bureau of Labor Statistics, "Handbook of Labor Statistic, 1985, Table 18.

Figure 7-4 Women are Holding a Growing Share of Managerial and Professional Jobs

Source: Adapted from William B. Johnston and Arnold E. Packer, *Workforce 2000* (Indianapolis: The Hudson Institute, 1987), p. 86.

to it; in the Orient, however, it is a highly successful product. As noted earlier, sushi bars tend to be more successful in the West, in areas that are highly populated by individuals of Japanese descent who are accustomed to and interested in purchasing the product. The growth of this product in some other locations in the United States has been much slower.

Social Class

Research scientists in the United States have developed a six-class system of social class: (1) upper-upper or old family; (2) lower-upper, or those newly arrived (in class); (3) upper-middle, which mostly includes professionals and more successful businesspeople; (4) lower-middle, which is the white-collar salaried class; (5) upper-lower, which are the basic wage earners and skilled worker group; and finally (6) lower-lower, which are the unskilled labor groups. Each group has been found to exhibit different buyer behavior.[19]

Figure 7-5 shows some psychological differences and contrasts between two different social groups encompassing the middle class and the lower

Middle Class	Lower Class
1. Points to the future.	1. Points to the present and past.
2. Embraces the long view of time.	2. Lives and thinks in a short expanse of time.
3. Has more urban identification.	3. Is more rural in identification.
4. Stresses rationality.	4. Is essentially nonrational.
5. Has a well-structured sense of the universe.	5. Has a vague and unclear structuring of the world.
6. Vastly extends or does not delimit horizons.	6. Sharply defines and limits horizons.
7. Has greater sense of choice making.	7. Has a limited sense of choice making.
8. Is self-confident, willing to take risks.	8. Is very concerned with security and insecurity.
9. Is immaterial and abstract in thinking.	9. Is concrete and perceptive in thinking.
10. Perceives itself as being tied to national happenings.	10. Perceives the world as revolving around family and home.

Source: Adapted from Pierre Martineau, "Social Classes and Spending Behavior," *Journal of Marketing*, vol. 23 (October 1958), p. 128.

Figure 7-5 Psychological Contrasts Between Two Different Social Groups

class. Consider how these contrasts might affect buyer behavior and your opportunities, as well as problems, in marketing to the two groups.

Other research has shown differences in information searches by different social classes, depending on **perceived risk**. For example, people in the highest social class reported using consumer guides "usually" or "sometimes" for high-risk purchases. But in the lowest social class, no one reported using this information source that frequently.[20]

For another example of the importance of social class, note the social status structure of food symbolism in Figure 7-6 and how social class affects preferences for qualities, attributes, and different foods.[21]

Reference and Face-to-Face Groups

Reference groups are individuals or groups of people whom consumers refer to or otherwise use as a point of reference when deciding which purchase decisions to make. A face-to-face group is a subset of a reference group that requires face-to-face contact.

One study of consumer perceptions in auto repair choice clearly demonstrated the importance of reference groups. Friends were used to obtain information about sources of repair as often as telephone calls were made to auto repair companies, and friends were used as a source far more frequently than actual company visits.[22] Another study looked at the importance of negative word-of-mouth comments by dissatisfied consumers. It found that dissatisfied customers would not only not repurchase, but would tell others.[23]

In general it has been found that reference group influence is very, very strong in an information vacuum, where the consumer has little or no direct knowledge about the attributes of a product or service. A most important factor is how conspicuous the product is. This means both visibility and noticeability. With a conspicuous product, reference group influence is usually the strongest.

170

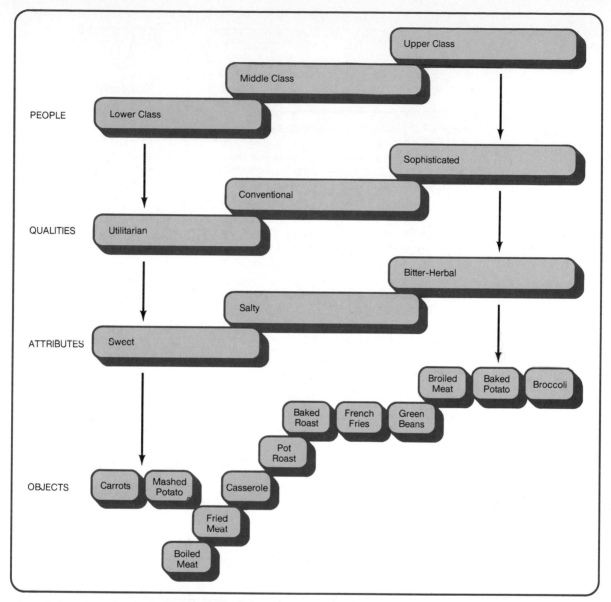

Figure 7-6 The Social Class Structure of Food Symbolism

Source: From Sidney J. Levy, "Interpreting Consumer Mythology: A Structural Approach to Consumer Behavior," *Journal of Marketing,* vol. 45 (Summer 1981), p. 57. Used with permission.

Family buying is a particular type of face-to-face reference group. Important considerations include

1. Who makes the purchase decision.
2. Who is the purchase agent.
3. Who is the ultimate user.
4. What the power positions are within the family.

Figure 7-7 Hierarchy of Effects Model of Food Shopping Goals and Behavior

Source: Mary Lou Roberts and Lawrence H. Wortzel, "New Life-Style Determinants of Women's Food Shopping Behavior," *Journal of Marketing*, vol. 43 (Summer 1979), p. 30. Used with permission.

Any of These Factors May Come into Play and Determine How the Product May Be Best Marketed to the Consumer

In recent years there has been a major controversy over the marketing of children's cereals via television and cartoon characters. Some critics maintain that all cartoon shows are really one long advertisement in which marketers consciously attempt to convince children to insist that their parents purchase a particular brand of cereal. That is, the assumption is that this is a classic model in which children are the decision makers as well as end users and the parents are the buying agents.

A different strategy might be to try to influence parents that a particular cereal is good for their children. You have probably seen advertisements for cereal that make this point. These advertisers make the assumption that it is the parents who are both purchase decision makers and purchase agents. In your family who makes the decision about what kind of iron to buy, what TV shows to watch, what brand of beer to buy (if your family drinks beer), or what brand of frozen foods to buy? One purchase model for foods even incorporates food preparation styles, as shown in Figure 7-7.[24] You can see how this information and the four factors stated previously would affect the direction of your marketing efforts.

Other Important Factors That Influence Consumer-Buyer Behavior

Other factors influence consumers' behavior. These include personality, attitude, learning, and willingness to adopt or innovate.

Personality. Personality pervades many aspects of the consumer behavior process. Various segmentations have been proposed and used, for example, life-style—how individuals live—and psychographics—how people think. In some cases psychological tests have been given to establish the boundaries of these segments. However, marketing managers should be cautious in utilizing data pertaining only to personality and relating it to consumer behavior. One major review of past studies concerning relationships between personality and consumer behavior concluded that only a very few studies confirmed a strong relationship between these two variables alone. Generally, there were other factors or combinations of factors that were more important than personality in having an impact on how the consumer behaved in buying.[25]

Attitude. Attitude consists of a predisposition to respond in a certain way. We are primarily interested in a customer's responding through purchase of a certain product or service. Some scientists theorize that attitude has three basic components: (1) an effective component, (2) a cognitive component, and (3) a behavioral component. The effective component is the aspect that evaluates an object on the basis of its goodness or badness. Thus, a particular consumer may have certain beliefs and judgments about a particular product, but they are not attributes unless he or she can attribute good or bad qualities or features to it that in turn result in a feeling of liking or disliking toward the product.

The cognitive component is that element of attitude that predisposes the consumer to perceive the product and differentiate it from others. Product differentiation as well as positioning, which will be discussed in our chapter on marketing strategy, are concepts based upon this particular aspect of consumer attitude.

The behavioral component predisposes the consumer to act toward the product or something representing that product in a certain way. Thus, a consumer with a positive attitude toward a product might be predisposed to defend it or, if possessing a negative attitude, to attack it. During the Persian Gulf Crisis of the 1990s, many consumers were predisposed to attack petroleum companies and their products due partially to this behavioral component. Other consumers might be predisposed to defend products such as, say, a Walt Disney movie, criticized by others for its lack of sophisticated dramatic contribution. It is said that music enhances a retail environment and the customers' predisposition to purchase. However, according to at least one study, this may not be so.[26]

In general, two different approaches might be used to take note of the influence of attitude. First, a marketing manager might attempt to change the attitude of the consumer, or second, a marketing manager might attempt to change the product or service to be more in conformity with the consumer's predisposition.[27]

Learning. Attitude is closely aligned with learning because attitudes can themselves be learned. Let's say we wanted to induce a repeat purchase through learning. We might initiate a sequence of events starting with product trial and then proceed to an initial purchase with little financial obligation. Next, we would induce a purchase with moderate financial obligation. For the final step, we would induce a purchase at the full amount. Psychologists call this shaping. The procedure and reinforcement introduced with this sequence of events are shown in Figure 7-8.[28]

How much can marketers "teach" consumers? Figure 7-9 shows that consumer learning through experience depends primarily on motivation, what they already know, and on the control the marketer has over the environment.[29]

Another example involving both learning and the psychological concept of association might be in an advertisement that depicts a man and woman enjoying dinner in a highly romantic atmosphere complete with appropriate room decor, dressy clothing, and an operating fireplace. The couple is enjoy-

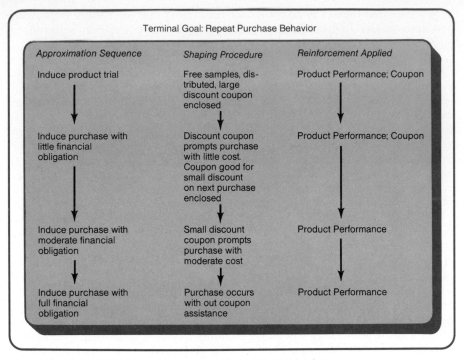

Figure 7-8   Application of Learning Theory to Marketing

Source: Adapted from Michael L. Rothschild and William C. Gaidis, "Behavioral Learning Theory: Its Relevance to Marketing and Promotions," *Journal of Marketing*, vol. 45 (Spring 1981), p. 72. Used with permission.

ing a wine, and the particular brand of wine is displayed prominently and conspicuously in the advertisement. The object here is to associate the brand of the wine with romance, so that the consumer making the purchase decision is not simply buying an alcoholic beverage but rather is buying romance. The obvious assumption is that this relationship or association can be learned.

Adoption.   One of the more challenging aspects of new product introduction, which will be discussed in a later chapter, is that of the adoption process, a very important aspect having to do with consumer behavior. One marketing scientist categorized people adopting a new product or service as innovators, early adopters, early majority, late majority, and laggards. Each group represents a percentage of the total population, as shown in Figure 7-10, and each group or category has certain characteristics. Innovators are the first to adopt, but because they adopt new ideas so much sooner than the average consumer, they are sometimes ridiculed by their more conservative associates. Early adopters furnish a disproportionate amount of formal leadership and perhaps as a result are respected as good sources of information about new products by their neighbors.

The early majority must be certain an idea will work before they adopt it, and they may look to the early adopters for their information. The late majority adopts new products or services after the average consumer has already

How motivated are consumers to learn?	What do consumers already know?	How much can experience teach?	
		Little (High Ambiguity Situation)	**A Lot** (Low Ambiguity Situation)
Highly Motivated	Unfamiliar	Learning is most susceptible to management.	Learning is spontaneous, rapid, and difficult to manage.
	Familiar	Formation of "superstitious" beliefs is possible. Existing beliefs inhibit suggestibility.	
Weakly Motivated	Unfamiliar	Learning is slow to start and difficult to sustain, but is susceptible to management.	Learning is difficult to initiate and once started difficult to manage.
	Familiar	Complacency inhibits initiation of learning, so experience is unresponsive to management.	

Figure 7-9   Consumer Learning Through Experience

Source: Adapted from Stephen J. Hoch and John Deighton, "Managing What Consumers Learn from Experience," *Journal of Marketing,* vol. 53, no. 2 (April 1989), p. 11.

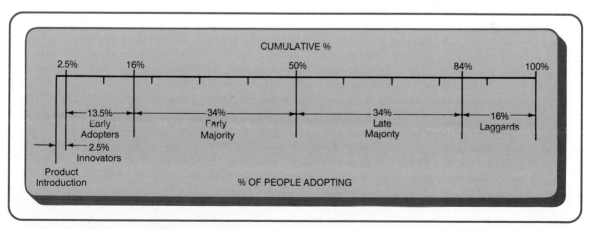

Figure 7-10   Groups Adopting New Products

Source: Adapted from Francis S. Bourne, "The Adoption Process," *The Adoption of New Products* (Ann Arbor: Foundation for Research on Human Development, 1959), pp. 1–8.

been using it. Although they participate less actively in formal groups, they may form the bulk of the membership in formal organizations. Finally, the last category, the laggards, participates least in formal organizations and other programs concerning groups; this category may include the nonadopters as well, if the new product or service is not adopted by everyone.[30]

Change in the Future of Consumer Behavior

The behavior of consumers is not a constant, and marketing managers must keep on top of those changes to be successful. Kathleen Keegan, a senior associate of Yankelovich, Skelly and White, has identified four themes underlying changes:

1. Tempering of traditional American optimism and confidence.
2. Cost-effectiveness emphasis by the consumer.
3. Focus on strategic thinking, action, and winning.
4. Rise in local identification.

Keegan made some predictions about the behavior of the consumer as a result of the trends she observed:

- Less impulse buying.
- Less response to novelty, change, and variety.
- More emphasis on quality, durability, and appropriateness.
- Increased trade-offs of time versus convenience in purchasing.
- Reduced store loyalty.
- Loyalty to brands with selective behavior among products.
- More time and thus more money spent on in-home shopping.
- A willingness to forgo present comforts for future benefits.
- More personal responsibility for making the right product choice.
- An emphasis on geographical/local products, brands, and those who influence their purchase.[31]

Whether Ms. Keegan's predictions prove to be accurate or not, they illustrate the kind of forward thinking marketing managers must do, in combination with research, to determine how the consumer is behaving in the marketplace.

Organizational Buyer Behavior

Although many students of marketing are primarily interested in consumer products, the fact of the matter is that total annual sales in organizational buying exceed those in consumer buying. But buyer behavior of organizational buyers and consumer buyers is not identical. For one thing, even though the number of the annual sales is greater with organizational buying, the number of organizations is much smaller. Thus, organizational sales on an individual basis tend to be much larger than consumer sales. An individual may buy a handful of light bulbs for his or her home, but the same buyer making purchases for a large company might require light bulbs numbering in the hundreds or even thousands. Furthermore, it has been discovered that while there are certainly psychological dimensions to organizational buying, there are other elements that must be considered. This is due to the following kinds of factors:

- There may be more than one individual making the purchase decision.
- Most individual buyers for organizations place the needs of their organization above their own.
- Organizations and individual consumers may have widely differing needs for similar products or services.

Thus, an individual consumer might have need of an automobile with certain attributes or features for transportation, whereas an operator of a fleet of taxis might need a similar vehicle that satisfies an entirely different list of needs.

The Organizational Buyer Behavior Process

The Three Elements of Organizational Buyer Behavior

Organizational buyer behavior can be categorized as having three separate and distinct elements. The first is the **psychological environment** of the individuals involved in making organizational buying decisions. The second element has to do with conditions that lead to joint decisions among these decision-making individuals. The last element is the process of **joint decision making** itself.[32]

Let's look at each of these in turn.

Psychological Environment. For many years marketing managers felt that organizational buyer behavior was characterized by rational choices made by a purchasing agent, as opposed to more emotional choices made by individual consumers. However, there is now doubt that this is always true. There are certain product expectations, and even these may have a psychological dimension. These expectations include product quality, delivery time, quantity of supply, after-sale service, as well as price.

Where a firm's performance exceeds customer expectations, it will cause an increase in repurchase intentions; performance that does not meet expectations may cause a decrease.[33] Also, differences in expectations between the buyer and provider have been found to have an adverse effect on postperformance evaluation, most recently in the services area.[34]

An even greater psychological dimension has been found in certain implicit criteria, including reputation, size of the firm and its location, the relationship between buyer and seller, personality, technical expertise, and sales-manship. Even the life-style of the sales representative is a criterion, not to mention the background of the buyer/decision makers, their past satisfaction or dissatisfaction with past purchases, and what might be the termed per-ceptual distortion—that is, the fact that each individual purchaser tries to make the objective information consistent with his or her own prior knowl-edge and expectations by systematically distorting it. Thus, with different and sometimes substantial differences in the goals and values of the purchase agents, engineers, production personnel, and managers, all of whom influ-ence and help to make the buying decision, we can expect to find, and in fact will find different interpretations of the identical information among this variety of individuals.[35] The influence due to the power of these individuals is situational and must take into account individual behavior, as well as buying center and other variables.[36]

Accordingly, it can be said that the organizational buyer or buyers some-times select a design or special part based more on psychological reasons and emotion rather than on rational fact. For example, a purchasing agent for a company making food products may have a choice between packaging the food in glass jars or in tin cans. The technical data are all available from the engineers. Glass engineers tell them that the glass can be recycled and that it has sales appeal because the product can be seen. Engineers who back canning tell the purchasing agent that the product can be used longer, that the packaging is unbreakable, and that it can be stored readily. Clearly, which packaging to adopt depends on the situation. Yet, one study found that there are some technical people who simply do not like glass, no matter how many practical and fashionable reasons are presented as absolutely relevant to their situation. A nonbiased purchaser would indicate that glass should be the definite and clear choice.[37]

As a consequence, marketing managers must consider the psychological environment in which the purchase decision is being made, as well as all psychological aspects of the individuals concerned with the decision. In fact, marketing scientists Edward Fern and James Brown recommend that the marketing manager consider the similarities between marketing to organi-zations and marketing to households as much as their differences.[38] Clifton J. Reichard, vice-president of commercial sales for the Ball Corporation's Glass Container Group, says, "Businesspeople are human and social as well as interested in economics and investments and salespeople need to appeal to both sides."[39]

Conditions That Lead to Joint Versus Individual or Autonomous Decisions. The organizational buying decision may be made by many in-dividuals at different locations, or in some cases the decision can be made by a single individual. The numbers and titles of these individuals vary from company to company and from situation to situation. In some cases hundreds of separate decision makers must agree before a particular product can be purchased. Let's say that you have developed a new oxygen breathing mask that is used by pilots in the Air Force when they are flying above 14,000 feet altitude. Such a product may require testing by various pilots at different Air Force bases around the country, representing different flying organiza-tions that might use your product. In Ohio, at a major development center for such equipment, various engineers, managers, production people, quality control supervisors, and cost people would all have an impact on the decision, not to mention the buying agent or contracting officer at this facility. Furthermore, the item would be tested in a laboratory, perhaps in Texas, or operationally in airplanes at some point of its development, someplace in New Mexico. Finally, after final approval of the adoption as being acceptable for Air Force use in quantity production, a purchase decision would come from an organization in Pennsylvania. In total, hundreds, perhaps thousands, of individuals would be involved in this particular purchase design for this single piece of new equipment. Note that this is not a case where the product has been approved for pilots in other branches of the armed forces including Navy, Army, or Marine Corps. Is it any wonder that the process is complex and time consuming—and yet critical?

What decides how many individuals, and who those individuals are, for a purchase decision for a new product or service in the organization? Professor Jagdeth Sheth, of the University of Southern California, has classified such factors into products-specific and companies-specific factors. Products-specific factors include perceived risk, type of purchase, and time pressure. Companies-specific factors include the company orientation, company size, and degree of centralization. In perceived risk, the greater the uncertainty in a buying situation, the greater the perceived risk and probably the more decision makers involved. Regarding type of purchase, is this a first purchase or a once-in-a-lifetime purchase? Such circumstances in consideration of increased risk might lead to greater joint decision making. On the other hand, if the purchase were routine and a purchase had been made many times before, fewer decision makers, or even a single one, might be involved. If there is little time, a single individual might make the decision versus more time for many other people to become involved.

It is important to see who's running the company. If a company is technically oriented and dominated by engineers, engineers will probably have a considerable impact on purchasing. If the company is very large, more decision makers will be available and will therefore probably become involved in the purchase decision. The greater the degree of centralization, the less likely it is that decisions will be jointly made. A small company or a unit of a large organization that is somewhat isolated from the rest of the organization tends to be highly centralized and will lead to autonomous decision making. There is little question but that organizational climate affects the chosen behavior of industrial buyers.[40,41]

In addition, it is frequently useful to stimulate an individual in the buyer's organization to take on the role of advocate. Research has demonstrated that these individuals can be motivated to adopt a more aggressive posture in their organizations in favor of a company's product or products and furthermore that these advocates can have a significant effect on the purchase decision.[42]

The Process of Joint Decision Making. Researchers have found that there is a common process in buyer purchase behavior. This process is very much affected by the assimilation of information, deliberations on it, and any conflict that results from the fact that the decision is made jointly.[43] It is also affected by what has been called script theory, a script being a coherent sequence of events in which an individual becomes involved either as a participant or an observer. The script defines what is expected by him or her.

According to this theory, professional buyers as well as salespersons have such scripts, which guide their thinking and behavior during the process of

CATEGORY/VARIABLE	EXAMPLES	
	TASK	NONTASK
INDIVIDUAL	Obtain lowest price	Personal values and needs
SOCIAL	Attend meetings to set specifications	Off-the-job socialization
ORGANIZATIONAL	Company policy to give preference to local suppliers	Promotion
ENVIRONMENTAL	Anticipated rise in prices	Political climate in an election year

Figure 7-11   How Variables Influence the Organizational Purchase Decision by Category

Source: Adapted from Frederick E. Webster, Jr. and Yoram Wind, "A General Model for Understanding Organizational Buying Behavior," *Journal of Marketing,* vol. 36 (April 1972).

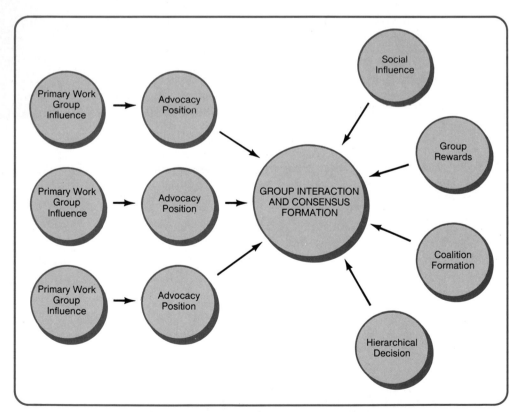

Figure 7-12   A Model of Group Consensus for Organizational Buying

Source: Adapted from Paul F. Anderson and Terry M. Chambers, "A Reward/Measurement Model of Organizational Buying Behavior," *Journal of Marketing,* vol. 49 (Spring 1985), p. 10.

the purchase decision.[44] Finally, the decision is affected by characteristics of the organizational buying center, including the degree of formal structure, the relative power positions of the members, the relative strengths of the task and nontask interdependencies, the permanence of the group interaction, and the size of the group.[45]

These variables affecting the process can be classified by task and non-task—that is, those actually related to the buying decision and those not, as well as by individual, social, organizational, and environmental categories. These are shown as a matrix in Figure 7-11. These factors must be considered by the marketing manager in planning for and executing a marketing campaign for any product or service to an organization.[46]

How this process works in practice can be conceptualized as shown in Figure 7-12. Note how such factors as social group influence, group rewards, coalition formation, hierarchical decisions and primary work group influence and advocacy positions act to effect group interaction and consensus formation.[47]

The Eight Stages of the Purchase Process

The purchase process for organizations can be divided into eight definite stages:

1. Anticipation or recognition of a problem (need) and a general solution.
2. Determination of characteristics and quantity of needed item.
3. Description of characteristics and quantity of needed item.
4. Search for and qualification of potential sources.
5. Acquisition and analysis of proposals.
6. Evaluation of proposals and selection of suppliers.
7. Selection of an order routine.
8. Performance feedback and evaluation.[48]

While all of these steps are important, steps 4 and 5 require some additional explanation.

The Acquisition of Information by the Organizational Buyer

The acquisition of product or service information by the organizational buyer is of importance to the marketing manager in the same way that it is important to those who are marketing to consumers: it provides insights as to how best to market the product to the organization and affects both strategy and tactics. Furthermore, as novelty and importance to the purchasing organization rise, more information is sought by members of the decision-making unit.[49] Information sources can be classified as personal and impersonal. Personal sources include salespeople, trade shows, an information systems department, top management, a using department, terminal users, outside consultants, colleagues, and a purchasing department. Impersonal users include advertising in trade publications, sales literature, news publications, trade associations, and rating services.[50] A study that included surveying 319 companies resulted in a relative perceived importance of these information sources, as shown in Figure 7-13.[51]

Source	Avg. Value on Scale
Information systems department	5.011
Using department	4.688
Top management	4.213
Salespeople from manufacturer	3.862
Actual terminal operators	3.767
Sales literature	3.446
Colleagues in other companies	3.220
Rating services	2.848
News stories in trade publications	2.684
Trade association data	2.510
Advertising in trade publications	2.290
Outside consultants	2.090
Purchasing department	1.675

Source: Adapted from Rowland T. Moriarty, Jr., and Robert E. Spekman, "An Empirical Investigation of the Information Sources Used During the Industrial Buying Process," *Journal of Marketing Research*, vol. 21 (May 1984), p. 141.

Figure 7-13   Perceived Importance of Information Sources for Organizational Buying (ranked on a scale where 1.0 = not very important and 6.0 = very important)

Use of the Proposal in Organizational Buying

Note that stage 5 refers to proposals. In many cases a proposal is necessary in marketing to organizational buying units. A proposal consists of documented information regarding the product or service, its price, delivery conditions, and other pertinent information. A proposal may be extremely complex and consist of many volumes and thousands of pages, such as a proposal to develop a new spacecraft for NASA. Or a proposal can simply be a single letter describing the basic elements of the sale. In many cases the buyer of the product or service will specify the context of the proposal. Hence, when a proposal is used, especially if there are multiple bidders for a particular organizational purchase, it must be considered that the proposal is part of the purchase decision process and is in fact a sales document partially upon which the decision to buy is made. The final selection process is dependent on the number of proposals actually received and justification for single versus multiple choices for the purchase.[52]

Summary

In this chapter we've seen that there are both problems and opportunities in buyer behavior and that buyer behavior is one of the more psychological dimensions of marketing. Buyer behavior is usually categorized into consumer buyer behavior and organizational buyer behavior, inasmuch as the two processes are somewhat different and different factors are primary in influencing them.

Many important factors influence consumer purchasing behavior. These consider basic motivations as conceived by Maslow's hierarchy of needs, as well as elements of a social-psychological model, including culture and sub-culture, social class, reference group, and face-to-face groups, and the importance of family decision making. Other important factors that interact and must be considered in consumer buying patterns include the personality of the buyer, attitude, learning, and the process of adoption of new products. As a process, consumer buying behavior is not fixed and is subject to change.

Organizational buying behavior has been characterized as involving many more decision makers and decisions based on much larger purchases and units of sale, with far fewer units making up the total category of decision maker. Three basic elements of the process include the psychological environment of the buyer, the conditions for joint decision making, and the process of joint decision making itself. Eight separate buying stages have been identified in the organizational buying situation. These are (1) anticipation or recognition of a problem (need) and a general solution, (2) determination of the characteristics and quantity of the item needed, (3) description of the characteristics and quantity of the needed item, (4) search for and qualification of potential sources, (5) acquisition and analysis of proposals, (6) evaluation of proposals and selection of suppliers, (7) selection of an order routine, and finally (8) performance feedback and evaluation.

Any study of buying behavior must conclude that both consumer buyer behavior and organizational buyer behavior are complex and must be analyzed by the marketing manager to take advantage of the opportunities and avoid the threats inherent in the marketing situation.

Questions

1. You are a product manager developing a new soap product for the consumer market. What important aspects of buyer behavior must you consider?

2. You are the product manager of a new soap product for the organizational market. What important aspects of buyer behavior should you consider?

3. Consider the model of the consumer buying process in Figure 7-2. What do you see in this model that can be categorized as opportunities you may take advantage of in your marketing campaign? What elements in the model can you see that might be categorized as problems or threats you must be aware of for your marketing campaign?

4. In Joe Karbo's famous advertisement, "The Lazy Man's Way to Riches," which of Maslow's hierarchy of needs are implied by the words in the headline?

5. Reference group influence is likely to be stronger or weaker depending upon available information and the conspicuousness of the product. State whether you think reference group influence would be strong or weak with the following products: light bulbs, gasoline, lawn mowers, instant dessert mix, toothpaste, aspirin, tennis rackets, lawn chairs.

6. You are a restaurant owner whose restaurant is perceived as being a place to go for a good time, where prices are low and the atmosphere is informal. Quality, however, is perceived as being only average. In what ways could you change the attitude toward your restaurant to attract an upper-class clientele?

7. Assume the four themes of consumer behavior change, and that predictions likely to take place over the next ten years or so are accurate. How would this affect the following industries: electronics, automobile, fast-food, and airlines?

8. You are the product manager responsible for a new microprocessor used in a variety of industrial applications. Who are some of the decision makers likely to affect whether your new microprocessor is purchased by various organizations?

9. Using the task and nontask examples of variables influencing organizational buying decisions illustrated in Figure 7-11, how might you take advan-

tage of the opportunities and handle the problems inherent in selling training seminars to an organization?

10. How does knowing the various phases in the buying process help you in marketing to organizations?

Ethical Question

You've hired a highly trained marketing scientist who is reputed to be unbeatable in consumer behavior. One day he rushes excitedly into your office. "Incredible news," he says. "I've just discovered what to add to the appearance of any product, so that through subliminal persuasion, anyone who sees it must buy it." Assuming your employee isn't exaggerating, what do you do about this discovery?

Endnotes

1. James B. Forkan, "Professional Karate Heads Yup-ward," *Advertising Age* (March 18, 1985), p. 37.
2. Robert D. Hay and C. P. Rao, "Football Coaches Rank Factors Impacting Attendance at Games," *Marketing News* (June 22, 1984), p. 5.
3. Thomas J. Stanley, "Feeding on the Rich," *Success*, vol. 35, no. 6, (July–August, 1988), pp. 54–55.
4. M. Joseph Sirgy, "A Conceptualization of the Consumer Behavior Discipline," *Journal of the Academy of Marketing Science*, vol. 13 (Winter 1985), p. 107.
5. Jack A. Lesser and Marie Adele Hughes, "The Generalizability of Psychographic Market Segments Across Geographic Locations," *Journal of Marketing*, vol. 50 (January 1986), p. 1.
6. John A. Quelch, "Why Not Exploit Dual Marketing?" *Business Horizons*, vol. 30 (January–February 1987), p. 53.
7. Robert Ferber, "What Do We Know About Consumer Behavior?" Selected Aspects of Consumer Behavior (Washington, D.C.: National Science Foundation, 1975), pp. 521–529.
8. Robert M. Cosenza, "Family Decision Making Decision Dominance Structure Analysis—An Extension," *Journal of the Academy of Marketing Science*, vol. 13 (Winter 1985), p. 99.
9. Ferber, loc. cit.
10. Ibid.
11. Gordon C. Bruner, II, and Richard J. Pomazal, "Problem Recognition: The Crucial First Stage of the Consumer Decision Process," *The Journal of Services Marketing*, vol. 2, no. 3 (Summer 1988), p. 44.
12. Stewart H. Rewoldt, Martin R. Warshaw, and James R. Taylor, *Introduction to Marketing Management*, 5th ed. (Homewood, Ill.: Irwin, 1985), pp. 126–127.
13. Richard L. Oliver and John E. Swan, "Consumer Perceptions of Interpersonal Equity and Satisfaction in Transactions: A Field Survey Approach," *Journal of Marketing*, vol. 53, no. 2 (April 1989), p. 33.
14. Abraham H. Maslow, "A Theory of Human Motivation," *Psychological Review* (July 1943), pp. 370–396.
15. Philip Kotler, "Behavioral Models for Analyzing Buyers," *Journal of Marketing*, vol. 29 (October 1965), pp. 40–41.
16. Jack Burton, "Women in Japan: A Growing Force," *Advertising Age* (January 14, 1985), p. 40.
17. William B. Johnson and Arnold E. Packer, *Workforce 2000* (Indianapolis: Hudson Institute, 1987), p. 86.
18. Alan L. Otten, "People Patterns," *Wall Street Journal*, 16 October 1989, p. B1.
19. W. Lloyd Warner and Paul Lunt, *The Social Life of a Modern Community* (New Haven: Yale University Press, 1950).
20. Paul Hugstad, James W. Taylor, and Grady D. Bruce, "The Effects of Social Class and Perceived Risk on Consumer Information Search," *Journal of Services Marketing*, vol. 1 (Summer 1987), p. 51.
21. Sidney J. Levy, "Interpreting Consumer Mythology: A Structural Approach to Consumer Behavior," *Journal of Marketing*, vol. 45 (Summer 1981), p. 57.
22. Gabriel J. Biehal, "Consumer Prior Experiences and Perceptions in Auto Repair Choice," *Journal of Marketing*, vol. 47 (Summer 1983), p. 87.

23. Marsha L. Richins, "Negative Word-of-Mouth by Dissatisfied Consumers: A Pilot Study," *Journal of Marketing*, vol. 47 (Winter 1982), p. 76.

24. Mary Lou Roberts and Lawrence H. Wortzel, "New Life-Style Determinants of Women's Food Shopping Behavior," *Journal of Marketing*, vol. 43 (Summer 1979), p. 30.

25. Harold H. Kassarjian, "Personality in Consumer Behavior: A Review," *Journal of Marketing Research*, vol. 8 (November 1971), pp. 409–418.

26. Richard Yalch and Eric Spangenbeg, "Effects of Store Music on Shopping Behavior," *Journal of Services Marketing*, vol. 4 no. 1 (Winter 1990), p. 36.

27. John J. Wheatley and Sadaomi Oshikawa, "Learning Theories, Attitudes in Advertising," *University of Washington Business Review* (Summer 1968), pp. 24–33.

28. Michael L. Rothschild and William C. Gaidis, "Behavioral Learning Theory: Its Relevance to Marketing and Promotions," *Journal of Marketing*, vol. 45 (Spring 1981), p. 72.

29. Stephen J. Hoch and John Deighton, "Managing What Consumers Learn from Experience," *Journal of Marketing*, vol. 53, no. 2 (April 1989), p. 11.

30. Francis S. Bourne, "The Adoption Process," *The Adoption of New Products* (Ann Arbor: Foundation for Research on Human Development, 1959), pp. 1–8.

31. "Social Changes Provide Valuable Clues to Consumer Behavior in the Marketplace," *Marketing News*, 2 March 1984, p. 21.

32. Jagdish N. Sheth, "A Model of Industrial Buyer Behavior," *Journal of Marketing*, vol. 37 (October 1973), p. 51.

33. J. Joseph Cronin, Jr., and Michael H. Morris, "Satisfying Customer Expectations: The Effect on Conflict and Repurchase Intentions in Industrial Marketing Channels," *Journal of the Academy of Marketing Science*, vol. 17, no. 1 (Winter 1989), p. 47.

34. Teresa A. Swartz and Stephen W. Brown, "Consumer and Provider Expectations and Experiences in Evaluating Professional Service Quality," *Journal of Academy of Marketing Science*, vol. 17, no. 2 (Spring 1989), p. 194.

35. Sheth, op. cit., p. 52.

36. Ajay Kohli, "Determinants of Influence in Organizational Buying: A Contingency Approach," *Journal of Marketing*, vol. 53, no. 3 (July 1989), p. 61.

37. Ernest R. Dichter, "Psychology in Industrial Marketing," *Industrial Marketing* (February 1973).

38. Edward F. Fern and James R. Brown, "The Industrial/Consumer Marketing Dichotomy: A Case of Insufficient Justification," *Journal of Marketing*, vol. 48 (Spring 1984), p. 68.

39. Clifton J. Reichard, "Industrial Selling: Beyond Price and Resistance," *Harvard Business Review*, vol. 63 (March–April 1985), p. 128.

40. Sheth, op. cit., p. 55.

41. William J. Qualls and Christopher P. Puto, "Organizational Climate and Decision Framing: An Integrated Approach to Analyzing Industrial Buying Decisions," *Journal of Marketing Research*, vol. 26, no. 2 (May 1989), p. 190.

42. Robert E. Krappfel, Jr., "An Advocacy Behavior Model of Organizational Buyers' Vendors Choice," *Journal of Marketing*, vol. 49 (Fall 1985), p. 57.

43. Sheth, op. cit., p. 54.

44. Thomas W. Leigh and Arno J. Bethans, "A Script Theoretic Analysis of Industrial Purchasing Behavior," *Journal of Marketing*, vol. 48 (Fall 1984), p. 22.

45. Michael H. Morris, Wilbur W. Stanton, and Roger J. Calantone, "Measuring Coalitions in the Industrial Buying Center," *Journal of the Academy of Marketing Science*, vol. 13 (Fall 1985), p. 19.

46. Frederick E. Webster, Jr., and Yoram Wind, "A General Model for Understanding Organizational Buying Behavior," *Journal of Marketing*, vol. 36 (April 1972), p. 15.

47. Paul F. Anderson and Terry M. Chambers, "A Reward/Measurement Model of Organizational Buying Behavior," *Journal of Marketing*, vol. 49 (Spring 1985), p. 10.

48. "Industrial Marketing: All Eyes Are on the Buyer," *Sales Management* (October 15, 1967), pp. 71–78.

49. Daniel H. McQuiston, "Novelty, Complexity, and Importance as Casual Determinants of Industrial Buyer Behavior," *Journal of Marketing*, vol. 53, no. 2 (April 1989), p. 76.

50. Rowland T. Moriarty, Jr., and Robert E. Spekman, "An Empirical Investigation of the Information Sources Used During the Industrial Buying Process," *Journal of Marketing Research*, vol. 22 (May 1984), p. 140.

51. Ibid., p. 141.

52. Niren Vyas and Archie G. Woodside, "An Inductive Model of Industrial Supplier Choice Processes," *Journal of Marketing*, vol. 48 (Winter 1984), p. 44.

Forecasting

8

CHAPTER OBJECTIVES

- Understand the importance of forecasting to the marketing manager.

- Know the different categories of forecasting and the application of each.

- Know the different methods of forecasting, including their advantages and disadvantages, and be able to choose the appropriate method according to the situation.

- Be able to use forecasting as a part of marketing planning.

There's Gold in Them There Department Stores

Once upon a time, retailer J. C. Penney shunned jewelry as a highly specialized, slow-moving business. Not any more. Now, J. C. Penney has made jewelry its most highly promoted item, and this department store has become the fourth largest retail jewelry merchant in the United States, part of a $13-billion-per-year business. How did this happen? Since 1965 spending on jewelry and watches has risen steadily from 4.1 to 5.3 per cent of the total outlays for consumer durables. Marriages are on the rise. More working women are investing in jewelry for their wardrobes. Finally, men are wearing more jewelry, including mostly high-priced watches and rings.

Trend analysis has shown that the potential has increased by 30 per cent in four years. When J. C. Penney and other department store retailers realized that the standard 300 per cent markup of the regular jewelry stores could be beaten by their own smaller margins, they leaped into the business.[1]

TRW's $1.9 Billion Forecast Is Mostly Air

Charles Miller is the president of Occupant Restraint Systems, a subsidiary of the $7 billion TRW industrial giant. TRW Occupant Restraint Systems is the conglomerate's fastest-growing segment, with sales of three-quarters of a million dollars in 1989. According to Miller, sales by the early 1990s will be almost $2 billion. The main cause is Federal Motor Vehicle Safety Standard 208. This standard requires mandatory passive restraints—that is, seatbelts that surround the person automatically, or air bags—on all cars sold in the United States. Miller persuaded TRW to invest heavily. "We anticipate dramatic annual growth over the next five years, and plan to have at least 40 per cent of this business by 1992," he said. Obviously, Miller's future as well as that of this TRW subsidiary depends heavily on his forecast.[2]

The Drug Wars

Mylan Laboratories, Inc., is a generic manufacturer of drugs. Recently earnings jumped 166 per cent, to $12.5 million, in a single year, and its stock soared 800 per cent in 18 months. The reason for this success was lower R&D costs and new rules from the government that no longer require time-consuming testing once developers prove generic drugs are chemically equivalent to brand-name drugs already on sale. As a result, cheaper generic drugs have soared from 30 per cent to 50 per cent of the entire $17.5-billion-a-year market. Mylan's R&D costs, for example, are only 9 per cent of its operating cost, which is considerably below the approximately 15 per cent typical for brand-name manufacturers. Thus, brand-name manufacturers are having to take a hard look at their forecasting and the strategies that will have to result from the fact that brand names of proprietary drugs provide the highest profits.

The short-run solution among brand-name producers has been cost cutting, and Hoffmann-LaRoche, Inc., the U.S. unit of a Swiss drug manufacturer, had to fire 1,000 of its work force of 8,000. It forecast a deterioration in profits after its patent on Valium expired, which allowed generic drug companies to manufacture it. The threat as well as the opportunity is defined by forecast.[3]

What Is Forecasting?

Forecasting is predicting the future by analyzing the past. This does not necessarily mean that what happened in the past will also happen in the future, only that analysis of the past begins the process. Why is it important? Through forecasting the marketing manager is able to do the following: determine markets for products; plan corporate strategy; develop sales quotas; determine the need and number of salespeople; decide on distribution channels; price products and services; analyze products and product potential in different markets; decide on product features; determine profit and sales potential for different products; help to determine advertising budgets; determine the potential benefits of sales promotion programs; and decide on the use of various elements of the marketing mix. Not only does forecasting have a central role in marketing, but it is also important for the planning and production, finance, and other operational staff areas of corporate activity.[4] Forecasting is so important, its control is one of the primary variables on which the power of the marketing department within the firm is dependent.[5] Harry S. Dent, author of *Our Power to Predict* says that it is "critical to the development of effective business plans and strategies.[6]

Market Potential, Sales Potential, and Sales Forecast

Three terms are frequently used in forecasting: market potential, sales potential, and sales forecast. These terms are not synonyms. Conceptually this is shown in Figure 8-1. Market potential is the total potential sales of a

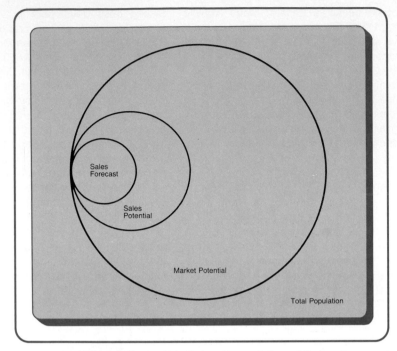

Figure 8-1 Market Potential, Sales Potential, and Sales Forecast

product or a service or a group of products in a specified period of time. Thus, it relates to the total capacity of the market to absorb the entire output of a specific industry, be that industry commercial airliners, pencils, or marketing textbooks.

Sales potential is differentiated from marketing potential in that it is the ability of the market to absorb or purchase the output from a single firm. Thus, it could be the airliners manufactured by a specific manufacturing company, the pencils manufactured by a pencil manufacturing company, or the marketing textbooks printed and published by the Macmillan Publishing Company.

Finally, we must differentiate sales forecast from sales potential. Whereas potential represents the maximum ability of the market to absorb a product from the entire industry or from a single firm, forecast is a prediction of the actual sales that are expected in whatever time period is decided upon.

Let's look at an example. The total potential for jewelry might be $50 billion a year for an entire industry. The total potential of the products that one firm manufactures may be $10 million. Yet the sales forecast for that one firm might be only $5 million. Why the difference between $5 million and $10 million? For various reasons the company may not seek to attain full potential for the product. Perhaps limited resources are available for marketing, or only a limited number of products can be manufactured. Also, there is the "law of diminishing returns," which says that as we try to achieve 100 per cent of anything, the marginal cost for each additional percentage becomes greater and greater. As a result, it would be better to forgo 100 per cent of sales potential for one product in order to use the resources to go after the sales for other products with overall greater profits. Finally, some unexpected environ may change, causing us to fall short of the sales potential possible.

Market Potential

Sometimes it is possible to find market potential published for various industries or various products. The research has been done by someone else. Frequently, we must derive our own market potential for the products we may consider. One way of deriving this is through the use of a chain ratio method. With the chain ratio, we try to connect related facts to develop the total market potential we desire.

Some years ago the author was required to derive the market potential for bulletproof vests used by foreign military forces worldwide for possible export from the United States. Because at that time only a few countries used bulletproof vests or body armor, this market potential had to be derived from the few facts that were known. The number of units of body armor used by the U.S. military forces was available from the U.S. government publication *Commerce Business Daily*. From the orders published in the *Commerce Business Daily*, an average number of body armor units per year could be obtained and calculated. The average size of the U.S. army during this same period was also available from published U.S. government sources as well as the number of U.S. infantry troops that were most likely to use the body armor.

From these two facts—that is, the total annual sales of body armor to the U.S. army and the average size of U.S. infantry forces during the same period—a ratio of body armor units per infantryman could be developed. Next, the *Almanac of World Military Power* was consulted. This almanac listed sizes of infantry forces for every country. Because this was an export military item with sales controlled by the U.S. government, only candidates likely to be approved by the government were included. Summing the total, a worldwide total of infantry candidates for the product was calculated. The ratio of body armor units per infantryman developed earlier was then applied. In this way a figure for the total market potential of military body armor worldwide was obtained.

Let's look at another example. Let's say that a supermarket in your area wants to know what the potential for frozen foods is. Your first step is to find the total population in the area that the supermarket serves. If the area determined is five miles in circumference, then that's the area for which we want to know the population. Such population figures for census tracts can be obtained through the Department of Commerce and the census surveys, and sometimes locally through a Chamber of Commerce or through state or local governments. The next step is to find out the per capita expenditure for food per year. Again, government surveys might provide the answer or food industry surveys available from trade associations and trade magazines. You would have to be careful here to make sure that the geographic factor was included because frequently expenditures differ among geographical regions. Multiplying the population in the five-mile area by the per capita expenditure on food per year will give you the total annual expenditure on food for the area per year. However, because you are only interested in frozen food, the final step would be to find the percentage of total food that was spent on frozen food. Once you multiply this percentage times the previous result, you would have the total potential or market potential for frozen foods on a yearly basis for the supermarket in the area indicated.

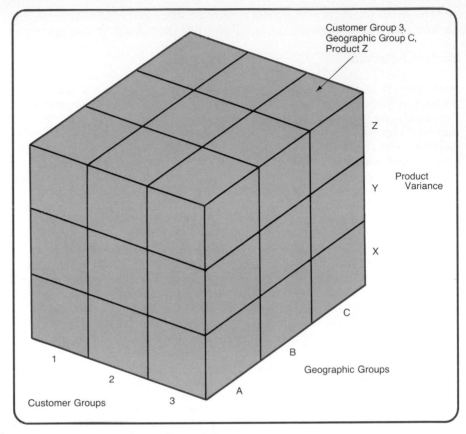

Figure 8-2   Categories of Potential

Various categories of potential must be considered when calculating this. Refer to Figure 8-2, in which we have customer groups, product variance, and geographic groups. In this case, there are three of each or twenty-seven different market potentials that might be of interest to us and therefore could be investigated.

The Index Method

Sometimes market potentials can be calculated for their consumer or industrial goods through estimating, after indexes have been constructed from basic economic data. For example, *Sales and Marketing Management* magazine publishes a survey of buying power indexes in July and October each year for consumer markets and in April for industrial and commercial markets. The commercial indexes developed through combining estimates of population, income, and retail sales result in a composite indicator of consumer demand according to the U.S. Census Bureau regions by state or by the Bureau's organized system of metro areas, by counties, or even by cities with populations of 40,000 or more. It is important to recognize that this **buying power index**, or **BPI**, is a relative value only, not an absolute one. It therefore must be multiplied times national sales figures to obtain the market potential for any local area.

A major advantage of this method is that the data required are readily available to the marketing manager. In fact, you can use this method easily even if you are working in a small company where large investments of time and money are not possible.[7]

Look at Figure 8-3. Let's say that the national sales for a particular brand of camera was expected to be ten million units. If you wanted to calculate the market potential for the city of Bakersfield in Figure 8-3, you would take the BPI of .001916 listed and multiply it times ten million. Your answer is a market potential of 19,160 for Bakersfield. Note that when multiplying, we multiply times .001916, and not .1916, as it appears in the figure. This is because the figure as it appears is .1916 *per cent*.

What if you are introducing a **new product**? How then would you calculate the BPI? First, decide on the demographic, economic, and distribution factors that are important for your product in accordance with the segmentation in the "Survey of Buying Power" in the magazine. Let's say your product is a new sports car. Demographically, you decide that your target market is in the age group twenty-five to thirty-four and that economically your target market earns between $35,000 and $49,999. Furthermore, you want to calculate the index for the Anaheim/Santa Ana region. That would be group C in the figure. You would select the automotive distribution category. Now you must assign a relative weighting among the three factors so that they equal 100 per cent, which will tell you the relative importance of each factor in targeting your market with your new product.

Let us assume that you decide on a weighting of demographics at 20 per cent, economic group at 30 per cent, and distribution at 50 per cent. Calculation for your special BPI, therefore, equals 0.2 times X per cent plus 0.3 times Y per cent plus 0.5 times Z per cent.

Now let's calculate the values for X, Y, and Z.

X, or the demographic factor, equals the market population of ages twenty-five to thirty-four divided by the total U.S. population. Because you're looking at Anaheim/Santa Ana in Figure 8-2, the population at twenty-five to thirty-four is given as 18.7 per cent. This is multiplied times the total population for that area of 2,129,400 and divided by the total U.S. population for this age group of 40,541,000. Thus, the value for X is 0.0098.

Y is the economic group that we selected, where earnings are $35,000 to $49,999. Again, for the Anaheim/Santa Ana area, the percentage given is 23.8 per cent, times the number of households in the area of 780,600, divided by the total number of U.S. households in this income bracket of 14,511,800. This equals 0.0128, which is the value for Y.

For Z you must go to automotive distribution. Sales for automobiles listed in the figure for the Anaheim/Santa Ana area are divided by the national figures. This equals 0.0104 and is the value for Z.

Plugging this into the equation, BPI $= 0.2 \times 0.0098 + 0.3 \times 0.0128 + 0.5 \times 0.0104 = 0.011$. This figure can be used as a relative indicator to compare the potential buying power of the market you have targeted for your product, repeating the sequence for each market targeted. Remember that the total U.S. BPI equals 100.000.

CALIFORNIA

CAL. S&MM ESTIMATES — POPULATION— / RETAIL SALES BY STORE GROUP

METRO AREA / County / City	Total Population (Thousands)	% Of U.S.	Median Age of Pop.	% of Population by Age Group: 18–24 Years	25–34 Years	35–49 Years	50 & Over	Households (Thousands)
ANAHEIM - SANTA ANA	**2,129.4**	**.9041**	**30.8**	**13.6**	**18.7**	**20.2**	**22.0**	**780.6**
Orange	2,129.4	.9041	30.8	13.6	18.7	20.2	22.0	780.6
• Anaheim	236.6	.1005	30.2	15.0	19.4	18.5	22.2	88.8
Buena Park	67.2	.0285	29.5	15.0	17.4	20.3	20.2	23.1
Costa Mesa	88.4	.0375	30.4	17.3	22.8	18.2	21.4	36.0
Cypress	44.9	.0191	30.2	12.8	14.7	26.0	16.9	14.5
Fountain Valley	55.4	.0235	30.4	10.4	15.2	27.9	15.1	16.7
Fullerton	109.9	.0467	30.9	16.2	18.7	18.5	23.9	42.1
Garden Grove	129.3	.0549	30.2	14.1	18.1	19.0	22.3	45.4
Huntington Beach	186.6	.0792	30.0	13.8	20.3	22.0	18.0	69.0
Irvine	74.3	.0315	29.9	12.0	23.9	24.1	13.6	26.4
La Habra	48.0	.0204	31.1	14.6	17.3	18.2	25.1	18.1
Newport Beach	68.3	.0290	37.2	13.1	17.8	22.1	31.4	31.3
Orange	99.9	.0424	30.6	13.6	18.2	20.3	21.6	35.7
• Santa Ana	223.2	.0948	27.6	15.5	21.0	15.9	18.6	72.5
Westminster	74.8	.0318	30.8	12.8	17.2	21.0	21.7	26.3
SUBURBAN TOTAL	1,669.6	.7088	31.4	13.2	18.4	21.0	22.4	619.3
BAKERSFIELD	**443.4**	**.1883**	**29.8**	**12.5**	**17.3**	**17.2**	**23.7**	**156.8**
Kern	443.4	.1883	29.8	12.5	17.3	17.2	23.7	156.8
• Bakersfield	121.3	.0515	29.3	13.6	20.3	16.7	21.8	46.3
SUBURBAN TOTAL	322.1	.1368	30.0	12.1	16.3	17.4	24.4	110.5

METRO AREA / County / City	Total Retail Sales ($000)	Food ($000)	Eating & Drinking Places ($000)	General Mdse. ($000)	Furniture/ Furnish./ Appliance ($000)	Automotive ($000)	Drug ($000)
ANAHEIM - SANTA ANA	**13,972,616**	**2,958,436**	**1,566,344**	**1,979,738**	**673,843**	**2,107,252**	**374,620**
Orange	13,972,616	2,958,436	1,566,344	1,979,738	673,843	2,107,252	374,620
• Anaheim	1,356,810	289,508	195,112	113,378	110,508	173,300	40,091
Buena Park	583,257	140,801	41,002	146,045	18,440	99,835	19,571
Costa Mesa	1,479,281	114,986	103,770	436,613	82,210	313,132	8,642
Cypress	209,660	85,013	31,172	13,068	6,738	15,138	5,855
Fountain Valley	296,437	87,719	25,332	56,413	23,613	5,883	10,242
Fullerton	701,368	108,352	87,747	155,267	23,728	128,366	26,524
Garden Grove	616,405	192,780	79,021	30,266	22,147	125,638	25,449
Huntington Beach	1,172,626	300,185	107,217	137,507	45,107	175,424	32,882
Irvine	348,009	97,126	61,218	3,676	5,268	56,416	6,845
La Habra	306,183	45,613	26,948	33,873	14,760	107,770	6,445
Newport Beach	777,298	120,059	171,947	79,956	17,443	178,416	17,245
Orange	919,441	98,882	61,079	180,324	48,469	128,507	12,996
• Santa Ana	1,547,475	269,169	161,360	144,875	67,835	246,977	56,111
Westminster	904,847	132,701	64,338	242,185	85,047	116,107	7,974
SUBURBAN TOTAL	11,068,331	2,399,759	1,209,872	1,721,485	495,500	1,686,975	278,418
BAKERSFIELD	**2,444,657**	**693,275**	**250,345**	**211,605**	**89,729**	**334,365**	**100,935**
Kern	2,444,657	693,275	250,345	211,605	89,729	334,365	100,935
• Bakersfield	1,384,641	345,796	131,787	175,084	68,947	233,686	76,597
SUBURBAN TOTAL	1,060,016	347,479	118,558	36,521	20,782	100,679	24,338

CAL. S&MM ESTIMATES — EFFECTIVE BUYING INCOME

% of Hslds. by EBI Group: (A) $10,000–$19,999 (B) $20,000–$34,999 (C) $35,000–$49,999 (D) $50,000 & Over

METRO AREA / County / City	Total EBI ($000)	Median Hsld. EBI	A	B	C	D	Buying Power Index
ANAHEIM - SANTA ANA	**28,206,195**	**32,715**	**16.6**	**28.3**	**23.8**	**21.8**	**1.1396**
Orange	28,206,195	32,715	16.6	28.3	23.8	21.8	1.1396
• Anaheim	2,850,531	28,886	19.7	31.0	21.9	16.1	.1156
Buena Park	787,169	32,391	15.8	31.4	26.2	17.7	.0374
Costa Mesa	1,139,635	28,329	20.1	31.7	20.3	16.0	.0694
Cypress	581,740	38,967	10.6	25.2	29.8	28.6	.0216
Fountain Valley	709,070	41,548	9.3	22.6	32.0	32.6	.0274
Fullerton	1,515,198	31,274	17.5	28.8	21.7	21.4	.0596
Garden Grove	1,489,831	31,053	17.3	31.2	25.2	16.2	.0586
Huntington Beach	2,554,557	34,533	14.7	28.3	25.5	23.6	.1003
Irvine	1,213,880	43,393	7.8	23.2	28.9	36.7	.0412
La Habra	591,949	30,209	17.9	31.5	24.0	16.1	.0245
Newport Beach	1,489,592	38,587	13.5	22.8	18.5	36.1	.0574
Orange	1,245,329	32,058	17.5	27.9	24.3	20.0	.0585
• Santa Ana	2,086,824	26,409	21.8	33.2	21.1	10.2	.1029
Westminster	911,506	33,361	15.8	28.7	27.0	19.4	.0488
SUBURBAN TOTAL	23,268,840	34,140	15.5	27.5	24.4	23.9	.9211

S&MM ESTIMATES — EFFECTIVE BUYING INCOME

% of Hslds. by EBI Group: (A) $10,000–$19,999 (B) $20,000–$34,999 (C) $35,000–$49,999 (D) $50,000 & Over

METRO AREA / County / City	Total EBI ($000)	Median Hsld. EBI	A	B	C	D	Buying Power Index
BAKERSFIELD	**4,294,002**	**23,628**	**24.2**	**30.3**	**17.5**	**10.1**	**.1916**
Kern	4,294,002	23,628	24.2	30.3	17.5	10.1	.1916
• Bakersfield	1,357,537	26,249	21.1	30.3	20.2	12.1	.0745
SUBURBAN TOTAL	2,936,465	22,638	25.4	30.4	16.4	9.2	.1171
CHICO	**1,404,070**	**17,930**	**30.2**	**28.1**	**10.9**	**5.4**	**.0617**
Butte	1,404,070	17,930	30.2	28.1	10.9	5.4	.0617
• Chico	235,052	15,119	27.9	25.2	8.4	4.6	.0151
SUBURBAN TOTAL	1,169,018	18,487	30.6	28.9	11.4	5.6	.0466
FRESNO	**5,351,877**	**22,689**	**25.3**	**29.8**	**16.3**	**10.0**	**.2318**
Fresno	5,351,877	22,689	25.3	29.8	16.3	10.0	.2318
• Fresno	2,452,246	21,204	25.9	29.0	15.9	7.9	.1172
SUBURBAN TOTAL	2,899,631	24,145	24.5	30.8	16.8	12.0	.1146
LOS ANGELES - LONG BEACH	**84,749,032**	**25,280**	**22.0**	**28.5**	**17.9**	**14.4**	**3.5274**
Los Angeles	84,749,032	25,280	22.0	28.5	17.9	14.4	3.5274
Alhambra	715,447	23,529	24.9	32.0	17.1	9.3	.0323
Arcadia	725,480	34,862	16.2	24.2	21.2	28.6	.0334
Baldwin Park	361,573	23,775	22.8	38.2	16.1	5.6	.0157

Figure 8-3

Source: *Sales and Marketing Management.*

Two Categories of Sales Forecasting Methodology

There are two basic categories of sales forecasting methodology. These are bottom-up and top-down. With bottom-up, the sequence is to break the market into segments and then calculate separately the demand in each segment. The total is obtained by summing the segments to arrive at a total sales forecast.

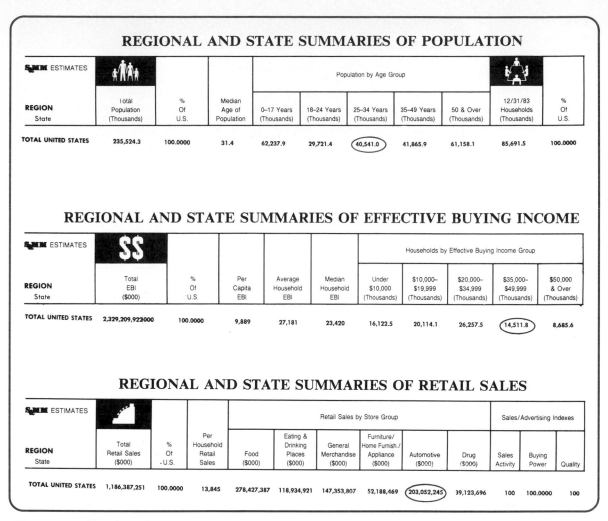

REGIONAL AND STATE SUMMARIES OF POPULATION

REGION / State	Total Population (Thousands)	% Of U.S.	Median Age of Population	0–17 Years (Thousands)	18–24 Years (Thousands)	25–34 Years (Thousands)	35–49 Years (Thousands)	50 & Over (Thousands)	12/31/83 Households (Thousands)	% Of U.S.
				Population by Age Group						
TOTAL UNITED STATES	235,524.3	100.0000	31.4	62,237.9	29,721.4	40,541.0	41,865.9	61,158.1	85,691.5	100.0000

REGIONAL AND STATE SUMMARIES OF EFFECTIVE BUYING INCOME

REGION / State	Total EBI ($000)	% Of U.S.	Per Capita EBI	Average Household EBI	Median Household EBI	Under $10,000 (Thousands)	$10,000– $19,999 (Thousands)	$20,000– $34,999 (Thousands)	$35,000– $49,999 (Thousands)	$50,000 & Over (Thousands)
						Households by Effective Buying Income Group				
TOTAL UNITED STATES	2,329,209,922000	100.0000	9,889	27,181	23,420	16,122.5	20,114.1	26,257.5	14,511.8	8,685.6

REGIONAL AND STATE SUMMARIES OF RETAIL SALES

REGION / State	Total Retail Sales ($000)	% Of U.S.	Per Household Retail Sales	Food ($000)	Eating & Drinking Places ($000)	General Merchandise ($000)	Furniture/ Home Furnish./ Appliance ($000)	Automotive ($000)	Drug ($000)	Sales Activity	Buying Power	Quality
				Retail Sales by Store Group						Sales/Advertising Indexes		
TOTAL UNITED STATES	1,186,387,251	100.0000	13,845	278,427,387	118,934,921	147,353,807	52,188,469	203,052,245	39,123,696	100	100.0000	100

Figure 8-3 (Continued)

Bottom-Up Forecasting

Typical methods used for **bottom-up forecasting** are sales force composites, industry surveys, and intention-to-buy surveys.

Although bottom-up forecasting appears fairly simple, there are problems that can seriously affect accuracy with two results. If the survey is done by a salesperson, the survey probably won't be his or her number one priority. Selling is. Also, because sales forecasts eventually lead to sales quotas, the salesperson may tend to underestimate the sales potential of the segments. Other salespeople, eternal optimists, may tend to overestimate.

Figure 8-4 shows a survey made of 202 separate sales and marketing executives regarding their agreement with statements concerning salesperson participation in forecasting. Note that only slightly more than a third—that is, 38 per cent—feel that their salespeople forecast just about right. The remainder indicate varying degrees of inaccuracies in their forecasting.[8]

% Agreeing	Statement
1%	My salespeople typically forecast low so they can earn more money.
20	In general, my salespeople are inaccurate forecasters because they lack the information about the company's plans needed to accurately estimate their future sales.
24	In general, my salespeople forecast high because their optimism outweighs their business judgment.
16	In general, my salespeople are inaccurate forecasters because they lack the necessary insight into the economic factors that impact their customers' need for our products.
38	In general, my salespeople forecast just about right.

Source: Adapted from Thomas R. Wotruba and Michael L. Thurlow, "Sales Force Participation in Quota Setting and Sales Forecasting," *Journal of Marketing*, vol. 40 (April 1976), p. 15.

Figure 8-4   202 Sales and Marketing Executives Opinions Concerning Salesperson Participation in Forecasting

For various reasons, industry surveys and intention-to-buy surveys by customers may also be in error. Companies may report erroneous information. Customers may tell researchers what they think they would like to hear or respond in a way that they think they should rather than what they would actually do when it comes to the purchase decision.

Top-Down Forecasting

Top-down forecasting is the most widely used, except for industrial applications. In the top-down sequence, the sales potential is first estimated, sales quotas are developed, and then a sales forecast is constructed.

The problems with top-down forecasting concern the correlation of economic variables and quantity demanded, as well as the assumption that this observable relationship will continue. Also, whichever indexing methodology is used to develop quantity of product demanded must work.

Typical methods used in top-down forecasting are executive judgment, trend projections, a moving average, regression, exponential smoothing, and leading indicators.

The Executive Judgment

With executive judgment, also known as the jury of executive opinion methodology, the marketing manager merely surveys executives who have expertise in the area being surveyed. Perhaps the most sophisticated of the executive opinion methodologies is that of Delphi, in which experts are asked their opinion on various questions having to do with forecasting events or the future. However, the process does not stop with the reception and analysis of the answers from a single round; the results of the round are divulged to the respondents and the questions are asked again. This process is repeated

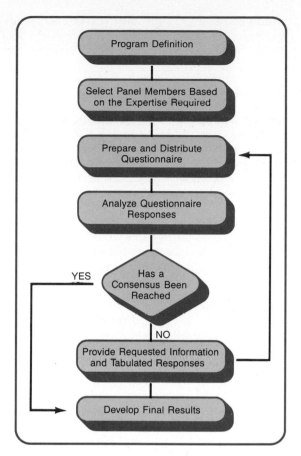

Figure 8-5   The Delphi Method of Forecasting

Source: Adapted from Raymond E. Taylor and L. Lynn Judd, "Environmental Forecasting for Direct Marketing," *Journal of Direct Marketing Reseach*, vol. 1, no. 2 (Spring/Summer 1987), p. 119.

several times until a group consensus of the results converges to give the answers sought. This process is shown in Figure 8-5.[9]

Sales Force Composite

As indicated earlier with the sales force composite, each individual salesperson is assigned the duties of forecasting for a particular territory. These territorial estimates are then summed up to arrive at an overall forecast.

Trend Projections

In its simplest application, trend analysis involves the examination of what has happened in the past. Historical values of a sales variable are analyzed to determine a value that can be projected into the future. Perhaps observation of recorded sales over the last five years may reveal that sales have increased 10 per cent on the average every year. A simple trend projection would forecast another 10 per cent increase for the following year.

Moving Average

Moving average is a more sophisticated type of trend projection. This approach assumes that the future will be an average of past performance rather than follow a specific linear percentage trend. The problem with the simple trend projection is randomness—that is, the random event or element that can create a major impact on the forecast. The moving average minimizes the impact of randomness on individual forecasts because it is an average of several values rather than simply a linear projection. For example, let us say that year 1 sales were $100,000; year 2, $300,000. The average of these two would be $200,000, and this would be our forecast. Thus, the moving average equation is basically summing up the sales in a number of past periods and dividing by the number of periods.

Industry Survey

Industry survey involves surveying the various companies that make up the industry for a particular item. Such a survey may include users or manufacturers. For example, if you want to forecast the number of computers that will be sold in a future year, you could survey all the computer manufacturers this year. In the same fashion, if you are interested in any product, you could survey the companies manufacturing the product or those interested in buying it. The industry survey method that is a buildup method of forecasting has some of the same advantages and disadvantages of the survey of executive opinion and sales force composites. For example, the executives may answer inaccurately.

Regression

A regression may be linear or multiple. With linear regression a relationship between sales and a single independent variable is developed and used to forecast sales data. With multiple regression, relationships between sales and a number of different independent variables are used. Usually the latter is accomplished with the help of a computer. Sales predictions are made by estimating the values for the independent variables and incorporating them into the multiregression equation. Thus, if a relationship can be found among various independent variables—let's say the number of college students, average family income, and part-time employment and the number of portable typewriters purchased—a multiple regression equation can be developed and used to predict sales for the coming year.

Intention-to-Buy Survey

The intention-to-buy survey is accomplished prior to the introduction of a product or service. Again, the main problem here is that the individuals in the target market will not always give accurate information regarding the intention to purchase new products or services. For one thing, the product or service may not be adequately explained or may be misunderstood by the respondent; other various psychological factors enter the responses, as when individuals respond as they think they should respond or are expected to respond. One informal survey asked university students to state their feelings about attending plays versus movies. Although a surprisingly high percentage felt that plays were to be preferred over movies for their cultural value, the facts were that few students had attended plays during the previous month, while many had attended movies.

Finally, environmental factors may act between the time the survey is accomplished and the product is introduced to invalidate the survey. For example, a technological breakthrough may immediately make the product obsolete, or economic conditions may mean that the product is no longer viable due to its high price.

Exponential Smoothing

Exponential smoothing is a time-series approach similar to the moving average already discussed. But instead of a constant set of weights for the observations made, an exponentially increasing set of weights is used. The result is that more recent values receive more weight than do older values. This is exponential smoothing in its most basic form. More sophisticated models include various adjustments for such factors as trends and seasonal patterns.

Leading Indicators

Many marketing students will already be familiar with leading indicators and their use in predicting recessions and recoveries from their study of economics. Leading indicators are the key issues found to have forecasting value by the National Bureau of Economic Research. Typical leading indicators reported by the National Bureau of Economic Research include prices of five hundred common stocks, new orders for durable goods, index of net business formation, corporate profits after taxes, industrial materials prices, and the change in consumer installment debt. The problem is in relating these values with specific products. When relationships are found, a multiregression model can be constructed, as explained earlier.

Comparison of Forecasting Methods

Usage

Some methods of forecasting are more popular than others. One survey of 175 different firms showed utilization of sales forecasting methods, as shown in Figure 8-6. Note that in this survey the jury of executive opinion and sales force composite were the two most popular methods used.[10]

Method	Regular Use (%)	Occasional Use (%)	Never Used (%)
Jury of executive opinion	52%	16%	5%
Sales force composite	48	15	9
Trend projections	28	16	12
Moving average	24	15	15
Industry survey	22	20	16
Regression	17	13	24
Intention-to-buy survey	15	17	23
Exponential smoothing	13	13	26
Leading indicators	12	16	24

Source: Adapted from Douglas J. Dalrymple, "Sales Forecasting Methods and Accuracy," *Business Horizons,* vol. 18 (December 1975), p. 71.

Figure 8-6 Utilization of Sales Forecasting Methods by 175 Firms

A more recent study compared the use and perceived accuracy of forecasting. Partial results are shown in Figure 8-7. In the study additional methods were noted, some of which do not appear in the figure. The most frequently used methods were individual subjective probability assessment and scenario development. That is, the manager in charge put down his or her best guess. This was once again followed by the sales force composite and jury of executive opinion.[11] A larger study came to the same conclusion.

Method	Mean Perceived Accuracy	Percentage of Firms Using Method
Individual Subjective Probability Assessment	3.53	93
Scenario Development	3.33	93
Sales Force Composite	2.81	91
Jury of Executive Opinion	3.32	90
Econometric Methods	3.48	63
Regression	3.40	61
Leading Indicators	3.50	58
Moving Average	2.92	42
Delphi Method	2.73	40
Single Exponent Smoothing	3.20	25

Perceived accuracy was measured on a scale of 1 to 5, where 1 = not accurate and 5 = very accurate.

Source: Adapted from Essam Mahmoud, Gillian Rice, and Naresh Malhotra, "Emerging Issues in Sales Forecasting and Decision Support Systems," *Journal of the Academy of Marketing Science,* vol. 16, nos. 3, 4 (Fall 1988), p. 56.

Figure 8-7 Usage and Perceived Accuracy of Sales Forecasting Methods

Methodology	Past Time Horizon	Costs	Accuracy	Time to Obtain	Ease of Interpretation
Moving average	Short	Low	Low	Short	Difficult
Exponential smoothing	Short	Low	Low	Short	Difficult
Regression	Medium to long	Medium	Medium	Medium	Medium
Econometric models	Medium to long	High	Medium to high	Long	Easy
Surveys	—	Variable	Medium to high	Variable	Easy
Leading indicators	Short	Low	Medium to high	Short	Difficult

Source: Adapted in part from Steven C. Wheelwright and Spyros Makridakis, *Forecasting Methods for Management*, 3rd ed. (New York: Wiley, 1980), pp. 206–207.

Forecasting Methods Compared

Sales force composite and jury of executive opinion are the most widely used methods of forecasting, even if they are less accurate than quantitative methodologies.[12]

Choosing a Method for Forecasting

The method selected for sales forecasting should not be based merely on popularity or who uses the method the most, but rather on situational factors, including feelings about the company's sales force, how quickly the forecast can be made, cost, accuracy, and so forth. Different forecasting methodologies have been measured against different factors, as shown in Figure 8-8.[13] David M. Georgoff and Robert G. Murdick of Florida Atlantic University prepared a chart to assist managers in selecting forecasting methods that contained twenty different approaches and variations of approaches to forecasting; the approaches were arrayed against sixteen evaluation dimensions, so the number of choices, even for relatively slight variations in the situation, are actually quite wide.[14] Frequently, different methods can be used simultaneously and the results compared to improve the reliability and confidence in the forecast. However, no one method is the best or even the most accurate under all conditions.[15]

The Supreme Importance of Judgment

The marketing manager should never forget that, whether the model used for forecasting is quantitative or not quantitative, sophisticated or unsophisticated, in the final analysis it is he or she who is ultimately responsible. It is his or her good judgment that is of supreme importance. Alvin Toffler, author of *Future Shock* and *The Third Wave*, recently said, "You can use all the quantitative data you can get, but you still have to distrust it and use your own intelligence and judgment."[16]

Summary

In this chapter we have seen the value of forecasting and the central part it plays in marketing and other business functions. We have seen that the terms *market potential, sales potential,* and *sales forecasting* are not the same. Market potential has to do with the total capacity of a market, sales potential has to do with the total capacity of a single firm in that market, and sales forecasting has to do with the forecast of the product actually to be sold in that market. We have seen that market potential can be calculated in various fashions: the chain ratio, in which one factor is linked to another to arrive at an ultimate potential, and in indexing methods, such as those developed in *Sales and Marketing Management* magazine.

Forecasting methodology is generally classified according to whether it is bottom-up or top-down. Bottom-up means starting with market segments, calculating the demand for each, and summing all to arrive at a total; top-down begins with a calculation of sales potential, proceeds to a calculation of a sales quota, and finally ends up with the forecast itself. Neither top-down nor bottom-up forecasting is without disadvantages. Either category may be appropriate, depending on the situation.

We have also looked at some of the most frequently used methods of forecasting: jury of executive opinion, sales force composite, trend projection, moving average, industry survey, regression, intention-to-buy survey, exponential smoothing, and leading indicators. The theme throughout is that no one single method works best under all conditions. Therefore, the judgment of the marketing manager is supreme in deciding which method or methods to use. This in turn requires that the marketing manager achieve sufficient mastery over the different methodologies to make this decision.

Questions

1. What means of forecasting might be used to confirm a future need for restraint systems in automobiles?
2. How might sales forecasting be used by firms producing proprietary drugs in competing with those manufacturing generic drugs?
3. Explain how sales forecasting would be used in planning corporate strategy.
4. It has been said that sales forecasting assists in deciding on the use of various elements and their proportions in the marketing mix. How might sales forecasts do this?
5. Explain how you would obtain market potentials for the following products, using likely sources of information and chain relationships, as appropriate: a karate studio in a local area; a book on how to repair Volkswagen "beetles"; a smoker's toothpaste; a product to assist in dieting; a new type of pump for the recovery of petroleum that is 20 per cent more efficient than the current type; a new computer game.
6. How would the decision be made in each case for determining whether to use bottom-up or top-down forecasting for each of the products listed in question 5?
7. Assume that all the products in question 5 are new. State explicitly how you would convert the market potential to a sales forecast in each case.
8. You are forecasting using the sales composite method. What can you do to minimize inaccuracies in the forecast?
9. You were recently hired to be a marketing manager in a small company. In the past in this company, the president has always made the sales forecast for the forthcoming year based on his own judgment. Although the accuracy of his judgment has never been measured precisely, apparently it's reasonably good because this has gone on for a number of years. How might you convince the president to change to a different method of sales forecasting?
10. Alvin Toffler says, or seems to be saying, that in-

telligent judgment is more important than quantitative data. If so, why should any quantitative type of sales forecasting be performed? And if you feel that quantitative sales forecasting is important, how should this be combined with a marketing manager's judgment?

Ethical Question

You work in a firm that does marketing and sales forecasts for client firms. Recently an old friend, who has given you considerable business in the past, asked you to forecast the future demand for lightweight portable oxygen systems for personal use in case of fire. He asks for an interim verbal report as soon as you get any data at all. Your standard modus operandi is to use two different methods, one quantitative and one qualitative, to cross check your results and report on both. You complete the quantitative analysis, which shows considerable growth in demand. You report this to your client. He tells you he is relieved because his job is on the line. If there were no demand, he'd be on the street. Three weeks later, you look over the results after using the Delphi method. It shows the exact opposite of your quantitative analysis. You call your friend and tell him the bad news. He gives you additional funds to do another Delphi. You do and get the same results. He asks you not to include the results of the two Delphi analyses in your formal report to his company. What should you do?

Endnotes

1. "Chain Stores Strike Gold in Jewelry Sales," *Business Week* (February 6, 1984), pp. 56–58.
2. Stanley J. Modic, "TRW Bets Big on Air Bags and Belts," *Industry Week*, vol. 238, no. 10 (May 15, 1989), p. 27.
3. Christopher S. Eklund, "Generics Grab More of the Drug Action," *Business Week* (May 13, 1985), pp. 64–68.
4. Spyros Makridakis and Steven C. Wheelwright, "Forecasting: Issues and Challenges for Marketing Management," *Journal of Marketing*, vol. 41 (October 1977), p. 24.
5. Nigel F. Piercy, "The Power and Politics of Sales Forecasting: Uncertainty Absorption and the Power of the Marketing Department," *Journal of the Academy of Marketing Science*, vol. 17, no. 2 (Spring 1989), p. 116.
6. Harry S. Dent, Jr., "Easy Forecasting," *Small Business Reports* vol. 15, no. 7 (July 1990), p. 68.
7. Gary Brockway and W. Glynn Mangold, "The Sales Conversion Index: A Method for Analyzing Small Business Market Opportunities," *Journal of Small Business Management*, vol. 26, no. 2 (April 1988), p. 35.
8. Thomas R. Wotruba and Michael L. Thurlow, "Sales Force Participation and Quota Setting in Sales Forecasting," *Journal of Marketing*, vol. 40 (April 1976), p. 15.
9. Raymond E. Taylor and L. Lynn Judd, "Environmental Forecasting for Direct Marketing," *Journal of Direct Marketing Research*, vol. 1, no. 2 (Spring–Summer 1987), p. 119.
10. Douglas J. Dalrymple, "Sales Forecasting Methods and Accuracy," *Business Horizons*, vol. 18 (December 1975), p. 69.
11. Essam Mahmoud, Gillian Rice, and Naresh Malhotra, "Emerging Issues in Sales Forecasting and Decision Support Systems," *Journal of the Academy of Marketing Science*, vol. 16, nos. 3, 4 (Fall 1988), p. 56.
12. Dalrymple, op. cit., p. 38.
13. Steven C. Wheelwright and Spyros Makridakis, *Forecasting Methods for Management*, 3rd ed. (New York: Wiley, 1980), pp. 206–207.
14. David M. Georgoff and Robert G. Murdick, "Manager's Guide to Forecasting," *Harvard Business Review*, vol. 64 (January–February 1986), p. 111.
15. Steven P. Schnaars, "Situational Factors Affecting Forecast Accuracy," *Journal of Marketing Research*, vol. 21 (August 1984), p. 296.
16. Bernie Whalen, "Toffler on Marketing," *Marketing News* (March 15, 1985), p. 31.

Ozark Counselors: Proposals for Funds

Ozark Counselors, a regional drug and alcohol abuse treatment organization in the southwestern part of the country, is contemplating engaging in a capital fund-raising campaign for the acquisition of new physical facilities. This move has become necessary to allow Ozark Counselors to cope with the increasing demand for their services, and to meet the growing competition from both profit and non-profit organizations providing similar services. Initial estimates indicated the cost of the new facility to be in the range of $750,000 to $1,200,000. It is hoped that this amount can be raised during a 1985–1986 fund-raising campaign; yet, at the present time (June 1984), plans for the campaign are sketchy. Time is running out, and it is imperative that Ozark Counselors develop a strategic plan for its fund-raising activities.

Organization Background

Ozark Counselors is a nonprofit social service organization that provides state certified alcohol and drug abuse treatment programs. Their services include alternate-care setting, nonmedical detoxification, residential care, and an aftercare program. Fees are negotiable, based primarily on the ability of the patient to pay, although no one is denied admission because of an inability to pay. The services are available to both of-age and underage individuals, with the stipulation that underage individuals receive parental consent. After a decade of operation, it has reached the point where an expansion of the physical facility is necessary to meet increased demand and match competition.

The geographic segment served by Ozark Counselors is primarily a four-county area: a diverse mix of both rural and urban. The urban population totals in the vicinity of 125,000, distributed in the six major communities of city A (46,000), city B (25,000), city C (21,700), city D (18,600), city E (11,300), and city F (1989).

Philanthropic Environment of the Area

It is well recognized that the success of any major fund-raising campaign is primarily a function of the philanthropic environment. Traditionally, the geographic area of interest has not been a particularly giving segment, but recent data seem to indicate that this may be changing.

The United Fund campaign is the area's largest annually held fund-raising effort. Typically, it is well supported and to a degree provides insight into the donation potential of the region. Table 1 presents the major communities, present and projected populations (1990), and each community's 1985 United Fund goals.

As evidence of the increased interest in giving, the United Fund goals of city C have risen from $80,000 in 1981 to $250,000 in 1985. Likewise, the United Fund campaign of city B surpassed its $132,000 goal by $28,000 in 1984.

Additionally, several recent capital fund-raising efforts have been successful in the area. Notable among these successes were a social services center in city

Developed by C. P. Rao and Mark C. Hall, University of Arkansas, Fayetteville, Arkansas. Used with permission.

Table 1   United Fund Estimates

Community	Present Pop.	Projected Pop.	United Fund Goal (1985)
City A	46,000	52,700	425,000
City B	25,000	32,000	150,000
City C	21,700	27,000	260,000
City D	18,600	22,500	110,000
City E	11,300	13,900	90,000
City F	1,989	—	—
TOTAL			1,035,000

D, an adult development center in city E, and a recent Salvation Army physical facility expansion in city A. Generally speaking, the philanthropic environment seems to be improving.

Not-for-Profit Peculiarities

Ozark Counselors is a not-for-profit entity and consequently operates in a domain somewhat different from profit making firms. These peculiarities need to be considered in any actions taken by Ozark Counselors.

First, not-for-profit entities don't typically have the direct line of accountability prevalent in profit-oriented organizations. In a more indirect fashion, they have accountability to voluntary workers, outside organizations, and the administrative hierarchy.

Second, not-for-profit organizations are in the unique position of having to satisfy two target markets: a source of funds market and a receiver of services market. Seeking donations from the source market is a relatively complex process of identifying likely donors (both large and small), defining their characteristics (psychological and demographic), and determining what causes them to give. The receiver market consists of those who benefit from the efforts of the nonprofit entity. The "marketing" to this group consists of identifying the specific needs, identifying the characteristics of those who benefit, and developing a plan for reaching the group.

Third, the effectiveness of a not-for-profit organization is difficult to assess due to the little interest placed on the bottom line. Instead of profit, the organization is likely to have goals of social benefits and services.

Finally, not for profit organizations are typically subject to more public scrutiny than are for-profit entities. When individuals and organizations make donations, they are generally quite concerned with results.

Fund-Raising Principles

Recent research and writings in the area of fund raising suggest that the feasibility of any major fund-raising effort depends on a number of critical factors. These factors can be regarded as the "principles" of fund raising: those issues generic to virtually all fund raising and essential to its success.

The first issue concerns the *case* for the fund-raising effort. The case may be the single most important element of a fund-raising campaign as it delineates the reasons why potential donors should support a fund-raising agency. In some situations different cases need to be prepared to appeal to different constituencies.

Second, the *relationship with other major fund-raising organizations* is a critical factor. To a certain extent, not-for-profit organizations directly or indirectly compete with each other for donated funds. The short- and long-term implications of this competition may dictate the appropriate strategy.

Multiple sourcing is another principle often employed in fund raising. Generally, all conceivable sources are solicited for funds. These sources may entail private and public foundations, other social service agencies, local businesses, and individual citizens.

Even though all sources are critically assessed, typically fund raising gets the greatest share of funds from a small number of donors. In this regard, it is often appropriate to employ a *sequential strategy.* Large potential donors are first identified and cultivated, followed sequentially with those less likely to give, or to give in smaller amounts. This approach is often successful as the first few donors "set the pace" for the rest. The multiple sourcing and sequential strategies often require the development of a number of mini or subcampaigns.

Organizational leadership and structure are also requisites for successful fund raising. The leadership establishes, and is the primary proponent of, the "case" of the soliciting organization; consequently the success of a campaign is heavily dependent on their ability to convey the message. This is especially important in the one-to-one interaction often necessary to solicit funds from major donors.

Managing a fund-raising effort is often impossible without a hierarchical organizational design. If donors are segmented either on a geographic (community) or potential basis, then it may be in the best interest of the soliciting firm to appoint segment-specific committees to oversee activities.

Generally, it is impossible (and undesirable) for the soliciting organization to utilize its own employees to head up these committees. Consequently, local prominent citizens and business leaders are often called upon to fill these leadership positions.

A final consideration is the two-dimensional phenomenon of *image.* First, a particular organization has an "image" in the area within which it operates. This image may be a function of its previous success and methods of operation or its relative standing to other organizations providing similar services. Second, the "cause" for which the organization is in existence has an image. The appeal of certain social issues is subject to change over time and public sentiments.

Current Situation

The principle problem facing Ozark Counselors is in identifying the most effective and efficient method of raising the needed capital funds. To develop a plan to accomplish this, Ozark Counselors has determined that it needs to address the essentially "strategic" issues brought to light in the last section, and also needs to answer questions of a more operational nature.

These operational issues involve identifying the size and characteristics of potential donor groups, assessing the donation potential of these groups, and determining donors' intentions with regard to different types of donations. Also, there is a question as to the relative effectiveness of alternative persuasion methods.

If Ozark Counselors does find enough potential to make feasible a fund-raising effort of this magnitude, then a final set of issues needs to be addressed. These are primarily the questions of staffing, costs, appreciation of donors, and the establishment of specific target-segment goals. The cost issue is of particular concern, as experts typically estimate that campaign costs vary between 5 and 10 per cent of the campaign target. A significant portion of this cost may be incurred "up front", and Ozark Counselors needs to give serious consideration as to the sources of these funds.

Given the magnitude of the task, and the relative inexperience of Ozark Counselors in this type of activity, they decided to undertake a feasibility study of the proposed campaign.

Feasibility Study

A marketing and management consultant was employed by Ozark Counselors to assess the feasibility of the proposed campaign. As it was felt that all possible sources of funds should be closely looked at, the consultant approached the study in a multistep fashion, initially focusing on the larger environment, and ultimately moving to a polling of individual citizens and businesses.

Data were collected in three ways. First, in-depth interviews were conducted with community leaders and other social service organizations. Next, both mail questionnaires and personal interviews were used to elicit responses from affluent households and businesses. Finally, mail contact was made with eighty-four major philanthropic foundations to assess their willingness to support Ozark Counselors efforts.

Reactions of Community Leaders and Social Organizations

Ozark Counselors is currently a part of the United Fund Group, an organization that works closely with local chambers of commerce in their fund-raising efforts. Consequently, Ozark Counselors is particularly concerned with both groups reactions to a fund-raising campaign of this magnitude.

During initial interviews, it was made clear that the United Fund does not look with favor on any organization that is a participant in the group to solicit funds on its own. The United Fund may be flexible on this issue only if the planned fund-raising campaign is a one-time capital fund type and if any possible conflicts in terms of timing are resolved.

The local chamber of commerce groups also seemed to be hesitant to sanction the Ozark Counselors proposal. The particular concern of this group is the adverse effect that too many fund-raising activities will have on the community's ability and willingness to donate.

Discussions with these organizations clearly indicated some reluctance to lend active support for the proposed campaign. Given this, two options seemed apparent. First, Ozark Counselors could attempt to elicit cooperation of these groups by convincing them that their activities wouldn't interfere with the established groups' activities. This could be done by stressing the unique "case" of Ozark Counselors and/or spreading the fund-raising activities over a number of years so as to minimize direct competition for funds. The second option would be a direct confrontation with the established organizations. Given the fact that the established community organizations represented the social and economic elite of each community, this option on the surface seemed risky.

Reactions of Households and Businesses

The second phase involved personal interviews and mail surveys of affluent households and businesses. These two groups were initially perceived as the primary donor target markets. Generally, it was thought that the business segment would be the more important and generous of the two groups. The personal interviews were structured to gain an in-depth understanding of the respondents' donation behavior, while the mail questionnaires were designed to cover a representative spectrum of the donating population of each segment. Twenty-five households and 15 business organizations were interviewed, while 135 households and 55 businesses were approached via mail survey.

Mail Survey Results

Results from the affluent-household mail survey indicated that both alcohol and drug abuse are perceived as relatively important problems. Survey results also indicated that about 30 per cent of household respondents presently give high levels of support to programs of the Ozark Counselors type; yet almost 54 per cent would be favorably disposed to support such an agency if they are approached. The type of support that households would provide was overwhelmingly cash donations, as opposed to volunteering of services, noncash contributions, or assuming leadership positions on committees. Awareness among the affluent households of the Ozark Counselors' mission was generally quite low. In fact, 63 per cent of the 135 households had never even heard of Ozark Counselors.

In a fashion similar to the household segment, the mail survey of businesses indicated that drug and alcohol abuse were considered important social issues and problems that may affect business productivity. This acknowledgment of importance didn't seem to carry over well into action, as only 23 per cent of the organizations presently rated their support as either high or very high. Relative to the household segment, a smaller percentage of businesses (38 per cent) would be favorably disposed to support a drug- and alcohol-abuse program if asked. With regard to the type of support they would be willing to provide, more than one-fifth of the businesses indicated they would likely provide executive services. Awareness of Ozark Counselors and its mission fared somewhat better among organizations when compared to households; yet 55 per cent of the polled businesses were unaware of Ozark Counselors activities.

Appendixes A and B contain the complete mail survey findings for households and businesses, respectively. Additionally, a representative subset of comments and open-ended responses from each group is provided.

Personal Interview Results

The mail survey responses from both households and businesses indicated a predisposition to be more supportive of fund raising for purposes of paying operating expenses and for procurement of equipment than for a building. This finding was refuted in both business and household interviews, where a definite preference was expressed for concrete evidence of fund usage.

Personal interviews with the two constituencies reinforced the mail survey findings that the social problems remedied by Ozark Counselors were generally perceived as important. On the other hand, a number of interviewed individuals and organizations made a distinction between what they considered "nature-inflicted" and "self-inflicted" problems. Self-inflicted problems (which alcohol and drug abuse were often perceived to be) were often viewed as being an individual's responsibility and not society's.

Although Ozark Counselors did in fact provide services somewhat different from other drug- and alcohol-rehabilitation programs in the area, the differences in programs were generally not well perceived. Consequently, both constituencies felt that too many organizations in the area were providing the same type of service. Both individuals and organizations felt a need to "draw the line," and this often occurred after donations were made to the United Fund.

Business interviews showed them to be strongly committed to the United Fund efforts but generally not restricted to just that agency in their giving. In fact, discussions with business leaders suggested that the particular cause an organization supports largely depended on the personal preferences of key people within the organization.

Philanthropic Foundations

The final phase involved mail contact with eighty-four major philanthropic foundations. In selecting these foundations, two criteria were used. First, some foundations were selected on the basis of their known support to various social causes in the region. Second, a few foundations were also selected from the national directory of foundations, if the scope of their support typically included alcohol- and drug-abuse treatment.

To receive funds from these foundations, it was generally required that a fairly elaborate application procedure be followed. Initial contact did indicate some interest from the various foundations, and for planning purposes it was hoped that approximately 20–25 per cent of the necessary funds could be raised this way.

DISCUSSION QUESTIONS

1. What are the critical issues that need to be addressed prior to the proposed fund-raising effort?
2. What specific recommendations and proposals would you present to Ozark Counselors?
3. How representative of the total business and household population do you think the sample is?
4. What additional information would be useful in analyzing this situation?

APPENDIX A HOUSEHOLD SURVEY RESPONSES

Table A1   Household Evaluation of the Relative Importance of Alcohol- and Drug-Related Problems as Social Problems

Importance Rating	No.	Percentage
Very important	87	54.4
Important	64	40.0
Somewhat important	9	5.6
Not important	0	0.0

**Table A2   Extent of Support to Nonprofit Alcohol-
and Drug-Treatment Services Agencies in the Area**

Extent of Support	No.	Percentage
Very high	13	8.1
High	36	22.5
Moderate	66	41.2
Low	28	17.5
Very low	17	10.6

**Table A3   Household Predisposition to Support
a Nonprofit Alcohol- and Drug-Treatment Agency
in the Area**

Degree of Predisposition	No.	Percentage
Very favorable	10	6.3
Favorable	75	47.5
Slightly favorable	63	39.9
Unfavorable	10	6.3

**Table A4   Types of Support Households Are Likely to Extend to a Nonprofit
Alcohol- and Drug-Treatment Services Agency**

Type of Support	Likelihood of Household Support							
	Very Likely		Likely		Somewhat Likely		Unlikely	
	No.	%	No.	%	No.	%	No.	%
Volunteering my services	7	4.6	29	18.9	45	29.4	72	47.1
Assume a leadership role on a committee	4	2.6	17	11.2	40	26.5	90	59.6
Making cash contribution	4	2.6	52	33.5	66	42.6	33	21.3
Making noncash contribution	6	6.2	20	20.8	22	22.9	48	50.0
Others	—	—	—	—	—	—	—	—

Table A5 Household Awareness of Ozark Counselors as a Nonprofit Alcohol- and Drug-Treatment Services Agency

Degree of Awareness	No.	Percentage
Very Aware	13	8.2
Aware	20	12.6
Somewhat aware	25	15.8
Unaware	100	63.3

Table A6 Likelihood of Households Supporting Various Purposes of Fund Raising by Nonprofit Social Services Agencies

Purpose of Fund Raising	Likelihood of Household Support							
	Very Likely		Likely		Somewhat Likely		Unlikely	
	No.	%	No.	%	No.	%	No.	%
To meet the day-to-day expenses	8	5.3	41	27.3	56	37.3	45	30.0
Funds for a major project like a new building	4	2.7	25	16.7	55	36.7	66	44.0
Funds for limited purpose projects like special equipment	5	3.3	36	24.0	71	47.3	38	25.3
Others	—	—	—	—	—	—	—	—

Table A7 Households' Evaluation of the Relative Effectiveness of Alternative Methods of Persuasion in a Fund-Raising Campaign

Methods of Persuasion	Effectiveness Rating							
	Very Effective		Effective		Somewhat Effective		Ineffective	
	No.	%	No.	%	No.	%	No.	%
Personal approach	55	35.5	77	49.7	18	11.6	5	3.2
Direct-mail soliciting	1	0.6	26	16.7	72	46.1	57	36.5
Telephone soliciting	1	0.6	23	14.7	48	30.8	84	53.8
Mass media appeals	8	5.2	36	23.2	75	48.4	36	23.3
Special events	14	9.2	64	42.1	47	30.9	27	17.8
Others	—	—	—	—	—	—	—	—

Table A8   Households' Evaluation of Return Benefit Expectations of Household Donors

	No.	Percentage
Do you think that people expect *something in return* for their support to a nonprofit social service organization?		
Yes	46	29.1
No	86	54.4
Not sure	26	16.5

Table A9   Households' Evaluation of the Relative Effectiveness of Alternate Methods of Appreciating Household Donors

Method of Appreciation	Effectiveness Rating							
	Very Effective		Effective		Somewhat Effective		Ineffective	
	No.	%	No.	%	No.	%	No.	%
Membership in the organization	4	8.2	21	42.8	16	32.6	8	16.3
Certificates of appreciation	5	10.0	21	42.0	15	30.0	9	18.0
Publishing the names of supporters	6	11.8	25	49.0	15	29.4	5	9.8
Appreciation functions (lunches, dinners, etc.)	5	10.0	22	54.0	15	30.0	3	6.0
Award of recognition plaques	8	16.7	21	43.7	13	27.1	6	12.5
Others	—	—	—	—	—	—	—	—

Table A10   Comments by Household Respondents

My only real problem with this is that I firmly believe that you are attempting a social solution to a spiritual problem.

In too many cases more is spent on administrative expenses than actually reaches the people involved. This is my own evaluation of such organizations.

Is this a new name for an old organization like 215 Club? I know absolutely nothing about it.

I know this work is important. I just don't think it is as important as several other causes. Matter of personal priority.

Need to get information concerning your organization and location to all area physicians. I cannot believe you've been active ten years and I didn't know about you!

I have been here for nine years, but I have not been informed about Ozark Counselors. A nice brochure or pamphlet would be helpful. Before I would give in any way I would need to make an inquiry about the agency.

Table A10 **(Continued)**

I am unaware of this organization—though I feel there is a great need for support of this type project. There is a need for research and care of these individuals with problems.

The reason I checked low on everything is I feel any government-related nonprofit projects don't do as good as privately owned projects because of political sways. But I do think it's a problem that needs to be solved.

APPENDIX B BUSINESS SURVEY RESPONSES

Table B1 **Business Organizations' Evaluation of the Relative Importance of Alcohol- and Drug-Related Problems as Social Problems**

Importance Rating	No.	Percentage
Very important	33	44.6
Important	36	48.6
Somewhat important	4	5.4
Not important	1	1.4

Table B2 **Extent of Support to Nonprofit Alcohol- and Drug-Treatment Services Agencies in the Area**

Extent of Support	No.	Percentage
Very high	5	6.7
High	12	16.2
Moderate	36	48.6
Low	13	17.6
Very low	8	10.8

Table B3 **Business Organizations' Predisposition to Support a Nonprofit Alcohol and Drug-Treatment Agency in the Area**

Degree of Predisposition	No.	Percentage
Very favorable	3	4.2
Favorable	24	33.8
Slightly favorable	28	39.4
Unfavorable	16	22.5

Table B4   Types of Support the Business Organizations Are Likely to Extend to a Nonprofit Alcohol- and Drug-Treatment Services Agency

Type of Support	Likelihood of Business Support							
	Very Likely		Likely		Somewhat Likely		Unlikely	
	No.	%	No.	%	No.	%	No.	%
Donating executive services	3	4.2	16	22.5	23	32.4	29	40.9
Executives assuming leadership role on a committee	3	4.2	17	23.9	18	25.3	33	46.5
Making cash contribution	3	4.3	12	17.1	32	45.7	23	32.9
Encouraging employees to make cash contributions	2	2.8	9	12.7	18	25.3	42	59.1
Making a noncash contribution	3	6.2	14	29.2	7	14.6	24	50.0

Table B5   Business Organizations' Awareness of Ozark Counselors as a Nonprofit Alcohol- and Drug-Treatment Services Agency

Degree of Awareness	No.	Percentage
Very aware	8	10.8
Aware	10	13.5
Somewhat aware	15	20.3
Unaware	41	55.4

Table B6   Likelihood of Business Organizations Supporting Various Purposes of Fund Raising by Nonprofit Social Services Agencies

Purpose of Fund Raising	Likelihood of Household Support							
	Very Likely		Likely		Somewhat Likely		Unlikely	
	No.	%	No.	%	No.	%	No.	%
To meet the day-to-day expenses	2	3.1	13	20.3	22	34.4	27	42.2
Funds for a major project, like a new building	2	3.1	12	18.7	17	26.6	33	51.6
Funds for limited-purpose projects, like special equipment	1	1.6	15	23.8	26	41.3	21	33.3
Others	—	—	—	—	—	—	—	—

Table B7   Business Organizations' Evaluation of the Relative Effectiveness of Alternative Methods of Persuasion in a Fund-Raising Campaign

Methods of Persuasion	Effectiveness Rating							
	Very Effective		Effective		Somewhat Effective		Ineffective	
	No.	%	No.	%	No.	%	No.	%
Personal approach	18	25.0	36	50.0	11	15.3	7	9.7
Direct mail soliciting	2	2.8	14	19.7	22	31.0	33	46.5
Telephone soliciting	1	1.4	7	10.0	32	45.7	30	42.9
Mass media appeals	1	1.4	20	28.6	19	27.1	30	42.9
Special events	5	7.0	25	35.2	25	35.2	16	22.5
Others	—	—	—	—	—	—	—	—

Table B8   Business Organizations' Evaluation of Return Benefit Expectations of Business Donors

		No.	Percentage
Do you think that businesses expect *something in return* for their support to a nonprofit social service organization?			
	Yes	25	33.8
	No	38	51.3
	Not sure	11	14.9

Table B9   Business Organizations' Evaluation of the Relative Effectiveness of Alternate Methods of Appreciating Business Donors

Method of Appreciation	Effectiveness Rating							
	Very Effective		Effective		Somewhat Effective		Ineffective	
	No.	%	No.	%	No.	%	No.	%
Permanent recognition as patrons	5	20.0	9	36.0	9	36.0	2	8.0
Certificates of appreciation	3	12.0	7	28.0	13	52.0	2	8.0
Publicity in mass media	9	36.0	11	44.0	4	16.0	1	4.0
Award of recognition plaque	3	12.5	10	41.7	10	41.7	1	4.1
Others	—	—	—	—	—	—	—	—

Table B10   Comments by Business Respondents

Those businesspeople whose lives have been touched by drugs or alcohol will certainly respond more positively—the personal approach will certainly mean more to them, as well as the corporate head who should consider in dollars and cents the losses he incurs because of drug-related illness among his employees and executives. Mass media could have some influence on the latter group, as could some form of corporate recognition (above and beyond tax incentive).

Some companies relish public recognition of their giving. Many more others, I would think, will give but shun publicity because they wish to avoid being pestered by every "do gooder" with a cause.

We participate very actively in the United Fund—including executive participation, employee solicitation, and corporate gift. We do not get involved in individual agency drives.

Why not go through the United Way? That is what the organization is supposed to do.

I know most programs are not working. Why should I support this one?

Because we do contribute to United Fund: Ozark Counselors is a UF agency, we would probably not make an additional donation unless it was for a special project (equipment, etc).

Large companies are frequently patrons of the arts and patrons of social service programs. It is a feather in their cap, tax deductible, and improves their civic image. Small businesses usually are just scraping by and every dollar they donate is one less they have for paying bills and just staying even. It is far harder to get much money from small businesses. It would probably make more sense to concentrate on companies large enough to be able to afford large contributions for their prestige value. Another thought would be to have fund raisers like the Fire Department's pancake breakfasts, chili suppers, spaghetti suppers, ice cream socials, etc. ad infinitum.

CASE 5

Da-Roche Laboratories, Inc.

In December, the officers of Da-Roche Laboratories, Inc., met to discuss the company's sales and advertising plans to re-launch their new product, Dapper-Diaper. The focus of the meeting was the strategy to be used in the marketing of the new product which had recently been approved by the Food and Drug Administration (FDA). They were particularly interested in the possible methods of promoting the product and in the channels of distribution to be used in distributing Dapper-Diaper.

This case is from Kenneth L. Bernhardt and Thomas C. Kinnear, *Cases in Marketing Management,* 4th ed. (Plano, Tex.: Business Publications, Inc, 1987). Used with permission.

Da-Roche Laboratories, Inc., was established in Jackson, Michigan, to develop and market a new antibiotic baby product, Dapper-Diaper. Dapper-Diaper was composed of an aqueous solution of the antibiotic neomycin sulfate, which was placed in a 10-ounce aerosol can. Neomycin inhibited odors in the animal kingdom, and Mr. Roy Crutchfield thought that the antibiotic could be used to eliminate odors from baby diapers. Dapper-Diaper kills bacteria which cause the decomposition of urea and thereby prevents ammonia from forming in diapers.

Da-Roche Laboratories convinced selected doctors to do some initial testing of its new product and the results were very encouraging. Doctors discovered that when sprayed on diapers in the diaper pail, Dapper-Diaper solved the odor problem. In addition, if sprayed on a clean diaper before it was worn by the baby, it appeared to stop or prevent diaper rash on the baby.

Gaining FDA Approval

With a great deal of encouragement from the doctors involved in the initial testing of their new antibiotic product, Mr. D. R. Wiley, then president and general manager of Da-Roche Laboratories, along with Mr. Crutchfield and Dr. John B. Holst, the company's consulting MD, went to Washington and informed the FDA that they had discovered a new gift to mothers which they wished to begin marketing immediately. The FDA did not agree and told the Da-Roche personnel that they would have to do studies to show that the product actually did what it claimed to do, and at the same time show that there were no harmful side effects from using the antibiotic product.

Thus, while they thought they could go through the Food and Drug Administration (FDA) for approval of a new cosmetic-type product, the Da-Roche executives discovered that they had actually created what was termed a new drug which had to be approved by the New Drug Division of the FDA.

Although the one active ingredient in Dapper-Diaper was neomycin sulfate, which had been known and widely used for about 15 years as one of a number of antibiotic products, the ingredient had never been mixed with water and other chemicals and placed in a pressurized spray can for sale over the counter. It appeared that it was due to the packaging and marketing plans for the new product, rather than its active ingredient, that it was declared a new drug, subject to FDA jurisdiction.

Consequently, what started out to be a new cosmetic product which would not have had to prove that it did any good as long as it did not do any harm, ended up being a new drug under FDA regulations. As a result, both the efficacy of the product and the absence of any harmful effects had to be proven to the satisfaction of the FDA committee of doctors. This effort required approximately four years and the expenditure of nearly $500,000 in testing costs alone.

Three basic steps had to be taken to get the required certification by the federal Food and Drug Administration. First, research of all the available literature was undertaken to see what kinds of problems should be researched in experimental situations. Animal testing (toxicity) was next conducted, including autopsy reports of white mice to be sure there were no harmful effects from continued use of the new product. The third step in the testing procedure involved clinical tests on infants using a placebo (the product minus the active ingredient) with double blind and double blind crossover techniques whereby aerosol spray cans labeled X and Y were tested both for safety and for efficacy. The doctors and nurses involved in these clinical observation studies did not know which cans contained the aqueous solution of neomycin sulfate and which contained the placebo, in order to ensure their objectivity throughout the duration of the study. Culture studies of diapers and the babies' skin were made and it was found that the bacteria which produced odor and diaper rash were gradually eradicated in the diaper with no effect on the resident flora (normal balance of bacteria) of the babies' skin.

Finally, at the end of four years, and after 30 visits to Washington and 25 label changes, the FDA approved Dapper-Diaper for over-the-counter sale. Since the machinery for producing the new antibiotic had been purchased and inspected about one and one-half years before the FDA approval had been received, Da-Roche was now able to begin production immediately.

Distribution

The original plan was to obtain distribution in Michigan and then use the capital generated by sales in this area to expand into adjacent markets. This plan was to be repeated until Dapper-Diaper was distributed throughout the United States. To obtain regional distribution as fast as possible, Da-Roche hired a broker's broker. This man had formerly sold to brokers and he was well acquainted with the food and drug brokers in Michigan and knew what it would take to get them to handle the company's product. The brokers, in turn, sold to large wholesale drug companies such as McKesson-Robbins and Hazeltine-Perkins, and to large grocers such as A&P, Kroger, Food Fair, and even to smaller "Mom and Pop" stores in some areas. The brokers also sold to some discount chains such as Kmart. It was felt that established brokers would be much more effective in bargaining with large accounts than salesmen from a new, unfamiliar company.

By March 1, the new product was on the market in many of these retail outlets, and a concerted effort was being made to get every drugstore in Michigan to carry the product as well. This objective was pursued by sending a free sample can of Dapper-Diaper to every major druggist in the state of Michigan. While this plan entailed giving away free more than 2,000 full-size cans of Dapper-Diaper, it also allowed Da-Roche to claim that its product could be found in every major drugstore in the state of Michigan. At the same time, it acquainted all of Michigan's druggists with the new product. By June, brokers had managed to obtain distribution in 80 per cent of the stores in eastern Michigan, but distribution in the western part of the state was much slower, with only about 20 per cent of the stores stocking Dapper-Diaper.

Pricing

It was estimated that if the same amount of neomycin as was contained in one 10-ounce can of Dapper-Diaper were to be bought by prescription, it would cost from $5 to $8. After talking with retailers, brokers, and doctors, it was decided that the "suggested retail price" of Dapper-Diaper would be $1.98. The Da-Roche executives, however, expected that it would sell for between $1.60 and $1.70 within four to six weeks after introduction. And, in fact, it was selling for $1.69 in Kroger and other supermarkets as of April 1. The product sold as low as $1.39 in some stores, and the average retail price was about $1.80.

Cost

The average retail price allowed the company enough margin to promote the product properly. The average retail price was about six times the cost of goods sold, which was normal for the drug industry. After discounts and allowances to wholesalers and retailers, the proceeds to the company were about $1 per can. Administrative and overhead costs were $100,000 per year exclusive of marketing costs.

Market Potential

In determining the size of the total market for Dapper-Diaper, Da-Roche executives first found out that there were approximately 8 million babies in diapers in the United States. (There were 350,000 babies in the company's initial marketing area.) A 10-ounce can of Dapper-Diaper was expected to last one month. Da-Roche executives reasoned that they would be able to get 10 per cent of the total market to use Dapper-Diaper, resulting in sales of 9.6 million cans per year.

Use of Personal Selling Through Ethical Channels to Get Intensive Distribution

The original strategy called for personal selling through five detail men. These men were to call on people in all medical professions to explain the benefits of the new product, how it was used, and where it could be obtained. In addition, small-size free samples were left with the doctor so he could recommend the product to a patient and be able to give her a 10-day supply of Dapper-Diaper as well.

Da-Roche's executives were immediately faced with the problem of how to get the detail men in to see a doctor, especially since they represented a new company with only one product. To solve this problem, the five detail men were each given an hourglass which was timed for three minutes. The detail men then went into the doctor's office and started the sand in motion, asking for three minutes of the doctor's time. Only the essential facts were given to the doctor in the three minutes, after which some free samples were distributed and the detail men attempted to leave. At this point, Da-Roche executives declared 9 out of 10 doctors asked for more information about Dapper-Diaper before the detail man could leave. The following points were made about the new baby product: It is certified by the federal Food and Drug Administration; it is an antibiotic; its active ingredient is neomycin; it is sold over the counter (no prescription needed); it is safe, because it is made from one of the most nearly perfect drugs known; and it is time saving, economical, easy to use, and it really works.

The use of detail men was selected over consumer advertising for the initial promotional job, because the Da-Roche executives believed that if the product was recommended by doctors, women would surely use Dapper-Diaper and tell their friends about it, too. This would give the new product the most desirable kind of promotion possible—word of mouth.

Another consideration which favored personal selling over consumer advertising was the fact that during the first week of February, when promotion of Dapper-Diaper by the company's detail men was first begun, distribution of the product was just beginning too. If consumer advertising had come in at the same time, the Da-Roche executives believed that much of it would have been wasted because the product was not yet available. It was felt that by April 1 this problem would be remedied and a consumer advertising campaign could be launched at this time. With only a limited amount of money available for advertising, it was important that distribution be achieved before the advertising commenced, in order that the advertising would not be wasted.

Dapper-Diaper Consumer Advertising Campaign

To be consistent with their intensive distribution policy within the introductory selling regions, the Da-Roche executives had planned a consumer advertising campaign which was to begin April 1. They believed that by waiting until April 1, they could be sure that Dapper-Diaper could be readily available to most stores by the time the consumer advertising campaign would begin. Discussion with brokers, people in the trade, and Da-Roche's agency, the La Vanway agency in Jackson, Michigan, resulted in an advertising budget of $50,000 for the first 13 weeks. After that time, advertising would be budgeted at 25 per cent of net sales. It was decided that to get maximum reach and frequency, the company should use 30-second and 60-second radio spots, with some 10-second IDs; IDs and 60-second spots on television, with some advertising in trade journals and newspapers.

In anticipation of the FDA's approval of the new use for Dapper-Diaper, which was expected in the near future, the company's advertising was based largely on the diaper and not exclusively on the narrower diaper pail use for which the product was currently certified by the FDA. A picture of a baby wearing a top hat, which appeared on the can, became known as "The Happy Baby" and was used in the company's introductory advertising campaign. All advertising carried the line, "Do your baby a favor, ask your baby's doctor."

Protection from Competition

It was hoped that eventually Dapper-Diaper would become almost a generic name, since it would be the first on the market and likely enjoy the status of being the only such product for at least one more year. This protection, it was felt, would be afforded by the patent which was pending on the new product, the trademark and copyrighted Dapper-Diaper name, and the fact that any competitor would have to do extensive testing of the type that took Da-Roche four years, in order to get its product approved by the FDA as a new drug.

Pursuing New Uses

While Da-Roche was still in the process of introducing Dapper-Diaper into its first region, which included all of Michigan and part of Ohio and Indiana, it was also engaged in more clinical testing. The product had received FDA approval only as a diaper pail spray. Knowing that it had no harmful effects on babies and that it would inhibit bacteria growth which caused ammonia burn or diaper rash, Da-Roche was seeking FDA approval to promote Dapper-Diaper as a diaper spray as well. For this new purpose the product would be sprayed on a clean diaper before it was to be worn by the baby. Much of the extensive testing which had already been conducted by Da-Roche indicated that when diapers were sprayed in the diaper pail, the diapers became clinically clean prior to washing and helped inhibit the growth of ammonia-producing bacteria, preventing odor and diaper rash.

Dr. J. D. Holst, M.D., Da-Roche's medical liaison with the FDA, explained that with the tests that had already been done, it would only require about six months of tests to return to the FDA requesting permission to use a broader label describing Dapper-Diaper as a diaper spray as well as a diaper pail spray. This additional use for the product could then be promoted by the company's detail men in talking to doctors and in the company's consumer advertising. Thus, while at the time of introduction Dapper-Diaper was only an antibiotic diaper pail spray which would limit the number of bacteria to control odor, its rash-prevention benefit was a by-product which the Da-Roche executives believed might soon become an equally important use for the new product.

Beyond the new use of Dapper-Diaper in controlling ammonia burn, the nature of the product itself and the way in which it worked suggested a variety of entirely new uses for which the new product might be equally well suited. The active ingredient, neomycin, was extremely effective in reducing or completely eliminating bacterial odor, and for this reason it might be used for eliminating all odors caused by organic decomposition. Examples would include a garbage pail or pet spray.

Consideration of a Full Baby-Product Line

Da-Roche executives also considered introducing companion products, such as baby powder and paper diapers, which would help better entrench the company as a producer of a more complete line of baby products and perhaps speed the translation of the brand name Dapper-Diaper into almost a generic concept. Another advantage would be that these companion products, as they were developed, could be promoted along with the Dapper-Diaper spray by the company's detail men as they called on doctors and left free samples and literature.

Results, April–December

The company ran into significant problems as Dapper-Diaper was being introduced. A batch of 180,000 three-ounce cans to be used as samples and distributed to doctors was not approved by the FDA. A change in the can design had resulted in valves which did not fit properly. The company therefore had to use trade cans for samples to distribute to the doctors, and, due to the greater cost of the full-size cans, a smaller number of samples was distributed.

After the product had been distributed to the retailers and had been on the shelf for a short period of time, problems with the full-size can became evident. Some of the ingredients in the product were interacting with the can, causing the can to rust. As the can rusted, the pressure in the aerosol leaked out, making it impossible to get the product out of the aerosol can. The company replaced bad cans, as they were found, with good ones, but then even the good ones turned bad. Finally, the source of the problem was discovered and a change in Dapper-Diaper's formulation had to be developed. Da-Roche then had to get FDA approval on the new formulation and on the new can. In effect, the company had to start all over.

The Present Situation

In December, the company finally received approval from the FDA to again begin marketing Dapper-Diaper. Da-Roche executives were now considering several alternative ways of marketing the product. First, they could follow exactly the same strategy that they followed with the initial launching of the product. This would entail both detail men and consumer advertising with distribution through drugstores, supermarkets, and discount stores.

A second alternative was to take a marketing approach similar to that used for ethical drugs. Thus, the company could use established outlets that do not require the high cost of familiarizing people with the product. Instead, detail men would be used to encourage doctors to recommend the product, and people would therefore become familiar with the product through their doctor's recommendation. This would eliminate the need for a significant amount of consumer advertising required to support a product which is to be distributed through supermarkets and discount stores.

Da-Roche's executives came upon a third alternative after reading an article in *Time* magazine. The article quoted the president of The American Diaper Service Association describing the smell of the diaper pail as diaper services' biggest single problem. The urea content of a new baby's urine is not very heavy, but as the baby gets older, the urea gets heavier. Therefore, after the baby becomes about three months old, the smell in the diaper pail significantly increases. Diaper services supply pails with neoprene bags, and therefore the diapers cannot be soaked. The diapers are usually picked up only once a week so there are 50 to 100 by that time. Mothers, therefore, began to buy diapers and wash them themselves three to four times per week.

The Associated Diaper Services of America and the other trade organization, The National Institute for Diaper Services, have members who make 83 million contacts per year where money changes hands. With the help of these two associations, Dapper-Diaper could be made known to millions of women through diaper service distributors. Da-Roche executives felt that either of the diaper services could sell 2 million cans per year with a minimum of effort. The company executives stated that Da-Roche would be very profitable at that volume.

Da-Roche executives had also made contact with a manufacturer of institutional clothing. This company sold very high-quality sleeping garments for babies and mentally retarded children in hospitals and training schools, and other garments for hospitals, penitentiaries, and other institutions. The manufacturer would distribute Dapper-Diaper along with his other products. As the institutions have a large problem with odor, Da-Roche's executives thought that this method of distribution would yield a large market.

Da-Roche executives were also considering one further alternative. A cosmetic broker—the best known in the country—with offices in Dallas, New York, and Chicago, had become interested in Dapper-Diaper. This broker employed over 100 people and distributed products of such well-known companies as Schick, Alberto-Culver, Revlon, and Tampax. The broker told Da-Roche's executives that if they could give him $1 million for advertising, he could guarantee them $3 million in sales with the company's present label (Dapper-Diaper had still not been approved for anything except use as a diaper pail spray).

Arizona Soccer Camp

In 1985, Ron Walters, Alan Meeder, and Steve Gay opened the Arizona Soccer Camp at Orme School in Orme, Arizona. In 1988, a second facility was opened at Cochise Community College. This new location is south of Tucson, near Douglas, Arizona. Since 1985, Steve Gay has removed himself from the partnership, leaving Meeder and Walters to make critical decisions about the product, price, place, and promotion of the Arizona Soccer Camp. Presently, a new situation faces Meeder and Walters. Changes have occurred in the public's enthusiasm toward soccer and in the types of life-styles pursued. Competition has increased, the profile of the Arizona soccer camper has changed in many respects, and the financial status of the Arizona Soccer Camp has reflected these changes. Meeder and Walters feel that a total reassessment of the camp's environment is necessary to determine the future directions of the camp.

Changes in Soccer Enthusiasm

Soccer has become the world's most popular sport. Recent articles have estimated that more than two billion people watched the 1986 World Cup on television. To the international media, the World Cup soccer playoffs are equivalent to the Olympics, and multinational firms have been quick to obtain marketing rights in anticipation of the World Cup profits. Marketing rights give a company in a particular field the exclusive right to the promotion of a product, trademark, or intangible within a certain medium and for a particular event.

Despite international fervor, however, professional soccer in America is struggling. Fan support is low and many teams are going bankrupt. The 1980s saw the demise of the North American Soccer League, and the Major Indoor Soccer League has been reduced to eight teams. The situation has been called a "depression," with two hundred professional players unemployed at the start of the year.

One reason for pro soccer's demise is the changing consumption patterns in the United States. The *Federal Reserve Bulletin* shows that discretionary income, stated in 1979 dollars, has increased by $142 billion in the past five years. However, there seems to have been a change in the consumption patterns of many consumers. Consumers have become less willing to part with their hard-earned dollars. Furthermore, ticket prices have increased to meet rising costs. Examples of these costs include player acquisitions, player salaries and operating expenses such as transportation costs.

Despite the decrease in fan support for professional soccer, amateur soccer has increased in popularity in America. A recent article, "New Recruits for the Most Popular Sport," (*Fortune*) reported that amateur soccer is the fastest-growing team sport in this country. This increased interest in amateur soccer can be seen at all age levels.

Evidence indicates that soccer participation is high among youths. For example, the article pointed out that Dallas youths are playing more soccer than baseball

This case was prepared by Richard F. Beltramini, associate professor of marketing and advertising, and John Schlacter, professor of marketing, both at Arizona State University, and Nancy De Rogatis, research assistant, as a basis for class discussion rather than to illustrate either effective or ineffective handling of an administration situation. Certain dates and facts have been slightly altered for the sake of case development. Copyright Richard F. Beltramini, 1989.

and football combined. Twenty years ago, in New York, the Long Island Junior Soccer League was founded; currently more than 100,000 youths actively participate in its leagues.

On the college level, the National Collegiate Athletic Association has announced that currently more colleges have varsity soccer teams than football teams. Soccer clubs are also prevalent on most college campuses.

Adults are also becoming active soccer participants. The Parks and Recreation Department in Mesa, Arizona, has three soccer leagues. The Arizona State Adult Men's Soccer League has a total of sixty participants. The Coed League has twelve teams of fifteen players each, and the Men's League consists of eight teams of fifteen players each. In total, there are 360 participating adults. Soccer participation has grown steadily in Mesa and the Parks and Recreation Department anticipates adding more soccer fields to its facilities within the next five years.

The U.S. Soccer Federation (USSF) is the United States division of the Federation International Football Association. This organization consists of both pro and amateur soccer players of all ages. The USSF sets the rules of soccer in America. All soccer players in America are encouraged to register as members, and the USSF, headquartered in New York, reports that registrations have been growing by 20 per cent a year for the past several years.

Changes in Life-Styles

Life-style is a common reason why most residents are attracted to Arizona. Exhibit 1 shows that the sports participation and outdoor enthusiast categories ranked high among all categories from the Western Savings *Foresight Eighty* survey of

**Exhibit 1   Arizona Soccer Camp
Life-Styles in Maricopa County**

	Metro Total	Glendale	Phoenix	Tempe	Mesa	Scottsdale	Sun City
Population	1,650,400	122,400	904,700	130,400	317,000	123,000	52,900
Occupied Households	597,500	42,200	328,700	45,300	107,200	45,100	29,000
*Lifestyles**							
Socially active	45%	47%	42%	56%	40%	56%	
Family oriented	42	58	39	57	43	42	
Church oriented	41	38	37	44	48	40	
Outdoor enthusiast	38	47	38	46	39	38	
Sports participant	37	39	32	56	38	48	
Sports fan	34	37	22	49	29	43	
Arts involved	16	10	15	27	11	25	
Entertainment	13	10	13	26	10	14	
Civically involved	10			10		14	

*Sixty activity and attitude questions in the study were grouped to form ten life-style categories. The level of participation or agreement with a concept within each life-style category determined whether that household was placed in a particular life-style. With this method, some households may be in more than one group.

Source: Western Savings & Loan Association, *Foresight Eighty*.

Activity	Per Cent	No. of Adults	Median Age
Bicycling	45%	505,400	35.5
Racquetball	19	208,400	29.0
Swimming	69	776,200	34.4
Running/Jogging	32	354,100	31.0
Amateur Sports Event	31	340,800	34.2
Professional Sports Event	26	295,500	36.1

Source: Phoenix Newspaper, Inc., *Inside Phoenix.*

the Phoenix Metropolitan Statistical Areas sampled. This report indicated that a large segment of the Scottsdale population is very sports oriented, with over 20,000 of these households reporting themselves as sports participants. More than 25,000 of the Tempe households reported that they lead life-styles heavily involved in family, sports, and social activities. These figures decline somewhat for residents in the central city of Phoenix. Still, a high proportion of these residents consider themselves to be outdoor enthusiasts. Thirty-eight per cent of the Mesa residents surveyed reported life-styles that are heavily involved in sports participation. Almost 50 per cent of the Glendale residents surveyed categorized themselves as outdoor enthusiasts. Thirty-nine per cent are sports participants; 37 per cent are sports fans.

The fact that a large number of Phoenix area residents' leisure activities are recreational in nature is supported by another study. The Phoenix Newspaper, Inc., *Inside Phoenix 1989* report noted that 69 per cent of those households surveyed reported swimming as a leisure activity in which they have participated within the last twelve months. Exhibit 2 shows that 45 per cent indicated that they had been bicycling and 32 per cent indicated that they had been jogging. Very vigorous sports such as racquetball were most popular with younger adults. These figures indicate that a large proportion of Phoenix area residents enjoy and participate in outdoor activities.

Changes in Competition

When Meeder and Walters originally assessed the external environment in 1985, the soccer camp market had been untapped. At that time, no soccer boarding camps were in existence in Arizona, and only one soccer day camp was operating. Since 1985, both direct and indirect competition have increased considerably. Although the Arizona Soccer Camp is the only soccer boarding camp in the area, several day camps have begun operations. Boarding camps provide sleeping arrangements for campers, while day camps do not. Both types of soccer camps can be considered as directly competing in that both provide training to improve soccer skills.

The Phoenix Infernos are a professional soccer team in Phoenix, Arizona, whose Soccer Camp '89 boasted 960 participants in the twenty-four sessions. These three-hour, one-week sessions were conducted in the morning and the afternoon. Both boys and girls could participate and both advanced and beginning sessions were offered. This camp distinguished itself by offering soccer balls, T-shirts, autographed bumper stickers, camp attendance certificates, and $25.00 discounts on Inferno season tickets to all camp participants. The total cost for each one-week session was $85.00. There were ten players to every Inferno coach, with four coaches available at all times. The one-week session consisted of three hours each day, in either the morning or afternoon.

Phoenix Inferno players also coach at competing youth soccer camps. The co-sponsored Arizona State University and Tempe Soccer Club 1989 Clinics are one such example. Phoenix Inferno players were heavily advertised and helped the camp to draw one hundred and fifty youths. Two clinics were offered, with each lasting four hours each day for a week. A $100.00 cost included all instruction plus lunches for each participant.

A third competitor is the Tucson Pro Soccer Camp, located in Tucson, Arizona. It has been operating for three years. Because of its location, this camp directly competes with Meeder and Walters' camp at Cochise College. The Tucson camp is headed by Wolfgang Weber, head coach for the Arizona Youth Soccer Association, and features half-day instruction for five days at a cost of $50.00 per player. The number of sessions has varied from year to year, as have the camp sites, but Weber advertises one coach for every ten players and a sixty-space limit for each week. In 1989, Weber offered three sessions, with one week devoted entirely to girls. The "girls' only" session was a first for the Tucson Pro Soccer Camp, but with a turnout of fifty girls, Weber plans to continue this session in 1990. Although all other sessions have been coeducational, Weber reports that each year 90 per cent of the players have been boys and that the majority of the players have been between the ages of eight and eleven. Boys and girls between the ages of seven and seventeen are eligible to attend the camp. The Tucson Pro Soccer Camp does not offer different skill-level sessions, but does group the children according to skill level, size, and age on the first day of each session. Weber feels that there is a good market to support an expansion. He reached this conclusion after participating as a soccer coach in the 1989 Arizona State University Soccer Camp. Weber's camp directly competes with the Arizona Soccer Camp.

The Arizona Soccer Camp indirectly competes with other youth programs that do not emphasize soccer. The Tempe YMCA, located in Tempe, Arizona, is one example of the various programs that are available for youths. This YMCA offers two summer camps. One of these is located in Mayer, Arizona. It emphasizes horseback riding and arts and crafts for twelve- to fifteen-year-olds. A second camp is located in Prescott, Arizona. Eight- to thirteen-year-olds are encouraged to attend this camp. Swimming, arts and crafts, riflery, and horseback riding are the planned activities for these campers. A fee of $135.00 covers all expenses for seven days at either camp. Transportation by bus is provided to all campers at no extra charge.

The summer program offered by the Phoenix Parks and Recreation Department is another type of opportunity available to youths. Special summer courses, ranging from acting to swimming to dancercize, are available for all ages. The price for most courses is under $30.00. Courses are scheduled for one hour each day, three days a week for eight weeks. There is usually one teacher for every ten students. Courses are available in the afternoons and evenings.

These examples indicate that both direct and indirect competition are present. Meeder and Walters must consider this fact when determining the future direction of the Arizona Soccer Camp.

Exhibit 3   Arizona Soccer Camp
Youths in Arizona

Age	Arizona	Maricopa County	Yavapai County
7–9	130,313	69,639	2,655
10–13	174,898	94,254	3,760
14	44,675	23,969	989
15	47,962	25,926	1,055
16	49,303	26,596	1,156

Source: Summary Data, Census of Population.

Changes in Youth Soccer Participants

The *Summary Data of the Census Population* shows that there are 447,141 youths in Arizona between the ages of seven and sixteen (see Exhibit 3). It is estimated that 50,000 youths in Arizona are soccer players. This number has doubled from 25,000 soccer players in 1985. The Arizona Youth Soccer Association (AYSA) is the largest youth soccer organization in the state, with 25,000 registered players in 1989. AYSA President Kay Seuss feels that their organization is representative of the youth soccer population. She says that the popularity of soccer among youths has grown tremendously in the past five years but sees a declining interest in the game.

Soccer's growth rate among youths in Arizona has slowed since 1987. The market may be saturated, but I really feel that economic conditions have caused the decline in our registrations. Parents have become less willing to spend their dollars on a soccer program for their children.

AYSA has registered approximately 50 per cent of all Arizona youth soccer players each year (see Exhibit 4), and they have consistently found the largest age group to be ten- to thirteen-year-olds. Three-quarters of all participants each year have been boys and Seuss feels this is representative of the total Arizona youth soccer population. The majority of all registrations are from the Phoenix

Exhibit 4   Arizona Soccer Camp
Number of Youths Playing Soccer

Year	Estimated No. of Youth Soccer Players	AYSA Registrations in Arizona	AYSA Registrations in Maricopa County
1985	20,000	10,000	4,000
1986	30,000	15,000	7,000
1987	40,000	18,000	9,000
1988	45,000	22,000	12,000
1989	50,000	25,000	14,000

Source: Kay Seuss, President of Arizona Youths Soccer Association; interview.

Exhibit 5   Arizona Soccer Camp Participant Characteristics

Year	Total No. of Children	Total No. of Boys	Total No. of Girls	Total No. of Returning Boys	Total No. of Returning Girls	No. of Campers with Basic Skills	No. of Campers with Advanced Skills	No. of Campers with Very Advanced Skills
1985	112	112	0	12	0	112	0	0
1986	255	255	0	70	0	255	0	0
1987	432	382	50	160	0	277	155	0
1988	551	481	70	125	25	396	155	0
1989	603	546	57	125	23	363	185	55

Source: Company records.

metropolitan area, with the largest percentage of these coming from northwest Phoenix. Seuss cites a larger youth population in this area as the explanation for this phenomenon. Strong soccer participation can also be found in the Tucson and Sierra Vista areas.

Changes in Arizona Soccer Camp Participants

The type of participant attracted to the Arizona Soccer Camp has changed throughout the years. These changes are illustrated in Exhibit 5. As can be noted from these statistics, no advanced skill sessions were offered to boys until 1987. These sessions have been sold out every year since that time. Fifty girls were attracted to the first coeducational session in 1987. In 1988, the number increased, but in 1989, fewer girls attended the sessions. Advanced skill sessions were offered to girls in 1989 and thirty-five enrolled.

With the introduction of both girls and boys advanced sessions and a boys very advanced (select) session, the number of participants in the basic skills level declined. The statistics indicate a possible trend toward a growing demand for advanced sessions and slowing demand for fundamental sessions.

Meeder and Walters recommend that all first-time campers enroll in the beginning skills session. Those who have already attended this session and who are between the ages of ten to sixteen are placed in the advanced session. Male soccer enthusiasts who have completed the advanced session and are between eleven and seventeen years old may enroll in the boys' select session. Exceptions are made when coaches recommend that a youth be placed at a particular skill level. Walters notes that campers usually cooperate with this system, "Campers want to enroll at the right skills level so that they can participate on a competitive basis with the other kids."

Throughout the years, skill level has been closely related to the age of the participant. For those with basic skills, 50 per cent of the campers have traditionally been between the ages of eight to ten years. Most predominant in the advanced skill sessions have been the twelve-year-olds. Thirteen- to sixteen-year-olds were most often found enrolling in the select session in 1989.

**Exhibit 6   Arizona Soccer Camp
Changes in Variable Costs**

Year	Cost per Counselor	Cost per Coach	Cost per Nurse
1985	$ 0.00	$125.00	$100.00
1986	0.00	150.00	100.00
1987	78.00	200.00	300.00
1988	78.00	275.00	300.00
1989	100.00	350.00	300.00

Source: Company records.

Financial Changes

Financial expenses have increased since the camp first opened in 1985. Fortunately, these increases and the inflation rate have been offset by the growing number of children attending the camp each year.

Examining the variable cost for the Arizona Soccer Camp, one sees that the cost-per-coach for one week has increased from $125.00 in 1985 to $350.00 in 1989. The cost of one nurse has increased from $100.00 in the first year of camp operations to $300.00 in 1989. Meeder and Walters offered to pay all expenses for counselors in 1987 but incurred an additional expense in 1989 when they agreed to let the children of counselors attend the camp at no charge. Exhibit 6 shows a year-by-year progression of the variable payroll costs.

Fixed costs have also increased throughout the years. While rental costs have averaged a 10 per cent increase each year, Cochise College facilities have consistently remained $10.00 per child—less expensive than the facilities at Orme School. Insurance has increased by 1 per cent each year and advertising has increased approximately 5 per cent each year. Legal and accounting services have increased in cost to $900.00 in 1989. The previous cost for these services was $500.00. Office and video expenses have remained constant. Video expenses include the cassettes, equipment, and processing costs associated with taping scrimmages at the camp.

Profits declined sharply from 1986 to 1987. The graph in Exhibit 7 shows that profits remained stable in 1988 but have recently turned upward.

**Exhibit 7   Arizona Soccer Camp
Profit/Loss for the Arizona Soccer Camp**

Year	Profit/Loss
1985	(2,626)
1986	4,365
1987	12,457
1988	11,650
1989	14,500

Source: Company records.

In the near future, Meeder and Walters are considering hiring an independent consultant to handle the marketing and promotion of their product. It is anticipated that $500 a month will pay for the salary and promotional materials of this consultant. How this money will be allocated has not been determined. Meeder and Walters are currently faced with the problem of financing this expenditure, as there is no reserve fund. Immediate cash flow may be generated through preregistration, or Meeder and Walters may tap their personal funds until the regular registration period, when cash flow improves. It is hoped that the increased revenue from greater promotion will more than offset the cost and expenses of the consultant. Should this not occur, Meeder and Walters' profits may decline again in 1990.

Throughout the years, modifications have been made in the product, price, place, and promotional strategy for the Arizona Soccer Camp. Meeder and Walters feel they must reassess these decisions as they look toward new developments and question their future directions.

The Product and Responses to Change

Meeder and Walters realize that their product offering has many attributes, but they are in disagreement as to the salient features relative to their markets served. Meeder believes that they are marketing soccer skills, improvement, and quality instructors. Walters believes that their product is a vacation for the parents away from the children, a social camp experience for youths, and high-quality sports competition. Meeder and Walters realize that they must decide on the most relevant product attributes for the target markets they select.

The daily camp schedule reveals both social and competitive skill aspects of the camp. Considerable free time is scheduled each day for the participants. Friendships that develop on the soccer field may become closer during free recreational periods. The majority of the day, however, is devoted to sports competition in the form of soccer scrimmages and skill drills. The daily format for the Arizona Soccer Camp has not been changed since 1985 because Meeder and Walters have found the schedule well liked by all campers.

One component of the schedule that has changed considerably since 1985 is the soccer skills sessions. Boys' fundamental sessions were the only sessions available until 1987, at which time an experimental boys' advanced session was organized. In this same year, a coeducational course was also offered. In 1989, both an advanced girls and boys' select session were added. Exhibit 8 indicates

**Exhibit 8   Arizona Soccer Camp
Types of Sessions Offered**

Year	Coed Fundamental Sessions	All Boys Fundamental Sessions	Boys Advanced Sessions	Girls Advanced Sessions	Boys Select Sessions
1985		X			
1986		X			
1987	X	X	X		
1988	X	X	X	X	X

Source: Company records.

the years when specific sessions were offered. It can be seen that the Arizona Soccer Camp has become somewhat more diversified in recent years.

Another part of the Arizona Soccer Camp's product offering is the quality of the instructors. Meeder and Walters emphasize the teaching aspect of their camp and therefore prefer to employ coaches and professional players with teaching experience. This is another aspect of the product that has not changed since the camp began operations in 1985 and 1987.

Expansions in Camp Locations

In 1985, the Arizona Soccer Camp ran a one week session at Orme School. Since that time, both the number of sessions offered and the number of camp locations have been expanding.

Orme School

Orme School is a private boarding school located about ninety miles north of Phoenix. Located on a 40,000-acre ranch, its facilities include five soccer fields, a recreational room, and a swimming pool. This facility accommodates 150 campers at one time. Because the cooks at Orme School live on the premises throughout the year, they have been providing meals each summer for the campers. The cost of the meals has been included in the rental fee for the facilities. Meeder and Walters have been renting this facility for three weeks each summer for the last three years. In 1986, the facilities were rented for two weeks; in 1985, one week was rented at Orme School. Meeder and Walters are contemplating renting five weeks for Summer 1990. Orme School has been most successful in attracting campers from Maricopa County and especially from the Phoenix metropolitan area. Exhibit 9 indicates that more children are currently being attracted from Tempe and Scottsdale than in the past, while the opposite pattern exists for Phoenix and Glendale participants.

Cochise College

Cochise College is located southeast of Phoenix near Douglas, Arizona. Its facilities include three soccer fields, an Olympic size pool, modern dorms, and a

Exhibit 9   Arizona Soccer Camp (B)
Profile on Campers Attending Orme School

Year	% of Campers from Phoenix, Glendale	% of Campers from Tempe, Scottsdale, Mesa, Chandler	% of Campers from Other Areas
1985	80%	10%	10%
1986	80	10	10
1987	80	10	10
1988	70	20	10
1989	60	30	10

Source: Company records.

Exhibit 10   Arizona Soccer Camp (B)
Profile on Campers Attending Cochise College

Year	% of Campers from Tucson	% of Campers from Douglas, Sierra Vista, New Mexico	% of Campers from Phoenix Area
1988	80%	10%	10%
1989	80	10	10

Source: Company records.

large gym where indoor soccer can be played. This facility can accommodate one
hundred and ten campers at one time. Meeder and Walters have been renting
these facilities for three weeks each summer for the past two years. Of the 220
campers to attend Cochise in 1989, 80 per cent were from Tucson (see Exhibit
10). The remainder of the children came from Phoenix and Sierra Vista areas.
Some children were attracted from New Mexico. Although fairly close for Tucson
and Sierra Vista residents, Cochise College is a five-hour drive for Phoenix residents. To promote this location with Phoenix residents, Meeder and Walters are
considering developing a new marketing strategy. If enough campers are interested, a bus will be chartered in 1990 to transport campers from Phoenix to
Cochise. One concern is that this convenience may draw campers from the Orme
School facility. If this were to occur, Meeder and Walters may defeat their original
purpose of attracting new campers. However, since the rent at Cochise is $10.00
per child less expensive, Meeder and Walters might enjoy a greater profit margin
at this camp site. Since Cochise College has expressed a willingness to rent more
weeks to the Arizona Soccer Camp, it might be very profitable to entice potential
Orme School campers to Cochise.

Sedona

Meeder and Walters have recently been presented with the opportunity to purchase forty acres of land directly adjacent to and currently owned by the Valley
Verde School, a private school in Sedona, Arizona. The expectation would be that
a portion of the acreage could be developed into a permanent site for the Arizona
Soccer Camp. The camp would require twenty acres of this land. There are several
investment options available to Meeder and Walters. They could buy all forty
acres, develop them, and then sell off the land they do not need, or others could
invest in and develop the land, after which time Meeder and Walters could buy
the needed twenty acres. The latter would require an initial investment of
$80,000.00. While the site is being constructed, the current Valley Verde facilities
could be rented. However, Valley Verde does not have a swimming pool or soccer
fields. To return their original investment in the land, Meeder and Walters would
have to operate the camp for ten to twelve weeks each summer for several years,
in addition to the current weeks of operation at Cochise and Orme School. Walters
and Meeder are concerned that the present population will not support this
investment.

Exhibit 11   Arizona Soccer Camp (B)
Direct-Mail Promotional Program

Year	No. of Brochures Printed	No. of Newsletters	% of Preregistrations	Costs for All Printing
1985	3,000	125	30%	$1,400.00
1986	3,000	275	30	1,600.00
1987	3,000	450	30	1,800.00
1988	3,000	575	30	1,800.00
1989	3,000	625	30	2,500.00

Source: Company records.

Promotional Programs

Since its inception five years ago, the Arizona Soccer Camp has conducted a series of promotional programs. Direct mail has been utilized each year to inform and interest potential campers. As shown in Exhibit 11, approximately three thousand brochures have been printed and mailed each year. Registration materials have been included in the direct-mail package for convenience. As an incentive, the Arizona Soccer Camp has offered a free camp picture to all campers who make their full tuition payments during preregistration. Thirty per cent of the campers each year take advantage of this offer.

Ron Walters has been responsible for generating mailing lists for the direct-mail campaign. In 1985 and again in 1986, he secured the Tempe YMCA and West Town Soccer Club mailing lists. By the end of 1989, Walters had mailing lists accounting for the names of 30,000 soccer enthusiasts; however, whenever possible, Walters delivers the brochures directly to the clubs to decrease mailing costs. These clubs include the Rose Land Soccer Club in Phoenix, the Moon Valley Soccer Club in Phoenix, the Arcadia Soccer Club in Phoenix, the Tempe YMCA, and the West Town Soccer Club in Glendale, Arizona. Walters feels additional sources may still be available. A bulk mailing permit has been used to mail brochures at ten cents each.

In addition to the brochure, the Arizona Soccer Camp has sent out newsletters to returning campers. The purpose of the newsletter is to further promote the

Arizona Soccer Camp (B)
Mailing Costs for Newsletters

Year	No. of Newsletters Mailed	Total Cost for Mailing
1985	112	$ 1.80
1986	255	10.50
1987	432	31.50
1988	551	35.10
1989	603	36.40

Source: Company records.

**Exhibit 13   Arizona Soccer Camp (B)
Promotional Budget**

Year	Budget
1985	$1,390.00
1986	2,825.00
1987	3,655.00
1988	3,830.00
1989	3,865.00

Source: Company records.

Arizona Soccer Camp and to inform past campers about the recent accomplishments of their coaches. The newsletter is mailed in the fall of each year. It is sent by first class mail. The cost associated with this mailing is shown in Exhibit 12.

During the summer of 1989, Club Med and the Arizona Soccer Camp co-sponsored the First Annual Skills Contest and Drawing. The two grand prizes were free vacations for the entire families of the winners. The vacations included air transportation from Phoenix, accommodations, meals, entertainment, and various sports activities at Club Med's newest resort location in Ixtapa, Mexico. A special feature was that the vacation package included soccer coaching in Ixtapa by two Phoenix Inferno soccer players. The vacation package was offered to all Arizona Soccer families at a total cost of $527.00 per child twelve years and under and $708.00 per adult.

The promotional budget for each year can be seen in Exhibit 13. The categories of advertising, postage, and office expense make up the promotional budget. The advertising and office expense allocations must cover all printing and artwork costs for the brochures and newsletters. Because direct mail is expensive, Meeder, and Walters have been questioning its effectiveness.

As Meeder and Walters consider the future they are faced with a number of questions:

1. What markets should be targeted and what is the potential of these markets?
2. What attributes of the offering are most important to each of the defined target markets, and how does the Arizona Soccer Camp rate on these attributes relative to the competition?
3. Should the Arizona Soccer Camp seek a single, permanent location? Should it seek ownership or continue renting facilities at Cochise and Orme? Is some combination of the above feasible?
4. How can the Arizona Soccer Camp promote to its markets most effectively and efficiently? What should be its message?
5. What is an appropriate pricing strategy, given the nature of the camp's competition and its present cost structure?
6. Where do additional marketing opportunities lie?

Jupiter Computers

Background Information

In the spring of 1988, Harley and Sue Hanson purchased a personal computer dealership that is authorized to sell the Jupiter line of personal computers. Jupiter is a competitively priced, domestic brand that commands approximately 20 per cent of its targeted market. Under their stewardship, the dealership's sales of the Jupiter line, and in particular, the Jupiter "Probe" series, which uses the powerful 386 chip, have been steady, and about where the Hansons forecast them to be when they took over the franchise.

Marketing Information

Jupiter sales have been about equally divided between individuals and businesses. To date, only about a dozen sales transactions with businesses have involved multiple units. All of these have been made on a negotiated basis, mostly to small businesses such as insurance agents, real estate agents, and larger restaurants. Thus, the Hansons have no experience with selling under conditions of competitive bidding. As a result, the Hansons are somewhat unsure as to how best to proceed as they approach their first opportunity to win business via the competitive bid. Their problem is how to respond to an invitation by the City Board of Education to bid on the board's requirement of 100 personal computers for use in the city's three high schools.

The Competition

There are five competitors who are nearly certain to respond to the bid invitation. One of these is a unit of a nationally franchised computer sales organization. Another is a unit of a chain owned by a major computer company. The other three known likely bidders are independent computer stores who act as PC brokers for a variety of companies.

Financial Information

As Sue and Harley prepare the bid they will submit to the Board of Education, they turn first to data that Sue, who handles the accounting function for the business, has assembled on recent sales of the Jupiter Probe model. This is the product they feel best meets the requirements defined in the school board's invitation to bid. The essence of these data are shown in Table 1. As shown there, the Hansons calculate a total average computer cost of $2,940.00. The $150.00 of fixed overhead is the customary charge that the Hansons have been using

This case was prepared by Nabil Hassan and Herbert E. Brown, Wright State University, Dayton, Ohio, and is intended to be used as a basis for class discussion rather than to illustrate either effective or ineffective handling of the situation.

Presented and accepted by the refereed Midwest Society For Case Research. All rights reserved to the authors and the Midwest Society for Case Research. Copyrighted © 1989 by Nabil Hassan and Herbert E. Brown.

Table 1

Average Realized List Price	$3,200
Cost allocated to normal sale:	
Dealer cost from manufacturer	$2,500
Fixed overhead	150
Shipping costs from manufacturer	100
Preparation charges	50
Sales commission	5%

since opening the store. Because the 100 computers would be a special sale, no sales commission will have to be paid. Thus, Jupiter's apparent total out-the-door costs of a standard Probe computer was $2,800. This number does not include any profit.

As she worked up these numbers, Sue was unsure as to how to decide which costs should be included and which should not. So she turned to an accounting book where she read the following:

In order to determine the price of a product, all manufacturing costs (direct materials, direct labor, and manufacturing overhead) and all nonmanufacturing expenses (administrative, financial, marketing, and R&D expenses) should be included in the total costs, to which a markup percentage is added. These costs, whether they are fixed or variable, should be considered (included) in determining the final selling price.

Business firms use several different formulas in determining their markup on costs. Among these are

1. $\text{MU\%} = \dfrac{\text{Target Profit}}{\text{Total Manufacturing and Nonmanufacturing Exp}}$

2. $\text{MU\%} = \dfrac{\text{Target Profit} + \text{Total Administrative, Financial and Research and Development Expenses}}{\text{Total Cost of Material, Labor and Overhead}}$

3. $\text{MU\%} = \dfrac{\text{Target Profit} + (\text{Total Fixed Manufacturing Costs}) + (\text{Total Administrative, Financial and Research and Development Expense})}{\text{Total Variable Manufacturing Cost} + (\text{Total Variable, Administrative, Financial, Marketing and Research and Development Costs})}$

All manufacturing costs (direct materials, direct labor, and overhead) are included in the product costs (whether they are variable or fixed)

All nonmanufacturing expenses (administrative, financial, marketing, and R&D, whether variable or fixed) are included in the determination of targeted markup profit.

The Proposal

Harley and Sue believe that they need to submit a bid for the computers at more than the $2,800 unit cost in order to earn a profit on the contract, should they win the bid. They would like a $150 profit on the sale of each computer. However, they suspect that a bid of more than $280,000 will not be low enough to be successful.

In view of this, the Hanson's begin to think seriously about making a "buy-in" bid. A buy-in bid involves bidding low with full recognition that the result be low profit, and possibly, no profit, or even a loss of money, on the bid sale, with a plan to make money on later follow-on business. The more they think about this idea the more certain they feel that if they win the bid, the follow-on business from the high school will be substantial and profitable. Harley had heard in fact that the average revenue from a buyer of a personal computer was approximately 38 per cent of the price of the computer over the first 36 months. Approximately 30 per cent of this 38 per cent follow-on revenue was thought to come in during the first year after the sale, 40 per cent during the second, and 20 per cent during the third. Harley's information also suggested that the average markup-on-cost on the merchandise this revenue represented was usually about 100 per cent.

The Hansons also reasoned that the area high schoolers who learn on computers supplied by the Hansons might also represent a major source of future revenue. Though it was pure speculation, because they could find no data concerning the issue, the Hansons felt that if they put together the proper type of follow-on marketing program to the high school's seniors, they should be able to sell, at approximately $25 per unit selling cost, at least 75 special "go-to-college" Probe personal computers to senior class members in each of the next five years. The Hansons' purchase cost of these computers was estimated to be $350. They planned to sell them for $750. These sales were sales the Hansons felt they wouldn't be able to make without the presence of the more expensive Probe line in the school, which in turn, depended on success on the bid proposal they were considering.

This is the school's first major request for bids on personal computers. In the past, PCs have been bought one at a time. Furthermore, many of the school's current inventory of PCs represent gifts from individuals and businesses who are friends of the school. Competitive bidding is a very familiar process to the purchasing arm of the school. However, there is evidence that the personnel in the school feel very unsure of themselves where computers are concerned and fear making a major mistake with this purchase. They are very much under the gun, so to speak, to hold the cost of the district's education program down to the very lowest level. They are also sure that the competitors will be very interested in who gets the bid, and in all likelihood will publicly challenge the board's decision if the sale does not go to the lowest bidder.

The Hansons look to you for advice on the what and the whys of what they should do.

Butterick Fashion Marketing Company

Butterick Fashion Marketing Company's sales of See & Sew, a new product, were higher than expected, but total company and industry sales continued to decrease. Mr. John Dodson, a Butterick sales manager, felt better understanding of product demand was needed to aid both corporate and sales planning.

Company Operations, History, and Marketing Development

The Butterick Fashion Marketing Company made and distributed home sewing patterns. Its product line consisted of Butterick patterns, Vogue patterns, and See & Sew patterns. Three companies dominated the industry—Butterick, Simplicity, and McCall's.

One evening in 1863 in Sterling, Massachusetts, Ellen Butterick remarked to Ebenezer, her husband, that her sewing projects would be easier if she had patterns to go by. Ebenezer, a tailor and inventor, soon began publishing practical and fashionable pattern designs, and by spring he was selling graded paper patterns in boxes of 100. The boxes sold at $10 wholesale and $25 retail. In 1864 he opened a New York City sales office. Pattern sales continued to increase, keeping pace with the then new acceptance of home sewing machines. By 1868 the pattern package consisted of the tissue pieces folded together in a neat rectangular package somewhat smaller than today's pattern envelope. The label carried the picture, some simple directions without diagrams, the price, and other pertinent data.

Butterick went into partnership with two other men in 1867 under the name Butterick & Company. The same year the first issue of *The Ladies' Quarterly Report of Broadway Fashions* appeared, the earliest of many Butterick magazines aimed to serve specific markets.

Butterick expanded to 100 offices and 1,000 agencies throughout the United States and Canada and in 1876 opened offices in London, Vienna, and Paris. In 1905 Butterick erected a sixteen-story building in Manhattan, which is still the company's headquarters.

For years Butterick practiced selective distribution, offering its products in certain department and dry goods stores and refusing to sell in variety stores. This provided an opportunity for competitors, and other pattern companies entered the market (Simplicity was among them) offering good products at slightly lower prices. Simplicity and the others first offered their lines in variety stores, then entered department stores.

The Great Depression left its mark on Butterick. By the early 1940s the company was almost bankrupt. It owed the Paragon Press more money than it had in assets. A retired banker, Leonard Tingle, bought the company for about ten cents on the dollar.

The World War II years, 1941 through 1945, were good for the industry. Limited selections of fashion merchandise in the stores caused more and more women

This case is reprinted from *Cases in Marketing* by Richard R. Still and Thomas H. Stevenson (Englewood Cliffs, N.J.: Prentice-Hall, 1985) with the permission of the authors.

to turn to home sewing. But Butterick did not benefit as much as Simplicity. Simplicity was able to receive larger allotments of supplies due to its resources, and from then on Simplicity led the industry.

Butterick's strategy during the 1950s was to have a strong sales force to gain distribution in the many independent fabric shops emerging nationwide and to gain a foothold in the new suburban shopping center department stores. In 1958 Butterick tried to penetrate the variety store market, having developed a revolving rack with 112 styles, in all sizes. The rack gave variety stores the chance to sell patterns without maintaining a large pattern inventory and to receive the costly support publications (counter catalogs, *Fashion News*). For the first time in many years, Butterick's market share reached 12 per cent. This was considered to be a turning point for the company. Meanwhile, Simplicity signed up the J. C. Penney and W. T. Grant accounts, two of the largest fabric retailers.

In the 1960s Butterick developed a small selection of styles for supermarkets, for sale through wholesalers with in-store maintenance programs. The fixture featured fashion and sewing notions. The program peaked with distribution in 10,000 stores and over $1.2 million in annual sales but rack fixtures in supermarkets were short-lived, and the program diminished in value each year.

Harry Howard, a Wharton M.B.A. and Leonard Tingle's son-in-law, became president in the mid-1950s. Recognizing a good opportunity, he approached Condé Nast, publisher of *Vogue* and other magazines, and suggested that Condé Nast's *Vogue* pattern be added to Butterick's product line. Condé Nast could not continue to make *Vogue* patterns, as production was too costly for the limited distribution, so it sold to Butterick.

In 1968 American Can Company bought Butterick and named the company Butterick Fashion Marketing Company. *Vogue, Glamour,* and American Can's capital enhanced the Butterick image as never before.

Two important things happened in the 1970s—the development of polyester knits and the proliferation of national and regional fabric chains. Polyester knits were easy to sew, and the versatile fabric facilitated pattern design. Home sewing and the pattern industry boomed. Butterick fielded a larger sales force than the much larger Simplicity and McCall's, whose strengths were in the national chains (Sears, Penney, Ward's, Woolworth, Kresge, etc.). The proliferating independent fabric shops diluted the department store and national chain businesses, and Butterick became the strongest supplier to the stores doing most of the business—the fabric shops. Butterick doubled its sales force from seven to fourteen—seven district managers and seven salespersons. Managers were responsible for supervising and motivating the salespersons as well as for selling and servicing their own accounts.

The Butterick sales force made both personal and telephone sales. Usually, phone sales were contacts or renewals of existing accounts. Members of the sales force were paid salaries plus bonuses for sales over quotas. Typically, the sales effort included cold calls to potential customers and attempts to persuade existing customers to reorder or to increase current orders.

The peak year for home sewing was 1975. The tremendous success of polyester knits caused nationwide proliferation of not only thousands of fabric shops, but led to the creation of regional and national fabric chains. Butterick increased its market share because it had distribution in places where consumers were shopping (see Exhibit 1).

After 1975 technological advances brought down retail polyester knit prices from $6.98 to $1.00 per yard, and many independent stores closed their doors. The major regional and national fabric chains became very strong. During 1976 and

Exhibit 1   Distribution of Pattern Business, Butterick Company

Type of Outlet	1960 Sales %	Type of Outlet	1980 Sales %
Department stores	35	Department stores	15
National dry goods chains	45	National dry goods chains	20
Fabric shops, others	20	Regional and national fabric chains	45
		Independent fabric shops, other	20

1977, Butterick held its unit sales constant due to improved pattern styling and catalog presentation, but Simplicity and McCall's began to record declining sales. The late seventies saw a new trend in fashion—blue jeans.

In 1977 Butterick launched a multimillion-dollar research program to determine consumer satisfaction/dissatisfaction with price points, styles, service, and out-of-stock situations. At the same time management analyzed the number of styles retailers sold versus the number carried. A key finding was that pattern sales were highly unprofitable for the mass merchandise and dry goods chains, because of the large inventories required and high costs for support material and freight. The large inventory resulted in average annual inventory turnover of less than one half. In addition, all the pattern companies had so increased their prices that pattern retailing did not fit the images of low-price stores.

Then Butterick developed a new product, the See & Sew pattern, to retail at $.99 per unit. It was first distributed in 96 styles made up of two home sewing categories—Misses and Children. Each style was available in two sizes: A (for size 8, 10, and 12) and B (for size 14, 16, and 18). A self-service fixture was designed for displaying the patterns. The total inventory for the retail store consisted of 576 units worth $570 at retail. Stores were memo-billed (account outstanding, no interest) and paid only for units sold between calls or reorders.

The Butterick sales force placed See & Sew racks in independent fabric shops and handled rack servicing. Each salesperson serviced up to 120 racks, for which they received flat bonuses, some of which amounted to $6,000. Later, an outside firm took over rack servicing. This firm's representatives dusted the racks, cleaned them, and took inventories. Inventories were sent to Butterick offices where they were computer-compared to a model, creating orders for the accounts represented. Each account was visited an average of four times a year, at an approximate cost of $30 per visit.

See & Sew patterns also became a part of the Butterick line, providing automatic sales to 9,000 existing accounts. By the end of 1979, See & Sew accounted for less than 10 per cent of the Butterick selection but over 22 per cent of its sales. In January 1980 the company decided to take See & Sew out of the Butterick pattern book and develop it as an additional line, using self-service fixtures in the existing accounts. Most of the largest fabric chains accepted this concept wholeheartedly, as stocking costs for See & Sew were a pittance compared to total pattern inventory costs, averaging $6,000 to $7,000 per store. By February 1980, 1,850 accounts had been sold (see Exhibit 2); See & Sew inventory turnover was predicted at twice per year.

238

**Exhibit 2 Breakdown of See & Sew Sales
(as of February 1980)**

Retailer	No. of Accounts
Cloth World	250*
House of Fabrics	500*
Fabric Center	500*
Hancock Fabrics	200*
Independent retailers	400

*Expected to sell 2,000 units/fixture/year.

Future Directions

Reflecting on the success of the See & Sew line within the overall fabric of Butterick's marketing program, Mr. Dodson recognized the need to position the company for further growth. He knew this would be difficult in the face of continuing socioeconomic changes. He hoped to rely on See & Sew without worrying about competitive retaliation, but he felt the need for better understanding of the demand for Butterick's products.

QUESTIONS

1. What were the major determinants of demand trends in the pattern industry?
2. How should Butterick have responded to these trends?
3. Was the See & Sew line likely to continue to grow? Why or why not?

PART THREE

Organizing and Planning Strategic Marketing Activities

Marketing activities cannot be successful without a strategic orientation. This section of the text will show you how to organize and plan marketing actions so that their probability of success is greatly increased. This part begins with Chapter 9, The Marketing Organization. Without the marketing organization, you cannot get anything done. Many marketing managers find that they either must build a new marketing organization from scratch or must reorganize extensively what they have. This chapter will help you to do both. The following chapter, Chapter 10, Concepts of Marketing Strategy, will give you new insights into strategy. Many of the experts, both practitioners and academics, who read this material were impressed. They felt that it provided a powerful new slant on being able to understand and apply strategy. You can judge for yourself. The final chapter in this section, Chapter 11, The Strategy of New Product Development, starts out by showing you the extreme importance of this function of the marketing manager. As you will see, hundreds of millions of dollars are on the line, and large corporations can fail or succeed just as readily as small companies. You are led through every step of the new product development process, with your alternatives and trade-offs explained along the way. Finally, alternatives to the strategy of new product development are discussed. From this section of the text, you will learn to be a master marketing organizer and planner.

The Marketing Organization

9

CHAPTER OBJECTIVES

- Understand the importance of the marketing organization to accomplishing marketing objectives.
- Know the alternatives for organizing marketing activities and under what circumstances each is used.
- Be able to design a marketing organization.

There Are Profits in Organizations

T-Bar is a 20-year-old company that was established to market proprietary communication switch designs. For years all went well and there was little competition. Then suddenly other companies entered the scene with similar products. Many of these companies were founded by former T-Bar employees. The solution was reorganization, according to its company president, "from a technology- to a market-driven company."

A marketing department that formerly consisted of only seven people who specialized in only two functions—advertising and product management—was replaced with what has been called a Marketing Operations Department. With a staff of thirty, it is responsible for applications engineering, customer and sales force training, field service and product planning, and pricing. And the new organization has worked. Sales in the six months after reorganization were over $19 million, up by almost 13 per cent from the previous year. T-Bar hopes for $100 million in sales within four years.[1]

Reorganizing Big Blue

The world calls IBM "Big Blue." Big Blue may be the one company that is respected by everyone, including IBM's hard-driving Japanese competitors. Yet, in recent years IBM's growth has slowed, and it no longer has double-digit growth rates. Many analysts wonder whether a gigantic company with 387,000 employees can move quickly enough to compete with smaller, faster competitors. John F. Akers, the fifty-four-year-old chairman and CEO of IBM, attempted to overcome this perception through reorganization. He reorganized the core company, IBM USA, into seven autonomous business units: PCs, mainframes, minicomputers, communications, microchip manufacturing, programming, and software. An eighth unit does marketing for the seven others. At the same time, he took 20,000 staff and laboratory personnel and moved them to the sales force. This not only resulted in increased customer contact, but positioned them to affect revenue directly. Says *Fortune* magazine, "A vast army in dark suits and white shirts chanting, 'Just say yes,' would be a force to reckon with—anywhere on the globe."[2]

High-tech Marketing Calls for High-tech Marketing Organizations

Two professors at Kent State University in Ohio, William L. Shanklin and John K. Ryans, Jr., investigated over 125 high-technology companies. Among the things they discovered were the unusual organizational aspects of successful high-tech marketing organizations. For example, in roughly three quarters of the companies they sampled, the high-tech development strategy group consisted of the CEO or president, marketing, R&D, and production. In a majority of the high-tech companies in the survey, the senior financial officer played no central role in product development and planning and only occasionally was the corporate council represented.[3] Furthermore, according to Bernard A. Goldhirsh, publisher of *Inc.* and *High Technology* magazines, "It is not simply big companies that mean success for high technology." IBM missed the minicomputer market and allowed Digital Equipment Corporation to become a giant in its own right. NCR Corporation missed the shift from electromechanical point-of-sales terminals to purely electronic machines. . . . In times of rapid technological change, it's only the entrepreneurial sector that can bring new products to market within the time frames required to be competitive.[4] ●

How a firm is organized for marketing can have a major impact on its success. One reason is that the quality of the customer-employee interface can have a dramatic impact on perceived quality and value of what is offered as well as on customer satisfaction.[5] In this chapter we're going to look at a number of different types of **marketing organizations** and the effectiveness and efficiency of each, depending on conditions. To be effective means that you accomplish your marketing objectives; the efficiency component denotes how well that you do this, how quickly, and how well you use the resources that are available to you as a marketing manager. Thus, while effectiveness has to do with doing the right things, efficiency has to do with doing things right. Both go hand in hand to help determine your marketing organization's contribution to the company's performance.

—————— Marketing Organization: The Objective

Marketing As a System

A system is a group of interacting and interdependent elements forming a unified whole. Thus, a marketing organization can be viewed as a system, and it has been suggested that as a system, the systems approach should be followed for organizing marketing activities. The systems approach simply means choosing a course of action by systematically investigating, analyzing, and including not only the correct marketing objectives, but also cost effectiveness, risks, and other important alternatives. Figure 9-1 represents such

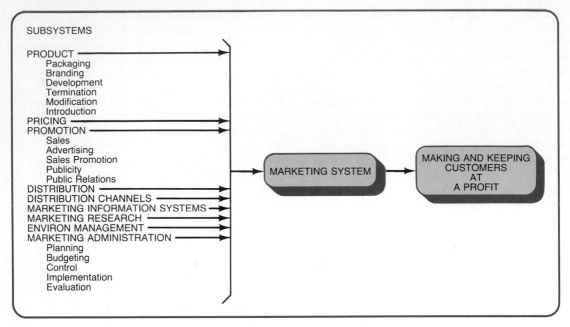

Figure 9-1 A Marketing System and Subsystems

Source: Adapted from Lee Adler, "Systems Approach to Marketing," *Harvard Business Review*, vol. 45 (May/June 1967).

a marketing system. Note the subsystems of the marketing system, including product functions, new product development, distribution channels, physical distribution, field sales, marketing intelligence, marketing administration, advertising, sales promotion or merchandising, and publicity and public relations.[6]

This **marketing system** can be considered to be a general one. A specific company could have a somewhat different marketing system based on its specific objectives, its environment, and the subsystems that it might have to work with. Thus, no one type of marketing organizational structure is right for all conditions. However, through organizational optimization, it is possible to improve the effectiveness of interaction among different marketing specialties and with specialties outside of marketing. This, in turn, leads to more effective and efficient task, project, and mission performance.[7]

The Concept of the Traditional Organization

Traditional organizational theory evolved over several thousand years. Basic to it is the concept of line and staff, an understanding of which is essential to structuring any organization. **Line personnel** are those individuals who take actions and make decisions that are related directly to the objectives of the organization. Accordingly, in the traditional concept of organization, line personnel form a chain of command in which decisions and orders are passed down successfully from the top of an organization to lower levels—finally to the very bottom working or "grunt" level. The ideal is that responsibility and authority are very explicit and clear cut. There is no doubt who reports to whom or about what authority or responsibility marketing managers at any level might have.

Staff personnel are not the same as line personnel. In traditional organizational theory they provide advice, assistance, and recommendations to line personnel but are not in the chain of command. According to traditional organizational theory, any executive who is not line is staff.

Many companies and marketing organizations are organized along traditional concepts of organization.

The Personal Staff. Personal staff members under traditional organizational theory are individuals who are assigned to a particular manager but have no specific duties or responsibilities except those as assigned by the individual to whom they report. "Assistants to," for example, have no official authority except that which derives from the authority of their manager. A secretary would also be considered part of the personal staff. Such an office has no authority of its own; however, if a manager instructs a secretary or an "assistant to" to arrange a meeting of all senior subordinate managers, within the limits of that assignment the secretary or "assistant to" has the authority to give such orders as are necessary as to complete the assignment.

Specialized Staff. Members of specialized staff differ from personal staff in that they perform certain necessary functions that require special skills, training, education, or experience. In addition, they may have authority over their own specialty areas. Yet the function of these specialties is not directly related to the organization's business. For example, specialized functions include finance, personnel, law, contracts, and so forth. The specialized staff does develop and execute plans and projects pertaining to a specialized function. And these functions are obviously very important to the enterprise. This allows line managers to be free to concentrate on day-to-day operations and make use of the data developed and provided by the staff as appropriate. Thus, specialized staff can advise line managers in the organization on a continuing basis, and in addition such members of the specialized staff may be assigned certain particular tasks by line managers pertaining to their specialties. For example, in a company with a sales division, but no division responsible for marketing, the manager of R&D might be directed to conduct some specific type of marketing research.

It should also be noted that certain of the specialized staff may be staff to a larger organization but line in accomplishment of its own function. Thus, a manager of product development might advise the president about product development matters, while within his or her own product development organization he or she manages people, capital, equipment, and facilities and heads a chain of command to execute and perform the technical function of developing new products. Therefore, the product development manager of a company might at once be operating as a line manager and as a staff adviser.

Principles of Traditional Organizational Theory

Seven main principles of organizational theory have evolved for the traditional organization over the years:

1. Responsibility should be given only with a commensurate amount of authority.
2. Every position in the organizational chain of command should report to only one other position, so that every individual has but one boss.
3. At every level of the organization, clear lines of authority must exist from the top to the bottom.
4. A limited number of individuals should report to any one supervisor. The number that one individual could control effectively typically was thought to be nine or less. This concept is known as "span of control."
5. The requirements of the position should determine the selection of personnel, rather than personnel determining what jobs are assigned.
6. Responsibility and authority for carrying out a specific task should not be given to more than one individual.
7. The supervisor may delegate authority for accomplishing a task, but responsibility cannot be delegated.

A Traditional Organization

A traditional marketing organization is the **functional organization** shown in Figure 9-2. Note that each functional area of marketing reports to the vice-president of marketing and that the division of labor is built around the various operating functions. This organization has characteristics that may either assist or hinder you in accomplishing your objectives, depending upon your unique circumstances. These include the following:

- Division of labor in a functional organization often leads to greater efficiencies than would be possible for other organizations. Because there is no duplication of effort, individuals in every function work organizationwide.
- There is more professional synergism in a functional organization, because professionals in any one functional area interact with one another.
- Performance evaluation is likely to be more accurate in a functional organization because each organization in each unit is supervised by a specialist qualified in that function.
- Functional organizations have more difficulty in coordinating, scheduling, and integrating their activities with other functional organizations in the company. This is because of role conflict and competition between

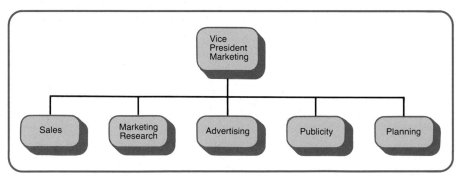

Figure 9-2   **A Functional Marketing Organization**

different organizations, as well as the lack of an overall manager to resolve these problems, except at the higher levels.

- Functional organizations tend to be more formal and less flexible; thus, conflicts may be more difficult to resolve because of the rigid relations between levels of authority within the organization and between different organizations.
- New tasks or activities that fall outside the domain of the established functional organization may require new organizations to be established because the old organization may resist taking on new responsibilities.

The Need for Alternative Marketing Organizational Structures

The modern practice of management, including marketing management, has found various problems associated with the traditional approach to organizing activities. These include the following:

- Demands on individuals are at odds with their psychological needs. One example is that a narrow specialization of tasks inherent in a traditional organization may be incongruent with an individual's desire for a variety of challenges in his or her work life.
- The principles of traditional organizational theory are derived from a basic assumption that may not be correct—that is, the idea that people dislike work responsibility and therefore must be closely supervised if they are to perform organizational tasks properly. The fact is, it's been observed that many people do seek responsibility and do enjoy work. Therefore, the principles derived from theory, to the contrary, cannot take advantage of the maximum potential inherent in every individual for doing work he or she likes.
- The traditional organizational structure provides for no communication between the manager and the organization as a whole, only between the manager and the intermediate subordinates in the chain of command. Therefore, information going from top to bottom or from bottom to top is by necessity filtered. Communications research has demonstrated that such filtered information is usually modified—sometimes significantly from its original form and content—and may not represent a true picture of what the original communicator intended.
- Many dimensions of managerial and employee behavior are not integrated with traditional theory. For example, leadership and motivation are treated as separate entities to be mastered and manipulated, rather than as a part of the organizational structure itself.
- Traditional organizational theory assumes that human beings act rationally. A manager issues a directive, it proceeds through the chain of command, and it is ultimately carried out as intended. But in real life we know that individuals do not always act in a rational manner. Thus, a directive put in at one end of the system does not always result in the desired action coming out at the other end. Informal organizational structure and "politics" are the norm, rather than the exception. Thus, marketing managers may be wasting their time if they try to achieve

goals by making people fit into their rational model of the world as they see it.

- Another assumption of traditional organizational theory is that human beings prefer the security of clearly defined paths as against the freedom to determine their own approach. But the fact that many individuals flourish in a less structured atmosphere means that, while this assumption may be true for some people, it is not true for all of the people and not all of the time.

- Finally, organizations built on traditional theory leave little question as to who has authority. Authority is always at the top of an organization. Levels of management below the top can only attain authority as it is delegated downward. But even this reasonable-sounding assumption has been found to be untrue at times within modern organizations. A type of authority may exist by virtue of a person's expertise, or even personality, as well as his or her position within the organization.[8]

The Product Management Solution

Product management is one response to the organizational problem of providing sufficient attention to individual products and/or brands when there are so many that a single marketing manager or marketing executive cannot coordinate all aspects of all of them either effectively or efficiently. The **product manager concept** began more than fifty years ago. It became increasingly popular after the 1950s. With this concept, a division containing a group of product managers reports to the vice-president of marketing. Each product manager is responsible for a separate product or brand. Supporting the product manager are a variety of other organizations, such as sales, marketing research, and new product planning. Each of these organizations also reports to the vice-president of marketing or the overall director of the marketing organization. Individuals support each particular product or brand in a matrix-type fashion, as will be discussed shortly. In many ways, the product manager system is in tune with current organizational theory. It emphasizes cooperation among different groups, plus participative decision making and a deemphasis on hierarchy authority patterns.[9] It is one solution to the complex problem of traditional marketing organizations.

However, the product manager system is not without its potential cost to the individual and the organization. Studies have shown that role pressures on the product manager may lead to tension, dissatisfaction, lower performance, and a high risk of burnout.[10] The organization can help by establishing clear procedures to resolve conflicts before they arise, having clearly written job positions, and keeping product managers informed of changes in company policy and the reasons for them. Companies should exercise care in recruiting for these positions, and individuals should understand the risks before accepting them.[11]

Eight Different Areas of Necessary Cooperation but Potential Conflict Between Marketing Organizations and Manufacturing Organizations

One marketing scientist found eight different problem areas in which it is extremely important that marketing and manufacturing cooperate, and where the potential for conflict exists.[12] These are contained in Exhibit 9-1.

- *Capacity planning and long-range sales forecasting.* Marketing wants to ensure that the company has the capacity to produce the item that is being planned; manufacturing is concerned about accurate sales forecasts so that neither an over- nor an undercapacity results.
- *Production scheduling and short-range sales forecasting.* Marketing is extremely concerned with delivery time and therefore wants a much faster response than exists; manufacturing is concerned with change of commitments and stops and starts, which cost money and waste resources in the manufacturing functional area.
- *Delivery and physical distribution.* Marketing is concerned with having the right merchandise in inventory; manufacturing demands accurate order input, inasmuch as limited space means that overinventory costs money.
- *Quality assurance.* Ideally marketing would like to have excellent quality at low cost; manufacturing is concerned with the rejection rate and the cost of obtaining the quality specified.
- *Breadth of product line.* Marketing is seeking the greatest variety of products possible to satisfy the maximum number of customers; manufacturing would like to repeat the same item over and over again for cost and efficiency reasons—too broad a line requires many production runs, which are shorter and less economical.
- *Cost control.* Marketing wants as low a cost as possible, so that the final price will be competitive; manufacturing is faced with the problem of producing at low cost, along with the desirability of fast delivery, high quality, and meeting other requirements.
- *New product introduction.* Marketing is probably the functional area within a company that is a new product's greatest proponent; manufacturing recognizes that all changes increase cost and therefore may be prohibitively expensive.
- *Adjunct services such as spare parts, inventory support, installation, and repair.* Manufacturers tend to view installation as a final manufacturing operation; marketers view it as a customer-service function.

Source: From Benson P. Shapiro, "Can Marketing and Manufacturing Coexist?" *Harvard Business Review,* vol. 55 (September–October 1977).

These eight areas of contention between marketing and manufacturing illustrate well the need for an organizational structure to deal with and resolve complex organizational issues.

One technique for analyzing and improving product management organizations is the product management audit. This audit surveys product managers with the following questions:[13]

- What per cent of your time do you usually spend on each activity?
- Rate how you like each of these activities.
- Rate the degree to which you expect to be supported in each activity.
- Rate the degree to which you expect to be rewarded for each activity.
- What percentage of your time would you ideally spend on each activity to build the business?

- If you could free up ten hours each week of what is now busy work, to which activity would you reallocate them?
- Rank the top five activities in which you would like training or teaching to help you do your job better and prepare you for a higher-level job.

Three Dimensions of Organizational Structure

Certain dimensions of the organizational structure have trade-offs that should be considered:

1. Centralized versus decentralized organizations
2. Formal versus nonformal organizations
3. Specialized versus nonspecialized organizations

Centralization Versus Decentralization

Centralized decision making means making decisions at the highest level of the organization. An example of centralization is a large firm with many plants in which all basic decisions and policies are made at the headquarters. The advantages of centralization are that important decisions are generally made by those people in the organization who are most qualified to make them—assuming, of course, that the most competent and experienced people in the organization are located at the top. Usually the decision makers in a centralized organization will be located where they are readily accessible to one another; thus, coordination is easier; it increases the likelihood that the decision will support overall company interests rather than the interests of any one group or division within the company or the organization.

Centralized organizations also require less total staff because general staff support can come from headquarters, rather than each suborganization being allocated its own staff. Other forms of duplication can also be eliminated, as many functions can be performed at the central location. Finally, centralization permits various types of standardization, which may be advantageous. Thus, if a company has standardized operating procedures throughout its organization, managers can be more easily transferred from one division to another. Less time will be needed to familiarize them with new procedures.

In a decentralized organization, responsibility for decision making is delegated to subunits of the overall organization. One of the primary advantages of decentralization is that the individuals who are most directly concerned with the work can make the decisions related to it. Thus, decisions are made by people who have greater knowledge of specific conditions and problems. Also, under decentralization there is a much more rapid response to changing situations. In a centralized organization, it takes time to collect the information required for a decision and send it to the higher headquarters to request additional information as appropriate. The information must then be collected and sent back. Finally, higher headquarters must make the decision and send it down to the subordinate unit for action. If the situation changes during the process, more reiterations may be necessary, thus causing more delay. In a decentralized organizational structure, decisions can be made much more rapidly for this reason.

Formalization Versus Nonformalization

Formalization involves a structured environment of rules and procedures that are required and must be followed in the day-to-day implementation of marketing tasks. The advantages of a formalized organization include a firm commitment by top management to the value and importance of the tasks being required, assurance that procedures will be adhered to that in the past led to success, and less chance of something being left out during the day-to-day operations that might be important for task accomplishment. Finally, standardization and routinization of activities brought about through formalization can increase efficiency under many conditions. The advantages of nonformalized organization include increased interaction; less conformity, which is desirable under some creative tasks; an increased flexibility; and ability to respond more easily to changes in the environment.

Specialization Versus Nonspecialization

Specialization involves breaking up an organization into unique elements. Thus, employees in highly specialized organizations focus on very limited ranges of activities. As a result there may be specialties in marketing research, in sales, and in new product development, as opposed to generalists and nonspecialists who are accomplishing all these tasks. The advantage of specialization is in-depth knowledge and understanding of certain types of more difficult problems. A greater adaptability to changing conditions occurs within that specific environment, along with the ability to discover new ways of doing things within that specialty. Nonspecialists and marketing generalists tend to attempt to do everything. The advantages with nonspecialization include flexibility, each individual operating a diversity of tasks, and a broader viewpoint in problem solving.

As we will see shortly, these variables must be manipulated in the construction of an organizational structure for marketing.

The Solution:
_____ Alternative Marketing Structures

The complexity of the process of marketing as well as the demands of marketing's goals and objectives means that modern organizations must use various optimized types of organizations under different conditions. As a result, certain structures of organizations have evolved to fulfill specific needs of the situation. Three such structures that have been designed to solve specific

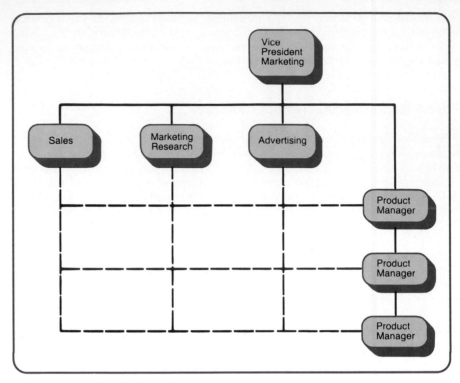

Figure 9-3   A Matrix Marketing Organization

marketing problems are the matrix organization, the goal- or task-centered organization, and market centering.

Let's take a look at each.

The Matrix Organization

Perhaps the best example of the **matrix organization** is the product management organization to which we referred earlier. A typical product management organization is shown in Figure 9-3. Note that each product manager has total responsibility for his or her product. Yet, in most cases, the individuals that work on the project and do the tasks necessary to enable the product manager to manage the product do not report to him or her but to functional managers. A marketing researcher, for example, reports to the marketing research manager, salespeople report to the sales manager, engineers working on new product development may report to an engineering manager, and so forth. Thus, these individuals violate a principal tenet of traditional organizational philosophy: they have more than one boss. They report to their functional manager as well as the product manager on whose program they're working.

The advantages of the matrix organization include flexibility and a focus on objectives. Individuals working for a functional organization may also work in the support of more than one product. It is the product manager who ensures focus on getting the job done for his or her product. In addition, there is little duplication of effort because functional areas supply overall support to all product managers.

Before a matrix marketing organization can be adopted, certain preconditions must be met. There must be a sufficiently large functional organization to service a reservoir of personnel to be assigned to the various components of the matrix organization. There must also be a need for multiple projects. In the case of the product management organization, the company must have more than one product that it is attempting to market. Finally, the matrix manager must get his or her power from somewhere. The mere establishment of the matrix organization by itself may not provide sufficient authority to stand against and win out over a functional department manager. Unlike the manager of the typical functional department, the head of a matrix organization has limited authority over the personnel working for him or her. Authority is over the project only. One common method for increasing the matrix manager's authority is through product funding. Funds are allocated to the matrix manager who in turn "buys" services from the various functional departments. In this way the functional departments are made dependent on matrix organization "funds" for their existence.

Another difficult problem for matrix organizations is that of esprit de corps. This common spirit of organization oneness can inspire great enthusiasm and devotion to group goals and can be most important in task accomplishment and success in marketing a product, brand, service, or anything else. Esprit de corps is much more difficult to foster in an organization that is only one of several to which an individual belongs. Thus, it is much more difficult to establish and maintain esprit de corps in a matrix organization than in an organization to which members are assigned fully and permanently.

Venture teams can also be examples of matrix organizations, as shown in Figure 9-4. Just as the various functional areas are matrixed in support of the product manager, various functional areas such as R&D, manufacturing, marketing, engineering, and finance can be matrixed to support a venture team.[14]

The Goal- or Task-oriented Organization

The goal or task organization is organized around what the organization is set up to achieve. This can be different products, different geographical areas, different categories of customers, or even different projects. However, although a matrix organization is organized around a project, it differs from the matrix organization in that each division of a goal-oriented organization is more or less self-contained and can operate relatively independently. Thus, each such organization probably has its own engineering, manufacturing, and marketing subunits.

Goal-oriented organizations, being self-contained, permit informal contact between different specialties with the result of reduced need to refer conflicts to higher authority for decision, as is possible and sometimes happens with matrix organizations. However, this attribute is also a weakness. There will be duplication of personnel, of skills, and of equipment for every goal- or task-oriented organization, whereas one group with each set of functional skills could be sufficient to support the same level of effort in several subordinate organizations in another company. Other drawbacks include the

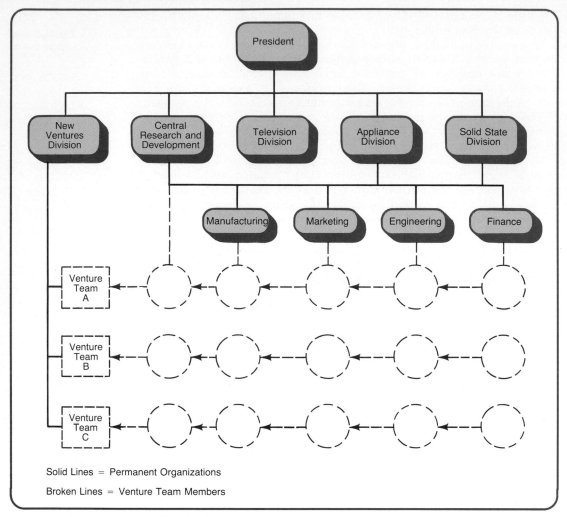

Figure 9-4 Venture Team Matrix Organization

Source: Adapted from Richard M. Hill and James O. Hlavecek, "The Venture Team: A New Concept in Marketing Organization," *Journal of Marketing*, vol. 36 (July 1972), p. 47.

fact that when there is no work within the goal-oriented organization, the marketer or marketing specialist cannot be easily directed elsewhere without a change of supervision or change in organization. There is also less professional synergism because specialties in the goal-oriented organization are dissimilar and have more difficulty accurately assessing the performance of specialists.

However, the major advantage with the goal-oriented organization, which can outweigh all the drawbacks, is that the organization is focused on achieving a goal rather than on day-to-day work routines of the functional organization. It operates without the conflicts inherent between different organizations in the matrix organization. Accordingly, when the emphasis is on the satisfactory accomplishment of a specific project or task, where schedules

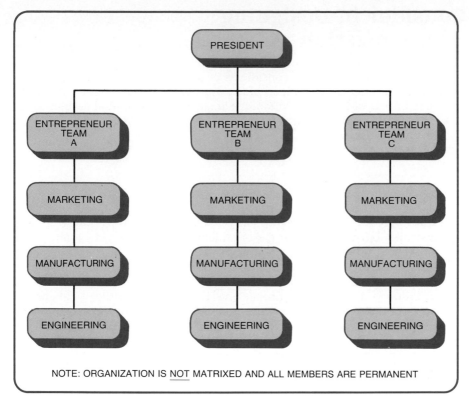

NOTE: ORGANIZATION IS <u>NOT</u> MATRIXED AND ALL MEMBERS ARE PERMANENT

Figure 9-5   **Entrepreneurship Team Organization**

absolutely must be met when unique problems are being solved—that is, when organization effectiveness is primary—the goal orientation design may work better than other organizational structures.

A typical example of the goal or task orientation is an entrepreneurship team. An entrepreneurship team differs from the venture team mentioned previously in that it is a separate profit center, reports to a high level in the firm, and is self-contained in itself; that is, all elements necessary to success are within the entrepreneurship team itself and are not matrixed or furnished from other organizations in the company. A special organization of several entrepreneurship teams is shown in Figure 9-5. Note how this differs from the venture team in Figure 9-4.

Market Centering

Market centering is a concept in marketing organization structuring where companies seek to organize their operations around the market to be served rather than around the production or the other functions within the company. Thus, it is perhaps the example par excellent of the marketing concept. Doing this, proponents of market centering say, helps to ensure that their customers' needs always come first. The basic key to organizational structuring here is simple: organize so that your major markets become the centers around which your various organizational divisions are constructed.[15]

Factors to Consider in Designing a Marketing Organization

Five basic factors should be considered in designing a marketing organization. These are the authority level of the organization; individual capabilities of the members of the organization; the stage of organizational development; the company's environment, philosophy, and culture; and, finally, the organization's objectives.

The Authority Level

The **authority level** determines not only what kind of organization structures are possible, but also whether the organization structure can be altered at all. If you are at the top of the organization, the president or a vice-president of a division or of marketing, you clearly have greater freedom to organize as you wish, although it still may be necessary to convince others that the organization you desire is the proper one. But you have authority to change from a functional organization to a goal-oriented one or vice versa, or to establish a matrix organization; a lower-level manager of marketing may not have this authority. Thus, design depends on the art of the possible and the authority level at which you are managing.

Individual Capabilities of the Members of the Organization

Individual capabilities are important. If you do not have qualified individuals to fill the organization you have constructed, it will not perform properly. An example might be a matrix organization in which you have a need for product managers. If you do not have individuals that can handle this extremely demanding type of job, it may be well to carry on with a traditional functional organization even though in the theoretical sense this is less than optimal, considering other factors in your situation.

Stage of the Organization's Development

The organization passes through three general stages of development, at any one of which it can remain for an indefinite period. These are the start-up stage, the functional stage, and the diversification stage. The start-up stage is the initial stage of the organization. It is characterized generally by a direct influence by the organization's manager. It may include a limited product line or service and limited expertise in functional areas. This means that in the start-up stage the members of the organization frequently wear several different hats. In the start-up stage, the best organization tends to be a goal-oriented structure because there are insufficient members for a functional organization, because the small size of the organization can foster the attainment of a particular goal, and because the size permits maximum impact by the manager's personality on all other personnel in the organization.

256

The Functional Orientation Stage

In this, the second stage of the development of the marketing organization, the responsibilities of the organization have increased, additional personnel are brought into the organization, and the organization tends to be larger. As a result, it is more difficult for the marketing manager to exert his or her personality over and control the number of people reporting to him or her directly. Also, it is no longer necessary for the manager or other members of the organization to be responsible for more than one function. In fact, it is more efficient to organize along the division of labor by specialty. This leads to the functional organization because the increasing depth of responsibility of the organization cannot be handled easily by the nonspecialized staff. There also are too many different responsibilities for the members to perform multiple functions simultaneously. Also, the increasing number of specialized personnel permits a functional organization. Finally, the size of the organization no longer allows the marketing manager to derive much advantage from one-on-one contact with all his or her personnel, even if this were possible.

The Diversification Stage

The diversification stage is the final stage in the organization's development. Here, the responsibilities of the organization have become even more diverse than before. The marketing manager is still operating with a functional organization and finds that he or she must now make general decisions that cut across all functional organizational lines. At the same time the number of decisions has increased to an extent where it may well be impossible to make optimal decisions in all cases. The manager cannot keep on top of all the different areas simultaneously. The reality is that the manager is losing control. As a result, at this point decentralization may occur, returning to a goal orientation in which some of the general decision making may be delegated to submarketing managers in charge of semiautonomous units. This stage is goal oriented because it permits delegation of some general decision-making authority to submanagers, giving the marketing manager of the overall organization more time and greater control in consideration of his or her increased responsibilities. Such an organization also represents a return to the entrepreneurial flavor, or intrapreneurial, to use the common terminology, in that each of the other subunits may now be viewed as being in the start-up stage themselves.

Thus, the stages of the marketing organization imply a cycle: goal oriented, functional, and goal oriented once again. However, some organizations progress to one stage of development and progress no farther. Other organizations, due to various changes in the environs, retrogress. A matrix organization might be introduced at any stage, either the functional orientation stage or the diversification stage, as an alternative or in conjunction with the goal-oriented structure of the diversification stage.

Company Environment, Philosophy, and Culture

The woefully inadequate attention paid to the human side of marketing organizations has been observed and documented.[16] In fact, the organizational structure selected must consider these elements. Every organization is different, different not only in industry, personnel, product, or service offered, but also in environment and its philosophy and culture. If the philosophy tends to be loose and freewheeling, with a considerable amount of decentralized decision making, it's going to be extremely difficult and probably a mistake to reorganize suddenly as highly centralized and formalized. In the same vein, if matrix management appears to be desirable, yet the company culture has not bred managers accustomed to operating without clear lines of authority over people, it may be better to seek some other organizational structure for getting the job done. Thus, it is preferable to do the best you can with a theoretically nonoptimal organizational structure. In fact, a theoretically optimal structure may be stymied by the environment, philosophy, and culture of the organization.[17] A customer-oriented organizational culture is always desirable and, some have argued, is a prerequisite for service firms.[18]

Structural Characteristics	Organizational Form
	Bureaucratic Form
Centralized, formalized, nonspecialized	Appropriate usage context • Conditions of market failure • Low environmental uncertainty • Tasks that are repetitive, easily assessed, requiring specialized assets
	Performance characteristics • Highly effective and efficient • Less adaptive
	Examples in marketing • Functional organization • Company or divisional sales force • Corporate research staffs
	Organic Form
Decentralized, nonformalized, specialized	Appropriate usage context • Conditions of market failure • High environmental uncertainty • Tasks that are infrequent, difficult to assess, requiring highly specialized investment
	Performance characteristics • Highly adaptive • Highly effective for nonroutine, specialized tasks • Less efficient
	Examples in marketing • Product management organization • Specialized sales force organization • Research staffs organized by product groups

Source: Adapted from Robert W. Ruekert, Orville C. Walker, Jr., and Kenneth J. Roering, "The Organization of Marketing Activities: A Contingency Theory of Structure and Performance," *Journal of Marketing*, vol. 49 (Winter 1985), p. 20.

Figure 9-6 Two Archetypical Marketing Structures Classified by Form and Structure

Achieving an organization's objective is perhaps the primary factor considered in the design of the marketing organization. Exactly what are you trying to accomplish and what are the parameters of achieving your objective? One study on marketing planning showed that the organizational structure and design were closely correlated with the results and success of the planning. A major conclusion was that although centralization is a generally appropriate and widely used component of bureaucratic control in organizations, it is clearly inappropriate in the context of this particular objective—planning.[19]

A Contingency Theory for Marketing Organizations

Recently a contingency theory of marketing organizations was developed that incorporates much of our previous discussion. This contingency theory incorporates the three dimensions of organizational structure: centralization versus noncentralization, formalization versus nonformalization, and specialization versus nonspecialization. At the same time, four archetypical marketing structures are documented. Two of them, the transactional form and the relational form, have to do with the external organization of the marketing activity. The other two, the bureaucratic form and the organic form, have to do with the internal organization of the activity.

Figure 9-6 shows the two internal forms, the bureaucratic and the organic, contrasted against two different sets of classes of structural characteristics: a class that is centralized, formalized, and nonspecialized and a class that is decentralized, nonformalized, and specialized. The appropriate usage context, performance characteristics, and examples in marketing are given in each case in the figure. Figure 9-7 shows the task characteristics and environmental characteristics of these two organizational forms, organic and bureaucratic.[20]

Bureaucratic Form	
Task characteristics	• Routine and frequent
	• Performance easily assessed
	• Requires some specialized knowledge or investment
Environmental characteristics	• Stable, noncomplex
	• Small number of potential suppliers
Organic Form	
Task characteristics	• Nonroutine
	• Hard to assess performance
	• Requires specialized knowledge or investment
Environmental characteristics	• Complex, uncertain
	• Small number of potential suppliers

Source: Adapted from Robert W. Ruekert, Orville C. Walker, Jr., and Kenneth J. Roering, "The Organization of Marketing Activities: A Contingency Theory of Structure and Performance," *Journal of Marketing*, vol. 49 (Winter 1985), p. 21.

Figure 9-7   Task Characteristics and Environmental Characteristics of Two Organizational Forms

Summary

In this chapter we have looked at the marketing organization and how it impacts on the achievable results. We first looked at the marketing organization as a system and noted what we were trying to accomplish; then the concept of the traditional organization was discussed, including line and staff, the principles of traditional organizational theory, and the prime example of traditional organization, the functional organization. Next, we looked at the need for alternative marketing organizational structures. The problems with traditional organizational theory were discussed, including cases where basic assumptions supporting theory do not always hold true. This difficulty was heightened by the complexity of modern marketing organizations, a prominent example of which is the concept of the product manager. Areas in which cooperation is necessary between marketing and other organizations within the firm—such as manufacturing—but in which the potential for great conflict exists were noted. From the complexity of major organizations, we extracted three major dimensions of organizational structure, each of which concerns major trade-offs in organizational design. These are centralization versus decentralization, formalization versus non-formalization, and specialization versus nonspecialization.

To solve this difficult problem of various conditions under which marketing managers must perform their function, the solution of alternate marketing structures was proposed. Three major organizational concepts of alternative structures were discussed, including the matrix organization, the goal- or task-oriented organization, and market centering.

Five factors were cited as being primary in considering the design of marketing organizations: authority level; individual capabilities of the individuals to be members of the organization, the stage of the organization's development; the company's environment, philosophy, and culture; and the objectives of the specific marketing organization under analysis. Finally, a contingency theory of organizational structure was discussed, and examples of two of the four organizational forms developed were illustrated.

In this chapter we see that the marketing organization is not simply an institution to which the marketing manager may belong and/or control and direct. In itself and in the way it is put together can have a major impact on the results of the marketing manager's efforts.

Keep in mind that what works today may not be optimum at all for tomorrow. According to Peter Drucker, the typical business organizational structure of the future may bear more resemblance to a hospital, university, or symphony orchestra than many organizations we see today.[21] If so, it will be because these models will have been found to be more effective in achieving marketing objectives.

Questions

1. Under the traditional concept of organizational theory, is a vice-president of marketing part of line or staff? A marketing research manager? A manager of new product development?

2. Traditional organizational theory says that responsibility should be given only with a commensurate amount of authority. Is this the case with a product manager? Defend your position.

3. Why is there a greater likelihood of organizational efficiency in a functional or a matrix organization than in a self-contained goal- or task-oriented organization?
4. How would you rank the three types of organizational structure—functional, goal- or task-oriented, or matrix—regarding their ability to focus on the objective? Which do you think would be most effective? The least?
5. The text notes eight different areas of necessary cooperation between marketing and manufacturing. What type of organizational structure would be best suited either to prevent and/or resolve the potential conflict?
6. IBM has established goal or task organizations for seven different product lines. What problems or advantages might accrue if, instead of this particular organization, a matrix-type organization were established?
7. What drawbacks might exist in establishing in-trapreneurship-type goal or task orientation organizations for IBM?
8. Are there any disadvantages you can think of to market centering?
9. One major factor to consider in designing a marketing organization is the stage of the organization's development. Can you think of a disadvantage in attempting to keep pace in changing the organizational structure as the organization matures through the stages of development discussed?
10. A contingency theory of organization states that an organization's structure should depend on the various characteristics and situational factors inherent in every situation. Can you think of any disadvantage to having a number of different organizations within a company all organized according to the conditions under which they operate?

Ethical Questions

A veteran senior marketing manager is no longer working to the level of his or her previous performance. This individual is given a small staff and "promoted" to head a specially created organization, "Futuristic Products." Is this an ethical solution to the problem? Why or why not?

Endnotes

1. "T-Bar Discovers Marketing," *Sales and Marketing Management* (September 10, 1984), pp. 27–28.
2. Joel Dreyfuss, "Reinventing IBM," *Fortune*, vol. 120, no. 4 (August 14, 1989), pp. 30–35, 38–39.
3. William L. Shanklin and John K. Ryans, Jr., "Organizing for High-Tech Marketing," *Harvard Business Review* (November–December 1984), p. 165.
4. "American Entrepreneurs Seizing Power in a Bloodless Coup," *Marketing News* (December 21, 1984), p. 12.
5. Michael R. Bowers, Charles L. Martin, and Alan Luker, "Trading Places: Employees As Customers, Customers As Employees," *Journal of Services Marketing*, vol. 4, no. 2 (Spring 1990), p. 55.
6. Lee Adler, "Systems Approach to Marketing," *Harvard Business Review*, vol. 45 (May–June 1967).
7. See, for example, Robert W. Ruekert and Orville C. Walker, Jr., "Marketing's Interaction with Other Functional Units: A Conceptual Framework and Empirical Evidence," *Journal of Marketing*, vol. 51, no. 1 (January 1987), pp. 1–19.
8. William A. Cohen, *High Tech Management* (New York: AMACOM, 1986), pp. 23–24.
9. Victor P. Buell, "The Changing Role of the Product Manager in Consumer Goods Companies," *Journal of Marketing*, vol. 39 (July 1975), pp. 3–11.
10. Steven Lysonski, Alan Singer, and David Wilemon, "Coping with Environmental Uncertainty and Boundary Spanning in the Product Manager's Role," *Journal of Services Marketing*, vol. 2, no. 4 (Fall 1988), p. 22.
11. Ibid. p. 21.
12. Benson P. Shapiro, "Can Marketing and Manufacturing Coexist?" *Harvard Business Review*, vol. 55 (September–October 1977).
13. John A. Quelch, Paul W. Farris, and James M. Olver, "The Product Management Audit," *Harvard Business Review*, vol. 65 (March–April 1987), p. 30.
14. Richard M. Hill and James D. Hlavecek, "The

Venture Team: A New Concept in Marketing Organization," *Journal of Marketing*, vol. 36 (July 1972), pp. 46–47.

15. Mack Hanan, "Reorganize Your Company Around Its Markets," *Harvard Business Review*, vol. 52 (November–December 1967), pp. 63–74.

16. A. Parasuraman and Rohit Deshpande, "The Cultural Context of Marketing Management," in Russell W. Belk et al., eds., *1984 AMA Educator Proceedings* (Chicago: AMA, 1984), pp. 176–179.

17. Cohen, op. cit., pp. 36–39.

18. A. Parasuraman, "Customer-oriented Corporate Cultures Are Crucial to Services Marketing Success," *Journal of Services Marketing*, vol. 1 (Summer 1987), pp. 39–46.

19. George John and John Martin, "Effects of Organizational Structure of Marketing Planning on Credibility and Utilization of Plan Output," *Journal of Marketing Research*, vol. 21 (May 1984), pp. 179–180.

20. Robert W. Ruekert, Orville C. Walker, Jr., and Kenneth J. Roering, "The Organization of Marketing Activities: A Contingency Theory of Structure and Performance," *Journal of Marketing*, vol. 49 (Winter 1985), pp. 13–25.

21. Peter F. Drucker, "The Coming of the New Organization," *Harvard Business Review*, vol. 66, no. 1 (January–February 1988), p. 45.

Concepts of Marketing Strategy

10

CHAPTER OBJECTIVES

● Understand the basic concepts that underlie all successful marketing strategies.

● Know the importance of well-thought-out marketing strategy to succeed in the competitive environment of business.

● Be able to explain the concepts of mass marketing, product differentiation, market segmentation, market strategy positions, market share strategies, and positioning.

Highest-Quality GM Car Rejected

NUMMI is the acronym that stands for New United Motor Manufacturing, Inc., a joint venture of General Motors and the Toyota Motor Company. NUMMI lost $80 million in 1988, due primarily to the small car known as Nova. Yet J. D. Power and Associates, a well-known researcher in the automotive industry, gave Nova the highest quality rating among all GM cars. At NUMMI the average worker produces sixty-three cars per year. That's more than at any U.S. plant, and 40 per cent above the average. If the product was terrific and manufacturing practices more so, what went wrong? NUMMI president Kan Higashi says that one problem was that Nova's styling was unappealing, compared with the Corolla and many of its other competitors. GM president Robert C. Stem-

pel drove the point home: "There's no lack of high quality, fuel-efficient, safe small cars." Does this mean that high quality, excellent manufacturing practices, and fully committed workers can't guarantee success? That's right. It takes something called marketing strategy.[1]

Can You Solve This Strategic Problem?

Take a look at Figure 10-1. Here's a chance to test yourself to see what kind of strategist you are. The 20,000 infantry and 2,000 mobile forces represented within the circle are yours. To your immediate rear is a river. Facing you in the formation indicated are 70,000 infantry, in three broad rectangular lines, and 2,000 mobile troops positioned at either flank. In just three minutes, these enemy forces almost four times your numbers are going to attack you. You cannot cross the river at your back; you cannot escape parallel to the river in either direction due to hills. Neither you nor your adversary has air, naval, missile, or any forces other than those noted. How would you position your 20,000 infantry and 2,000 mobile forces to meet this attack? Or would you take some other action? Take a few minutes to consider what you would actually do. You've got the ball, General. What's your decision? Take a few minutes to work out your solution.

One General's Solution

This problem in strategy actually arose more than 2,000 years ago in 216 B.C. at the Battle of Cannae in which the Carthaginian general, Hannibal, opposed the Romans led by General Varro. Hannibal won because he developed and executed a well-thought-out plan based on a decisive and innovative strategy. The strategy was executed in two phases. In phase 1, as shown in Figure 10-2, Hannibal divided his forces into an advanced weak center and very strong forces positioned at both of his flanks and anchored on natural terrain obstacles by the river. His cavalry was also posted on both flanks, but with a stronger force of his cavalry at his left and a weaker holding force to his right. His center was ordered to withdraw slowly as the Romans advanced, but his flanks were to remain fixed in position. His stronger cavalry force on the left was ordered to destroy the enemy's cavalry opposing them and then to circle behind the enemy's infantry forces. The remaining Roman cavalry on the opposite flank was caught between the two Carthaginian cavalry forces.

This initial action was executed exactly as planned. The Carthaginian center slowly withdrew toward the River Autidus as the Carthaginian cavalry first destroyed Roman cavalry on one flank and then on the other. Varro, the Roman general, smelled victory when he saw the Carthaginian center retreating, and he ordered his mass of infantry to advance at an

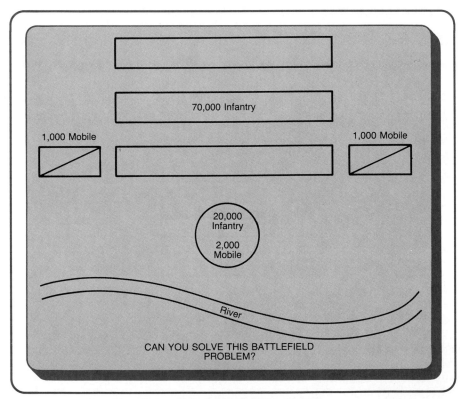

Figure 10-1   Can You Solve This Battlefield Problem?

264

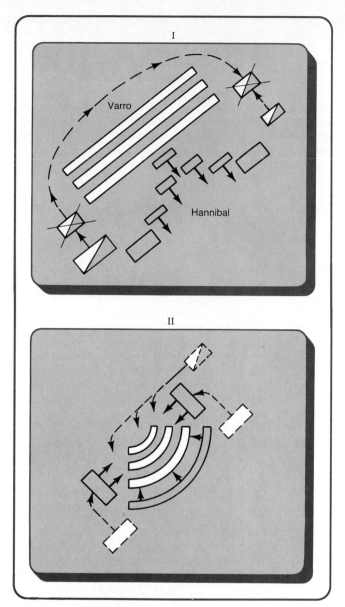

**Figure 10-2   The Battle of Cannae in 2 Phases:
A Lesson in Strategy**

increasing pace. In ever-increasing numbers and density, the Romans rushed into the Carthaginian center to take advantage of what they perceived to be disintegrating Carthaginian forces. Phase 2 is also shown in Figure 10-2.

At the critical point, with the Roman infantry forced so close together they were unable to wield their short swords effectively, Hannibal ordered his previ-

ously retreating center to the attack. At the same time, he ordered his strong forces at either flank to wheel in on the enemy. The Carthaginian cavalry, now unopposed by any remaining Roman cavalry, struck unopposed at the Romans' infantry rear. Thus, the trap was closed. Attacked from all sides, the Romans were massacred in great numbers, and the result was the most decisive battle in the history of warfare. Of the original Roman forces of 72,000, 60,000 were killed on the field of battle. The Battle of Cannae went down in history as one of the outstanding examples of strategy and decisive victory by an inferior against a superior force.

What are the marketing lessons in the Battle of Cannae? First, we can see that superior strategy can be more important than superior resources. Hannibal won his victory even though he was greatly outnumbered. Also, Hannibal had a well-thought-out plan that covered all the details of his strategy. It was not an off-the-cuff, off-the-top-of-his-head solution that depended on "feel" or luck. Finally, to implement the strategy required coordination among large numbers of troops and different units. Yet everything fit together to work to reach the overall objective. It was not a case of "everyone doing his best." It was a case of everyone doing his best to support the overall strategy and a single objective.[2] ●

This chapter opened with an example from military strategy because many of the concepts embodied in military strategy and developed over the millennia are very similar, if not directly applicable to marketing strategy. Consider Chrysler's comeback from near disaster. Chrysler was on the verge of bankruptcy. There was $700 million in stockpiled inventory of unsold Dodges, Plymouths, and Chryslers. Most of Chrysler's American plants were in various states of disorganization, and subsidiaries abroad were losing money every year. Product quality was so bad that cars were coming off the assembly line with doors that were falling off or didn't fit. Even *The Wall Street Journal* ran an editorial in which it stated that Chrysler should give up and "die with dignity." Only four years later, Chrysler was the example of what is right with America. Sales volume was up 20 per cent in a single year. Chrysler obtained 11 per cent of the North American car market. Chairman Lee Iacocca's book became a national best-seller. How did this miracle, this Cannae, happen at Chrysler?

It wasn't a U.S. government bailout. Chrysler didn't get money from the U.S. government. Instead, it got federal guarantees that allowed the firm to go public and borrow in public credit markets at interest rates up to 15 per cent. The government became the co-signer of Chrysler's notes, and the bottom line was that Chrysler paid the U.S. government money—more than $300 billion. Chrysler, like Hannibal, succeeded because of a strategy. There was a corporate grand strategy and also a marketing strategy, and that marketing strategy contributed significantly to Chrysler's victory.

Chrysler executed a strong positioning strategy against a redefined target market. Chrysler positioned itself as the quality car for young, affluent, upwardly mobile consumers. In support of this overall strategy and the objective of "We don't want to be the biggest, just the best," Chrysler made product quality a top corporate priority. At the same time it invested $9.5 billion through 1988 in product innovation and development. In some cases the results were immediate: Chrysler gained an enhanced reputation for quality in the marketplace and at the same time was able to slash its warranty costs about 45 per cent over a five-year period. Over the same period, Chrysler's advertising campaigns, featuring Chairman of the Board Lee Iacocca, emphasized the message that Chrysler intended to be the best. The overall result of this well-planned, well-coordinated, well-executed strategy was, as in the case of Hannibal, a resounding success.[3]

As with other human activities and endeavors, the ability to develop marketing strategies that are successful are not inherent at birth but rather can be learned. In this chapter we will see how this is done.

What Is Strategy?

The definition of strategy can be fairly simple. It is the actions that we take to achieve the objectives that we set. As already noted, there are basically three different levels of strategy. First, there is strategic marketing management accomplished at the corporate level. This was discussed in Chapter 2. The next level is marketing strategy. It is accomplished by marketing organizations and will be covered beginning with this chapter. Finally, there are marketing tactics, which are executed in support of the marketing strategy and are accomplished by various subordinate units within marketing. These are the familiar "4 Ps of marketing. Marketing strategy is of particular importance because it is the link between operational actions accomplished by a firm's marketers and overall corporate strategy. Furthermore, all marketing organizations are involved in marketing strategy. While subordinate marketing organizations may not be directly involved in strategic marketing management, and top corporate executives may not be involved with marketing tactics, all levels are involved with the marketing strategy that ties the two together.

The central objective of any strategy is to be stronger at the decisive point.[4] But it is also important to recognize that a point is defined by a time, by a location, and by a position relative to the competition. Thus, the marketing manager must be cautious regarding the dynamics of the situation, in that even a specific market or markets may be a temporary vehicle for growth— a vehicle that must be used and then abandoned as circumstances dictate and as the decisive point changes.[5]

Marketing strategy focuses explicitly on the quest for a long-run competitive advantage in a particular marketing situation.[6] **Competitive advantage** means that you have a differential advantage over your competition such that you are stronger—and stronger when and where it counts—at the decisive point.

Let's look at a specific example. Some years ago a small company with fewer than eighty employees, ICS, Inc., took on IBM as a competitor in the automatic typewriter market. For a particular niche of the market, ICS, Inc., was stronger—stronger because of the innovation of its design and its willingness to give personalized attention. ICS, Inc., had a competitive differential advantage and at this point ICS was successful in forcing IBM out of that particular market niche. Yet, note that, over all, IBM had far superior resources available.

Military Strategy and Marketing Strategy

We opened this chapter with a discussion of a military example of strategy. In fact, there is great similarity in application between military strategy and marketing strategy. Many marketing scientists noticed this similarity, beginning back in 1959 and perhaps even earlier. Why the similarity? In marketing strategy as with military strategy, critical decisions must be made under conditions of risk and uncertainty, with limited resources, while facing severe competition.[7,8]

Given our extensive experience at making war, a considerable body of practical, as well as theoretical knowledge of military strategy exists. This knowledge has been documented by military thinkers and strategists going back as far as the Chinese general, Sun Tzu, who wrote *The Art of War* more than 2,300 years ago, a treatise still in print and being studied. Business in general and marketing in particular already owe much to ideas borrowed from the military, including concepts of planning and organization. It is not surprising, then, that captains of industry occasionally search military strategy for lessons applicable to business operations.

An extreme example of this was in 1982. *A Guide to Strategy*, written by Miyamoto Mushashi, a seventeenth-century Samurai warrior reputed to have killed more than sixty men in personal combat by the age of thirty was published as a business book. It sold more than 100,000 copies, making it a best-seller.

For marketing strategists who wish to explore military knowledge for lessons that can be applied to marketing, probably no concept is better known or more celebrated by military strategists than the so-called "principles of war." About these principles Napoleon said, "They have regulated the great captains since the beginning of recorded warfare." Twelve of those principles that have a direct applicability to marketing have been called "the principles of marketing strategy."[9,10] These are described in Exhibit 10-1.

Despite these and other applications of military concepts, it is a mistake to think that adapting military strategy is simply a matter of giving military terms to marketing actions—for example, referring to a marketing action as "an attack" or "guerilla warfare." By this thinking, you could apply technical terms from many different disciplines to marketing. Thus, removal of the product from the marketplace could be called a "productectomy," in pseudomedical terms, and a changing of target markets a "pirouette," in dance terms. However, there is much about military strategy that applies to marketing strategy.

Consider the two principles of concentration and economy of resources, one says to concentrate resources at the decisive point and the other to allocate lesser or no resources to points where they are less important. This corresponds closely with a principle of marketing strategy that we will be discussing shortly called marketing segmentation. In it the resources of a company are concentrated against a single market segment, with few resources expended elsewhere, rather than trying to sell to every segment of the total market.[11]

Exhibit 10-1   The Principles of Marketing Strategy

1. *Objective.* The principle of the objective states that every strategy must have an objective. The objective must be the attainment of a specified and decisive goal. The objective should be specified so it is clearly understood by everyone responsible for or participating in the goal's or objective's attainment. It should be decisive so that the cost in resources and time is minimized.
2. *Initiative.* Initiative implies action instead of reaction and underscores the advisability of maintaining an offensive attitude to control the time and place of action. A defensive posture should be considered a temporary expedient only, which exists until a counteroffensive can be initiated.

Exhibit 10-1 (Continued)

269

Concepts of Marketing
Strategy

3. *Concentration.* This principle, also called the principle of mass, is considered by some to be the fundamental concept because it involves allocating resources to achieve a competitive advantage at a decisive point. It was summarized by Confederate General Nathan Bedford Forrest who said that winning battles was a matter of "getting there firstest with the mostest."

4. *Economy of Resources.* No organization can be strong everywhere, and no marketing executive should squander his or her resources but rather should concentrate them against the decisive objective. Minimum resources should be allocated to secondary efforts.

5. *Maneuver.* Maneuver refers to positioning resources to assist in accomplishing the objective. It can be applied to economical or psychological factors as well as geographics, and it incorporates the concept of timing.

6. *Unity of command.* For every assigned mission there should be one responsible manager. This ensures unity of effort that is necessary to get maximum power from available resources.

7. *Coordination.* Coordination emphasizes cooperation among the company organizational units, the integration of tasks, and planning the overall marketing strategy as well as implementing it. It minimizes the danger of suboptimization of subordinate units while facilitating economy of force and concentration.

8. *Security.* Competitors should never be allowed to acquire an unpredicted advantage. Security requires accurate intelligence about the competition as well as in-house security that guards both physical objects and information about your capabilities and intentions.

9. *Surprise.* Surprise may emanate from deception, secrecy, variation methods, innovation, audacity, or speed of action, and it can compensate for inferior resources just as its principle assisted Hannibal at the Battle of Cannae. Total ignorance of your intentions is not necessary and probably impossible, but you must be able to accomplish your purpose before your competitors can react effectively.

10. *Simplicity.* Simple direct plans are necessary because operational conditions and pressures make even the most simple strategy difficult to execute.

11. *Flexibility.* "Everything that can go wrong will go wrong" is an old maxim, and therefore problems and opportunities must be thought about before a strategy is implemented so that alternative actions can be planned before they are necessary.

12. *Exploitation.* General George S. Patton said, "Pursue the enemy with the utmost audacity." This principle refers to maintaining forward momentum; that is, when winning, don't relax but continue to maintain pressure until maximum success is achieved.

Important Marketing Strategies

Mass Marketing

Mass marketing predated much of the present thinking regarding marketing strategy. In very basic terms, mass marketing means marketing to the masses—that is, selling the same product to the great mass of any population.

From the previous discussion of strategy, you may immediately recognize weaknesses in adopting such a strategy. However, it is also important to recognize that there are also advantages associated with a mass marketing strategy and that, in certain instances, mass marketing of a product may actually be desirable. The biggest advantage of mass marketing is the potential size of the market that can be served. If everyone in the United States is considered a candidate for a product, we are talking about a market of 250-million-plus consumers. But you must also consider the disadvantages in such a strategy.

Adoption of a mass marketing strategy begins with an assumption. The assumption is that all individuals in this market think alike, act alike, and in other ways are the same with respect to the product's use and purchase. For example, we have said 250-million-plus consumers; thus, we are including infants in this market. Also, there is a question of the size of the market. If it is this large, can we actually reach it through our advertising or other promotions? When would a mass marketing strategy be advisable? These are conditions when a product is so much of a commodity that it is needed by everyone, or nearly everyone. Certain commodities, such as food or gasoline, might be successfully mass marketed when the resources of the firm are sufficient and the competition nonexistent.

Also, the product and environment should be such that we have a product or service desired or needed by nearly everyone of all ages, incomes, geographic locations, and other groups. Certain utilities, such as electricity, gas, water, or telephone services might fall into this category.

However, in general, there are more problems than opportunities in mass marketing. One does not concentrate resources with this strategy. Thus, two principles of marketing—concentration and economy of force—are violated. Except with technological breakthrough products, there is almost always some kind of direct competition. Furthermore, it is doubtful that many groups of consumers are served well by a mass marketing approach. It is highly unlikely that one single product can best serve all groups. Therefore, if other specialized offerings are available, major shares can be lost to competitors, just as ICS, Inc., chiseled out a niche for itself and concentrated its resources to take a part of IBM's market. For most firms under most conditions, strategies other than that of mass marketing must be adopted.

Product Differentiation and Market Segmentation

Product differentiation and market segmentation are popular strategies. They are frequently viewed as alternatives, although they may also be implemented simultaneously; and of course product differentiation can be a means of implementing market segmentation.[12] Basically, a strategy of product differentiation involves promoting product differences to the target market. Market segmentation is a strategy that recognizes the market is not one single mass of look-alike, act-alike prospects, but rather various submarkets, each of which is composed of potential consumers with certain characteristics in common that make them better candidates for the particular product or service being marketed. These differences and how they relate to the basic concept of strategy are shown in Figure 10-3.

According to Silicon Valley marketing guru Regis McKenna, differences are becoming more and more important: "Gone is the convenient fiction of

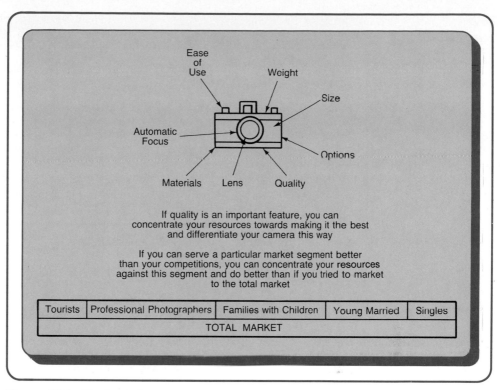

Figure 10-3   Product: Camera
Both Product Differentiation and Market Segmentation Illustrate the Basic Concept of Strategy: To Be Stronger at the Decisive Point

a single, homogeneous market. The days of a uniformly accepted view of the world are over. Today diversity exerts tremendous influence. . . ."[13]

Variables of Segmentation

The number of product differences that can be promoted to the consumer is infinite—and so are the characteristics by which a total market might be segmented. Still, there is a basic requirement that the segment or submarket must be large enough to make going after that segment worthwhile. In addition, a target submarket must be reachable. That is, it makes little sense to identify a submarket with common characteristics if such a submarket is located where we cannot reach it with efficient methods of advertising or distribution. Once these requirements are met, segmentation can be accomplished based on demographics—that is, on age, income, education, or other factors; on geographical locations; on psychographics, or the way people think, including both their responses and behavior; and on life-style, or the way people live.[14] One example of how **life-style segmentation** can be accomplished is based on the life-style dimensions shown in Figure 10-4 and classified according to activities, interests, and opinions, as well as demographics.[15,16] There isn't a one best way to segment markets. Every approach

Activities	Interests	Opinions	Demographics
Club membership	Achievements	Business	Age
Community	Community	Culture	City size
Entertainment	Family	Economics	Dwelling
Hobbies	Fashion	Education	Education
Shopping	Food	Future	Family size
Social events	Home	Politics	Geography
Sports	Job	Products	Income
Vacation	Media	Social issues	Occupation
Work	Recreation	Themselves	Stage in life cycle

Source: Adapted from Joseph T. Plummer, "The Concept and Application of Life-Style Segmentation," *Journal of Marketing*, vol. 38 (January 1974), p. 34.

Figure 10-4   Segmentation by Life-Style Dimensions

has its advantages and disadvantages, merits and limitations. So the method of segmentation should be determined by the marketing manager, based on the product and market being considered, as well as on his or her own objectives in segmenting.[17]

An example of a segmentation strategy that also uses product differentiation is Pepsi's caffeine-free product called Pepsi Free. Pepsi noted that the "fitness craze" and concern over unnatural food ingredients caused caffeine awareness among the general public to jump from 32 per cent in 1968 to 90 per cent in the 1980s. Additional research revealed that regular cola users comprised 75 per cent of soft drink consumers, with 24 per cent expressing a definite purchase interest in caffeine-free cola. Diet cola users only make up 25 per cent of this category but show a stronger purchase interest of 34 per cent. Analyzing these data, Pepsi estimated that the volume potential among regular users would be about twice that of diet users, but that the size of both segments would be large enough to support both the regular and sugar-free version of the new product. Thus, the caffeine-free cola segment was calculated to be 5 to 15 per cent of the total category, or between $1 billion and $3 billion of the total $21 billion soft drink industry.

To implement this segmentation strategy, Pepsi communicated that its cola's taste wasn't sacrificed because of the caffeine-free benefit with two different versions, both the regular and a sugar-free version. Pepsi's estimates were $200 to $250 million in sales the first year, but actual results were more than double this, a successful new introduction of a product using a market segmentation strategy.[18]

Product Differentiation and Market Segmentation as Alternative Strategies

As noted earlier, product differentiation and market segmentation are frequently considered to be alternative strategies. Product differentiation and market segmentation can be employed simultaneously, but they are usually applied in sequence, in response to changing market conditions. This is because successful product differentiation results in giving the marketer a horizontal share of a broad and generalized market. Successful market segmentation tends to produce greater sales through a depth of market for the market segment chosen.[19] Both attempt to coordinate the market and the product: one, market segmentation, by finding the correct market for the product, and the other by an attempt to change the product, either in actual or imaginary ways, to differentiate it from other products and thus to find the correct product for the market.

As alternatives, different conditions tend to call for one strategy or the other. Six major factors have been identified in determining which strategy might be more appropriate.

1. *The size of the market.* If the market or market segment served is already small, further segmentation through a market segmentation strategy may reduce the potential number of buyers to such a degree that a market segmentation strategy is unattractive.
2. *Consumer sensitivity.* In some cases the consumer may be insensitive to product differences, or it may be that product differences are very difficult to explain or promote. An example might be garden tools or pocket combs. On the other hand, other products are such that the consumer is very sensitive to product differences, such as for laundry detergent or perfume.
3. *Product life cycle.* We have already mentioned the product life cycle and the fact that products can be considered to have different phases of life, just as do living things. Each phase of the life cycle implies certain strategies that may be more successful than others. For example, when a product is first introduced, an objective may be to capture as large a share of the market as possible to establish the product in the marketplace. At the same time, if similar products are already in the market, and they are in an introduction or growth stage, a product differentiation strategy is probably advisable. On the other hand, let's say that this new product is introduced into a market that is already very mature and saturated. In this case a market segmentation strategy might help to establish itself by concentrating resources against a specific market segment.
4. *Type of product.* Some products are basically like all other products. They are known as commodities, as opposed to products that are distinctive, and may be changed significantly, if desired. The computer, a VHS, and a FAX machine are distinctive products, whereas gasoline, salt, and sugar are commodity products. You might think that because commodity products are basically alike they cannot be differentiated; the contrary is true. Because differences in commodities that can be easily perceived do not exist, differences that can be promoted stand out; distinctive products can be more easily changed and modified to be particularly useful and acceptable to a particular market segment.
5. *The number of competitors.* When there are a lot of competitors in the marketplace, it is much more difficult to differentiate a product. Thus, a large number of competitors calls for a market segmentation strategy.
6. *Competitor strategies.* When there are many competitors that are using market segmentation, it is very difficult to counter with a product differentiation strategy—that is, attempting to sell to all segments by differentiating your product. After all, you can't be all things to all people. Your best bet, then, is probably to choose your target market segments

USE PRODUCT DIFFERENTIATION — USE MARKET SEGMENTATION

	Emphasis on Promoting Product Differences	Strategy Selection Factors	1	2	3	4	5	6	7	8	9	10	Emphasis on Satisfying Market Variations
MARKET	Narrow	Size of Market							A			B	Broad
MARKET	High	Consumer Sensitivity to Product Differences			B					A			Low
PRODUCT	Introduction	Stage of Product Life Cycle							A			B	Saturation
PRODUCT	Commodity	Type of Product	B								A		Distinct
COMPETITION	Few	Number of Competitors		B					A				Many
COMPETITION	Product Differentiation	Typical Competitor Strategies			B	A							Market Segmentation

A Home Computers

B Sugar

Figure 10-5 Strategy Selection Chart

Source: Adapted from R. William Kotrba, "The Strategy Selection Chart," *Journal of Marketing*, vol. 30 (July 1966), p. 25.

along with your competitors. But what about a large number of competitors using a product differentiation strategy? In this case a market segmentation strategy in which you pick a particular segment of the market to concentrate your resources against makes a lot of sense.[20]

Based on these six factors, a strategy selection chart was developed. This chart, presented in Figure 10-5, shows product differentiation and market segmentation strategies as different alternatives. It assists in showing when to choose one strategy or the other.[21]

Marketing Strategy Positions

Another important strategic concept has been developed based on a product situation/market situation matrix—the product being new, modified, or ex-

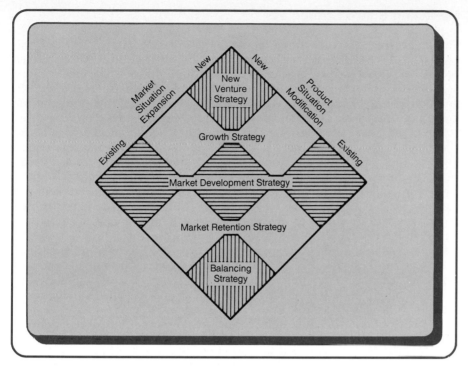

Figure 10-6 Marketing Strategy Positions

Source: Adapted from David W. Cravens, "Marketing Strategy Positioning, *Business Horizons*, vol. 18 (December 1975).

isting and the market situation being existing, expansion, or new. Depending on the location in this matrix, as shown in Figure 10-6, five different strategies are possible: (1) a **new venture strategy**, (2) a **growth strategy**, (3) a **market development strategy**, (4) a **market retention strategy**, and (5) a **balancing strategy**. The new venture strategy position represents a totally new undertaking by the organization. The growth strategy, either a new product or a new market, is involved in combination with market expansion or product modification. Market development strategy works basically with existing products in existing markets; nevertheless, it requires extending an enterprise beyond existing market product commitments. A market retention strategy means simply holding on to what you already have. A product is modified or a market is being expanded, but you work with existing markets and products. Finally, there is the balancing strategy. Here a firm seeks to balance revenue cost flows to achieve desired profit and market share targets. In this case, with minimum risk, the marketing organization attempts to do the best with what already exists, with little or no change.

Sometimes a position shift is required after selecting a strategy because of environmental threats, unsatisfactory performance, identification of potential opportunities, innovations, or other reasons. In all cases the marketing manager must reassess in current situations where he or she wants to go and then select from among the five different strategies to do this.[22]

Marketing Share Strategies

The **marketing share strategy** focuses on increasing market share to the exclusion of all else. Such a strategy may not always be called for, either because of the necessity of a defensive posture or because a firm can be more profitable overall while maintaining a small share of the market for a specific product. But large share does have advantages, including the potential for lower costs, improved corporate image, and synergism with other businesses at the corporate level. A market share gain strategy should be considered when the current market position is poor—that is, when share must be gained to increase profitability and profit volume—and new products are being launched directly against strong competitors; when significant losses in share have been suffered at the hands of competitive actions; when a recent acquisition permits the potential for increased share; or when competition has become vulnerable due to its own actions, environmental changes, or something you have done.[23]

However, a share gain strategy is not for everyone. As mentioned earlier, a product can be extremely profitable with a smaller share of the market. Also, share expansion requires more risk and resource allocation. Finally, the fact that share gain is planned as a strategy does not automatically make it successful. In fact, strategies based on market share might not be only inappropriate, but detrimental. Remember, your resources are always limited. The resources spent fighting for share may be better used in entering a new market or in introducing a new product.[24] Therefore, the marketing manager should consider alternative strategies, including integration with other marketing strategies. Note that a share gain strategy is implied in three of the five positioning strategy alternatives mentioned previously: market development, growth strategy, and new venture.

Positioning

Positioning has to do with consumer perceptions of how various brands differ.[25] It was further defined by Al Ries and Jack Trout, two advertising agency executives, during the 1970s. They stated it quite simply: "you position the product in the mind of the prospect."[26] Thus, positioning requires no actual product changes but rather where the potential customer or consumer sees the product in his mind relative to other competing products. It is differentiation of a perception. Let's look at some examples.

Over the last ten years or so, wearers of jeans have been treated to images of status, fashion, cowboys, and artistic designers. Recently, V.F. Corporation, the parent company of Lee Jeans, came out with something different. The ad for V.F. Jeans said, "If you could own only one pair of jeans, this would be the pair." And the jeans were called "The best made jeans in the world." The ad went on to document features that supported this contention. Furthermore, the jeans were priced at $47 to $50, compared with $10 to $14 for an average pair of jeans at the time. Remember, these jeans are not designer jeans. Why should the consumer pay so much for a nondesigner-type product? According to Bob Stec, Lee vice-president of merchandising, "Consumers are willing to pay for a rational benefit if it is tied to an emotional need, in this case superior quality and the need to express it." Very clearly,

V.F. Corp. has positioned its jeans as the "Rolls-Royce," the top of the line, of all jeans.[27]

Let's look at a different product. Schiefflin & Company has sold a product called Blue Nun, a white German wine. Over the years it has followed three different positioning strategies. At first, the product was positioned as being perfect with every dish. This strategy was extremely successful, in fact so successful that other wineries soon followed suit. According to Brand Manager Laurie Millman, "By the end of the 1970s, people were drinking white wine with everything." Schiefflin then changed positioning. The new positioning was Blue Nun goes everywhere, suggesting that consumers take the product on picnics and to other occasions. Note the difference. Not just as the wine that goes with everything, but the wine that goes everywhere. Finally, the most recent positioning is that of a wine sold by the glass. Meanwhile, its success with positioning strategies has led to the introduction of a new Blue Nun wine, Blue Nun red. It is positioned as two wines in one, promoted as being light and fruity when chilled, or full-bodied when served at room temperature.[28]

For a positioning strategy to work, it is extremely important that the positioning chosen be distinctive, so that potential consumers will not feel that the product or the brand is easily replaceable by similar products or brands. This is especially important when the product has a higher price tag. Otherwise, it can be replaced by lower-priced alternatives. Also, the positioning chosen must be relevant—that is, it must be important to people. The position chosen can be the people's car, like the Volkswagen beetle once was, or it could be the automobile for those who have everything, top of the line, the Rolls-Royce. Either way, this positioning must be relevant to the target market sought. Finally, the position must be determined by a number of different tactical moves working together in a coherent fashion. For example, the price and promotional aspects on the product must all work together to reinforce one another; otherwise, the consumer will be confused and the positioning will lack clarity.[29]

Why does the positioning strategy work? One reason is the partial insulation that a successful positioning strategy gives from the competitive pressures of other firms. This differentiation reduces the degree to which it will be viewed by consumers as substitutable with other products or services. These competitive barriers give the firm greater latitude within which to develop customer loyalty.[30]

Six Steps for Positioning

Trout and Ries suggest a six-step question framework for successful positioning:[31]

- What position do you currently own?
- What position do you want to own?
- Whom you have to defeat to own the position you want?
- Do you have the resources to do it?
- Can you persist until you get there?
- Are your tactics supporting the positioning objective you set?

Developing Marketing Strategy in a Crisis

One of the most difficult problems for a marketing manager is developing strategy when a crisis situation forces the abandonment of previous plans and strategies. Researchers have found three major factors that impact on successful strategy development in crisis situations.[32] You might not have too much control over the first: it is to ensure that the marketing managers in place are of the "right stuff," appropriate to handling these types of crisis situations.

The other two are to be prepared and to immediately take action to regain control after the crisis hits. However, there is something you can do proactively to encourage successful outcomes. Because decision time in crisis situations is generally short, prepare with crisis drills. What do you do if a competitor unexpectedly introduces a technological breakthrough product? How about international political problems that cut you off from a key material component of your product? What if rumors about your product based on isolated instances of product failure threaten to destroy your entire market? You can't anticipate every crisis, but you can gird yourself so that when the real thing happens you are prepared to shift gears into alternative strategies that still support your strategic marketing management objectives.

To regain control, take marketing action specifically aimed at this objective. Tylenol took its product off the market at once when its crisis hit. It started a new product development program that eventually corrected the danger of product tampering. When Exxon had its crisis, it delayed acting to regain control and is still suffering for it.

Future Dimensions of Marketing Strategy

Quantifying the Unquantifiable

The many elements of strategy—including the environs of the situation, internal company resources and variables, and external variables dependent on the competition and on others—make for a marketing situation that rarely repeats itself in exactly the same manner. Also, many elements, because they concern people, are extremely difficult to quantify. But for some years, researchers have worked with **PIMS** (**Profit Impact of Market Strategy**), in which empirical information supplied by companies on resource inputs, strategies, and results is collected from many companies, analyzed, and published. In addition, some attempts at quantifying military strategic concepts for application to marketing have been attempted by marketing scientists.[33,34] Thus, one important future dimension of marketing strategy is likely to concern a greater association between strategic concept and numbers in devising guidelines for marketing managers.

The Military Connection

Another likely direction of future marketing strategy is the further adaption and application of historical military concepts of strategy to marketing. For

Opportunity or Threat_____			
	Description of Outcome	Magnitude of Effect (1–5)	Significance to Firm's Marketing Objectives (1–5)
Most Desirable Outcome			
Most Probable Outcome If No Special Action Taken			
Least Desirable Outcome			

Figure 10-7 **Strategic Center of Gravity Analysis**

Source: William A. Cohen, "A Methodology for Developing International Marketing Strategies Using a Strategic Center of Gravity Analysis," in Erdner Kaynak, editor, *Managing the International Marketing Function: Creative Challenges of the Eighties* (Halifax, Nova Scotia: World Marketing Congress, 1983), p. 105.

example, consider the strategic center-of-gravity concept developed originally by Clausewitz, a nineteenth-century German military theorist and thinker. According to this concept, in every situation there exists a strategic center of gravity. If this strategic center of gravity can be identified and dominated, the entire situation will fall under the control of the dominating organization. If this concept is applicable to marketing, following it and allocating superior resources to the center of gravity will result in success over one's competitors. The concept has been further developed, and a matrix for locating the strategic center of gravity, based on the opportunities or threats in the environment constructed, is shown in Figure 10-7. It is likely that work in the area of applying this type of concept to marketing will continue.[35]

Integrative Strategy

A final direction that marketing strategy is taking is that of integration among disciplines and among the other major categories of strategy in business—that is, strategic marketing management and corporate strategy on one end and marketing tactics on the other, integrated with marketing strategy and other functional business areas.[36]

Six Criteria of Sound Strategy

Potential strategies developed by the marketing manager should be measured against criteria that are most likely to lead to success. Six such criteria for measurement follow:

279

1. *Internal consistency.* Are all elements consistent with one another internally? Are they supportive and synergistic?
2. *Consistency with the environment.* Is the strategy selected consistent with the environs of the marketplace that the marketing manager faces?
3. *Appropriateness in the light of available resources.* Any strategy may fail, no matter how defensible from a "textbook approach," if appropriate resources are not available to implement it. Therefore, sometimes the second-best strategy is the best strategy for a particular situation due to appropriateness.
4. *Satisfactory level of risk.* Again, a best strategy in which the risk is the very survival of the firm may not be worthwhile; in all cases benefits versus cost must be measured.
5. *Reasonable time horizon.* Time, as pointed out earlier, is a crucial element involving the application of resources at the decisive point. Therefore, time horizons, both for preparation and implementation, are crucial.
6. *Workability.* Is the strategy working, considering all previous criteria?[37]

Finally, the marketing manager must analyze the strategies selected as to the critical issue of why there is the potentially sustainable competitive advantage for the corporation and whether it is at the decisive point considering time, place, and position.[38]

Summary

In this chapter we have looked closely at the basic concepts of marketing strategy, including a definition of strategy—that is, how we go about achieving our objectives. We have also looked at where marketing strategy fits in with strategic marketing management conducted at the corporate level and at marketing tactics conducted by lower units of the marketing organization. The central objective, or concept, of strategy is to be stronger at the decisive point, the point incorporating time, place, and positioning. This is accomplished in marketing terms as a competitive differential advantage is achieved, and this advantage is achieved when and where it counts.

A discussion followed concerning military strategy and marketing strategy, showing their similarities and why much of what has been done and will be done in the future in marketing is borrowed from military strategy. The principles of marketing strategy were then noted, including the principles of the objective, initiative, concentration, economy of force, maneuver, unity of command, coordination, security, surprise, simplicity, flexibility, and exploitation. Although various military strategy concepts are extremely valuable for marketing, it was shown that blindly applying military terms to marketing offers minimal gain.

We next turned to important marketing strategy concepts, including mass marketing, product differentiation and market segmentation, marketing strategy positions, marketing share strategies, and finally the strategy of positioning.

We also looked at the future dimensions of marketing strategy, including quantifying marketing strategies, further adaptation of historical military strategic concepts—such as the strategic center of gravity analysis—and integration of marketing strategies throughout the corporation. Finally, we looked at six important criteria for a successful marketing strategy. Strategy is one of the marketing manager's main tasks and main responsibilities. In this chapter you have been introduced to basic concepts that will allow you to develop alternatives that work best under various environmental conditions and organizational situations.

The marketing manager is key to defining need, sensing opportunity, and conceptualizing how the firm's resources might be restructured to take advantage of an opportunity.[39] Thus, there is little question but that the successful marketing manager is a master strategist.

Questions

1. How might you go about finding the decisive point in a marketing situation?
2. Can you think of examples in marketing to illustrate each of the principles of marketing strategy: objective, initiative, concentration, economy of force, maneuver, unity of command, coordination, security, surprise, simplicity, flexibility, and exploitation?
3. It has been said that, in any marketing situation, one or more of the principles of marketing conflict with one another. Do you agree with this statement? If so, what explanation might you have for this and what could you, as a marketing manager, do about it?
4. How might you use the principles of marketing strategy to develop marketing strategy?
5. Give examples of companies that have used product differentiation and marketing segmentation.
6. What would have been the likely outcome if those of your examples using product differentiation had used market segmentation, and vice versa?
7. For each of the following products, state whether market segmentation or product differentiation would be the better strategy and why: fly swatters, gasoline, lawn chairs, personal computers for consumers, business computers, real estate, toothpaste, life insurance.
8. State the condition of product and of market for each of the following marketing strategy positions: new venture, growth, market development, market retention, and balancing.
9. It has been stated that a product always occupies a position in the consumer's mind, whether one actively intends this or not. Does this mean that every marketing manager automatically follows a positioning strategy? Why or why not?
10. Two firms compete in the same market with similar products. From what you have learned about marketing strategy in this chapter, when would it make sense for (a) one firm to concentrate on a certain niche in the marketplace or (b) one firm to attempt to dominate the entire market with the products it offers?

Ethical Questions

You are the product manager of a new brand of cleanser. You have spent six months and hundreds of thousands of dollars developing a unique positioning strategy. You plan to spend a lot more when you roll out a national advertising campaign. Before you can do this, one of your employees drops a package on your desk. It contains the complete marketing plan for your main competitor's new product. It is going to be introduced at the same time as your product. The plan indicates that, by making some changes in your advertising theme and by a slight repositioning, you can demolish his campaign and practically ensure that his product will fail. You ask your employee where he got the package. He answers "Don't ask." What do you do?

Endnotes _____

1. Robert D. Hof and James B. Treece, "This Team-up Has It All Except Sales," *Business Week* (August 14, 1989), p. 79.
2. William A. Cohen, *Winning on the Marketing Front* (New York: Wiley, 1986), pp. 1–2.
3. "Chrysler's Comeback Called 'Blueprint for Success,'" *Marketing News* (March 1, 1985), p. 26.
4. William A. Cohen, "The Application of Historical Military Strategy Concepts to Marketing Strategy," in John C. Rogers III et al., eds., *Development in Marketing Science* (Logan, Utah: Academy of Marketing Science, 1983), pp. 263–265.
5. Derek F. Abell, "Strategic Windows," *Journal of Marketing*, vol. 42 (July 1978), p. 26.
6. Yoram Wind and Thomas S. Robertson, "Marketing Strategy: New Directions for Theory and Research," *Journal of Marketing*, vol. 47 (Spring 1983), p. 12.
7. Harry L. Hansen, "Creative Marketing Strategy," *Boston Conference on Distribution* (Boston: International Marketing Institute, 1959).
8. Philip Kotler and Ravi Singh, "Marketing Warfare in the 1980s," *Journal of Business Strategy* (Fall 1980), pp. 67–81.
9. William A. Cohen, "Historical Military Strategy Principles Advocated for Winning Marketing Wars," *Marketing News* (April 12, 1985), p. 23.
10. These principles may have applicability in other fields. See William A. Cohen, "Are There Generic Principles of Strategy?" *1990 AMA Educators' Proceedings* (Chicago: American Marketing Association, 1990), pp. 330–334.
11. William A. Cohen, "War in the Marketplace," *Business Horizons* (March–April 1986).
12. Peter A. Dickson and James L. Ginter, "Market Segmentation, Product Differentiation, and Marketing Strategy," *Journal of Marketing*, vol. 51 (April 1987), pp. 1–2.
13. Regis McKenna, "Marketing in the Age of Diversity," *Harvard Business Review*, vol. 66, no. 5 (September–October 1988), p. 88.
14. Henry Assael and A. Marvin Roscoe, Jr., "Approaches to Marketing Segmentation Analysis," *Journal of Marketing*, vol. 40 (October 1976), p. 74.
15. Joseph P. Plummer, "The Concept and Application of Life-Cycle Segmentation," *Journal of Marketing*, vol. 38 (January 1974), p. 36.
16. William Wells and Doug Tigert, "Activities, Interests and Opinions," *Journal of Advertising Research*, vol. 11 (August 1971), pp. 27–35.
17. Rajiv Grover and V. Srinivasan, "A Simultaneous Approach to Market Segmentation and Market Structuring," *Journal of Marketing Research*, vol. 24 (May 1987), p. 139.
18. "Pepsi Targets Projected Three Billion Segment of Cola Market with Carefully Plotted Entry," *Marketing News* (December 9, 1983), p. 16.
19. Wendell R. Smith, "Product Differentiation and Market Segmentation as Alternative Marketing Strategies," *Journal of Marketing* (July 1956), pp. 3–8.
20. R. William Kotrba, "The Strategy Selection Chart," *Journal of Marketing*, vol. 30 (July 1966), p. 23.
21. Ibid., p. 25.
22. David W. Cravens, "Marketing Strategy Positioning," *Business Horizons*, vol. 18 (December 1975), p. 60.
23. C. Davis Fogg, "Planning Gains in Market Share," *Journal of Marketing*, vol. 38 (July 1974), p. 30.
24. Robert Jacobson, "Distinguishing Among Competing Theories of the Market Share Effect," *Journal of Marketing*, vol. 52, no. 4 (October 1988), p. 78.
25. Lewis Alpert and Ronald Gatty, "Product Positioning by Behavioral Life-Styles," *Journal of Marketing*, vol. 33 (April 1969), p. 65.
26. Al Ries and Jack Trout, *Positioning: The Battle for Your Mind* (New York: McGraw-Hill, 1981), p. 2.
27. Pat Sloan, "Jeans Marketers Tune Up Toney Pitches," *Advertising Age* (May 27, 1985), p. 12.
28. "Schiefflin Tests Dual-Positioned Red Wine," *Marketing News* (November 11, 1983).
29. "Sacrifice Is the Penance Paid for Effective Positioning," *Marketing News* (November 23, 1984), p. 3.
30. John W. Schouten and James H. McAlexander, "Positioning Services for Competitive Advantage: The Case of Duds 'N Suds," *Journal of Services Marketing*, vol. 3, no. 2 (Spring 1989), p. 70.
31. Ries and Trout, op. cit., pp. 214–221.
33. Terry Clark, "The Concept of Marketing Crisis," *Journal of the Academy of Marketing Science*, vol. 16, no. 2 (Summer 1988), p. 47.
33. Victor J. Cook, Jr., "Marketing Strategy and Differential Advantage," *Journal of Marketing*, vol. 47 (Spring 1983), pp. 68–75.
34. Victor J. Cook, Jr., "Understanding Marketing Strategy and Differential Advantage," *Journal of Marketing*, vol. 49 (Spring 1985), pp. 137–142.
35. William A. Cohen, "A Methodology for Developing International Marketing Strategies Using a Strategic Center of Gravity Analysis," in Erdener Kaynak, ed., *Managing the International Market-*

ing Function: Creative Challenges of the Eighties (Halifax, Nova Scotia: World Marketing Congress, 1983), pp. 99–108.

36. Wind and Robertson, op. cit., pp. 12–25.

37. Seymour Tilles, "How to Evaluate Corporate Strategy," in Richard G. Hamermesh, ed., *Strategic Management* (New York: Wiley, 1983), p. 77.

38. Robin Wensley, "Strategic Marketing: Betas, Boxes, or Basics," *Journal of Marketing*, vol. 45 (Summer 1981), p. 181.

39. Michael D. Hutt, Peter H. Reingen, and John R. Ronchetto, Jr., "Tracing Emergent Processes in Marketing Strategy Formation," *Journal of Marketing*, vol. 52, no. 1 (January 1988), p. 16.

11

The Strategy of New Product Development

CHAPTER OBJECTIVES

● Understand new product development as a marketing strategy and why companies adopt it.

● Know the six stages of the product development process and what is required for the management of each stage.

● Understand what is required to increase the new product development success rate.

● Know the major alternatives to internal new product development and when they should be used.

RCA's Slipped Disc

RCA finally threw in the towel and wrote off $580 million of investment in video disc players. This ended a four-year battle to introduce a new product that RCA once touted as the most important consumer electronics product of the decade. Originally, RCA had expected to sell 500,000 video disc players in the very first year. Yet, after four years, it had sold only 840,000 of the eight million video cassette recorders (VCRs) sold up to that time. During the battle to get the video disc accepted, prices were cut in half, and more advanced models were introduced. Millions of dollars were spent by RCA to develop a library of discs. Promotion was not slighted. Promotional efforts included not only a major ad campaign featuring Gene Kelly, but also no finance charges on term purchases, a free disc with each player, and a money-back guarantee. Finally, technical advantages of the videodisc over the VCR were not insignificant. They included convenience, ease of storage (in fact videodiscs were not much larger than an ordinary audio record), and the price—which was only $14.95 to $35.95, with an average price of $26, much lower than video cassettes. But the video disc player was a flop.[1]

Can You Say BMW, Mercedes Benz, and Toyota in a Single Breath?

The Japanese luxury cars are here. First was the Toyota Lexus, selling at a base price of $35,000. The Japanese spent six years and over $5 million at Toyota developing the Lexus, and it is targeted directly at luxury-buying consumers in the United States. The Japanese didn't consider introducing luxury cars in the U.S. market until taxes on big autos, amounting to 23 per cent of the wholesale price, were eased. According to Chief Engineer Ichiro Suzuki, once the decision was made to introduce a new product, "Compromise was unacceptable, and we had to push the engineers to achieve the vision we wanted to create." The first prototype engine only got 20.5 miles per gallon. That wasn't enough. So the entire engine was redone, redesigned, and improved until design goals were met. Hard decisions, such as whether to go with a smooth design or a high rear deck that improves aerodynamics but looks ungainly, had to be made. So did other important trade-offs between looks and performance. Existing Toyota dealers appeared inappropriate to sell this car because they were volume sellers. So an entirely new distribution system had to be set up. An appropriate name also seemed called for. The name Lexus was finally selected. The owner of a computerized legal information service called Lexis got a temporary injunction against the use of the name. Eventually an out of court settlement was reached, and the name "Lexus" stood. While this was going on, the head of the American Lexus operation quit to go back to General Motors. Toyota executives picked his second in command to replace him. Close behind Toyota's Lexus is Nissan's Infiniti Q45, which will sell for slightly more. Says Wall Street's best-known automotive deal analyst, Mary Ann Keller, "I have no doubts about Lexus and Infiniti being ultimately successful, but I don't think this is a market conducive to instant success."[2]

Hard on the Outside, Soft on the Inside

Not so long ago, all cookies crunched when their consumers took a bite. But several years ago, major food marketers, including Nabisco Brands, Procter & Gamble, Frito-Lay, and Keebler, introduced soft and chewy cookies that they predicted would eventually command as much as $775 million annually. That's 25 per cent of the $3.1 billion cookie market. Currently, the category is almost there, with Nabisco Brands' Almost Home in the forefront with 37 per cent of the retail market share. But though Nabisco Brands is in the lead, the competition has far from thrown in the towel. Frito-Lay, while trailing the pack, spent $2.2 million for advertising to introduce its products. A totally new category of cookie was firmly established in the U.S. market.[3]

Why did the video disc product fail at such great financial and other costs to RCA while other companies successfully introduced a totally new concept in cookies? Could the problems associated with failing products have been anticipated and avoided? Or should these products have been introduced at all? What actions should companies take to prevent failures in the future?

This chapter will help you both to answer these questions and to exercise one of the most exciting, yet demanding functions as a marketing executive: managing the strategy of new product development.

But RCA's video disk is only one of many examples of product failure that many sources feel to be as high as eight or nine out of every ten products introduced. In fact, the cost of new product introduction is horrendous. Over the last five years, R&D spending has increased at an average 14.4 per cent per year.[4] Three measures of the top fifteen companies in R&D spending from a single year are shown in Figure 11-1. From these figures you can see the tremendous amounts of money involved. With a failure rate as high as nine out of ten, why should companies invest in new product development and R&D of new products at all?

Source: Alan Hall, "Where R&D is Strong and Getting Stronger," *Business Week* (Special Issue March 22, 1985), p. 164.

Why Companies Adopt the New Product Development Strategy

Companies may adopt a new product development strategy for many reasons. Sometimes a company is forced into it by the competition. If you are a cookie company and a competitor introduces a soft, chewy cookie, you may need to introduce a similar product to protect your share of the overall market. The product life cycle, which will be discussed in more detail in the next chapter, is a concept that describes the life of a product in terms of a cycle. This means that, at some point, your product goes into decline. A company that knows its marketing will always have new products on the way to replace those at the end of their life cycles. What would you do if all your company's products were in section B of the product life cycle shown in Figure 11-2?

Sometimes new laws or changes to old laws will force companies to innovate with new products. Thus did legislation force automobile manufacturers to develop cars with lower gas consumption. Excess capacity may encourage companies to look for new products that they can market to allow them to make fuller use of production equipment and facilities. Some companies embark on new product development to diversify into new markets; others seek merely to take advantage of new developments in technology. Increasing market share is the primary way in which many companies experience growth. One study showed a direct relationship between spending on research and development and sales. As one increased, so did the other. This relationship is illustrated in Figure 11-3.[5]

Increased profits are always a valid reason for adopting a new product development strategy. Milton D. Rosenau, Jr., now a consultant, but formerly

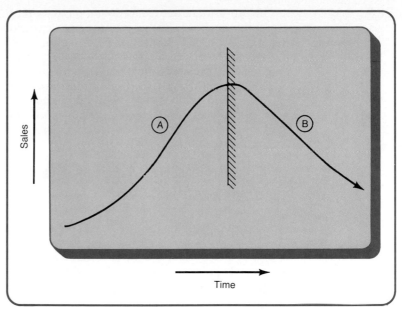

Figure 11-2 If All of Your Company's Products are in Section B of the Product Life Cycle Curve, the New Product Development Strategy is Crucial!

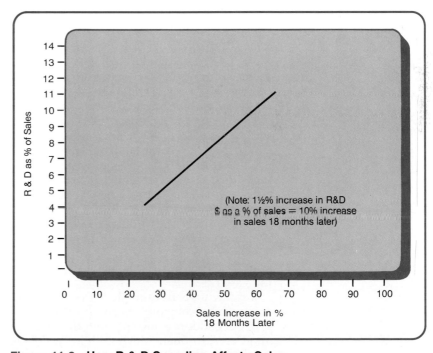

(Note: 1½% increase in R&D $ as a % of sales = 10% increase in sales 18 months later)

Figure 11-3 How R & D Spending Affects Sales

Source: Adapted from "The More They Spend on R & D the Faster They Grow," *Inc.* (August, 1981)

vice-president of Science Technology, a multinational *Fortune* 500 industrial company, says, "If this is not the basic reason that your company is engaging in new product development, you should seriously ask yourself whether it is worth the effort."[6]

Many firms recognize that new product development is worth tremendous investment despite the high failure rate, and the result of this effort is seen again and again. One recent study showed that 19 per cent of the million-dollar-a-year brands sold in food stores in 1981 were new since 1970. In health and beauty aids, 38 per cent were new over this period; for dry grocery nonfoods, 29 per cent; for frozen and refrigerated foods, 16 per cent; and for dry grocery foods, 15 per cent. In health and beauty aids, 50 per cent of brands with annual sales of $2.5 million to $5 million first appeared during the previous twelve years.[7]

The New Product Development Process _____

There are seven steps in the new product development process. These are illustrated in Figure 11-4. The process begins with **idea acquisition** and proceeds to **screening**, **business analysis**, and **concept testing**, which are sometimes combined. Next, **product development** itself is begun. When development is complete, **market testing** is initiated, and if all goes well, finally there is the **introduction** of the product. Note that the process is interactive. Products may reach one stage, encounter problems, and go back one or more stages to begin again. Let's look at each of these steps in turn.

Idea Acquisition

Ideas for new products may come from many different sources. These include

- *Customers.* According to the marketing concept, the focus of marketing should be on the customer and customer need satisfaction. Therefore, the customer is a major source for new product ideas either revealed through market research, or through other processes. One survey indicated that of 267 mentions of major external sources for new product ideas, customers represented 28 per cent.[8] For industrial companies, the percentage was even greater. In another study, 77 per cent of the sample of 111 scientific instrument innovations and 67 per cent of a sample of 49 process machinery innovations came from the customer.[9] As mentioned previously, this sometimes comes from market research, but the customer can also assist in new product development ideas through research of customer letters, including complaints, and even customer buying patterns.

   A rather unusual example of this is provided by entrepreneur Joe Cossman, whose company, E. Joseph Cossman and Company, sold various types of children's novelties and toys. One of his products was a "potato spud gun" through which a child could shoot a small bit of potato. It was a harmless toy because potatoes are mostly water. Cossman sold over a million of these products in a single year. A significant portion

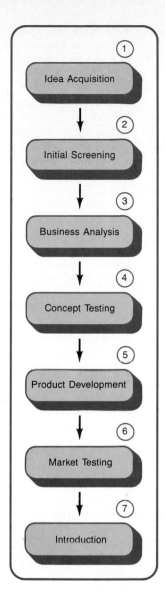

**Figure 11-4 The Seven Steps in the New
Product Development Process**

was sold in grocery stores, a few of which had originally ordered the
gun to be used as a premium to be given away with each sack of potatoes.
Cossman found out about it in reviewing his orders. He asked the question, "Why would a grocery store want to buy potato spud guns?" When
he discovered the answer, he launched a full-fledged promotional campaign in which he convinced grocery store owners to sell the gun and
give a bag of potatoes away as a premium.[10]

- *The Competition.* The competition is also an excellent source of new
  product development ideas for many companies. In the $675 million
  dentifrice industry, Lever Brothers was the first to introduce a gel in

1969 with the Close-Up brand. The gel idea caught on, and a few years later Lever brought out another gel called Aim. Beecham, Inc., noted this success and introduced Aqua-Fresh, a striped combination that included both gel and paste in 1979; and then Procter & Gamble, and Colgate-Palmolive both introduced their own versions of gels in Crest and Colgate, their old standbys.

Many companies study every new product introduced by the competition for its potential. If it does appear to have potential, they decide whether to introduce a similar product that does the same thing. If they do, they must do it without violating a patent or other protected rights of the company that introduced the product. Sometimes that means developing an entirely new product to do essentially the same thing that the competitor's product does.

A study of 107 firms found that almost 30 per cent used an analysis of competitive products as a source of new product ideas.[11] Noted marketing professor Theodore Levitt of Harvard has recommended what he calls "innovative imitation" as a strategy.[12]

- *Salespeople.* Salespeople, dealing with the consumer, with resalers, or with company buyers, are excellent sources of new product ideas. And those ideas are based on their firsthand experience with their contacts, who purchase from them. As a matter of fact, salespeople tend to be advocates for the customer and as such should be given the same attention, just as if the customer were speaking.

  One cautionary note, however. Information from a single salesperson should be checked with other salespeople and against other market intelligence before resources are committed to new product development. Some companies, small and large, err by listening to a single salesperson who may be particularly articulate and persuasive. Such individuals may convince top company decision makers to allocate resources to a particular project based on their input, without going through the initial screening and business analysis stages. The results have been major failures, and worse, failures that might have been foreseen and avoided.

- *Top management.* Top management is also a source of new product ideas in many firms. This tends to be both because of their experience with a particular product and also because of their perspective. Top management sees a broader picture of the overall market and the company's environment. Top management may sometimes spot an unfulfilled need or demand in the marketplace missed by other managers within the company who are too close to the problem. However, middle managers responsible for new product development must be cautious in handling ideas emanating from this source.

  One particular company run by an engineer, who himself had previously headed the new product development organization, unwittingly wasted resources and caused cost overruns and slippages and other difficulties within his new product development organization simply because of his own propensity to "suggest" ideas. Because of his position as president, these suggestions were taken as directives, and new programs were started and stopped with great frequency until the organization was so demoralized and the new product development output so poor that an extremely strong new product development manager had to be brought in to revitalize the organization.

Research and Development Department. Sometimes new product ideas will come from the R&D organization itself, with little contact with the customer or the competition. This is especially true with innovative organizations that have considerable R&D talent who are on the very cutting edge of the state of the art and technology. As a result, these individuals will think up new products based on their knowledge of what is possible, rather than what is demanded in the marketplace.

Examples of technology leading the marketplace include everything from the airplane to hand-held calculators to the home computer—all cases where an ongoing demand didn't exist until the product first was invented. It was then that the marketplace became aware of the possibilities.

Such a situation is sometimes noted as a fallacy in the marketing concept because in focusing totally on the customer, one overlooks the potential of developing demand by demonstrating the feasibility of what was not even considered by the potential customer. However, others would argue that this merely supports the marketing concept: that what is really being accomplished is to satisfy the needs of the marketplace, which existed but were not recognized at the time the product was introduced. Regardless of whether one supports the theory of new product initiation from R&D being a phenomenon of the marketing concept or an exception to it, it is clear that important ideas can come from R&D departments and the engineers, scientists, and other technologists developing products within them, even though, in some cases, their contact with the marketplace is scant or nonexistent.

Screening and Deciding Among New Product Development Opportunities

Screening and methods of comparing different new product opportunities are considered together, although their purposes may be somewhat different. Screening implies go/no-go criteria that may be quantitative or have to do with the fit of a product into a product line, acceptability of a product in the marketplace, or other criteria. A comparison among various opportunities, all of which have passed the go/no-go screening test, will indicate some products that are more attractive in a business sense to a company than others. Accordingly, a business analysis must be performed to see which products are more desirable, considering the business criteria decided upon as important for the company. However, some business analyses could also be screening criteria. For example, a company may have a policy of a certain minimal return on investment or sales potential, or a new product development will not be undertaken. At the same time, return on investment or sales potential may be compared among potential new products to see which is more favorable.

Screening Questions. Typical screening questions, which any company might ask, may be categorized by having to do with company operations, potential market, concept marketability, engineering and production, and financial and legal influences. These are summarized in Exhibit 11-1.[13]

Exhibit 11-1 Typical Screening Questions

Company Operations

- How compatible is the concept with the current product lines?
- Does it represent an environmental hazard or threat to our production facility and to the facilities of our neighbors?
- Would it unreasonably interrupt manufacturing, engineering, or marketing activities?
- Could we meet the after-sale service requirements that would be demanded by customers?

Potential Market

- What is the size of the market?
- Where is the market located?
- What would be our potential market share?
- How diversified is the need for the product? Is it a one-industry or multi-industry product?
- How fast do we anticipate the market for the concept to grow?
- How stable would such a market be in a recession?

Concept Marketability

- Who would be our competitors?
- How good is their product?
- How well capitalized are potential competitors?
- How important is their product to the survival of their business?
- How is our product differentiated from the competition's? Will the differentiation provide a market advantage?
- Could we meet or beat the competition's price?
- Is the product normally sold through our current distribution channels, or would we have to make special arrangements?
- Do we have qualified sales personnel?
- Do we have a suitable means by which to promote the product?
- What would we anticipate to be the life expectancy of the product? Is it going to move through the various life-cycle stages in 6 months, 6 years, or 60 years?
- Will the product be offensive to the environment in which it will be used?

Engineering and Production

- What is the technical feasibility of the product?
- Do we have the technical capability to design it?
- Can it be manufactured at a marketable cost?
- Will the necessary production materials be readily available?
- Do we have the production capabilities to build it?
- Do we have adequate storage facilities for the raw materials and completed product?
- Do we have adequate testing devices for proper quality control of the product?

Financial

- What is our required return on investment?
- What is our anticipated ROI for this product?

Exhibit 11-1 (Continued)

293

The Strategy of New
Product Development

- Do we have the available capital?
- What would be the pay-back period?
- What is our break-even point?

Legal

- Is the product patentable?
- Can we meet legal restrictions regarding labeling, advertising, shipment, and the like?
- How significant are product warranty problems likely to be?
- Is the product vulnerable to existing or pending legislation?

Source: Adapted from Tom W. White, "Use Variety of Internal, External Sources to Gather and Screen New Product Ideas," *Marketing News* (September 16, 1983), p. 12.

Methods for Screening and Business Analysis

Return on Investment (ROI) Analysis. Return on investment is a measure of the profitability with which economic resources required for a particular product under development are employed. While the ROI definition is clear, different ratios have been employed in business to represent what ROI means. But ROI is essentially a cost-benefit analysis in which we compare costs—in this case our investment with benefits, or profits, to the firm.

One way to calculate ROI would be to consider the total anticipated profit over the lifetime of the product divided by the total anticipated investment. The total anticipated investment would include the development cost, outlays for capital equipment, marketing cost, and any other expenditures required to achieve the level of profits forecasted. Thus, for a potential new product in which the total anticipated profit was $10 million and investment was $2 million, the ROI would be $10 million divided by $2 million, or 500 per cent. Of course, more meaningful results could be obtained by discounting both the numerator and the denominator for the time value of money, using capital budgeting techniques, as will be discussed later.

Pay-back Analysis. Pay-back, or pay-back period, is the time required for the earnings to pay back the cost of the investment. Pay-back is computed by dividing the investment by the annual profit expected. Thus, it represents the number of years required for the gross earnings on the project to pay back the original cash outlay, or investment. If, for example, one new product development opportunity had required a $5,000 investment and the annual profit was estimated to be $1,000 per year, the pay-back period would be $5,000 divided by $1,000, or five years.

The pay-back is used in many companies to compare projects; however, it should be noted that it does not tell which products among those compared are more profitable, only how soon the original investments will be returned. The pay-back figures used also can be discounted due to the time value of money using capital budgeting techniques.

Time, Cost, Sales, and Profit Goal Comparisons. Time, cost, sales, and profit goal comparisons may be quite arbitrary, but they can be used as both the screening and comparative techniques to determine the relative acceptability of products that are under consideration for development. Time goals, for example, may be set up because a new product is needed within a certain time to meet a competitive introduction of a similar product. Cost criteria may be important because of available resources within the company to develop new products. In the same fashion, sales and profits goals can be compared as indicators of effectiveness and the achievement of company objectives.

Capital Budgeting Techniques. Capital budgeting techniques can also be used to assist in deciding the relative merit of different new product candidates. With these techniques, the cash flow of each product is developed, including the new product development cost, capital equipment, expenditures for marketing, and profits. Because these outlays and inflows of cash do not occur in the same year, they must be discounted over a period of time, considering the fact that the money can be put to alternative uses. For example, instead of investing in the new product development and introduction, the money could be in the bank to earn interest. Considering the risk factor of introducing new products, if the interest rate were identical to the annual profits as a per centage of the investment earned through developing the new product, if no other factors were considered, it would make more sense to put the money in the bank.

There are two different methods for using capital budgeting techniques for analyzing new product development alternatives. First, you can discount the cash flow over a period of years of the life of the product, from initial expenditure through its life cycle, until the product is withdrawn. This cash flow, of course, would include all expenditures, as well as receipts. Those products with the highest net present value would be those that we would select over those that have lower net present values.

An alternative methodology would be to select products with higher internal rates of return. The internal rate of return would be the average annual per centage that we are receiving from our investment.[14]

Cost Prediction Formula Analysis. Cost prediction formulas predict the investment required to complete individual new product development. They use relevant related parameters such as sales forecasts and historical data. For example, you could derive a cost formula based on the historical ratio of cost to sales for successful products in your organization. Thus,

$$\text{cost} = \frac{\text{historical cost for successful projects}}{\text{historical sales for successful project}} \times \text{predicted sales}$$

There are, however, two problems with this approach. First, it assumes a relationship between development and marketing costs and sales for future products in your company as they were in the past. This may or may not be true. Second, of course, to do such forecasting, you must have a model from your company based on a product that has gone through its life cycle to calculate a costs-to-sales ratio.

Scoring, Weighting, and Ranking Methods. Scoring, weighting, and ranking methods can be used with a combination of other methods that we have discussed. With this approach, simply rank the potential products according to some list of criteria that are important in your company. Select products from the top to the bottom of the list until a cutoff point is reached—when you run out of products to develop because of budget limitations. Numerous criteria can be considered, including product life cycle, patentability, and strength of competition.

Economic Allocation Methods. Economic allocation methods are perhaps among the most sophisticated for different methods of new product development selection. These methods address themselves to the question of how much should be spent for each product rather than just to the question of which product should be developed. Complex models can consider such factors as the likelihood of success in development; the payoff in sales and profits if successful; and the risk of the competition developing a similar product. For a comprehensive review of this method of calculating funding levels for new products, see the *Economics of Defense in the Nuclear Age* by Charles J. Hitch and Roland N. McKean (New York: Athanenum, 1965).

The method, or combination of methods, to use in deciding among competing potential new products for development depends on the situation. It depends on what is important for your company at a particular time. To accomplish new product development analysis and screening, first document the alternative opportunities with the attendant facts. Decide which method or methods of analysis are relevant to your situation. Accomplish the analyses and compare alternative projects. Select those for development continuance. Review your analyses periodically as conditions change and whenever other new product opportunities are to be considered.

Concept Testing

Concept testing involves testing the market acceptance of the new product concept or comparing the market acceptance of competing concepts to determine those that have the greatest appeal. Concept testing is usually done after the initial screening. However, it could be a part of the initial screening or of the comparative analysis phase of the selection of new products for development.

With concept testing, consumers are asked to react to a concept—that is, a synthesis provided in a verbal or visual description of the product idea— usually without an example of the product itself.

The Objectives of Concept Testing. The objectives of concept testing are several. First and foremost, of course, is to see whether the concept is acceptable to the market as anticipated—due to prior marketing research and internal company analysis. Several concepts may be presented during concept testing. The company doing the testing would like to see which concepts are the better ones. Sometimes a company wants to learn what modifications should be made to the product concept prior to development, when changes or modifications are less expensive, rather than during development, when they are more so. The testers may wish to learn and obtain clues on

Exhibit 11-2 Sample Concept Testing Questions

1. What do you think of the product concept?
2. Would you buy it?
3. How much do you think it should sell for?
4. How often would you purchase it?
5. Where would you expect to purchase it?
6. What additional features should the product have?
7. What features should be eliminated?
8. How would you expect to learn about the product's availability?
9. How large should the product be?
10. What color should the product be?
11. How would you use the product?
12. Are there benefits of this product over competing products or products that it might replace?
13. Would you buy this product to replace the current product you are using?

distribution channels, promotional appeals, pricing, or other aspects of the marketing mix. Also, a company may want to learn additional uses or modifications of the uses of the product to understand better not only about development, but also about how to present the product to the consumer. And, finally, those doing concept testing may wish to learn what target markets or market segments would be better for the proposed new product concept.

Sample Concept Testing Questions. To achieve the foregoing objectives, various questions are constructed to be answered by consumers, either in focus groups or in larger numbers. Typical questions are shown in Exhibit 11-2.

Inherent Dangers of Concept Testing. Perhaps the greatest inherent danger in concept testing is that individuals who were surveyed do not answer truthfully. Because as many as 70 to 90 per cent of companies introducing new products may use concept testing incorporating purchase intention, this can be a major problem. In fact, studies attempting to relate purchase intention to actual purchase behavior have found substantial variation between the two.[15]

Respondents usually do not answer truthfully, not because of any malicious intent, but rather because people give the answers they think are expected of them. For example, a survey to decide on the construction of a playhouse in a small town was misled by the number of respondents who indicated that they would see a play or opera were it performed locally. As noted previously, plays and operas are indicative of culture to many people. Therefore, to give a negative response was perceived as demonstrating a lack of culture. The timing of the research can also be important.[16] What is true today may not be true, or as true, tomorrow. At times the only true test of purchase is when consumers actually spend their money to purchase any given product or service. This is why test marketing is still needed, even after marketing research and concept testing.

Still, concept testing is important because it is done relatively early in the development process; as a result it can not only assist in eliminating unprofitable products or products that would fail later in the marketplace, but can accomplish this before greater R&D expenditures in developing the new product are made.

Product Development

Product development may be under the direct control of a product manager or other marketing manager with a similar title, or it may be done by a technical manager reporting to the marketing manager directly, or a technical manager reporting to a nonmarketing executive at a higher level. In any case, the marketing manager must be involved in the new product development process. Any problems either with scheduling or slippage, cost, or achieving the performance intended will affect marketing planning, strategy, and relationships with consumers, suppliers, resalers, and other groups involved in the marketing process.

Planning. The key to successful product development is in planning. Four aspects should receive particular attention:

1. Defining objectives
2. Establishing the project organization
3. Installing controls
4. Coordinating

Defining Objectives. Objectives must be defined from the very beginning of the project, before any money is spent on development. Objectives should be defined not only in terms of performance goals, but also in timing when the product is needed and what it will cost to develop.

Establishing the Project Organization. The basic principle of project organization for development of the new product is that the project head has the authority commensurate with the responsibility to accomplish his or her task. This may either be done by assigning responsibilities to an established functional organization for product development in which all individuals report to the individual with the authority to establish the project, as in Figure 11-5, or it may be accomplished using a matrix organization of product development, as in Figure 11-6. In any case, it must be clearly established who is going to do what—what organizations are reporting directly to the product development manager or matrixed into his or her organization. It is highly desirable that the new product organization be separate from the group responsible for existing products.[17]

Installing Controls. Performance controls must be installed so that product development can be monitored continually. No new product development will go exactly as planned. The larger and the more complex the project, the more opportunity for problems to occur. Accordingly, the key to solving these problems is spotting them sufficiently early. Otherwise they can become major bottlenecks that can delay or destroy the development program and terminate the product even before it enters the market. To do this,

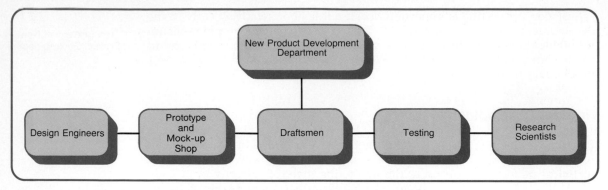

Figure 11-5   New Product Development Using a Functional Organization

controls must be instituted that enable the product development manager to keep a continual pulse on the timing, scheduling, and cost of each aspect of the product development as performance goals are reached.

Coordination. The development of a new product in a company involves the coordination of many different functional areas. Monies have to be available at various times for expenditures in development. Materials must be on hand to build prototypes. Resources that are on hand too early cost the company money due to storage or the fact that they could have been used

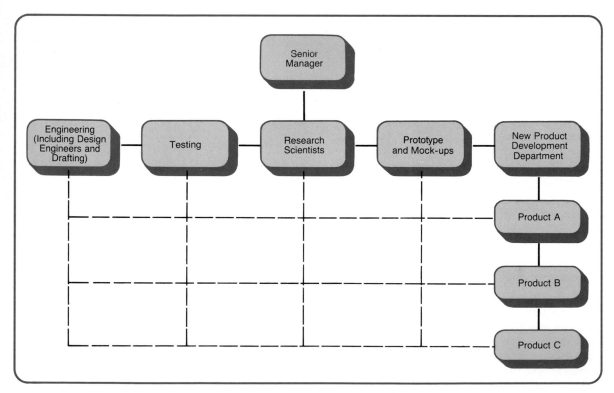

Figure 11-6   New Product Development with a Matrix Organization

298

elsewhere in the company to contribute to profit. The product design developed by the engineers must be able to be produced later on in quantity by the manufacturing division. Further, it must be able to be manufactured at the price planned. Because of the foregoing, no new product development can be planned in a vacuum only by the product manager and his or her staff. Every phase must be coordinated with many other organizations within the company, and this coordination must be continued throughout the development process.

Such coordination is no small problem in new product development, and its complexity can be easily demonstrated. A framework for assessing marketing's interaction with other functional areas during new product development is shown in Figure 11-7. It outlines relationships considering situational dimensions, structural and process dimensions, and outcomes. Note that the interactions of fourteen dimensions are identified and that they lead to five separate outcomes, all of which are crucial.[18]

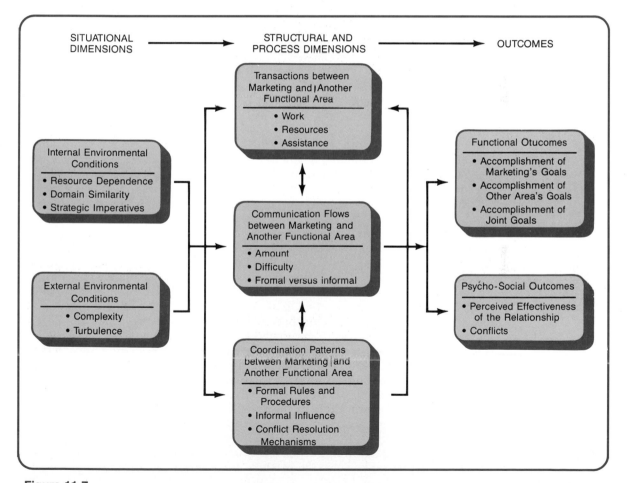

Figure 11-7

Source: Adapted from Robert W. Ruekert and Orville C. Walker, Jr. "Marketing's Interaction with other Functional Units: A Conceptual Framework and Empirical Evidence," *Journal of Marketing* Vol. 51 No. 1 (January 1987) p. 1.

TASK	MONTHS AFTER PROJECT INITIATION											
	1	2	3	4	5	6	7	8	9	10	11	12
DESIGN MODULE												
Eng. Dept.	10,000	5,000	5,000	5,000	5,000							
PROTOTYPES												
Eng. Dept.					2,000	2,000	1,000	1,000	500			
Prototype Shop						10,000	5,000	3,000	2,000			
Drafting Dept.					1,000	1,000						
TESTING												
Eng. Dept							500	500	500	500	500	
Testing Dept.							1,000	1,500	1,500	2,000	1,000	
TOTALS	10,000	5,000	5,000	5,000	8,000	13,000	7,500	6,000	4,500	2,500	1,500	$68,000

Figure 11-8 Product Development Schedule

Product Development Schedule. A simple device for use in controlling, coordinating, and managing any new product development is a product development schedule, shown in Figure 11-8. Note that the first column is entitled "Tasks." Every task necessary to develop the product is listed under this column. Also, across the top of the product development schedule are time periods from the month that the project was initiated until the product development is complete. Departments having a responsibility in completing a task are listed under the task. And going horizontally to the right, on a monthly basis, from initiation until completion of that task, dollars to be expended are noted. In this way, the entire project can be planned, including its cost on a total, as well as a monthly basis. When actually implemented, the same schedule can be used to measure progress with each month's actual expenditures compared with those planned. In this fashion, product development can be controlled from inception to completion.

Terminating New Products During Development. One of the most difficult, yet necessary functions of a new product development manager or marketing manager is deciding to terminate a new product's development. This may be necessary due to the product's technical failure to achieve its required performance characteristics, to its costing more to develop than was anticipated, to changing conditions in the marketplace, or to advancing technology making continuing its development unwarranted. Termination may also be necessary because the product is no longer related to the firm's objectives or goals.

The decision to terminate product development can be as important as the decision to initiate product development because the resources—financial,

300

material, and human—always have alternative uses to which they can be put in developing other new products that can benefit the company.

Market Testing

Once all the other gates have been passed, market testing is frequently used as the final trial before committing the bulk of financial resources to introducing the product. With market testing, the company comes closer to realizing what will actually happen when the product is introduced nationally or internationally than anything that has gone before. Thus, market testing is worthwhile when it can save money, and this is the primary reason for undertaking it. The relatively small expenditure, even if this expenditure is several million dollars, is definitely worthwhile if it can save $100 million or more later because a product that was introduced nationally failed.

Drawbacks with Market Testing

Despite the benefits of spending a little to learn a lot, there are, however, some drawbacks that must be considered before the decision is made to market test a new product: market testing may reveal actions to the competition prematurely, there may be additional costs, there may be a delay in getting the product fully established in the market, and the market test may not be a good predictor of success. To maximize the chances of the market test being a good predictor, select your test area carefully. Ensure that the site selected will lead to projectable and accurate results. Also, you should test long enough to achieve meaningful results. According to A. C. Nielsen, the advertising research company, the ratio of forecasting accuracy in test marketing is only one out of seven, or 13 per cent after two months of testing—but it's five out of six after ten months.[19] Watch the competition. Competitive actions in the test area can invalidate your results. Finally, study past test campaigns for similar products before you start. History tends to repeat itself, and costly basic mistakes may be avoided.

Because of the potential drawbacks, a **cost-benefit analysis** should always be undertaken before the decision is made to market test. If the advantages outweigh the disadvantages, market testing should be accomplished; if not, risks may need to be accepted and introduction accomplished without testing.

The Introduction Phase

The introduction phase, which is also known as commercialization, involves taking a product that has been successfully developed through the preceding steps and establishing it in the marketplace. Strategies for new product development during this phase are discussed in other chapters. However, it should be understood by all marketers that it does not require a technological breakthrough to have a successful product in the marketplace. Most successful new products simply build on past successes and on products already in general use.

For example, a recent product that has been extremely successful was introduced by Minnesota Mining and Manufacturing Company. The product is simply an improved scratch paper, but it is scratch paper with a difference. It has a thin strip of adhesive on the back so that it can be stuck on telephones, desks, walls, office reports, and other objects to get one's attention and to be a constant reminder to the individual who put it there.[20]

The success of this product demonstrates that some of the best new products are obviously ones that marketers somehow overlooked. In fact, many successful products and big winners, including disposable diaper liners, razors, home smoke detectors, and small briefcase-sized folding umbrellas, are products that could have been developed relatively easily and did not represent a gigantic leap forward in technology. This demonstrates once again that the primary aspect in the success of new products in the marketplace is marketing and the value of the product fulfilling a need, rather than the state of the art of technology that the new product represents. It is perhaps for this reason that the process of "new product diffusion" depends not only on the product but also on the interaction of communication channels, time, and the social system.[21]

Increasing the Success Rate

Marketing experts have sought ways of increasing the success rate for developing new products for many years. One study distilled the reasons for failure down to eight factors:

1. Product lacked meaningful uniqueness
2. Poor planning
3. Bad timing
4. Overenthusiasm that caused facts to be disregarded
5. Product failure in the marketplace
6. Absence of a product champion
7. Company politics
8. Unexpectedly high product cost[22]

Another study looked at 114 new industrial products in 101 firms. Four general reasons for failure were found, as shown in Figure 11-9. Note the importance of sales, profit margins, and development costs.[23] Certain management mistakes should be avoided like the plague. These include an incomplete overall strategy; not communicating this strategy to everyone involved in any way with the new product; organizational confusion regarding who is responsible for what, when, and where; poor communications across the marketing/R&D interface; not actively seeking the generation of ideas; poor financial evaluation; misuse of marketing research; poor tracking from test marketing; delusion, self-deception, and overconfidence; and, finally, lack of a new product abandonment program.[24] Implementation of a new product development strategy inevitably means that the marketing manager has his or her hands full.

A summary of factors and subfactors desirable in new products is shown in Figure 11-10.[25] Booz, Allen, Hamilton, the management consulting firm,

	Percentage of Product Failures		
Reason	Main Reason	Contributing Reason	Main or Contributing Reason
Sales fell below expectations	63.2%	14.9%	78.1%
Profit margins fell below expectations	21.1	23.7	44.7
Development costs exceeded expectations	19.3	21.1	40.4
Investment exceeded expectations	4.4	8.8	13.2
All others	4.4	0.0	4.4

Source: Adapted from Robert G. Cooper, "Why New Industrial Products Fail," *Industrial Marketing Management,* vol. 4 (1975).

Figure 11-9   General Reasons for New Industrial Product Failure

completed a major study of 13,000 new products from more than 700 U.S. manufacturers. Factors that in some way contributed to success from this study are illustrated in Figure 11-11.[26] Yet another approach at finding the keys to new product introduction success looked at products as their results clustered around certain scenarios. The "synergistic 'Close-to-Home' prod-

I. Marketability
   A. Relation to present distribution channels
   B. Relation to present product lines
   C. Quality-price relationship
   D. Number of sizes and grades
   E. Merchandisability
   F. Effects on sales of present products
II. Durability
   A. Stability
   B. Breadth of market
   C. Resistance to cyclical fluctuations
   D. Resistance to seasonal fluctuations
   E. Exclusiveness of design
III. Productive Ability
   A. Equipment necessary
   B. Production knowledge and personnel necessary
   C. Raw materials availability
IV. Growth Potential
   A. Place in market
   B. Expected competitive situation—value added
   C. Expected availability of end users

Source: Adapted from J. T. O'Meara, "Selecting Profitable Products," *Harvard Business Review* (January–February 1961), pp. 84–85.

Figure 11-10   What Attributes Should New Products Have?

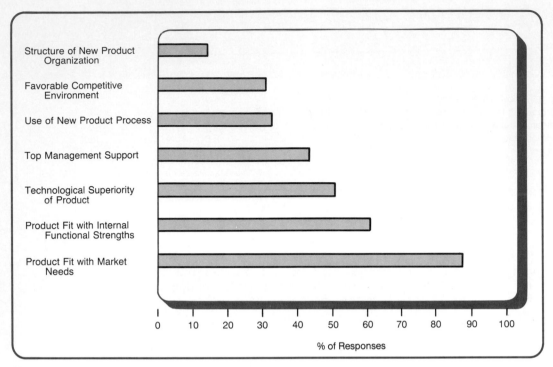

Figure 11-11 Factors Contributing to the Success of New Products

Source: Adapted from *New Product Management for the 1980s* (New York: Booz, Allen, Hamilton, Inc., 1982), p. 16.

uct," the "innovative superior product with no synergy," and the "old but simple money saver" clusters of products appeared to have the best chance for success. The "better mousetrap with no marketing," the "me too" product with no technical/production synergy," and the "innovative mousetrap that really wasn't better" had little to no chance of succeeding.[27]

Another word of caution regarding success is that the marketing manager must be suspicious of myths about what has an effect on winning and what does not. For example, an investigation of new industrial products found that factors that had little impact on whether the product was successful included

- Being first into the market.
- The mere existence of a strong competitor.
- Production capability by itself.
- Product technical complexity.[28]

Another major reason for new product failure is consumer resistance to innovation. Researchers have identified five barriers in two major classes that must be overcome. The first class consists of functional barriers due to current practice, the value placed on the innovation by the potential buyer, and risk. The second class consists of psychological barriers. They are tradition due to the cultural change caused by the barrier and image due to the origin of the innovation.[29] These barriers must be overcome for a successful new product introduction.

304

Developing products with one's own internal resources and organization is not always the best alternative to take. It is sometimes far better to consider acquiring the right to market new products from someone else. The two major alternatives to doing this are to (1) license the right to sell or (2) purchase the right. In licensing, the company is only borrowing these rights and they may be limited. A company can license the exclusive rights to manufacture and sell a product, or it can license a nonexclusive right, which would allow the owner to grant the same rights to a competitor at the same time. The company pays a royalty or certain percentage for each unit sold in return for this right. In the acquisition of rights through purchase, the rights to manufacture are usually bought in their totality and belong to the purchaser from then on.

The Advantages of Licensing or Purchasing New Products

There are several advantages to a company **licensing** or purchasing new products rather than developing them internally.

Save Company Time. The time to develop a new product may be considerable. Thus, if your competitor has introduced a new product that is making inroads in your market share, you need a new product immediately. A one- to three-year development and introduction time may be unacceptable. It may be far better to license or purchase the rights to a similar product, if available, than to develop one internally and accept the disadvantages inherent in this long lead time.

Save the Company Money. Some companies have the resources to accept the financial cost and risks of new product development. Others do not. Furthermore, if a company is getting into an area in which the technology is totally different, enormous costs can be associated with the purchase of new equipment, the acquisition of trained and experienced personnel, and the acquisition of facilities. Even patenting can be a costly process.[30] As a result, it may be far more cost effective either to license or buy the technology for a new product from some other company that is already operating in that field.

Acquisition of Know-How. Closely involved with costs is know-how. If know-how and proprietary information are not available internally, it must be developed. This affects both time and money, and such time and money penalties may not be cost effective, or the company may not have the resources available. In these cases, it may be wiser to spend the money for know-how, especially if the product is not going to change the orientation of the firm such that additional products of the same type will be required in the future.

Targets of Opportunity. Targets of opportunity consist of new products that have not necessarily been considered by the company. They may also consist of products that have been considered and are even into development, but for which suddenly the opportunity to obtain a fully developed product becomes available. Analysis is necessary to determine whether it is better to proceed with internal development or to take advantage of the immediate availability of this product of opportunity.

Summary

In this chapter we looked at the strategy of new product development. We saw that new product development is absolutely necessary, despite its attendant risk and current high failure rate, to survive in the marketplace. We next looked at the alternatives in the entire new product development process, including idea acquisition, initial screening, business analysis, product development, market testing, and introduction.

Beginning with idea acquisition, sources of new product ideas were explored, including customers, competition, salespeople, top management, the R&D department, and marketing research department of a company.

Then we looked at screening and business analysis together and saw how the success rate of new product introduction can be improved through proper screening, as well as determining which screening method to use based on the situation and the value of concept testing for finalizing this screening process. The development process itself was explored and the importance of planning emphasized. Guidelines for planning were listed, including defining objectives, establishing the project organization, installing controlling mechanisms, and coordinating the overall efforts. We then discussed when and under what conditions to terminate new product development and warning flags to alert us that termination should at least be considered. We turned our focus on test marketing—the advantages as well as the disadvantages—and the trade-offs that must be considered as to whether to proceed with test marketing or to exclude it from a particular new product development campaign. Finally, we surveyed introduction or commercialization of a new product as part of the new product development process.

Having completed the six steps in the new product introduction process, we examined some of the reasons for success and some of the reasons for failure. In conclusion, we considered alternatives to internal development, primarily licensing or acquisition from outside the company.

The strategy of new product development is clearly one of the major responsibilities with which a marketing executive is concerned. Your success as a marketing manager will in no small part be determined by your ability to master this strategy.

Questions

1. Consider RCA's video disc. Why do you think this product failed? What did you learn in this chapter that might have prevented the failure or the product's introduction?

2. Why do companies adopt the new product introduction strategy despite the risks?

3. Which step in the new product introduction process do you think is the most important? Why?

4. Considering the sources of new product ideas, under what conditions are some sources to be preferred over others?
5. What screening questions do you think are most important? Why?
6. Discuss different methods of screening and comparing potential new products for development and discuss the advantages and disadvantages of each.
7. Why can't concept testing be used in every case?
8. What warning flags might alert you to the possibility of terminating a new product that is under development prior to its introduction?
9. When should alternatives to developing new products be considered?
10. Can you think of any problems you might have in recommending termination of a new product to your boss? How might these problems be overcome?

Ethical Question

You are the director of new products. You must analyze all new product proposals for development and present your recommendations to your company's new product screening board. The company has no fixed criteria for comparison, so you can compare the new product proposals any way you like. Because different methods of comparison may lead to different preference rankings, is it ethical to use only those methods that favor the new products you personally believe in and wish to see pursued?

Endnotes

1. "RCA's Slipped Disc," *Fortune* (April 30, 1984), p. 7.
2. Alex Talor, III, "Here Come Japan's New Luxury Cars," vol. 120, no. 4 *Fortune*, (August 14, 1989), pp. 62–66.
3. Laurie Freeman, "Cookie Marketers Keep Mixing It Up," *Advertising Age* (February 23, 1986), p. 12.
4. Alan Hall, "Where Spending Is Strong and Getting Stronger," *Business Week* (Special Issue March 22, 1985), p. 164.
5. "The More They Spend on R&D, the Faster They Grow," *Inc.* (August 1981).
6. Milton D. Rosenau, Jr., *Innovation* (Belmont, Calif.: Lifetime Learning Publications, 1982), p. 7.
7. The Editors of New Products Newsletter, *New Products* (Point Pleasant, N.J.. Point Publishing, 1982), p. 102.
8. William S. Sachs and George Benson, *Product Planning and Management* (Tulsa, Okla.: PennWell Books, 1981), p. 210.
9. Eric Von Hippel, "Successful Industrial Products from Customer Ideas," *Journal of Marketing* (January 1978), p. 45.
10. Personal conversation with E. Joseph Cossman, 1981.
11. Leigh Lawton and A. Parasuraman, "The Impact of the Marketing Concept on New Product Planning," *Journal of Marketing*, vol. 44 (Winter 1980), p. 23.
12. Theodore Levitt, "Innovative Imitation," *Harvard Business Review*, vol. 44 (September–October 1966), p. 67.
13. Tom W. White, "Use Variety of Internal, External Sources to Gather and Screen New Product Ideas," *Marketing News* (September 16, 1983), p. 12.
14. William A. Cohen, *Principles of Technical Management* (New York: AMACOM, 1980), pp. 148–149.
15. Linda F. Jamieson and Frank M. Bass, "Adjusting Stated Intention Measures to Predict Trial Purchase of New Products: A Comparison of Models and Methods," *Journal of Marketing Research*, vol. 26, no. 3 (August 1989), p. 336.
16. Roger A. More, "Timing of Market Research in New Industrial Product Situations," *Journal of Marketing*, vol. 48 (Fall 1984), p. 93.
17. David W. Nylen, "New Product Failures: Not Just a Marketing Problem," *Business Magazine* (September–October 1979), p. 140.
18. Robert W. Ruekert and Orville C. Walker, Jr., "Marketing's Interaction with Other Functional Units: A Conceptual Framework and Empirical Evidence," *Journal of Marketing*, vol. 51, no. 1 (January 1987), p. 3.

19. Richard F. Chay, "How to Improve Your Chances for Test Market Success," *Marketing News* (January 6, 1984).

20. Lawrence Ingrassia, "By Improving Scratch Paper, 3M Gets New Product Winner," *Wall Street Journal*, 31 March 1983.

21. Vijay Mahajan, Eitan Muller, and Frank M. Bass, "New Product Diffusion Models in Marketing: A Review and Directions for Research," *Journal of Marketing*, vol. 54, No. 1 (January 1990), p. 1.

22. C. Merle Crawford, "Marketing Research and the New Product Failure Rate," *Journal of Marketing*, vol. 41 (April 1977).

23. Robert G. Cooper, "Why New Industrial Products Fail," *Industrial Marketing Management*, vol. 4 (1975), p. 318.

24. C. Merle Crawford, "Product Development: Today's Most Common Mistakes," *University of Michigan Business Review* (January 1977), pp. 2–6.

25. J. T. O'Meara, "Selecting Profitable Products," *Harvard Business Review* (January–February 1961), pp. 84–85.

26. New Products Management for the 1980s (New York: Booz, Allen, Hamilton, 1982), p. 16.

27. Roger Calantone and Robert G. Cooper, "New Product Scenarios: Prospects for Success," *Journal of Marketing*, vol. 45 (Spring 1981), p. 52.

28. R. G. Cooper, "The Dimensions of Industrial New Product Success and Failure," *Journal of Marketing*, vol. 43 (Summer 1979), p. 102.

29. S. Ram and Jagdish N. Sheth, "Consumer Resistance to Innovations: The Marketing Problem and Its Solutions," *Journal of Consumer Marketing*, vol. 6, no. 2 (Spring 1989), pp. 7–9.

30. Ronald D. Rothchild, "Making Patents Work for Small Companies," *Harvard Business Review*, vol. 65 (July–August 1987), pp. 24–30.

Associated Foods, Incorporated

Associated Foods processes and sells a wide grocery product line of 30 product categories and approximately 320 individual products. Its sales have increased over the past few years due to new product introductions. In 1978 sales reached $258 million, 30 per cent of which were from their four major categories: cereals, cake mixes, puddings, and pancake mixes.

Competition

Because of the stiff competition in the food industry, most companies depend on new products for major increases in profit. However, companies are beginning to imitate each other's successes, which tends to drive prices down, decreasing sales profits. There is stiff competition among retail food processors for shelf space at the grocery store or supermarket. Since Associated has such a wide product line, it competes with many of the larger food processors like General Foods, Corn Products Company, Nabisco, Pillsbury, Procter & Gamble, Quaker Oats, and Standard Brands.

Marketing Organization

The marketing function of Associated comes under the direction of Scott Davis, the vice-president of marketing. Reporting to Davis are the national marketing and national sales managers (see Exhibit 1). The five divisional marketing managers, who represent five geographical divisions of the company, report to the national marketing manager. Their job is to tie together all the company activities with respect to their products and to build sales volume and profits. The divisional marketing manager is responsible for determining which products to emphasize through advertising, sales promotion, and pricing discounts, both for the company and for his division. He has no power over the sales organization. He is expected to develop a broad five-year marketing plan for his division and a comprehensive annual plan. These plans usually include written statements with supporting details such as a statement of current market share position on each product, current strengths and weaknesses in each area, and expected market trends. A statement of objectives including market share, volume, revenue, expenses, profit contribution, and subobjectives, such as geographical penetration and distribution penetration, is also developed. Finally a recommended marketing program based on evaluation of the alternatives available to achieve objectives has to be set forth.

Sales Organization

The sales organization comes under the direction of the national sales manager. Under her authority are five divisional sales managers who are in charge of the sales force in the five geographical divisions. Each division has six regional sales managers. Within a region there are four district managers, each with approxi-

This case was developed by Professor Charles M. Futrell, Texas A&M University. The company's name has been changed.

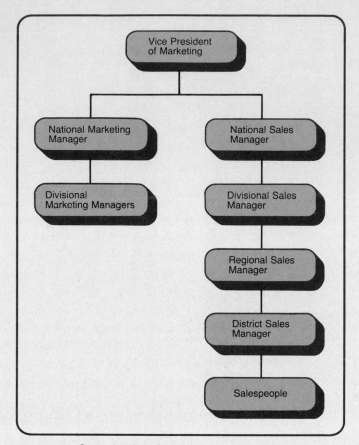

Exhibit 1   Organization Chart

mately twelve salespeople. The main responsibility of the sales organization is to reach the overall sales goals set in the annual marketing plans. They also provide feedback to the marketing managers on the effect of sales promotions.

Problem Definition

Bob Smith, marketing manager for the Houston division was perplexed over current trends in the food industry and in his region. Trying to come up with a five-year plan and an annual plan of action for 1979, Smith found three things that puzzled him. One was the introduction of private label brands in leading supermarket chains. Another was the trend toward committee buying: another, the continued growth of discount supermarkets. The latest reports showed that certain product categories in the Houston division were not meeting their market share objectives. These included cereals (-6.5 sharepoints), cake mixes (-2.0), puddings (-1.8), and pancake mixes (-3.8). Other product categories that were expected to show signs of significant improvement were showing only nominal improvement. Smith developed data on these trends for the size of the markets and Associated's market share for these four products. From this data he projected sales for the next year, 1979, as shown in Exhibit 2. It appeared that sales for

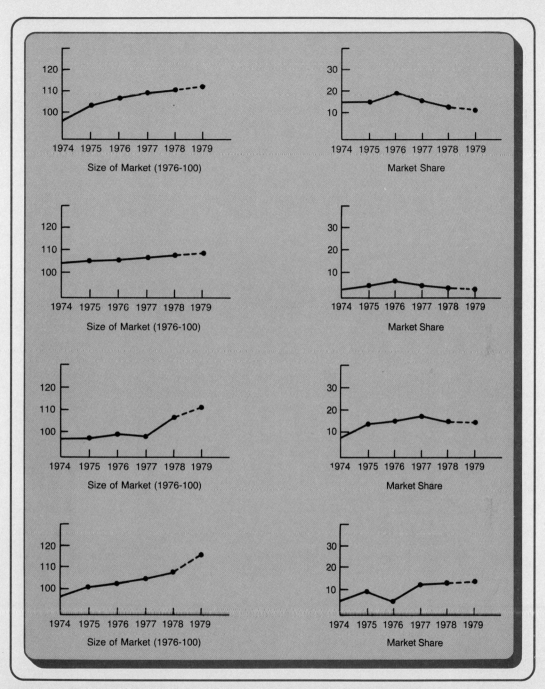

Exhibit 2   Houston Division's Trends in Market Size and Market Share[a]

311

the four product categories could be expected to increase. However, Associated sales would not increase proportionately. In fact, he felt there might be some decreases. Smith felt that his performance was evaluated based on the cost of obtaining sales in his division, and he knew Scott Davis would be disappointed in the sales on cereals, cake mixes, pancake mixes, and puddings because these products accounted for 30 per cent of sales.

Among the immediate problems Smith saw in the Houston division was a change in the operating behavior of the retail outlets and a weak brand image of Associated Foods products. There are thousands of retail stores in the Houston division with many major national and local chains. Recent changes in the operating behavior of the retail food stores has reduced shelf space in most of them because of the addition of private label brands and the deletion of the slow-moving products. Many grocery chains have buying committees that have stopped the practice of some stores buying entire product lines. Each product has to be approved individually.

Smith felt Associated's brand image for quality was low because the company offered trade discounts. He felt retailers thought of Associated Foods products as discount items and often featured them in mass displays as a loss leader. However, other divisions did not feel they had an image problem.

There seemed to be a direct correlation between total sales and number of deals offered. In addition, because of the discount operations of some retail food outlets, prices to consumers at nondiscount food stores did not reflect trade discounts. Occasionally the discounters did this. For example, if there was a one-dollar-a-case discount for price reduction and a fifty-cent advertising allowance, some retailers would sell the products at the regular price, not promote, and pocket the money.

With these thoughts in mind, Smith set about tackling the problem of developing a marketing plan for the next year that would increase both the volume of sales and brand awareness for Associated Foods products. He decided to discuss his suggestions for improving sales with Rex Harris, the Houston divisional sales manager.

QUESTIONS

1. What is the main problem in the Houston region?
2. What should the Houston divisional marketing manager, Bob Smith, do?

Perpetual Care Hospital: Downtown Health Clinic

In mid-April 1986, Ms. Sherri Worth, assistant administrator at Perpetual Care Hospital (PCH) in charge of PCH's Downtown Health Clinic, uncovered an unsettling parcel of news. During a call on the employee benefits director at a downtown department store, she was told that a firm was conducting a study to deter-

From Roger A. Kerin and Robert A. Peterson, *Strategic Marketing Problems: Cases and Comments,* 4th ed. (Boston: Allyn & Bacon, Inc., 1987). Reprinted with permission.

mine whether or not sufficient demand existed for a clinic located five blocks north of PCH's Downtown Health Center. The description of the clinic's services sounded similar to those offered by PCH's Downtown Health Center, and the planned opening date was May 1987.

As Ms. Worth walked back to her office, she could not help but think about the competitive clinic. Upon arriving at her office, Ms. Worth called Dr. Roger Mahon, PCH's administrator, to tell him what she had learned. He asked her to contact other employee benefit directors and query patients to see whether or not they had been surveyed. He expressed concern for two reasons. First, a competitive clinic would attract existing and potential patients of the Downtown Health Center. Second, a competitive clinic that provided similar services could hamper the Downtown Health Clinic's progress toward achieving its service and profitability objectives. They concluded their talk with Dr. Mahon suggesting that Ms. Worth summarize the Downtown Health Clinic's performance to date so that he could speak to members of the board of trustees' executive committee on what action, if any, the DHC should take to compete for patients. He concluded their discussion by saying, "Who would have thought ten years ago that a hospital administrator would be making decisions not unlike a retail chain store executive's. But I guess it comes with the territory these days."

Health Care and the Hospital Industry

Health care, and specifically the hospital industry, has undergone a dramatic transformation in the last decade. Until the 1960s, hospitals had been largely charitable institutions that prided themselves on their not-for-profit orientation. Hospitals functioned primarily as workshops for physicians and were guided by civic-minded boards of trustees.

Federal legislation introduced in the 1960s created boom times for the hospital industry. The Hill-Burton Act provided billions of dollars for hospital construction, to be repaid by fulfilling quotas for charity care. Additional funds were poured into expansion and construction of medical schools. Medicare and Medicaid subsidized health care for the indigent, disabled, and elderly. These programs reimbursed hospitals for their incurred costs plus an additional return on investment. The 1960s also saw dramatic increases in commercial insurance coverage, offered as employee fringe benefits and purchased in additional quantities by a more affluent public. Accordingly, health care became accessible to an overwhelming majority of U.S. citizens, regardless of where they lived or their ability to pay. Federal intervention had changed the concept of health care services from *privilege* to *entitlement.*

By the mid-1970s, however, skyrocketing health care costs had forced the federal government to reassess its role in health care. Stringent controls were placed on hospital construction and expansion, and utilization and physician review programs were implemented to ensure against too-lengthy inpatient stays. By the end of the decade, hospitals were initiating voluntary cost-cutting programs to stave off additional government intervention. Despite all efforts, however, health care expenditures continued to outpace the Consumer Price Index. In 1981 Americans spent close to 10 per cent of the gross national product on health care, and the government's portion was 43 per cent of the $287 billion tab. Only 11 per cent of all hospital services were paid for by individuals; the balance were financed by third-party payors, such as insurance companies.

The 1980s ushered in a very different health care environment, and hospitals particularly have been hard hit by the changes. On the one hand, the federal government has sought to reduce health care costs through cutbacks in subsidy programs and cost-control regulations. On the other hand, innovations in health care delivery have severely reduced the number of patients serviced by hospitals. Two of these innovations are preventive health care programs and the increase in the number of ambulatory health care services.

Preventive health care programs fall into two categories: (1) Health Maintenance Organizations (HMOs) and (2) Preferred Provider Organizations (PPOs). HMOs surfaced in the mid-1970s. An HMO encourages preventive health care by providing medical services as needed for a fixed monthly fee. HMOs typically entered into contractual relationships with designated physicians and hospitals and have been successful in reducing hospital inpatient days and health care expenditures. PPOs, which emerged in the early 1980s, have contractual arrangements between health care providers (physicians and/or hospitals) and large employer groups. Unlike HMOs, PPOs generally offer incentives for using preferred providers rather than restricting individuals to specific hospitals or physicians. PPOs are likely to have the same effect on inpatient days and health care expenditures as HMOs and Dr. Mahon had planned to design a PPO for Perpetual Care Hospital using the Downtown Health Clinic as a link to large employers in the downtown area.

A second and farther-reaching innovation is the use of ambulatory health care services and facilities. Ambulatory health care services consist of treatments and practices that consumers can use on an episodic or emergency basis. Examples include physical examinations; treatment of minor emergencies (e.g., for cuts, bruises, minor surgery); and treatments for common illnesses (e.g., colds and flu).

Ambulatory health care facilities are split into two categories: (1) minor emergency centers, known by names and acronyms such as FECs (Free-Standing Emergency Clinics) and MECs (Medical Emergency Clinics) and (2) clinics that focus on primary or episodic care.[a] Although regulation is nominal, if a clinic positioned itself as an emergency care center, expressing this focus in its name, it generally was required (or pressured by area physicians) to be staffed twenty-four hours a day by a licensed physician and to have certain basic life-support equipment.

Ambulatory health care services are the fastest-growing segment of health services.[1] The first no-appointment, walk-in clinic opened in Newark, Delaware, in 1975. By 1985 there would be at least twenty-five hundred similar facilities in the United States, not including group-practice physician arrangements and HMOs. Ambulatory health care services have siphoned away a large portion of the care offered by physicians and have forced hospitals to deal increasingly with only the most acutely ill and severely injured patients.

Three factors have accounted for the growth of ambulatory health care services. First, advances in medical technology, miniaturization, and portable medical equipment have made more diagnostic and surgical procedures possible outside the traditional hospital setting. Second, consumers have adopted a more proactive stance on where they will receive their health and medical care. Consumers are choosing the hospital at which they wish to be treated, and the incidence of "doctor shopping" is on the rise. Third, the mystique of medical and health care has been

---

[a]*Primary care* is the point of entry into the health care system. It consists of a continuous relationship with a personal physician who takes care of a broad range of medical needs. Primary-care physicians include general practitioners, internal medicine and family practice specialists, gynecologists, and pediatricians.

altered with the growth of paramedical professionals and standardized treatment practices.

Most of the early centers emphasized quick, convenient, minor emergency care. A new wave of centers have positioned themselves as convenient, personalized alternatives to primary-care physicians' practices. These operations typically employ aggressive, sophisticated marketing techniques, including branding, consistent logos and atmospherics, promotional incentives, and mass media advertising (giving rise to vernacular designations such as "Doc-in-the-Box" and "McMedical"). Although ambulatory care facilities vary considerably among communities and owners, the following characteristics appear to be universal: (1) branding, (2) extended hours, (3) lower fees than emergency rooms, (4) no appointments necessary, (5) minor emergencies treated, (6) easy access and parking, (7) short waiting times, and (8) credit cards accepted.

Even though these facilities have tapped a market need, not all have been successful. Failure rates are as high as 25 per cent in some areas of the country. Many areas were already saturated with many MECs fighting aggressive market share battles.[2] According to one industry estimate, the average MEC is open sixteen hours per day, seven days per week, with two physicians on each eight-hour shift. The average visit is fifteen minutes, and the average break-even volume lies between thirty and forty-five visits per day.

Perpetual Care Hospital

Perpetual Care Hospital is a 600-bed, independent, not-for-profit, general hospital located on the southern periphery of a major western city. The hospital is one of six general hospitals in the city and twenty in the county. It is financially stronger than most of the metropolitan-based hospitals in the United States. It is debt-free and has the highest overall occupancy rate among the city's six general hospitals. Nevertheless, the hospital's administration and board of trustees have had serious concerns about its patient mix, which reflected unfavorable demographic shifts. Most of the population growth in the late 1970s was occurring in the suburban areas to the north, east, and west. These suburban areas were attracting young, upwardly mobile families from the city. They were also attracting thousands of families from other states—families drawn to the area's dynamic, robust business climate.

As suburban hospitals have sprung up to serve the high-growth areas, the hospital has found itself becoming increasingly dependent on inner-city residents, who have a higher median age and higher incidence of Medicare coverage. Without a stronger, stable inflow of short stay, privately insured patients, the financial health of the hospital would be jeopardized. Accordingly, in the summer of 1984, the board of trustees authorized a study to determine whether to open an ambulatory facility in the downtown area about ten blocks north of the hospital.

Downtown Health Center

The charter for the Downtown Health Center (DHC) contained four objectives:

1. To expand the hospital's referral base
2. To increase referrals of privately insured patients

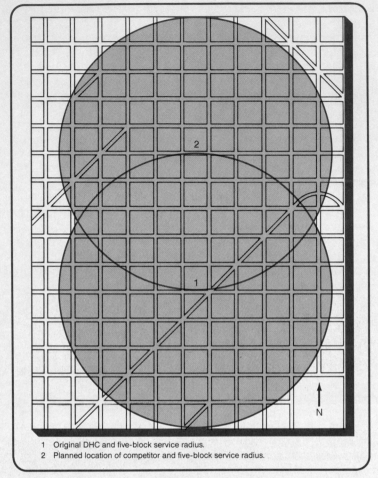

1 Original DHC and five-block service radius.
2 Planned location of competitor and five-block service radius.

**Exhibit 1   Present and Planned Locations of Downtown
Health Centers and Service Areas**

3. To establish a liaison with the business community by addressing employers'
   specific health needs
4. To become self-supporting three years after opening

The specific services to be offered by the DHC would include (1) preventative
health care (e.g., physical examinations and immunizations); (2) minor emergency
care; (3) referral for acute and chronic health care problems; (4) specialized employer services (e.g., preemployment examinations, worker's compensation injuries); (5) primary health care services (e.g., treatment for common illnesses); and
(6) basic X-ray and laboratory tests. The DHC would be open 260 days per year
(Monday-Friday) from 8:00 A.M. to 5:00 P.M.

The location for the DHC would be in the Greater West Office and Shopping
Complex situated on the corner of Main and West streets (see Exhibit 1). This
location was chosen because a member of the board of trustees owned the
Greater West Complex and was willing to share construction, design, and equipment expenses with the hospital.

Item	Expenditure
Physician coverage/260 days/8 hrs./5 days—$33/hr.	$ 68,640
Professional fees	21,360
Lease	38,250
Supplies	23,447
Utilities	3,315
Personnel, including fringe (director, nurse, laboratory, X-ray technician, receptionist)	84,188
Amortization	15,324
Annual expenditure	$254,524

Note: Expenditures were based on the assumption that the DHC would have four visits per hour, or thirty-two visits per day, when operating at full capacity.

During the fall of 1984, construction plans for erecting the DHC were well underway, and the expense budget was developed (see Exhibit 2). During the winter months, PCH commissioned a study to (1) determine the service radius of the DHC, (2) estimate the number of potential users of the DHC, (3) assess responsiveness to the services offered by the DHC, and (4) review the operations of suburban ambulatory-care clinics. The results indicated that the service area would have a five-block radius, since this was the longest distance office workers would walk. Discussions with city planners indicated the service area contained 11,663 office workers during the 9:00-5:00 Monday-Friday work week. The population in the area was expected to grow 6 per cent per year given new building and renovation activity. Personal interviews with 400 office workers, selected randomly, indicated that 50 per cent would use or try the DHC if necessary and that 40 per cent of these prospective users would visit the DHC at least once per year (see Exhibit 3 for additional findings). Finally, the study of suburban ambulatory care facilities revealed the data shown in Exhibit 4. Given their locations in suburban areas, these facilities were not considered as direct competition, but did indicate that "the city's populace was attuned to ambulatory health care facilities," remarked Ms. Worth.

These results were viewed favorably by the board of trustees and "confirmed our belief that an ambulatory facility was needed downtown," noted Ms. Worth. The DHC was formally opened May 1, 1985. However, except for the publicity surrounding the opening, no advertising or other types of promotion were planned. "Several members of the hospital staff shied away from advertising or solicitation since it hinted at crass commercialism," noted Ms. Worth.

Performance: May 1985–March 1986

A financial summary of the DHC performance through March 1986 is shown in Exhibit 5. According to Dr. Mahon:

We are pleased with the performance to date and hope the DHC will be self-supporting by April 1987. We are getting favorable word-of-mouth from satisfied patients that will generate both new and repeat patients. We expect 410 patient visits in April (1986). In addition, we have taken steps to improve our financial standing. For example, our bad debts have been

Exhibit 3   Profile of DHC Service Area Based on City and Survey Data

1984 Population Estimate (Source: City Planning Department)

Total office worker population in five-block radius	11,663
Expected annual growth, 1984–1989	6.0%/yr.

Sex breakdown in five-block radius:

Male	40%
Female	60%

Results from Personal Interviews (January 1984)

Would use/try DHC if necessary for personal illness/exams	50%

Expected frequency of DHC use for personal illness/exams among
those saying would use/try if necessary[a]:

Once every other year	60%
Once per year	25%
Twice per year	10%
Three or more times per year	5%

Selected Cross-Tabulations

	Sex		
Would use or try DHC if necessary:	Male	Female	Total
Yes	88[b]	168	256
No	72	72	144
Total	160	240	400

	Have Regular Physician (Excluding Gynecologist)		
Would use or try DHC if necessary:	Yes	No	Total
Yes	58	198	256
No	130	14	144
Total	188	212	400

[a]No difference between males and females on frequency of use.
[b]Eighty-eight of the 160 males (55 per cent) interviewed would use the DHC; 88 of the 256 interviewees (34 per cent) who said they would use the DHC were male.

costing us 4 per cent of gross revenue. With a better credit and collection procedure established just last month, we will reduce this figure to 2 per cent. We plan to initiate an 8 per cent across-the-board increase in charges on May 1 and will experience only a 5 per cent increase in personnel and professional services expenses next year.

Records kept by PCH revealed that the DHC was realizing its objectives. For example, the referral objective was being met since the DHC has made 105 referrals to PCH and produced slightly over $189,000 in revenue and an estimated $15,000 in net profit. Almost all of these patients were privately insured. The service mix, though dominated by personal illness and examinations, did indicate that the DHC was being used for a variety of purposes. A breakdown of the reasons for patient visits for the first eleven months of operation is as follows:

Personal illness exams	53%
Worker's compensation	25%
Employment/insurance physical exams	19%
Emergency	3%
	100%

Exhibit 4 Suburban Ambulatory Care Clinics: Operations Profile

Operations	EMERCENTER #1	EMERCENTER #2	Adams Industrial Clinic	Health First	MEDCENTER
Opening	March, 1980	November, 1982	June, 1980	May, 1982	June, 1983
Patients/year	9,030	6,000	8,400	5,700	8,661
Hours of operation	10:00 A.M.–10:00 P.M. Monday–Friday	10:00 A.M.–10:00 P.M. Monday–Sunday	8:00 A.M.–5:00 P.M. Monday–Friday	5:00 P.M.–11:00 P.M. Monday–Friday; 10:00 A.M.–10:00 P.M. Saturday–Sunday	8:00 A.M.–8:00 P.M. Monday–Sunday
Physicians/8-hour shift	2	2	2	2	2
Estimated patient visits/ hour	3.8/hour	3.4/hour	5.0/hour	3.0/hour	3.0/hour
Estimated average charge per visit	$30.00	$31.00	$38.00	$31.00	$32.00
Services provided:					
Preventive health care			X	X	X
Minor emergencies	X	X	X	X	X
Employer services			X		
X-ray/lab tests	X	X	X	X	X
Miscellaneous	X	X		X	X
Use direct mail advertising	X	X		X	X

Exhibit 5 Downtown Health Center Financial Summary

	1985								1986			Total Year to Date
	May	June	July	Aug	Sept	Oct	Nov	Dec	Jan	Feb	Mar	
Gross revenue	4,075	8,387	8,844	9,697	11,206	11,406	11,672	11,758	12,846	13,879	14,715	118,485
Variable expenses												
Bad debt	163	355	354	388	448	456	467	470	513	555	588	4,757
Medical/surgical supplies	6,591	798	935	643	1,063	1,213	1,661	612	976	1,580	1,078	17,150
Drugs	159	54	65	52	305	93	0	56	186	253	76	1,299
Office supplies	647	222	596	718	315	(190)	24	281	467	0	64	3,144
Total variable expense	7,560	1,429	1,950	1,801	2,131	1,572	2,152	1,419	2,142	2,388	1,806	26,350
Contribution	(3,485)	6,958	6,894	7,896	9,075	9,834	9,520	10,339	10,704	11,491	12,909	92,135
Fixed expenses												
Personnel	7,816	7,459	6,670	5,900	6,816	11,490	7,320	6,249	6,705	8,995	7,644	83,064
Professional services[a]	10,009	6,945	7,732	7,158	7,385	6,800	7,200	7,450	7,242	7,078	7,187	82,186
Facility[b]	3,222	2,537	2,890	2,905	2,622	2,655	2,620	2,613	2,836	2,622	2,719	30,241
Miscellaneous	705	107	133	140	238	45	111	76	106	123	57	1,841
Amortization	1,277	1,277	1,277	1,277	1,277	1,277	1,277	1,277	1,277	1,277	1,277	14,047
Total fixed expense	23,029	18,325	18,702	17,380	18,338	22,267	18,528	17,665	18,166	20,095	18,884	211,379
Net gain (loss)	(26,514)	(11,367)	(11,808)	(9,484)	(9,263)	(12,433)	(9,008)	(7,326)	(7,462)	(8,604)	(5,975)	(119,244)
Number of patient visits	109	231	275	277	322	320	321	366	383	463	423	3,490
Number of working days	22	21	21	22	20	23	22	20	22	21	23	237

[a]Includes professional fees paid (see Exhibit 2).

[b]Includes lease payments, utilities, and maintenance.

Patient records indicated that 97 per cent of all visits were by first-time users of the DHC, and 113 visits were by repeat patients. Approximately 5 per cent of the visits in each month from October, 1985 through March 1986 were repeat visits. "We are pleased that we are already getting repeat business because it shows we are doing our job," Ms. Worth commented. The average revenue per patient visit during the first eleven months was $33.95.[b] A breakdown of the average charge by type of visit follows. The average charge would increase 8 per cent on May 1, 1986.

Personal illness/exams	$25 per visit
Worker's compensation	$39 per visit
Employment/insurance physical examination	$47 per visit
Emergency	$67 per visit

In an effort to monitor the performance of the DHC, patients were asked to provide selected health care information as well as demographic information. This information was summarized monthly, and Exhibit 6 shows the profile of patients visiting the DHC for the first eleven months of operation. In addition to this information, patients were asked for suggestions on how the DHC could serve the downtown area. Suggestions typically fell into three categories: (1) service hours, (2) services, and (3) waiting time. Thirty per cent of the patients suggested expanded service hours with an opening time of 7:00 A.M. and a closing time of 7:00 P.M. One half of the female patients requested that gynecological services be added. A majority of the patients expressed concern about the waiting time, particularly during the lunch hours (11:00 A.M.-2:00 P.M.). A check of DHC records indicated that 70 per cent of patient visits occurred during the 11:00 A.M.-2:00 P.M. period and that one-half of the visits were for personal illnesses.

Ms. Worth believed all three suggestions had merit and had already explored ways to expand the DHC's hours and reduce waiting time. For example, the reason for her call on the employee benefits director at a local department store was to schedule employee physical examinations in the morning or late afternoon hours to minimize crowding during the lunch hour. Nevertheless, she believed a second licensed physician might be necessary, with one physician working the hours from 7:00 A.M. to 3:00 P.M. and the other working between 11:00 A.M. and 7:00 P.M. The overlap during the lunch period would alleviate waiting times as well, she thought. Expanding from nine- to twelve-hour days would entail a 33 per cent increase in personnel costs, however, as well as the cost of another physician.[c]

Ms. Worth believed that scheduling was more of a problem than she or the PCH staff had expected. "You just can't schedule the walk-ins," she said, "and pardon me for saying it, but the people coming in with personal care needs have really caused the congestion." She added that the problem would get worse because the mix of patients was moving toward personal illnesses and examinations. "If the trend continues, we should have 20 per cent more personal illness visits next year than last year."

Ms. Worth believed that gynecological services[d] would be a plus since 70 per

[b]The average charge per patient visit includes the charge for basic X-ray and laboratory tests when appropriate.

[c]Expanded hours would be staffed by part-time personnel who would receive the same wages as full-time personnel.

[d]*Gynecology* is that branch of medicine dealing with the female reproductive tract.

**Exhibit 6   Profile of Downtown Health Center Patients:
Personal Illness/Exam Visits Only**

Occupation		
Clerical	48%	
Professional/technical/managerial	23	
Operators	19	
Other	10	100%
Sex		
Male	30%	
Female	70	100%
Referral Source		
Friends/colleagues	35%	
Employer	60	
Other	5	100%
Patient Origin		
Distance:		
One block	25%	
Two blocks	28	
Three blocks	22	
Four blocks	15	
Five blocks	8	
More than five blocks	2	100%
Direction:		
North of DHC—10%, south of DHC—25%		
Northeast of DHC—5%, southwest of DHC—15%		
East of DHC—20%, west of DHC—10%		
Southeast of DHC—10%, northwest of DHC—5%		
Have Regular Physician		
Yes	18%	
No	82	100%

cent of the visits were made by women and almost all were under thirty-five years of age. She said:

Women will or should see a gynecologist regularly at least once a year and often twice a year. We could add an additional 2,000 visits per year with a hospital gynecologist working at the DHC two eight-hour days a week by appointment. An average charge per visit would be about $52 including lab work, and the physician cost would be $35 per hour.

Ms. Worth had also given some thought to how the DHC could improve its relations with the business community. Currently, business-initiated visits (worker's compensation and employment/insurance physical examinations) accounted for 44 per cent of the DHC's visits. Construction in the downtown area had stimulated worker's compensation activity and growth in employment in the five-block service radius had contributed to employment physicals. Ms. Worth believed worker's compensation visits would stabilize at about 81 per month and then decline with slowed building activity. Employment physicals accounted for 50 visits per month and were expected to remain at this level given current operating hours. Insurance physicals were not expected to increase beyond current activity levels, nor were emergency visits.

Commenting on her calls on businesses, Ms. Worth remarked:

I have actively called on businesses under the guise of community relations because the PCH staff has not sanctioned solicitation. My guess, after talking with business people, is that we could get virtually every new employment physical if we didn't interfere with employment hours and scheduled them before 8:00 A.M. or after 5:00 P.M. Given net new employment in the area and new employees due to turnover, I'd guess we could schedule an additional 65 employment physicals every month—that is, 115 a month.

Ms. Worth added that she had also received approval to run an "informational advertisement" in the downtown weekly newspaper each week next year, provided the advertisement did not feature prices or appear to be commercial in its presentation. The weekly advertisement would cost $5,200 per year.

Competitive Clinic

Ms. Worth's calls on local businesses and patient interviews indicated that a survey was being conducted. She believed that MEDCENTER, a privately owned suburban ambulatory facility, was the sponsor. MEDCENTER appeared to be successful in its suburban location (see Exhibit 4) and had a reputation for being an aggressive, marketing-oriented operation. Even though MEDCENTER did not provide employer services at its suburban location. Ms. Worth thought the fact that an employee benefits director had been interviewed suggested that such services might be offered.

The location for the new clinic was five blocks directly north of the DHC. Based on the research for the DHC, Ms. Worth estimated that the number of office workers within a five-block radius of the competitive clinic would be 11,652 in 1987 and 13,590 in 1988, and would grow at an annual rate of 7 per cent through 1995 because of new construction and building renovation. Ms. Worth believed the competitor's service area had the same socioeconomic profile, and the same usage and employment characteristics as the DHC's service area.

The overlap in service areas was due to the layout of the downtown area and the availability of high-quality street-level space. According to Ms. Worth, "It is possible that a third of our current personal illness/exam patients from the northern portion of our service area will switch to the new clinic and about 40 per cent of potential personal illness/exam patients in this area will go to the new location." Ms. Worth went on to say that the overlap in service areas would actually cover 3,424 existing office workers in 1986.

The effect of the competitive clinic on emergency, worker's compensation, and employment/insurance exam volume was more difficult to assess. Ms. Worth did feel, however, that worker's compensation visits would not be materially affected because most construction was being undertaken in areas south, east, and west of the DHC. Emergency visits were so random that it was not possible to assess the effect of the competitive clinic. Projected employment and insurance physical volume could change with the addition of a competitive clinic, however. Ms. Worth guessed that, "At worst, we would see no increase in these types of visits over last year since we have not gotten many visits from this area."

A week after she first heard about the possibility of a competitive clinic, Ms. Worth and Dr. Mahon met to review the information on the DHC. Just before Ms.

Worth completed her overview, Dr. Mahon's administrative assistant interrupted to tell him he had to leave to catch a plane for a three-day conference dealing with health care marketing. As he left the room, he asked Ms. Worth to draft a concise analysis of the DHC's position. He also asked her to specify and evaluate the alternatives for the DHC assuming MEDCENTER did or did not open a facility. "Remember," Dr. Mahon said, "PCH has a lot riding on the DHC. Making it work not only involves dollars and cents, but our image in the community as well."

QUESTIONS

1. How big a threat is the opening of MEDCENTER to the Downtown Health Clinic?
2. How would you classify the service being offered by Downtown Health Clinic? Why?
3. How would you rate the Downtown Health Clinic's performance so far?
4. What will happen if the Downtown Health Clinic makes no changes to its current operations?
5. If you were Downtown Health Clinic's management, what would you do?
6. How would you implement the changes you've suggested?

NOTES

1. "FECs Pose Competition for Hospital EDs," *Hospitals* (March 1984): 77–80; *Immediate Care Centers: Fast Medicine for the '80s* (Washington, D.C.: U.S. Department of Health and Human Services, November 1984).
2. See, for example, "Urgent Care Centers Seek Niches," *Modern Health-care* (April 1984): 110–12.

United States Football League (USFL)

The entrepreneur behind the USFL was David F. Dixon, a 59-year-old New Orleans art dealer who observed that this country had an insatiable appetite for football. Dixon informed the would-be owners how much they could lose, but he also told them that an investment of $1.5 million could someday be worth $50 million.

The original goals of the USFL were clearly defined and understood. The premise was to establish a competitive but minor league summertime diversion to provide a relatively low-cost type of television programming. The USFL televised games were to replace some of the marginal spring sports. The league was to limit itself to players no higher than an NFL fourth-round draft choice. It was not to raid or entice players away from the NFL with high salaries.

A substantial number of the original investors were wealthy, and USFL teams were well financed. Each team contributed $1.5 million to a league kitty that would

This case was written and developed by John B. Clark, professor of marketing, California State University-Sacramento. Used with permission.

Table 1   United States Football League Key Statistics, 1983–1985

	1985	1984	1983
Number of teams	14	18	12
Losses (millions)	$60	$63	$40
Average loss per team (millions)	$4.3	$3.5	$3.3
Average attendance (regular season)	24,494	27,126	28,824
TV ratings[a]			
ABC Sports	4.1	5.5	6.0
ESPN	2.0	2.9	3.3

[a]Each rating point = 90,000 viewers.

Sources: USFL, ABC Sports, ESPN.

be used to protect the league and financially troubled teams. Another $4.5 million was set aside by each team to cover anticipated losses. First-year franchises sold for $1.5 million. Original estimates were that each team would lose $6 million over the first three years. The league planned for heavy losses in its introductory stage.

The formation of the USFL was announced at a press conference in New York City on May 12, 1982. Some of the significant events that occurred before the opening game on March 6, 1983, were hiring of big-name coaches such as Chuck Fairbanks, "Red" Miller, George Allen, and John Ralston. USFL teams signed agreements to play in major sports stadiums such as the Liberty Bowl, Super-dome, and Silverdome. Heisman Trophy winner Herschel Walker was also signed.

United States Football League, 1983 Season

Estimated losses for 1983 were $40 million. The league champions, the Michigan Panthers, incurred a $6 million loss, and only one team, the Denver Gold, had a minimal profit. The TV rating of 6.0 was sufficient for the ABC network to earn a profit (5.0 was the break-even point), but below the desired 7.0 rating. Average attendance was 25,000—lower than the desired 35,000. The ground rules were broken with the signing of Herschel Walker, which resulted in escalating player salaries. At the end of the first year, many people characterized the league as being shaky (see Table 1).

1984 Season

The 1984 season had a number of changes. The league was expanded to 18 teams with 6 new teams joining the league and the Boston Breakers becoming the New Orleans Breakers (see Table 2). Six of the original 12 teams changed hands. Ownership of the New Jersey Generals exchanged hands for $6 million, followed by the Chicago Blitz for $7 million and Washington Federals for $8 million. Despite a 9 per cent increase in average attendance, the average loss per team continued to increase and television ratings continued to decrease (see Table 1). The league continued to stray from its original goals and signed several big-name

Table 2   Location of USFL Teams, 1983–1986

	1983	1984	1985	1986
Arizona Wranglers	X	X	X	X
Birmingham Stallions	X	X	X	X
Boston Breakers	X			
Chicago Blitz	X	X		
Denver Gold	X	X	X	
Los Angeles Express	X	X	X	
Michigan Panthers	X	X		
New Jersey Generals	X	X	X	X
Oakland Invaders	X	X	X	
Philadelphia Stars	X	X		
Tampa Bay Bandits	X	X	X	X
Washington Federals	X	X		
Pittsburg Maulers		X		
New Orleans Breakers		X		
Memphis Showboats		X	X	X
Jacksonville Bulls		X	X	X
Houston Gamblers		X	X	
Oklahoma Outlaws		X		
San Antonio Gunslingers		X	X	
Baltimore Stars			X	X
Portland Breakers			X	
Orlando Federals			X	X
Total	12	18	14	8

Source: USFL, *Media Guide*.

players, including Mike Rozier and Steve Young. Team payrolls leaped from an averaged $1.8 million to $2.8 million, representing 40 per cent of the average team's budget.

1985 Season

The significant preseason events were the signing of Doug Flutie with the New Jersey Generals, the appointment of Harry Usher as the new league commissioner, and the reduction of the league from 18 to 14 teams (see Table 2). Table 1 illustrates the continuing eroding statistics of the league.

1986 Season

In 1986 the USFL was scheduled to field only eight teams (see Table 2). An 18-game schedule beginning September 14 and ending with a championship game February 1, 1987, was planned; however, the departure from a spring-summer schedule to a fall schedule precipitated a series of events that led to the USFL's demise on August 4, 1986, when the team owners voted to suspend play.

The shift to a fall schedule left the league without a television network, except for ESPN. ABC televised the USFL's games on Sunday during 1983, 1984, and

1985 and had an option for 1986. But the network stated that it would not pick up that option if the USFL switched from its spring-summer schedule. The other networks, NBC and CBS, had contracts with the NFL. During 1985, the networks (ABC, NBC, and CBS) paid approximately $420 million to the NFL. This constituted approximately 60 per cent of their gross revenues.

On May 12, 1986, the USFL filed a $1.3 billion antitrust case against the NFL. The league contended that the NFL conspired to pressure the three networks into keeping USFL games off television in 1986, thus closing off its largest source of potential income, and sabotaged its efforts to operate franchises in large cities.

The NFL argued that it conspired with no one and did nothing to harm the new league, that the USFL was really suing to force a merger, and that the USFL was in financial trouble through its own doing—poor management and excessive spending.

On July 29, 1986, the United States Football League won a hollow victory against the National Football League. The federal court jury ruled that the NFL did have a monopoly on the overall professional football market. It also concluded that the NFL did not monopolize the market for fall football telecasts and did not exert pressure on the three major television networks to stop them from offering

Table 3 Comparison of Marketing Mix and Other Selected Factors for the NFL and USFL

	NFL	USFL
Number of teams	1973, 26 1985, 28	1983, 12 1984, 18 1985, 14
Market potential of U.S. population (target market)	1974, 60% 1985, 70%	1983, 30% 1984, 40% 1985, 25%
Average paid attendance (customers)	1975, 50,000 1984, 60,000	1983, 24,824 1984, 27,126 1985, 24,494
Average television revenue per team	1975, $1 million 1985, $15 million	1983, $1.5 million 1984, $2.3 million 1985, $2.5 million
Time	Fall	1983-1985, spring–summer 1986, fall
Rules of the game (product)	Standard	Basically, same as NFL
Location (distribution)	Big cities Large television markets	1983, most NFL cities 1985, only 5 NFL cities
Players (product)	Superstars, 12-15 Blue Chip players, 30 fill-ins	Raided NFL and colleges for superstars, Heisman Trophy winners, 2–3 blue chip players, rest fill-ins
Promotion	Strong	Strong
Pricing	Competitive	Competitive

Sources: National Football League, United States Football League.

a contract to the USFL for a 1986 fall schedule of games. The jury awarded the USFL only $1 in damages, asserting that the USFL's problems stemmed mostly from its own blundering.

QUESTIONS

1. Was there really a market for another football league such as the USFL?
2. How was this product (USFL) originally positioned in the market?
3. Did the league stay with its original goals?
4. Were sustained losses properly planned for in the league's introductory stage?
5. Should the USFL have modified its game (rules of the game) so that it was not basically the same as the NFL (see Table 3)?
6. What steps did the USFL take to establish credibility and improve its image?

PART FOUR

Strategy Alternatives

Part IV of the text gets into some real strategy alternatives. It begins with Chapter 12, "Strategy Development: Use of the Product Life Cycle." In this chapter, you will learn not only how to respond to your life cycle environment depending on the stage that you are in, but how to control the product life cycle. Through special techniques, you will learn how to determine what stage of the life cycle a product is in, and how to predict and change life-cycle shapes. You will also be exposed to some entirely new thoughts about product life cycles. In Chapter 13, we return again to how to deal with the competition. The chapter is called "Strategy Alternatives: The Competitive Environment." In it you will receive some amazing ideas about competitive strategies from some of the world's foremost strategic thinkers. You will find that some "facts" you thought you knew just aren't true. Chapter 14, "Strategy Alternatives: The International Environment," takes on some rather interesting issues that are plaguing marketing thinkers. One such is the current dialogue between those supporting international marketing and those recommending what is called global marketing. Did you think both terms are the same? Chapter 14 will not only explain the issues, it will provide you with new ideas about how you, as a marketing manager, can exploit the opportunities available in this important environment. In the final chapter in this section, we will examine strategy under different economic conditions. The final chapter in this section takes you into the economic area. Chapter 15, "Strategy Alternatives: The Economic Environment," makes it clear that this environ is constantly changing. You can be successful under any economic condition, if you now understand the underlying forces and have the necessary strategy tools in your repertoire. This chapter will give you these tools.

12

Strategy Development: Use of the Product Life Cycle

CHAPTER OBJECTIVES

● Understand the product life cycle concept and the characteristics of each of its stages.

● Know the strategy implications of each stage.

● Be able to use the product life cycle to develop marketing strategies.

● Understand the importance of managing the product life cycle as one of the marketing manager's responsibilities.

New Disks on an Old Cycle

With worldwide revenues of $21 billion, the disk drive business has always been competitive. Now that it's in a mature life cycle, things are a lot worse. The number one producer, Seagate Technology, cut prices 20 per cent. To avoid the effects of Seagate's price cutting, a number of competitors—including Miniscribe, Maxtor, and Micropolis—tried concentrating on producing higher-margin drives, which in the past had been a safer niche. The general outlook, however, was bleak. Sales trends for personal computers indicated continuing problems for the companies making the disk drive subsystems. One estimate was that sales of personal computers would be on a steep decline, down 9 to 24 per cent from two years earlier. It was no surprise that analysts expected disk drive entry sales and earnings to fall as well. But for the older floppy disk drive makers, it was really bad news. The laptop computer models and higher-powered 32-bit machines were based on the 80386 microchip from Intel Corporation. They all used 3½-inch drives. James N. Porter, president of the market research firm of Disk/Trend, Inc., said, "Companies with new products are growing like weeds. Those with out-of-date product lines are suffering." And while 3½-inch disk drives were forecast to be in the growth stage of the product life cycle through 1992, the 5½-inch disk drives were in decline.[1]

330

When Pickett Slid

Pickett was once the world's leading manufacturer and developer of slide rules. For the uninitiated, slide rules are mechanical calculators that predated electronic calculators. They were once of absolute necessity to engineers, scientists, physicists, and many other professionals. This mechanical device was as much as a foot long and three inches wide. It was made in four pieces, with each element calibrated, and three of them have the general appearance of rulers. Two of these "rulers" were fixed and the third was movable and moved between the other two. Both sides were calibrated on many models, allowing many different calculations, including not only multiplication and division, but also log computations and other scientific calculations. And there were other special applications for special models.

To read the device, the fourth component was a cross-hair index mounted in clear plastic. It, too, was movable along the track of the three rulers. With the cross-hair index one read from one ruler to an answer on another, after making various manipulations with the central ruler. Naturally, accuracy was limited, and if the cross hair was slightly off center, as it frequently was, an erroneous answer would result. Also, more complex calculations required several different motions with the slide rule. Thus, the answer was not always immediate and forthcoming, and errors were easy to make. However, despite these drawbacks, use of these slide rules was popular because they were far quicker than doing the calculations manually, and they permitted a mobility that one did not have with a device such as a desk-mounted adding machine.

Thousands of slide rules were sold worldwide every year out of metal or expensive bamboo. Manufactured to close tolerances, they sold for up to $100 each. Every engineering student taking undergraduate or graduate courses was equipped with one. But as a generic product, slide rules had been around for a long time. Pickett failed to realize that the slide rule as a class of products was already in the mature stage of its product life cycle and that other products on the horizon could create rapid decline through technological obsolescence.

In 1973 this happened, and the electronic calculator made the slide rule more obsolete than the buggy whip. In a few months Pickett lost its market. There may be a few advantages to being the "Rolls-Royce" of buggy whips today, but there are no advantages to being the Rolls-Royce of slide rules.

The electronic calculators that replaced the slide rule exhibited life cycles of much shorter duration. In 1973 the author purchased an electronic calculator from Commodore. In addition to the basic mathematical functions, it also included a percentage key and had a memory. It cost $85 and was the size of a small brick. Nevertheless, it was entirely satisfactory in that it could fit in the inside pocket of a suit jacket, even though it gave the wearer the appearance of being armed and sometimes ripped out the jacket lining. Yet, it was a considerable improvement over the previous models. As if to demonstrate the confidence the manufacturer had in its product, it came with an insurance policy covering repair for a ten-year period. Only a year later it was given to the children to play with to destruction. So rapidly was technology advancing, and so shortened was its life cycle, that an electronic calculator with many more features that was far more compact could be purchased at less than half the price. Today, many product life cycles later, we are using calculators that have similar functions and are the size of credit cards. Furthermore, they don't use batteries, but gather energy automatically from the sun or lamplight. Yet the many companies that enter and leave this industry attest to the fact that while some are aware of the product life cycle and use it to help them formulate strategy, others do not.

How DuPont Wrapped Up a Success

E.I. du Pont de Nemours totally dominated the market for cellophane until the end of World War II. At this time polyethylene film was introduced. Polyethylene is far superior to cellophane. It is less sensitive to cold and is lower in cost. The obvious happened. Cellophane began losing market share to polyethylene. Here was a product that had left the mature stage and was going into decline. What to do? DuPont wrapped up a success by an entirely different strategy, suggested by the product life cycle. Years before, when the product had just entered the mature stage, DuPont began its research. Thus, when polyethylene was introduced, DuPont already had new modifications and coatings ready to go. These were introduced. They increased the ability of cellophane to protect food and enabled use for other purposes, for which polyethylene was unsuited. The net result was that the market for cellophane actually increased. Furthermore, in addition to this product extension strategy, DuPont took the profits from the increased cellophane sales and used them to acquire large shares of the polyethylene market while the product was still in its growth stage. The result was control of both markets. Success was due to smart marketing and knowledge and use of the product life-cycle concept. ●

The Product Life Cycle—What It Is and What It Can Do for You

What is this product life cycle to which so many companies owe their successful strategies? We've alluded to it in earlier chapters. Stated quite simply, the product has a cycle of life from birth to death, just like a living organism. Just as a man or woman goes through different life-cycle stages from infancy to being a toddler, through youth to being a teenager, a young adult to middle-age, and finally old age, so does a product progress through similar stages of life. These stages are introduction, growth, maturity, and decline. Figure 12-1 traces the classical shape of profits and of sales of a product as it progresses through introduction, growth, maturity, and decline. Note that the profits peak in the growth stage, level off, and then begin declining during the maturity stage. Meanwhile, sales continue to increase and peak out during the maturity stage before they, too, begin to level off and then decline. The product life-cycle concept can be used for plotting the life-cycle curve for a single product, a class of products, or an entire industry.

Why does the curve have the shape that it does? During the introduction stage, sales start naturally at point zero and are generally low because full

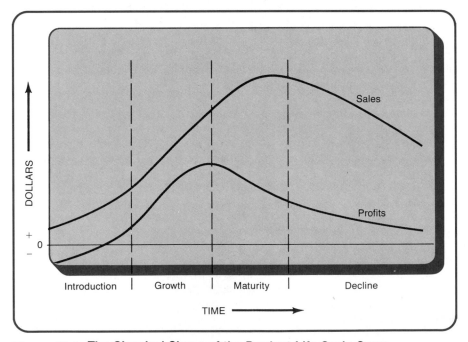

Figure 12-1 The Classical Shape of the Product Life Cycle Curve

332

acceptance by the market has not yet been achieved. Also there are very high expenses during this stage because the number of units manufactured may be low and the marketing and sales expenses usually high. As sales increase during the growth stage, profits also grow; as noted earlier, they reach their peak during this stage. However, this growth does not go unobserved. Success always attracts competition and competitors rush to enter this market with similar products. Accordingly, prices begin to be driven down due to the competition, even while sales continue to rise. Thus, the product enters the maturity stage where sales peak and then begin to decline. During this stage, profits are declining even more. Strong price competition and competition in other ways will begin to force weaker competitors to drop out. Finally, the product enters its decline stage. Now the sales begin to fall more rapidly along with profits. The decline stage may come about for a variety of reasons, including new technology, a change in social trends, or a change in consumer behavior. During this stage, the phase-out of the product is begun and only the strongest competitors remain to the very end.

The Uses of the Product Life Cycle

The product life cycle can be used by the marketing manager for many purposes, including forecasting, pricing, advertising, product planning, and strategy formulation.[2] Models developed based on the product life-cycle concept force a disciplined approach to estimating market potential both in absolute terms and for the various stages of the life cycle.[3] Industrial manufacturers have also used the product life cycle for procurement—that is, for purchasing raw materials and services needed to manufacture the various products they manufacture. The life cycle is used for procurement planning as well as in negotiating the purchase.[4] The product life cycle has also been used to analyze competitors and the industry, to plan corporate growth, and to practice strategic marketing management. Its use has been linked to the Boston Consulting Group's four-cell matrix discussed in Chapter 2.[5,6]

Three Basic Roles in the Formulation of Strategy

The product life-cycle analysis serves several different basic roles in the formulation of strategy:

- An enabling condition
- A moderating variable
- A consequence of strategic decisions[7]

The various stages of the product life cycle either assist or detract from the ability of companies to enter the market, create or eradicate the opportunity for profits or markets, and in general help to enable the problems, threats, and opportunities that exist in any marketing situation.

The product life cycle is also a moderating variable. Depending upon the stage of the life cycle, it influences the value of market share position and therefore the profitability possibilities of various decisions made by the firm. For example, the competitive value of market share for a product varies with its stage in the product life cycle. If you doubt this, consider the value of market share for buggy whips versus the value of market share for a high-technology product just being introduced.[8]

Finally, the product life cycle is a consequence of strategic decisions in that, as we will see shortly, the product life cycle can be managed and caused to react to actions that we or our competitors may take.

What You Need to Know to Exploit the Product Life Cycle

As a marketing manager seeking to control and exploit the product life cycle, you must know the answer to the following three questions:

1. To what extent can the shape and the duration of the life cycle be predicted?
2. How can you determine what stage of the product life cycle your product or product line is in?
3. How can this information be effectively used in formulating strategy?[9]

Let's look at the answer to each of these questions in turn.

To What Extent Can the Shape and Duration of the Product Life Cycle Be Predicted?

It would be nice if the shape shown in Figure 12-1 were the only shape for all product life cycles and the duration of all product life cycles was identical. Unfortunately, they are not. A study by the Management Science Institute of over one hundred product categories found that only 17 per cent of product classes and 20 per cent of individual brands have the shape shown in Figure 12-1. In fact, many different shapes of the product life cycle exist.[10] Nine shapes are shown in Figure 12-2 resulting from various special conditions as indicated.[11]

The high-learning product life cycle takes quite a bit longer than the ordinary product to get off the ground. Thus, the introduction and growth stages take longer than normal.

The missing link, or low-learning product, is just the opposite. Its introduction and growth phases are combined. It's steep right from the start, and there's no kink at the transition between introduction and growth.

The fad curve only has two stages: nearly straight up, and then even more nearly straight down. However, if there is a significant residual market, it will manage three stages—the third being a sort of extended decline.

The instant bust goes up and down before it even gets out of the introduction stage. A new prime-time TV show that gets cut due to poor ratings only a couple weeks after being introduced is an example.

The market-specialty product peaks in the mature stage. Although the mature stage is the longest with a conventional product life-cycle curve, this product's maturity stage goes on and on.

The pyramided product hits periods of regrowth. Franchises such as McDonald's sometimes demonstrate this cycle.

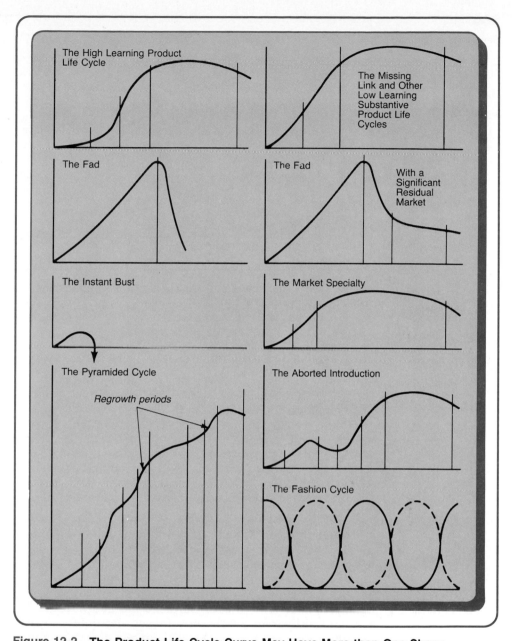

Figure 12-2 The Product Life Cycle Curve May Have More than One Shape

Source: From Chester R. Wasson, *Dynamic Competitive Strategy and Product Life Cycles*, 3rd ed. (Austin, TX: Austin Press Division of Lone Star Publishers, 1978). Used with permission.

The aborted introduction is a product whose backers back off, but then come back and support it again before the product dies. Have you ever heard of the book *Your Erroneous Zones*, by psychologist Wayne Dyer? After selling two thousand copies the first year, the publisher stopped promoting the book and sales fell to near zero. Then Dr. Dyer took his summer leave from his

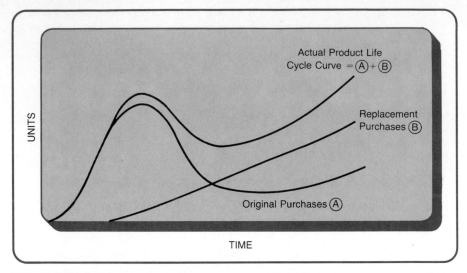

Figure 12-3   The Shape and Duration of the Product Life Cycle Curve Must Consider Replacement Purchases

Source: Adapted from Stephen G. Harrell and Elmer D. Taylor, "Modeling the Product Life Cycle for Consumer Durables," *Journal of Marketing, vol. 45 (Fall 1981), p. 70.*

university to traverse the country promoting the book on his own. Sales increased dramatically. His publisher started promoting again, and more than a million copies were sold the second year.

Finally, we have the fashion cycle. The curve for a new garden hose, lawn mower, or snow remover would duplicate this curve. Many other additional shapes have been discovered.[12] Furthermore, the shape of the product life-cycle curve observed will be altered depending upon replacement sales, as shown in Figure 12-3.[13,14] That is, for products that wear out or are used up, additional quantities will be purchased that can affect the product life cycle.

The Product Life Cycle Isn't What It Used to Be. In the introduction to this chapter, we noted that with electronic calculators, the product life cycle had become extremely short in duration. This is true with a variety of products. Way back in the mid-1930s, the Douglas Aircraft Corporation introduced a revolutionary transport aircraft that cruised at a little over a hundred miles per hour. This amazing airplane was known as the DC-3. It remained a leading airliner for fifteen years. In fact, almost fifty years later the airplane is still in use. Yet, a later Douglas airliner, the DC-7, remained a first-line airliner for fewer than five years. Although one may argue the various merits of the DC-3 as compared with the DC-7, the amount of time that products take to go through their entire life cycle is definitely decreasing. These shorter cycles are evident in many different types of products. Table 12-1 shows the lengths of introductory and growth stages for thirty-seven household products through three different periods: 1922–1942, 1945–1964, and 1965–1979.[15] Why is this so? The full explanation for this trend is extremely complex. It is not fully known or understood for all products.

**Table 12-1 The Lengths of Introductory and Growth
Stages for 37 Household Products**

Period	Number of Products	Introductory Stage Duration (Years)	Growth Stage Duration (Years)
1922–1942	12	12.5	33.8
1945–1964	16	7.0	19.5
1965–1979	9	2.0	6.8

Source: Milton D. Rosenau, Jr., "Speeding Your New Product to Market,"
Journal of Consumer Marketing, vol. 5, no. 2 (Spring 1988), p. 24.

Some of the reasons confirmed include an increasing rate of technological advancement, an increasing number of consumers that are able to use such new products as computers; more favorable attitudes held by consumers toward innovations; differences in the level of penetration achieved by products; differences in the character of products; and technological improvements in communication and distribution. A short duration of the life cycle has important implications for the marketing manager and his or her development of strategy. It's especially important for the marketing manager to pay more attention to the timing of entry into the market. There also may not be sufficient time required to execute some strategies that might once have been an option. In general, the marketing manager must move much more quickly in response to this shortened cycle.[16]

The Service Cycle

Another important concept sometimes overlooked by marketers is that of the service cycle. The product service cycle lags behind its life cycle. As the life cycle enters the maturity stage, the product's service cycle is just beginning to really get under way. This is illustrated in Figure 12-4. Many things can go wrong if the marketing manager fails to consider the product service cycle. There can be either a deficient or excessive spare parts inventory, poor service pricing strategy, a mislocation of manpower resources, or a premature or late shutdown of product improvement programs. At one company, almost 70 per cent of service revenues for a product came when the product was in the maturity and decline stages.[17] Therefore the marketing manager must track and control both the service and the product life cycles.

You Can Predict and Change the Shape of the Product Life Cycle.
Despite the complications caused by variable shapes and other limitations noted, marketing scientists have discovered that one can reliably predict the shape of the product life cycle for many types of goods by manipulating the ratio of the mean adoption to mean interpurchase times and the depth of the repeat purchase.[18] But perhaps more important, the shape of the product life cycle itself can be altered as a result of strategy influences. In fact, so

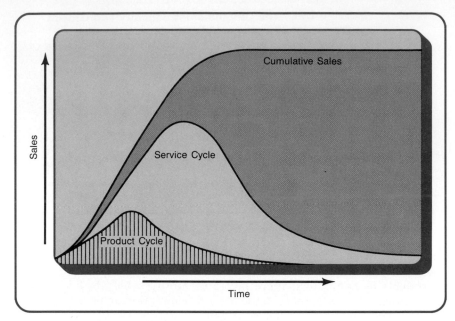

Figure 12-4   The Product and Its Service Cycle

Source: Adapted from George W. Potts, "Exploit Your Product's Service Life Cycle," *Harvard Business Review* Vol. 66 No. 5 (September–October 1988) p. 33.

important is strategy on the shape of the life-cycle curve that some marketing scientists feel that a brand or product is not predestined to mature and die but can be kept profitable by proper adaption to the marketing environs, as they evolve almost indefinitely.[19]

An example of this is the product extension strategy for baking soda, a product formerly used only in the baking process. But one manufacturer, Arm and Hammer, was successful in promoting the product for an entirely different purpose: as a food odor absorber for refrigerators. This **product extension strategy** altered the shape of the product life-cycle curve for baking soda. In the same fashion, use of the DC-10 transport aircraft, originally developed and used as an airliner, as a missile launcher for the Air Force was a product extension strategy. The product extension strategies employed as the products entered the mature stage of their life cycles change the shape of the curves, as shown in Figure 12-5.[20]

How Can We Determine What Stage of the Product Life Cycle a Product Is In?

One of the more difficult problems is how to determine what stage of the product life cycle a product or product line or a brand is in. We can do this if we can identify the common characteristics peculiar to each cycle.

The Introduction Stage. In the introduction stage, there are few or no competitors of importance. Profits are negligible due to high production, R&D, and marketing costs. As a general rule, pricing is set high to attempt

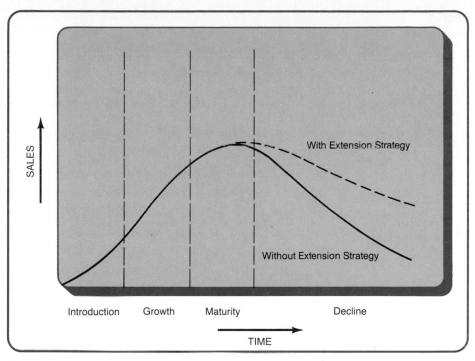

Figure 12-5 Changing the Shape of the Product Life Cycle Curve with a Product Extension Strategy

to recover these costs of introduction. But as we will see, this is not always so. As we learned earlier in Chapter 7 on buyer behavior, during this introduction stage there is a certain amount of buyer inertia. Customers must be convinced to try the product, and strategies must be developed to accomplish this objective. This requires a particular emphasis on promotion, and thus marketing costs are high. In this stage manufacturing has an overcapacity. Production runs tend to be short, and there is a high-skill labor content that contributes to the high production costs. There may be some attempt at export in this stage, but usually such efforts are limited. Channels of distribution are probably limited due to the limited resources available, and thus the first channels opened are selected very carefully.

The Growth Stage. In the growth stage, the product has survived its birth and has become established in the market. Its success attracts increasing numbers of competitors. Profits reach peak levels during this stage as prices are increased to take advantage of increasing demand. There is an increased number of potential buyers during this stage, and because of the demand for the product, these buyers may accept less than perfect quality and even delays to obtain the product. Marketing costs are still high during this stage, but they are lower as a percentage of sales than in the earlier introductory stage. Manufacturing, however, has changed from an overcapacity to an undercapacity, and there is less skilled-labor content. There is more of a shift toward a mass production of the product. Exports increase greatly during this stage, and distribution becomes intensive as multiple

339

channels are used to expand market share. Sales are growing rapidly. During this stage the firm could be cash poor. It will therefore be seeking additional capital to finance expansion to meet market demand. If so, financial planning to support growth is essential.

The Maturity Stage. In the maturity stage many competitors are competing for increasingly smaller shares of the market. The result is increased price competition and a general shake-out, with less efficient competitors dropping out and no longer producing the product. Profits are significantly lower due to lower margins. Prices are falling due to the competition. At this point there is repeat buying, which, as mentioned earlier, may alter the shape of the curve. Marketing efforts are needed to broaden the product line and seek out new customers. Manufacturing returns to some overcapacity, although lower labor skills are maintained. There tend to be lower production runs during this stage, with stable techniques employed for production. Exports begin to decline. In fact, in some cases significant imports may begin due to lower production costs abroad. Sales level off in this stage and begin to decline, but distribution is continued intensively, although some channels may be dropped to improve margins.

The Decline Stage. In the decline stage few competitors remain. Profits decline rapidly as declining sales volumes push costs up to higher levels. Prices continue to fall. Eventually they will fall so low the marketing manager can no longer ignore quick liquidation of the inventory as an option. The buyers at this point are fairly sophisticated and can make choices among different products based on intelligent use over a period of time. Marketing expenditures during this stage are much less, but there is a substantial overcapacity in manufacturing, exports drop to zero in most cases, and there are significant imports. There is no question that sales are down and the remaining distribution channels are only those few that are still profitable. Finally, like the buggy whip or the slide rule, the product disappears.

A summary of the conditions during the various stages classified according to market structure variables, organization and performance variables, and strategy variables is presented in Figure 12-6.[21,22]

There are two methods we can use to determine the stage of the product life cycle we are in by knowing the characteristics of each stage of the product life cycle. First, we can compare these characteristics with the ones that we are experiencing with our own product. Second, we can look at a history of similar products and the unique characteristics that occurred during each stage of their life cycle. In this way, we can trace a probable product life-cycle curve for our product and our probable position on it.

How Can the Information Available Be Used Effectively to Formulate Strategies?

Researchers have discovered that each stage of the product life cycle has certain characteristics that favor the use of particular strategies. Thus, if we can establish the shape of the life-cycle curve and where we are on that curve, we can then look at various strategies that might be most appropriate for this location. Let's look at the different stages and at various strategies we might employ, depending on the stage of the product life cycle.

Market Structure Variables	Organization and Performance Variables	Strategy Variables
Degree of market innovation	Cash flow	Advertising objectives
Entry and exit of competition	Emphasis on productivity and financial control	Breadth of product line
Incidence of mergers and acquisitions	Market research needs	Degree and nature of market segmentation
Industry capacity utilization rate	Market share objectives	Distribution channel strategy
Intensity of competition	Patent protection	Intensity of distribution
Intensity of price competition	Unit gross profit margins	Level of customer service
Industry exports		Marketing expenditures
Market concentration		Number and form of new product introductions
Nature of customers		Package changes
Number of competitors		Price changes
Number of customers		Private branding
		Product quality
		Relative importance of advertising, promotion, and sales force expenses
		R&D expenditures
		Vertical integration

Source: Adapted from Hans B. Thorelli and Stephen C. Burnett, "The Nature of Product Life Cycles for Industrial Goods Businesses," *Journal of Marketing*, vol. 45 (Fall 1981), p. 99.

Figure 12-6   Strategy, Structure, and Performance Variables That Vary Over Different Stages of the Product Life Cycle

Strategies for the Introduction Stage. In the introduction stage our basic purpose is to establish market share and persuade the early adopters to buy our product. On an international basis, the Japanese companies have been strong competitors by their understanding of this strategy and their willingness to take initial losses to establish their product in the marketplace. Thus, when the Datsun was first introduced in the United States, it was priced low—a tremendous bargain. However, when the quality of the car and its features were accepted in the American marketplace and demand grew, the price was raised.

To establish share and persuade early adopters to buy, R&D and engineering are key functions. But various combinations and use of product, price, promotion, and distribution variables are all useful. In general, we want to have as short an introductory period as possible. This is highly desirable because the resources required during the introduction are so extensive. A short introductory period will reduce negative impacts on both earnings and cash flow. Also, of course, a short introductory period will dispel any uncertainty we may have about the ultimate success of the product; thus, it may be easier for us to get additional resources to continue our marketing of the product. The duration of this stage, however, is largely determined by characteristics of the product and the nature and amount of resource commitment. The newer the class of product, the harder it may be to get it accepted. Recall the problem that the Wright brothers had, as recorded in an earlier chapter.

To overcome this problem of newness, we try to maximize acceptability through product design. Thus, a beep in a calculator may be important to the user even though unnecessary, simply because users have in the past used machinery that made noise. Noise attested to the fact that the machines were still working. The beep was needed psychologically for the same purpose. In the same fashion, microwave ovens were supplied with a browning option. The meat was fully cooked, although not "browned," but over several thousands of years, people had become used to the fact that if meat was not brown it was not fully cooked. Because marketing is important, we may need to spend more money to disseminate information about products and their newness.

A new armor material developed by Phillips Petroleum never did sell well, partially due to an unwillingness to spend additional money for marketing after R&D. On the other hand, E. I. du Pont de Nemours developed a cloth product called Kevlar that has five times the tensile strength of steel and is used in automobile tires. It displaced a billion-dollar ballistic nylon industry as an armor material because of DuPont's willingness to spend the money after the R&D for marketing.

The more complex the product, the slower the acceptance. This is one reason why personal home computers began moving slowly, picked up speed, and then slowed down again. They are evidently more complex than the average individual is willing to accept in a home-use product.

Environs can, of course, slow down the introductory stage. Although it may be difficult to believe today, automobiles took some twenty years from their invention to their general acceptance by the population. The environ in this case was the fact that no paved highways existed, which made it difficult to use the new method of transportation over the old-fashioned horse and buggy. In the same way, color televisions were not widely purchased in the early 1950s, although they were technologically feasible. More color programming was needed to make the purchase of a color television set attractive to the consumer.

A clear and significant competitive differential advantage over older products can shorten the introduction stage. This means either superior performance, superior quality, or significantly lower prices. In general, the higher the cost of the product, the larger this advantage must be.

Strategies for the Growth Stage. The growth stage is critical because it is important to penetrate as many markets as possible. What can be captured in this stage can be held. The key is to stay ahead of the competition. As competitors are just entering one market, you should be already opening up additional markets. This is also a good time to keep ahead of the competition by continuing to improve the product. New channels of distribution should also be sought during the growth stage of the product life cycle. Finally, price and quality trade-offs can be manipulated easily during the growth stage to satisfy the demand of the market. This is not to encourage poor value for the money. Even though quality may be lowered, the overall value may be raised because of a much lower price. In any case this ratio is an important consideration, as the marketing manager seeks to satisfy needs and meet the competition. It is also possible to raise the price to meet the competition, a technique that will be discussed in a later chapter.

Strategies for the Maturity Stage. In the maturity stage we must defend the markets we have obtained and prevent the competition from establishing inroads. We have the advantage because, unless we are not satisfying our customers' needs, it can be very difficult for competitors to break in. Controlling costs is extremely important during this stage. Product differentiation may be an excellent strategy to emphasize the unique advantage we have. It is very important that we continue to search for new markets and new uses of the product. What else can we do with the product? This is important whether we are making an odor absorber from a product that was originally a cooking component or a missile carrier from what was once a passenger aircraft. In one study of 567 successful innovations—modifications to an existing product—it was found that two-thirds cost less than $100,000.[23] Thus, modifying a product can be very cost effective. We can look to DuPont for another example of this kind of strategy. During World War II, DuPont became the leading manufacturer of nylon parachutes. At the end of the war, DuPont consulted its products' life-cycle curve to help in strategy formulation. Nylon was clearly in the mature stage. DuPont modified its product using an extension strategy: it sought new markets and new uses, going into the consumer industry for women's hosiery, tires, vehicles, and various nylon composites. The result was a dramatic increase in nylon sales. In fact, it was estimated that if DuPont had continued to produce nylon only for the markets it served during World War II, sales would have been about fifty million pounds of nylon fifteen years later. Instead, it was ten times this figure.

One other strategy for the mature stage is for the leader to go against weaker competition by significantly lowering price. Through this strategy, markets that have been established earlier can be maintained.

Strategies for the Decline Stage. In the decline stage it's essential that the marketing manager prepare for product removal. Such an elimination can be slow, or it can be fast. The alternatives must always be weighed. One important concept is to milk or harvest all possible benefits, while keeping costs low. Thus, advertising may be minimized during the decline stage. Camel cigarettes were advertised extensively after their introduction in 1913 and throughout the majority of this product's life cycle. But in the decline stage, even before some cigarette advertising was curtailed by law, Camels at one time competed with 170 other brands, and with no advertising maintained its position in seventh place with sales of $250 million.

If any remaining markets are still profitable, the product can be concentrated in them. Finally, the product is withdrawn or liquidated. Decline and deletion must be managed with consideration for the reseller. Dropping a product abruptly and without warning may leave retailers with heavy inventories of a product that cannot be sold. This may have a negative impact on other products marketed through the same channel in the future.

The focal point of the strategy during the decline stage of the product life cycle is how well the end is met. There are always reasons for killing off weaker products immediately, including better profits elsewhere and better uses of scarce resources, not the least of which may be the time of the marketing manager. Concurrently, there may be reasons for retention, including effects on other product lines and image—or even societal effects if it is desirable that certain plants remain open and continue to produce—while the markets for new products are being developed.

Condition	Introduction	Growth	Maturity	Decline
Competition	Little or none	Some emulators	Many	Few
Overall strategy	Market establishment	Market penetration	Defense of position	Preparation for removal; harvesting
Profits	Negligible	Highest levels	Declining from peak	Declining to zero
Retail prices	High	High	What the traffic will bear	Low enough to liquidate inventory
Distribution	Selective	Intensive	Intensive	Selective
Advertising strategy	Target needs of early adopters	Mass market awareness of benefits	Vehicle for product differentiation	Emphasize low price
Advertising emphasis	High	Moderate	Moderate	The minimum required for phase-out
Customer sales and promotion expenditures	Heavy	Moderate	Heavy	Minimal

Source: Adapted from Nariman K. Dhalla and Sonia Yuspeh, "Forget the Product Life-Cycle Concept," *Harvard Business Review* (January–February 1976), p. 104.

Figure 12-7   Conditions and Strategy and Tactics Implications of the Product Life Cycle According to Stage

A summary of various strategies and other attributes of stages of the product life cycle is shown in Figure 12-7.[24]

How to Use the Product Life Cycle and Manage It Simultaneously

To use the product life-cycle curve and at the same time manage it, it is necessary to plot the curve and locate our position in it, as noted earlier. To do this, follow these seven steps.[25]

1. Develop historical trend information for a period of three to five years, or longer. Information that we particularly want to look at are unit and dollar sales, profit margins, total profit contribution, return on investment capital, market share, prices, and other quantifiable measures of trends having to do with the product.
2. Check recent trends regarding the number and the nature of competitors, including their market shares, rankings of competing products, quality and performance advantages, distribution channel shifts, and relative advantages and disadvantages of competitive products in each channel.
3. Look at short-term competitive tactics, including announcements of new products, plans for expansion, production capacity, and similar recent actions of competitors.
4. Update historical information available on the product life cycles of similar products or products related to the product under analysis.
5. Project sales for the product over the coming three to five years, based on information we have obtained. As an aid, estimate an incremental

344

profit ratio for the product during these years. This ratio is a ratio of direct costs, including manufacturing, advertising, product development, sales, distribution, and other applicable costs to pretax profits. This ratio measures the number of dollars required to generate each additional dollar of profit. In general, the ratio tends to become lower as the product enters the growth period; it begins to rise as the product approaches maturity. In the decline stage, it begins to rise very sharply.

6. Estimate the number of profitable years remaining in the product's life cycle, based on the information you have analyzed.

7. Using the shape of a life-cycle curve from a similar or related product that has completed its cycle, and for which information is available, to plot its curve; adjust this curve's shape based on the information you have analyzed, and plot your product's position on this curve.

New Thoughts on the Product Life Cycle

In recent years the product life-cycle concept has come under attack. The basic criticism is that the model of the product life cycle fails to represent what actually happens. According to this viewpoint, the concept is overly simplistic in expecting sales plotted as a function of time in and of itself to result in a curve that relates accurately to a product's performance from birth to death. One alternative model offered is that of an evolutionary approach containing "patterns," rather than stages:[26]

1. *Divergence.* Divergence is the beginning of a new product type. The term is used inasmuch as the product is usually not an entirely new concept, but rather a modification or combination of existing products or technologies. Thus, it is a divergence from a line of product evolution.

2. *Development.* In this pattern, product sales increase rapidly, and the product is increasingly adapted to the consumer.

3. *Differentiation.* During this pattern, the product is differentiated to suit a variety of consumer demands and interests.

4. *Stabilization.* The stabilization pattern is characterized by a few minor changes in the product category, but by numerous changes in packaging, accessories, service skills, and other ancillary aspects.

5. *Demise.* Demise occurs when the product no longer meets consumer expectations or no longer satisfies consumer demand.

The originators of this Product Evolutionary Cycle (PEC) model believe that it will be more useful in the planning of marketing strategies. The major premise is that product growth is partly the result of the strategy adopted and not the reverse. Empirical support for this notion has been demonstrated.[27]

Thus, a profitable brand is not predestined to mature and die following chronological stages but can be maintained as a profitable business endeavor by proper adaptation to the environs of the marketplace.

Another approach is that of market evolution, using population ecology as a model. According to this concept, as a market evolves, three processes are set in motion. These three processes are the main movers in changing competitive structure and performance:

1. New markets attract increasing numbers of competitors. This leads to an increasing level of population density until the space for resources is filled and a shake-out of firms occurs.
2. Every group of entrants introduces new structures and strategies in response to changes in the availability of resources.
3. Competitive conditions change over time, the tendency being toward less risk and uncertainty and higher intensity of competition.

These processes, in turn, cause the development of distinct niche configurations. These have been categorized as embryonic, developing, and maturing configurations. As resource conditions change and new niche categories develop, the resulting market structure and resource profile are altered. They require different optimum responses in the same way as the stages of the product life cycle.[28]

Summary

In this chapter we have seen how some companies have successfully used the product life-cycle concept to help formulate strategies that were extremely successful in the marketplace, while others, which ignored the product life cycle and its implications, were displaced by successful competitors. We have noted that the basic concept of the product life cycle is no more than that a cycle of life exists for a product or a service or a brand or a product line just as for any living thing. The concept is useful because of common characteristics of the four stages of the product life cycle: introduction, growth, maturity, and decline.

With the help of the shape of the curve and knowledge of where a product or service is located relevant to these stages, the product life cycle can be used for a variety of purposes: forecasting, pricing, advertising, product planning, strategic marketing management, and especially the formulation of strategies. To exploit the product life cycle properly, however, it is necessary to have the answers to three basic questions: To what extent can the shape and duration of the product life cycle be predicted? How can we determine what stage of the product life cycle we are in? And, finally, how can this information be effectively used? All three questions were answered through our discussions. We saw that the so-called typical shape really is not typical, that various other shapes of the product life cycle exist, and that the duration of the product life cycle has been shortened, may be different, and must consider replacements. We also considered the separate service life cycle. However, we can still predict shapes by considering of a number of relevant factors and comparing the product life cycle of past similar products. Through an analysis of many factors, we can also locate the stage of our product in its life cycle. We can then turn around and use this information to formulate strategies, depending upon the stage of the cycle. Inasmuch as the stage and the shape of the life cycle can be changed by our strategy, as proved through product extension, we are both using and managing the product life cycle simultaneously.

Recently, some researchers proposed different approaches to a product cycle rather than a life cycle. The evolutionary approach has five patterns, rather than four stages. Another approach depends on population ecology for its model. Only the future can tell us whether the life-cycle concept has completed its own life cycle. However until such time that the concept is displaced, its use provides considerable aid to the marketing manager.

Questions

1. Is there any purpose to plotting the life cycle of a competitor's products? How might you use this information?
2. Your company has five successful products in the mature stage of their product life cycles. All are well defended and profitable. What does this position imply regarding strategy, and what recommendations would you make to the management of your company?
3. IBM and other companies have successfully terminated successful products in the mature stage. Is there any situation you can think of where you might want to terminate a successful product in the growth stage?
4. What can a company like Pickett do when it finds its product in the mature stage being replaced by a technologically superior product?
5. Because profits are highest in the growth stage, is there any way of keeping a product in the growth stage of the product life cycle indefinitely?
6. Can a competitor alter the shape of your product's life cycle?
7. It is said that the duration of the life cycle is shortening. From your own observations, state examples of this shortening and note in what stages it is occurring.
8. Because product modification generally costs so much less than completely developing a new product, why isn't changing the shape of the life cycle through product modification always a good strategy?
9. In plotting the life cycle of our products, we look at past life cycles of similar or related products. Is there any problem in doing this?
10. What are the advantages of the evolutionary approach to product growth explained in this chapter as an alternative to the product life-cycle concept?

Ethical Question

Sometimes an analysis of a product's life cycle is subject to different interpretations. Is there anything wrong with interpreting the results of such an analysis to support the particular case you are trying to make? If so, how do you handle this problem of various interpretations?

Endnotes

1. Robert D. Hof, "How Disk Drive Makers Gummed Up the Works," *Business Week* (October 17, 1988), pp. 106, 110.
2. John E. Smallwood, "The Product Life Cycle: A Key to Strategic Marketing Planning," *MSU Business Topics* (Winter 1973), p. 35.

3. Douglas Tigert and Behrooz Farivar, "The Bass New Product Growth Model: A Sensitivity Analysis for a High Technology Product," *Journal of Marketing*, Vol. 45 (Fall 1981), p. 90.

4. David R. Rink and Harold W. Fox, "The Role of Product Life-Cycle Theory in Formulating Industrial Procurement Strategy: An Empirical Analysis," in Russell W. Belk, et al., eds., *1984 AMA Educators' Proceedings* (Chicago: AMA, 1984), pp. 162–166.

5. John A. Weber, "Planning Corporate Growth with Inverted Product Life Cycles," *Long-Range Planning* (October 1976), pp. 12–29.

6. Shekhar Misra, "Price and Advertising Effort over the Product Life Cycle: The B.C.G. and Dorfman-Steiner Approaches," Jon M. Hawes and George B. Glisan, eds. *Developments in Marketing Science*, vol. 4 (Akron: Academy of Marketing Science, 1987), p. 288.

7. George S. Day, "The Product Life Cycle: Analysis and Applications Issues," *Journal of Marketing*, vol. 45 (Fall 1981), p. 65.

8. Bernard Catry and Mike Michel Chevalier, "Market Share Strategy and the Product Life Cycle," *Journal of Marketing*, vol. 39 (October 1974), p. 31.

9. Theodore Levitt, "Exploit the Product Life Cycle," *Harvard Business Review* (November–December 1965), pp. 81–84.

10. David R. Rink and J. E. Swan, "Product Life-Cycle Research: A Literature Review," *Journal of Business Research*, vol. 7 (September 1979), pp. 219–242.

11. Chester R. Wasson, *Dynamic Competitive Strategy and Product Life Cycles*, 3rd ed. (Austin, Tex.: Austin Press Division of Lone Star Publishers, 1978).

12. Gerard J. Tellis and C. Merle Crawford, "An Evolutionary Approach to Product Growth Theory," *Journal of Marketing*, vol. 45 (Fall 1981), p. 126.

13. Vijay Mahajan and Eitan Muller, "Innovation to Fusion and New Product Growth Models in Marketing," *Journal of Marketing*, vol. 43 (Fall 1979), p. 65.

14. Stephen G. Harrell and Elmer D. Taylor, "Modeling the Product Life Cycle for Consumer Durables," *Journal of Marketing*, vol. 45 (Fall 1981), p. 70.

15. Milton D. Rosenau, Jr., "Speeding Your New Product to Market," *Journal of Consumer Marketing*, vol. 5, no. 2 (Spring 1988), p. 24.

16. William Qualls, Richard W. Olshavsky, and Ronald E. Michaels, "Shortening of the PLC—An Empirical Test," *Journal of Marketing*, vol. 45 (Fall 1981), p. 80.

17. George W. Potts, "Exploit Your Product's Service Life Cycle," *Harvard Business Review*, vol. 66, no. 5 (September–October 1988), pp. 32–33.

18. David F. Midgley, "Toward a Theory of the Product Life Cycle: Explaining Diversity," *Journal of Marketing*, vol. 45 (Fall 1981), p. 114.

19. Tellis and Crawford, op. cit., p. 131.

20. Ben M. Enis, Raymond La Garce, and Arthur E. Prell, "Extending the Product Life Cycle," *Business Horizons*, vol. 20 (June 1977).

21. Hans B. Thorelli and Stephen C. Burnett, "The Nature of Product Life Cycles for Industrial Goods Businesses," *Journal of Marketing*, vol. 45 (Fall 1981), p. 99.

22. Nariman K. Dhalla and Sonia Yuspeh, "Forget the Product Life-Cycle Concept," *Harvard Business Review* (January–February 1976), p. 104.

23. Donald G. Marquis, "The Anatomy of Successful Innovation," ed. by the staff of *Innovation* magazine, *Managing Advanced Technology*, vol. 1 (New York: AMA, 1972), p. 42.

24. Dhalla and Yuspeh, loc. cit.

25. Donald K. Clifford, Jr., "Managing the Product Life Cycle," in Roland Mann, ed., *The Arts of Top Management: A McKinsey Anthology* (New York: McGraw-Hill, 1971), p. 225.

26. Tellis and Crawford, op. cit., p. 129.

27. Susan L. Holak and Y. Edwin Tang, "Advertising's Effect on the Product Evolutionary Cycle," *Journal of Marketing*, vol. 54, no. 3 (July 1990), p. 16.

28. Mary Lambkin and George S. Day, "Evolutionary Processes in Competitive Markets: Beyond the Product Life Cycle," *Journal of Marketing*, vol. 53, no. 3 (July 1989), pp. 13–14.

Strategy Alternatives: The Competitive Environment

13

CHAPTER OBJECTIVES

● Understand the importance of competition in the marketplace.

● Know how to overcome stronger competitors with the appropriate strategy.

● Be able to apply important competitive strategies in varying situations.

A Big Mac Attack . . . with Pizza

McDonald's in the pizza business? Unbelievable . . . but true. Chief executive of McDonald's, Michael R. Quinlan, thought pizza was too great an opportunity to pass up. Americans have been gobbling down $20 billion worth of pizza a year, and growth in sales has been running at 11 per cent annually. In McDonald's mainstream $31 billion hamburger business, the growth has been only 8 per cent per year. McDonald's entry is 14 inches in diameter and cut into eight slices. It comes in four varieties (cheese, sausage, pepperoni, and deluxe), ranging in price from $5.84 to $9.49. So McDonald's is targeting the same segment as their regular burgers. But the competitive environment is hot, and McDonald's has lots of worries. In addition to established armed-and-ready competitors, including a Pizza Hut spokesperson who

said about McDonald's pizza: "Our people have been all over it," McDonald's has to ensure that it can maintain its efficiency and quality with this new product as well as take care that it doesn't cannibalize its nighttime sandwich sales. Domino Pizza Inc.'s marketing vice-president, Mike Raymond, maintained that "this will be a real challenge for them."[1]

Being Big by Targeting Small

A little firm in Chattanooga, Tennessee, called Chattem is making its name by taking from large companies brands that failed and turning them into winners. As a result, since 1976 this company has grown at a compounded rate of 18 per cent every year, while profits have advanced 22 per cent. What kinds of products does Chattem sell that larger companies can't cope with? One such product was Sun-In, a peroxide hair lightener developed by Gillette. At $500,000 annual sales, Gillette did not feel it was much of a winner for its then $1-billion-plus sized company. But Chattem acquired the product and within three years sales were at $4 million. Another product acquired was a facial cleanser named Mudd. Its annual sales before Chattem got hold of it were only $90,000 per year. In seven years Chattem boosted those sales to $3 million. Other loser products that have been turned into winners came from American Cyanamid Company and SmithKline Beckman Corporation. How does Chattem do it? What's the secret of its success? Very simply, Chattem's strategy, often repeated by its managers, is "To be big in small markets."[2]

David 1; Goliath 0

A thirty-six-year-old Canadian named Lewis Steiner, working in the United States as an accountant, went into a joint venture with a friend to sell aluminum strips to venetian blind manufacturers in the United States. He found an incredible demand for miniblinds. Miniblinds are made of aluminum strips and are much thinner than the normal-sized venetian blinds. Miniblinds had been growing at about 30 per cent a year. At the time of Mr. Steiner's venture, the market had reached an astronomical $500 million, with the leading company doing an estimated $100 million a year. But Steiner noted that 90 per cent of the sales for these miniblinds were for custom-made blinds, with customers waiting as long as five weeks for the made-to-order blinds to arrive. The remaining 10 per cent in the market were ready-made blinds of grossly inferior quality. Steiner felt there was a real market for quality blinds that were ready-made, if something could be done about the cost of installation. Steiner's solution was to make quality blinds in stock sizes that people could buy and, with directions supplied with the blinds, take home and install themselves. At the end of the first year, sales of his blinds were $2 million, with a projected growth rate of 300 per cent. As one company officer said, "We are in a position to increase volume quite a bit, with almost no increase in overhead." The success of Lewis Steiner's Rainbow Window Fashions, Inc., demonstrates that a new company just entering the market can capture, hold, and expand its market share by offering something that large, well-entrenched competitors do not offer.[3]

In this chapter we will see how small organizations with sometimes limited resources can face competitors that are far stronger and better established in the market, and win. Sometimes these small organizations are in reality tiny subdivisions of the giants. Yet, for various reasons, at various times, and due to some overall corporate strategies, these divisions have limited resources. Thus, for all practical purposes, the subdivisions of larger firms are in the same situations as small companies facing large competitors. Therefore, instead of looking at alternative strategies that consider small companies taking on larger companies, we will examine alternate strategies that consider the organizational strengths of small organizations competing with large organizations. To sum up the contents of this chapter, we will see how David can fight and win against Goliath, as well as what Goliath can do to defend himself against such an attack.

The Fundamentals _____

As stated in an earlier chapter, the fundamental principle of strategy is to concentrate superior resources at the decisive point. To secure a competitive advantage, according to Bruce Henderson, founder and CEO of the Boston

Consulting Group, you must "Induce your competitors not to invest in those products, markets, and services where you expect to invest the most."[4]

Accordingly, says Henderson, there are six different **diversion and dissuasion** action categories that may be used by a firm to accommodate this fundamental rule. A firm can appear to be unworthy of attention with its action. For example, it can very quickly cut off a part of the market that may be too small to justify a major response from a larger competitor. After this has successfully been accomplished, it can repeat the same action. In some cases a smaller firm or organization can appear to be unbeatable. Notice that the emphasis here is on appearance. The idea is to convince competitors that if they do the same thing you're doing—that is, if they follow your lead and your actions—they will be unable to gain success, because you will equal or better any actions they take or resources they commit. A smaller firm or organization can avoid attention. This is accomplished by following the principle of security mentioned in Chapter 10. Competitors are not forewarned about new products, strategies, capabilities, or policies until they are actually taken, or until it is too late for them to respond effectively to them. Another of Henderson's diversion and dissuasion concepts involves redirecting attention. Here the organization focuses competitive attention not on high-potential areas of interest, but on major volume areas of company sales. In this fashion the competitor is encouraged to be concerned with the organization's areas of current activity, rather than those of future intentions. Another diversion and dissuasion approach is to attract attention but to discredit the significance of the action to which the attention is attracted. One method of doing this is to overstate and overpublicize the potentials of the action, whether it is a new policy or a new strategy. Finally, an organization can appear to be irrational; remembering that this is diversion and dissuasion, an organization can take actions that on the face of it appear to be illogical, due to their impulsive or emotional content. As a result, the competitor is encouraged to hesitate because the attractiveness of the investment is disconfirmed by the irrationality of the behavior.

When William Randolph Hearst began to build his newspaper chain, he was spending so much money his accountant told him that he was losing more than a million dollars a year and must stop. Hearst replied that because his wealth exceeded $100 million, it would be more than one hundred years

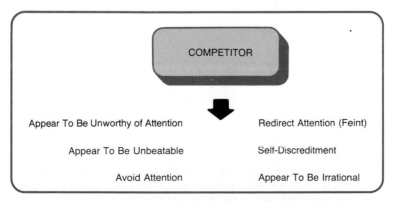

Figure 13-1   Six Diversion and Dissuasion Action Categories

Source: Adapted from Bruce D. Henderson, *Henderson on Corporate Strategy* (New York: Abt Books, 1979), pp. 14–15.

before he would be out of business. His comment was widely reported at the time. How would you react if you were a potential investor in a newspaper or chain of newspapers potentially competing with Hearst?

The six diversion and dissuasion categories are summarized in Figure 13-1.[5] All strategies that primarily consider the relative strength of the competition—that is, where a weaker firm is facing one or more stronger competitors—must emphasize one or more of these six basic diversion and dissuasion action categories.

Giant Smashing: The Small Organization versus Larger Competitors

Small Organizations Can Have Advantages Over Larger Ones

Organizations facing larger competitors frequently see the advantages of the larger organization without stopping to consider that their own small organization may have advantages as well. Some of the advantages that a smaller organization may have in a contest with larger competitors include the ability to move faster, to be closer to the customer, to focus on a target objective of choice using strengths unique to the organization, and to develop a stronger commitment to success, given that jobs or fortunes may be on the line, or simply due to greater interest. A recent study found that effective strategies under different competitive environments are far more similar for smaller firms than larger ones.[6] Because there is a price associated with changing strategies and reallocating resources, this also constitutes an advantage for smaller firms.

All these potential advantages of small organizations over larger ones must be weighed against the superior resources and clout or power that larger organizations inherently have. The objective for the small organization is to emphasize its advantages and make the advantages of the larger organization irrelevant. By doing this, a smaller organization can overcome its disadvantages to win out against a larger competitor. In his book *The Mind of the Strategist*, Kenichi Ohmae, managing director of the Tokyo office of the consulting firm of McKinsey & Company, pointed out how this is done.

In the home appliance market, not one, but three large companies—Matsushita, Toshiba, and Hitachi—paid incentives to its dealers in strict proportion to their captive dealers' total sales in yen, the Japanese monetary equivalent of the dollar. Thus, a smaller competitor with a significantly smaller volume, trying to compete with these major companies, had major disadvantages even before it began. Its dealers would be paid inferior incentives to sell its products. However, one small company saw in this problem an opportunity. It calculated its incentives not on absolute volume, but on a graduated percentage basis, thus making incentives variable by guaranteeing its dealers a larger percentage of each appliance sold. This brilliant solution had the additional attraction that the larger competitors could not afford to offer such higher percentages across the board without seriously eroding their profitability. The result was the small upstart company whipped three large competitors and established itself in the market.[7]

Strategy	Advantages	Disadvantages

Be first	Learning/experience curve
	Customer inertia
	Initiative and momentum
	Opportunity to dominate market
		Extreme concentration of effort
		  required
		Substantial and continual work
		  to maintain
		Must eventually cut price

Be early	Reduced risk Knowledge of what works and what doesn't Most of market opportunity remaining	May need to overcome barriers Market opportunity not as great
Be late	Include technological improvements Better terms from suppliers May be able to offer lower prices Choose point of entry	May need to overcome barriers Market opportunity could be much reduced

Figure 13-2   Entry Strategies Summarized

Entry into the Marketplace

There are three **entry strategies** that should be considered by any organization attempting to enter a new market. These strategies, conceptualized by Peter Drucker, are summarized in Figure 13-2. They are (1) being first, (2) being early, and (3) being late. Let's take a look at these strategies.

Being First

Being first is inherently attractive to many; after all, it connotes leadership, innovation, and being number one. There are advantages to being first, and they are not to be discounted. For one thing, a company that is first is the first to benefit from its learning curve. That is, as it gains experience and knowledge in manufacturing and marketing products, its cost of doing business goes down. Thus, when competitors attempt to enter the market, the company that is first has a tremendous cost advantage. It can be translated into a price break for the customer and into increased resources for advertising, distribution, and other tactics to boost its overall strategy. Also, there is a certain customer inertia, which we discussed earlier in Chapter 7. As long as the firm is satisfying its customers, it is going to be difficult for a competitor to woo those customers away. Third, being first gives that "first" a certain initiative and momentum as its competitors' attempt to catch up with a similar product or service. The firm that is first can be moving on, either with product improvement or to additional markets. Thus, the initiative is with the firm that is first, and it has the edge always to be just a little bit ahead of its competition. Probably the greatest attractiveness of being first is the opportunity to dominate the market. This can happen for a variety of reasons associated with the factors already noted. Under some conditions an advantage is created from the process by which consumers learn about brands and form their preferences. This process can produce a preference structure that favors the first entrant. The first entry is perceived as close to the ideal, and all other brands are compared with it. This makes it difficult for later entrants to capture share from the first entry in the market.[8]

Being first is not without its problems. As Peter Drucker points out in his book *Innovation and Entrepreneurship,* being first requires extreme concentration of effort. It must have one clear-cut goal and concentrate all efforts on it just to succeed. Once successful as being first, substantial and continuing efforts are necessary to maintain leadership or all that has been invested will be lost. Finally, the firm that is first must cut the price of its own product, process, or service, or risk encouraging and protecting competitors as they attempt to enter the market.[9]

The advantages of being first, according to strategist Michael Porter of the Harvard Business School, follow:

1. The reputation that a firm gains.
2. The position that the firm preempts in the market.
3. The cost of switching from the first firm to other firms once the initial purchasing has been done.
4. The firm's choice of channels for distribution.
5. The learning curve discussed earlier.
6. Favorable access to facilities, imports, and other scarce resources.
7. Definition of standards that later competitors may be forced to adopt.
8. Institutional barriers to competition, such as patents or special status and agreements with customers or regulatory agencies such as those controlled by governments.
9. High early profits due to the unavailability of the product, service, or process from other sources.[10]

Being Early

Being early does not mean being first, but it does mean being one of the first in the market after the first firm has entered the market. Sometimes early entry is really not by intent, but simply because two firms are both vying to be the first and the company that was "early" really came in second in the race to be first. When this happens, there is usually a strong fight due to the previous commitment of resources and actions put in motion by both firms. This type of early entry requires some readjustment before proceeding and will have most of the disadvantages of being first without the advantages. On the other hand, early entry can be advantageous if the organization has the resources effectively to fight the firm that is the leader. But be cautious here. A weak second entry will invariably lead to defeat and will be conveniently swallowed up by the leader.[11]

However, if the firm has the resources and the proper strategy to take on the first entrant, an early entry can be successful and beneficial. It has the following advantages over the firm that was first.

- *Reduced risk.* The major disadvantage of being first has to do with risk— risk in demand, risk in technological obsolescence, and risk in many other different areas of things that can go wrong. It is because of this high risk that many firms do not choose to adopt a first-into-the-market strategy; it is also the reason that many firms that do are unsuccessful.

- *Knowledge of what works and what does not.* Because another firm has pioneered the effort, observation as to what has occurred in the marketplace gives the early entry "free" information as to what will work and what will not. It allows for a more optimum strategy with less wasted time, and, more important, fewer wasted resources.
- *Coincident with a lower risk, most of the opportunity of the marketplace still exists.* Because the demand for the product or service has been established and as yet few other competitors are in the marketplace, it is still largely untapped. Significant portions of the market have not yet been satisfied, as will be the case when the product grows more mature.

As a result, being an early entry, as opposed to being first, is an attractive alternative for many organizations. But there are two disadvantages. Certain barriers to entry must be overcome, and the market opportunity may be slightly less.

Being Late

Being late involves entering the market after it is already established and other competitors are already it. Yet there are advantages to lateness. These include the following:

- While earlier entries are already committed to their previous investments, new entrants can include the latest technological improvements in products or processes.
- Late entrants may be able to achieve greater economies of scale than those that entered at an early stage. This is due to the fact that the size of the market and the demand for the product can be established more accurately. Thus, a larger optimal size of plant is probable, and as the size of the plant increases, corresponding cost decreases per unit sold.
- Late entrants may be able to obtain better terms from suppliers, employees, or customers because earlier entrants may be locked into higher costs due to negotiation accomplished when the market was still at risk.
- With reduced cost for R&D and fewer marketing investments and resources wasted, late entries may be able to offer lower prices than firms already in the marketplace. As noted earlier, early entrants are obligated to reduce prices or provide a protective umbrella for new competition to enter. Yet, late entrants may be able to do this more easily or at least cancel out the advantages provided by the earlier entry going through the experience curve.
- As mentioned earlier, one of the advantages small firms have is particularly evident with a late entrant to a market. That is, the late entry can attack a particular weak link, while those firms already in the market must be strong everywhere and may not be able to anticipate attack by shoring up defenses in a particular place. Furthermore, an effective defense may require upsetting the incumbent's entire marketing system.[12]

Again, disadvantages are barriers to entry and the fact that the market opportunity could be much reduced, especially if the product has entered the maturity or even the decline stage of its life cycle.

Drucker advises two possible substrategies to the late-entry strategy. These he calls **creative imitation** and entrepreneurial judo. Creative imitation, the term coined by Theodore Levitt, involves a strategy that is imitative in its substance yet creative in that it makes better use of the basic innovation than those who innovate it.[13]

Melvin Powers is the president of the Wilshire Book Company, a small publisher of books in various specialty fields. At any one time Melvin Powers has about four hundred books in print, all soft cover (known as "trade paperbacks"). Some of these are original works, and some are books that were previously published elsewhere in hard cover. For example, the Wilshire Book Company sold more than three million copies of *Psycho-Cybernetics* by Maxwell Maltz and more than one million copies of *Think and Grow Rich* by Napoleon Hill. Several years ago Melvin noted that books on *The New York Times* best-seller list included health and fitness books such as *How to Flatten Your Stomach* by Coach Jim Overroad and other books with sexual topics. Using creative imitation, Melvin imitated the idea of a book on health and fitness combined with sex through a spoof he wrote in fewer than two days called *How to Flatten Your Tush* by "Coach Marge Reardon." Melvin's creative imitation was his combining the two concepts of proven demand in the marketplace and putting them together in a single humorous volume. His spoof sold more than 250,000 copies in fewer than six months. Creative imitation works!

Entrepreneurial Judo

According to Drucker, **entrepreneurial judo** is the catapulting of a company into a leadership position in an industry against the efforts of entrenched established companies by sidestepping its strength. For an example he cites the transistor. Developed in 1947 by Bell Laboratories, it was recognized that eventually it would replace the vacuum tube; the estimated date of replacement being about 1970. Meanwhile, Akio Morita, president of Sony in Japan, read about the transistor and went to the United States and bought a license for only $25,000. Two years later the first Sony portable transistor radio entered the market. Within eight years the Japanese had captured the radio market all over the world.

Drucker says that entrepreneurial judo is enabled by the following five bad habits of entrenched firms:

1. The **NIH (not invented here) syndrome**, in which companies believe that a product cannot be good unless they thought of it.
2. The tendency to take only the high-profit part of a market and to ignore smaller users.
3. Misdefining quality as what the manufacturer puts in, rather than what customers actually receive that is of use to them.
4. The delusion of maintaining a premium price to achieve a higher profit margin.
5. Maximizing rather than optimizing a product—that is, attempting to satisfy every single user through the same product or service by adding to it rather than optimizing a product for specific groups of users.[14]

Niching

Early in 1981, Outlet Company's women's specialty store division was in bad shape, having just posted its first annual loss of $1.9 million. Forecasts were for sales to decline. The alternatives considered were bankruptcy or selling out. To get the chain in shape or sell, Gerald A. Gura was called in to run the division. He renamed it CWT Specialty Stores, and rather than continue to offer the traditional conglomeration of high-priced apparel, children's clothes, cosmetics, lingerie, and other departments, he concentrated on a certain niche. The niche was younger shoppers who bought their latest styles in name brands. "The two expressions that curdled our blood," said a senior vice-president, "were 'My mother shops here' or 'My mother used to love this company.'" A year later the company was well on its way back. Recently, CWT earned $4.5 million on sales of $80.5 million. Profits increased almost 600 per cent in five years. Success came due to competent management by Mr. Gura and a brilliant marketing strategy of niching.[15]

In a similar fashion, the retail business for personal computers became so crowded that those firms hoping to survive sought niches. Niches for these specialty computer stores, as opposed to department stores or mass marketers, include those more serious about their computing: business and professional users and to some extent institutional and educational markets. What the specialty stores can supply that the department stores cannot are service and support. The result is that while department stores may continue to sell computers in the years to come, they will be moving low-end products; the specialty stores will dominate the medium- to high-end products' sales through niching.[16] With more than six thousand software products for computers vying for space on the shelves of computer dealers, software manufacturers are also seeking to succeed in the marketplace through a niching strategy.[17]

What is niching? Niching simply means finding a distinguishable market segment—identifiable by size, need, and objective—and seeking to concentrate on fulfilling the needs of this niche and no other. The strategy works because it may not be worth a larger competitor's effort to expand the resources to compete in the niche. Therefore, the organization practicing a niching strategy may be small, but in the niche it is "king." It concentrates its resources in the niche and controls that segment of the market.

Peter Drucker has identified three separate niching strategies. These are illustrated in Figure 13-3 and are (1) the **toll gate strategy**, (2) the **specialty skill strategy**, and (3) the **specialty market strategy**.[18]

The Toll Gate Strategy. With the toll gate strategy, the firm attempting to control a niche seeks to establish itself such that potential customers cannot do without the company's or organization's product. To do this requires meeting three basic demands. The product must be essential, the risk of not using it must be infinitely greater than the cost of the product, and the market must be so limited that whoever occupies it controls it and preempts others from entrance. Perhaps the product is a device used in a medical operation. The use of the device increases the chances for survival and success. Thus,

Strategy	Control of Niche	When Used	Loss of Control
Toll gate	Unique toll position	Essential product risk of not using greater than cost-control preempts	Obsolescence of toll device
Specialty skill	Unique skill	New industry, market, trend	Skill not continually improved
Specialty market	Unique market	Needs not currently filled	Market becomes larger and therefore more attractive to larger competitors

Adapted from Peter F. Drucker, *Innovation and Entrepreneurship* (New York: Harper & Row, 1986), pp. 233–242.

Figure 13-3 Niching Strategies

it can be considered essential to the process. At the same time, risk of loss of life is greater than the cost of the product. Therefore, the risk in not using it is greater than the cost. Finally, because we are assuming that it is applicable only to a certain type of operation—say, an appendectomy—the market is limited sufficiently so that whoever occupies it first will probably preempt it. The control may be enhanced by patent protection, reputation, or contacts, but it mainly comes from being first in a small market.

The Specialty Skill Strategy. The specialty skill strategy is useable when a niche occurs because an organization has a specific specialty skill that other organizations do not have. Therefore, the specialty skill niche must involve something new or something new that is added. For example, Bruce Henderson, when he founded the Boston Consulting Group, had a specialty skill: the structured approach to developing corporate strategy for a company. Previously, consultants had counseled top management regarding corporate strategy. But Henderson's was the first successful structured approach to this. (This structured approach was discussed in Chapter 2.)

In the same fashion, Martin Baker of England developed a specialty skill by developing and manufacturing ejection seats for military aircraft. The ejection seat catapults the pilot clear of a high-speed jet aircraft in the event of an emergency in which the aircraft is in imminent danger of crashing. This skill was developed to such an extent that many different companies in many different countries use Martin Baker ejection seats.

The special skill strategy as a class of niching strategy is usually available in the early stages of a new industry, market, or trend. Thus, in every new and rapidly evolving situation, there are special opportunities for the specialty skill niche. Please note, however, that the specialty skill niche must in fact involve a skill that is different from similar skills offered by others and that it must continually improve once the niche is occupied.

The Specialty Market Strategy. Just as the specialty skill strategy requires a skill that is unique and different, so the specialty market strategy requires a market that is unique and different and whose needs are not being filled by other, perhaps larger, firms. Specialty market niches are carved out of larger markets dominated by giants when the smaller competitor can identify the needs of a niche and serve it better. Thus did Adam Osborne carve out a major specialty market for portable computers and expand his company

358

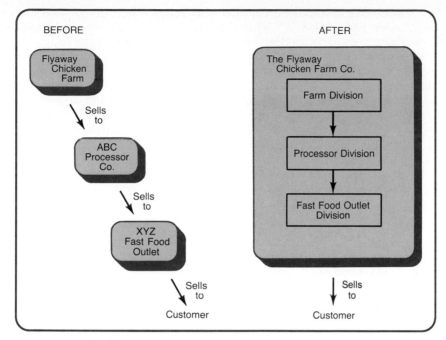

BEFORE   AFTER

Flyaway
Chicken
Farm

Sells
to

ABC
Processor
Co.

Sells
to

XYZ
Fast Food
Outlet

Sells
to

Customer

The Flyaway
Chicken Farm Co.

Farm Division

Processor Division

Fast Food Outlet
Division

Sells
to

Customer

Figure 13-4 An Example of Vertical Integration

in size in one year, starting from zero to a thousand employees. Yet, only a year later, Adam Osborne's company collapsed, partially due to what Drucker terms the greatest threat to the specialty market position: success to such an extent that the specialty market becomes a larger and therefore more attractive market to larger competitors.

Vertical Integration

Vertical integration is a combination under a single ownership of two or more stages of production or marketing that are usually separate.[19] Thus, as shown in Figure 13-4, a farm that has formerly sold its chickens to a food processor that in turn sells the prepared chickens to a retail food store instead opens its own fast-food chicken outlets direct to the consumer and starts to process the chickens in its own plant. Or perhaps a company that manufactures soft drinks in formerly purchased bottles from a bottle manufacturer instead buys the company and begins to manufacture its own bottles. Both are examples of vertical integration.

Vertical integration has both advantages and disadvantages. First, vertical integration amounts to a deepening of a niche. It therefore can retain many of the benefits of a niching strategy. In certain classes of markets, this narrow focus on this vertical niche enables easier and more effective management. Economies of scale and combined operations may reduce costs and increase profitability. There may also be a reduction in transaction costs due to buying, selling, and negotiating by a single organization. Because of more stable relationships with suppliers, the supply of raw materials, subcomponents, and other needed products is also stabilized. There may be additional cost reductions due to improved coordination, scheduling, control, and reduced duplication of function. A higher entry barrier due to these economies and cost advantages, as well as greater control over the product and its marketing, will exist to keep out potential competitors. Finally, greater control over all aspects of marketing will enable more opportunities for differentiation. Disadvantages include the potential loss of specialization, reduced incentives for efficiencies in the acquisitions of raw materials within the organization, a greater difficulty in avoiding suboptimization, reduced access to outside input, increased capital investment requirements, higher exit cost, reduced flexibility, increased fixed costs, and the need to overcome the entry barriers to integrate vertically.[20,21,22]

In summary, we can say that the strategy of vertical integration can be highly successful. A cautionary note is that the company should have a strong enough position in the market to support the costs associated with it.[23]

Market Share Decisions

Five Basic Share Strategies

As shown in Figure 13-5, there are five basic share strategies. These are (1) **expansion**, (2) **maintenance**, (3) **harvesting**, (4) **risk reduction**, and (5) **share reduction**. In the expansion strategy, our aim is to expand our share of the market. With maintenance, we wish merely to hold on to what we have. With harvesting we are going to get everything we can out of the share that we own, with the intent of ultimately getting out of the market.

In the risk reduction strategy, the company wants to adopt strategies that reduce the risks of the high market share they own without reducing this share. Share reduction is reducing market share, but with no intention of leaving the market entirely.[24,25]

It is important to recognize that a large share is not necessary for success in the marketplace. In fact, there are certain market characteristics that help

Strategy	Objective	Examples When Used
Expansion	Increase market shares	Market not adequately served by competition
Maintenance	Maintain status quo in market	Demand stable competitors attempting entry or to expand share
Harvesting	Extract maximum benefit while exiting market	Market profitability declining
Risk reduction	Reduce risk associated with market share without reducing shares	Market volatile and unstable
Share reduction	Reduce market share	Cost of maintaining current shares too high

Figure 13-5   Five Basic Market Share Strategies

to create the climate for successful low-share businesses. One is low-growth markets, where products don't change frequently; products are frequently standardized, with few extra services; markets are for industrial components or supplies; products and supplies are of the type that are purchased frequently; and industries are those in which products have high value added.[26]

To succeed with low market share, marketing researchers have found four primary ingredients for success. These are (1) careful market segmentation, (2) efficient use of R&D funds, (3) satisfaction in remaining small in the market chosen, and (4) the persuasive influence of the CEO throughout the organization.[27]

Elements of Strategies of Low-Share Businesses

In nearly 90 per cent of the cases researched, successful low-share businesses exhibited strategies that incorporated the following elements:

1. A strong focus was tailored to environmental differences with highly focused strategies. These organizations didn't try to do everything but competed in carefully selected ways, according to their particular environment.
2. High-quality products were offered. Also, this high quality was perceived as such by buyers.
3. Associated with the high quality were medium-to-low prices relative to similar products.
4. There was a heavy emphasis on achieving low total cost. This was achieved in part by concentrating on a narrow line of standardized products. In this fashion overall, less was spent on advertising, promotion, new product introduction, and even R&D, although the resources allocated were used very efficiently.[28]

—————————— The Dangerous Fight for Market Share

A major issue with any size company is market share expansion usually coupled with a goal of dominating the market. As we have seen previously, high share is not required for high profitability. But dominating the market does have advantages, and it is important to understand when this is a worthwhile goal and when it should be avoided.

The basic reason for seeking large market share is based on the Boston Consulting Group and its message of the experience curve. The experience curve says that, as we produce and market more and more of a product, we learn better how to do it. Therefore, the associated costs to do this are reduced. Accordingly, a competitor holding the greatest market share and thus producing and selling more units would go through a steeper experience curve. Unit costs would be lower, and there would be a potential for greater profits. As a corollary, competitors holding smaller shares would likely be less profitable, even unprofitable until they could gain larger market shares.[29]

However, in practice, there are various problems with this theory. For one thing, cost differentials among competitors tend to diminish as the market

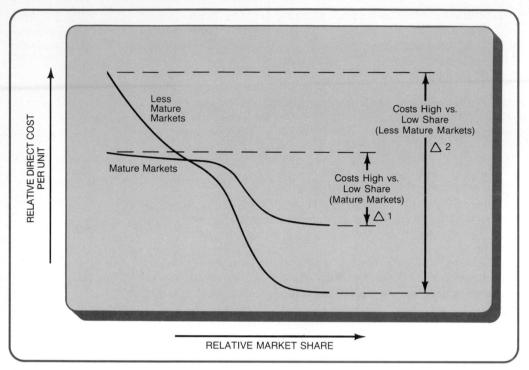

Figure 13-6 **Relative Market Share and Relative Costs**

Source: Adapted from Robert D. Buzzell, "Are There Natural Market Structures?" *Journal of Marketing,* vol. 45 (Winter 1981), p. 49.

matures due to imitation of the market leaders' processes and equipment. This is shown in Figure 13-6.[30] Note how Δ1 (mature markets) differs from Δ2 (less mature markets). Also, there may be thresholds of market share size at which market share becomes more or less relevant as a determinant of profitability.[31]

In addition, the experience curve itself is a product of underlying scale technology and learning effects. Its relevance depends on whether these effects are influential features of the particular environment under consideration. In addition, there's a growing recognition that there is a family of experience curves, each addressing various issues that are separate, regarding cost and price forecasting.[32] Finally, the experience curve does not come into play automatically. Actions must be taken to reduce costs, and the rate of improvement depends on the actions taken by the organization. Thus, while it may be true that reduction in costs can be used to result in increased profits, reduce prices, or additional resources to spend, say, on advertising, it is not certain that reduced costs will come from high market share.

In recent years the whole idea of the experience curve has been balanced by a quite different concept made possible by modern high technology. This is the concept of flexible manufacturing, with an emphasis on fast machinery set-up changes. These fast set-up changes make smaller quantities and even individual customization economically feasible. They also make "just-in-time" inventory control techniques possible. The end results are competitive advantages and more feasible profitability in small market share positions.

There are definite risks associated with being a high-share company, in addition to the problems associated with the experience curve. First, companies that have a high market share are more vulnerable to various types of actions by small companies that are not as effective against companies of equal size or smaller. One example is private antitrust suits. Also, a high-share company is seen as the target that stands in the way of increasing profitability by all competitors and potential competitors. Therefore, they are more likely to be attacked than small companies might be. The third risk of the high-share company is posed by consumerism. A high-share company has much greater visibility than one with a lower share. If consumer groups are concerned with a problem that they are trying to correct, it is the high-share company and not the low-share company they will go after. For similar reasons, the high-share company usually has more problems with the government, including antitrust initiatives.[33]

When Does a High-Share Strategy Work?

It should be obvious that a high-share strategy is not for every marketing organization in every conceivable situation, and the marketing manager must always consider all the alternatives. When does the high-share strategy work? Research has discovered that a high-share strategy based on the experience curve works when financial resources are adequate; when the company's position will be viable, even if the fight for market share is stopped; and finally, when government regulations do not interfere.[34]

Researcher Pankaj Ghemawat recommends asking the following ten questions before deciding on a high-share strategy.:

1. Does my industry exhibit a significant experience curve?
2. Have I defined the industry broadly enough to take into account interrelated experience?
3. What is the precise source of cost reduction?
4. Can my company keep cost reductions proprietary?
5. Is demand sufficiently stable to justify using the experience curve?
6. Is accumulated output doubling fast enough for the experience curve to provide much strategic leverage?
7. Do the returns from the experience curve strategy warrant the risks of technological obsolescence?
8. Is demand price sensitive?
9. Are there well-financed competitors who are already following an experience curve strategy or are likely to adopt one if my company does?
10. Is there a significant antitrust risk?[35]

As noted earlier, it is important to recognize that a high-share strategy does not always work and will sometimes result in a low return on investment to those organizations that attempt it. In one study of 112 market share leaders, the results of 41 low-performing market share leaders was contrasted with 71 high-performing market share leaders. The results indicated certain characteristics of low-return market share leaders. These included the fact that low market share leaders were more often located in regional and fragmented markets, that the market environments of low-return leaders were more unstable, that market conditions in the markets of low-return leaders appeared to be deteriorating, that the value added factors associated with low-return leaders was lower than that of high-return leaders, that customer service and professional support were very important for these organizations, that these firms were more often suppliers of capital goods and less often connected with materials and components, and that low-return leaders tended to have a worse reputation for quality, to charge higher prices, and seemed to shoulder heavier costs than did competitors. Also, the strategy of low-return leaders appeared to fit poorly with the environments they faced. Finally, the marketing resources were less focused against a specific target and were spread out more over various parts of the organization.[36]

When to Look for Trouble

Any organization seeking to reach its objectives through high-share strategy must be able to anticipate competitive attack. In-depth analysis of twenty-

---

External Forces
1. Government or environmental challenge
2. Random catastrophe for leader
3. Change in status of industry technology
   a. Substitute technology emerges
   b. Patents expire
4. New "personality" enters the industry
   a. New corporate parent
   b. Competition from related industry

Market Structure and Characteristics of the Leader
1. No strong number 2 role
2. The leader is expensive
   a. Price skimming
   b. High-quality image to maintain
   c. High-cost producer
3. New positioning opportunity emerges
4. Leader is relatively small
5. Number 2 can expand geographically

Leader's Behavior
1. Lethargic leadership
   a. "Conservative"
   b. Financial goals
   c. Relatively inconsequential market
   d. Afraid to cannibalize
   e. Preoccupied or diverted
2. Significant strategic weakness
3. Alienating key distributors

Source: Adapted from Stanley F. Stasch and John L. Ward, "When Are Dominant Market Leaders Likely to Be Attacked?" in Russell W. Belk et al., eds., *1984 AMA Educators' Proceedings* (Chicago: 1984), p. 225.

Figure 13-7   When the Market Leader Is Likely to Be Attacked

three cases of when dominant market leaders in mature markets will most likely face marketing challenges was performed by two marketing scientists at Loyola University in Chicago. These three general situations involving twelve specific circumstances that existed when long-established leaders were attacked by newly aggressive competitors are shown in Figure 13-7.[37]

Note that the three general situations involve external forces such as a change in one or more of the marketing environs, the structure of the market and characteristics of the market leader, and finally how the market leader behaves. When a market leader notes one or more of the twelve circumstances listed, it is time for immediate action to prepare for or avoid the threat posed by competitors.

Summary

In this chapter we have seen that David can still take on Goliath and win. That is, a small organization can defeat a large one with more resources. However, there are actions that Goliath can take to defend himself. In all cases, the idea is to be stronger at the decisive point in the marketing situation. One way of accomplishing this is by inducing competitors not to invest in those products, markets, and services where we intend to concentrate. Various categories of diversion and dissuasion are available to assist us in accomplishing this.

Although these concepts hold for all organizations, small organizations have certain advantages over large ones. These include the ability to move faster, their closeness to their markets, focus, commitment, and the choice of objective. These must be weighed against the superior resources and clout of the larger organization. We next looked at three potential entry strategies—being first, being early, and being late—and noted the advantages and disadvantages of each, as well as the barriers associated with entry that must be overcome. We then examined the case of expansion into additional markets and the very important corollary strategies of niching and vertical integration. We investigated market share decisions, including five basic share strategies: expansion, maintenance, harvesting, risk reduction, and share reduction. We saw that large share is not necessary for success, and that low-share companies can be quite profitable. Along these lines, we analyzed several strategies for low-share businesses. We probed the popular strategy of dominating the market and becoming the market share leader. Finally, we reviewed when conditions indicate that a company is vulnerable to attack by others.

This chapter is important because a marketing manager will not always agree that sufficient resources are available to challenge the competition successfully. Yet, as noted in Chapter 10, superior resources are not necessary. A small organization can successfully win out against a large one. Large organizations that must defend themselves against such strategies must recognize when this may occur and what they can do about it.

It should be noted that developing strategy in a competitive environment does not mean ignoring the customer. Even in a situation where competition is of major importance, there is a direct relationship between market orientation and performance.[38]

Questions

1. You are an entrepreneur who has control over a new PC that is technologically better than products of the market leader and other similar products in the marketplace. What advantages do you have over your main competitor? What advantages does your main competitor have over you?
2. There are six categories listed for diversion and dissuasion in the text of this chapter. Can you think of an example of each that actually occurred?
3. There are advantages as well as disadvantages to being first in the marketplace with a new product. However, if you are a small company or marketing organization, do you have a choice? Explain your answer.
4. Being early means being one of the first organizations in a particular market but not the first. How could your entry be timed to be an early entry but to avoid being the first entry?
5. Sometimes a company that intends to be early in the market ends up being late. How would your allocation of resources and strategies change based upon an unintended late entry?
6. If you were the entrepreneur described in question 1, what barriers would exist to your entry into the market and how would you go about overcoming them?
7. Niching is frequently recommended for a small company or a later entry into a mature market. What situations might exist that would lead you to decide against a niching strategy?
8. Describe some examples or situations in which a vertical integration strategy would be appropriate.
9. Is vertical integration for big companies only, or can small companies use this strategy as well?
10. Describe the theory behind a large-market-share strategy.
11. Why doesn't a large-market-share strategy necessarily work?
12. What strategies should low-share businesses pursue?

Ethical Question

Are diversion and dissuasion actions ethical? Why or why not?

Endnotes

1. Brian Bremner, "Two Big Macs, Large Fries, and a Pepperoni Pizza, Please," *Business Week* (August 7, 1989), p. 33.
2. Bill Abrams, "Stressing Neglected Markets, Firm Ends Its 60-Year Slump," *Wall Street Journal*, 19 August 1982, p. 19.
3. Sanford L. Jacobs, "How Entrepreneur Exploited Chance the Big Firms Ignored," *Wall Street Journal*, 1 March 1982, p. 23.
4. Bruce D. Henderson, *Henderson on Corporate Strategy* (New York: Abt, 1979), p. 11.
5. Ibid., pp. 14–15.
6. Radha Chaganti, Rajeswararao Chaganti, and Vijay Mahajan, "Profitable Small Business Strategies Under Different Types of Competition," *Entrepreneurship: Theory and Practice*, vol. 13, no. 3 (Spring 1989), p. 31.
7. Kenichi Ohmae, *The Mind of the Strategist* (New York: McGraw-Hill, 1982), p. 134.
8. Gregory S. Carpenter and Kent Nakamoto, "Consumer Preference Formation and Pioneering Advantage," *Journal of Marketing Research*, vol. 26, no. 3 (August 1989), p. 298.
9. Peter F. Drucker, *Innovation and Entrepreneurship* (New York: Harper & Row, 1985), p. 209.
10. Michael E. Porter, *Competitive Advantage* (New York: Free Press, 1985), pp. 186–189.
11. Subhash C. Jain, *Marketing Planning and Strategy*, 2nd ed. (Cincinnati: Southwestern Publishing Company, 1985), pp. 607–611.
12. George S. Yip, "Gateways to Entry," *Harvard Business Review*, vol. 60 (September–October 1982), p. 89.
13. Drucker, op. cit., p. 220.
14. Ibid., p. 225.
15. Hank Gilman, "CWT Specialty Stores Story: An Anatomy of a Turnaround," *Wall Street Journal*, 22 July 1985, p. 19.

16. Betsy Gilbert, "Retailers Key in on Niches," *Advertising Age*, February 7, 1985, p. 14.

17. ————, "Producers Need 'Niche' to Survive in Crowded Computer Software Field," *Marketing News* (March 29, 1985).

18. Drucker, op. cit., pp. 233–240.

19. Robert D. Buzzell, "Is Vertical Integration Profitable?" *Harvard Business Review*, vol. 61 (January–February 1983), p. 93.

20. Michael E. Porter, *Competitive Strategy* (New York: Free Press, 1980), p. 302.

21. Buzzell, op. cit., pp. 93–94.

22. Michael P. Seashols, "Increased Profits, Dominate Segments by Using Vertical Marketing Strategy," *Marketing News* (September 16, 1983), p. 19.

23. Buzzell, op. cit., p. 102.

24. Robert D. Buzzell, Bradley T. Gale, and Ralph G. M. Sultan, "Market Share—A Key to Profitability," *Harvard Business Review* (January–February 1975).

25. Paul N. Bloom and Philip Kotler, "Strategies for High-Market-Share Companies," *Harvard Business Review* (November–December 1975), pp. 63–72.

26. Carolyn Y. Woo and Arnold C. Cooper, "The Surprising Case for Low Market Share," *Harvard Business Review*, vol. 60 (November–December 1982), pp. 108–110.

27. Richard G. Hamermesh, M. Jack Anderson, Jr., and J. Elizabeth Harris, "Strategies for Low-Market-Share Businesses," *Harvard Business Review* (May–June 1978), pp. 95–102.

28. Woo and Cooper, op. cit., pp. 111–113.

29. Barry Hedley, "A Fundamental Approach to Strategy Development," *Long-Range Planning*, vol. 9 (December 1976), pp. 2–3.

30. Robert D. Buzzell, "Are There Natural Market Structures?" *Journal of Marketing*, vol. 45 (Winter 1981), p. 50.

31. Michael Minor, "The Market Share Effect: A Review and Consideration," in Paul Bloom, et al., eds. *AMA Educators' Proceedings: Enhancing Knowledge Development in Marketing* (Chicago: AMA, 1989), p. 131.

32. George S. Day and David B. Montgomery, "Diagnosing the Experience Curve," *Journal of Marketing*, vol. 47 (Spring 1983), p. 56.

33. Bloom and Kotler, op. cit., p. 65.

34. William E. Fruhan, Jr., "Pyrrhic Victories in Fights for Market Share," in Richard G. Hamermesh, ed., *Strategic Management* (New York: Wiley, 1983), pp. 124–125.

35. Pankaj Ghemawat, "Building Strategy on the Experience Curve," *Harvard Business Review*, vol. 63 (March–April 1985), p. 149.

36. Carolyn Y. Woo, "Market-Share Leadership—Not Always So Good," *Harvard Business Review*, vol. 62 (January–February 1984), p. 50.

37. Stanley F. Stasch and John L. Ward, "When Are Dominant Market Leaders Likely to Be Attacked?" in Russell W. Belk et al., eds, *1984 AMA Educators' Proceedings* (Chicago: AMA, 1984), p. 225.

38. Stanley F. Slater, John C. Narver, and Seong Park, "Competitive Environment and External Emphasis in a Market Orientation," *1990 AMA Educators' Proceedings* (Chicago: AMA, 1990), p. 314.

14

Strategy Alternatives: The International Environment

CHAPTER OBJECTIVES

⬤ Develop an appreciation for the advantages and disadvantages of a firm's marketing internationally.

⬤ Understand the barriers to international business.

⬤ Understand how the general principles of marketing strategy are applied on an international basis.

⬤ Understand the major issues pertaining to the international environment.

Go Overseas, Young Man, Go Overseas

Who's making it big in the international marketplace recently? Believe it or not, it's the smaller companies. And just when it appeared that the major players had reached some sort of export plateau, a new class of smaller companies moved into the field to boost exports. A good example is Dan Hanna, who at the tender age of eighteen started off with a single car wash on the outskirts of Portland, Oregon, and over the years built it into a regional chain. With high sales in the United States, Hanna decided to practice some international marketing. Today his sales are over $100 million a year, not from giving car washes but from the car wash systems he perfected. In total he has sold his systems to seventy-one countries, in-

cluding the Soviet Union and China. "My survival instinct led me into the international arena," he says. Out of a total of a hundred thousand exporters in the United States today, only about 10 per cent are small- and medium-sized companies like Hanna's. But the sales of these smaller companies are growing rapidly. You don't need to be a large company or an old one to be successful in the international marketplace. You just have to understand international marketing.[1]

Black and Decker Goes Global

Black and Decker Manufacturing Company manufactures and markets power tools and household appliances. Now, for the first time in this industry, this firm

368

is employing global marketing techniques, selling the same product in the same way and with essentially the same advertising as it is sold here in the United States. In the past, Black and Decker, or B&D, followed an international marketing strategy, and with it, it claimed a 50 per cent market share worldwide in power tools and a 25 per cent share in household products. But tough international competition from companies using global strategies forced a reassessment. In accordance with its new plans, all international advertising is consolidated at one U.S. location. B&D introduced an array of new models of power tools overseas, all with the same packaging and the same specifications in every country in which the products were introduced.[2]

Where VW Ran Off the Road

Once upon a time, the VW's "Beetle" conquered the world. It was the most popular car in history, and had sales in the United States alone of more than five million units. Not so today. Losses have been reported over past years. Operations in the United States have been a disaster. In a six-year period, during which Volkswagen invested $750 million in the United States, losses exceeded $250 million, while sales of one model dropped to less than 100,000 copies. What did VW do wrong? After being first in the United States with a small car, how did VW get so badly beaten not only by the Japanese, but by American companies producing larger cars?

Some analysts say that VW failed to market using international marketing techniques. These experts say that the Germans failed to spot the move in America toward more expensive cars with modern styling, elaborately furnished interiors, and other features having little to do with basic transportation. According to these analysts, the Japanese analyzed the American market and grabbed and maintained huge shares of it—not only with a quality product, but also with a product that features smooth lines and dashboard gadgetry.

On the other hand, other experts say that the failure of VW was not in international marketing, but rather in not practicing global marketing. The company went too far. It made too many concessions to the American consumer, when, in fact, important features such as durability, handling, performance and value—which were felt to be VW's strong suits—would have sold the car anywhere. And this would have been without the additional expense of a country-specialized vehicle. Meanwhile, VW fights for survival in a country in which it was once king.[3]

Advantages of Marketing Internationally

Why should an American marketing manager be interested in international trade? For every firm, the answer may be different, but there are significant advantages for marketing on an international basis through which many companies can benefit. These include the following:

- *New markets.* New markets may be desirable when markets at home are saturated, such as the personal computer market in 1985. It may also be extremely important for expansion, even when markets in the United States are doing well.
- *Increased sales.* Increased sales may be important for economies of scale. It may be possible, through selling internationally, to increase the number of units sold without substantially increasing the overhead. Thus, profits are also increased.
- *Outlet for excess capacity.* In many industries there is an up and down cycle of purchasing. During the down cycle, companies have an overcapacity. Having markets abroad enables a company either to eliminate or greatly reduce this undesirable situation, by increasing international sales during a downcycle period.

- *Risk diversification.* Selling in many different markets enables a marketing manager to stabilize his or her operations better over all than if he or she has to depend on a single or on only a few markets. Risk is further reduced because of the ability to reduce the amplitude of undesirable cycles during the periods of overcapacity noted previously.
- *Product life-cycle extension.* As mentioned in Chapter 12, products can be viewed as going through cycles of life, as with a living thing. Profits are usually greatly reduced in the mature and decline stages of this cycle, but if the cycle can be extended, sales as well as profits can be maintained at a higher level. International trade is one method of extending the product life cycle.
- *Favorable taxation.* Most countries encourage exporting to maintain the most favorable balance of trade that they can. Various tax deductions are usually available that are not available to individuals selling only domestically. Tax savings is real money and increases the profitability of those products sold internationally.
- *Additional income sources.* Marketing internationally may provide sources for additional income. For example, the product or service may be licensed or franchised abroad, and this investment may bring a much higher rate of return than local marketing alternatives.
- *Competition with foreign firms.* Competition is still the most dangerous environ, and one strategy to counter a foreign firm selling on your turf is to repay the honors by foreign sales on his.[4]

In this chapter we're not only going to examine the what, when, how, why and where of international trade, but also one of the major decisions faced by marketing managers today: the alternative concepts of international versus the global approach to marketing internationally.

Barriers to International Trade

Four Categories of International Trade Barriers

Studies have shown that only about 7 per cent of U.S. manufacturers export, despite the many advantages just listed. The reason is that real barriers prevent or discourage many U.S. firms from any type of international marketing. These barriers may be considered in four different categories: (1) financial, (2) legal, (3) cultural, and (4) psychological. Financial barriers include shipping costs, tariffs, limited mass communication systems abroad, limited transportation systems, the cost of adapting various products to individual countries, and credit and currency risks. Legal barriers include **protectionism**, foreign legal restraints, foreign government interference, required government participation in business transactions, and home country government actions such as antitrust laws or restrictions dealing with corrupt practices. Cultural barriers include nationalism, differences in mores, different business relationships and practices, potential advertising differences due to mores, differing structures of distribution from those in the United States, and differing roles for women. Psychological barriers include **ethnocentrism**, which is a belief in the superiority or importance of one's own group;

FINANCIAL 1	LEGAL 2
Shipping Costs	Protectionism
Tariffs	Foreign Legal Restraints
Limited Mass Communication Systems	Foreign Government Interference
Limited Transportation Systems	
Cost of Individual Country Adaptation	Required Government Participation
Credit and Currency Risks	Home Country Government Actions

CULTURAL 3	PSYCHOLOGICAL 4
Nationalism	Ethnocentrism
Cultural Differences	Racial and Ethnic Prejudice
Different Business Relationships and Practices	Risk Aversion
Potential Advertising Differences Due to Culture	Focus on Short Term Performance
Differing Structures of Distribution	
Differing Roles of Women	

Figure 14-1 Barriers to International Trade

Source: Adapted from Taylor W. Meloan and John L. Graham, "International Marketing Course Should Stress Trade Barriers, Small-Firm Exporting/Importing," *Marketing News* (August 5, 1983), p. 12.

racial and ethnic prejudice; risk aversion; and a focus on short-term performance rather than on longer-term international investments. These barriers are summarized in Figure 14-1.[5]

Researchers have identified various other problems that make multinational marketing—that is, marketing by corporations that have a direct investment in more than one country—more difficult:

- Lack of qualified international personnel
- Lack of strategic thinking and long-range planning at the subsidiary level
- Lack of marketing expertise at the subsidiary level

- Too little relevant communication between headquarters and the subsidiaries
- Insufficient utilization of multinational marketing experience
- Restrictive headquarters' control of the subsidiaries
- Excessive headquarters' control procedures
- Excessive financial and marketing constraints
- Insufficient participation of subsidiaries in product decisions
- Insensitivity of headquarters to local market differences
- Shortage of useful information from headquarters
- Lack of multinational orientation at headquarters

These problems can be classified according to problems identified by headquarters' executives and problems identified by subsidiary executives. These two classes of problems and their ranking by importance are shown in Figures 14-2 and 14-3.[6]

Barriers and problems can be overcome. In some cases it is a certain critical mass from economies of scale that makes entry possible.[7] In others the major barriers are simply identifying attractive foreign markets and locating the right foreign distributors.[8] This can be accomplished. At other times the barrier may exist due to an inability to enforce contractual arrangements. But even this barrier may be overcome through increased vertical control, such as ownership of foreign firms.[9]

When the barriers are insurmountable in any other way, trading companies that purchase goods from one country and exchange them for other goods for sale in yet a third may have a significant role to play.[10]

Global Versus International Marketing ——————

Global and International: Not the Same

Today in marketing, global and international are not synonyms. Rather, they describe two completely different concepts of marketing to foreign markets. In international marketing the marketer adapts products, services, and methods of marketing, depending on each country's unique situation and the markets presented. In **global marketing** the identical products, services, and methods of marketing are standardized, or nearly standardized, for every country. You can see the two compared in Figure 14-4. Let's take a closer look at both concepts.

International Marketing

As noted, in international marketing, every market is considered differently—with different needs, consumers, and ways of thinking, acting, and purchasing. Those who recommend **international marketing** state that it best represents the marketing concept because the focus is on each market and the product is adapted to the needs of the consumer in that market. Figure 14-5 shows obstacles to standardization.

	Rank (out of 182)		Rank (out of 182)

Lack of qualified international personnel

	Rank (out of 182)
Getting qualified international personnel is difficult.	1
It is difficult to find qualified local managers for the subsidiaries.	1
The company can't find enough capable people who are willing to move to different countries.	15
There isn't enough manpower at headquarters to make the necessary visits to local operations.	22

Lack of strategic thinking and long-range planning at the subsidiary level

	Rank (out of 182)
Subsidiary managers are preoccupied with purely operational problems and don't think enough about long-range strategy.	3
Subsidiary managers don't do a good job of analyzing and forecasting their business.	5
There is too much emphasis in the subsidiary on short-term financial performance. This is an obstacle to the development of long-term marketing strategies.	13

Lack of marketing expertise at the subsidiary level

	Rank (out of 182)
The company lacks marketing competence at the subsidiary level.	4
The subsidiaries don't give their advertising agencies proper direction.	8
The company doesn't understand consumers in the countries where it operates.	8
Many subsidiaries don't gather enough marketing intelligence.	17
The subsidiary does a poor job of defining targets for its product marketing.	20

Too little relevant communication between headquarters and the subsidiaries

	Rank (out of 182)
The subsidiaries don't inform headquarters about their problems until the last minute.	5
The subsidiaries do not get enough consulting service from headquarters.	13
There is a communications gap between headquarters and the subsidiaries.	31
The subsidiaries provide headquarters with too little feedback.	33

Insufficient utilization of multinational marketing experience

	Rank (out of 182)
The company is a national company with international business; there is too much focus on domestic operations.	25
Subsidiary managers don't benefit from marketing experience available at headquarters, and vice versa.	28
The company does not take advantage of its experience with product introductions in one country for use in other countries.	36
The company lacks central coordination of its marketing efforts.	45

Restricted headquarters control of the subsidiaries

	Rank (out of 182)
The headquarters staff is too small to exercise the proper control over the subsidiaries.	8
Subsidiary managers resist direction from headquarters.	17
Subsidiaries have profit responsibility and therefore resist any restraints on their decision-making authority	38

Source: Adapted from Ulrich E. Wiechmann and Lewis G. Pringle, "Problems That Plague Multinational Marketers," *Harvard Business Review,* vol. 57 (July–August 1979), p. 120.

Figure 14-2   Key Problems Identified by Headquarters Executives

	Rank (out of 120)		Rank (out of 120)
Insensitivity of headquarters to local market differences.		**Excessive headquarters control procedures**	
Headquarters management feels that what works in one market should also work in other markets.	2	Reaching a decision takes too long because we must get approval from headquarters.	2
Headquarters makes decisions without thorough knowledge of marketing conditions in the subsidiary's country.	12	There is too much bureaucracy in the organization.	5
Marketing strategies developed at headquarters don't reflect the fact that the subsidiary's position may be significantly different in its market.	13	Too much paperwork has to be sent to headquarters.	6
		Headquarters staff and subsidiary management differ about which problems are important.	17
The attempt to standardize marketing programs across borders neglects the fact that our company has different market shares and market acceptance in each country.	27	Headquarters tries to control its subsidiaries too tightly.	22
Shortage of useful information from headquarters		**Excessive financial and marketing constraints**	
The company doesn't have a good training program for its international managers.	7	The emphasis on short-term financial performance is an obstacle to the development of long-term marketing strategies for local markets.	1
New product information doesn't come from headquarters often enough.	22	The subsidiary must increase sales to meet corporate profit objectives even though it operates with many marketing constraints imposed by headquarters.	7
The company has an inadequate procedure for sharing information among its subsidiaries.	27		
There is very little cross-fertilization with respect to ideas and problem solving among functional groups within the company.	27	Headquarters expects a profit return each year without investing more money in the local company.	10
Lack of multinational orientation at headquarters		**Insufficient participation of subsidiaries in product decisions**	
Headquarters is too home country oriented.	17	The subsidiary is too dependent on headquarters for new product development.	13
Headquarters managers are not truly multinational personnel.	17	Headquarters is unresponsive to the subsidiaries' requests for product modifications.	22
		New products are developed centrally and are not geared to the specific needs of the local market.	22
		Domestic operations have priority in product and resource allocation; subsidiaries rank second.	31

Source: Adapted from Ulrich E. Wiechmann and Lewis G. Pringle, "Problems That Plague Multinational Marketers," *Harvard Business Review*, vol. 57 (July–August 1979), p. 122.

Figure 14-3 Key Problems Identified by Subsidiary Executives

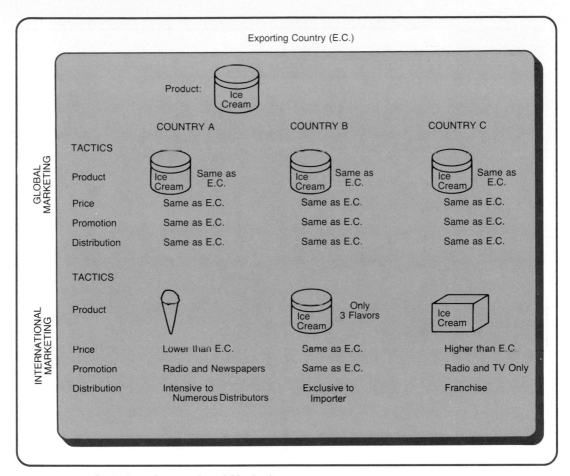

Figure 14-4   Global vs. International Marketing

Along the vertical axis are factors limiting standardization. These include the market characteristics of physical environment; state of economic and industrial development; cultural factors; industry conditions, including the stage of the product life cycle in each market; competition; market institutions, including the distributive system, advertising media, and agencies; and, finally, legal restrictions. Across the horizontal axis are elements of the marketing program, including product design, pricing, and distribution; the sales force; and advertising promotion, branding, and packaging. For example, obstacles to product design standardization are climate and the conditions of product use.[11]

That consumers have different perceptions of different marketing approaches can be seen from an investigation into Finnish consumer attitudes toward the products and marketing practices of the United States, Japan, and various European countries. Finnish consumers had significantly more positive responses to products and marketing activities from West Germany and Japan.[12]

Other evidence that argues against global marketing has to do with countries as they develop into a major world market. In this decade more than 90 per cent of the world's population growth will occur in developing coun-

Factors Limiting Standardization	Elements of Marketing Program				
	Product Design	Pricing	Distribution	Sales Force	Advertising and Promotion, Branding and Packaging
Market characteristics					
Physical environment	Climate Product use conditions		Customer mobility	Dispersion of customers	Access to media Climate
Stage of economic and industrial development	Income levels Labor costs in relation to capital costs	Income levels	Consumer shopping patterns	Wage levels, availability of manpower	Needs for convenience rather than economy Purchase quantities
Cultural factors	"Custom and tradition" Attitudes toward foreign goods	Attitudes toward bargaining	Consumer shopping patterns	Attitudes toward selling	Language, literacy Symbolism
Industry conditions					
Stage of product life cycle in each market	Extent of product differentiation	Elasticity of demand	Availability of outlets Desirability of private brands	Need for missionary sales effort	Awareness, experience with products
Competition	Quality levels	Local costs Prices of substitutes	Competitors' control of outlets	Competitors' sales forces	Competitive expenditures, messages
Marketing institutions					
Distributive system	Availability of outlets	Prevailing margins	Number and variety of outlets available	Number, size, dispersion of outlets	Extent of self-service
Advertising media and agencies			Ability to "force" distribution	Effectiveness of advertising, need for substitutes	Media availability, costs, overlaps
Legal restrictions	Product standards Patent laws Tariffs and taxes	Tariffs and taxes Antitrust laws Resale price maintenance	Restrictions on product lines Resale price maintenance	General employment restrictions Specific restrictions on selling	Specific restrictions on messages, costs Trademark laws

Source: Adapted from Robert D. Buzzell, "Can You Standardize Multinational Marketing?" *Harvard Business Review*, vol. 46 (November–December 1968), pp. 108–109.

Figure 14-5 Obstacles to Global Marketing

tries. The United Nations notes that by the year 2000, 79 per cent of the world's population will be in such countries. It has been observed that those countries, as they develop, progress through different stages. One such concept involves fives stages, from "dependence" to "seekers" to "climbers" to "luxury and leisure" and, finally, to "rocking chairs."

In countries in the dependent stage, women average five or more children during their lifetimes, but one out of ten dies at birth, and life expectancy may be only forty years. The term **dependence** was given to this stage because countries in it are dependent upon other countries and are not yet full partners in international trade.

In countries at the **seekers** stage, both the birth rate and the infant mortality rate are reduced, and life expectancy is about sixty years. Seekers are actively seeking investments from foreign countries and markets for their own goods.

Next come the **climbers**, where women average two or three children each, and life expectancy continues to grow, resulting in an aging population. Climbers are the primary home of the emerging middle class. The **luxury and leisure phase** includes women who have only about two children on the average, and the population has stopped growing. Maximum longevity may be reached during this phase. Because of the smaller families, consumers have more money to spend on each family member and on luxury and leisure. Finally, we have the **rocking chairs**, where women have fewer than two children each, and life expectancy has already peaked and will be unlikely to improve further. Such a society has a high proportion of older people in its mature years.

Note that even with the limited demographics described in these five phases for emerging countries, the opportunities and needs that can be fulfilled differ. To fulfill these needs effectively requires different strategies in every case, or international and not global marketing.[13]

As Professors Allan Reddy and C. P. Rao have noted, RCA Corporation researchers would probably not be wildly enthusiastic about designing a hand-cranked phonograph. However, in villages near the Sahara Desert, potential purchasers of recorded music, with no access to electricity and few opportunities to purchase batteries, might consider a hand-cranked phonograph high technology.[14]

Global Marketing

Although the idea of having standardized products and methods of marketing is not new, the idea of globalization as a concept whereby companies operate as if the world were one large market, ignoring regional and national differences, was proposed by Theodore Levitt in an article in *Harvard Business Review* only fairly recently. Levitt said, "Only global companies will achieve long-term success by concentrating on what everyone wants, rather than worrying about the details of what everyone thinks they might like." And, furthermore, "Corporations geared to this new reality benefit from enormous economies of scale and production, distribution, marketing, and management. By translating these benefits into reduced world prices, they can decimate competitors that still live in the disabling grip of old assumptions about how the world works."[15] More recently, Levitt said, "Today's modern, professionally managed multinational corporations are actually in decline and headed for profound transformation or euthanasia. If they don't transform, they won't survive." Levitt went on to describe successful global marketing strategy as consisting of a common brand name, packaging, and communications. He stated that a movement toward global marketing has been going on for some time, citing the Beatles as a product of global marketing, unlike Mozart, who had an audience limited to the wealthy classes in Europe. Such global marketing is possible because, due to modern travel and communications, people all over the world have homogenized tastes, preferences, and motivations.[16] This argument has gained momentum among leading European and Japanese multinational firms.[17]

It is important to recognize that even proponents of global marketing strategies don't claim them to be automatically successful. A company adopting a global strategy must be superior in effectiveness, have superior cost advantages, and pay attention to two other important factors: timing and financial resources. Timing is crucial because a company embarking on a global strategy must use its cost or distribution advantage to make it disadvantageous for a competitor to respond until it is too late to do so. The financial aspect is particularly important because global marketing requires a major investment. Therefore, it can be said that the global marketing strategist is playing for big stakes and will fail to reap the benefits of global strategy if the requirements of it—superior effectiveness, cost advantage, timing, and financial resources—are not met.[18]

Cheskin and Masten, a research consulting company, surveyed the opinions of more than 120 senior marketing executives from major U.S. corporations. Only 9 per cent said their companies are officially pursuing a global marketing strategy, and only 19 per cent strongly agree that their company's packaging has been designed to be sold worldwide. Although many executives thought that consumer taste is becoming increasingly similar across cultures, most believe that individuals' strategies must be considered on a country-by-country or regional basis. Also, certain categories of products were felt to be more appropriate for global marketing than others: photography equipment, heavy equipment, and machine tools. Those thought less appropriate included beer, household cleaners, toiletries and food, confections, and clothing.[19]

Global and International Marketing Alternatives

Strategy Approaches

Considering all the alternatives, five strategic options are available to the company seeking to expand its base internationally into other markets. These include the following:

- Product/communications extension
- Product extension/communications adaption
- Product adaption/communications extension
- Dual adaption
- Product invention

Product/communications extension involves selling the same product with the same advertising and promotional themes as in the United States. That is essentially a global marketing strategy.

Product extension/communications adaptation is used when a product fills a different need or serves a different function under different use conditions in the international market. The only adjustments made are in marketing communications and advertising. For example, bicycles or outboard motors may fill a recreational need in the United States but are a real transportation need in some foreign countries.

Product adaptation/communications extension involves a case where the product will serve the same function in foreign markets as in the United States, but under different use conditions. The same communications appeal can be used, however; thus, the formulation for a soft drink or soap may be changed to adapt to local conditions, but the same basic advertising and communications approaches are used.

Dual adaptation is used when there are differences in both the environmental conditions of use and in the function that the product serves. It is a combination of the preceeding two strategies.

The final strategy is **product invention**—that is, serving a need by inventing an entirely new product. This may be necessary because the consumer can't afford the product, or for some other reason cannot use it. A hand-wound audio player of records would fall into this class.[20] Which strategy to follow depends primarily on the situation with which a company seeking international trade finds itself. Examples under various country conditions are shown in Figure 14-6.[21]

An alternative framework for the development of strategies is the so-called **EPRG framework**, an acronym for **ethnocentric**, **polycentric**, **regiocentric**, and **geocentric**. An ethnocentric framework involves overseas operations that are viewed as being secondary to those done within national boundaries; they are used primarily to dispose of excess or surplus goods from domestic production. A polycentric framework involves subsidiaries established in overseas markets. Each subsidiary operates independently. A regiocentric framework considers a certain region as being homogeneous and ignores national boundaries; strategies are developed on such a basis. Finally, we have a geocentric framework, in which the entire world is viewed as one potential market. This, then, is global marketing. Ethnocentric, polycentric, and regiocentric are all basically international marketing strategies. The approach to take involves not only the objectives of the firm, but also its size, experience in overseas markets, size and degree of heterogeneity of the potential market, and the nature of the product itself.[22]

For the present, the decision to take an international or a global marketing approach may be situational, and sometimes a hybrid strategy may be indicated. For example, a study of energy conservation products found that while there were market segments of similar attitudes and behavior across countries where a global strategy would be effective, a single global strategy for all countries would not.[23]

To what extent can standardization be accomplished? A framework for determining this is shown in Figure 14-7. It considers not only inputs such as target market, market position, the nature of the product, the environment, and organizational factors, but also the observed performance in the target markets. Note that the process is iterative. The inputs from the various factors serve as a point of departure. But once you have observed performance,

Strategy	Product Function or Need Satisfied	Conditions of Product Use	Ability to Buy Product	Recommended Product Strategy	Recommended Communications Strategy	Relative Cost of Adjustments	Product Examples
Product/communications extension	Same	Same	Yes	Extension	Extension	1	Soft drinks
Product extension communications adaptation	Different	Same	Yes	Extension	Adaptation	2	Bicycles, motor scooters
Product adaptation/communications extension	Same	Different	Yes	Adaptation	Extension	3	Gasoline, Detergents
Dual adaptation	Different	Different	Yes	Adaptation	Adaptation	4	Clothing, Greeting cards
Product invention	Same	—	No	Invention	Develop new communications	5	Hand-powered washing machine

Source: Adapted from Warren J. Keegan, *Multinational Marketing Management*, 2nd ed. (Englewood Cliffs, N.J.: Prentice-Hall, 1980), p. 280.

Figure 14-6 Global and International Marketing Alternatives

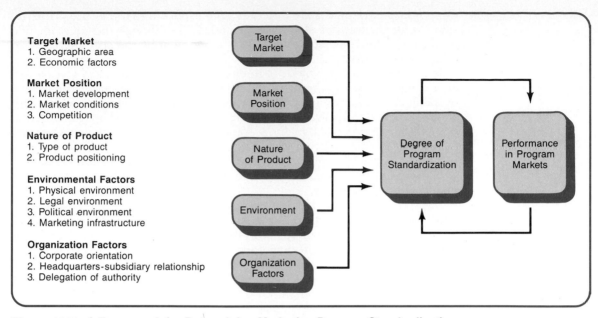

Target Market
1. Geographic area
2. Economic factors

Market Position
1. Market development
2. Market conditions
3. Competition

Nature of Product
1. Type of product
2. Product positioning

Environmental Factors
1. Physical environment
2. Legal environment
3. Political environment
4. Marketing infrastructure

Organization Factors
1. Corporate orientation
2. Headquarters-subsidiary relationship
3. Delegation of authority

Target Market

Market Position

Nature of Product

Environment

Organization Factors

Degree of Program Standardization

Performance in Program Markets

Figure 14-7   A Framework for Determining Marketing Program Standardization

Source: Adapted from Subhash C. Jain, "Standardization of International Marketing Strategy: Some Research Hypotheses," *Journal of Marketing* vol. 53, no. 1. (January 1989), p. 72.

you have an even more important input to modify the extent of your standardization.[24]

In the future, global marketing may yet win out. To quote Robert D. Buzzell's observation written twenty-five years ago:

There is no doubt the differences among nations are still great, and that these differences should be recognized in marketing planning. But the experiences of a growing number of multinational companies suggest that there are also some real potential gains in an integrated approach to marketing strategy. Standardization of products, packages, and promotional approaches may permit substantial cost savings, as well as greater consistencies in dealing with customers. The harmonization of price policies often facilitates better internal planning and control. Finally, if good ideas are scarce, and if some of them have universal appeal, they should be used as widely as possible.[25]

Expansion into Foreign Markets

For a company seeking to expand into foreign markets, there are three basic entry modes that may be followed. These include **export entry**, **contractual entry**, and **investment entry**. This choice is not inconsequential. There is evidence that once a decision is made, it tends to be reinforced as new products are introduced. Thus, a less than optimal choice may be continued, if for no other reason than the high costs of changing.[26] The export entry mode may be indirect, whereby the firm merely sells to an exporter who takes title to the goods while they are still in the United States. It may be direct through an agent or distributor, or it may be direct through a branch or a subsidiary.

Contractual entry modes are different from export in that they are primarily vehicles for the transfer of knowledge and skills, although they may include product as well. They require no equity investment by the firm interested in international entry.

One contractual entry mode is **licensing**, where the company gives a foreign company the right to use certain of its industrial property, know-how, or trademarks in return for some compensation. **Franchising** is another with somewhat greater involvement. The franchiser also assists the franchisee in his or her operations. Usually a franchise is a permanent arrangement, whereas a licensing agreement may not be. Other contractual entry modes include technical agreements, service contracts, management contracts, construction and **turnkey** contracts, and contract manufacturer and **co-production agreements**.

Co-production is a form of joint venture, but without an equity investment. Thus, one partner may furnish the knowledge and technology and another the manufacturing, or perhaps both furnish the manufacturing of different subelements of the same product. Investment entry modes involve ownership investment by the company. This may be through the establishment of a new company abroad, acquisition of a company or a business abroad, or a **joint venture** with a foreign company.

Each entry mode has advantages and disadvantages. For example, while licensee or technical agreements may require minimum investment, and thus a far greater return on investment, ultimately they may involve transferring the technology to a foreign firm that will eventually become a competitor. Similarly, while it may seem that to either acquire or establish a new firm is a significant investment, due to local environs, this may be far more profitable than attempting to export the product as manufactured in the home country.[27]

Stages of Entry

Entry strategies into foreign markets are categorized by three states of market competition:

1. Entering a product market
2. Developing and penetrating a product market
3. Maintaining an established position in a product market[28]

All three stages are crucial for long-range success. A good example is Nissan, which entered the American market for sports cars in 1970 under the name Datsun, with the 240Z, at a price that was far lower than that of the competition. Over the years this market was further developed and expanded as the price was raised. Ultimately, Nissan controlled a major share of the market and had an established position in it.

Rate of Entry

The rate of expansion into foreign markets is also of major importance in achieving a firm's overall objectives. Two basic strategies have been identified. The first is a strategy of **market concentration**. Market concentration is characterized by a slow and gradual rate of growth in the number of markets

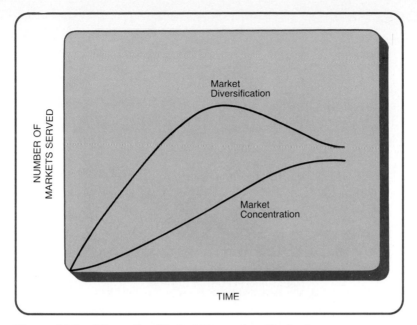

Figure 14-8　Alternative Market Expansion Strategies

Source: Adapted from Igal Ayal and Jehiel Zif, "Market Expansion Strategies in Multinational Marketing," *Journal of Marketing*, vol. 43 (Spring 1979), p. 86.

served. The other strategy alternative is that of diversification. Diversification is characterized by a very fast rate of growth in the number of markets served at the early stages of expansion.[29] These alternative strategies are shown in Figure 14-8.

Research has shown that, under different conditions, one or another of these alternative strategies for rate of entry is preferable. For example, if the growth rate of each market is low, a diversification strategy is preferable; if high, a concentration strategy is preferable. If demand for the product in the market is unstable, risk can be spread through the use of diversification. Similarly, if the firm is only slightly ahead of its competition, a diversification strategy is important to beat the competition in as many markets as possible. If there is a spillover from one market to another, a diversification strategy is preferred.

Other situations in which a diversification strategy is preferred include those where there is little need for either product or communication adaptation to the market, where economies of scale and distribution are low, where there are few or low requirements for program control, as might be required with an R&D program, and where the extent of other constraints is low. Where these conditions do not exist, a **concentration strategy** is preferable.

A diversification strategy is also preferable if the sales response function curve is concave, as shown in Figure 14-9. If it is an S-curve, then a concentration strategy would be more productive. The concave response function, as shown in Figure 14-9, implies that the best return on the marketing effort is at the lower levels of effective effort. As additional funds and effort in marketing are spent, market share does increase. But due to increased effort

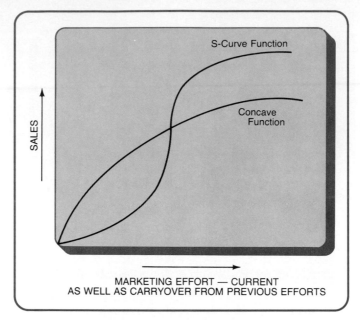

Figure 14-9   Alternative Market Share Response Functions

Source: Adapted from Igal Ayal and Jehiel Zif, "Market Expansion Strategies in Multinational Marketing," *Journal of Marketing,* vol. 43 (Spring 1979), p. 88.

by competition, each increase costs more and more per unit. The S-curve response function contains the implicit assumption that small-scale efforts of penetration into a new market will not count for much. Increases in share and coincidental profitability will only be made after a concentrated marketing effort is accomplished.[30]

When to use one strategy or the other and its coincidental and implied slow or rapid rate of growth into the market is summarized in Figure 14-10.[31]

Product/Market Factor	Prefer Diversification if	Prefer Concentration if
1. Sales response function	Concave	S-curve
2. Growth rate of each market	Low	High
3. Sales stability in each market	Low	High
4. Competitive lead time	Short	Long
5. Spillover effects	High	Low
6. Need for product adaptation	Low	High
7. Need for communication adaptation	Low	High
8. Economies of scale in distribution	Low	High
9. Program control requirements	Low	High
10. Extent of constraints	Low	High

Source: From Igal Ayal and Jehiel Zif, "Market Expansion Strategies in Multinational Marketing," *Journal of Marketing,* vol. 43 (Spring 1979), p. 89. Used with permission.

Figure 14-10   Alternative Strategies Based on Product/Market Factors

Foreign Market Analysis
Methodologies

Various techniques can be used to analyze foreign market for potential entry. These techniques include **shift share analysis**, anthropological surveys, and **environmental segmentation**.

Shift Share Analysis

One relatively new method of foreign market analysis is known as shift share analysis. Shift share analysis is different in that it identifies growth differentials based upon changes that have occurred in market shares in the market being analyzed over time. This is in contrast to most other forms of trend analysis, which, as we have seen in Chapter 8, express growth in terms of absolute or per centage changes.

To accomplish the shift share calculation, measurements are accomplished on a variable of interest. This might be an imported product in each country being considered as a potential target market. Using the numbers of products imported, an expected growth figure is calculated for each target group member for a specified period based on the average growth of all members in the system. Each country's expected growth for this product is then compared with its actual growth during the period. The difference is the net shift, and it will be positive for members gaining market share over the period and negative for members losing market share. The magnitude of the gain or loss represents the difference between actual performance and the performance it would have had, had its growth rate been equal to the average of the entire system. The percentage net shift provides a picture of growth or shrinkage among the members of the group being analyzed. Percentage net shift is calculated by dividing the net shift for each unit by the total positive or negative net shift, and multiplying by 100. The procedure is illustrated in Figure 14-11.

This technique can be useful in reducing a large number of products and market combination export alternatives to a relatively smaller set that can be subjected to an intensive analysis based on other criteria the firm deems important or in combination with other types of analyses.[32]

Anthropological Surveys

In emerging countries another problem exists that must be considered. While the major existing markets for many goods are generally in large metropolitan areas, huge potential markets many times their size may exist elsewhere. Yet, because they are not in cities, data on these markets are not usually available. One solution to this problem is an anthropological research method. With this method, a firm can outmaneuver the competition and enter the hinterlands, establishing itself as a monopoly and controlling the best positions in the market with the right product before the competition. This method requires a review of anthropological data taken from secondary research sources.[33]

An example of the use of this method may be seen by considering Figure 14-12. This figure illustrates fifteen different steps, each one progressing to

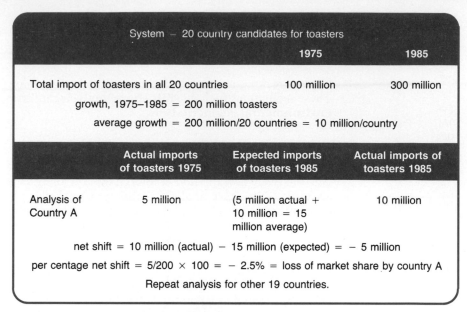

Figure 14-11   An Example of Shift Share Analysis

Step Number	Item Content
1.	Named and autonomous locality group.
2.	One or more governmentally designated officials; more than one street.
3.	One or more organizations in village.
4.	A church.
5.	A school building; a government organization; mass said in the village more than annually.
6.	A functional school.
7.	Has access to a railroad or informant voluntarily includes railroad in list of village needs.
8.	Access to electric power; informant estimates that a majority have electricity; six or more streets.
9.	Railroad station; four or more bus or train trips daily.
10.	School has four or more grades.
11.	Village has a public square; village market patronized by people in other villages.
12.	Doctor; priest resides in village; ten or more streets; school has six or more grades; six or more stores; two or more television sets in village; public monument.
13.	Has one or more telephones.
14.	Forty per cent or more have radios; settlement area one square mile or more.
15.	Secondary school; 20 or more stores.

Source: Adapted from Richard P. Carr, Jr., "Identifying Trade Areas for Consumer Goods in Foreign Markets," *Journal of Marketing,* vol. 42 (October 1978), p. 77.

Figure 14-12   Fifteen Steps from Least Likely to Most Likely Candidacy for Marketing in 24 Villages

a greater likelihood of a market for a specific product. For example, step 1 merely is a named and autonomous locality group, whereas step 15 is a secondary school and twenty or more stores. The procedure in using the anthropological research method involves comparing a successful market at the desired level with each succeeding step. If necessary, this must be tested in the country being considered for expansion, until the proper step level is ascertained. Once this is accomplished, the data are extrapolated to other markets in the country under analysis. Thus, it may be determined for a specific product; once an area has one or more telephones, as in step 13, it has become a viable candidate for expansion into this hinterland market-place.[34]

Environmental Segmentation

Environmental segmentation analysis involves consideration of three major variables: (1) economic, (2) political, and (3) cultural. This is important for analysis because the factors having to do with the product have been found to correlate with their acceptability by a potential import country.

For example, in Figure 14-13, the environmental segmentation model is represented on the horizontal axis by "a poor country," "neither poor nor

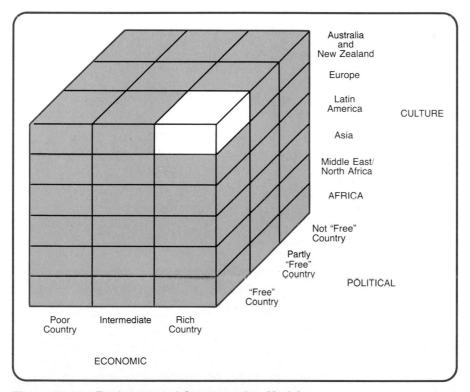

Figure 14-13 Environmental Segmentation Model

Source: Adapted from Chi-Kang Wang and Charles W. Lamb, Jr. "The Impact of Selected Environmental Forces Upon Consumers' Willingness to Buy Foreign Products," *Journal of the Academy of Marketing Science*, vol. 11 (Winter–Spring 1983), p. 80.

1. Skill ratio (professional and skilled workers as a per centage of the total labor force)
2. Labor intensity (payroll divided by value added)
3. Value added per employee
4. Wage bill per employee
5. Shipments per employee
6. Capital per employee
7. Economies of scale measurements
8. Concentration (combined market share of four largest firms)
9. Vertical integration (value added divided by shipments)
10. Average tariffs of major industrial countries
11. Index of incidence of nontariff barriers in major industrial countries

Source: Adapted from Igal Ayal, "Industry Export Performance: Assessment and Prediction," *Journal of Marketing*, vol. 46 (Summer 1982), p. 57.

Figure 14-14   Typical Characteristics as Potential Performance Indicators

rich," or "a rich country"; politically by "not a free country," "partially free," or "a free country"; and culturally by six different continental cultures. Research by Americans has shown that products from countries close to the shaded segment of Figure 14-13 are generally perceived favorably, and that marketers may be able to exploit this advantage in their strategy, development, and expansion. When a product's foreign origin is distant from the shaded segment, special marketing strategies may have to be designed to overcome or minimize this impact of a negative bias.[35] Potential performance as an importer can also be assessed through other quantifiable characteristics, such as those shown in Figure 14-14.[36]

More sophisticated analysis methodologies will increasingly be used to select potential markets for foreign expansion, as the importance of marketing products on an international or global basis grows.

Summary

In this chapter we have seen the advantages of marketing our products internationally, including new markets abroad to overcome saturation locally, to increase sales, as an outlet for excess capacity, as risk diversification, as product life-cycle extension, as favorable taxation treatment, as additional income, and as world strategy competition with foreign marketers. We have also seen that there are various barriers to international trade that must be overcome, not only to establish a beachhead in a foreign market, but also to become successful. Currently, two different concepts of foreign marketing are being given a great deal of thought by marketing experts and theoreticians.

First is the traditional international marketing, whereby every market is treated differently and the product, as well as the marketing, optimizes for that market. The other concept is global marketing, where economies of scale are sought through standardization.

At the present time, it is felt that while both concepts can work, trade-offs must be made considering the specific situation in which the company finds itself versus its products and markets sought—although the future probably favors global marketing. There are three basic expansion modes: investment, contractual, and export. The stages of expansion that must be considered in strategy development are entry, penetration, and establishment and maintenance of position. Rate of entry was also found to be important and dependent upon whether the marketing manager chooses a concentration strategy, characterized by a slow and gradual rate of growth, or a diversification strategy, characterized by a fast rate of growth. Major analysis methodologies are used to assist in selecting and evaluating target markets. Shift share analysis, anthropological surveys, and environmental segmentation were discussed.

Technology is exercising a continual and increasing influence on marketing a product outside of a country's domestic boundaries. This influence, including not only transportation betterment, but also new systems, including satellites and teleconferencing, can only enhance the importance of marketing on an international basis. Thus, marketing in an international environment is and will continue to be an important subject for the marketing manager.

Questions

1. This chapter describes the advantage of marketing internationally. Are there disadvantages? If so, what are some of them?
2. How might you handle each of the problems identified by headquarters executives and subsidiary executives shown in Figures 14-2 and 14-3?
3. Do you think a small company is better suited to international marketing or global marketing concepts?
4. Is global marketing in accordance with the marketing concept?
5. There are advantages and disadvantages to each mode of foreign market entry. State the advantages and disadvantages of investment, contractual, and export modes.
6. Stages of entry into a foreign market have been categorized as that of entry, penetration and development, and establishment and maintenance of position. Which of these three phases, or categories, do you think, will require the greatest amount of resources? Justify your answer.
7. Is there a limiting factor having to do with rate of entry not mentioned in the chapter that may affect your decision to go with a strategy of diversification or concentration?
8. It has been said that a critical mass from economies of scale may be needed before export. Should an entry ever be attempted before a critical mass exists?
9. If trading companies are international exporters in world trade, why would it not always be advisable to sell to an international trading company rather than to export on one's own?
10. Anthropological surveys were cited as a method by which potential markets in the hinterlands of developing countries might be evaluated. Can you think of any drawbacks to this method of market analysis?

Ethical Question

U.S. law makes payoffs for bribes illegal. Yet, in some countries such bribes are considered the normal way of doing business. Being aware of U.S. laws, a foreign businessman with whom you have done business in the past proposes a joint venture in which you will manufacture the product and he will be responsible for all marketing in his country. It is understood that this will include payoffs, if required. Even if this successfully circumvents U.S. law, is this an ethical thing to do or not?

Endnotes

1. William J. Holstein and Brian Bremner, "The Little Guys Are Making It Big Overseas," *Business Week* (February 27, 1989), p. 94.
2. Wendy Kimbrell, "B&D Turning to Global Marketing," *Advertising Age* (October 29, 1984), p. 52.
3. Chris Wells, "How VW Got in the Slow Lane," *Los Angeles Times* 12 February 1984, part 5, p. 1.
4. Luu Trankiem, *Introduction to Import/Export* (Los Angeles: Trident, 1979), pp. 4–6.
5. Taylor W. Meloan and John L. Graham, "International Marketing Course Should Stress Trade Barriers, Small Firm Exporting/Importing," *Marketing News* (August 5, 1983), p. 12.
6. Ulrich E. Wiechmann and Louis J. Pringle, "Problems That Plague Multi-National Marketers," *Harvard Business Review*, vol. 57 (July–August, 1979), pp. 120, 122.
7. Vern Terpstra, "Critical Mass and International Marketing," *Journal of the Academy of Marketing Science*, vol. 11 (Summer 1983), p. 280.
8. S. Tamer Cavusgil, "Exporters Wrestle with Market and Distributor Selection Problems in Penetrating New Markets," *Marketing News* (December 23, 1983), p. 10.
9. Saul Klein, "A Transaction Cost Explanation of Vertical Control in International Markets," *Journal of the Academy of Marketing Science*, vol. 17, no. 3 (Summer 1989), p. 253.
10. Richard H. F. Kao and Moonsong David Oh, "The Development of General Trading Companies for Export Promotion in Developing Countries: The Cases of Korea and Taiwan," in K. Malhotra, ed., *Developments in Marketing Science*, vol. 8 (Miami: Academy of Marketing Science, 1985), p. 78.
11. Robert D. Buzzell, "Can You Standardize Multi-National Marketing?" *Harvard Business Review*, vol. 46 (November–December 1968), p. 108.
12. John R. Darling and Danny R. Arnold, "The Competitive Position Abroad of Products and Marketing Practices of the United States, Japan, and Selected European Countries," *Journal of Consumer Marketing*, vol. 5, no. 4 (Fall 1988), p. 68.
13. Doris L. Walsh, "Demographic Trends, Transition Phases Suggest International Marketing Opportunities, Strategies," *Marketing News* (September 16, 1983), p. 16.
14. Allan C. Reddy and C. P. Rao, "Beware These Pitfalls When Marketing U.S. Technologies in Developing Countries," *Marketing News* (March 1, 1985), p. 3.
15. Theodore Levitt, "The Globalization of Markets," *Harvard Business Review*, vol. 61 (May–June 1983), pp. 92–102.
16. "Levitt: Global Companies to Replace Dying Multi-Nationals," *Marketing News* (March 15, 1985), p. 15.
17. Masaaki Kotabe, "Corporate Product Policy and Innovative Behavior of European and Japanese Multinationals: An Empirical Investigation," *Journal of Marketing*, vol. 54, no. 2, (April 1990), p. 19.
18. Thomas Hout, Michael E. Porter, and Eileen Rudden, "How Global Companies Win Out," *Harvard Business Review* (September–October 1982), p. 104.
19. Nancy Giges, "Executives Say Global Strategies Are Limited," *Advertising Age* (June 3, 1985), p. 56.
20. Warren J. Keegan, *Multi-National Marketing Management*, 2nd ed. (Englewood Cliffs, N.J.: Prentice-Hall, 1980), pp. 273–281.
21. Ibid., p. 280.
22. Yoram Wind, Susan P. Douglas, and Howard V. Perlmutter, "Guidelines for Developing International Marketing Strategies," *Journal of Marketing*, vol. 37 (April 1973), pp. 19–21.
23. Bronislaw J. Verhage, Lee D. Dahringer, and Edward W. Cundiff, "Will a Global Marketing Strategy Work? An Energy Conservation Perspective," *Journal of the Academy of Marketing Science*, vol. 17, no. 2 (Spring 1989), p. 135.
24. Subhash C. Jain, "Standardization of International Marketing Strategy: Some Research Hypotheses," *Journal of Marketing*, vol. 53, no. 1 (January 1989), p. 72.
25. Buzzell, op. cit., p. 113.
26. Erin Anderson and Anne T. Coughlan, "International Market Entry and Expansion via Independent or Integrated Channels of Distribution," *Journal of Marketing*, vol. 51 (January 1987), p. 80.
27. Franklin R. Root, *Foreign Market Entry Strategies* (New York: AMACOM, 1982), p. 7.
28. Philip Kotler and Liam Fahey, "Japanese Strategic Marketing: An Overview," in Howard Thomas and David Gardner, ed., *Strategic Marketing and Managing* (New York: Wiley, 1985), p. 442.
29. Igal Ayal and Jehiel Zif, "Market Expansion Strategies in Multi-National Marketing," *Journal of Marketing*, vol. 43 (Spring 1979), p. 85.
30. Ibid., p. 89.
31. Ibid., p. 88.
32. Robert T. Green and Arthur W. Allaway, "Identification of Export Opportunities: A Shift Share Approach," *Journal of Marketing*, vol. 49 (Winter 1985), p. 84.
33. Richard P. Carr, Jr., "Identifying Trade Areas for

Consumer Goods in Foreign Markets," *Journal of Marketing*, vol. 42 (October 1978), p. 77.

34. Ibid.

35. Chih-Kang Wang and Charles W. Lamb, Jr., "The Impact of Selected Environmental Forces Upon Consumers' Willingness to Buy Foreign Prod-

ucts," *Journal of the Academy of Marketing Science*, vol. 11 (Winter–Spring 1983), pp. 80, 82.

36. Igal Ayal, "Industry Export Performance: Assessment and Prediction," *Journal of Marketing*, vol. 46 (Summer 1982), p. 57.

15

Strategy Alternatives: The Economic Environment

CHAPTER OBJECTIVES

- Know the major categories of economic conditions under which a marketing manager must direct marketing activities.

- Know the strategies that a marketing manager may use when operating under varying economic conditions and when to employ them.

- Understand the variability of economic conditions and how the marketing manager deals with this uncertainty.

- Understand that marketing success does not come under one economic condition but can be achieved under any such condition with the right strategy.

What Do You Do When Costs Go Up and You Can't Raise Prices?

Did you know that newspapers priced at 25 cents were once pretty common? Now pressures are pushing newspapers toward the 35-cent mark. The problem is that prices are rising. Newspapers expect a 6.5 per cent increase in the price of newsprint. That accounts for about 29 per cent of publishing costs for large newspapers and 16 per cent for smaller ones. It is true that advertising rates have gone up, but only by about 8 per cent, and advertisers are beginning to complain about that increased rate. Additional increases will probably cause advertising volume to

fall. The bottom line is that many industry experts feel that newspapers must raise their prices and shift more of their costs to their readers in order to remain competitive with other media that carry advertising. But there are also some problems with raising prices. Circulation for morning newspapers has increased about one per cent a year for the past two years. The rule of thumb is that a newspaper that raises its prices expects a 4 to 5 per cent decline in circulation, which it eventually regains over time. But advertising revenues are very important, and they have increased about 15 per cent over last year. The newspaper industry would like to hold on to these gains. A declining readership due to price increases will have a negative impact on advertising. Thus, publishers are extremely reluctant to raise prices at a time when the twenty-year downward trend in circulation is finally showing signs of a turnaround. Newspapers are between a rock and a hard place. The call will probably be made based on the state of the economy.[1]

Would You Like to Trade a Coke for a Tube of Tomato Paste?

Economic conditions in various countries have left them short of cash. How, then, do you sell your product? Well, a senior vice-president of Coca-Cola's West Germany subsidiary sells Coke in eastern and southern Europe by operating a tomato paste factory in Turkey and selling Polish beer in the United States, and currently he is thinking about selling Yugoslav wine in Japan. This vice-president's unique marketing efforts typify what has been growing throughout the world in recent years under unstable economic conditions and stagflation. The most direct way to do business when cash problems exist may be to barter, or exchange, your goods for other goods. One estimate is that 10 percent of world trade involves bartering, with many large companies involved in it. For example, Goodyear Tire and Rubber Company uses countertrade, or bartering, as a sales tool, trading tires for minerals, textiles, agricultural products, and other products. General Electric and PepsiCo International are also involved. In fact, GE's Takis Argentinis, who heads up its bartering operations, says that almost a third of the world's two trillion dollars of trade involves some type of barter deal, compared with less than 2 per cent ten years ago. But bartering involves some unique marketing techniques, as well as cautionary notes. Control Data Corp., which once became involved in exporting Soviet Christmas cards, found few buyers for religious cards stamped "Made in the USSR."[2]

Supermarkets Say Inflation Is What They Want

Although high inflation is not desirable for many businesses, supermarkets increase profits when inflation is high because they are able to increase prices and profit margins faster than operating costs rise. As a consequence, in an economy in which inflation is not prevailing, profits decline significantly. Kroger's earnings fell 31 per cent in a recent quarter and 34 per cent for the year, despite sales gain increases during both of those accounting periods. Standard and Poor's tracked thirty-eight supermarket chains and found a 7 per cent decline in profit margin as a group. Labor is one problem, and the treasurer for Lucky Stores, Inc., a West Coast chain, says that it's because sales don't increase at the same level as the wages built into labor contracts. As a result, many chains are trying to reduce this, their biggest operating cost. But reducing labor is not easy. When Jewel Food Stores in Chicago attempted to control labor expenses by decreasing the benefits of 15,000 employees, a $25-million lawsuit resulted. Thus, some chains close stores when they cannot obtain labor concessions. More problems may exist in the future, with a nominal rate of inflation, because low population growth may dim real sales gains prospects. Retailing experts seem to agree that real growth must come through larger market share. But the problem here is that to reach a larger market share may require lower prices, and thus lower margins. Another tactic is to increase the stock of higher margin products, especially food and health and beauty aids. A lower rate of inflation has resulted in enormous pressures on supermarkets. Supermarket retailers will have to change their traditional strategies in order to survive.[3]

Booming Sales in Automobiles Are No Good

You would think that everyone would be in favor of high sales, but under some economic conditions that's not so. The automobile industry had severe problems when there was a shortage of the product. So, output was increased. In fact, at one point it was kicked up 28 per cent. Yet, by the time the new models were introduced, the problems were still severe. In simple terms, it was because the Detroit manufacturers were unable to catch up with economic recovery—primarily they were reluctant about boosting capacity too much and risking overshooting demand. And this demand has been extremely volatile. At Ford Motor Company, sales ran 40 per cent higher than the previous year. As the production line of older models had already been shut down, dealers were in a severe shortage and attempted as best they could to match their available inventories to what customers would purchase. But as one dealer said, "I can't sell from an empty shelf." How are such problems prevented when an environ like the economy can't be controlled and rarely can be predicted?[4] ●

393

Economics Can Affect Selection of Optimal Marketing Strategies

The preceding examples implicitly and explicitly demonstrate that a single marketing strategy is not optimal for all economic conditions. America may not be meeting the challenge of competition under varying economic conditions adequately. John A. Young, president and CEO of Hewlett-Packard, was chairman of the President's Commission on Industrial Competitiveness. Speaking on the human dimension of this problem, Young came to exactly this conclusion: "the unhappy reality is that we aren't meeting the test of competitiveness."[5]

To be competitive, certain economic conditions require special marketing strategies. These economic conditions include the following:

- Growth
- Shortage
- Inflation
- Recession
- Stagflation

A conceptual framework for the relationships among the economic environment, business, and the consumer is shown in Figure 15-1. Note how the changes in the economic environment—including growth, shortage, inflation,

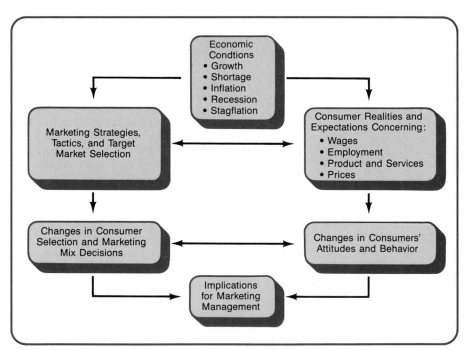

Figure 15-1 A Conceptual Framework of the Interrelationships Among Economic Conditions, Business Consumers, and Implications for Marketing Management

Source: Adapted from Avraham Shama, "Management and Consumers in an Era of Stagflation," *Journal of Marketing*, vol. 42 (July 1978) p. 44.

recession, and stagflation—affect marketing strategy, tactics, and target market, as well as consumer realities and expectations, both of which are interrelated. Marketing strategy, tactics, and target markets, in turn, affect changes in consumer selection and marketing mix decisions; consumers' reality and expectations affect changes in their attitudes and behavior. Again, both are interrelated, both inputs result in implications for you as a marketing manager.[6]

_____ **Growth**

For many who grew up after World War II, regular economic growth seemed to be the norm. It seemed the norm, but was not, even though continuous growth was an economic reality from the end of World War II until about 1973. The characteristics of an economic environ of continuous growth include rapid real growth of the gross national product (GNP), a low rate of inflation, generally low unemployment, an increase in consumer spendable income, general overall buying, and the fact that markets are expanding.

Under these conditions, marketing cynics might say that there is not much that the marketing manager can do wrong, except not to take advantage of the opportunities. And, in fact, were it not for other environs—such as that very dangerous environ we have discussed previously, competition—this might be 100 per cent accurate. But because of competition and other environs, the marketing manager's job is still challenging, even during a period of growth and rapid expansion. He or she must take advantage of opportunities while avoiding threats and overcoming obstacles and problems.

Depending on the environs during growth, a wide product line is generally suggested. The line should include many products and heavy expenditures for R&D. Pricing is set according to corporate objectives and the demand of the consumer. For most products, this demand will be high. During growth, a heavy emphasis on promotion, especially advertising, is recommended, and the marketing manager generally seeks to use every distribution channel possible. As for targeting the market, every reasonable market the company can afford is usually fair game.

But as noted earlier, serious mistakes can still be made, just as in any other economic condition. Prior to World War II, Montgomery Ward and Sears Roebuck were close competitors. But after the war, the chairman of the board of Montgomery Ward, Sewell Avery, sat on his resources and failed to invest. He expected a worldwide depression. Meanwhile, Sears launched a major expansion drive that followed the general strategic guidelines mentioned in the previous paragraph. The result is that today Sears Roebuck is the industry leader and Montgomery Ward has never recovered its prewar competitive position.

Even if growth is a period of relatively easy decision making, like the other economic conditions, it will eventually change to make life more challenging for the marketing manager. As Philip Kotler, the famous Northwestern University marketing professor once noted, "We had the Booming Sixties and Stagnant Seventies, but now we're in the Sluggish Eighties. Competition has markedly increased, with companies fighting over shares of a pie that isn't growing very much."[7] We're out of the Sluggish Eighties and into the Nifty Nineties. If you've noted signs of growth, stand by for change.

Shortage

Shortage occurs as an economic condition when demand is greater than supply at the available price of products, services, and other goods. Other goods include raw materials, and if there are no raw materials, manufacturers can't manufacture. This, in turn, leads to or exacerbates product shortages. Shortage can be characterized as being permanent, quasi-permanent, or temporary.[8] If the shortage is due to a strike, for example, it may be considered temporary. On the other hand, some shortages are permanent, or almost so. The oil shortage would be in this category. So would the shortage of certain types of products, such as diamonds, which are caused by strict control over supply.

One study of six African countries found economies likely to remain a sellers market for some time to come. For all practical purposes, these countries will be in conditions of shortage for some time.[9]

Shortage has two basic causes. The first is inadequate productive capacity. That is, the manufacturer is unable to produce due to a lack of machinery or people to run the machinery. A second shortage cause is inadequate natural resources. A comparison of the two causes is shown in Figure 15-2. Note that the conditions are characterized by more differences than similarities.[10]

A framework for shortage analysis is shown in Figure 15-3. There are seven important factors for analysis. The first is the shortage itself, including its cause, permanence, duration, severity, and abruptness. Next is the breadth of the shortage—that is, the extent to which it affects individual members of an industry, including whether the impact is on one firm, all firms, or the whole industry. The third factor is the industry—its nature, seller concentration, product differentiation, ease of entry, and cost structure. The fourth is the firm itself—its marketing objectives, competitive position, and internal conditions. The fifth factor is competitive strategy; the sixth, the market—the nature of product substitutability—and its social significance—the demand and the buyer. The seventh, and final factor is the environs—political, legal, economic, technological, and cultural.[11]

Cause	Duration	Firms Affected	Reasons Behind Occurence	Nature	Societal Interest
Inadequate productive capacity	Usually short term	Usually one or a few	Financial, technical, underestimation of demand, etc.	Internal—thus largely controllable	Relatively low
Inadequate resources	Usually long term	Usually a whole industry	Natural limitations	External—thus largely uncontrollable	Relatively high

Source: Adapted from Nicolas G. Papadopoulos, "Shortage Marketing: A Comprehensive Framework," *Journal of the Academy of Marketing Science,* vol. 11 (Winter–Spring 1983), p. 43.

Figure 15-2 **A Comparison of the Two Causes of Shortage**

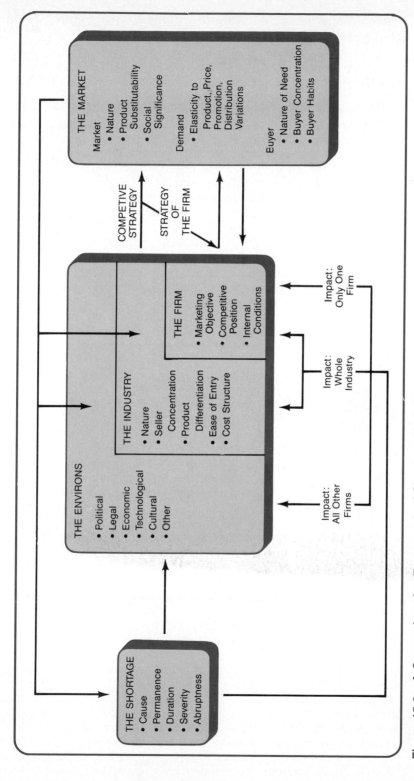

Figure 15-3   A Comprehensive Framework of Shortage Marketing

Source: Adapted from Nicolas G. Papadopoulos, "Shortage Marketing: A Comprehensive Framework," *Journal of the Academy of Marketing Science, vol. 11 (Winter–Spring, 1983), p. 47.

Three Major Areas of Marketing and Reprogramming During the Economic Condition of Shortages

There are three major areas where marketing managers might readjust programming to meet the challenges of the shortage period. These include the product mix, the customer mix, and the marketing mix.

The product mix includes all of the various products offered to the customers. In many cases it may be advantageous to switch raw materials and fuels to products that have higher profitability. To do this we must identify product lines and products and their relative profitability. This can be accomplished by establishing those criteria that are most important for our situation. For example, ROI is such a criterion, and the products we currently manufacture can be ranked accordingly. We can also look at sales growth and see what the potential is, not only for the immediate future, but also after the shortage ends.

The customer mix refers to the fact that some customers are more profitable to deal with than others during the period of shortage; customers can be segregated accordingly. It is a fact that some customers are always better than others, shortage or not, and that it is wiser to direct most of our time at those customers that result in the highest profitability. During a period of a shortage, it is critical to accomplish this. So, again, an analysis should be done and conscious decisions made as to which customers we should continue to service and which we must drop or, at least, cut back our effort toward.

The marketing mix refers to our allocation of resources among the four Ps—product, price, promotion, and place or distribution. Naturally this tactical allocation is always of importance to the marketing manager, but during shortages some elements are especially important.[12] For example, the price of the product line is important during a shortage. Pricing is a key variable because the definition of a shortage always includes the availability of products, services, or raw materials at specific available prices. Profits are largest when the firm produces products and orders that generate the largest contribution per unit of scarce resources used. There are basically two options that can be adopted to achieve this:

1. Maintain the current price and allocate scarce resources across the product line in the most effective manner.
2. Increase the price and allow an anticipated decrease in demand to allocate the resource.[13]

These alternatives are illustrated in Figure 15-4, a decision flowchart of product-line pricing under conditions of scarce resources. Note that the marketing manager must maintain current prices or consider alternative solutions. If he or she maintains prices, that completes the decision-making process. However, if alternative decisions are made, the marketing manager can specify the price schedule or specify estimates of the price-volume relationships. This leads to the two alternatives discussed: either to maintain the price and allocate scarce resources across the product line, or to increase the price and allow the anticipated decrease in demand to allocate the scarce resources. Whichever decision is taken leads to a new product-line price schedule and then the additional decision either to continue or terminate the analysis. If the analysis is continued, once again the marketing manager has

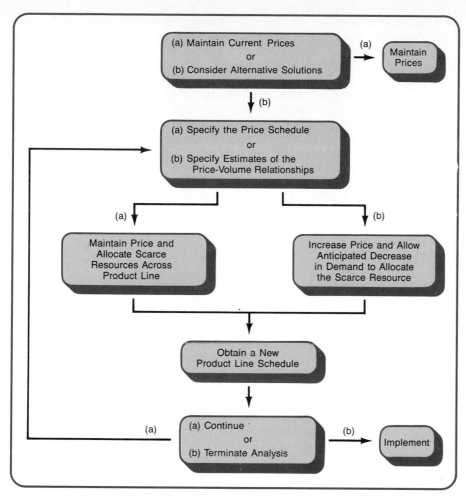

Figure 15-4   Decision Flow Chart of Product-line Pricing with Scarce Resources

Source: Adapted from Kent B. Monroe and Andris A. Zoltners, "Pricing the Product Line During Periods of Scarcity," *Journal of Marketing*, vol. 43 (Summer 1979), p. 52.

the option fo specifying either the price schedule or estimates of the price-volume relationships. If the analysis is completed, the final action is implementation.[14]

Inflation

Inflation is an economic condition of generally rising prices for raw materials, products and services, and other factors of production. In general, three types of inflationary economic conditions have been identified. The first is where an excess of demand exists because the aggregate demand grows more rapidly than the economy's full employment output potential. The second type of inflation is known as bottleneck inflation. Bottleneck inflation results from changes in the structure of demand. The third type of inflation is cost-push inflation, which is caused by economic groups in society that have the power to force up prices.[15] These three types of inflationary conditions are important because they affect consumers and businesses differently, although all three may be present in an inflationary economy in various amounts.

For the corporation, inflation does not mean happy times. The profits stated in the earnings report are not actually available for growth. Peter Drucker points out that the figures that firms see on their profit and loss statements lie, and that few businesses, if any, can really be making a profit at all.[16] Strategist Bruce Henderson cautions that inflation causes a shortage of funds and chokes off growth. Business policies are required just to survive.[17]

Success Strategies

In a major study of sixty-four of the largest companies in eight different industries under intensified inflation, William Hall, vice-president of North American operations at Cummins Engine Company and a former professor at the University of Michigan, found that the sixteen most successful companies followed one or both of the following strategies:

1. Attempted to achieve the lowest delivered cost relative to the competition, coupled with both an acceptable quality and a pricing policy set to gain profitable volume and market share growth
2. Attempted to achieve the highest product/service/quality differentiated position relative to the competition, with an acceptable delivered cost structure and a pricing policy intended to gain margins sufficient to fund reinvestment in product/service differentiation[18]

Industry	Low Delivered Cost	Differentiation	Simultaneous Use of Both Strategies
Steel	Inland Steel	National	
Tire and Rubber	Goodyear	Michelin	
Heavy Duty Trucks	Ford	Paccar	
Construction and Materials Handling Equipment		John Deere	Caterpillar
Automotive	General Motors	Daimler-Benz	
Major Home Appliances	Whirlpool	Maytag	
Beer	Miller	G. Heileman Brewing	
Cigarettes	R.J. Reynolds		Philip Morris

Source: Adapted from William K. Hall, "Survival Strategies in a Hostile Environment," in Richard G. Hameresh, ed. *Strategic Management* (New York: John Wiley and Sons, Inc., 1983), p. 159.

Figure 15-5 Competitive Strategies by Leading Companies Under Hostile Economic Conditions with Inflation

Examples of companies employing these strategies, along with their industries, are shown in Figure 15-5.

Hall also discovered that marginal or failing competitors also exhibited certain factors in common. For example, historical actions that these companies had pursued placed them in unstable positions prior to the arrival of serious inflationary conditions. They were all high-cost producers in their particular segments, and all had a product that not only was largely undifferentiated, but also could be considered below average in quality and in performance. Although certain external pressures were claimed by these companies as significant, such as "unwarranted regulation" and "unfair foreign competition," these unfavorable environs appeared to be simply the final blows. Many of these marginal companies had held low-cost or differentiated positions in their earlier years, but during reinvestment decisions they had made significant errors; they had failed to continue one or both of these strategies into the inflationary period.[19]

The Importance of Pricing

Pricing was found to be as important a key during inflationary times as during a period of shortage. Yet, while pricing may be one of a firm's most important strategy tools, price control by the government could limit the firm's ability to maneuver. One solution was to raise quality much higher than the competition. Quality, in turn, then, could be used as a rationale for higher prices. According to Professor Mary Louise Hatten at Boston College, this strategy has the potential to keep customers happy while satisfying the government and maintaining high profitability.[20]

Recession

A recession is a condition in the economy of decreasing demand for raw materials, products, or services. Because labor is a service, there is less demand for it. This reduced demand results in lower income, which in turn decreases demand even more, and prices fall. If demand is depressed sufficiently, "price" as income no longer becomes the issue, as a result of widespread unemployment. Just having a job may be of primary importance to many wage earners; thus does a recession deepen into a depression in which there are soaring bankruptcies, business failures, defaults, and foreclosures.[21]

Yet, fortunes have been made during both recessions and depressions. A leading multimillion-dollar importer of high-priced cigars today traces its founding to the onset of the Great Depression of 1929 to 1941.

In a recession or depression, there are two basic strategies for the marketing manager to consider. One strategy is to stimulate demand in falling markets. The second is to seek out new markets with higher demand. Although an obvious recession strategy may be to stimulate demand, to find demand and satisfy it where it exists may be less obvious. A recession accompanied by falling prices can benefit certain groups. These may include creditors and fixed-income receivers. Thus, for some market segments, higher prices can work as a strategy even as overall prices fall.

	Shortage	Inflation	Recession
Product	• Narrow product line • Offer cheaper, more functional products • Purchase materials carefully and strategically • Get maximum use from materials • Invest in researching substitute materials and introduce • Avoid quantity discounts	• Narrow product line • Offer cheaper, more functional products • Purchase materials carefully and strategically • Use less-expensive or lower-grade material • Invest in researching substitute materials • Avoid quantity discounts	• Narrow product line • Offer cheaper, more functional products • Cut top of product line • Use fewer raw materials • Offer quantity discounts
Price	• Raise prices • Adjust prices upward periodically • Adjust price within product line to decrease demand for shortage goods • Tighten credit • Centralize price decisions • Stop price discounting	• Raise prices • Adjust prices frequently • Change price differential among products to decrease total demand • Stop price discounting • Tighten credit • Centralize price decisions	• Lower prices when possible • Offer price discounts • Loosen credit • Centralize price decisions
Promotion	• Demarket • Decrease promotion of shortage goods • Increase promotion of more available products	• Demarketing • Decrease advertising and personal selling • Push the more profitable products	• Remarketing • Increase promotion to stimulate demand • Cultivate all potential accounts • Motivate salesforce to sell more
Place	• Limit quantity per customer • Limit distribution to make products less available	• Limit quantity per customer • Limit distribution to make less available • Differentiate with higher price	• Increase distribution outlets • Motivate middlemen • Offer direct to consumer
Target Mkt	• Analyze effect on consumers • Where possible drop marginal accounts • Selective treatment to maximize loyalty	• Analyze effect on consumers • Where possible drop marginal accounts • Selective treatment to maximize loyalty	• Analyze effect on consumers • Cultivate marginally profitable accounts • Selective treatment to maximize sales
Other	• Innovate • Increase productivity • Diversify	• Innovate • Increase productivity • Diversity	• Innovate • Increase productivity • Diversify
Overall	• Demand reduction in short-run and demand adjustment in the long run	• Demand reduction	• Demand increase

Source: Adapted from Avraham Shama, "Management and Consumers in an Era of Stagflation," *Journal of Marketing*, vol. 42 (July 1978), p. 47.

Figure 15-6   Strategies and Tactics in Shortage, Inflation, and Recession

**Strategies and Tactics During Shortage,
Inflation, and Recession**

403
Strategy Alternatives:
The Economic
Environment

A summary of strategy and tactics implied under the various economic conditions of shortage, inflation, and recession is shown in Figure 15-6, along with their applicability to various target markets. Note that in many cases, the same actions are implied for each of these different economic conditions. Still, different combinations of the marketing mix, product mix, or the customer mix will be required in order to reach an optimal solution.[22]

Stagflation

Stagflation has been defined as a stagnant economy experiencing inflation. The post-World War II growth days are long gone. Commodities prices are no longer expected to soar. The late 1980s saw a good deal of oversupply. Forecasts of world consumption for some commodities, such as metals, are conservatively low for the future.[23] This is one type of stagflation.

Stagflation has four different categories resulting from combinations of any two or all three of the economic conditions: shortage, inflation, and recession. The four different types of stagflation follow:

1. Inflation–shortage
2. Inflation–recession
3. Recession–shortage
4. Inflation–recession–shortage[24]

Watch Your Target Market

During stagflation there are four specific tendencies that become more intense among consumers: the conservation ethic, the desire for a simpler way of life, planned shopping, and the desire for greater value.

The conservation ethic results in a consumer who is demanding smaller cars, smaller houses, and other products or services that imply saving or conservation as opposed to luxury, comfort, and large size. The desire for a simpler way of life is exemplified by growing one's own fruits and vegetables in a home garden, home baking, and sewing one's own clothes. Planned shopping means a reduction in impulse buying and an increased tendency on the part of the consumer to plan on shopping for certain items at particular times and at particular places. Finally, we have the desire for greater value caused by reduced financial resources, leading to the consumer's desire to obtain a greater level of functionalism in all purchases.[25]

Professor Avraham Shama surveyed 969 consumers and found that they reacted to stagflation in various ways within these four tendencies:

- Changed their habits and preferences
- Judged products and services in a new way
- Became more comparative shoppers
- Became less wasteful
- Became more energy-conscious

- Weighed purchase decisions more with spouses
- Argued about financial matters
- Became insecure about their jobs[26]

He found that marketing managers responded to stagflation as shown in Figure 15-7. Note that, once again, pricing was used as an important part of marketing strategy in this economic condition, whereas promotion and place were used less frequently.[27]

Use of Barter

One somewhat unusual, but widespread marketing solution to these changes during stagflation is bartering. Bartering, which is also called nonmoney marketing, can help in six ways. First, it can help ensure a supply of raw materials

Marketing Mix	Percentage of Managers Reporting Action				
	Very Much	Much	Somewhat	Little	None
Price					
Frequent price adjustments	30.8	38.5	19.2	9.6	1.9
Stronger emphasis on profit margin	26.0	36.5	19.2	10.6	5.8
Competitive pricing	7.7	28.8	26.0	26.9	7.7
Stricter credit	11.5	47.1	26.0	12.5	2.9
Extra services to justify higher prices	1.9	7.7	30.8	36.5	21.2
Consumers					
Avoiding marginal accounts	10.6	44.2	24.0	13.5	6.7
Better servicing of faithful accounts	12.5	37.5	27.9	9.6	10.6
Consumer research	5.8	18.3	17.3	25.0	32.7
Carrying marginally profitable products to satisfy customers	3.8	17.3	27.9	32.7	15.4
Capitalizing on new markets	2.9	8.7	30.8	27.9	27.9
Product					
Product line reduction	13.5	25.0	37.5	15.4	8.7
Increased R&D	6.7	31.7	26.9	24.0	10.6
Developing alternative raw materials	9.6	25.0	28.8	26.9	8.7
Promotion					
Discounted slow-moving products	21.2	29.8	27.9	16.3	4.8
Increased use of coupons	15.4	32.7	22.1	17.3	11.5
Increased promotional budget	4.8	11.5	31.7	27.9	24.0
Broadened salesforce responsibilities	1.0	15.4	48.1	23.1	12.5
Place					
Reexamining distribution channels	7.7	34.6	24.0	16.3	15.4
Receptiveness to selling wholesale to consumers	1.0	4.8	11.5	17.3	63.5

Source: Adapted from Avraham Shama, "Management and Consumers in an Era of Stagflation," *Journal of Marketing*, vol. 42 (July 1978), p. 50.

Figure 15-7   How 104 Marketing Managers Responded to Stagflation

vital for plant operation. Second, bartering can unload excess inventory. Third, bartering can raise production capacity. Fourth, bartering can help liquidate discontinued items. Fifth, bartering can help introduce new products by permitting the manufacture of high numbers and the bartering of the excess. Finally, bartering can help conserve the firm's cash.[28]

What To Do?

Because the combination of the three economic conditions resulting in stagflation (shortage, inflation, and recession) are so complex, few best strategies for all contingencies are possible. Still, the research of Professor Shama and others have demonstrated that under conditions of stagflation, consumer research is most critical to the redefinition and modification of target markets. While conditions are more dynamic and complex during conditions of stagflation, greater resource allocation to research and conscious and rapid retargeting and redeployment of marketing resources can give a competitive edge.

Summary

In this chapter we have talked about a major environ of the marketplace and various strategies the marketing manager might use when faced with conditions of growth, shortage, inflation, recession, or that combination of other conditions known as stagflation. We can see that this economic condition intensifies other factors in the marketplace, especially buyer behavior. Thus, depending upon which economic condition prevails, the marketing manager must consider the alternatives available to apply workable solutions that will not only maximize the profit position of his company during that economic condition, but also in the new economic condition that will follow. Thus, during growth, typically heavy investment for R&D, a wide product line, promotion, and maximum distribution channels are used to satisfy a wide range of markets and consumers. A firm's failure to invest in such a situation can lead to serious consequences in its competitive position, even if it prospers. During a shortage, the marketing manager must closely focus on three major areas of reprogramming, including the product mix, the customer mix, and the marketing mix. Within the marketing mix, price must be looked upon as a key variable, with two basic alternatives being to maintain the price and allocate scarce resources across the product line in the most effective manner, or to increase price and allow the anticipated decrease in demand to allocate the resource. During inflation, to be successful, a strategy should focus on three options. The marketing manager can work toward achieving the lowest delivered cost position, relative to the competition, along with acceptable delivered quality and a pricing policy set to gain a profitable volume and market share growth. Alternatively, he or she can attempt to achieve the highest product/service/quality differentiated position, relative to the competition, with an acceptable delivered cost structure and a pricing policy to gain a sufficient margin to fund reinvestment in product/service differentiation. Finally, a combination of both of these strategies is possible. Again, pricing must be considered a key element. In a recession, you must either stimulate demand in the existing markets, or seek out new markets where higher demand exists. Remember that under these conditions, some markets are less affected or even favorably affected. Finally, there is the condition of stagflation. Here, the key is to focus on an ongoing analysis of the consumer in order to keep up with complex and changing conditions and to allocate resources accordingly. Pricing is once again a primary tactical tool for supporting strategy. For the large firm with international marketing operations, barter is a profitable, perhaps even a desirable way of doing business under these conditions.

Questions

1. What is a normal economic condition for a firm in its marketing environment? What are the implications of your answer for the marketing manager?
2. A conceptual framework of relationship—considering the economic environ, the business, and the consumer—involves several major elements, beginning with the changes in the economic environment. Trace the implications of these changes for the marketing manager, according to this framework, as illustrated in Figure 15-1.
3. During a period of economic growth such as existed in the United States from the end of World War II until 1973, generally favorable economic conditions prevailed. Under such conditions, what can the marketing manager possibly do wrong?
4. The 1980s have been referred to as the "Sluggish Eighties." In which category of economic conditions were they?"
5. Figure 15-2 illustrates two different types of shortage. There is a different level of societal interest for each type. What are the implications of this difference for the marketing manager?

6. Figure 15-3 shows a comprehensive framework for shortage marketing. Note that the shortage can affect all other firms, impact the whole industry, or only one firm. What is the importance of these differences for the marketing manager?
7. The text describes three major areas of marketing reprogramming during a period of shortage: product mix, customer mix, and marketing mix. Which area do you think should take priority if you are suddenly faced with these economic conditions?
8. Peter Drucker has stated that few businesses can actually be profitable during inflation. Assuming this is true, why is it true? What can a business do to become and remain profitable during inflation?
9. When demand is low during a recession, or tremendously low as during a depression, how can a firm such as the cigar manufacturer mentioned in the text get a successful start and actually grow?
10. If you could state one basic action for a marketing manager to take to be successful during a stagflation, what would that action be?

Ethical Question

Is it ethical to introduce a product such as a luxury cigar during a period of general economic depression, when millions are out of work?

Endnotes

1. William F. Gloede, "Two-Bit Papers Disappearing," *Advertising Age* (December 31, 1984).
2. Everett G. Martin and Thomas E. Ricks, "Countertrading Grows as Cash-Short Nations Seek Marketing Help," *Wall Street Journal*, 13 March 1985, p. 1.

3. ————, "How Low Inflation Stings the Supermarkets," *Business Week* (March 19, 1984), p. 34.
4. ————, "Detroit's Latest Problem Is Booming Sales," *Business Week* (August 20, 1984), pp. 45–48.
5. John A. Young, "The Human Side of Industrial Competitiveness," *Harvard Business Review*, vol. 66, no. 6 (November–December 1988), p. 74.
6. Avraham Shama, "Management and Consumers in an Era of Stagflation," *Journal of Marketing*, vol. 42 (July 1978), p. 45.
7. Bernie Whalen, "Kotler: Rethink the Marketing Concept," *Marketing News*, vol. 18 (September 14, 1984), p. 1.
8. Nicolas G. Papadopoulos, "Shortage Marketing: A Comprehensive Framework," *Journal of the Academy of Marketing Science*, vol. 11 (Winter–Spring 1983), p. 41.
9. Kofi Q. Dadzie, "Demarketing Strategy in Shortage Marketing Environment," *Journal of the Academy of Marketing Science*, vol. 17, no. 2 (Spring 1989), p. 164.
10. Papadopoulos, op. cit., p. 43.
11. Ibid., p. 47.
12. Philip Kotler, "Marketing During Periods of Shortage," *Journal of Marketing*, vol. 38 (July 1974), pp. 22–28.
13. Kent B. Monroe and Andris A. Zoltners, "Pricing the Product Line During Periods of Scarcity," *Journal of Marketing*, vol. 43 (Summer 1979), pp. 56–58.
14. Ibid., p. 52.
15. Thomas F. Dernbury and Duncan M. McDougall, *Macro Economics*, 2nd ed. (New York: McGraw-Hill, 1963), p. 219.
16. Peter F. Drucker, *Managing in Turbulent Times* (New York: Harper and Row, 1980), p. 10.
17. Bruce D. Henderson, *Henderson on Corporate Strategy* (New York: Abt Books, 1979), pp. 128–131.
18. William K. Hall, "Survival Strategies in a Hostile Environment," in Richard G. Hamermesh, ed., *Strategic Management* (New York: Wiley, 1983), p. 158.
19. Ibid., pp. 161–164.
20. Mary Louise Hatten, "Don't Get Caught with Your Prices Down: Pricing in Inflationary Times," *Business Horizons*, vol. 25 (March–April 1982), pp. 27–28.
21. Maurice Smith, "When the Next Recession Comes, Will You Be Ready?" *Small Business Reports* (January 1990).
22. Shama, op. cit., p. 47.
23. Gerald Pollio and Charles H. Riemenschneider, "The Coming Third World Investment Revival," *Harvard Business Review*, vol. 66, no. 2 (March–April 1988), p. 113.
24. Shama, op. cit, p. 45.
25. Zoher E. Shipchandler, "Keeping Down with the Joneses: Stagflation and Buyer Behavior," *Business Horizons*, vol. 25 (November–December 1982), pp. 36–37.
26. Shama, op. cit., pp. 51–52.
27. Ibid., p. 50.
28. Jack G. Kaikati, "Marketing Without Exchange of Money," *Harvard Business Review*, vol. 60 (November–December 1982), p. 72.

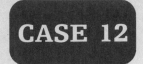

CASE 12

Rogers, Nagel, Langhart (RNL PC) Architects and Planners

It was August 1984. John B. Rogers, one of the founders and a principal stockholder in RNL, had just completed the University of Colorado's Executive MBA program. Throughout the program John had tried to relate the concepts and principles covered in his courses to the problems of managing a large architectural practice. In particular, he was concerned about the marketing efforts of his firm. As he put it, "Marketing is still a new, and sometimes distasteful, word to most architects. Nevertheless, the firms that survive and prosper in the future are going to be those which learn how to market as effectively as they design. At RNL we are still struggling with what it means to be a marketing organization, but we feel it's a critical question that must be answered if we're going to meet our projections of roughly doubling by 1989, and we're giving it lots of attention."

RNL

In 1984, with sales (design fees) of approximately $3,300,000, RNL was one of the largest local architectural firms in Denver and the Rocky Mountain region. The firm evolved from the individual practices of John B. Rogers, Jerome K. Nagel, and Victor D. Langhart. All started their architectural careers in Denver in the 1950s. The partnership of Rogers, Nagel, Langhart was formed from the three individual proprietorships in 1966 and became a professional corporation in 1970.

In 1984 the firm provided professional design services to commercial, corporate, and governmental clients, not only in Denver but throughout Colorado, and, increasingly, throughout the western United States. In addition to basic architectural design services, three subsidiaries had recently been formed:

- Interplan, which provides prearchitectural services, programming, planning, budgeting, scheduling, and cost projections utilized in corporate budgeting and governmental bond issues.
- Denver Enterprises, formed to hold equity interests in selected projects designed by RNL and to take risk by furnishing design services early in a project and by participating in the capital requirements of a project.
- Space Management Systems, Inc. (SMS), which provides larger corporations with the necessary services (heavily computer system supported) to facilitate control of their facilities with respect to space, furnishings, equipment, and the cost of change.

In 1984 the firm had seventy-two employees. John Rogers served as the chairman and Vic Langhart served as president. Nagel had retired in 1976. (See Exhibit 1 for an organization chart.) Development of broad-based management had been a priority since 1975. The firm had seven vice-presidents. Two of these vice-presidents, Phil Goedert and Rich von Luhrte, served on the board of directors, together with Rogers and Langhart.

Growth was financed through retained earnings. In addition, a plan to provide for more employee ownership, principally through profit sharing (ESOP in 1984),

This case was prepared by H. Michael Hayes, professor of marketing and strategic management, University of Colorado at Denver, as the basis for class discussion, rather than to illustrate either the effective or ineffective handling of an administrative situation.

Exhibit 1   **Organization**

409
Cases

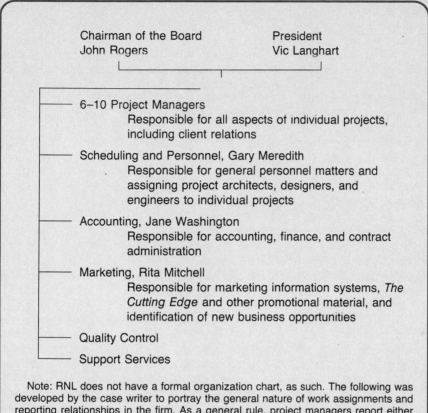

Chairman of the Board   President
John Rogers   Vic Langhart

— 6–10 Project Managers
  Responsible for all aspects of individual projects,
  including client relations

— Scheduling and Personnel, Gary Meredith
  Responsible for general personnel matters and
  assigning project architects, designers, and
  engineers to individual projects

— Accounting, Jane Washington
  Responsible for accounting, finance, and contract
  administration

— Marketing, Rita Mitchell
  Responsible for marketing information systems, *The
  Cutting Edge* and other promotional material, and
  identification of new business opportunities

— Quality Control

— Support Services

Note: RNL does not have a formal organization chart, as such. The following was developed by the case writer to portray the general nature of work assignments and reporting relationships in the firm. As a general rule, project managers report either to John Rogers or Vic Langhart. Most administrative staff functions report to Vic Langhart. At the operational level, Interplan and SMS projects are handled similarly to RNL projects.

was initiated in 1973. Rogers and Langhart held 56 per cent of RNL stock and 66 per cent was held by the four board members. The Colorado National Bank Profit Sharing Trust held 12 per cent in its name. The remaining 22 percent was controlled by twenty-three other employees, either personally or through their individual profit-sharing accounts. It was a goal of the firm to eventually vest stock ownership throughout the firm, in the interest of longevity and continuity.

The firm's principal assets were its human resources. Rogers and Langhart, however, had significant ownership in a limited partnership that owned a 20,000-square-foot building in a prestigious location in downtown Denver. In 1984 RNL occupied 15,000 square feet. Use of the remaining 5,000 square feet could accommodate up to 30 per cent growth in personnel. Through utilization of automation and computers, RNL felt it could double its 1984 volume of work without acquiring additional space.

Architectural Services

architecture: the profession of designing buildings, open areas, communities, and other artificial constructions and environments, usually with some regard to aesthetic effect. The professional services of an architect often include design or selection of furnishings and decorations, supervision of construction work, and the examination, restoration, or remodeling of existing buildings. (Random House Dictionary)

Demand for architectural services is closely tied to population growth and to the level of construction activity. The population in the Denver metropolitan area grew from 929,000 in 1960 to 1,620,000 in 1980, and it is estimated to grow to 1,958,000 by 1990. Denver's annual population change of 3.4 per cent in the decade 1970–1980 ranked tenth for major American cities (Dallas and Phoenix ranked one and two). The projected population growth for the Denver metropolitan area from 1978 to 1983 ranked third in the nation, and Colorado was predicted to be one of the ten fastest-growing states during the 1980s.

Commercial construction permits grew from 340 in 1970, with an estimated value of $70,818,000, to 1,235 in 1980, with an estimated value of $400,294,000. This growth was not steady, however. Year-to-year changes in dollar value of commercial construction varied from 0.2 to 91.6 per cent and the number of permits dropped from a high of 2,245 in 1978 to 1,235 in 1980. Similar patterns of growth and variation characterized industrial construction.

Translating construction growth into estimates of demand for architectural services is difficult. One rule of thumb holds that each additional person added to the population base required 1,000 square feet of homes, schools, churches, offices, hospitals, manufacturing facilities, retail and shopping facilities, and transportation facilities. In the Denver Metro area alone this could mean 338 million square feet. At $50 on average per square foot, total construction expenditure over the decade could reach $16,900,000,000 involving as much as $845 million in design fees during the 1980s.

The past and projected growth in demand for architectural services was accompanied by a significant growth in the number of architects in Colorado. From 1979 to 1982, the number of state registrations of individual architects grew from 1,400 to 3,381, an increase of 141.5 per cent. Over one hundred architectural firms compete actively in the Denver market. (Over five hundred architects are listed in the Yellow Pages of the Denver Metro Area phone directory.) In recent years a number of national firms (e.g., Skidmore, Owens and Merrill) have opened offices in Denver. Other major firms come to Colorado to do one job and then return to their home offices (e.g., Yamasaki for the Colorado National Bank Office Tower, TAC for Mansville World Headquarters, etc.). Of the twenty-six major firms working on thirty-eight selected jobs in Denver in 1983, sixteen, or 61.5 per cent, are Denver based. Of the other ten, which have headquarter offices elsewhere, all but two have offices in Denver.

Major categories of customers for architectural services include

```
Industrial
Commercial
    Owner
    Developer
Government
    Federal
    State
    Municipal
Residential (Note: RNL did not compete in this market)
```

Within these categories, however, not all architectural work is available to independent firms and not all architectural work on a project is awarded to one architect. A recent survey, for example, indicated that of forty-nine commercial jobs under construction with a known architect, eleven were handled by an "inside" architect. Of the remaining thirty-eight jobs, twenty included shell and space design, whereas eighteen involved space design only. In the eighteen space designs, only 50 per cent were actually done by architects.

The rapid growth in the construction market in Denver came to an abrupt halt in February 1982. Triggered by the broad realization that the oil boom was over, or had at least had slowed significantly, project after project was put on hold. Construction of office space literally came to a halt. Of particular concern to RNL, which had just completed negotiations for a $1 million contract with Exxon, was the Exxon announcement of the closing of its Colorado Oil Shale activities at Parachute, Colorado.

It was against the backdrop of these changes that RNl felt the pressing need to review its marketing activities.

Marketing of Architectural Services

The basis of competing for architectural work has changed dramatically over the past several decades. As John Rogers recalled:

At the beginning of my practice in 1956, you could establish an office, put a sign on your door, print calling cards, and have a "news" announcement with your picture in the *Daily Journal* that you had established a new practice of architecture. Beyond that, it was appropriate to suggest to friends and acquaintances that I was in business now, and I hoped that they might recommend me to someone they knew. The Code of Ethics of the American Institute of Architects, like many other professions at the time, prohibited any kind of aggressive marketing or sales effort as practiced in recent times.

In fact, after convincing one school board member (an artist) in Jefferson County that design was important, and then being awarded a commission to design an elementary school, which led to another and another, it was not surprising to read in the *Daily Journal* that the school board had met the previous evening and had elected me to design a new junior high school, one that I hadn't even known about. I called and said, "Thank you." Marketing expense was zero, with the exception of an occasional lunch or courtesy call here and there.

Today, the situation is vastly different. We have to compete for most jobs, against both local firms and, increasingly, large national firms. Clients are becoming more sophisticated regarding the purchase of architectural services (see Exhibit 2 for a brief description of buyer behavior). Promotion, of some kind, and concepts such as segmentation have become a way of life.

During the 1960s, development of an architectural practice was a slow process, characterized by heavy reliance on word of mouth regarding professional experience and expertise. Overt communication about an architect's qualifications was limited to brochures. Personal acquaintances played a significant role in the development of new clients. Personal relations between principals and clients were an important part of continuing and new relations. This method of practice development tended to favor local firms, whose reputation could be checked out on a personal basis, and small firms, whose principals could provide personal management and design of client projects.

As Denver grew, the market changed. The advantage of being a successful local architect and knowing the local business community diminished. Newcomers

Exhibit 2   Buyer Behavior

Purchase of architectural services is both complex and varied. Subject to many qualifications, however, there seem to be a number of steps that most buying situations have in common.

- Development of a list of potential architects.
- Identification of those architects from whom proposals will be solicited for a specific job. (Usually called the "short list.")
- Invitations to submit proposals.
- Evaluation of proposals and screening of final candidates.
- Selection of a finalist, based on proposal evaluation, or
- Invitations to finalists to make oral presentations to an evaluation group.

From a marketing standpoint, the focus of interest is the process of getting on the short list and the process by which the final selection is made.

The Short List

Prospective clients find out about architects in a variety of ways. Those who are frequent users of architectural services will generally keep a file of architects, sometimes classified as to type or practice. Additions to the file can come from mailed brochures, personal calls, advertisements, press releases or, in fact, almost any form of communication. When a specific requirement develops, the file is reviewed for apparent fit. With many variations, a short list is developed and proposals are solicited.

Those who use architects infrequently tend to rely on various business or social networks to develop what is in essence their short list. In either case, a previously used architect is almost always on the short list, provided that past experience was satisfactory.

As the largest single customer for architectural services, agencies of the federal government follow a well-defined series of steps, including advertisement in the *Commerce Business Daily* and mail solicitation of local firms.

The Selection Process

The selection process is significantly influenced by the nature and scope of the work and its importance to the firm. Architect selection on major buildings is usually made at the highest level in the organization, by a principal or the president in a private organization or by various forms of boards in not-for-profit organizations such as churches. In some instances the principal, president, or board is actively involved in all phases of the process. In others the management of the process is delegated to those who develop recommendations to the decision makers. On smaller jobs, and those of an ongoing nature (e.g., space management), the decision is usually at lower levels and may involve a plant engineer or facilities manager of some kind.

Regardless of the level at which the selection process is made, there seem to be two well-defined patterns to the process. The first, and predominant one, evaluates the firms on the short list, taking into principal consideration nonprice factors such as reputation, performance on previous jobs, and current work load. Based on this evaluation, one firm is selected and a final agreement is then negotiated as to the scope of the work, the nature of the working relationship, the project team, and specific details as to price.

Exhibit 2 *(Continued)*

413
Cases

The second, and of limited but growing use, attempts to specify the requirements so completely that a firm price can accompany the proposal. In some instances the price and the proposal are submitted separately. Evaluation of the proposals includes a dollar differential, and these dollar differentials are applied to the price quotation to determine the low evaluated bidder.

Regardless of the process, there appear to be three main criteria on which firms are evaluated:

- The ability of the firm to perform the particular assignment. For standard work this assessment is relatively easy and relies on the nature of past work, size of the organization, current backlogs, and so forth. For more creative work, the assessment becomes more difficult. Much importance is put on past work, but the proposal starts to take on additional importance. Sketches, drawings, and sometimes extensive models may be requested with the proposal. In some instances there may actually be a design competition. Much of this evaluation is, perforce, of a subjective nature.
- The comfort level with the project team that will be assigned to do the work. For any but the most standard work, there is recognition that there will be constant interaction between representatives of the client's organization and members of the architectural firm. Almost without exception, therefore, some kind of evaluation is made of the project team, or at least its leaders, in terms of the client's comfort level with the personalities involved.
- Finally, there is the matter of cost. While direct price competition is not a factor in most transactions, the cost of architectural services is always a concern. This has two components. First, there is concern with the total cost of the project, over which the architect has great control. Second, there is growing concern with the size of the architect's fee, per se.

At least some assessment of the reputation of the architect with respect to controlling project costs is made in determining the short list. Once final selection is made, there is likely to be much discussion and negotiation as to the method of calculating the fee. The traditional method of simply charging a percentage of the construction price seems to be on the wane. Increasingly, clients for architectural services are attempting to establish a fixed fee for a well-defined project. The nature of architectural work, however, is such that changes are a fact of life and that many projects cannot be sufficiently defined in the initial stages to allow precise estimation of the design costs. Some basis for modifying a basic fee must, therefore, be established. Typically this is on some kind of direct-cost basis plus an overhead adder. Direct costs for various classes of staff and overhead rates obviously become matters for negotiation. In the case of the federal government, the right is reserved to audit an architect's books to determine the appropriateness of charges for changes.

to Denver tended to rely on relationships with architects in other cities. For local architects there wasn't time to rely on traditional communication networks to establish relationships with these newcomers. The size of projects grew, requiring growth in the size of architectural staffs. Personal attention to every client by principals was no longer possible.

Concomitantly, there was a growing change in the attitude toward the marketing of professional services. New entrants in the fields of medicine and law, as well as architecture, were becoming impatient with the slowness of traditional methods of practice development. A Supreme Court decision significantly reduced the restrictions that state bar associations could impose on lawyers with respect to their pricing and advertising practices. In a similar vein, the American Institute of Architects signed a consent decree with the Justice Department that prohibited the organization from publishing fee schedules for architectural services.

Perhaps of most significance for architects, however, was the start of the so-called "proposal age." Investigations in Maryland and Kansas, and other states, had revealed improper involvement of architects and engineers with state officials. Financial kickbacks were proven on many state projects. Formal proposals, it was felt, would eliminate or reduce the likelihood of contract awards made on the basis of cronyism or kickbacks. Starting in the government sector, the requirement for proposals spread rapidly to all major clients. In 1984, for example, even a small church could receive as many as twenty detailed proposals on a modest-sized assignment.

Marketing at RNL

In 1984, RNL was engaged in a number of marketing activities. In addition to proposal preparation, major activities included

- Professional involvement in the business community by principals, which provides contacts with potential clients. This included memberships in a wide variety of organizations such as the Downtown Denver Board, Chamber of Commerce, Denver Art Museum, etc.
- Participation in and appearances at conferences, both professional and business oriented.
- Daily review of the *Commerce Business Daily* (a federal publication of all construction projects), along with other news services that indicate developing projects.
- Maintenance of past client contacts. (RNL found this difficult but assigned the activity to its project managers.)
- Development of relationships with potential clients, usually by giving a tour through the office, plus lunch.
- VIP gourmet-catered lunches for six invited guests, held once a month in the office. These involved a tour of the office and lively conversation, with some attempt at subsequent follow-up.
- Participation in appropriate local, regional, or national exhibits of architectural projects.
- Occasional publicity for a project or for a client.
- The Cutting Edge[1]

[1]*The Cutting Edge* is an RNL publication, designed to inform clients and prospects about new developments in architecture and planning and about significant RNL accomplishments (see Exhibit 2 for a typical issue).

- An assortment of brochures and information on finished projects.
- Special arrangements with architectural firms in other locations to provide the basis for a variety of desirable joint ventures.

RNL participated in a number of market segments, which it identified as follows, together with its view of the required approach:

Segment	Approach
Government	
City and County Governments	Personal selling, political involvement
School Districts	Personal selling (professional educational knowledge required)
State Government	Political involvement, written responses to RFPs (Requests for Proposals, from clients), personal selling
Federal Government	Personal selling, very detailed RFP response, no price competition in the proposal stage
Private Sector	Personal selling, social acquaintances, referrals, *The Cutting Edge*, preliminary studies, price competition
Semiprivate sector (Includes utilities)	Personal selling, *The Cutting Edge*, referrals, continuing relationships, some price competition

Net fee income and allocation of marketing expenses by major segments are given in the following table. The general feeling at RNL was that there is a lapse of six to eighteen months between the marketing effort itself and tangible results such as fee income.

	Net Fee (in $) 1982	Marktg. Exp. (in $)	Net Fee (in $) 1983	Marktg. Exp. (in $)	Net Fee (in $) 1984 (est.)	Marktg. Exp. (in $)	Net Fee (In $) 1985 (est.)	Market. Exp. (in $)
Government	800	104	1,220	101	1,012	150	1,200	140
Private	1,376	162	1,261	140	1,200	195	1,616	220
Semiprivate	88	11	118	24	100	25	140	30
Interiors	828	40	670	30	918	100	1,235	110
Urban design	95	20	31	10	170	30	220	40
Total	3,187	337	3,300	305	3,400	500	4,411	540

Salient aspects of budgeted marketing expense for 1985, by segment, were

- Government. Heavy emphasis on increased trips to Omaha (a key Corps of Engineers location), Washington, and other out-of-state, as well as in-state, locations, plus considerable emphasis on participation in municipal conferences.

- Private. Personal contact at local, state, and regional levels with corporations, banks, developers, and contractors, plus local promotion through Chamber of Commerce, clubs, VIP lunches, *The Cutting Edge,* promotion materials, and initiation of an advertising and public relations effort.
- Semiprivate. Increased level of personal contact and promotional effort.
- Interiors. Major allocation of salary and expenses of a new full-time marketing person to improve direct sales locally, plus other promotional support.
- Urban design. Some early success indicates that land developers and urban renewal authorities are the most likely clients. Planned marketing expense is primarily for personal contact.

Additional marketing efforts being given serious consideration included

- A more structured marketing organization with more specific assignments.
- Increased visibility for the firm through general media and trade journals—paid or other (e.g., public relations).
- Appearances on special programs and offering special seminars.
- Use of more sophisticated selling tools, such as videotapes, automated slide presentations, etc.
- Increased training in client relations/selling for project managers and other staff.
- Hiring a professionally trained marketing manager.
- Determining how the national firms market (i.e., copy the competition).
- Expansion of debriefing conferences with successful and unsuccessful clients.
- Use of a focus group to develop effective sales points for RNL.
- Training a marketing MBA in architecture versus an architect in marketing.

RNL Clients

RNL described its clients as

1. Having a long history of growing expectations with respect to detail, completeness, counseling, and cost control.
2. Mandating the minimization of construction problems, including changes, overruns, and delays.
3. Having an increased concern for peer approval at the completion of a project.
4. Having an increased desire to understand and be a part of the design process.

Extensive interviews of clients by independent market researchers showed very favorable impressions about RNL. Terms used to describe the firm included

- Best and largest architectural service in Denver.
- Innovative yet practical.
- Designs large projects for "Who's Who in Denver."
- Long-term resident of the business community.
- Lots of expertise.
- Designs artistic yet functional buildings.

RNL's use of computer-aided design systems was seen as a definite competitive edge. Others mentioned RNL's extra services, such as interior systems, as a plus, although only 35 per cent of those interviewed were aware that RNL offered this service. In general, most clients felt that RNL had a competitive edge with regard to timeliness, productivity, and cost-consciousness.

Two major ways that new clients heard about RNL were identified. One was the contact RNL made on its own initiative when it heard of a possible project. The other was through personal references. All those interviewed felt advertising played a minor role and, in fact, several indicated they had questions about an architectural firm that advertises.

Clients who selected RNL identified the following as playing a role in their decision:

- Tours of RNL's facilities.
- Monthly receipt of *The Cutting Edge.*
- Low key selling style
- RNL's ability to focus on their needs
- Thoroughness in researching customer needs and overall proposal preparation and presentation.
- RNL's overall reputation in the community.
- Belief that RNL would produce good, solid (not flashy) results.

Clients who did not select RNL identified the following reasons for their decision:

- RNL had less experience and specialization in their particular industry.
- Decided to stay with the architectural firm used previously.
- Decided to go with a firm that has more national status.
- Other presentations had more "pizazz."

Overall, clients' perceptions of RNL were very positive. There was less than complete understanding of the scope of RNL services, but their current approach to clients received good marks.

Marketing Issues: The Views of the Founders

Vic Langhart started his practice of architecture in 1954 and has taught design in the architecture department of the University of Colorado. He was instrumental in developing new services at RNL, including Interplan and SMS, Inc., and was heavily involved in the training of the next level of management. In 1984 he supervised day-to-day operations and also served as president of Interplan and SMS, Inc. Looking to the future, Vic observed:

Our toughest issue is dealing with the rate of change in the profession today. It's probably fair to say there are too many architects today. But this is a profession of highly idealistic people, many of whom feel their contribution to a better world is more important than dollars of income and so will stay in the field at "starvation wages." We wrestle with the question of "profession or business?," but competition is now a fact of life for us. The oil boom of the 1970s in Denver triggered an inrush of national firms. Many have stayed on, and we now have a situation where one of the largest national firms is competing for a small job in Durango. We're also starting to see more direct price competition. Digital Equipment recently prequalified eight firms, selected five to submit proposals that demonstrated understanding of the assignment, and asked for a separate envelope containing the price.

Our tradition at RNL has been one of quality. I think we're the "Mercedes" of the business and in the long haul an RNL customer will be better off economically. A lot of things contribute to this—our Interplan concept, for instance—but the key differentiation factor is our on-site-planning approach.

In 1966–1968 we were almost 100 per cent in education. Then I heard that they were closing some maternity wards and we decided to diversify. Today we have a good list of products, ranging from commercial buildings to labs and vehicle maintenance facilities. In most areas the only people who can beat us are the superspecialists, and even then there's a question. Our diversification has kept our minds free to come up with creative approaches. At Beaver Creek, for example, I think we came up with a better approach to condominium design than the specialists. Plus, we can call in special expertise, if it's necessary.

Over the past several years we've had a number of offsets to merge into national, or other, firms. We decided, however, to become employee owned. Our basic notion was that RNL should be an organization that provides its employees a long-time career opportunity. This is not easy in an industry that is characterized by high turnover. Less than 10 per cent of architectural firms have figured out how to do it. But we're now at 35 per cent employee ownership.

I'm personally enthusiastic about Interplan. It has tremendous potential to impact our customers. In Seattle, for instance, a bank came to us for a simple expansion. Our Interplan approach, however, led to a totally different set of concepts. We've had some discussions about expansion. Colorado Springs is a possibility, for instance. But there would be problems of keeping RNL concepts and our culture. We work hard to develop and disseminate an RNL culture. For example, we have lots of meetings, although John and I sometimes disagree about how much time should be spent in meetings. A third of our business comes from interiors, and there is as much difference between interior designers and architects as there is between architects and mechanical engineers.

In a somewhat similar vein, John Rogers commented:

In the 1960s RNL was primarily in the business of designing schools. We were really experts in that market. But then the boom in school construction came to an end and we moved into other areas: first into banks and commercial buildings. We got started with Mountain Bell, an important relationship for us that continues today. We did assignments for mining companies and laboratories. In the late 1960s, no one knew how to use computers to manage office-space problems, and we moved in that direction, which led to the formation of Interplan. We moved into local and state design work. One of our showcase assignments is the Colorado State Judicial/Heritage Center.

In the 1980s we started to move into federal and military work, and this now represents a significant portion of our business. We have done some developer work, but this is a tough market. It has a strong "bottom-line orientation," and developers want sharp focus and expertise.

As we grow larger, we find it difficult to maintain a close client relationship. The client wants to know who will work on the assignment, but some of our staff members are not good at the people side of the business.

Currently we're still doing lots of "one of a kind" work. Our assignment for the expansion of the Rocky Mountain News building, our design of a condominium lodge at Beaver Creek, our design of a developer building at the Denver Tech Center are all in this category. A common theme, however, is our "on-site" design process. This is a process by which we make sure that the client is involved in the design from the start and that we are really tuned in to his requirements. I see this as one of our real competitive advantages. But I'm still concerned that we may be trying to spread ourselves too thin. Plus, there's no question that there is an increased tendency to specialization. "Shopping center architects", for example.

We need to become better marketers, but we have to make sure that we don't lose sight of what has made us the leading architectural firm in Denver: service and client orientation.

Medical Services, Inc.

Dr. Jane Shea was thoughtfully reviewing her notes after completing a strategy review of the medical practice that she shared with two partners, Dr. Fred Hughes and Dr. John Lehmann. The three physicians, upon completion of their internships in a local hospital in 1983, purchased a family practice that was enlarged by opening a minor emergency clinic. Two years later, the combined practice was barely breaking even. One of the more disappointing aspects was the sparse utilization of the emergency clinic.

Dr. Shea had recently attended a short course at the nearby university titled "Strategic Planning for Services." Now she was trying to apply some of the course concepts to her own professional situation.

Product/Market Description

Products Offered

The products are the medical services offered by three doctors of osteopathy. (See Appendix 1 for a description of osteopathic philosophy and training.) These services are distributed from a converted house located on a main street in a midwestern city of some 400,000 residents. Two different distribution systems are used: a private practice office and a minor emergency clinic.

From these units, Medical Services, Inc., offers general health care as well as the following medical specialties: pediatrics, internal medicine, surgery, OB/GYN, emergency medicine, orthopedics, and geriatrics. In addition to the pure medical services, the doctors attempt to provide many convenience services. These include personable physicians with experience in health care for the entire family; maintenance of office hours that extend past normal business hours; a flexible appointment policy to fit patients' needs; minor emergencies treated at a fraction of the cost of a hospital emergency room; worker's compensation injuries treated; doctors available 24 hours a day for emergency calls; payment by Visa, MasterCard, personal check, or cash; and assistance in filing insurance and Medicare forms.

Their prices are generally about 17 per cent lower than those of competitors for a standard office visit ($25 vs. $30). Many prices are fixed by the cost of the use of an outside facility, such as one of the local hospitals. See Table 1 for a list of fees. The doctors use a hospital because it can provide services and use of equipment less expensively than they can provide it themselves. As they become more prosperous, they will buy more of their own equipment. Currently the doctors have the equipment and facilities to handle approximately 90 per cent of their patients' needs. For the remaining 10 per cent they have made arrangements to use outside services at reasonable rates.

This case was prepared by James W. Cagley and Lester A. Neidell, both professors of marketing, University of Tulsa, Oklahoma. This case has been made possible by the cooperation of a medical service that wishes to remain anonymous.

Distributed by the Case Research Association. All rights reserved to the authors and to the C.R.A. Permission to use this case should be obtained from the authors and the C.R.A.

Copyright © 1986 by James Cagley and Lester Neidell.

Table 1 Family Medical Services Typical Fees

Office visit	$21.00–$25.00
Routine physical examination	$25.00
Extended physical exam	$30.00 and up depending on services
Electrocardiogram	$25.00
Xrays	$30.00–45.00 depending on part
Small lacerations	$35.00–50.00

Market Situation

The markets that Medical Services, Inc., targets include three segments. These are the on-campus students at a mid-sized (6,000 students) private university, townspeople within a 2-mile radius of the MSI clinic, and the small businesses within that same radius. Details on each of the market segments are as follows:

1. The on-campus university student.
   The doctors realize that the faculty and staff have their own health care service, but the bulk of the on-campus student population does not. The office and clinic are two blocks from the campus, handy for students without cars and for minor emergencies such as minor athletic injuries, cuts, and burns. The clinic's payment policy is flexible and facilitates insurance collections. This should encourage students to utilize MSI's services. Making the students aware of the clinic appears to be a major task.

2. The townspeople within a 2-mile radius of the clinic.
   Realistically many of a doctor's patients come from referrals and personal contact. In addition to students there are many older people who live in the vicinity. The close proximity of the clinic is an asset which should encourage the local people to use MSI. There are approximately 23,500 residences in the target market, with a median of 2.1 persons per household. Over 10 per cent of these are minorities. The median age of the target market is over 45, with more than 58 per cent over 45 years old. Over 17 percent of these are married couples with one or more persons under 18 living in the house. The median education level of the target market is 12.5 years. The median income is in the low-middle category. This area's method of payment is generally either Medicare or some form of company insurance. The clinic's policy is to assist in filing insurance and Medicare claims, and the doctors encourage patients to use those methods of payment.

3. The small businesses within the same radius of the clinic.
   The doctors feel that with adequate promotion through personal and written contact, this market is wide open for them. There are approximately 4,000 businesses in the target area. While they hesitate to offer "special deals" on medical service, their business policies and close proximity make the clinic attractive to worker's compensation claims and on-the-job minor emergencies. And, as employees come to the office for those reasons, they will also get accustomed to coming in (and bringing their families) for other ailments. Service contracts are not being used for small businesses, but this option is currently being considered.

Exhibit 1 Location of Competing Services

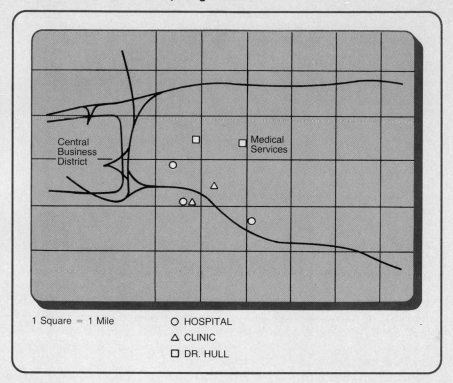

1 Square = 1 Mile

O HOSPITAL
△ CLINIC
□ DR. HULL

Central Business District

□ Medical Services

Competitive Situation

Major competitors for MSI's targeted market segments include three hospitals: Johnson Clinic, Inc., Nelson Clinic, Inc., and Dr. Ashley W. Hull (see Exhibit 1). The three hospitals, each located within 2 miles of MSI, represent the major threat to MSI's minor emergency operation. Each hospital has far greater capability to handle emergencies than does the clinic. There are some negative aspects concerned with the hospitals' emergency care, such as cost and customer waiting time. MSI's prices for minor emergencies are substantially lower than those of the hospitals. In general, the MSI doctors can treat patients much more quickly than can the typical hospital emergency room.

Johnson Clinic, Inc., specializes in family practice and surgery and is located about 1½ miles southwest of MSI, close to both hospitals. Dr. Kenneth Johnson is a medical doctor (as opposed to D.O.). The hours of the Johnson Clinic cover the normal business hours of 7 A.M. to 4 P.M., Monday through Friday. MSI covers these normal business hours, but additionally is open late Monday through Thursday until 7 P.M. and is open four hours on Saturday. Nelson Clinic's hours and services are identical to those of the Johnson Clinic.

Doctor Ashley W. Hull operates an office within one-half mile of MSI. Dr. Hull is a doctor of osteopathy, whose office hours are Monday through Friday from 8 A.M. to 5 P.M., except on Thursdays when he is open only until noon.

While there are several minor emergency clinics and hundreds of doctors (D.O. and M.D.) in the town, due to the narrow geographically defined target markets, these are considered only peripheral competitors.

The Macroenvironment

Macroenvironmental factors that could impact on MSI include demographic characteristics and trends, such as population growth, age distribution, urbanization, education, affluence, and governmental policies intended to reduce health care access inequities.

The city's population growth is slowing. Located in one of the ten fastest-growing states in the United States during the 1970s and early 1980s, with annual population increases close to 10 per cent, projections are for very slow growth in the next decade. The city's birth rate is also decreasing. The median number of persons per household in the target market is 2.1, down from the number ten years ago. This declining population growth will affect the local health care system in many ways. This could, for example, mean that obstetric units may be under pressure to close due to low occupancy, the demand for pediatrics will decline, and there will be less demand for general health services.

The city population, in general, is older. This has some positive demand effects as older persons tend to need more health care. A growing percentage of the population is over 65 years old, and 58 per cent of the target market is over 45 years old. Physician visits are more frequent for older patients (average 7.4 times a year compared to less than 5 times a year for patients ages 17–24 years). Hospital admission rates are also higher for elderly people, and they require longer recuperation and rehabilitation time.

The United States is becoming increasingly urbanized and suburbanized. City dwellers are more prone to acute respiratory diseases. Medical Services, Inc., is located in the central city. The SMSA's center of population is 7 or 8 miles to the southeast and moving farther out each year.

The United States is becoming more highly educated; better-educated people use health care services to a greater extent. The median educational level in the target market is 12.5 years, which suggests a high level of health care use. Increasing affluence levels and the reduction (not elimination) of poverty has had a positive dramatic impact on health problems. But affluence creates new health hazards, such as stress-related problems.

With Medicare and Medicaid, health care is rapidly becoming a right rather than a privilege. Medical Services. Inc., is located in a low-middle-income area and these insurance methods can be utilized to a great degree.

Strategic Situation Analysis

In the planning course that Dr. Shea had attended, the concept of a strategic situation analysis was introduced and discussed. Dr. Shea looked over her notes on the product/market situation and on the competitive and macroenvironments. She was aware that one of the missing factors was specific information about how patients chose a specific doctor or clinic. In general, she knew that people decide on a specific doctor on the advice of family or friends, from work relationships, by hospital reference, or by reference through another doctor.

It had been a long day. Dr. Shea was the physician on call at the clinic, and this review of the competitive environment was perplexing. She and her two partners needed to devise a strategy for increasing the utilization of the practice and emergency clinic. She decided to review the strategic situation analysis according to the format developed in the short course. (This is contained in Appendix 2.)

Appendix 1: Osteopathic Medicine

Physicians trained in osteopathic medicine integrate all accepted treatment modes for disease and injury: drugs, surgery, physical therapy, and manipulation. A distinctive feature of osteopathic medicine is the belief that symptoms of functional disease may be found in the patient's musculoskeletal system. Osteopathic physicians try to treat irregularities of this system. Emphasis is on the total condition of the body; osteopathic management promotes health by releasing people's natural abilities to fight disease-causing stresses.

Students enrolling in osteopathic education are required to have a minimum of three years of college; in fact, 95 per cent of entering osteopathic students have received a B.A. or B.S. degree. Osteopathic medical training requires a basic four-year program in all branches of medicine and surgery, which qualifies graduates for the D.O. (doctor of osteopathy) degree. A 12-month internship in an approved teaching hospital follows receipt of the degree. Specialty training can then be undertaken, which requires three to five years additional study.

Practicing D.O.s must be licensed by state agencies. In many states the licensing exams are identical for D.O.s and M.D.s. D.O.s and M.D.s often practice at the same hospitals, but there are a number of D.O. hospitals, which are evaluated rigorously by the American Osteopathic Association. D.O.s are eligible for membership in the American Medical Association (AMA).

Opinion studies in many parts of the United States have revealed that the majority of Americans do not know that osteopathic medicine treats the full scope of human illness and injury. D.O.s are sometimes labeled as "quacks," and are often confused with chiropractors, whose medical practice is limited to manipulation of body joints. These studies also demonstrate that preference for a D.O. is relatively small, but that users of D.O.s rate their willingness to talk to patients about an illness as the most important feature of their physician-patient relationship.

Appendix 2: Strategic Situation Analysis

Strengths

The doctors' medical education is comprehensive and continually being kept current through postgraduate training in family medicine at the local osteopathic hospital.

Extended hours at the clinic offer more convenience for patients.

The doctors inherited many of the files and patients of the previous physicians.

There are several methods of payment available for patient convenience.

Patient cost is low in relation to alternative sources of health care.

The image of osteopathic doctors is better than in the past.

Weaknesses

The clinic has a weak history in promoting its services, and there is no advertising budget.

While there is potential for financial success, currently the clinic is struggling due to lack of patients.

Management's (the doctors') general business and marketing background is limited.

The street sign, while informative, is not eyecatching, and the gray building is easy to miss while driving by.

Doctors of osteopathy must continually fight inherited image problems.

The doctors are young and relatively inexperienced.

There is little money for advertising and promotion.

Opportunities

The on-campus students at the university can be considered a "built-in" market.

The many small and medium-size businesses in the area potentially can use a nearby medical facility for low-cost minor emergency care with insurance worker's compensation capabilities.

There are few competitors in the target area, so market potential should be good.

Threats

The target markets are unproven and may be more limited in size than previously estimated.

Within a mile outside the targeted area, the number of competitors drastically increases. Associated with the hospitals are physicians' buildings, each containing dozens of doctors.

QUESTIONS

1. What do you believe are the problems and opportunities facing MSI?
2. What is the "product" that MSI is offering?
3. How should MSI prioritize their possible target markets?
4. In what ways are strategy decisions for services different from those for products? How are they the same?

Porsche AG

Peter Schultz seemed to have everything going his way. In the three years since he became president of Porsche AG, the Porsche model 944 had become a resounding success. It was introduced in mid-1982, and Porsche sales in the United States had more than doubled. Nevertheless, Mr. Schultz had expressed concerns about Porsche's distribution effort in the United States and was contemplating a change.

This case is from Roger A. Kerin and Robert A. Peterson, *Strategic Marketing Problems*, 4th ed. (Boston: Allyn & Bacon, Inc., 1986). Used with permission.

Since 1969, Volkswagen of America (VWoA), a subsidiary of Volkswagenwerk AG, had handled all aspects of Porsche's automotive business in the United States, including importing, advertising, sales, and service when it established a Porsche-Audi Division. VWoA sold the Porsche line through 323 independent franchised dealers. These dealers also sold Audis, produced by a Volkswagenwerk AG subsidiary. According to industry sources, VWoA made $40 million importing Porsches into the United States in 1983.

Porsche's contract with VWoA was due to expire in August 1984, and Mr. Schultz felt the time was right to make the "single most important decision in the company's entire history": whether to change the way Porsche sold, warehoused, and repaired its cars in the United States. Several factors combined to lead Mr. Schultz to consider a change. First, he had heard that successful dealers in need of cars often had to buy Porsches from other dealers at premium prices, which inflated the price paid by customers. Second, he felt a mass market retailer such as a Porsche-Audi dealer was the wrong outlet for low-volume, high-priced ($21,400–$44,000 list price) Porsche cars. Third, he believed the Japanese would soon enter the high-performance sports car market in the United States, and Porsche needed a distribution system that would compete against them. These factors led him to conclude that a new distribution arrangement was necessary to bring the Porsche factory closer to its customers. Furthermore, he believed sales in the United States would increase if customers could be assured of getting cars more readily with the special features they desired.

The new distribution plan envisioned by Mr. Schultz contained four major points:

1. Porsche AG would withdraw from its contract with VWoA in August 1984 and would stop selling its cars through the VWoA dealer network.
2. Porsche would recruit and use agents to sell its cars rather than Porsche-Audi dealers. These agents would not have to buy cars and inventory them at a fixed location as dealers do. Therefore, they would not have to tie up cash in a car inventory, incur interest costs on that inventory, and operate a dealership.
3. Porsche would operate two warehouses in the United States, one in Reno, Nevada, and the other in Charleston, South Carolina.
4. Forty distribution and repair centers would be operated in the United States, where the Porsche population was highest. These forty distribution centers would also sell Porsches. The distribution company would be called Porsche Cars North America.

The Company

Porsche AG was founded by Ferdinand Porsche in 1931. Based in Stuttgart, West Germany (Federal Republic of Germany), Porsche AG is primarily engaged in the development, manufacturing, and marketing of sports cars, in four-, six-, and eight-cylinder models, both for domestic consumption and for export. Porsche AG is also well known for its development of racing car models. For example, in 1983 Porsche cars swept nine of the first ten places at LeMans.

Porsche AG recorded net sales of $841 million with record earnings in fiscal 1983. One of the factors in this recent success was the Porsche 944—a high-performance model with an enticing $18,450 price, well below the $33,000 average sticker prices for Porsche cars. Another factor in Porsche's record year was a more prosperous U.S. economy, since 53 per cent of company sales came from

Exhibit 1   Porsche AG Financial Statement Summary (in DM 1,000)

Income Statement Summary
(for the Year Ended July 31, 1983)

Net sales	DM	2,133,679
Gross margin		758,674
Other income		43,066
Depreciation and amortization		71,148
Operating expenses		449,919
Taxes		124,945
Net income	DM	69,600

Balance Sheet Summary
(as of July 30, 1983)

Assets:		
Current assets	DM	511,098
Fixed assets (including participatives and deferred charges)		355,452
Total assets	DM	866,550
Liabilities and equity:		
Current liabilities	DM	630,105
Long-term debt		15,700
Equity		220,745
Total liabilities and equity	DM	866,550

Note: For analysis purposes, $1.00 U.S. = DM 2.54. DM is the abbreviation for Deutschemark, the monetary unit of West Germany.

the United States. The introduction of the Porsche 944 and the rebound in the U.S. economy resulted in sales of 21,831 cars in the United States in 1983, compared with 14,407 cars in 1982 and only 11,200 cars in 1981. Summary financial statements for fiscal 1983 are shown in Exhibit 1.

Distribution Plan

The plan envisioned for the distribution of Porsche cars in the United States was based in part on consumer research indicating that the Porsche buyer was different from the so-called typical car buyer. For example, Porsche owners were not impulse buyers but, rather, approached the decision to buy a Porsche in a deliberate manner. They compared products and considered the purchase of a Porsche as an investment. Furthermore, Porsche owners were viewed as working sixty to eighty hours per week, having high standards of excellence and high expectations, and earning at least $75,000 per year. These data buttressed Mr. Schultz's opinion that Porsche customers could be better served by a different distribution arrangement. He was quoted in *Automotive News* (February 20, 1984, p. 1) as saying:

It is our firm belief that Porsche cannot hope to be viable as a manufacturer of high-technology, high-performance sports cars that are distributed by a traditional automotive marketing organization that is basically structured to serve a volume market with traditional service and sales activities.

He added: "It must be as much fun to acquire a Porsche as it is to drive one." Details of the plan follow.

Agents Versus Dealers

A central element of the new distribution plan was the change from conventional car dealers to agents who would represent Porsche Cars North America. Under the arrangement with VWoA, Porsche was inventoried and sold through Porsche-Audi dealers, which typically received a 16–18 per cent margin on new Porsche cars. In addition, these dealers operated (1) a service department for routine and other car maintenance and repair needs and (2) a preowned, or used, car lot.

Under the new plan, Porsche Cars North America would sell its cars through agents that would be formed as limited partnerships. Every current Porsche dealer would be offered the opportunity to become an agent. These agents would receive an 8 per cent commission on new cars sold. Each agent would receive four Porsches for demonstration purposes as part of the limited-partnership fee, but would not inventory new Porsches or operate used car lots. An agent could offer car servicing or rely on Porsche Cars North America distribution centers to perform Porsche service. Agents would be allowed to set prices for new cars; but the forty distribution centers located in areas of high Porsche ownership would list a suggested retail price and sell its cars only at the list price. According to a Porsche executive, the establishment of a fixed list price would mean that "A customer that is aware [of the list price] doesn't have to pay over list price; he has an alternative."

Distribution Centers

A second element of the new distribution plan included distribution centers. Forty distribution centers were planned, to be located in areas of high Porsche ownership. The distribution centers would assume many of the functions performed by conventional car dealers, including preparation, delivery, and service of new cars. In addition, distribution centers would operate a used car program for buyers wishing to purchase a preowned Porsche. However, used cars sales would not be handled in the usual way. The major difference would be that Porsche Cars North America would refurbish the cars for the purpose of increasing their value.

Warehouse Locations

West Coast and East Coast warehouses would be operated for new cars and parts. The West Coast warehouse would be located in Reno, Nevada, and the East Coast warehouse in Charleston, South Carolina. Reno, Nevada, would also house the corporate offices of Porsche Cars North America.

Each warehouse would be situated on the premises of an airport, since parts are shipped by air and plans were under way to ship cars by air as well. The plan involved transporting 250 cars per week via Boeing 747 cargo planes. Five flights per week were planned. These cars would serve as a buffer stock for distribution centers and agents. A schematic representative of the proposed distribution system is shown in Exhibit 2.

Buyer and Agent Ordering

The ordering of new or used cars would proceed as follows. A customer would go to an agent or distribution center and arrange to buy a car. Once a car was sold, a request for the model would be made through a computer link to Reno or Charleston. The customer would then go to either location or pick up the car and drive it home. Alternatively, an agent or distribution center employee could pick up the car for the buyer.

Exhibit 2   Porsche Cars North America Three-Tiered Distribution System

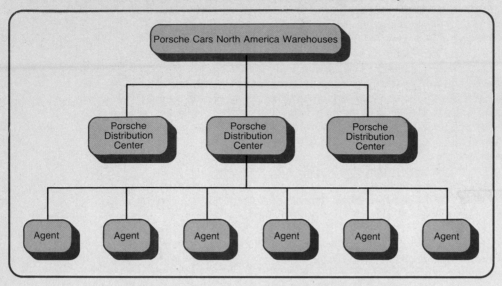

Cost

The total cost associated with the new system would include the costs of operating the two warehouses and distribution centers as well as importing, advertising, and servicing Porsche cars in the United States. It is estimated that Porsche AG would have to invest $350 million to start the operation and hire at least 275 people. Approximately $22 million would be spent to set up the Reno, Nevada, warehouse alone.

Distribution Plan Issues

The plan outlined by Peter Schultz represented a significant departure from past practices and could affect long-standing relationships with Volkswagenwerk AG. For example, the management of Porsche AG and Volkswagenwerk AG shared numerous family ties. Ferdinand Porsche, the company's founder, designed the Volkswagen "Beetle" that established Volkswagenwerk AG. Ferdinand Porsche's son, Ferry, is chairman of the board of Porsche AG; his son-in-law, Anton Piëch, was Volkswagenwerk's first chairman of the board. Anton Piëch's widow and children are still active in Volkswagenwerk affairs and own a Volkswagen distributorship and retail outlets in Austria. Ferdinand Porsche's grandson, Ferdinand Piëch, is director of research and development at Volkswagenwerk's Audi subsidiary. In short, a break with Volkswagenwerk could mean severing family ties.

Another issue was the response by Porsche-Audi dealers in the United States and VWoA. When Peter Schultz presented his idea to 300 Porsche-Audi dealers on February 15, 1984, in Reno, Nevada, the response was cool. According to a *Fortune* magazine report (April 16, 1984, p. 64) "the dealers felt betrayed by the abolition of franchises and insulted by Schultz's invitation for them to invest in limited partnerships that would finance Porsche centers." Within a month of Mr. Schultz's announcement, Porsche AG was put on notice that it could face legal action by Porsche-Audi dealers totaling over $1 billion in penalties. In addition,

VWoA filed protests against Porsche AG with the California and Nevada Departments of Motor Vehicles.

By April 1984, Mr. Schultz had to decide whether or not to proceed with his original plan or some variation. He was fully aware of the fact that the August 31 date for renewing the distribution contract with VWoA was quickly approaching.

QUESTIONS

1. How would you characterize the relationship between VWoA and Porsche AG in terms of marketing channel leadership, power, and conflict?
2. How do you think present and potential Porsche customers will react to the plan envisioned by Mr. Schultz? How will Porsche-Audi dealers react?
3. Would you favor the plan Mr. Schultz has outlined? Why or why not?

Positioning Wright State University

CASE 15

Positioning Wright State University

Background Information

In 1967, with five thousand students, Wright State University emerged from the status of a branch campus of Ohio State University and Miami University to become Ohio's twelfth state-assisted university. By 1989 it had grown to an enrollment of nearly 18,000 and was fully accredited, offering more than a hundred undergraduate majors, twenty-seven master's degree programs, and programs of study for the MD, Psy.D., Ed.S., and Ph.D. degrees, as well as a variety of certification programs.

The university is located in metropolitan Dayton, Ohio, an area that contains approximately one million people. It is situated in a very attractive suburban location. And, although physically distant (eight miles) from the hustle and bustle of downtown Dayton, it is exceptionally accessible from all parts of the region, being located adjacent to a major beltway. It even has its own beltway access ramps that literally dump drivers onto its beautifully wooded, 600-plus acre campus.

As a state-assisted university, Wright State has always maintained an open admissions policy and is committed to enrolling both outstanding traditional and nontraditional students, as well as those bound by place, time, economic, or other personal constraints. Most Wright State Students (12,000 undergraduate and 6,000 graduate) are commuters, with about 96 per cent traveling regularly to campus for classes. Ninety-six per cent of the students are from the four contiguous counties that contain the Dayton, Ohio, metropolitan area. About one-third of the university's classes are taught at night.

This case was prepared by Paula M. Saunders and Herbert E. Brown, Wright State University, Dayton, Ohio, and Roger W. Brucker, Odiorne Industrial Advertising, and is intended to be used as a basis for class discussion, rather than to illustrate either the effective or ineffective handling of the situation.

In 1987 WSU constructed some exceptionally attractive, on-campus housing for approximately 1,200 students. This is located in a wooded area only a few hundred yards from classroom buildings. Quasi-university housing—controlled to a degree by the university and contiguous to the university—has been provided in ample supply by private builders. The campus has sororities, fraternities, and a large variety of clubs available to students who desire to join them. The university also has a very active student government for students to get involved in, as well as a student-run radio station and newspaper. A large university center provides a variety of recreational activities, ranging from swimming to handball and the like. In the very best sense of the word, Wright State is a "complete" university.

The university's physical facilities are excellent. It has a new 12,000-seat, all-purpose stadium under construction. It can boast of major, and new, buildings for its college of business, its medical school, and its college of science and mathematics, as well as major additions to what was already one of the most modern libraries in the nation. All of the university's major facilities are linked together by miles of spacious, well-lighted tunnels, making interbuilding travel very easy, whatever the weather, and also making the campus extremely attractive to handicapped students.

The university's overall sports program is judged by most to be respectable and rapidly improving. It won a Division II national basketball championship in the middle 1980s, moved up to Division I in 1988, and has bright prospects for success at this level. Football has been discussed, but given current thinking and resources, prospects for adding this sport are slim. All of the other intercollegiate sports, such as baseball, soccer, swimming and the like are well established—for both men and women.

Economic Environment

The Dayton metro area is very prosperous, having had, for several years, the lowest unemployment rate in the state of Ohio, and one of the lowest of any region in the nation. This is due in large measure to the area's rapid conversion, in the late 1970s and early 1980s, to high technology-oriented industry, as employment shrank in basic manufacturing industries—cash registers, automobiles, etc. The conversion was so dramatic that, by 1989, it was thought that the Dayton, Columbus, Cincinnati triangle, linked together by I-70, I-71, and I-75, has as much "hi-tech" activity as such areas as the Silicon Valley in California and the Route 128 area in Massachusetts. A regional group, called Challenge 95, is, in fact, preparing a program to market the region as an ideal location for new and growing high-tech firms.

The Competition: Other Area Colleges and Universities

The Dayton area can boast of seventeen other colleges and universities. This set includes the University of Dayton, an established, 6,000-student, parochial university that was solidly entrenched in the Dayton community long before Wright State came to town. Many of its graduates are established leaders in the community and are known to "look to it first" for consultants, for new hires, to make donations, and the like. Sinclair Community College, a 23,000-student institution, located in downtown Dayton, was also well established long before Wright State, and is recognized as doing an excellent job in its two-year associate degree granting role. It also serves as a feeder to Wright State and other four-year institutions in the area and elsewhere.

Wright State also "competes" for the Dayton area's top students with several large, nearby institutions such as Miami University—a highly respected state-assisted school long known for its academic excellence; Ohio State—the flagship of the Ohio system; the University of Cincinnati (all of which are about sixty miles away); and other, more distant schools. The group of suppliers to the area's education market also includes smaller, but well-established institutions such as Wittenberg University—a highly respected liberal arts institution; Antioch College—an institution with a very rich history dating back to Horace Mann; Cedarville College—a Baptist-affiliated institution; and Wilmington College—a Quaker-affiliated institution.

The Air Force Institute of Technology (AFIT), located literally across the street from Wright State, on Wright-Patterson Air Force Base, offers Ph.D. degrees in several engineering areas, as well as master's degrees in logistics management, to highly select students from throughout the U.S. armed services and to armed services personnel from other countries, as well. These programs are not available to the general public, but they unquestionably add to the educational "climate" of the area. Wright Research and Development Center, a government-operated, two-billion-dollar-a-year R&D organization located at Wright-Patterson, also adds to the intellectual climate of the Wright State area.

The Need for a Marketing Communications Plan

Wright State has not been suffering from an enrollment problem. In fact, the fall of 1989 saw Wright State's enrollment continue to grow—at a 3 per cent annual rate. Consequently, the attention of most administrative people has been focused not on enrollment growth, but on solving such growth-related problems as closed classes—the most frequently heard student complaint—and such other matters as recruiting and keeping qualified faculty and getting additional funding to support the educational and support-service demands of its ever-growing student population.

Within this growth scenario, the university's relatively new and visionary administration has managed to forge ahead and complete a long-term strategic plan for the university. A central pillar of the strategic plan is that the university would become an eminent metropolitan university. To this end, the university plans, among other things, to target selective instructional, research, and professional programs for distinction, to establish a coordinated and integrated program of outreach, to assume an active role in the economic development of southwestern Ohio, and to develop a stronger shared "sense of community" among faculty, staff, students, and alumni.

The "metropolitan university" that was referred to in the strategic plan was not well defined. However, the following definition seemed to capture its essence as the university administration understood it:

The metropolitan university has in common with all quality universities a central focus on the creation and dissemination of knowledge. It, like other quality universities, is also dedicated to excellence in teaching, to excellence in science (creation of new knowledge—from accountancy to zoology), and also to excellence in technology (application of science—from accountancy to zoology to real problems).

Critical to the metropolitan university concept is increased sensitivity and proactive responsiveness to the science and technology requirements of the region the university serves.

A metropolitan university is a major source of applied research, technology transfer, policy analysis, and other professional services to meet the manifold knowledge needs of its service area. A metropolitan university is identified with vision and dedication to change for better. It finds out what works and does more of it. It finds out what doesn't work and does less of it. It is fiercely pragmatic, strongly pluralistic, and dedicated to the community in every positive way.

However difficult it was to define, the metropolitan university concept being pushed by the university administration made clear that the administration did not plan for the university to emulate either the big "flagship" universities such as Ohio State or Indiana, or the "Ivy League" schools such as Princeton or Yale. It was also obvious, from the strategic plan, from the administration's touting of the metropolitan university concept, as well as from the existing reality at Wright State, that the liberal arts college or university was not an appropriate model for Wright State to follow in its pursuit of excellence. A new model was needed.

The Ad Hoc Marketing Communications Committee

The university's strategic plan also included a provision for developing a marketing communications plan. To this end, an ad hoc committee on marketing communications was formed. This committee was chaired by a marketing department faculty member. Other members of the committee included representatives from university communications, foundation and development, alumni affairs, government relations, admissions, faculty, students, and the business community. The faculty and student components of the committee varied from meeting to meeting.

The marketing communications committee met biweekly for nearly six months. During this time it worked to assemble information on the internal and external aspects of the university that seemed important to an understanding of Wright State's current market position and to develop a positioning concept for the university. The committee decided to perform its work in two major phases. It would first develop and recommend a positioning strategy to the president and the university's board of trustees. Only after a concept that had won the support of these leaders was found would the committee go to the second phase of its work: the preparation of the communications tools and programs needed to create the desired position for the university. Ultimately, all of this was to be pulled together in a written plan.

Facts Developed by the Committee

The written plan that was ultimately submitted to the president included the following positive facts about Wright State University.

1. WSU has a safe, accessible, and very comfortable physical plant—the tunnel system is a very positive aspect to many people.
2. WSU has a high-quality, caring, and student-oriented faculty and staff.
3. WSU has selected programs whose excellence attracts students from all over the country.
4. Selected WSU programs are excellent, e.g., theater, engineering, accounting, and urban studies, and the number of such programs is growing.
5. WSU has selected faculty with national, even international, reputations. The number of faculty in this category continues to grow.

6. WSU has an innovative campuswide writing-improvement program in place.
7. WSU has new, state of the art mathematics and statistics labs that are accessible to all students.
8. Access to PCs, mainframe computers, desktop publishing, and the like is greater at WSU than at any other university in the region.
9. WSU has a newly implemented, and strong, common curriculum in place.
10. An excellent "factual," philosophical, theoretical, critical thinking education is available at WSU.
11. A large percentage of WSU's student body could compete anywhere.
12. WSU students have a strong work ethic.
13. A large percentage of WSU students hold full- or part-time jobs, in addition to carrying a full academic load.
14. Students feel accepted at WSU—feel like real people.
15. Academic standards are as high at WSU as they are at most other institutions in the Midwest.
16. WSU's athletic program is comparable to most collegiate programs in the country, and superior to many, and is set for dramatic improvement with the opening of the Nutter Center—a large new sports and entertainment complex. "Academic institutions are known by the athletic company they keep," and WSU will be keeping good company.
17. WSU has a diverse student body, with students from all over the nation and the world in residence.
18. When an objective comparison is made, WSU has a very good "campus" life, as compared to other colleges and universities in the region.
19. WSU has a variety of programs designed to attract and hold minority students.
20. WSU has many, and very notable, examples of academic all-stars. However, these have not received very much recognition.
21. WSU alumni feel they received a very good education at WSU, even though most do not have the strong emotional ties to the university that alumni traditionally have.
22. WSU's on-campus child-care center is among the best in the country. It's gifted-children's program and research are nationally recognized.
23. Approximately two thousand WSU students live on or very near campus. This number is larger than the student body of most liberal arts college campuses and surpasses the critical mass experts say is needed for a university to offer its students a "true" campus life.
24. WSU currently offers the internal and external community a solid combination of cultural events—concerts, theater, lectures, etc.
25. WSU is located in the "Golden Triangle" of Dayton, Columbus, and Cincinnati, which contains all of the major elements of a "cosmopolitan environment."
26. WSU is located in the "Golden Triangle" of Dayton, Columbus, and Cincinnati, which is becoming a mecca for high-technology companies. Wright Research and Development Center at Wright-Patterson Air Force Base (with a research budget in excess of two billion dollars annually) is the "crown jewel" in this Golden Triangle. The area is being promoted as another Route 128 or Silicon Valley.
27. WSU students are consistently accepted and excel in the best, most visible graduate schools in the country.
28. Top-achieving WSU alumni are increasingly in evidence.

Given the above statements of fact, the committee concluded that WSU was already an excellent, and consistently improving, academic institution. However, the committee also discovered facts that strongly suggested that the university's image had not caught up with reality. For example, it was determined that the most common reaction from visitors to the Wright State campus was that WSU was the best-kept secret in Ohio. The committee also found that the information people thought they "knew" about Wright State was often either incomplete or inaccurate. The following *perceptions* (or misperceptions in the committee's view) of the university were held to a significant degree by all of Wright State's various audiences (current students, prospective students, alumni, potential donors, etc.):

1. Educational programming at WSU is rather basic, routine, and bland. There is nothing unusual to be experienced there. It is a generic school with no real character. It has a few "enclaves of excellence," but these are the exception, not the norm.
2. WSU offers its students too little "campus life." It offers a good "factual-philosophical-theoretical education," but not a true "college experience." It does not educate the "whole person." The school has no friendly student "ghetto," *à la* the University of Dayton. Many students remain anonymous in a crowd of commuters.
3. Wright State is a fast-growing, affordable, commuter, part-time, and night-time school where the "first generation," the economically strapped, and the place-bound go to college. (It recognized, however, that many Wright State students are place-bound by choice; they don't want to leave home.)
4. Wright State is the choice of students who haven't worked hard in high school. It is an extension of high school and a four-year version of Sinclair Community College. It is the last-resort college for the academically deficient. Students dream of going elsewhere, then come to WSU.
5. Typical Wright State students are less talented than students at other, more mature schools, such as Miami, Bowling Green, and OSU.
6. WSU is a young and immature University that is both literally and figuratively distant from Dayton.
7. WSU is not a significant participant in the life of the community, as compared, for example, with the University of Dayton.
8. Black students see WSU as being run for white students only—as a place where they will be uncomfortable.
9. Scheduling and advising services are not designed with students in mind. The university is not concerned about closed classes and the like.
10. "Bureaucracy-of-going-to-school" problems such as admissions, financial aid, registration, fee payment, drop dates, etc., are a major frustration for students, and neither faculty nor staff have a truly "problem-solving" attitude toward students who are having problems with the system.
11. The university does not have a shared sense of its mission—e.g., whether it is a teaching institution, a research institution, both, or what.
12. Wright State's campus is not a friendly one. It lacks the trappings of friendliness—signs, etc.
13. Wright State is primarily for handicapped students.
14. Most classes at WSU are taught by foreign teachers.
15. WSU's athletics are better than its academics.

There is, of course, some truth in all of the above described negative perceptions. However, when the committee combined the positive perceptions and the negative perceptions with objective reality, the major conclusion they drew was not that WSU had a negative image, but rather that it had a *diffuse* and *unclear* image. This, in turn, had led to significant audience indifference toward, and often, dismissal of, the institution. There were several important implications of this indifference and dismissal by the university's major stakeholders. Among the most important of these implications are

1. a tendency for the area's highest potential high school students to dismiss Wright State as an option in the sincere, but flawed, belief that they will get a better education elsewhere,

2. a tendency for many of Wright State's top students to leave after doing much of their work at WSU to graduate from a school with a better, or at least a different, reputation—producing a retention problem,

3. a tendency of both students and faculty to discount the ability of the Wright State student—leading to a poor self-image for both the faculty member and the student,

4. a business community tendency to overlook Wright State as a major resource in many areas when, in fact, it could be an extremely valuable resource, and finally,

5. a failure of the university to get the approbation and support that it needs from its many stakeholders to become the eminent university that it desires to be.

The committee decided that a solid, new positioning concept and implementation program were needed to deal with these problems.

Qualitative Description of Wright State Students

After examining the available information, the committee concluded several things about Wright State's current student body. Most WSU students are commuters. Most are first-generation college students, and most are economically strapped to some extent. Despite these characteristics, the committee also found that typical WSU students have talent, ability, and high (in fact, unlimited) potential— though many do not have outstanding (high school) records. Employers agree that WSU students are willing to work harder than students from other area schools. Most are holding down jobs, even full-time jobs, while still in school. As a group, they are determined to be very reality-based, committed to achievement, and excited about growth—both personal and professional. And, despite the fact that many students are juggling demands of jobs and families, the committee found that a large number of Wright State students have managed to do exceptional things and become nothing less than academic all-stars. The committee also found that the university can boast of a host of illustrious alumni. Included among these are acclaimed professors, college presidents, Wall Street whiz kids, and presidents of large businesses. Wright State students are also prone to start their own businesses. "Serious and talented, unlimited potential" students is the way one very successful Wright State professor described his students, many of whom were *sans* outstanding high school records, but who blossomed under his tutelage.

The committee determined that though the university needed to be much more so, WSU has been responsive to the needs of its type of student, offering them access to the kinds of real-world educational opportunities that prepare them for the challenges of the future. The educational opportunities offered include not only access to the content material of a good education, but also access to opportunities to develop critical thinking and communication skills students would need for success in the 1990s, and beyond.

Other Data Collected by the Committee

Other data collected by the committee include national enrollment statistics. Pertinent among these is the fact that public colleges and universities, which account for 77 percent of all undergraduate enrollments, peaked in 1983 at 6.3 million—nineteen years after the end of the baby boom in 1964. By 1987 enrollments had declined 3 percent, to 6.1 million. Projections of undergraduate enrollment in public colleges and universities show an additional 3.2 percent drop from 1987 to 1995, with enrollments falling below 5.9 million. Four-year institutions are forecast to lose 3.1 per cent of their estimated 1987 enrollments, while two-year institutions are projected to lose 3.4 per cent. (About six in ten undergraduates in public institutions attend four-year schools.) On the positive side, college enrollments are forecast to begin to cover some lost ground in 1996 and 1997, nineteen years after the end of the "baby bust"—a twelve-year period of declining births ending in 1976. (Source: Thomas Exeter, "Demographics Forecast: Sliding College Enrollment," *American Demographics,* vol. 11, no. 9, 1989, p. 71.)

QUESTIONS

1. Compare and contrast market segmentation, product positioning, and product differentiation as frameworks for understanding the communications task that appears to confront the ad hoc marketing/communications committee.
2. What are the rules of positioning that Wright State's ad hoc communications committee should follow as it constructs the university's positioning strategy?
3. Given the facts of the case and the rules of positioning, what is the most viable positioning for WSU?
4. Suggest ways a university could accomplish the positioning you have chosen for it to establish for itself.

PART FIVE

Organizing and Planning Tactical Marketing Activities

Until you implement marketing tactics, nothing gets done. In fact, even the most brilliant marketing strategy can fail if the tactics designed to support it are incorrectly conceived or executed. This section not only shows you the correct application of marketing tactics, but their integrated use for maximum effectiveness. Chapter 16, "Product and Service Tactics," introduces the concept of the product or service as a tactic, as opposed to a strategy alternative. You may be surprised to learn that introduction and modification are not your only options. Chapter 17, "Pricing Tactics," gives you an array of tactical techniques that, when used with other tactics, will help make your marketing strategy successful. In Chapter 18, "Channel and Distribution Tactics," you will learn when and what channels of distribution to use, as well as how to distribute through these channels. The advertising and publicity tactics analyzed in Chapter 19 have helped to make millions of dollars for those who have used them correctly. How to do this is fully explained. You may have thought that sales promotion tactics were reserved for certain specialized classes of products. Chapter 20, "Sales Promotion Tactics," shows you how some innovators are exploding that myth. Chapter 21, "Sales Management Tactics," will show you how to apply one of the most powerful tactics in your inventory. Finally, you are shown the cutting edge of your campaign in Chapter 22, "Implementation." This is the payoff.

Product and
Service Tactics

16

Color-Coded Food

In the future your refrigerated food may be color coded, courtesy of a new product from Reynolds Metal Company. Not so long ago, the gigantic conglomerate rolled out a new line of colored plastic food wrap in transparent shades of red, yellow, and blue. Their market research showed that women appreciated the product and were willing to buy it. The buyers for supermarkets are mostly men, however, and some didn't see the value at first. However, Reynolds hit on the idea of sending samples to the buyers' homes. The tactic worked. The male buyers noticed their wives' positive reactions. This convinced them that the product would sell. Ten weeks after introduction, colored Reynolds plastic wraps were in stores in 75 per cent of the country, and sales exceeded Reynolds' expectations. Although Reynolds' main business is making the aluminum used in cans and buildings—to the tune of $5.6 billion a year—it has built a nice $.5 billion sideline in products used to wrap today's foodstuffs, of which this new product is a part. President William O. Bourke made clear his vision for the firm: "We want to own that aisle in the supermarket."[1]

Nabisco's Hand Is in the Cookie Jar

The retail cookie market represents a $2.2 billion market. That's no small potatoes for Nabisco, which for years was the unchallenged champion of cookies. Then Procter & Gamble and Frito-Lay both entered with big guns and forced Nabisco Brands, Inc., to retreat. Frito-Lay introduced Grandma's Cookies, and P&G the Duncan Hines brand, both tasting as if they were made at home. Nabisco counterattacked with a fifteen-variety line, its own almost-like-homemade cookie called "Almost Home." It was the biggest cookie project by Nabisco in years, and it billed the product as "the moistest, chewiest, most perfectly baked cookies the world has ever tasted . . . well, almost." A Nabisco company sales representative said, "Nabisco's new cookie line was one of the best-kept secrets I've ever seen." Salesman didn't learn of the project until the last minute, when they were told to cancel any vacation plans and come to special meetings. Indications are that not only was the competition caught off guard, but that Nabisco Brands, Inc., has recaptured previously lost ground.[2]

They Lost at Monopoly, But Won at Trivial Pursuit

Back during the Great Depression, the creators of a little game called Monopoly attempted to sell the rights to the Selchow and Righter Company. But Selchow and Righter thought it was too risky during the Depression, and that the use of play money in the game could be perceived as encouraging gambling. As a result, Parker Brothers bought the game, and it went on to become the hottest-selling board game in history.

History sometimes repeats itself. Came the 1980s and Trivial Pursuit was offered to several game companies, among them Parker Brothers. Parker Brothers turned the game down. But this time, it was Selchow and Righter, a $40 million company, which in the past had produced mainly the games of Scrabble and Parcheesi, that bought the game. In the first year of marketing Trivial Pursuit, sales increased by a factor of 10 to $400 million. And that was only the first year. The second year, sales exceeded $700 million, with more games sold than any other board game, including Monopoly.[3]

Consumers Love Products, But Hate Services

Most experts agree that we are headed for a services-oriented society. If so, marketing managers really have their work cut out for them. Recently the Conference Board surveyed six thousand families. Each was asked to rate the value they received from thirty-eight major products and services. Nine out of the top ten receiving the highest "poor" ratings had to do with services. The services receiving those ratings included those from hospitals, attorneys, movie theaters, credit cards, banks, cable TV, health insurance, physicians, and the post office.[4] But as astute marketers, you probably recognize immediately that these results represent major opportunities for companies or nonprofit organizations that can satisfy customer needs and wants and change the perception of value received. In this chapter we are going to see how we can do this.

Product and service are variables we can control, not only to increase sales in an absolute sense, but to support major strategic objectives decided on at a higher level in the company. Tactical product/service decision making affects product differentiation, market segmentation, positioning, other marketing strategies, and ultimately strategic marketing management, as well.

The Product and Service Concept _____

A Product Is More Than a Tangible Object

The concept of a product includes more than simply flesh and bone or something that has weight and occupies space. A service can also be a product, such as the service performed by a doctor, an accountant, or a consultant. In fact, it is performance that distinguishes between the two. Goods businesses sell things. Service businesses sell performances.[5] And risk of not attaining the service performances advertised are perceived to be riskier than not attaining goods performances advertised by consumers.[6] But even considering this fact, the marketing of either a product or a service requires expanding the definition and concept of both considerably. Increasing the number of hours of operation of a bank or doctor's office changes the service. Physical products have accompanying service dimensions that make or break current and future sales. Maintenance service on a new automobile is an example.

In Los Angeles there is a company called Frieda's Finest that sells exotic foods. Currently, it sells about two hundred items from all over the world. Frieda Caplan, who founded this business, knows the product is not simply the exotic food itself. Frieda enhances the product with recipes and preparation instructions in every package. This not only expands the use of that food, but also creates a unique product that offers greater value than would otherwise be the case.[7] Over the years, the brand name "Frieda's Finest" has itself acquired value, and this is why even the brand name is considered part of the product.

A study of ethical drugs confirmed this not so long ago. Patents in the United States are good for only seventeen years, after which they go into the public domain, when the item can be produced by anyone. The interesting fact learned from the study was that many ethical (or proprietary) drugs maintain a dominant position in the market even after the patent expires. Furthermore, this dominant position could not be attributed to price, quality, or cost factors. Clearly, the brand name itself had acquired some important value to the consumer. Want an example? The patent for Listerine mouthwash expired more than a half-century ago.[8]

The brand name is associated with a certain product, and the consumer can react violently at any attempt at change. This was probably why the reaction was so strong when Coca-Cola made the decision to change the ninety-nine-year-old formula of Coke for New Coke. Market research showed that in blind tests, the public clearly preferred the taste of New Coke over old Coke and leading competitive brands. Yet, when Coca-Cola implemented the results of this research by changing the formula, the consumer public rebelled. Coca-Cola was eventually forced to reintroduce the old formula under the new name, Classic Coke. This illustrates that the product and the brand name are one and, moreover, that the product was not simply the taste, but the entire concept. Thus, to some extent, at least in the United States, changing the formula of Coke was like changing the concept of motherhood or apple pie. It just isn't done, and if it is, you no longer have the same brand.[9]

The Importance of Product Quality

High product quality has been found to be an important attribute of a product, and its effects can positively increase marketing results. We've talked about PIMS previously. Some important findings of PIMS research, which have to do with product quality, include the following:

1. Product quality is an important determinant of business profitability.
2. Product quality and market share are positively related.
3. Quality is positively and significantly related to ROI for almost all kinds of products and market situations.
4. High-quality producers usually charge premium prices.[10]

There is a cost to pay for product quality in terms of reduced short-run profitability. This is because consumers attach a value to product quality, as they do with any other attribute. Thus, for a given price and bundle of product attributes, quality could come at a cost to the consumer of a reduction of one or more of the other attributes. For example, we could furnish higher quality, but reduce performance. To provide high quality in this sense, we must increase quality without increasing price. It is in these terms that high quality has a positive effect on ROI.[11] The potential benefits versus costs of high quality are conceptualized in Figure 16-1.

The opportunities to increase product quality are almost unlimited. Eight different opportunities, or dimensions, of product quality are shown in Figure 16-2. Each dimension represents another opportunity to increase product quality and build a competitive advantage over competitors.[12]

One cautionary note is needed here, however. Inconsistencies in expectations and experiences can and do have an adverse effect on the evaluation of quality in service performance. That is, if a buyer has high expectations of quality, and only moderate quality is provided in actual performance, you may have problems.[13] The same thing has been observed in products sold

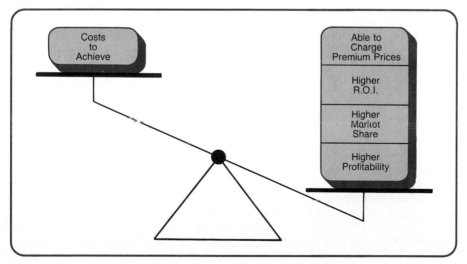

Figure 16-1   Product Quality: Costs vs. Potential Benefits

- Performance (primary product characteristics)
- Features ("bells and whistles")
- Reliability (frequency of failure)
- Conformance (match with specifications)
- Durability (product life)
- Serviceability (speed of repair)
- Aesthetics ("fits and finishes")
- Perceived quality (reputation and intangibles)

From David A. Garvin, "Product Quality: An Important Strategic Weapon," *Business Horizons*, vol. 27 (May–June 1984), p. 42. Used with permission.

Figure 16-2   Dimensions of Product Quality

through the mail. When the difference in quality between what was expected and what was received differs significantly, products are much more likely to be returned. Because mail-order business is heavily dependent on repeat sales, inconsistencies between expectancies and experiences can be deadly.[14]

The Definition of a Product

We are now in a position to define what we mean by product. A product is a set of tangible and intangible attributes assembled to satisfy the needs and wants of a potential buyer.

Note again that this definition of a product not only includes a physical object, but other attributes furnished with that product, including brand name, product name, quality, service, and other peripheral elements.

The importance of the product to the buyer can be classified in two categories.[15] **Instrumental importance** is temporary, based on the consumer's desire to obtain particular extrinsic goals deriving from the product's purchase or use. **Enduring importance** is long-term, based on the strength of the product's relationships to central needs and values. These two categories of importance are examined separately because alternate tactical decisions can be made depending upon the class into which a product falls. If a product is of enduring importance, a rejuvenation policy is generally more appropriate than discontinuance. On the other hand, products of the type that primarily have high instrumental importance around the time of purchase can be more advantageously introduced and discontinued frequently.

To contrast the two, consider a collector of antique cars. A magazine catering to such a collector would rarely be discontinued because of an enduring need for this type of product. Rather, the product would be rejuvenated, using techniques similar to those described earlier in extending the product life cycle. On the other hand, the purchaser of a motor vehicle in itself is probably choosing a product that has primarily instrumental importance. For such a product, new models may be introduced and the old ones discontinued every year.[16] In all cases, we are talking about satisfying the cus-

Table 16-1 Customer Satisfaction with Intangible Products

Service Industry	Outcome Sought by Buyer	Tactical Possibilities	Strategic Possibilities
Higher education	Educational attainment	Help professors to be effective teachers; offer tutoring	Admit better-prepared students (or provide the better preparation before entry, for a fee)
Hospitals	Health	Instruct patients in managing their current problem and preventing others	Market preventive medical services (weight loss, stress reduction etc.)
Banks	Prosperity	Offer money-management courses, management assistance to small business	Market expertise as well as money, probably by industry specialization
Plumbing repair	Free-flowing pipes	Provide instructions and supplies for the consumer to prevent further clogs	Diversify

Source: Adapted from Betsy D. Gelb, "How Marketers of Intangibles Can Raise the Odds for Consumer Satisfaction," *Journal of Services Marketing*, vol. 1, no. 1 (Summer 1987), p. 15.

tomer. There are many approaches to satisfying the customer, whether we are speaking of a tangible or an intangible product. Table 16-1 shows some examples of customer satisfaction with intangible products.[17]

Can the Marketing Concept Be Wrong?

The marketing concept emphasizes the customer, not the product, and states that marketers can have their greatest impact in satisfying a customer's needs, rather than first developing a product without research, and then attempting to sell it to the customer. However, in recent years, the marketing concept has come under attack in that such a focus on the customer and what the customer wants results only in minor improvements in a product without any major breakthroughs.[18] In fact, it has been claimed that strict adherence to the marketing concept has actually damaged American business.[19]

In an attempt to reconcile the fact of success through the marketing concept in satisfying the customer with the reality that significant breakthrough in new development and products can probably only come when initiated by the producer, David Gobeli of Oregon State University conceptualized a marketing concept matrix with three different themes, simulating the introduction of a new product. The themes are (1) opportunity driven, (2) market driven, and (3) competition driven, as shown in Figure 16-3, along with their orientation, market research approach, and market strategy pattern.[20]

The differences between product importance and the theme driving the introduction or development of a new product are situational. The selection

Theme	Opportunity driven	Market driven	Competition driven
Orientation			
Nature of consumer wants	Unknown	Known	Known
Markets	New	Expanded	Existing
Technology	New	Improved	Existing
Risk level	High	Moderate	Low
Market research approach			
Management involvement	High	Moderate	Low
Primary techniques	Qualitative	Quantitative	Quantitative
Researcher directives	Discover opportunities	Evaluate opportunities	Evaluate opportunities
Researcher background	Broad	Limited	Narrow
Marketing strategy pattern			
Functional synergy	High	Moderate	Low
Nature of products	Innovative	Competitive	Imitative
Role of products	Dominant	Equal	Subordinate
Role of marketing support	Subordinate	Equal	Dominant

Source: David Gobelli, "Recasting the Marketing Concept," in Patrick E. Murphy, et al., eds., *1983 AMA Educators' Proceedings* (Chicago: AMA, 1983), p. 320. Used with permission.

Figure 16-3   Marketing Concept Matrix

of alternative product decisions, product branding, or product packaging depends on the situation and the category of product importance, as well as on what is driving the introduction of the product into the marketplace.

Alternative Product Decisions

Product Processes

There are three actions, and three actions only, that you can take to change the situation of any product. You can introduce it, you can discontinue it, or you can rejuvenate it. Let's look at each of these actions in turn.

Product Introduction

Product introduction can be an important strategy, as discussed in Chapter 11. It can also be a tactical decision driven by any of the three categories of the marketing concept matrix, after overall strategy has been decided, and due to a changing marketing environment. For example, let's assume that our company has a new product development strategy that it has begun to implement. Suddenly our development is preempted by a competitor, who has introduced a similar product. We are now faced with a tactical decision: to introduce the new product or not to introduce it. A decision isn't made based on this one fact, of course, but after considering all other marketplace environs. A factor that novice marketing managers sometimes overlook is cannibalism—that is, the fact that the introduction of our new product, in addition to facing competition from a competitor, may compete with a product already in our product line. Those sales taken from our ongoing product are said to be cannibalized from it, and this factor, too, must be considered.[21] The decision at this point, however, is tactical and primarily in response to a competitor's actions.

Product Discontinuance

You may at first view product **discontinuance** as a negative act only, but it can have some important positive benefits to a firm. It may free up resources for more viable or profitable products. Furthermore, those resources may not only be in the form of money, but in the form of better use of marketing managers' and other managers' time. Product discontinuance may also produce a benefit such as reduction of inventory levels. As a bottom-line result, discontinuance can improve the product line and improve overall sales and profits.[22]

Many firms recognize the benefits of product discontinuance; as a result, 40 per cent of the firms surveyed in one study actually have formal programs to consider products that should be dropped.[23] Even so, having a formal program to consider this tactical alternative may not be required as long as the marketing manager does not forget it as an option.[24]

Failure to consider the possibility of discontinuance, even for a product that has been very profitable for a firm in the past, may lead to major problems and delays in the introduction of a replacement product. It should, therefore, be considered an ongoing option in the support of any overall marketing strategy. A summary of warning signals that indicate a product should be discontinued is given in Figure 16-4.[25]

- Absolute sales volume declining
- Sales volume declining as a percentage of total sales
- Market share declining
- Past sales volume not meeting projections
- Future sales projected lower than desired
- Future market potential outlook for class of products unfavorable
- Return on investment below minimum acceptable
- Variable costs exceeding revenues
- Costs as a per centage of sales consistently increasing
- More and more executive time and attention required
- Price must be constantly lowered to maintain sales
- Promotional budgets must be continually increased to maintain sales

Source: Adapted from Stanley H. Kratchman, Richard T. Hise, and Thomas A. Ulrick, "Management's Decision to Discontinue a Product," in Terry T. Ball, Robert W. Jefferson, Richard D. Nordstrom, and Paul C. Thistlethwaite, eds., *Marketing Readings* (Prospect Heights, Ill.: Waveland Press, 1979), p. 327.

Figure 16-4 Warning Signals That Product Discontinuance Should Be Considered

Product Rejuvenation

In many cases, a product that is in trouble need not be dropped, but may be rejuvenated. **Rejuvenation** is a viable tactical decision that can be extremely successful. Effective rejuvenation extends the product life-cycle curve, as was noted in Chapter 12.

The benefits of tactical decisions for rejuvenation of a product include the following:

- Being able to take advantage of customer goodwill and awareness that were associated with the product as it formerly existed
- Reducing the necessary promotional cost of introducing a new product because of consumer prior familiarization with the older product
- Reducing costs and time for new product development
- Reducing time and costs to obtain the cooperation and participation of trade channel members
- Reducing numerous associated and peripheral costs having to do with the product by capitalizing on past experience with the suppliers of equipment, raw materials, and components
- Being able to take full advantage of prior marketing and distribution experience with the product[26]

To take advantage of rejuvenation, there are four basic tactical alternatives that may be followed. These are indicated in Figure 16-5: recapture, redesign, refocus, and recast.[27]

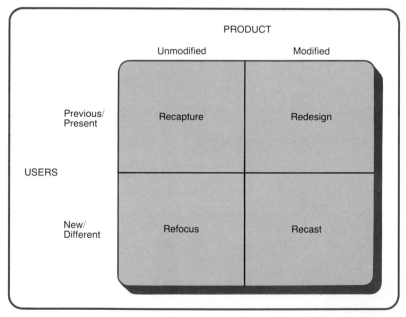

Figure 16-5   Four Tactical Alternatives in Implementing Rejuvenation

Source: Adapted from William Lazer, Mustaq Luqmani, and Zahir Quraeshi, "Product Rejuvenation Strategies," *Business Horizons*, vol. 27 (November-December, 1984), p. 22.

Recapture involves marketing an abandoned or declining product to previous or present users. Nonfiction books still in print can be repromoted, as can records or old radio recordings (Oldies But Goodies, Inc.). Redesign involves modifying a product, but selling it to the same or previous consumers. McDonnell-Douglas offered a stretched version of the Douglas DC-9 aircraft that permitted transportation of more passengers than the original model. Refocus involves an unmodified product, but offering it to new or different consumers. The tactical objective here is to focus on certain product characteristics that might be emphasized to classes and segments of consumers who have had little, if any, prior experience with the product, although they may be familiar with other aspects, such as the name. For years, Hewlett-Packard continued to sell its 3000 minicomputer, called obsolete by its many competitors because of its lack of power. But in 1985, Hewlett-Packard took the 14-year-old computer and packaged it as an integrator for PCs used in business. Thus, today, the Hewlett-Packard 3000 is the ultimate departmental computer, a low-cost machine that links personal computers used in the department with bigger machines used throughout the company. On the bottom line, whereas demand is shrinking for competitors of minicomputers, Hewlett-Packard expects to ship more than seven thousand units of this old model in its first twelve months of implementing this rejuvenation tactic.[28] Finally, we have recast, in which the product is modified and marketed to a new or different group of users. Thus, Sierra Engineering Company in California altered an earcup used in flyers' helmets it sold to the Air Force. By changing its color from Air Force gray to navy blue and adding some foam backing to allow it to fit better into a Navy helmet, it sold it to the U.S. Navy.

Product Branding

You may have heard of Sunkist oranges, Dole pineapples, and Chiquita bananas. All are branded fruits, and they command higher gross profit margins, 10 per cent to 60 per cent higher, than do generic produce. But oranges, pineapples, and bananas aren't the only fruits that can be branded. New breeding techniques and storage and package methods are enabling companies to introduce branded produce that tastes better and stays fresh a lot longer. One of the latest is Tom Ahtoes, developed by Natural Park Produce, Inc., whose current president, Jack M. Fox, branded Chiquita bananas while president of the United Fruit Company. As you may have guessed, Tom Ah toes sell for a bit more. Tom Ahtoes sell at about a dollar per pound, versus about 70 cents a pound for unbranded tomatoes.[29]

Why brand a product? Higher profit margins is only one reason. Another is image and identification. In fact, the brand name itself can help to position a product. You know that if a product carries a Rolls-Royce brand name, it is not basic transportation. On the other hand, if the brand name is "Volkswagen," that is exactly what you would expect. As a result, a product's brand has some important value as a part of the product. Research demonstrates that there is a positive and statistically significant relationship between brand name and perceived quality.[30] Studies have shown that when certain products

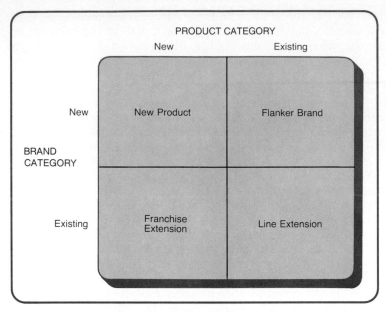

Figure 16-6   Four Branding Alternatives

Source: Adapted from Edward M. Tauber, "Brand Extension Franchise Extension: New
Product Benefits from Existing Brand Names," *Business Horizons*, vol. 24 (March-April,
1961), p. 37

are branded in such a way that they seem to imitate other already established
and successful products, the consumer assumes that this newer product has
similar or the same attributes.[31] It has also been shown that brands with a
larger share of users have a proportionately larger fraction of loyal buyers—
that is, buyers who return again and again.[32]

Brand Extension Versus Unique Brands

When a company introduces a new product, there are four possibilities regarding branding. These are illustrated in Figure 16-6. First, the company
can employ a new brand name with a new product or a new service in a
category completely new to the company. Second, the company can introduce a new brand, but in a category the firm is already marketing. This is
known as a **flanker brand**. Both the new product and the flanker brand are
unique brand strategies, but the company has two other options. A **line extension** represents use of the company's brand name in the firm's present
product category. A **franchise extension** takes the process one step farther.
A brand name that is familiar to the consumer is applied to products in a
category the firm is not presently marketing.[33]

Examples of a line extension would include a new get-well card in Hallmark's line of greeting cards, a new flavor for the Häagen-Dazs line of ice
cream, or a new kosher pickle for Vlasik's line of pickles. A franchise extension would be a Mr. Coffee brand of coffee, in that Mr. Coffee previously
was known to consumers as an appliance brand name. Or consider Ivory's
shampoo and conditioner, a franchise extension from Ivory soap.[34] Finally,

remember Dr Pepper, the soft drink? Amurol Products Company, a unit of the Wrigley Jr. Company of Chicago, has introduced Dr Pepper chewing gum that has a Dr Pepper soft drink flavor.[35]

The benefits of brand extension include the fact that the extension capitalizes on one of the company's most valuable assets. Thus, with the **good will**, brand name, awareness, and all other aspects and impressions that have been previously communicated by the brand, the company moves in with its new product from a position of strength. As a bonus, the expenses associated with attaining the brand-name recognition for the new brand are minimized—consumers are already familiar with the name. Also, further promotion of the brand name with the new product can lead to increased sales for the parent brand. Finally, there may be a reduced risk of failing with the new product when the brand name communicates the benefits of the new product that the company wishes to emphasize.[36]

But that's only one side of the story. Al Ries and Jack Trout have made a very strong case against brand extension in their book *Positioning: The Battle for Your Mind*. According to Ries and Trout, brand extension names are forgettable because they have no independent position in the mind. They point out that for a firm using a brand such as Cadillac to introduce an inexpensive car may cause a temporary increase in the sales of the new product, but it will ultimately damage the position and expensive image of other Cadillac automobiles.[37]

Accordingly, the use of a brand extension strategy, either with a franchise extension or a line extension, is dangerous if the extension between the new product and the old line is either too great—as with an "inexpensive" expensive-branded car—or there is little connection between the two. The connection between Mr. Coffee and the product coffee may be close enough, even though Mr. Coffee has been the brand name of an appliance. But how about Mr. Coffee greeting cards or Mr. Coffee automobiles? At the same time, the old product line may be hurt. In general, line extensions that are too great—either because of features, benefits, market segments, quality, distribution channels, or price differing greatly from the current line—argue for separate branding. A recent study shows that there may also be problems if the extension is too easy to make—for example, if the consumer perceives the extension as a blatant attempt to capitalize on a brand image to command higher than justified prices.[38]

Private Branding

Another decision the marketing manager must sometimes make is whether to agree to **private branding**—that is placing a distributor's brand, or some other company's brand name, on a product the marketing manager's company manufactures. Some very large distributors with lucrative orders may require their branding on a product your company manufactures. Products manufactured by a variety of different companies bear the brand name "Sears." It is especially tempting for a small company to agree to this. However, there is some danger.

First, if the private brand under which the product is labeled takes all or a large part of your production, you are in a situation of having all of your eggs in one basket. Should this firm suddenly decide to go elsewhere to produce the item, or to produce itself, not only have you lost considerable sales, but your product has been marketed to the public under a different brand name. Thus, all the promotion and advertising used to promote the product and gain public awareness and acceptance of it are attached to the brand and not to your product. If you now decide to market direct to the consumer, or to go to other channels, you do not have the advantage of brand awareness, even though your product may be bought in the millions.

In reality, there are only three tactical alternatives that can be taken regarding private branding. A firm can produce only private branding under the distributor's name. A firm can produce a brand only under its own name. Or a firm can follow a policy of private branding mixed with its own brand. The decision as to which tactical alternative to take is made by considering the following:

1. Risk in nonrecognition by consumers and a possible sudden loss in sales if the distributor stops selling the product
2. Potential gains in production by being able to sell more of a product
3. Additional intelligence information and feedback from distributors distributing under their private brand, which would not otherwise be available
4. Information from the distributors on their operations and how they reach and market to the consumer that might not otherwise be available

Naming the Brand

Picking a brand or product name is not an insignificant activity. In fact, there are consulting companies that do nothing but develop brand names for new products. Whether we are talking about products called Cheerios or Hush Puppies or a service known as Next Day Air, brand name can be an important tactic. Some criteria used in this brand-name selection from a survey of eighty-two firms are shown in Figure 16-7. From this survey, the major cri-

Criteria	Number Using	Percentage
Descriptive of product benefits	48	₃8.5%
Memorable	38	46.3
Fit with company image and other products image	38	46.3
Trademark availability	28	34.1
Promotable and advertisable	18	22.0
Uniqueness vs. competition	18	22.0
Length	13	15.9
Ease of pronunciation	12	14.6
Positive connotations to potential users	11	13.4
Suited to package	5	6.1
Modern or contemporary	3	3.7
Understandable	2	2.4
Persuasive	2	2.4

Source: Adapted from James U. McNeal and Linda M. Zeren, "Brand Selection for Consumer Products," *MSU Business Topics* (Spring 1981), p. 37.

Figure 16-7   Criteria Used in Brand Name Selection in 82 Firms

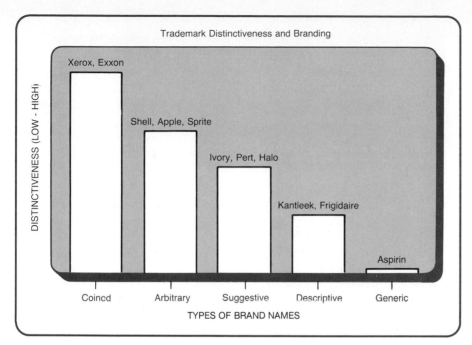

Figure 16-8   Trademark Distinctiveness and Branding

Source: Ronald F. Bush, Peter H. Bloch, and Claude F. Reynaud, "The Brand Trademark; A Valuable and Vulnerable Resource," in Russell W. Belk, et al., eds. *1984 AMA Educator Proceedings.* Used with permission.

terion used as a guide to naming the brand was a description of product benefits.[39]

Because brand names can be so valuable, companies are very careful to protect their brand name through the use of a **trademark**, which is legally registered to protect the company's ownership. However, simple registration doesn't in itself protect. A company must actually use the trademark, and it must police the market to ensure that the trademark of the brand name doesn't become generic. This is what happened with aspirin. At one time, aspirin was a unique name for a single product manufactured by the Bayer Company. As soon as individuals began spelling the word "aspirin" with a small "a," it became generic and Bayer lost control of the name. This is why corporate attorneys are kept busy when the publication of "Coke" with a small "c" is used to stand for Coca-Cola, or "xerox" is used as a verb meaning to photocopy.[40]

Distinctiveness has been found to be one of the major factors for maintaining control over a brand name through trademarking. As you can see from Figure 16-8, the most distinctive terms are those that are coined, such as Exxon and Xerox, followed by arbitrary, suggestive, and then descriptive names. With generic names, of course, control has already been lost.[41] To maintain control over brand names through trademarking, the seven rules contained in Figure 16-9 are recommended.[42]

Some firms find that their brand names are so sought after they can license their names to other companies. This generates additional income in royalties, as well as increased promotional exposure. For this reason, you may see

1. Distinguish from other words in print, even if only by capitalization.
2. Place trademark notice after the mark whenever possible.
3. Always use the trademark with the generic name.
4. Never use trademarks in the possessive form.
5. Always use the trademark in the singular.
6. Never use a trademark as a verb or a common adjective.
7. Identify ownership of the trademark by use of the company name.

Source: Adapted from Ellen M. Kleinberg, "Trademarks: The Care and Feeding of Brand Name Identities," *Industrial Marketing* (October 1980), p. 62.

Figure 16-9 Seven Rules to Maintain Control of Brand Names Through a Trademark

the famous Coca-Cola and Kellogg brands on everything from t-shirts to toys and "yuppie" telephones.

We've mostly talked about consumer product branding. Do organizational products use brand strategy? They certainly do. In fact, some companies sell to both the consumer and organization markets using the same basic product, but with different brand names and packaging. We'll see some additional examples of how this is done when we examine channel and distribution tactics in a later chapter.

Product Packaging

Packaging can be a major key to product success. Beechnut is hardly in the number one position in baby food, with Gerber holding 70 per cent of the market. But Beechnut doubled its sales in only five years, not from a technological breakthrough, but rather by new packaging in a product called Stages. Stages' products are color coded to correspond to different phases of an infant's development. That packaging is new and different, and of added value to the consumer.[43]

Packaging is more important than ever, with more than five thousand new items on grocery shelves every year. How can consumers tell the difference? Well, consumers do notice. In 1958 the R. J. Reynolds Tobacco Company simply removed a picture of a pyramid from its Camel cigarette pack. Sales plummeted and, according to the consumer, the cigarette no longer tasted the same. For this reason, packaging expert Saul Bass claims that packaging is the product.[44] When Borden Ice Cream can increase its brand identification by 400 per cent instantly by simply redesigning a container (which it did), it seems to support Bass's view.[45]

For this reason, we must consider product packaging to be not only a product tactical variable, but also a part of the promotional variable, which we'll talk about in Chapter 19. In fact, Campbell's Soups estimates that the average consumer sees its label seventy-six times a year in a supermarket. That is twice the number of exposures from television, for which it spends $30 million a year.[46]

As a result of all this, **packaging** is a $50-billion-a-year industry, accounting for more corporate spending than advertising.[47]

The Functions of Packaging

In addition to containing and protecting the product, the package also makes such products as Tylenol tamper resistant or tamper evident and, of course, performs the promotional function we noted earlier. The L'Eggs egg packaging would have been a disaster if customers and retailers had to chase it around a flat shelf. As a part of this function, the goals of packaging include product awareness, image formation, and incentive to purchase.[48] Confirming the importance of packaging as a communication vehicle, a study conducted by John A. Deighton at the Amos Tuck School of Business Administration at Dartmouth College delved into the reasons behind repackaging existing products. Among marketing respondents, results were as follows:

- Modernizing designs/graphics, 22 per cent
- Product positioning, 22 per cent
- Improving shelf impact, 19 per cent
- Cost savings, 11 per cent[49]

As does advertising, the package communicates whether the product is expensive or cheap, functional or aesthetic, high quality, nominal quality, or low quality. Therefore, positioning is determined, to a large degree, by packaging. One study performed at the University of Texas at Austin by Carl McDaniel and R. C. Baker revealed that a significant proportion of consumers perceive that potato chips in polyvinyl packages are crisper and tastier than are exactly the same potato chips in wax packages. Furthermore, a tightly sealed package is perceived as an important mechanism for maintaining product quality, even though it created frustration because it was difficult to open.[50]

On the other hand, ease of opening must be considered a trade-off. In an A. C. Nielsen Company study of 985 consumers, it was found that 19 per cent of consumers with packaging problems—such as having difficulty in opening a package—would not buy the same brand again; 24 per cent said they would shop around more cautiously or buy a different type of package in the future.[51]

Dissatisfaction with product packaging classified by product category is shown in Figure 16-10.[52] In every case, potential exists for an astute marketing manager to create a differential advantage over the competition by ensuring a package that does not irk the customer.

Packaging may also have important implications for rejuvenation. The d-Con Company is now offering a new weapon against ants and cockroaches. The weapon? A large felt-tipped pen filled, not with ink, but with an insecticide. This product, called Exact, allows you to draw exact lines on the wall, floor, or any other space where you can't spray easily that will kill those insects. The insecticide is not a breakthrough, nor is it advertised or promoted as such. Rather, the unique dispenser gives the product its competitive advantage over other products and has actually rejuvenated the insecticide as a product. In the same classification are toothpaste pump dispensers, which in one year captured 12 per cent of the $1 billion U.S. market for toothpaste. Or Brush Plus, introduced by Gillette, which contains one of

Lunch meat	77%	Noodles	49
Bacon	76	Lipstick	47
Flour	65	Nail polish	46
Sugar	63	Honey	44
Ice cream	57	Crackers	44
Snack chips	53	Frozen seafood	40
Cookies	51	Nuts	39
Detergents	50	Cooking oil	37
Fresh meat	50	Ketchup	34

Source: Bill Abrams, "Packaging Often Irks Buyer, But Firms Are Slow to Change," *Wall Street Journal* 28 January 1982, p. 25.

Figure 16-10   Customer Dissatisfaction with Packaging by Product Category

Gillette's standard shaving creams. The difference? In addition to rejuvenating the product, the product sells for about a third more than the same product in a can.[53]

As with other aspects of product tactical decisions, product packaging is not free. It costs money and uses up other critical company resources to design, manufacture, and produce packages for products. But the expert marketer can leverage this investment by benefits, not only in protecting and containing the product, but in using it to assist in accomplishing larger marketing strategies.

Product Warranties

Product warranties are another important element of the total product. According to the American Marketing Association, a **warranty** is a statement or promise to the customer that a product being offered for sale is fit for the purpose being claimed. The promise concerns primarily what the seller will do if the product performs below expectations or turns out to be defective in some way. The promise (warranty) may be full (complete protection) or limited (some corrective steps), under the terms of the Magnuson-Moss Act of 1975. It may also be expressed (orally or in writing) or only implied, and it may have time restrictions.[54]

Remember Joe Karbo's advertisement for "The Lazy Man's Way to Riches" in Chapter 7? His warranty was that if the buyer did not want the product for any reason, he or she could return it within thirty days and receive in return his or her original, uncashed, check. Strong guarantees or warranties are usually required when offering a product for sale sight unseen. This is necessary to lower the perceived risk to the prospective customer. Karbo's was one of the strongest.

What do product warranties accomplish? Here are some of the reasons for using them:

- Lower risk to consumer
- Signal high product reliability[55]
- Reduce buyer complaints and dissatisfaction with the product
- Generate feedback on an offering[56]

- Promote an emphasis on product quality within the company
- Signal the company's belief in customer satisfaction
- Provide an additional reason for the customer to use the product correctly

Warranties can be the source of considerable competitive advantage. As with other attributes, however, their cost must be considered. If they are used, they should be promoted to maximize the advantage to the company.

Summary

In this chapter we have seen how product is more than just an animal, vegetable, or mineral object. "Product" includes other important peripheral aspects—quality, service, name, and package—and how they are combined into a single unit. The "product" may also be an intangible service. First, we discussed alternative product/service decisions regarding product introduction, discontinuance, and rejuvenation, and we saw that each of these tactical decisions was appropriate under different market and product circumstances. We also considered alternative branding decisions, including brand extension versus unique brands, and the advantages and disadvantages of private branding for any manufacturer. Finally, we looked at product packaging and considered it not as an expense, but as a promotional variable with the power and efficacy of major advertising efforts. We saw that packaging not only contains and protects, but also has a role to play in product awareness, image formation, incentive to purchase, and even in the tactical deployment decision of rejuvenation.

Questions

1. Gasoline is a commodity product and, by smell, taste, appearance, and even performance, given a certain octane, is indistinguishable from other gasoline products. What tactics might you employ to create a competitive advantage over your competition?
2. Studies prove that quality results in greater profitability over the long run. Why, then, might you ever not want to introduce a product that has greater quality than does that of a competitor?
3. Give an example of an opportunity-driven product, a market-driven product, and a competition-driven product. When do you think each should control primary marketing decision making?
4. Give an example of a successful product that has been discontinued by a company. What advantages did the company presumably obtain by withdrawing this product from the marketplace?

5. There are significant advantages to rejuvenating a product over introducing a new product. Why, then, would we want to implement a new product introduction strategy if we have a product that can be rejuvenated?
6. Is there any reason that we would ever not want to brand a product?
7. Is there a way not discussed in the text by which we might have the advantages of brand extension without the disadvantages?
8. Why would/would not a company like Procter & Gamble agree to do private branding for a distributor?
9. Because packaging has an important promotional dimension, under which budget of a marketing department should packaging fall—promotion or new product development?
10. In research noted in your text, a tightly sealed

package was perceived as an important mechanism for maintaining product quality, even though the same package created frustration because it was difficult to open. Which fact is more important to you in marketing a product? How might you determine which is more important for the particular product you are trying to market?

Ethical Question

You are the vice-president of marketing for a firm that makes lawnmowers on which you have a ninety-day warranty for parts and service. A customer bought one of your lawn mowers about nine months ago. One of the blades broke recently and he demanded complete replacement or repair. It was explained that the warranty was only good for ninety days. His answer was: "Look, I don't care how long the warranty says. I bought the mower at the end of the summer last year. I only used it once. The second time I used it was this summer and the blade broke." A sales slip confirms the date of purchase, and signed statements from his neighbors confirm that this was only the second time the mower was used. Your lawyers advise you that if you honor his warranty, you may be setting a dangerous precedent for the company. What do you do?

Endnotes

1. Michael Schroeder, "Can Reynolds Wrap Up the Kitchen Market?" *Business Week* (May 29, 1989), p. 68.
2. Janet Guyon, "Nabisco's New Cookie Line Marks the Beginning of a Fierce Sales War," *Wall Street Journal* 17 October 1983, pp. 31, 49.
3. "Selchow and Righter: Playing Trivial Pursuit to the Limit," *Business Week* (November 26, 1984).
4. "Consumers Fault Services," *Sales and Marketing Management* (January 13, 1986), p. 34.
5. Leonard Berry, "Big Ideas in Service Marketing," *Journal of Services Marketing*, vol. 1 (Summer 1987), p. 5.
6. Keith B. Murray and John L. Schlacter, "The Impact of Services versus Goods on Consumers' Assessment of Perceived Risk and Variability," *Journal of the Academy of Marketing Science*, vol. 18, no. 1 (Winter 1990), p. 61.
7. Trish Hall, "Brand Name Produce Hits Stores— But Will It Really Taste Better?" *Wall Street Journal* 23 September 1985, p. 33.
8. Meir Statman and Tyzoon Tyebjee, "Trademarks, Patents and Innovations in the Ethical Drug Industry," *Journal of Marketing*, vol. 45 (Summer 1981), p. 76.
9. John Koten and Scott Kilman, "How Coke's Decision to Offer Two Colas Undid Four and a Half Years of Planning," *Wall Street Journal* 15 July 1985, pp. 1, 8.
10. Robert D. Buzzell, "Product Quality," in Roger A. Kerin and Robert A. Peterson, eds., *Prospectives on Strategic Marketing Management*, (Boston: Allyn & Bacon, 1983), p. 283.
11. Lynn W. Phillips, Dae R. Chang, and Robert D. Buzzell, "Product Quality, Cost Position and Business Performance: A Test of Some Key Hypotheses," *Journal of Marketing*, vol. 47 (Spring 1983), p. 41.
12. David A. Garvin, "Product Quality: An Important Strategic Weapon," *Business Horizons*, vol. 27 (May–June 1984), p. 42.
13. Stephen W. Brown and Teresa A. Swartz, "A Gap Analysis of Professional Service Quality," *Journal of Marketing*, vol. 53, no. 2 (April 1989), p. 98.
14. Richard T. Garfein, "Guiding Principles for Improving Customer Service," *Journal of Services Marketing*, vol. 2, no. 2 (Spring 1988), p. 37.
15. Peter H. Bloch and Marsha L. Richins, "A Theoretical Model for the Study of Product Importance Perceptions," *Journal of Marketing*, vol. 47 (Summer 1983), p. 71.
16. Ibid., p. 78.
17. Betsy D. Gelb, "How Marketers of Intangibles Can Raise the Odds for Consumer Satisfaction," *Journal of Services Marketing*, vol. 1, no. 1 (Summer 1987), p. 15.
18. Robert H. Hayes and William J. Abernathy, "Managing Our Way to Economic Decline," *Harvard Business Review*, vol. 58 (July–August 1980), pp. 67–77.
19. Roger C. Bennett and Robert G. Cooper, "The Misuse of Marketing: An American Tragedy,"

Business Horizons, vol. 24 (November–December 1981), p. 52.

20. David Gobeli, "Recasting the Marketing Concept," in Patrick E. Murphy et al., eds., *1983 AMA Educators' Proceedings* (Chicago: AMA, 1983), p. 320.

21. Roger A. Kerin, Michael G. Harvey, and James T. Rothe, "Cannibalism and New Product Development," *Business Horizons* (October 1978), p. 27.

22. Richard T. Hise, A. Parasuraman, and Ramaswamy Viswanathan, "Product Elimination: The Neglected Management Responsibility," *Journal of Business Strategy*, vol. 4 (Spring 1984), p. 56.

23. Ibid., p. 61.

24. George J. Avlonitis, "Product Elimination Decision-Making: Does Formality Matter?" *Journal of Marketing*, vol. 49 (Winter 1985), p. 51.

25. Stanley H. Kratchman, Richard T. Hise, and Thomas A. Ulrick, "Management's Decision to Discontinue a Product," in Terry T. Ball, Robert W. Jefferson, Richard D. Nordstrom, and Paul C. Thistlethwaite, eds., *Marketing Readings* (Prospect Heights, Ill: Waveland Press, 1979), p. 327.

26. William Lazer, Mushtaq Luqmani, and Zahir Quraeshi, "Product Rejuvenation Strategies," *Business Horizons*, vol. 27 (November–December, 1984), p. 22.

27. Ibid.

28. John W. Wilson, "A New Life for Hewlett-Packard's Old Mini," *Business Week* (July 15, 1985), p. 106.

29. Christopher S. Eklund, "Will a Tomato by Any Other Name Taste Better?" *Business Week*, (September 30, 1985), p. 105.

30. Akshay R. Rao and Kent B. Monroe, "The Effect of Price, Brand Name, and Store Name on Buyers' Perceptions of Product Quality: An Integrative Review," *Journal of Marketing Research*, vol. 26, no. 3 (August 1989), p. 351.

31. George Miaoulis and Nancy D'Amato, "Consumer Confusion and Trademark Infringement," *Journal of Marketing*, vol. 42 (April 1978), pp. 48–55.

32. S. P. Raj, "Striking a Balance Between Brand Popularity and Brand Loyalty," *Journal of Marketing*, vol. 49 (Winter 1985), p. 53.

33. Edward M. Tauber, "Brand Franchise Extension: New Product Benefits from Existing Brand Names," *Business Horizons*, vol. 24 (March–April 1981), p. 37.

34. Ronald Alsop, "Firms Unveil More Products Associated with Brand Names," *Wall Street Journal* 13 December 1984, p. 29.

35. Tom Bayer, "Dr. Pepper Gums Up Works," *Advertising Age* (August 12, 1985), p. 69.

36. Tauber, op. cit., p. 38.

37. Al Ries and Jack Trout, *Positioning: The Battle for Your Mind* (New York: McGraw-Hill, 1981), p. 143.

38. David A. Aaker and Kevin Lane Keller, "Consumer Evaluations of Brand Extensions," *Journal of Marketing*, vol. 54, no. 1 (January 1990), p. 38.

39. James U. McNeal and Linda M. Zeren, "Brand Name Selection for Consumer Products," *MSU Business Topics* (Spring 1981), p. 37.

40. Ellen M. Kleinberg, "Trademarks: The Care and Feeding of Brand Name Identities," *Industrial Marketing* (October 1980), p. 62.

41. Ronald F. Bush, Peter H. Bloch, and Claude F. Reynaud, "The Brand Trademark: A Valuable and Vulnerable Resource," in Russell W. Belk et al., eds., *1984 AMA Educators' Proceedings* (Chicago: AMA, 1984), p. 278.

42. Kleinberg, loc. cit.

43. Jaclyn Fierman, "Beechnut Bounces Up in the Baby Market," *Fortune* (December 24, 1984), p. 56.

44. Kathleen Day, "Packaging Emerges as a Key Selling Tool," *Los Angeles Times* 17 March 1985, pt. 5, pp. 1, 5.

45. Kevin Higgins, "Economic Recovery Presages Packaging Explosion," *Marketing News* (February 3, 1984), p. 2.

46. Ibid.

47. "Cost Cutting Inspires Many Repackagings, Study Finds," *Marketing News* (February 17, 1984), p. 15.

48. Ibid.

49. Ibid.

50. Carl McDaniel and R. C. Baker, "Convenience Food Packaging and the Perception of Product Quality," *Journal of Marketing*, vol. 41 (October 1977), p. 58.

51. Bill Abrams, "Packaging Often Irks Buyer, But Firms Are Slow to Change," *Wall Street Journal* 28 January 1982, p. 29.

52. Ibid.

53. Amy Duncan, "Want to Wake Up a Tired Old Product? Repackage It," *Business Week* (July 15, 1985), pp. 130, 134.

54. Peter D. Bennett, *Dictionary of Marketing Terms* (Chicago: AMA, 1988), p. 213.

55. Craig A. Kelley, "An Investigation of Consumer Product Warranties as Market Signals of Product Reliability," *Journal of the Academy of Marketing Science*, vol. 16, no. 2 (Summer 1988), pp. 72–78.

56. Christopher W. L. Hart, "The Power of Unconditional Service Guarantees," *Harvard Business Review*, vol. 66, no. 4 (July–August 1988), p. 58.

Pricing Tactics

17

CHAPTER OBJECTIVES

- Understand the importance of the pricing decision to marketing management decision making.

- Know how pricing tactics are used to reach a marketing objective in support of a higher-level marketing strategy.

- Know the major categories of price classification.

- Know and understand the major influences on price setting and the process by which a price is set.

In This Restaurant, the Customer Sets the Prices

There's a thirty-four-seat restaurant in the town of Warrendale, Pennsylvania, that has attracted a great deal of attention recently. After barely breaking even at first, receipts are now up by 25 per cent. Without question, this increase in receipts is due entirely to pricing. But in this restaurant, it is the customer who sets the price, for there are no prices on the menu. The customer simply places the order, and at the end of the meal, it is the customer who decides what the cost of the meal will be. According to owner Jerry Juliano, a former truck driver, only a few people have

been guilty of crass underpayment, and just two diners have not paid at all. In this case, says Mr. Juliano, "I just say, God bless you, and smile."[1]

The Good Deal That Wasn't

TeleFirst was the brainchild of ABC, Incorporated. Briefly, TeleFirst was an entertainment recording service that was supposed to provide significant advantages within noncable areas of the television market. Services included first-run movies transmitted months before they would become available elsewhere, the ability to record and pay for only those first-run movies that were wanted, and 60 hours of additional programming not generally available on subscription TV. The price was set at $75 for a one-time installation fee for a wire recording decoder box and a monthly subscription rate of $18 to $26, according to how many first-run movies were recorded. Tested in the Chicago area, TeleFirst got off to a good start. But only six months later, it went under due to insufficient subscribers. Why?

One reason was the failure to anticipate discount pricing trends in the videocassette rental industry. Rental rates dropped overnight from $3 to $5 per cassette to $1 to $2. Thus, the consumer had to ask why he or she should pay $26 a month for four first-run movies when a dozen or more could be rented for the same price. Then there was the $75 installation fee. But perhaps the major reason for TeleFirst's failure was the incorrect assumption that consumers would pay additionally for the convenience of not having to go to video stores to rent movies.[2]

Stellar Prices for Cellular Phones

It wasn't so long ago that a standard car phone cost about a thousand dollars, and a portable one needing no power source other than its one-hour battery cost twice that. Not any more. Prices have fallen to levels that analysts hadn't expected. Motorola, Inc., a market leader, is selling an older model for under $700. Satellite Technology Services, a direct-marketing newcomer, is promoting a new portable for under $700 via direct mail. Cellular phones are already becoming a shelf item for mass retailers, and a General Electric cellular phone is going for $199 plus a $100 installation charge. According to *Business Week,* incremental production costs generally represent 50 to 60 per cent of the cellular phone's wholesale price. These costs decline by up to 20 per cent each time the market doubles. This suggests that prices will drop at least 20 per cent a year in the next few years. The average cellular phone will sell for less than $500. The main obstacle now to even more rapid expansion is not the cost of the cellular phone itself, but rather of cellular calling. Most carriers are charging a monthly fee ranging from $25 to $35. That may not be too bad, but usage charges are going from 25 to 45 cents a minute, and for the average subscriber, that amounts to $125 to $150 a month. If that price comes down and sales continue to grow, cellular prices will fall even further.[3] ●

Pricing: The Revenue-Making Decision _____

Pricing is unique among the decisions that the marketing manager must make as a part of his or her work. It is the sole decision that generates revenue without generating costs.[4] Yet, amazingly, one important survey done some time ago indicated that only 50 per cent of marketing practitioners rated pricing as an important marketing decision.[5]

This is absolutely not true today. A recent study conducted by Fleming Associates of Columbus, Indiana, surveyed marketing executives at 125 U.S. corporations. These marketing executives were asked to rank sixteen pressure point issues on a scale of 1 to 10, with 10 representing the highest priority. Pricing was easily number one, the critical pressure point. It had a score of 8.57, outdistancing new product introductions with 7.67, internal staffing and training with 7.47, product differentiation with 7.43, and selling costs with 7.02.[6]

Perhaps one of the main reasons that pricing is considered such a critical issue in today's marketing arena is that pricing, as a decision that must be thought through and implemented by the marketing manager, is very much tied to change. Thus, when the change comes due to the introduction of a new product, or an environmental change such as an action by a competitor or the government, or even a technological breakthrough occurs, or a change in strategy is taken by the firm, or there is a change in the product line, a pricing decision is required. In the fast-paced marketing operations of the 1980s, with more changes than ever before, pricing is and will continue to be a critical issue that must receive the marketing manager's close attention.

Concepts of the Pricing Decision

Pricing New Products

As shown in Figure 17-1, three basic alternative pricing tactics may be followed in introducing a new product into the marketplace: (1) penetration pricing, (2) a meet-the-competition pricing, and (3) price skimming. Relative to the pricing of similar items in the marketplace, this pricing could be referred to as low, medium, and high. Let's look at each.

Penetration Pricing

With **penetration pricing**, the marketing manager seeks to enter a market with a low price to capture as large a share as possible. Pricing is emphasized as a major differential advantage over the competition. Once the product is established in the marketplace, the price can be raised to be more on a level with that of the competition, or the price can be raised even higher. A good example of this is Datsun/Nissan. Introduced into this country as a sports car in the early 1970s, the Datsun 240Z was underpriced, compared to similar sports cars offered by other manufacturers. Then, as market share was captured, and the product became well established in the U.S. market, the price was raised. Ten years after its introduction, its price was on the high side for its class.

In a similar fashion, Korean marketers prepared to enter and penetrate the American market for videocassette recorders in early 1985, taking on not primarily U.S. manufacturers, but Japanese multiconglomerates. One Korean firm, Sam Sung Electronics, shipped 600,000 VCRs to the United States. They priced them at $50 to $75 less than the comparable $400 mid-priced Japanese units. Dave Butterfield, president of the market research company Butterfield Communications in Cambridge, Massachusetts, pre-

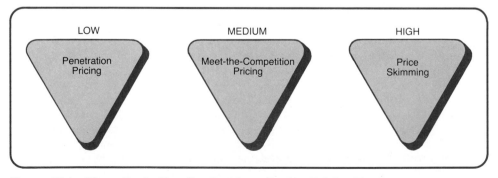

Figure 17-1   Three Basic New Product Introduction Pricing Tactics

dicted: "By the end of the decade, the Koreans could have 25 per cent of that market."[7]

One type of penetration pricing that may not be quite so obvious is couponing. The coupon permits a price discount in the early stages of introducing a new product. When the coupon expires, the consumer pays the regular price. Yet the regular price advertised never changed. It was the coupon that enabled the consumer to buy the product at a lower amount: a penetration price.

Meet-the-Competition Pricing

Meet-the-competition pricing means that the marketer will enter the market with the new product priced the same or approximately the same as those currently offered by competitors. If you use this particular tactic, you must then ask yourself why anyone would buy your product, which is both unfamiliar and unproven in the market. If the customer is purchasing a product that satisfies the same needs at the same price you have set, unless there is an additional advantage to your product, there is no reason to do so. Therefore, a marketing manager choosing a tactic of meeting the competition's price must add something to increase the value of the new product, or consumers will not switch.

One such technique for accomplishing this is called bundling. A company bundles customer benefits together to increase the value. Bundling occurred when Japanese automobile manufacturers included options such as tinted windows and white-wall tires as standard equipment, instead of charging additional amounts. The cost of this added value is much less than one would expect. At retail, tinted windows might cost the purchaser $50. But the typical cost to the manufacturer is only $3. The objective of bundling, therefore, is to add value while keeping cost increments small, and thus not to increase price for the added value.[8] One could, of course, also add value by additional service, higher quality, and more convenient store locations.

Price Skimming

Price skimming implies entering the market with a relatively high price for a new product. Usually the price is later reduced to be competitive as competitors enter the market. In theory the fact that a high price began the process means that the firm should have additional financial resources to use to fight the competition due to higher margins. This additional capital can be used for more promotion and additional channels of distribution, once the competition attempts market entry.

To introduce a product at a relatively high price means that the product must be relatively new and offer superior advantages to what is already in the marketplace. Consider the compact disc, or CD, products, thought to be the forerunners of a revolution in the staggering $11 billion worldwide audio business. The CD product involves laser-based digital audio disc technology. It is the first major advance in this type of equipment since the introduction of stereo, and it has the advantage not only of higher-fidelity music, but of far smaller and more versatile audio equipment. When this product was first introduced in 1982, it carried a $1,000 retail price, five times that of a high-quality conventional stereo record player. A year later the price came down to less than $900. In 1984 the price was less than $500, and in 1985 less than $300. Currently you can buy a CD player for a little over $100. In each case the producers reduced the price to meet additional competition, as well as to increase the level of sales.[9]

Although these three basic tactics can all be successful, some modifications at the proper times and under the proper circumstances can be equally so. Marketing genius Joe Cossman introduced the plastic hose lawn sprinkler system, which consisted of a single plastic tube with many holes in it. This was a product that, although highly innovative, was also easy to reproduce and copy and could not be protected through patent. During the first selling season, spring and summer, Cossman's product was the only one on the market, and at $5.95 a unit, his innovation was priced relatively high for that time. Thus, it was a price skimming tactic. Anticipating heavy competition the following year, Cossman actually increased the price and was successful. Here's how he did it. Cossman was wholesaling the product. He increased the recommended retail price while decreasing price to the retailer, which happened to be supermarkets. His several competitors, entering with either a meet-the-competition or a penetration price tactic, offered significantly lower margins to the retailer. As a result the retailers stayed with Cossman's product, and he was able to dominate this market for an additional year, which he probably could not have done otherwise.

Special Pricing Considerations

Promotional Versus Baseline Pricing

Two important concepts in pricing that must be differentiated from one another are promotional and **baseline pricing**. **Promotional pricing** is short term. It is not the regular price of the product, and it is used primarily to encourage potential consumers to try the product or the service when it is first introduced. Baseline pricing is the regular price decided on for the item. If the two become confused, serious problems can accrue. For example, an innovative snack product was priced at 79 cents, but promotional pricing made it available at 50 cents during introduction. Coincidentally, with the introduction increased costs pushed the baseline price to $1.00. However, at the end of the introductory period, it was impossible for the brand to be maintained at the new baseline price. The marketing manager must also be careful about forecasts made that are based on tests using the promotional pricing. These forecasts may or may not hold once the baseline price is implemented.[10]

The **loss leader** is a special type of promotional pricing. The intent is to increase sales of promoted items or other items offered. For example, a marketing manager could offer a videotape at $4.95 if a second were bought at the regular price. Or a store could offer any one video tape at $4.95 just for shopping at the store during a promotional period. Marketers selling through the mail frequently price an item advertised at a loss in order to acquire the customer, to whom similar items can be sold at a profit.

Do loss leaders always work? The answer is no. One study of loss leaders at two supermarkets found that most loss leaders had no effect on store profit, and those that did affect profit did so through their effect on store traffic, rather than on sales of the promoted items.[11]

Psychological Pricing Tactics

Another important concept in pricing is psychological: **odd/even pricing**. This is in many ways an aspect of consumer or buyer behavior. Many marketing students will already recognize the value of charging $3.99 or $6.98, in that the consumer perceives these prices as $3.00 and $6.00 rather than $4.00 or $7.00. There are other important psychological considerations. One is the **absolute** versus a **relative price difference**. At the $1.00 to $2.00 range, a 10 per cent difference may be perceived as significant by the consumer and may make a difference in sales. However, if the product is $30 or $40, a 10 per cent difference, although the same absolute percentage, may not be perceived as meaningful at all.[12] Another psychological consideration of some importance in pricing has to do with markdowns. A high markdown will favorably influence consumers and encourage them to purchase the product as long as there was perceived value for the product at the pre-markdown price.[13] However, as noted previously regarding promotional pricing, a high markdown, although it increases sales in the short run, may make it extremely difficult, if not impossible, to return to and maintain the original price.

The final psychological pricing tactic that should be understood by the marketing manager is **discount pricing**. This may be simply a lower price to induce a customer to buy. It is used by discount stores, which routinely discount their entire stock of merchandise. In such a store, the buyer expects merchandise to be discounted. A buyer expects that the more of a product purchased at the same time, the lower the price will be. There may be some very real reasons that a product can be discounted when ordered in larger quantities, such as a lower cost to the supplier. But the important point here is that the buyer will expect this to occur whether or not the supplier gets a cost break. An entrepreneurial supplier of a new type of pilot's kneeboard, which was used to provide a platform for writing notes while seated in flight in fighter-type aircraft, was proposed to the U.S. government and eventually ordered. Yet the inventor lost millions of dollars in contracts primarily because of his initial refusal to lower the unit price of the item when ordered in quantities of several thousand.

Earlier we talked about price bundling as potential technique for meet-the-competition pricing. But bundling may also be considered a special form of discount pricing. Examples include travel packages that include, in one price, travel, lodging, meals, and car rental; credit card memberships that include not only a credit card, but also a magazine subscription and life insurance; and health club memberships that include exercise classes, showers, massages, and use of the exercise equipment.[14]

Major Influences on Pricing

There are certain factors that influence pricing to such a degree that they can only be termed major. These include the **price-value relationship**, im-

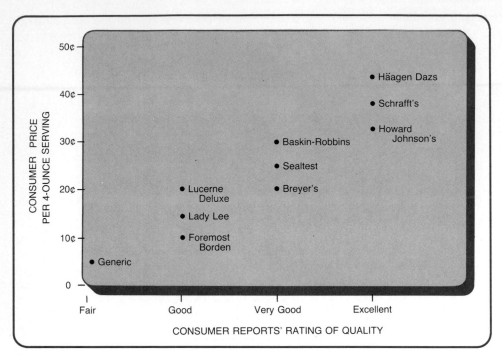

Figure 17-2　The Price/Value Relationship in Ice Cream

Source: Adapted from Elliot B. Ross, "Making Money with Proactive Pricing," *Harvard Business Review*, vol. 62 (November-December 1984), p. 149.

age, competition, cost, the buyer, company objectives and legal restraints.[15] Let's look at each of these factors in turn.

The Price-Value Relationship

As you can see in Figure 17-2, the **perceived value** of a product can be very important. In this figure, a variety of different brands of ice cream is shown. The consumer price for a four-ounce serving has been plotted against the consumer's reported rating of quality from fair through excellent. The results are that a generic ice cream product is rated only fair in quality, whereas Häagen-Dazs ice cream, which is priced the highest, receives a quality rating of excellent.[16] The implication is that better-quality ice cream has additional value for which the consumer is willing to pay. Inferring value or quality from price may be critical where information on quality is low, but its importance is high.[17]

But, in addition to perceived value, there is also an **economic value** to the customer that must be considered regarding the price that he or she is willing to pay, due to a variety of other factors. This economic value is illustrated in Figure 17-3, where two products, X and Y, are compared. Because of favorable start-up and postpurchase costs, as well as an additional incremental value of $100 for product X, the customer should be willing to pay twice as much for product X—that is, $600—as product Y. Furthermore, from the

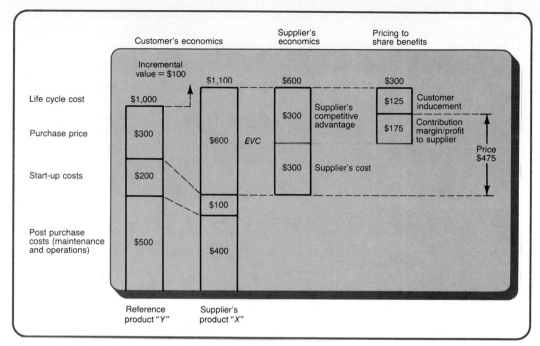

Figure 17-3 The Economic Value (EVC) to the Customer Concept

Source: From John L. Forbins and Nitin T. Mehta, "Value-Based Strategies for Industrial Products," *Business Horizons,* vol. 24 (May-June 1981), p. 33. Used with permission.

manufacturer's viewpoint, it costs $300 to produce product X. Therefore, any price in excess of $300 constitutes a profit. Now, because any price under $600 gives the customer a better deal than he or she can get from product Y, the supplier of product X has a $300 competitive advantage. In addition, supplier X could price the product to the customer at $475, which would result in $175 in profit, and a $125 advantage over product Y for the customer.[18]

Adding value in this way can also mean making the product easier to use, making it more attractive, making it more profitable to a supplier, or giving it some other value advantage. Without question, consumers as well as industrial buyers are willing to pay a premium in those instances where they perceive a significant value or benefit to them over competitive products. For example, five pounds of potatoes currently cost approximately forty cents. But Betty Crocker Au Gratin Potatoes Mix, for approximately the same weight of potatoes, sells for $2.88. Similarly, a whole fryer chicken per pound is 79 cents, while Tyson Frozen Breaded Breast Fillets of Chicken cost $4.92 per pound.[19]

Image

The image that a product or service has can have a very definite effect on the price that should be charged. Thus, identical consulting services may have a wide range of prices. One part-time consultant may bill at $50 per

465

hour, whereas another, performing exactly the same service, with exactly the same background and training, may bill at twice that. A survey of consulting in a particular specialty of marketing found fees charged clients for identical services by individuals with identical backgrounds varied from $50 to $250 per hour, depending primarily upon whether the consultant was working part-time or whether the consultant was an employee of a major national consulting firm.

Without question, higher prices suggest higher quality and may have little to do with the actual cost to the supplier or manufacturer. An expensive bottle of perfume costing several hundred dollars may only contain a few dollars' worth of scent. Cubic zirconium, highly touted as the new "counterfeit diamond," which actually cuts glass and is indistinguishable from a real diamond to all but an expert, sells for about $40 for a one-quarter carat in a handsome display case. Yet the case costs more than the diamond: 52 cents versus 42 cents. According to Gerald Katz, vice-president of Management Assistance Systems, Inc., a firm in Waltham, Massachusetts, "The higher you price certain products, like a Mercedes-Benz, the more desirable they become."[20]

Yet, another example of image pricing comes from the Japanese. Aprica is a baby stroller made in Japan and introduced in the United States in 1980. The manufacturer, Kassai, Inc., didn't follow the traditional Japanese strategy of capturing the low-priced, high-volume end of the market at all. Its line of baby strollers accounts for 8 per cent of the three million strollers sold in the United States each year, at a price of $100 to $300 per copy—well above the market average. Kassai has achieved this pricing by attaining a "Rolls-Royce" image for its product.[21]

The Competition

In earlier chapters we looked at the dangers of the competition as a marketplace environ, in that the competition can react to spoil a strategy we have initiated. The same holds true in tactics. We must anticipate the actions of our competitors, even as we plan the pricing tactics we will implement. But, in pricing, the fact of competition itself can have an effect on price, whether the competition chooses to take a specific action or not. One researcher looked at 356 industrial items sold to the government and priced under both sole-source conditions—where there was but a single supplier without competition—and under competitive conditions—with two or more suppliers. The mere fact of the presence of competition resulted in a price reduction of between 10.8 and 17.5 per cent.[22] Thus, competition has a significant effect on pricing, whether the competition chooses to do anything in response to our tactical pricing actions or not.

One approach to proactive pricing in anticipating actions that the competition might take in response to our own—and thus adjusting our tactics accordingly—is shown in Figure 17-4, "Guidelines for Tactical Pricing." Multiple matrices, one within the other, consider customer price sensitivity, knowledge of price action to the competition, relative market share, and cost. Depending on these factors and on the location of the product in these matrices determines the tactical alternatives of matching the competition's price, pricing above the competition, pricing below the competition, and either matching or raising the price or matching or lowering the price.[23]

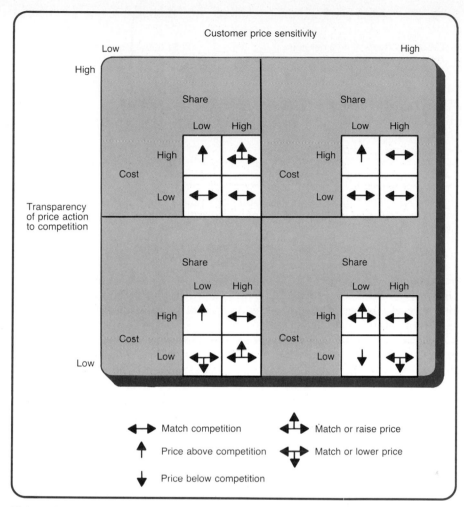

Figure 17-4   Guidelines for Tactical Pricing

Source: Elliot B. Ross, "Making Money with Proactive Pricing," *Harvard Business Review*, vol. 62 November-December 1984), p. 153. Used with permission.

Cost

As pointed out earlier, the cost of an item may have very little to do with its selling price. In fact, the markup may be several thousand per cent, as with the perfume or immitation diamonds discussed earlier.[24] However, cost does play one very important part in pricing. If we are going to make any money in a specific transaction, we must not price below our cost. Of course, it is possible to do this and make money through the back end—that is, through additional deals or other services from which we profit after the initial transaction. This is very much in contrast to the so-called **engineering method** of pricing, the method usually required by the U.S. government and some local and state governments and used by many industrial firms.

This method starts with the cost of materials and labor, permits an addition for overhead and "general and administrative expenses," and finally, a certain

Labor, 100 hours @ $10 per hour	$1,000
Overhead (burden) @ 75%	750
Cost of materials	250
Subtotal	$2,000
General and administrative expenses @ 20%	400
Subtotal	$2,400
Profit @ 10%	240
Final price	$2,640

Figure 17-5 The "Engineering Method" of Pricing Based on Cost and a Fixed Percentage for Profit—Price, 1,000 Widgets

"reasonable" fixed percentage for profit. This method of pricing is shown in Figure 17-5. Such a method disregards the price-value relationship, image, influence of competition, and other important factors. Therefore, it is only useful for establishing basic costs.

Because the number of items ordered has a most definite effect on the cost, we must consider the experience, or **learning curve**, noted earlier in our chapters on strategy. In this concept the cost of producing the one-thousandth item is a lot less than is producing the first item: we have learned how to produce and manufacture it more efficiently, and we order a larger quantity of raw materials. As a result, we can reduce the price. This must be incorporated into the basic costing illustrated in Figure 17-5.

One point of caution in using the experience curve in developing costs is that antitrust enforcers may see the final price derived from experience-curve pricing as predatory pricing and as an attempt to monopolize the industry, which is prohibited under section 2 of the Sherman Act of 1890, or even as an unfair method of competition, proscribed by section 5 of the Federal Trade Commission Act of 1914. The solution, however, is to maintain records to justify experience-curve costs forecasts. As long as prices exceed costs, there is probably little to fear.[25]

If you want to be successful in pricing, even though you must use cost as a baseline, consider the words of F. G. "Buck" Rogers. He spent thirty-four years at IBM before retiring as vice-president of marketing. His advice is to "understand the customer's requirements, have broad management coverage, and put together a cost-justified solution that truly conveys value-added marketing."[26]

The Buyer

We have already looked at some of the influences the buyer has on price, and they are extensive. The very successful Ford Mustang program initiated under Lee Iacocca when he was with the Ford Motor Company in the early 1960s can be viewed in the framework of discovering a market segment that valued sportiness in a car but was unwilling to pay the price for a sports car.

High Involvement
1. Spend a great deal of time shopping for the product.
2. Spend a great deal of time thinking about the purchase.
3. Find significant differences among brands.
4. Product is kept for a long period of time.
5. Poor choice is perceived as having serious consequences.

Low Involvement
1. Spend little time shopping for the product.
2. Spend little time thinking about the purchase.
3. Find few significant differences between brands.
4. The product will be used quickly and discarded.
5. It would be difficult to make a poor brand choice.

Source: Adapted from William Theodore Cummings and Lonnie L. Ostrom, "Measuring Price Thresholds Using Social Judgment Theory," *Journal of the Academy of Marketing Science*, vol. 10 (Fall 1982), p. 399.

Figure 17-6   High-Involvement vs. Low-Involvement Buyers

Thus, the Mustang strategy was most definitely buyer oriented. Other early detection of the differences in the way buyers value identical product benefits can be extremely important for a company establishing pricing tactics. Airlines that have managed to survive deregulation and remain profitable have done so because they recognized the differences among buyers in the benefits that each buyer segment valued. Thus, airlines were able to offer differentiated products, and not simply basic transportation from point A to B. A low-priced product was offered to the vacationer—if planning could be accomplished several months ahead. Another low price was sometimes offered at very short notice. Higher-priced products timed according to convenience were offered the business customer.[27]

Marketing researchers have also been able to identify categories of buyers, which results in more favorable tactics in pricing of one sort or another, depending upon high or low involvement in the buying situation. In one study subjects were designated as high involvement or low involvement in the buying situation, according to the definitions shown in Figure 17-6. Research findings suggested that it was far easier to pass on higher costs to high-product–involved customers; low prices were recommended for low-product–involved customers.[28]

Company Objectives

Another important influence on pricing has to do with the objectives of the company. In any specific situation, a marketing manager can price for far more complex reasons than profits or sales. Pricing objectives can be for maximum long-run profits, for maximum short-run profits, for market share, for ROI, for growth, for stabilizing the market, for desensitizing customers to price, for maintaining price leadership, for discouraging the entrance of competitors, for speeding the exit from the marketplace of marginal firms, for avoiding government investigation and control, for maintaining loyalty of middlemen and getting their sales support, in response to demands from suppliers, for enhancing the image of the firm and its offerings, for being regarded as fair by the ultimate customer, for creating interest and excitement about the product, for being considered trustworthy and reliable by rivals, for helping in the sale of weak items in the line, for discouraging others from cutting prices, for making a product conspicuous, for eventually obtaining a high price for sales of the business, and for building traffic.[29] Company pricing objectives also include payback period, where the company wants to recoup its investment in a certain number of years; or breakeven, where the company wants its investment to break even (zero profit, zero loss) at a certain number of units sold. As an objective, pricing may be strategic as well as tactical—for example, pricing for market share.[30]

Legal Restraints

There are also certain legal restraints on pricing. For example, under the Clayton Act of 1914, charging different prices to different buyers is prohibited. The Robinson-Patman Act of 1936 further restricts price discrimination of supplemental services and discounts. The Wheeler-Lea Amendment to the Federal Trade Commission Act outlawed false and deceptive advertising. This means that you can't advertise a price as a sale price unless a substantial amount of merchandise has been offered, and at a higher price. And you can't get together with other sellers to agree on prices either. That is known as price fixing and can land you in jail. Another action that can get you in trouble is low pricing to drive out a competitor. In fact, anything that threatens to lessen competition is probably covered under one or more legal restraints. Do governmental agencies convict only in case of flagrant violations? Maybe. However many situations are handled on a settlement basis, to avoid bad publicity and expensive court actions.[31] Ignoring legal restraints can have a detrimental effect on your company and on you personally. The best advice is not to forget this important environ as you formulate your pricing tactics.

Setting the Price _____

Who Sets the Price?

Partially because there are so many situations in which the marketing manager can be involved in setting a price, and partially because of the critical nature of the price as a part of the marketing mix, an individual with marketing responsibilities who becomes involved in price setting may have many different titles. Also, such a marketing manager will be involved with others outside the marketing discipline. Price may be set by the president of the company, by a vice-president with marketing responsibilities, by a product or brand manager, or by a committee made up of several different executives in the company. In some companies pricing tactics are delegated to salespeople. This last policy—that is, delegating the pricing authority to salespeople in the field as opposed to having sales representation on a committee arriving at the pricing decision—is generally not recommended.

One study of 108 firms giving salespeople the highest degree of pricing authority showed that the firms generated the lowest sales and profit performance.[32] What you as a marketing manager must recognize is that involvement in pricing and the pricing decision is almost inevitable. You can be solely responsible for the price set or share the responsibility with other marketing executives or other company executives outside of the marketing functional area.

The Procedure

The procedure for setting the price is accomplished in five steps: establishing and clarifying company objectives; determining cost; determining the demand at different prices; pricing to meet objectives, considering the relevant factors in the tactical situation; and testing the price and adjusting it if necessary.

We have already discussed setting objectives and determining costs. Let's take a look at how we determine demand for different prices, once the first two steps have been accomplished.

Determining Demand at Different Prices

Economists tell us that, all other things being equal, there is a downward-sloping demand curve. That is, if we plot demand against various prices on a vertical axis, the slope of the resulting curve at these different prices is downward, as shown in Figure 17-7. However, as you probably suspected, this is theoretical, and many other factors can affect the shape of the curve. Look at Figure 17-8. This is the **demand curve** for a prestige product such

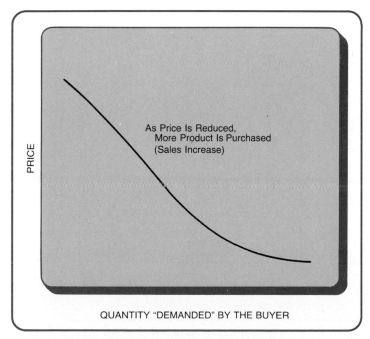

Figure 17-7 The Downward Sloping Demand Curve

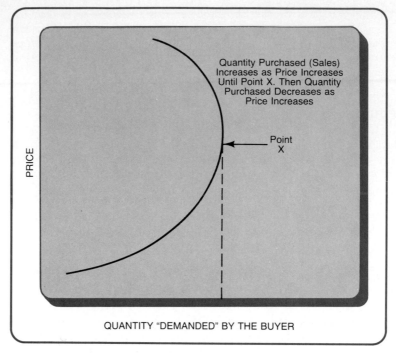

QUANTITY "DEMANDED" BY THE BUYER

Figure 17-8   Demand Curve for a Prestige Product

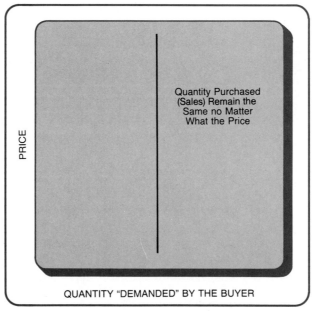

QUANTITY "DEMANDED" BY THE BUYER

**Figure 17-9   Demand Curve for a Product for Which
There is No Substitute**

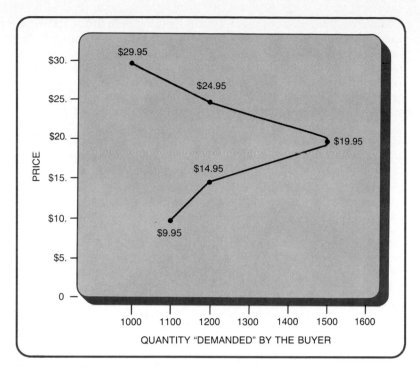

Figure 17-10   Demand Curve for an Actual Product as a Result of Testing

as a prestige perfume. Note that, as the price is increased, the quantity demanded actually increases as well, until it reaches a certain point, X. Then, as prices continue to increase, the quantity demanded decreases. This results in an inverse C shape for the demand curve.

Or look at Figure 17-9. There we have a demand curve for a product for which there is no substitute. Perhaps it is a drug that is the only cure for a fatal illness. Clearly, regardless of price, those needing the drug will pay almost any price for it. The demand for the product is price insensitive, and the curve is a vertical line. We say that this demand curve is perfectly inelastic because the demand doesn't vary at all with changes in price. Thus, we see for different products in different situations, there are differently shaped demand curves.

Now let's look at Figure 17-10. This is the curve that resulted from an actual test of the product at different prices. The product was a series of four booklets marketed through the mail and entitled *The Writer's Guide to Publication and Profit.* The initial price was $19.95. The marketer then reduced the price to $14.95. The quantity demanded declined. The price was then reduced to $9.95. The quantity demanded declined further. The price was then tested again at $19.95, whereupon the demand returned to approximately its former position. The price was then increased to $24.95. The quantity demanded declined. The price was then tested at $29.95, and it was found that the quantity demanded decreased even further. For this product, the optimum price, if maximization of the quantity sold is the sole criterion, is $19.95.

The most common approach to determining demand for an entire product line is to model the sales response function, as was done in Figure 17-10, and then to optimize each product separately within the product line. However, more complex and sophisticated models are available that permit solving simultaneous equations for all sales-response functions of products against demand within the product line. Optimal product pricing can be arrived at for all products within the line simultaneously.[33]

But whether pricing is done individually or simultaneously for all products within the product line, how does a marketer find the demand? One technique is simply to test empirically, as was done in Figure 17-10. Another is to use an estimation based on limited testing and/or the sale response to the price history of similar products or products that are being replaced by the new product being introduced. In this way a company introducing a new type of fountain pen that would replace older types would look at the price of the older types versus the demand to create a model for the sales response curve. In other cases where the product class or category is new, products that are being replaced are looked at. In 1972, when the hand-held electronic calculator was introduced, marketers looked at two other items in developing a sales response model. One was large table-model electronic calculators selling for $300 or more; the other was mechanical slide rules selling for between $30 and $150. Using historical pricing data, and pricing to meet their objectives, marketers came up with a new product pricing range of between $100 and $200 per unit.

What does a marketer do when a product is so new in its class that there is no direct replacement or similar product whose prices can be analyzed? One solution is to design experimental scenarios that simulate actual buying decisions. This simply means that various types of marketing research can be accomplished, as discussed in previous chapters, such as **focus groups** or one-on-one interviews in which the product and its function are described, and suggested prices are obtained from the participatory research subjects.[34]

Pricing to Meet Objectives Considering Other Relevant Factors

Once a demand curve has been determined for the product at different prices, the marketer must consider the objectives set by the firm and other relevant factors. Looking again at *The Writer's Guide to Publication and Profit* in Figure 17-10, if the objectives were to maximize sales or market share, the $19.95 price might be chosen. But as noted in an article aptly entitled, "Manage Customers for Profits (Not Just Sales)": "High sales volume does not necessarily mean high income, as many companies have found to their sorrow."[35] If the objective were per unit profitability, more per unit profit could be made by selecting a higher selling price on the demand curve. If total short-term profits are an issue, this would occur at $29.95. Other relevant factors, such as competition, must be considered. Will our tactic be to capture a large share of the market and then raise the price slowly, or do we want to enter with a skimming price and then reduce our price, using our profits to fight the competition later? This can make a difference in the ultimate price selected.

Testing and adjusting a price are always required. We enter a market with a certain price after our best efforts to discover what that price should be. But many times the price arrived at was through guesswork, forecasting, historical information, and other combinations of estimating research and judgment. But once in the marketplace, all bets are off. The competition may not react as planned. Or maybe the target market—which in a survey indicated a willingness to pay $50 for a product—was in fact only willing to pay $25 when it came to actually putting money down when the product was in the marketplace. Product introduction is itself a test, and price adjustments may be required. In addition, as the environs of the marketplace change, sometimes a change is also required in our pricing.

Elements of a Successful Pricing System

Important Elements to Consider

The following cautionary notes should be followed in any pricing system:

- Have as much information available as possible about market and customer characteristics, competitor capabilities, likely competitor actions and internal capabilities, competitor costs, and pricing.
- Collect and analyze price data for each product introduced by competitors early in the development process and throughout the product's life.
- Make certain that you are organized to take advantage of the latest data to support effective and optimal pricing.
- Maintain flexible and responsible organizations and systems for collecting and data.
- Ensure that competent people are assigned the task of collecting, analyzing, and dispensing price information.
- Maintain effective pricing control and feedback.[36]

Summary

In this chapter we have seen that pricing decisions are the sole revenue—as opposed to cost-oriented decisions—that the marketing manager makes. Pricing is being increasingly recognized as important in the marketing process not only because of the effect of pricing decisions on the overall outcome of the marketing campaign, but also because the marketing manager is fully responsible for pricing in a number of situations. These include new product introduction, action by the competition and the government, technological breakthroughs, product line changes, and, in fact, proaction and reaction to potential or actual changes of any environ of the marketplace. For new product introduction, there are basically three alternatives: penetration pricing, meet-the-competition pricing, and price skimming. The three work under different circumstances. The astute marketing manager must also consider special pricing alternatives, including promotional versus baseline pricing, psychological pricing, and discount pricing, as well as major influences, including the price-value relationship, image, the competition, cost, the buyer, and company objectives.

We have seen that the price-setting procedure is in five steps: setting objectives; determining costs; determining demand at different prices; pricing to meet objectives, considering other relevant factors; and testing and adjusting. In this fashion we arrive at a pricing system that is effective and efficient and will make a major contribution to the overall marketing mix.

But don't get hung up on fixed formulas or methodologies of pricing. As the noted marketing professor Joseph Kamen of Indiana University advises: "More important than the methods, however, is the mindset: the challenges of creativity devising new techniques, the excitement of tailoring pricing approaches in ways that others have overlooked, the feat of inventively linking the disciplines of psychology and economics, the exhilaration from successfully applying and melding analytical skills and creative talent."[37]

Questions

1. You are introducing a new marketing management textbook into the marketplace. What type of pricing should you use? What factors should you consider?

2. You are an established drug company with a brand name well known to physicians as well as to consumers. You introduce a new drug that will cure a heretofore incurable and dreaded disease. What pricing will you use? What factors should you consider?

3. Scientists in your company have invented a means of lowering your cost of manufacturing by 50 per cent. How will this affect the established baseline price of the product that you have been selling that uses this manufacturing process?

4. A recent law school graduate hangs out his shingle and decides to use a penetration strategy setting his fee at half that of his competitors. Do you see any problems with this?

5. You are a new marketing manager. One of the products for which you are responsible is of extremely high quality, compared with other products in the market. However, your product sells for a very low price. What is the problem with simply raising the price to that of other high-quality products being sold?

6. You have a product to which the customer is highly sensitive regarding price, and any action you take is clearly seen by the competition. You have a low market share, and the product manufacturing costs are fairly high. How should you price the product compared to the competition, according to the guidelines provided by the text? Explain the logic behind your pricing decision.

7. If a primary company objective in your firm is pay-back period, how might this affect your pricing?

8. If the demand curve for your pricing looks like the curve in Figure 17-8, how do you locate point X?

9. In theory what does the demand curve illustrated in Figure 17-9 say about the maximum price you might set? What are the reasons you would not actually want to do this?

10. What might cause the demand curve shown in Figure 17-10?

Ethical Question

It is illegal to advertise a sale price unless a substantial amount of the product has been offered previously at a higher price. You are the marketing manager for a publishing company selling business books for practitioners. You get a brilliant idea that you feel is totally legal, but that has the effect of a sale price. The regular price of the book is $19.95. You print this price on the dust jacket, along with the notation: "Real value, $29.95." Is this ethical, even if it is legal? Would there be any difference if your notation read: "Real value $1,995.00"? What if your notation read: "Compare at $29.95"?

Endnotes

1. Terrence Roth, "We Can Name Lots of Restaurants That Wouldn't Dare Attempt This," *Wall Street Journal,* 21 February 1985.
2. Bernie Whalen, "Why ABC's TeleFirst Didn't Last," *Marketing News* (November 9, 1984), p. 32.
3. John J. Keller, "Will Cheaper Cellular Put a Phone in Every Pocket?" *Business Week* (December 5, 1988), p. 142.
4. Kent B. Monroe and Albert J. Della Bitta, "Models for Pricing Decisions," *Journal of Marketing Research,* vol. 15 (August 1978), p. 427.
5. John G. Udell, "How Important Is Pricing in Competitive Strategy?" *Journal of Marketing* (January 1964), pp. 44–48.
6. "Pricing Competition Is Shaping Up as '84's Top Marketing Pressure Point," *Marketing News* (November 11, 1983), p. 1.
7. Susan Spillman, "Korea Triggers VCR Wars," *Advertising Age* (January 10, 1985), p. 3.
8. "Panelists Offer Pricing Strategy Advice for Consumer and Industrial Products," *Marketing News* (February 1, 1985), p. 10.
9. "Digital Audio Builds Toward a Sales Crescendo," *Business Week* (January 30, 1984), pp. 62–63.
10. "Panelists Offer Pricing Strategy Advice for Consumer and Industrial Products," *Marketing News* (February 1, 1985), pp. 1, 10.
11. Rockney G. Walters and Scott B. MacKenzie, "A Structural Equations Analysis of the Impact of Price Promotions on Store Performance," *Journal of Marketing Research,* vol. 25, no. 1 (February 1988), p. 51.
12. "Panelists Offer Pricing Strategy Advice for Consumer and Industrial Products," *Marketing News,* loc. cit.
13. Hershey H. Friedman, Phillip E. Weingarten, Linda Friedman, and Ralph Gallay, "The Effect of Various Price Markdowns on Consumers' Ratings of a New Product." *Journal of the Academy of Marketing Science,* vol. 10 (Fall 1982), p. 436.
14. Joseph P. Guiltinan, "The Price Bundling of Services: A Normative Framework," *Journal of Marketing,* vol. 15 (April 1987), p. 74.
15. Joel Dean, "Techniques for Pricing New Products and Services," in Victor Buell and Carl Heyel, eds., *Handbook of Modern Marketing* (New York: McGraw-Hill, 1970), pp. 5, 51.
16. Elliot B. Ross, "Making Money with Proactive Pricing," *Harvard Business Review,* vol. 62 (November–December, 1984), p. 149.
17. Gerard J. Tellis and Gary J. Gaeth, "Best Value, Price-Seeking, and Price Aversion: The Impact of Information and Learning on Consumer Choices," *Journal of Marketing,* vol. 54, no. 2 (April 1990), p. 44.
18. John L. Forbis and Nitin T. Mehta, "Value-Based Strategies for Industrial Products," *Business Horizons,* vol. 24 (May–June 1981), pp. 32–42.
19. Betsy Morris, "How Much Will People Pay to Save a Few Minutes of Cooking? Plenty," *Wall Street Journal* 25 July 1985, p. 21.
20. Jeffrey H. Birnbaum, "Pricing of Products Is Still an Art Often Having Little Link to Cost," in Benson P. Shapiro, Robert J. Dolan, and John A. Quelch, eds., *Marketing Management Readings,* vol. 3 (Homewood, Ill.: Irwin, 1985), p. 175.
21. Larry Armstrong and Judith H. Dobrzynski, "Aprica Kassai: A Last Ride into the U.S. with Status Symbol Strollers," *Business Week* (January 21, 1985), p. 117.
22. David N. Burt and Joseph E. Boyett, Jr., "Reduction in Selling Price After the Introduction of Competition," *Journal of Marketing Research,* vol. 16 (May 1979), p. 275.
23. Ross, op. cit., p. 153.
24. Birnbaum, loc. cit.
25. Alan R. Beckenstein and H. Landis Gabel, "Experience Curve Pricing Strategy: The Next Target of Antitrust," *Business Horizons,* vol. 25 (September–October 1982), p. 71.
26. Mary Karr, "The Case of the Pricing Predicament," *Harvard Business Review,* vol. 66, no. 2 (March–April 1988), p. 16.
27. Thomas Nagle, "Pricing as Creative Marketing," *Business Horizons,* vol. 26 (July–August 1983), p. 15.
28. William Theodore Cummings and Lonnie L. Ostrom, "Measuring Price Thresholds Using Social Judgment Theory," *Journal of the Academy of Marketing Science,* vol. 10 (Fall 1982), pp. 399, 406.
29. Alfred R. Oxenfeldt, "A Decision-Making Structure for Price Decisions," *Journal of Marketing,* vol. 37 (January 1973), p. 50.

30. Hugh M. Cannon and Fred W. Morgan, "A Strategic Pricing Framework," *Journal of Services Marketing*, vol. 4, no. 2 (Spring 1990), pp. 19–30.

31. Norton E. Marks and Neely S. Inlow, "Price Discrimination and Its Impact on Small Business," *Journal of Consumer Marketing*, vol. 5, no. 1 (Winter 1988), p. 37.

32. R. Ronald Stephenson, William L. Cron, and Gary L. Frazier, "Delegating Pricing Authority to the Sales Force: The Effects on Sales and Profit Performance," *Journal of Marketing*, vol. 43 (Spring 1979), p. 21.

33. David J. Reibstein and Hubert Gatignon, "Optimal Product Line Pricing: The Influence of Elasticities and Cross Elasticities," *Journal of Marketing Research*, vol. 21 (August 1984), p. 259.

34. Gordon A. Wyner, Lois H. Benedetti, and Bart M. Trapp, "Measuring the Quantity and Mix of Product Demand," *Journal of Marketing*, vol. 48 (Winter 1984), p. 108.

35. Benson P. Shapiro, V. Kasturi Rangan, Rowland T. Moriarty, and Elliot B. Ross, "Manage Customers for Profits (Not Just Sales)," *Harvard Business Review*, vol. 65, no. 5 (September–October 1987), p. 101.

36. Ross, op. cit., p. 154.

37. Joseph Kamen, "Price Filtering: Restricting Price Deals to Those Least Likely to Buy Without Them," *Journal of Consumer Marketing*, vol. 6, no. 3 (Summer 1989), p. 43.

18

Channel and Distribution Tactics

CHAPTER OBJECTIVES

⬤ Know the channel and distribution alternatives available to the marketing manager.

⬤ Understand how these tactics work together with other elements of the marketing mix to support marketing strategy.

⬤ Understand the importance of these tactics to success in the marketplace.

⬤ Know and be able to resolve the conflicts inherent in the use of these tactics.

Retail Power

There is a battle for power you may not know about. It is between the retailer and his supplier. The supplier wants shelf space and distribution. The retailer wants to remain competitive in his or her inventory assortments and wants a one-stop appeal to its consumers. So the retailer would rather deal with a number of different suppliers, while the supplier would like to have the retailer sell nothing but his product. According to Avijit Gosh, a New York University professor of marketing, this balance of power has definitely shifted toward retailers for several reasons. There is a lot of power concentrated in a relatively few very large retailing companies in the United States. How

did this come about? There was a tremendous retail expansion in the seventies and eighties. These large retail chains expanded their geographic regions to new territories. High technology has allowed major retailers to capture a great deal of purchase information with scanning devices. This allows them to be a lot more choosy about what products they order. Also, many large retailers have implemented direct product profitability analysis. Meanwhile strong competition between different suppliers allowed the retailer to play one supplier off against the other. "Just take a look at a company like Toys R Us, which controls roughly 25 per cent of the toy business in the United States," said Professor Gosh. "If they don't carry your toy, you are locked out of 25 per cent of the market from the start. The same power is now being used by Federated and Allied, which have begun to consolidate their buying with other divisions."[1]

Can a Ninety-Eight-Year-Old Woman Be Happy with a Twenty-Eight-Year-Old Rock Star?

A few years ago, a company called Collagen Corporation introduced a new product called Zyderm Collagen Implant, or ZCI. ZCI is a treatment for repairing scars and filling in wrinkles. But because this product must be injected by a doctor, its scientific credibility had to be established. To do this, Collagen spent $3.5 million on an advertising and publicity campaign through direct mail, ads in medical journals, and presentations at symposiums, to convince the nation's ten thousand physicians who specialize in dermatology and plastic surgery and similar cosmetic improvement work that their product was legitimate. Only after the physicians had been promoted did Collagen turn to the market segment targeted: women in the thirty-five to fifty-four age bracket with annual income above $25,000. The method used was to place low-key and nonsensational ads in moderate and noncontroversial magazines such as *Vogue.* As physicians' familiarity with and ability to use the product increased, Collagen tripled its initial year's advertising to the consumer with a $1.5 million advertising budget and increased its reach and mass appeal in additional magazines. As one analyst said, "Collagen didn't pull a fast one and go to the consumer first. If they had, it would have been absolutely disastrous." And as Collagen President Howard D.

Palefsky said, the last thing wanted was "headlines reading, 'Ninety-Eight-Year-Old Woman Gets Three CC of Collagen and Weds Twenty-Eight-Year-Old Rock Star.' "[2]

A Five-Million-Copy Best-Seller You Never Heard of

A best-selling book sold almost five million copies, and yet you probably never heard of it. The book was called *Olympic/Access,* and the reason it never appeared on any best-seller list is simple. It wasn't sold through the same channels as other books, such as bookstores. The number of books sold through bookstores determines which are best-sellers. Yet, *Olympic/Access* probably sold more copies than any other book the year it was published. This 96-page guide to the Olympic Games had an incredible first printing of 2.1 million copies. It was imprinted with the logo of Arco, the official gasoline sponsor of the games, which sold the books through its AM/PM Mini Markets. Another million books without the Arco logo were sold by Ken Mears Associates through gift shops, mass merchandisers, and the Boy Scouts of America. In this book, every Olympic event was described, including the rules of the games, information on the playing field, site maps, charts of world and Olympic records, and a great deal of other related information. If there are lessons here, they are that obvious channels of distribution for even well-known products may not always be the best and that much can be done with innovative channel and distribution tactics.[3] ●

Channels and Distribution: The Logistics of the Marketplace

In marketing, **logistics** is defined as "A single logic to guide the human process of planning, allocating and controlling financial and human resources committed to physical distribution, manufacturing support, and purchasing operations."[4] Although a marketing manager may be concerned with any of these functions, the major areas of concern for most marketing managers have to do with the **channels of distribution** and **physical distribution. Channels** are routes, or passages, or means, of distributing a product from producer to the ultimate buyer. **Physical distribution** consists of the materials management of incoming materials and supplies and the transportation and other associated activities. These include warehousing and inventory of physical goods, from the time they are produced until they reach the ultimate buyer. Therefore, channel decisions have to do with what routes, or means, to take and physical distribution decisions—for example, how to operate on that route.

481
Channel and
Distribution Tactics

Channel Decisions

There are six basic channel decisions with which the marketing manager must concern him- or herself, and for which he or she might be held responsible:

1. Direct or indirect channels
2. Single or multiple channels
3. Length of channel
4. Types of intermediaries
5. Number of intermediaries at each level
6. Which intermediaries[5]

These decisions are made by an overall planning analysis within five basic frameworks. First is economic orientation, which basically has to do with efficiency. It focuses on costs and economic outputs and is generally a short-term view. Second is a behavioral framework. This orientation is more social and looks to power and conflict. It is much longer range than the economic framework. Third is a political-economic framework. This is a newer orientation and looks at the distribution system, or channel, as a social system consisting of interacting sets of major economic and social political forces that affect behavior and performance.[6] Another framework is ecological. This approach focuses on the interaction between the firm and its environment. Finally, we have a strategic managerial system approach that emphasizes decision making and a developed system of strategy planning. Thus, this framework for looking at channel alternatives is concerned with the integrated and coordinated use of channel and marketing resources to achieve specific objectives.[7]

In considering the six basic channel alternatives, the marketing manager should consider these five analysis frameworks for decisions about the following tactical considerations: (1) evaluating the relative power of the various channel members, (2) organizing channel commitments formulating channel procedures, (3) accurately measuring channel performance, and (4) evaluating change potential within the channel and managing of the change when appropriate.[8]

Direct and Indirect Channels

A channel direct from the producer to the ultimate buyer offers advantages such as control over the product and marketing activities, including associated promotion, sales, and other marketing costs and reduced time spent in the channel. Under certain circumstances, a direct channel is very important for products such as perishables, including fresh fruits and dairy and other farm products. This channel may also be very important for specialty prod-

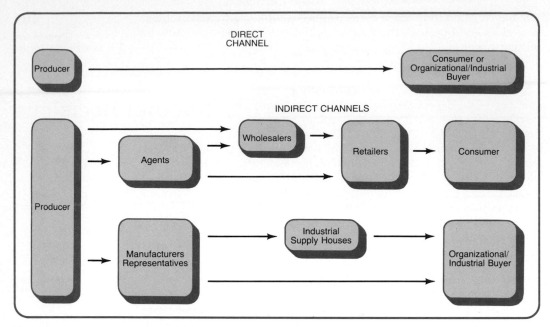

Figure 18-1 **Direct or Indirect Channels**

ucts that require a great deal of explanation and demonstration. Examples include certain types of cosmetics, encyclopedias, and other items sold directly, or face to face. However, there are some very important limitations in using direct channels. The main problem is achieving widespread distribution. The limited resources of a small firm may prohibit the use of a direct channel when it is selling to a large number of customers that are widely distributed. As a result, of the major channels for selling consumer goods, direct from manufacturer to consumer is the least used. On the other hand, it is the most popular channel for selling to organizations because unlike the consumer market, the organizational market consists of a smaller number of relatively large buyers, and, not infrequently, these organizational buyers are concentrated in specific geographic locations.

The use of indirect channels includes employing retailers, wholesalers and industrial supply houses. It also includes manufacturers' representatives, and other agents who do not actually take ownership of the products. Both are shown in Figure 18-1. The advantage in using each of these different agents will be discussed later, in the discussion of the types of intermediaries. But, in any case, one major advantage for all indirect channels are increased marketing opportunities and wider distribution potentials under varying conditions. In theory you might think that indirect channels invariably add cost. It is true that some manufacturers selling directly to consumers advertise that they have "the lowest prices by cutting out the middleman." In fact, because the cost per transaction tends to remain about the same in each sale, this is not necessarily true when costs are considered as a percentage of selling price. For example, a college student sought to make some money part-time by importing a bamboo cockroach trap made in the Orient. He profitably sold this item by an indirect channel (i.e., mail-order catalog houses). In this way he reached thousands of ultimate buyers for his product.

At an ultimate selling price to the consumer of $4 per unit, this student received $2 per unit from his intermediary, the catalog house. Thus, considering only an economic framework, had he gone directly to the consumer, he would have been able to sell at a lower price only if the cost of reaching each customer was $2 or less per unit.

Selling direct from an advertisement is usually so expensive that not only is a 400 per cent or better markup normal, but most direct-response advertisers make money only by selling the customer additional items after the initial sale. Opening a retail outlet (perhaps a booth at a weekend "flea market") would also require a high percentage of selling price due to the limited size of the market and, thus, numbers sold. It is probable that the cost of direct-response advertising necessary to sell each unit of this type of product or to rent a booth in a flea market would require a selling expense of at least $5 per unit. Thus, all other considerations aside, and to maintain the same profit margin, the price to the ultimate consumer under these circumstances would have had to have been $7 instead of $4.

Single and Multiple Channels

Multiple channels means using more than one channel simultaneously. Because the use of more than one channel obviously tends to provide additional outlets for sales and more chances for selling, you might think that use of multiple channels is always a good idea. There are several reasons why multiple channels may not be desirable. First, the economics of the situation has to be considered, including costs, profits, and available resources. Because resources are always limited—and this is especially true with a smaller firm—resources may only be available for a single channel, or a limited number of channels, as opposed to all available channels, due to the cost of operating through each channel. Thus, one distribution tactic that has been employed is distribution through a limited number of channels and expansion through additional channels using the profits from initial operations. A firm may distribute locally and later expand nationally.

Another reason why multiple channels may not be desirable is due to interchannel rivalry. A standard drugstore outlet selling your toothpaste product at its recommended retail price will hardly be delighted that the discount department store across the street is selling the product at 10 to 20 per cent less. A newspaper purchasing a news column from a syndicated columnist does not mind if other newspapers around the country print the same column, as long as other newspapers in the same geographic area do not print it. A mail-order house selling your product does not want to see the same product sold in retail stores. In every case the channel distributor would like to have exclusive distribution rights to your product.

Now you may say, so what? But if you choose to operate with multiple channels despite **interchannel rivalry**, a channel may not push your product or service aggressively. In fact, unless they have "an exclusive," some channels may refuse to sell your product at all.

Whether you as a marketing manager grant this or not is one of the decisions that must be made, for which you are responsible. At some times, the desires or even demands of the distribution channels must be considered as primary, and this gets especially into a behavioral and political economy approach to channel decision making. If the channel member has the power to affect your business significantly and negatively, should you choose to operate with competing channels, this certainly must be considered. In addition, there may be advantages in using a selective single channel.

In some cases a contractual relationship will enable a minimum number of units to be guaranteed to be sold. In others the mere fact of exclusivity will in itself provide sufficient encouragement for the channel member to provide far more attention to selling your item than would be the case were many different channels in operation.

In other cases use of multiple channels can be maintained in the face of interchannel rivalry. One manufacturer of a new skin care product, when faced by the demand of exclusivity by a chain of major department stores, responded as follows: "I won't guarantee that you will be the only stores to sell my product, but I will guarantee that if you order now, you will be the first." Another potential solution is to use special branding for different channels.

Upjohn, a well-known chemical company, introduced a new product that cured mastitis in cattle and decided to sell it through drugstores as well as supply it to veterinarians. Because of interchannel rivalry—because the veterinarians' customers could buy the product direct—the veterinarians refused to use the product, using instead a similar product produced by a competitor. Upjohn then rebranded the product under a new name for the

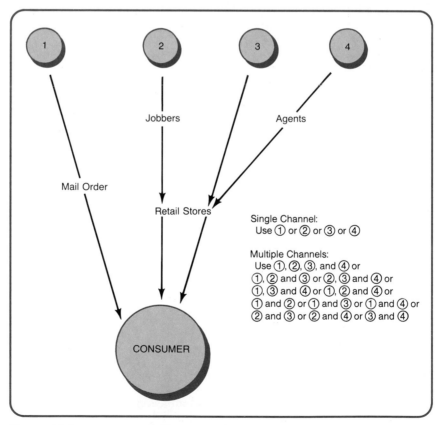

Figure 18-2   Single vs. Multiple Channel Concept

veterinarians and kept the original name for the drugstores, and sales increased dramatically.

Other solutions that enable using multiple channels, despite interchannel rivalry, include different packaging and different pricing. In some retail outlets, you may find a **private brand** in a different package and at a lower price than a name-brand product manufactured by the same producer. Also, the manufacturer's brand may be on different versions of a product, designed for different stores. This makes comparison very difficult. The single- versus multiple-channel concept is shown in Figure 18-2.

Length of Channel

The length of channel decision requires additional considerations regarding distribution, either indirectly or directly, to the ultimate buyer. Should the producer sell through a retailer and thence to the ultimate customer; or should the producer sell through a wholesaler, thence to a retailer, and thence to the customer; or should the channel be even longer, through use of a jobber and an agent or other intermediaries? There is no one fixed answer. Factors that should be considered include the financial strength of the manufacturer, the size and completeness of the product line, the average order size, the concentration of customers geographically, the seasonality of sales, the distance from the producer to the market, and the perishability of the product. The channels tend to be shorter when the manufacturer is strong financially, the product line is large and complete, the average order size is high, the customers tend to be concentrated geographically, there is little seasonality, the distance from producer to market is short, or the product is perishable.[9]

Types of Intermediaries

Retailers. Use of **retailers** with no other channel intermediaries is usually common when the number of retail outlets necessary to reach the ultimate consumer is limited, and these retail outlets buy in sufficiently large quantities to make the transaction profitable. Next to selling direct, it is the best way to stay close to the customer, and the quickest way of knowing what is going on in the marketplace.

Wholesalers. The use of a **wholesaler** is desirable when greater distribution is required over a wider area. A cost comparison would probably show that attempting to contact retail establishments directly over a wide geographic area would probably be more expensive due to the greater number of transactions and the greater distance from the producer. Thus, eliminating the wholesaler where wide distribution is needed should only be considered when the retailer buys in significantly large quantities. Along with straight wholesalers of consumer goods, **industrial supply houses**, which are wholesalers for organizational buying units, should also be noted. These houses provide not only widespread distribution, as with consumer wholesalers, but are also cost effective with low-cost, relatively standardized equipment, when a great deal of explanation is not required to make a sale.

Manufacturer's Representatives and Agents. Manufacturer's representatives and **agents** who represent the manufacturer, but are independent and do not take title to the goods sold, are most useful under certain conditions. They are very beneficial when the producer or manufacturer is small and has a narrow product line. Under these conditions, the manufacturer has insufficient resources to maintain and train its own internal sales force. Also, it may lack the marketing expertise in some cases or be too new to have contacts in the market. If the product line is very narrow, the cost for each sales contact may become inordinately high because the entire contact cost must be absorbed by the sale of a relatively few products.

To the agent representing several different companies with noncompeting products, this is no problem because multiple products can be shown at any single sales contact. As with a wholesaler, the use of an agent enables widely disbursed distribution of the product. Thus, a small manufacturer located anywhere in the United States can sell not only nationally, but internationally. For larger companies, the agent is also important in circumstances where either a great deal of explanation and time are needed to sell the product, or a great deal of understanding of the market or the customer is required. Examples of this are expensive farm machinery, airplanes used by airlines internationally, and exported military equipment. Sometimes agents are used because of their specific expertise and knowledge of the marketplace and the company, along with the company's own sales force and representative.

If you're wondering how to get agents and manufacturers' representatives to spend time selling your product instead of someone else's, you might consider some of the suggestions contained in Table 18-1. Remember, these market intermediaries may carry other product lines in addition to yours. When you are a small company, or have just entered the market, you can't expect to be among an agent's top lines.[10]

Franchising Operations. Franchising operations, whereby a producer or supplier, known as a franchiser, permits the franchisee the right to sell products and use the producer's or supplier's name and strategy in exchange for a percentage of the sales, is a relatively new concept in distribution. But, over the last twenty years, franchising sales have grown at better than 10 per cent per year, and currently exceed more than $430 billion a year. As a consequence, while there are limitations to franchising operations that must be considered, the franchising alternative is a proven tactical tool in the arsenal of the marketing manager. The characteristics of a successful franchise operation include the following:

- *High growth margin.* High growth margin is necessary in order that the franchisee can afford a high franchise fee that the franchisor needs to run the program successfully.
- *In-store value added.* Franchising tends to work better when a certain amount of the value is added in stores, be they fast-food outlets or automobile dealers.
- *Secret processes.* The franchise should involve certain unique processes that may be concepts, formulas, or products that cannot be obtained or duplicated anywhere else. This is the basis of Col. Sanders's Kentucky Fried Chicken franchise.
- *Real estate profits.* Real estate profits are necessary to generate income from ownership of property that is a significant source of revenue for the franchisor.

- Treat them like family.
- Outline your marketing program and ensure that the agent is comfortable with his or her role.
- Follow up fast in shipping brochures, etc.
- Make headquarters people available for field visits.
- Customize sales literature with the agent's name.
- Tell the agent which items to emphasize.
- Provide product training.
- Set your commission above competing lines.
- Pay a premium for landing new accounts.
- Don't cut commission when agent sales increase.
- Ship and pay promptly.
- Pay extra if an agent exceeds your target.
- Visit the agent on his or her territory at his or her convenience.
- Do on-the-spot coaching and make joint calls.
- Give agent accounts that you have made in his or her area.
- Listen to the agent's opinion and feedback from the customer.
- Make it easy to track the status of orders.
- Use cash incentives for short periods to achieve specific sales goals.
- Recognize agent achievements in sales verbally, in print (letters, newsletters, thank yous), and with awards.
- Put the agent's name, address, and phone number in your ads.
- Qualify sales leads thoroughly before forwarding them to your agents.
- Form an agents or reps council as a board to assist you with strategy and problems.
- Assure the agent that the territory is his or hers and will be in the future.

Source: Adapted from Martin Everett, "What to Do When You Are Tenth Out of the Bag," *Sales and Marketing Management Magazine*, vol. 141, no. 1 (January 1989), p. 37.

- *Simplicity.* Research has demonstrated that the most successful franchise operations are those in which the owner merely implements a program already thoroughly thought through and tested by the franchisor.[11]

What does it cost the franchisee? This varies from a few thousand dollars to several million. Table 18-2 shows the cost for a CelluLand, Inc., franchise. CelluLand is a franchised chain of retail stores that sell, install, and service cellular telephone products.[12]

You may be surprised to learn that there is a great deal of international franchising going on. In a recent year, 295 American companies had 23,524 franchising outlets worldwide, as shown in Figure 18-3.[13]

Number of Intermediaries at Each Level

The decision as to the required number of intermediaries at each level of distribution is based on many important factors. More intermediaries at each level are required when the unit value is low, the product is purchased frequently, there is high technical complexity in the product, service require-

Table 18-2 What Does It Cost the Franchisee?

Franchisor revenues	$6,700,000
Franchisor losses	950,000

Average start-up costs for franchisees:

● Franchise fee	$25,000
● Design fee	3,000
● Leasehold improvements	30,000 to 60,000
(including construction build-out, exterior sign, and interior graphics)	
● Inventory	20,000 to 30,000
(including display phones, accessories, opening inventory, and supplies)	
● Deposits	3,600 to 8,300
(including security deposits for leased equipment and site lease)	
● Prepaid business expenses	63,100 to 133,400
(including leased equipment, rent, insurance, license, legal, printing, promotion, training costs, and working capital)	
TOTAL ESTIMATED COSTS	$144,700 to 259,700

Monthly royalties: 5 per cent of monthly gross sales.
National marketing: 1.5 per cent of monthly gross sales.
Source: CelluLand Inc.

Source: Adapted from Echo Montgomery Garrett, "Breaking into the Big Time," *Success* (June 1989), p. 71.

ments are high, inventory investment is high, there is significant product differentiation, total market potential is high, geographic concentration is low, the manufacturer's current market share is high, the competition is intense, and lack of availability could significantly affect the customer's production process.[14,15]

Which Intermediaries?

The selection of specific intermediaries depends on both potential roles and role conflict for each potential distributor.

Figure 18-4 illustrates fourteen different **intrachannel conflict** issues. The selection of a specific intermediary can depend on any one or all of these. In general, it has been discovered that the conflict arising from both the administrative and product service issues indicated in the figure diminishes when the producer is perceived to exhibit a leadership style emphasizing participation, support, and direction in carrying out channel activities.[16]

The individual intermediary's role is also important to consider because it can have a major impact on marketing strategy. The distributor's role was found to vary as a function of several interrelated factors, including the pro-

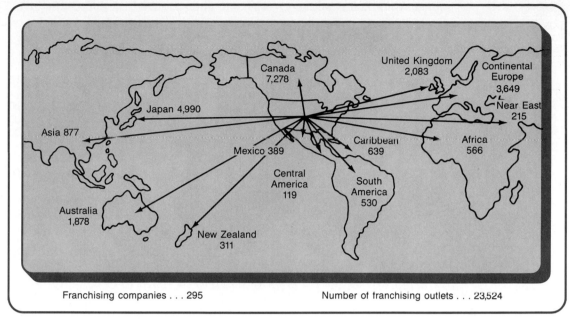

Franchising companies ... 295   Number of franchising outlets ... 23,524

Figure 18-3   International Franchising

Source: From Wray O. Candilis, *Franchising in the Economy* (Washington, D.C.: U.S. Department of Commerce, 1984), p. 6.

1. Bureaucratic red tape
2. Quality of sales training programs
3. General responsiveness of franchisor to franchise needs
4. Quality of meetings and conventions
5. Quality of intercity referral program
6. Local advertising assistance
7. Service and/or advertising fees
8. Contract terms or arrangements
9. Accounting information requirements
10. Initial franchise fees (or fees on additional new offices)
11. Sales promotion assistance
12. Quality of national advertising program
13. Quality of management training program
14. Exclusive territory arrangements

Source: Adapted from Patrick L. Schul, William M. Pride, and Taylor L. Little, "The Impact of Channel Leadership Behavior on Intrachannel Conflict," *Journal of Marketing,* vol. 47 (Summer 1983), p. 27.

Figure 18-4   Important Intrachannel Conflict Issues

ducer's marketing strategy—especially the producer's intended unique competitive advantage—the strength of the producer's position in the marketplace, the technical characteristics of the product, and the importance of immediate product availability to the customer (the latter is especially important with industrial or organizational-bought goods).[17]

For example, an intermediary may have strengths where they are unimportant, given the firm's intended competitive advantage, and weaknesses, given the technical characteristics of a particular product. As a result, an outstanding distributor may be the wrong one for certain manufacturers.

Selection Considerations

In addition the marketing manager should consider the following before deciding which intermediaries to use:

- *Market segment.* It is essential that the specific intermediary selected know and understand the customer and the specific market segment that has been targeted.
- *Changes during the product life cycle.* As noted in Chapter 12, different strategies are required in different stages of the product life cycle. The selling requirements for these strategies differ and may therefore require different intermediaries.
- *Producer-distributor fit.* Intermediaries are not members of your company or organization, and therefore you have less control over them. It follows that the policies, strategies, image, and other aspects of the distributor chosen should fit with the producers.
- *Qualification assessment.* Intermediaries must be examined as to their qualifications, and if the intermediary has a track record, this record of performance should be examined and confirmed by others who have done business with the intermediary under consideration.
- *Distributor training and support.* Before the channel is opened, you should know what training and support will be required by the producer.[18]

Evaluating Existing Distributors

In many cases the marketing manager, assuming responsibilities for a distribution channel or channels, will find a complete or, sometimes, a partially complete network of distributors already in place. He or she should never automatically assume that things are as they should be. He or she should evaluate existing distributors in terms of current market share, rate of penetration, territory, product, and market potential. The bottom line is that the market manager must effectively match products with distributors and then monitor the results.[19]

One approach to evaluating existing distributors is shown in Figure 18-5. In this distributor portfolio analysis, the company's share of the distributor's product line sales on the horizontal axis is plotted against the distributor's inflation-adjusted growth rate on the vertical axis. Other information is also displayed, including manufacturing costs, overhead recovery, deals and discounts, promotional allowances, and freight allowances. Depending upon the

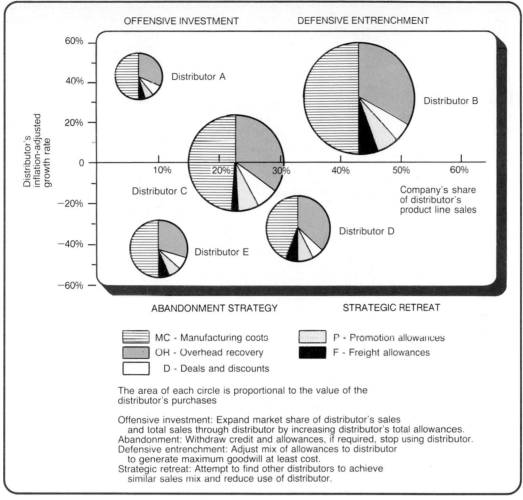

Figure 18-5 Distributor Portfolio Analysis

Source: From Peter R. Dickson, "Distributor Portfolio Analysis and the Channel Dependence Matrix; New Techniques for Understanding and Managing the Channel," *Journal of Marketing*, vol. 47 (Summer 1983), p. 38. Used with permission.

location of the distributor on this graph, offensive investment, defensive entrenchment, abandonment strategy, or strategic retreat is recommended.[20]

Figure 18-5 looks more complicated than it actually is. Let's say we're going to check out distributor A. First we find out our company's share of the distributor's total sales. In this case it's 8 per cent. Next we find the distributor's annual sales growth rate. He's growing pretty fast. Adjusting for inflation, it turns out to be 42 per cent. We plot these coordinates on the graph. Now we draw a circle. How big? That depends on how much a particular distributor sold. Of our five distributors, let's say we sell only one-sixth of that of our largest distributor (distributor B). In fact, we sell only about one-sixth as much. Then our circle should be only one-sixth as large as the circle drawn for distributor B. The circle is divided into segments representing the various costs incurred in selling the product. Distributor A falls in the area representing offensive investment. So we should seek to expand our share of the distributor's sales and to increase his or her total sales. We can do this by increasing his or her allowances.

Channel Management

Selection does not end the marketing manager's responsibilities regarding channels. In addition, the marketing manager must manage. Because the marketing manager usually will not have direct supervisory authority over distribution channels, channel management frequently takes the form of influence. The basic questions become how these channels might be influenced once selected and which influence strategies are more effective under different situations.

To be able to influence channel members is crucial to good marketing management. Phil Knight, CEO of Nike, Inc., directed a turnaround that nearly tripled profits to $101.7 million on $1.2 billion in sales of his famous Nike footwear. This feat was made possible through channel management and influence. For example, by pressuring more retailers to order six months in advance, he was able to cut production when necessary and avoid inventory buildup.[21] But how do you get channel members to do this kind of thing?

Take a look at a channel member's evaluation process in Figure 18-6. You can see that acceptance or rejection is based on the member's characteristics, the information presented, inferences on certain attributes, and the member's judgment of profit potential.[22]

Potential Influence Strategies

Gary Frazier and Jagdish Sheth at the University of Southern California have identified five categories of **influence strategies**:

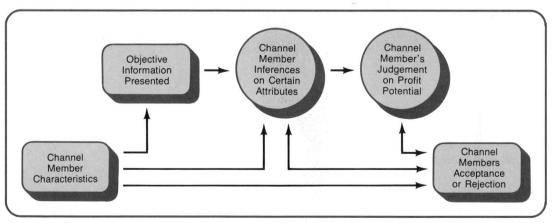

Figure 18-6   A Channel Member's Evaluation Process

Source: Adapted from Vithala R. Rao and Edward W. McLaughlin, "Modeling the Decision to Add New Products by Channel Intermediaries," *Journal of Marketing*, vol. 53, no. 1 (January 1989), p. 82.

1. **Indirect influence strategies**, whereby information is merely exchanged with channel member personnel
2. **Direct unmediated strategies**, where consequences of the acceptance or rejection of the channel program and/or its implementation are stressed, but consequences are based on a response from the market environment and not on a member of the producer organization
3. **Reward and punishment strategies**, where rewards or punishments are given to channel members and their firms
4. **Direct unweighted strategy or request**, where the producer's desires or wishes are communicated and no consequences of acceptance or rejection are mentioned or applied.
5. **Direct mediated strategies**, where a specific action is requested and consequences of exception or rejection are stressed and based on the producer's mediation[23]

A summation of the frequency of the use of various of these influence strategies is shown in Figure 18-7. Note that the most frequent strategy used is that of information exchange, with threats and legalistic pleas being the least frequently used.[24]

To understand the effectiveness, as well as the efficiency, of the use of one or more of these influence strategies, we must return to the concept of power. The effectiveness of any influence strategy depends on the power of the producer or supplier, as well as that of the channel member. On both sides power tends to be controlled by virtue of position—access to and control over scarce and limited resources.[25]

The specifics of the supplier or producer power are shown in Figure 18-8, including measures of power and sources of power.[26] For example, measures of power include control over retail pricing; choice of retail location; minimum order size; mix of units ordered; retail advertising; provision of credit to customers; ability to buy from other suppliers; salesperson training; salesperson hiring; physical layout of a store; participation in professional and trade associations; and selling policies, including territorial and customer restrictions. Note that the supplier or producer has varying control

	Mean Use	Most Frequently Used	Tied for Most Frequently Used	Never Used
Information exchange	49%[a]	62%[b]	6%	8%
Requests	27	13	7	11
Recommendations	19	8	7	23
Promises	15	4	9	37
Threats	10	1	5	53
Legalistic pleas	6	0	3	59

[a]The information exchange strategy was used in an average of 49% of typical monthly contacts.

[b]The information exchange strategy was the one most frequently used in 62% of the dyadic relationships.

Source: Adapted from Gary L. Frazier and John O. Summers, "Interfirm Influence Strategies and Their Application Within Distribution Channels," *Journal of Marketing*, vol. 48 (Summer 1984), p. 50.

Figure 18-7 Frequencies of Use of the Influence Strategies

Measures of Power	Measures of Power Sources	
Control Over	Economic	Noneconomic
1. Retail pricing 2. Choice of retail location 3. Minimum order size 4. Mix of units ordered 5. Retail advertising 6. Provision of credit to customers 7. Ability to buy from other suppliers 8. Salesperson training 9. Salesperson hiring 10. Physical layout of the store 11. Participation in professional and trade associations 12. Selling policies—territorial and customer restrictions	1. Financial assistance at start 2. Financial assistance on a current basis 3. Help in retail advertising 4. Assistance in store management 5. Provision of market information 6. Provision of sales leads 7. Promptness of delivery 8. Frequency of delivery	1. Selection of products 2. Assistance in training 3. Rate of development of new products 4. Backup by advertising 5. Level of expertise 6. Team association

Source: Adapted from Michael Etgar, "Selection of an Effective Channel Control Mix," *Journal of Marketing*, vol. 42 (July 1978), p. 56.

Figure 18-8 Measures of Power and Sources of Power in Distribution Channels

over these different measures, that the control will vary greatly depending on the situation, and finally that there will be no control in some situations.

These sources of power can be categorized as coercive or reward. Some examples, along with their classification as to unfavorable deviation, natural favorable limit, natural unfavorable limit, or favorable deviation, are shown in Figure 18-9.[27]

In general, a channel member's satisfaction is related to noncoercive sources and inversely related to coercive sources.[28] But this does not mean

Coercive Power Sources	Unfavorable Deviation	Natural Favorable Limit
Delay delivery	Infinite delay possible	↔ Instantaneous delivery
Take legal action	Infinite amount of legal action possible	↔ Absence of legal action
Charge high prices	Unlimited potential for high prices	↔ Free goods
Reward Power Sources	**Natural Unfavorable Limit**	**Favorable Deviation**
Provide service	No service	↔ Unrestricted amount of service possible
Provide advertising support	No advertising support	↔ Unlimited advertising support
Train personnel	No training	↔ Unlimited training

Source: Adapted from John F. Gaski, "The Theory of Power and Conflict in Channels of Distribution," *Journal of Marketing*, vol. 48 (Summer 1984), p. 23.

Figure 18-9 Coercive and Reward Power Sources and Potential Outcomes

that coercive sources are not more effective in various situations, only that channel members are less satisfied with this means of influence. The implications of this dissatisfaction over a longer period and in dynamic situations is one of the factors that must be taken into account by the marketing manager. However, long-term relationships do not only depend on the type of influence employed. Sound relationships can be developed and maintained when a producer provides products, services, and a modus operandi that meet or exceed distributor expectations and that are, over all, superior, or at least considered superior, to those available from alternative sources.[29] This generally means that the management of ongoing channels of distribution leans heavily on a behavioral, socially oriented model of decision making by channel members. It emphasizes the importance of a social contract in maintaining efficient exchange in long-run relationships that are vulnerable to alternative opportunities from other sources even if simple dependence is the crucial factor in the short run.[30,31,32]

Physical Distribution Management

Focus of Physical Distribution Management

Physical distribution management focuses on the means as well as ancillary activities required to get the physical product from the producer to the buyer along the channel. It includes considerations of warehousing, inventory carrying, inventory obsolescence, production or supply alternatives, cost concessions, transportation, communications and data processing, alternative facilities used, and the physical aspects of channel of distribution itself.[33] Peter Drucker calls it the last profit frontier.[34] It requires a considerable balancing of objectives—considering not only the many alternatives possible in physical distribution, but also the objectives of other functional areas such as manufacturing. The balancing of some typical conflicting objectives is shown in Figure 18-10.[35]

Customer service needs to be further amplified. Availability, timeliness, and the quality of physical distribution are benefits that customers value as much as product quality and a competitive price/benefit ratio.[36] Companies have failed to introduce new products successfully due to a delay in shipping to the channel intermediary. Ten thousand copies of one of this author's books for marketing practitioners were presold to bookstores. A paper shortage created a delay in production, and the books were shipped several months late, arriving shortly after Christmas. Because bookstores take books on consignment and have the right to return copies unsold, more than half of the books were returned to the publisher immediately. You can see that the importance of these trade-offs is not trivial.

Although, in the great majority of cases, there is little conflict between marketing managers and physical distribution managers, who are specialists in this area, there are exceptions. Inventory control and warehousing have been found to be the largest problem areas in balancing the objectives between these two marketing functional areas.[37]

Successful marketing logisticians must look at the costs of both inbound and outbound transportation—inbound because the transportation of raw

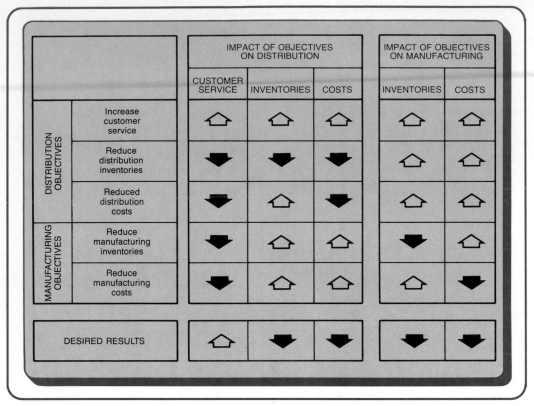

Figure 18-10 The Balancing of Conflicting Physical Distribution Objectives

Source: From Stephen B. Oresman and Charles D. Scudder, "A Remedy for Maldistribution," *Business Horizons* (June 1974), p. 66. Used with permission.

materials is tied to manufacturing, as outbound is tied to inventory control. They are juggling inventory turn rates, order cycle time, and of course, customer service.[38]

The weighing of the importance of sometimes conflicting objectives is always crucial. For example, one study showed that distribution service was second only to product quality in importance to the channel member. It was more important than price.[39] This demonstrates just how important physical distribution is and the weight that it must be given in allocating time and resources.

Physical Distribution Alternatives

There are only three basic decisions with which a marketing manager is concerned regarding physical distribution:

1. What physical distribution services are needed?
2. How should these physical distribution services be provided?
3. What resources are required?[40]

Deciding what physical distribution services are needed begins with the establishment of physical distribution objectives. To answer the question of how these services are to be provided requires a consideration of alternatives and their associated costs, as well as of environmental scanning and an analysis of the situation, as was discussed in Chapter 6. Recent trends that should be considered part of the analysis include the result of a recent National Council of Physical Distribution Management (NCPDM) survey of one hundred businesses, as shown in Figure 18-11.[41] Finally, required resources in money, people, and capital equipment to reach these objectives are

1. Better decision making will result from improved computer-based information.
2. Increased worker productivity will result from automation and computerization at all levels.
3. Competition in world markets will be increasingly difficult for U.S. corporations.
4. Control of logistics activities, integrated through computer-to-computer interface, will improve.
5. New capital will be needed to modernize facilities and plants.
6. Information will replace or reduce inventory as a supply/demand buffer.
7. The U.S. economic base will shift from smokestack industries to high-tech services.
8. There will be slow economic growth with relatively low inflation of 6% or less.
9. Off-shore sourcing of manufactured goods will increase.
10. Multinational corporations will be increasingly important in a worldwide economy.
11. Multimodal, full-service transportation companies (megacarriers) will emerge.
12. Emphasis on strategic planning will increase.
13. The prime interest rate will remain higher than 12%.
14. A more knowledgeable, better-trained labor force will emerge.
15. The decrease in transportation regulation by the federal government will continue.
16. The use of personal computers by all levels of management will grow.
17. Smaller, decentralized plants located closer to the marketplace will emerge.
18. Retail and wholesale deliveries will be reduced through more direct delivery.
19. Third World nations will play a greater role in the world economy both as producers and consumers.
20. The U.S. population will continue to shift from the Northeast to the Sunbelt.

Source: "Study Pinpoints Trends with Biggest Impact on Distribution Management," *Marketing News* (March 2, 1984), p. 10.

Figure 18-11 Twenty Trends with the Biggest Impact on Physical Distribution (in order of importance)

projected. In effect, the result is a physical distribution plan that is a subset of the overall marketing plan. And, like a marketing plan, there are clear objectives. One expert says that in physical distribution, his objectives are always "the right product, at the right place, at the right time, and in the right condition."[42].

Is is worth it? A study by Dr. Bernard LaLonde, professor of logistics at Ohio State University, surveyed the industry for logistics improvements. Here's what his respondants predicted:

- A 25 per cent reduction in time from order placement to merchandise receipt at the distribution center
- A doubling of merchandise turnover at the distribution center
- More than 60 per cent of vendor transactions accomplished through electronic means
- A dramatic increase in the use of bar code technology
- Ninety-eight per cent of sales transactions recorded by point-of-sale data[43]

Physical Distribution Optimization

Physical distribution optimization is limited only by the imagination, according to two experts in this field, Kenneth Ackerman, chairman of Distribution Centers, Inc., and Bernard J. LaLonde, of Ohio State University. In an important essay in the *Harvard Business Review*, they recommended improvements in one specialty area of physical distribution, **warehousing**.[44] Their recommendations might usefully be considered in all physical distribution areas to improve efficiency. The areas noted by these experts for emphasis were increasing the size of the units shipped, seeking round-trip opportunities where the transportation conveyance didn't travel empty, increasing the use of cubes and other efficient packaging methods for shipment, reducing the distances traveled, reducing the items handled, improving forecasting accuracy, freeing labor bottlenecks, smoothing the flow variation, and installing specific improvement targets.

But perhaps the most important area that bears on physical distribution optimization has to do with customer service. Researchers have found that customer service is a unifying factor for integrating marketing and logistics. According to Dr. Doug Lampert at the University of South Florida,[45] logistical factors rank high in determining customer satisfaction.[46] To reach full potential in this role requires greater emphasis on the physical distribution role within the firm. It is possible optimizing physical distribution will require the consolidation of logistical activities within the firm in the same manner as the consolidation of other marketing activities is required to obtain the full benefits of marketing.[47]

Summary

In this chapter we have noted the importance and power of channel and distribution decisions for implementing marketing strategy. Specifically, we have seen that channel decisions fall into six different areas: deciding on direct or indirect channels, single or multiple channels, the length of the channel, the types of intermediaries, the number of distributors at each level, and which intermediaries to use. Each area of decision making is interrelated and requires management analysis, judgment, and decision making to develop the optimal tactical channel mix. But even competent decision making doesn't ensure that the process will perform at its optimum. It must be managed. The basic questions are how to influence the process and which influence strategies are best under varying conditions and situations.

Once the channel has been established and is operating, it leads to the physical distribution management process, which focuses on the means and ancillary activities of moving the product through the channel. To accomplish this, we must consider which physical distribution services are needed, how they should be provided, and what resources are required to provide them. Once the physical distribution system is implemented, it can be optimized through considering improvements in various areas, which is limited only by the imagination. The entire process of channel and physical distribution management consists of far more than static goals and procedures. Channel and distribution tactics are dynamic concepts that change continually due to the changing of the environs in the marketplace. As a consequence, they must be continually reviewed and modified to meet the needs of the market.[48] One practitioner has noted: "Because distribution strategy often relies on channel members for execution, it's one of the most challenging areas facing marketing managers."[49]

Questions

1. What can you do about "retail power?"
2. What changes in the environs of the marketplace would need to occur that might cause the Collagen Corporation to change its tactics in distributing ZCI? How would Collagen's tactics change under the conditions you envision?
3. Can you think of situations in which a producer would have to select the alternative of selling direct, despite the advantages discussed in the chapter for selling indirect?
4. If it is more profitable to sell through one channel, what are some examples of situations in which a producer would choose to sell through additional or alternate channels, even though it is less profitable?
5. What are the major reasons why multiple channels cannot be used in every situation?
6. Give examples of when you would want to use a retailer, a wholesaler, an agent, manufacturer's representatives, wholesale industrial supply houses, franchisees.

7. You have engaged an agent to sell a product. You suspect that the agent is not selling as much as he or she could. How might you influence this agent to increase his or her sales?
8. Who has the most power in any situation, a producer or the channel member? Justify your answer.
9. A survey cited in the text indicates that distribution service is second only to product quality in importance to the channel member. It is noted as more important than product price. How much emphasis should you give this study in considering other marketing tactics, such as pricing?
10. The case of the Olympic book selling five million copies and yet being unknown in bookstores demonstrates that less well-known channels of distribution can be tremendously effective. Can you think of some unusual channels for distributing the following products: shoes, toothpaste, lobsters from Maine?

Ethical Question ────────────────────

As the president of a profitable and growing firm, you have only one problem: a continual shortage of operating capital. Accordingly, you habitually pay suppliers 60 to 180 days late. Although always late, you always pay. Your suppliers grumble about this, but none have refused you credit to date. Is it ethical to use suppliers as a source of what amounts to an interest-free loan?

Endnotes ────────────────────

1. Brent H. Felgner, "Retailers Grab Power, Control Marketplace," *Marketing News* (January 16, 1989), vol. 23, no. 2, p. 1.
2. "The Smooth Selling of a Wrinkle Remover," *Business Week* (March 5, 1985), p. 66.
3. "Publisher Garners Box Car Sales with a Dual Distribution Strategy," *Marketing News* (May 11, 1984), p. 15.
4. Peter D. Bennett, *Dictionary of Marketing Terms* (Chicago: AMA, 1988), p. 108.
5. Bruce Mallen, "Functional Spinoff: A Key to Anticipating Change in Distribution Structure," *Journal of Marketing*, vol. 37 (July 1973), pp. 19–20.
6. Louis W. Stern and Torger Reve, "Distribution Channels as Political Economics: A Framework for Comparative Analysis," *Journal of Marketing*, vol. 44 (Summer 1980), p. 53.
7. Ronald D. Michman, "Marketing Channels: A Strategic Planning Approach," *Managerial Planning* (November–December 1983), p. 39.
8. Donald J. Bowersox, M. Bixby Cooper, Douglas M. Lambert, and Donald A. Taylor, *Management in Marketing Channels* (New York: McGraw-Hill, 1980).
9. Michman, loc. cit.
10. Martin Everett, "What to Do When You Are Tenth Out of the Bag," *Sales and Marketing Management Magazine*, vol. 141, no. 1 (January 1989), p. 37.
11. Phillip D. White and Albert D. Bates, "Franchising Will Remain Retailing Fixture, But Its Salad Days Long Since Gone," *Marketing News* (February 17, 1984), p. 14.
12. Echo Montgomery Garrett, "Breaking into the Big Time," *Success*, vol. 36, no. 5 (June 1989), p. 71.
13. Wray O. Candilis, *Franchising in the U.S. Economy* (Washington, D.C.: U.S. Department of Commerce, 1984), p. 6.
14. Michman, op. cit., p. 41.
15. Frederick B. Webster, Jr., "The Role of the Industrial Distributor in Marketing Strategy," *Journal of Marketing*, vol. 40 (July 1976), p. 13.
16. Patrick L. Schul, William M. Pride, and Taylor L. Little, "The Impact of Channel Leadership Behavior on Intrachannel Conflict," *Journal of Marketing*, vol. 47 (Summer 1983), p. 27.
17. Webster, op. cit., p. 12.
18. James D. Hlavacek and Tommy J. McCuistion, "Industrial Distributors—When, Who and How," *Harvard Business Review*, vol. 61 (March–April 1983), pp. 97–100.
19. Ibid., p. 99.
20. Peter R. Dickson, "Distributor Portfolio Analysis and the Channel Dependence Matrix: New Techniques for Understanding and Managing the Channel," *Journal of Marketing*, vol. 47 (Summer 1983), p. 38.
21. Barbara Buell, "Nike Catches Up with the Trendy Frontrunner," *Business Week* (October 24, 1988), p. 88.
22. Vithala R. Rao and Edward W. McLaughlin, "Modeling the Decision to Add New Products by Channel Intermediaries," *Journal of Marketing*, vol. 53, no. 1 (January 1989), p. 82.
23. Gary L. Frazier and Jagdish N. Sheth, "An Attitude Behavior Framework for Distribution Channel Management," *Journal of Marketing*, vol. 49 (Summer 1985), p. 41.
24. Gary L. Frazier and John O. Summers, "Interfirm Influence Strategies and Their Application Within Distribution Channels," *Journal of Marketing*, vol. 48 (Summer 1984), p. 50.
25. Mary N. Lederhaus, "Improving Marketing Channel Control Through Power Exchange," *Journal of the Academy of Marketing Science*, vol. 12 (Summer 1984), p. 32.
26. Michael Etgar, "Selection of an Effective Channel Control Mix," *Journal of Marketing*, vol. 42 (July 1978), p. 56.
27. John F. Gaski, "The Theory of Power and Conflict in Channels of Distribution," *Journal of Marketing*, vol. 48 (Summer 1984).
28. Donald A. Michie and Stanley D. Sibley, "Channel Member Satisfaction: Controversy Resolved," *Journal of the Academy of Marketing Science*, vol. 13 (Winter–Spring 1985), p. 203.
29. James C. Anderson and James A. Narus, "A Model of the Distributor's Perspective of Distributor/

Manufacturer Working Relationships," *Journal of Marketing*, vol. 48 (Fall 1984), p. 70.

30. George John, "An Empirical Investigation of Some Antecedents of Opportunism in a Marketing Channel," *Journal of Marketing Research*, vol. 21 (August 1984), p. 287.

31. Erin Anderson, Leonard M. Lodish, and Barton A. Weitz, "Resource Allocation Behavior in Conventional Channels," *Journal of Marketing Research*, vol. 24 (February 1987), p. 95.

32. Janet E. Keith, Donald W. Jackson, Jr., and Lawrence A. Crosby, "Effects of Alternative Types of Influence Strategies Under Different Channel Dependence Structures," *Journal of Marketing*, vol. 54, no. 3, (July 1990), p. 30.

33. Raymond LeKashman and John F. Stolle, "The Total Cost Approach to Distribution," *Business Horizons*, vol. 8 (Winter 1965), pp. 34–36.

34. Brian S. Moskal, "Distribution: The Last Frontier," *Industry Week*, vol. 237, no. 3 (August 1, 1988), p. 63.

35. Stephen B. Oresman and Charles D. Scudder, "A Remedy for Mal-Distribution," *Business Horizons* (June 1974), p. 66.

36. John T. Mentzer, Roger Gomes, and Robert F. Krapfel, Jr., "Physical Distribution Service: A Fundamental Marketing Concept?" *Journal of the Academy of Marketing Science*, vol. 17, no. 1 (Winter 1989), p. 60.

37. Peter M. Lynagh and Richard S. Poist, "Managing Physical Distribution/Marketing Interface Activities: Cooperation or Conflict?" *Transportation Journal*, vol. 23 (Spring 1984), p. 42.

38. Moskal, loc. cit.

39. William D. Perreault, Jr., and Frederick A. Russ, "Physical Distribution Service in Industrial Purchase Decisions," *Journal of Marketing*, vol. 40 (April 1976), p. 7.

40. Lewis M. Schneider, "New Era in Transportation Strategy," *Harvard Business Review*, vol. 63 (March–April 1985), p. 120.

41. "Study Pinpoints Trends with Biggest Impact on Distribution Management," *Marketing News* (March 2, 1984), p. 10.

42. Gene R. Tyndall, "Determine the Right Levels of Service," *Marketing News*, vol. 23, no. 22 (October 23, 1989), p. 16.

43. Gene R. Tyndall, "Study Finds Innovative Retail Practices Gathering Steam," *Marketing News*, vol. 23, no. 14 (July 3, 1989), p. 13.

44. Kenneth B. Ackerman and Bernard J. LaLonde, "Making Warehousing More Efficient," *Harvard Business Review*, vol. 58 (March–April 1980), pp. 95–96.

45. Lloyd M. Rinehart, M. Bixby Cooper, and George D. Wagenheim, "Furthering the Integration of Marketing and Logistics Through Consumer Service in the Channel," *Journal of the Academy of Marketing Science*, vol. 17, no. 1 (Winter 1989), p. 63.

46. Gordon J. Bingham, "Research Crucial to Effective Distribution Strategy, Execution," *Marketing News*, vol. 23, no. 1 (January 2, 1989), p. 26.

47. Cornelia Droge and Richard Germain, "The Impact of the Centralized Structure of Logistics Activities on Span of Control, Formalization, and Performance," *Journal of the Academy of Marketing Science*, vol. 17, no. 1 (Winter 1989), p. 83.

48. Jehoshua Eliashberg and Donald A. Michie, "Volatile Business Goals Sets as Determinants of Marketing Channel Conflict: An Empirical Study," *Journal of Marketing Research*, vol. 21 (February 1984), p. 84.

49. Bingham, loc. cit.

19

Advertising and Publicity Tactics

CHAPTER OBJECTIVES

- Understand the concept of advertising and publicity as alternative as well as complementary tactics.

- Be able to consider relevant trade-offs and make decisions having to do with where, when, how, and the financial resources that should be expended in employing advertising and publicity.

- Understand the concept of direct marketing, its importance, and its differences in application from traditional methods and practices.

Advertising Can Be Sweet

Hershey Foods Corporation, the company that makes the Hershey's Milk Chocolate Bar, has had rough times in recent years. In the 1970s, it lost its number one spot as a candy seller to Mars, Inc., and in 1977, cocoa costs tripled and profits dropped. A good many customers left Hershey in 1979, when the price of the candy bar more than doubled from a dime to a quarter. But now, Hershey is on a roll. In a recent year, earnings were $100 million on sales of $1.7 billion, a 9 per cent jump in sales in a single year during a period in which prices remained the same while cocoa prices increased 20 per cent. With a health food emphasis that was antisugar, the real

growth in the candy market was a meager 1.7 per cent per year, hardly the secret to Hershey's recovery. But one doesn't have to look far to find the real reason.

In three years Hershey's advertising rose from $36 million, and 6.5 per cent of sales, to $137 million, and 8.8 per cent of sales. For a company that did no advertising at all until 1969, Hershey really came alive. The result is that Hershey is back in the ballgame with its major competitor, Mars.[1]

Mazda: The Japanese Luxury Car Company

Do you think "upscale" and "luxury" when you hear the name Mazda? Maybe not, but things are chang-

502

ing. Mazda came out with an ad campaign intended to create radically different thinking about itself. In fact, it wanted an entirely new personality that would identify it with upscale, luxury products and services. The new campaign emphasized Mazda's Japanese roots and its *kansei* engineering. In plain English, *kansei* means "harmony with the five senses." *Kansei* may not sound like much of a breakthrough, but Mazda threw its entire $150 million annual advertising budget behind the effort to promote it. Why the frantic effort to change its image? Mazda felt that it needed to reposition itself to boost both sales and reputation. Over the previous few years, sales became lackluster and flattened out. So the advertising campaign and the introduction of the sporty Miata, a roadster-style convertible were the first steps in repositioning the company. But Mazda's campaign was not without risk. It could easily alienate its current customers, and lose more of them than it gained. Nissan, another Japanese car company, was roundly criticized when it introduced a campaign with a similar "built for the human race" theme. Nissan's advertising campaign for the Infiniti, which hadn't even been introduced at the time, had already been the butt of endless jokes. Its advertising approach consisted of oriental screens and close-ups of pussy willows. But Richard Winger, a partner at the Boston Consulting Group, agreed with Mazda's advertising concept. "Potentially powerful strategy," he said. "Made in Japan stands for uncompromising quality, so they might as well take advantage of it."[2]

Man from Outer Space Promotes Book

When L. Ron Hubbard's science fiction masterpiece, *Battlefield Earth,* was published a couple of years ago, the publisher was somewhat concerned about the author's availability for publicity. There was a rumor that the author was no longer alive. But even if alive, he wasn't available and, as a billionaire, certainly didn't need the money. *Dianetics,* one of the author's nonfiction books, had sold more than seven million copies, and over a fifty-year period Hubbard had turned out about one book a month. If he was really continuing to write, he probably didn't have the time. The solution was a thirty-foot inflatable, touring the world on behalf of the author. The inflatable was named Terl, which was the antagonist in *Battlefield Earth.* Terl, the being from outer space, substituted for L. Ron Hubbard in more than fifty U.S. markets, as well as in a European tour through England, Scotland, and West Germany. This tour, arranged by Bridge Publications, Inc., which held the paperback rights to *Battlefield Earth,* was on target. Sales totaled 700,000 copies within a few months, and at $4.95 a copy, gross dollar value reached approximately $3.5 million.[3] ●

Advertising and Publicity: Why So Important

Advertising and publicity tactics are important because no matter how good the product or the service, if the potential buyer doesn't know about it, he or she can't and won't buy. That's the main object of advertising and publicity—to make the product or service known to the potential buyer and to present it in the best and most favorable light possible, in comparison to competitive offerings.

Unfortunately, the advertising and publicity tactic idea is such a good one that new marketing managers frequently misuse this tool simply because they misunderstand what it can accomplish and its associated costs. In this chapter we are going to explore advertising and publicity tactical decision making. We are going to look at such issues as where to advertise, how much to spend, when to advertise, what to say, and how to measure results. But before we do, let's look at five myths new marketing managers frequently hold concerning advertising, as shown in Figure 19-1.

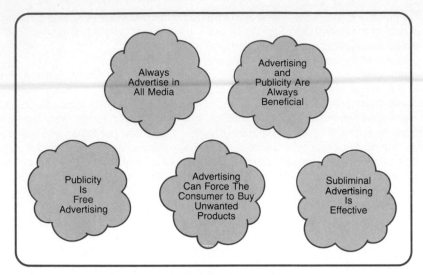

Figure 19-1   Five Advertising Myths

1. We'll do it everywhere.

One cannot advertise and publicize everywhere, using all potential media and methods, due to limited resources. Therefore, in using advertising and publicity to assist in promoting a product or a service, it is wrong to plan the automatic use of television, radio, newspapers, magazines, personal appearances, and publicity releases without considering their relevant costs and effectiveness. Sometimes only one type of advertising or publicity is possible. Sometimes none. Cost must always be considered.

2. Advertising and publicity are always beneficial.

Even if it were true that advertising and publicity are always beneficial, a marketing manager would have to measure the results before it could be determined whether they were worth the cost. However, the fact of the matter is that advertising or publicity may not be working at all. Cigarette advertising on television and radio came to a halt on January 2, 1971. Many cigarette manufacturers claimed that this would be the end of the cigarette industry in the United States. Yet, sales actually increased in the years following, until recently mainly due to a switch to print advertising, which was found to be a more-than-adequate substitute.[4] Furthermore, other analyses of cigarette brands have shown that more advertising sometimes results in reduced sales.[5]

3. Publicity is free advertising.

Publicity is sometimes called free advertising. But while publicity has certain advantages over regular advertising, including that the promotion is done by a third party—which gives what is said about the product or service more credibility—publicity is by no means free. Even a simple publicity release requires preparation and mailing costs. A publicity campaign such as the one conducted for *Battlefield Earth* cost a staggering $750,000. So while it may make sense to consider publicity together with advertising, it does not make sense to consider it without its associated costs.

4. Advertising can force the consumer to buy products that he or she really doesn't want.

In one view advertisers lie, cheat and steal, and trick potential buyers into buying things they really don't need, don't want, and can't use. For a variety of reasons, this is inaccurate. First, there are watchdog agencies, both non-governmental and governmental, that keep a close watch on advertising and determine that what is said is not misleading. Also, inaccurate advertising has little value over the long term. A firm might gain an advantage over its competition by outright lying in an ad, but if the product or the service does not live up to its claims, the customer will not purchase the item again. For repeated purchase, advertising that is untruthful will probably hurt the product. You can see this from the integrated information response model depicted in Figure 19-2. Note that advertising is the information source and initially results in low information acceptance, lower-order beliefs, and lower-order affect, which results in the trial of a new product. The trial results in direct experience. Only if this experience is favorable do advertising and information source result in high information acceptance, higher-order beliefs, higher-order affect, and commitment to use the product again.[6]

5. The most effective advertising is subliminal, and subliminal advertising can cause a potential buyer to purchase a product whether he or she wants it or not.

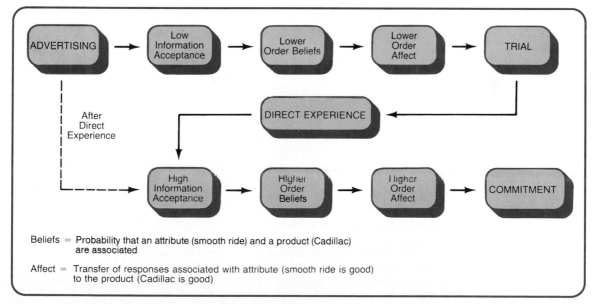

Figure 19-2 Integrated Information Response Model

Source: Adapted from Robert E. Smith and William R. Swinyard, "Information Response Models: An Integrated Approach," *Journal of Marketing*, vol. 46 (Winter 1982), p. 85.

For years, **subliminal advertising** has been exposed as the secret weapon that marketers use to rip off the public. A study undertaken in 1958 is sometimes cited. The study was supposedly accomplished by a marketing researcher named Jim Vicary. He claimed that he had developed a test at a movie theater in Fort Lee, New Jersey, at which two subliminal messages were flashed on the screen, one to buy Coca-Cola and one to buy popcorn. According to Vicary, sales of popcorn increased 57.8 per cent and of Coca-Cola 18 per cent. This early "experiment" was the basis for several best-selling books whose authors claimed that advertisers were unscrupulously using this device.

Though this experiment has been attempted again and again, the results of an increase in sales of any kind have never been replicated. And no wonder. For shortly after the initial experiment and results were announced by Vicary, Mr. Vicary admitted that he had fabricated the results of the test and done so because his business was failing and he hoped to increase it by the result of this so-called research. His admission was published in *Advertising Age*, back in 1958, but was never picked up by the general media.[7] Thus, although the fact that subliminal stimuli can have an effect is well established in psychology, and despite popular books such as *Subliminal Seduction* by journalism professor Wilson Brian Key, academic researchers have failed to find a single case of subliminal advertising effects in more than thirty years of serious research. The general conclusion has been that the potential effects of subliminal stimuli are masked by other, more important factors.[8,9]

Advertising and Publicity: Five Keys to Using Them

There are five keys to success in using advertising and publicity tactics, as shown in Figure 19-3:

1. Where to advertise or publicize
2. How much to spend
3. When to advertise or publicize
4. What to say
5. How to measure results

The answers to these questions depend on the overall objective for the advertising, the target market, and the five broad alternatives for reaching the objective and the financial resources we have for the campaign. The five broad alternatives for reaching the advertising objective are

- Stimulate **primary demand** for the product or service.
- Introduce previously unknown or new advantages or attributes.
- Alter the assessed importance of an existing product or service's attributes.
- Alter the perception of a product or service.
- Change the perception of competing products.[10,11]

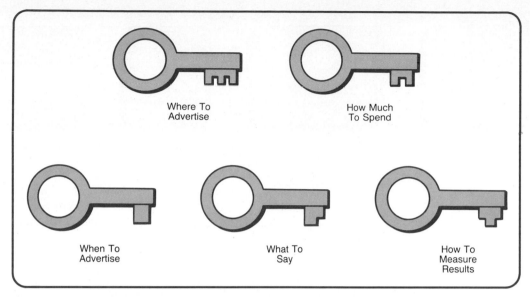

Figure 19-3   5 Keys to Success in the Use of Advertising and Publicity Tactics

Let us assume that our objective is to increase market share by 1 per cent in a single month in the target market we have selected. This target market consists of teenage girls ages fifteen to seventeen. The alternative that we have selected for reaching this objective is to stimulate primary demand for a new skin care product.

Now, in this case, the marketing share increase we aspire to is relatively large and the time to achieve it is short. Furthermore, unless we have geographic limitations, the target market itself is fairly large. The fact that we need to stimulate primary demand means maximum exposure of our product. This in turn probably will require a large advertising expenditure. Do we use TV? Do we use radio? Some cable channels might work well. But the number of potential customers reached in the target market would be limited with cable channels. Without very careful program selection, many of our advertising dollars are going to be wasted in general TV and radio advertising. These media reach too many market segments in addition to teenage girls ages fifteen to seventeen. We would have to pay for these additional market segments, even though they are not candidates for our new product.

How about magazines as a medium? Would *Boy's Life* be an appropriate vehicle? Probably not. Similarly, *Time* magazine or *Newsweek* probably would not work either. Again, they are too broad, with many other additional segments outside of our target market for which we would have to pay. *Seventeen* magazine probably would be a candidate, but with magazines we also have a timing problem. That is, because we have specified we want to increase the market share by 1 per cent in a single month, we would be limited to advertising in one issue only. If we do it, however, this says that probably we will need at least a full-page spread. Newspapers? Again, we have a large mass market audience, and we will have to pick out this segment—perhaps certain newspapers or certain sections in large-city newspapers.

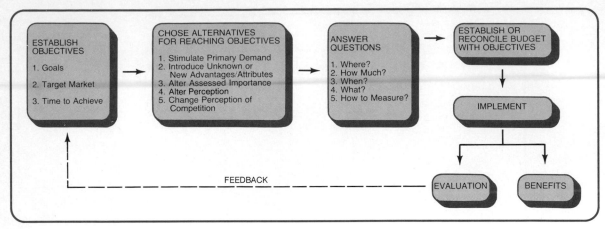

Figure 19-4 **The Advertising and Publicity Process**

Do we use a **direct-mail** campaign? Perhaps, if we can rent a list large enough. And what about publicity? Do we do a general new product publicity release? Do we have something really different, a breakthrough that can get us general news coverage? Again, the publicity media must be targeted, considering whom we can reach to influence, as well as the timing. And, of course, we must consider our budget throughout. This will affect our choices of media and how much advertising and publicity we can do. It may be that we cannot reach our objectives due to budget limitations. Then either the objectives or the budget must be modified.

You can see how the five keys to success work together, as well as our integration of overall objective, target market, available financial resources, and the five broad alternatives. If done right, there is great benefit. We can improve customer satisfaction, improve the firm's image, and, through feedback of the results of our campaign, improve the effectiveness of our advertising and publicity and gain additional insights into our buyers.[12]

The overall process is illustrated in Figure 19-4, starting with establishing objectives, proceeding to the evaluation of results, and recycling to the objective again at the same time it benefits from the advertising results.

Where to Advertise or Publicize

We've already seen some of the alternatives to where to spend for our advertising or publicity. These might include **print**, which would include newspapers, magazines, and direct mail; **broadcast advertising**, including radio, television, and cable television; **outdoor advertising**, such as billboards; **transit advertising**, such as the posters displayed in subways and buses; **specialty advertising**, in which the message is printed on such items as pens and key chains and are given away; **directories**, such as the telephone book; personal appearances; publicity releases; and press conferences. Which **media** and **vehicle** depend on our objectives, the alternatives available to reach our objectives, and the requirements for media and vehicle that will support these alternatives and are available considering our financial resources. This leads to another set of five questions that the marketing manager should consider:

1. What are the demographics of the media and the vehicle audience? The media and vehicle should match the target market. If we pick a medium such as a magazine and our target market doesn't read magazines, it won't purchase. Or, even if it reads magazines and we have the right medium, if we pick the wrong magazine or vehicle, our target market won't purchase either.
2. What is the reach of our media and vehicle? **Reach** has to do with how many households in our target market will receive our message.
3. What is the available **frequency** of our media and vehicle? Frequency has to do with how often our target market receives our advertising or publicity message. Increased exposure may enhance the effectiveness of a difficult appeal and decrease the effectiveness of an easy appeal.[13]
4. What are the costs? For many objectives, reach may be primary in importance, but in others, it is not cost per thousand of the target audience in itself, but cost per inquiry or value to us per inquiry that must be considered.[14]
5. What are other limitations or advantages of the medium or vehicle? An interesting fact is that **classified advertising** is generally the best medium in terms of profitability for a direct response. That is, for many products, a classified ad will result in more sales dollars per dollar invested for advertising. However, classified ads have a serious limitation. They are not read by as many of our target market as, say, a space ad in the same magazine. As a result, even though the cost of advertising may be higher in a space ad per sales dollar, the need for increased overall profits may require a more expensive method of advertising. The need for readership was confirmed by a study accomplished by Cahners Publishing Company and shown in Figure 19-5. The higher the ad readership, the more inquiries received.[15]

In direct-mail advertising, a medium of direct marketing that will be discussed later, the list of potential customers is the vehicle. The list can be twice as important as the offer and five times as important as the package used in the mailing.[16] Even with colorful, compelling copy and graphics, and a product of potential high demand and usefulness—such as a sophisticated and expensive machine for diagnosing disease—if the vehicle or list that you mail to isn't doctors or hospitals, your direct-mail advertising campaign will probably fail. Again, with the wrong medium or vehicle, your target market can't respond in sufficient numbers because it won't have seen your advertising.

The answers to the other four questions are equally important in selecting a medium and a vehicle. In addition, recent research suggests that the psychological response for each medium in various combinations with other media is different, and therefore that coordinated planning of the schedules and simultaneous use of different media and vehicles are also important factors in obtaining responses. Future measurements of advertising and effectiveness will likely include measurements of media and vehicle combinations.[17]

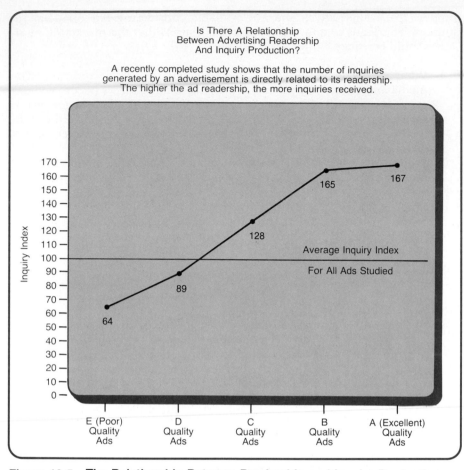

Is There A Relationship
Between Advertising Readership
And Inquiry Production?

A recently completed study shows that the number of inquiries
generated by an advertisement is directly related to its readership.
The higher the ad readership, the more inquiries received.

Figure 19-5   The Relationship Between Readership and Inquiry Production

Source: Cahners Advertising Research Report No. 150.1. *Is There a Relationship Between Advertising Readership and Inquiry Production?* (Boston: Cahners Publishing Company).

How Much to Spend

Objective and Task

Advertising budgets set by various methods for consumer and industrial products are shown in Figure 19-6.[18] Note that in this recent study, the **objective and task method** is the most frequently used for both consumer and industrial products. With this method, the marketing or advertising manager first establishes the objective of the advertising, as shown earlier. Next, he or she works out the alternatives and tasks necessary to reach this objective. Each alternative and task is associated with a cost, and the amount spent comes from whatever this campaign will cost to accomplish the objectives. If you have data that correlate past sales with levels of advertising in various media, you can see how it is possible to calculate this with some precision.

Method	Consumer	Industrial
Objective and task	62%	74%
Percentage of anticipated sales	53	16
Quantitative methods	51	3
Match competitors	24	21
Per unit of sales	21	2
Maximum affordable	20	33
Percentage of past year sales	20	23
Arbitrary	4	13

Source: Adapted from Vincent J. Blasko and Charles H. Patti, "The Advertising Budgeting Practices of Industrial Marketers," *Journal of Marketing*, vol. 48 (Fall 1984), p. 107.

Figure 19-6   Methods Used by Consumer and Industrial Marketers to Set Advertising Budgets (figures exceed 100 per cent due to multiple responses)

Of course, the method is not without its drawbacks. In some cases, it is extremely difficult, if not impossible, to relate the amount of advertising to sales or profits. But as you will see when we discuss how to measure results, advertisers are getting better at this. This may help to explain the high per centages of advertisers using this method to determine advertising budgets. Only fifteen years ago, a relatively small number of advertisers used the objective and task method.

Although many researchers consider the objective and task method to be the best method for general use, you can see from Figure 19-6 that other methods are also widely used. Of course, as noted in the figure, there is some overlap. For example, 51 per cent of the consumer firms and 3 per cent of the industrial firms used some sort of quantitative model in arriving at their advertising budget—and this quantitative method might have been associated with the objective and task, per centage of anticipated sales, or some other method. But let's look at some of the alternative methods and see why we might, or might not, want to use them.

Percentage of Sales or Units

We can lump per centage of anticipated sales, per centage of past years' sales, and per unit sales together. In some way we look at sales and then come up with our advertising budget. These methods are fast and easy to calculate. They can work reasonably well if the product or service is well established, the environs of the marketplace are not changing very much, and the advertiser doesn't have a very good handle on the effectiveness of the firm's advertising. However, a simple percentage of sales as a tactic doesn't really support a strategy that the marketing manager has decided upon. It really turns a variable over which the manager has some control into an environ that the market manager considers a given when making other tactical decisions. Of the three subsets, basing advertising budget on past years' sales is probably the poorest choice. This can result in what has been called "the going-out-of-business curve," under certain circumstances. Advertising budget is decreased based on percentage of sales during a bad year. This lowered advertising budget results in even lower sales. But once again budget is set on the last year's sales. The next year's sales are even lower, and this cycle continues until the firm is out of business.

Matching the Competition's Spending

Matching the competitor's budget may work if your strategy is one of neither advancing nor retreating—providing you can accurately estimate what your competitor's advertising budget is going to be, or if you use his or her last year's budget and it's not going to change. Usually this method means working from an industry average, sometimes raising it for an attempt at increasing market share or decreasing for share reduction. But be careful. You are implicitly assuming that every firm in your industry is like every other firm.

Maximum Affordable

Maximum affordable means that your budget is set to the maximum amount that you can afford to spend. In certain circumstances a firm, especially a small firm, may have no choice but to pursue this tactic. The problem is that the firm's expenditures aren't related to anything. It's possible that the firm might be better off not advertising at all, considering what this maximum amount might be. Also, a maximum affordable tactic too easily degenerates to the maximum amount that is left over after all other needs have been taken care of. It smacks too much of the engineering genius who spends millions developing his or her product and leaves no money at all for marketing, on the assumption that the product's advantages eliminate the need. It won't work.

Which Approach Should You Use?

Which approach should you use to determine advertising budgets? It all depends on your situation and what you are trying to do. If you are simply trying to hold on to the market share in an old, established market, just meeting the competition's spending or taking past or anticipated sales may work as well as carefully calculated financial modeling. On the other hand, if you are trying to penetrate a new market, or you have a precise sales figure you are trying to reach, it makes sense to calculate what it will take to do the job. Sometimes, even when you have the data to prove that your advertising can generate millions, you still can't do it. The money necessary for the campaign may just not be available. That's when the maximum affordable method begins to become acceptable. The only means that seems to make no sense at all is an arbitrary approach. "The moon was full last night, and $100,000 is a round figure, so let's use that." If you want to remain a marketing manager, better think again.

But regardless of methodology, amounts budgeted for advertising as a percentage of total sales differ among industry and country as well as consumer versus industrial classifications due to situational factors as well as customs, experience, and knowledge of the marketing managers involved. Typical country as well as consumer versus industrial product differences noted in

	United States		United Kingdom		Canada		Continental Europe	
	Consumer	Industrial	Consumer	Industrial	Consumer	Industrial	Consumer	Industrial
Advertising and promotion	5.08%	0.94%	8.15%	1.42%	4.49%	0.62%	12.66%	0.94%
Media advertising	1.91	0.22	3.80	0.29	1.99	0.10	7.91	0.10

Source: Adapted from Jehiel Zif, Robert F. Young, and Ian Fenwick, "A Transnational Study of Advertising-to-Sales Ratios," *Journal of Advertising Research*, vol. 24 (June–July 1984), p. 61.

Figure 19-7   Advertising as a Percentage of Sales in Several Countries

a recent survey are shown in Figure 19-7.[19] Advertising expenditures as a percentage of sales have also been found to be consistently high under certain situational variables of product market and competitive position.[20,21] Advertising expenditures tend to be high if the product is standardized, rather than produced to order; if there are many end users; if the typical purchase amount is small; if auxiliary services are of some importance; if sales are made through channel intermediaries, rather than direct to users; if the product is premium priced; if the product is premium quality; if the product is low or discount priced; if the manufacturer has a high contribution margin per dollar of sales; if the manufacturer has a relatively small share of the market or a very high share of the market; if a high proportion of the manufacturer's sales comes from new products; if the market is growing rapidly; if the product is very important to the firm's customers in terms of total purchases; and finally, if there is a broad product line.

When to Advertise or Publicize

As with other strategic and tactical decisions, timing is critical. In some cases all advertising should be held in abeyance during certain seasons or certain periods. In the United States, advertising, no matter how well planned or executed, would probably sell few Christmas decorations except in December, few snow shovels except during the period of October through April, and few lawn sprinklers outside of Florida and California except for May through September. In addition to halting all advertising during certain periods, other tactical alternatives are possible:

- Advertising heavily during your peak sales seasons only
- Maintaining a low level all year, with a major short-term increase during your peak season
- Advertising every other week during your peak season
- Advertising on one specific day of the week all year long[22]

Of course, combinations of the foregoing are possible (e.g., two days per week, every other month, and so forth). These alternatives are summarized in Figure 19-8.

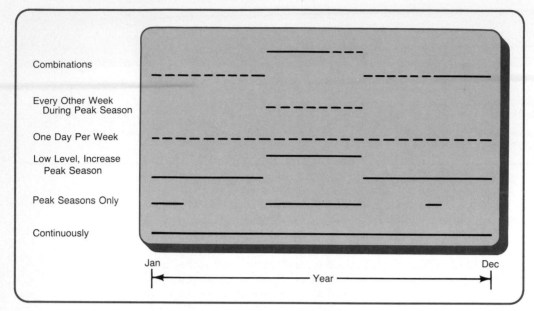

Figure 19-8   **Basic Tactical Alternatives When to Advertise**

The optimal alternative cannot be accurately predicted. The most effective and efficient combination can only be established by testing after the most likely has been used as a point of departure (no advertising of Christmas trees in July) and a tentative schedule has been established based on similar terms and on your own experience or that of your competitors.

Let's look at an example. Let's say you market memberships in a health studio. At first you advertise every day. To encourage prospects to sign up, as well as track results, you put a coupon in the newspaper worth a 10 per cent discount. You realize right away that advertising every day isn't bringing in sufficient clients to cover your cost of advertising plus providing the service. So you cut back to advertising on weekends only. At first this plan is profitable. Every week your advertising brings in new clients. However, after a couple of months, the numbers of clients the coupons bring in begins to fall off. Finally, the advertising isn't bringing you enough business to justify it, so you stop advertising for two months. When you start again, you find that your coupon ad is once again profitable. Now you pay attention and calculate a period for which you anticipate continual weekend advertising will be profitable. You use this model until you find that you must adjust it for seasonal effects.

What to Say

What to say in your advertising or publicity campaign incorporates a great many factors and elements, including the copy, graphics, photography, and layout design; it represents the work of many separate functional specialties

514

within the discipline. What you say in an ad can make a major difference. In **direct-response advertising**, where the results of different ads selling the identical product can be precisely measured, these differences have been found to affect results by 600 per cent and even more. Thus, what to say not only spells the difference in profitability, but also the difference between success and failure. The marketing manager must arm him- or herself with some basic facts, even though he or she may not be planning to write copy or prepare artwork or photography for an advertisement.

Once again, what is commonly thought to be fact is not always true. Did you think that a detailed technical description of a product in an advertisement would increase favorable response to the ad? Not necessarily so. An experiment conducted with 264 household consumers regarding technical contents of ads—their ability to retain the interest and attention of readers, believability, and evaluation of the product—showed that as the technical level of an advertisement increases, it may have an inverse effect to that desired by the advertiser, depending on the target audience. A summary of these findings is shown in Figure 19-9.[23]

Did you think that humor, sex, or color influence advertising results? If so, you're absolutely correct. In fact, even music can directly affect product preferences.[24] However, the influence of these factors can be negative as well as

- As the technical level of an advertisement rises, readers perceive the advertised product to be less durable, more difficult to operate, and higher priced.
- As the technical level of an advertisement rises, the ad is less likely to gain and hold the interest and attention of readers.
- The perceived believability of an advertisement is not significantly related to the technical content of the ad copy.
- Novices are most inclined to purchase when exposed to nontechnical content and least inclined when exposed to partially technical content.
- If the target audience has some considerable experience with the type of product, product rating varies directly with increasing technical content.
- If the target audience has considerable experience with the type of product, purchase intentions vary directly with increasing technical content.
- Overall evaluation of the product increases with technical content for those with some college and decreases for those with no college.
- Those with no schooling beyond high school are strongly motivated to intent to purchase by nontechnical ads and almost completely demotivated by others.
- Those with some college prefer nontechnical ads regarding motivation to intent to purchase.
- College graduates consider a purchase in direct proportion to technical content in the advertisement.

Source: Adapted from Rolph E. Anderson and Marvin A. Jolson, "Technical Wording in Advertising: Implications for Market Segmentation," *Journal of Marketing*, vol. 44 (Winter 1980), pp. 63–64.

Figure 19-9   The Result of Research Regarding Technical Wording in Advertising

- Good casting and story line combine to generate believable, sympathetic scenes and characters.
- A positive, light, happy mood is created by music and story line.
- Words and phrases such as love, care, and wonderful are used to establish a positive mood.
- A warm mood is established by the characters and the story line.
- An appropriate, credible spokesperson is used.
- The commercial is perceived as amusing (although commercials considered very amusing can irritate some, and slapstick or adult humor is more frequently perceived as irritating).
- The commercial is perceived as being informative.

Source: Adapted from David A. Aaker and Donald F. Bruzzone, "Causes of Irritation in Advertising," *Journal of Marketing*, vol. 49 (Spring 1985), pp. 55–56.

Figure 19-10 **Factors That Reduce Irritation in Television Ads**

positive; also, the cost paid for, say, humor, may not attain the objective that you wish.

Several years ago an advertisement for Wendy's featured eighty-year-old Clara Peller asking that famous question: "Where's the beef?" So popular was this ad campaign, which cost a clean $8 million, that the words themselves became a national slogan. But, according to John M. Kawula, vice-president of the Point of Purchase Advertising Institute in Fort Lee, New Jersey, despite the ad's popularity and its cost, the ad was a flop at producing sales. Kawula said that the reason was simple: "The commercial has committed the gravest sin in advertising: it has forgotten its purpose. It doesn't sell Wendy's fast food."[25]

At one time it was felt that a little irritation in advertising might be beneficial in gaining audience attention. Today we know that ads that irritate probably affect buyers' responses negatively more frequently than positively.[26] If you want to minimize irritation in television commercials, follow the guidelines contained in Figure 19-10.[27]

As the percentage of elderly people in the population increases, we ought to have more elderly people appearing as spokespersons in ads, right? Perhaps not. One researcher found that older spokespersons were not effective in appealing to older as well as young audiences; younger spokespersons effectively appealed to both. The researcher concluded that the seller must consider each case individually. He or she must consider patterns of adjustment to retirement, education, disposable income, health status, lifestyle, self-image, reference groups, the age with which the audience identified, as well as whether it was economically feasible to separate the targeted segment of elderly persons in the advertising from other segments.[28]

Are celebrities beneficial in promoting products through advertising? Maybe not. One study found that while consumers recognized and associated celebrities with the endorsed product, this was not related to ultimate purchase or nonpurchase.[29] Similarly, another study demonstrated physically that an attractive model in an ad failed to affect a reader's evaluation of the ad as believable, informative, or clear. It did, however, affect the reader's

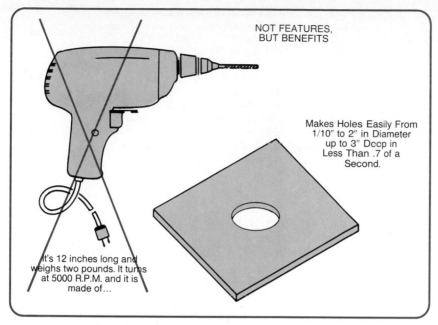

NOT FEATURES,
BUT BENEFITS

Makes Holes Easily From
1/10" to 2" in Diameter
up to 3" Deep in
Less Than .7 of a
Second.

It's 12 inches long and
weighs two pounds. It turns
at 5000 R.P.M. and it is
made of...

Figure 19-11   Not Features, But Benefits

willingness to buy the product. So whether you use a celebrity or a physically
attractive model in an advertisement may depend on what you are trying
to do.[30]

A major factor in the success of advertising regarding what is said may
simply be the advertiser's failure to present advertising that is easily understood by the target market. An investigation of television ads sponsored by
the American Association of Advertising Agencies discovered that viewer mis-
comprehension of television advertising was an amazing 30 per cent.[31] The
buyer is unlikely to buy if he or she can't even understand the proposition.

Perhaps the greatest criticism of an advertisment in general is when it
emphasizes attributes and fails to stress benefits. Of course, there is such a
thing as image, and an advertiser must always consider this element.[32] But,
a customer who wants to make a hole in a piece of wood is far more interested in the hole than in a description of the drill that makes it. This is
conceptualized in Figure 19-11. The difference between attributes and benefits was probably best expressed and illustrated by a famous copywriter, Victor O. Schwab, in a poem he wrote:

Tell Me Quick and Tell Me True
(Or Else, My Love, to Hell with You!)

I see that you've spent quite a big wad of dough
To tell me the things you think I should know.
How your plant is so big, so fine, and so strong;
And your founder had whiskers so handsomely long.

So he started the business in old 92!
How tremendously interesting that is . . . to you.
He built up the thing with the blood of his life?
(I'll run home like mad, tell that to my wife!)

Your machinery's modern and, oh, so complete;
Your "rep" is so flawless; your workers so neat.
Your motto is "Quality" . . . Capital "Q"—
No wonder I'm tired of "Your" and of "You."

So tell me quick and tell me true
(Or else, my love, to hell with you!)
Less—"how this product came to be";
More—"what the damn thing does for me!"

Will it save me money or time or work;
Or hike up my pay with a welcome jerk?
What drudgery, worry, or loss will it cut?
Can it yank me out of a personal rut?

Perhaps it can make my appearance so swell
That my telephone calls will wear out the bell;
And thus it might win me a lot of fine friends—
(And one never knows where such a thing ends!)

I wonder how much it could do for my health?
Could it show me a way to acquire some wealth?—
Better things for myself, for the kids and the wife,
Or how to quit work somewhat early in life?

So tell me quick and tell me true
(Or else, my love, to hell with you!)
Less—"how this product came to be";
More—"what the damn thing does for me."[33]

How to Measure Results ——————————————

Sales resulting from advertising are extremely difficult to measure, except
for one class of advertising, direct-response advertising, which we will discuss
shortly. This is because there are so many other factors that may influence
purchasing. These factors include not only the environs of the marketplace,
especially the competitor environ and what a competitor does during the
period of the advertising or publicity campaign, but also physical and geographic environment, which may even be as mundane as the weather. This
typically means that measures of advertising or publicity results have to be
accomplished with **recognition**, **recall**, **awareness**, and **attitude** and **opinion surveys**. Let's look at each of these in turn.

Recognition. Recognition, which is sometimes called readership, attempts to measure the frequency of an ad having been remembered by the
target audience. This is generally accomplished by showing the ad to a subject
and having the subject state whether he or she recognizes the ad.

Recall. Recall is of an order slightly higher than recognition, in that the
individual surveyed is asked to describe the advertisement or some contents
of it from memory.

Awareness. Awareness usually measures factors having to do with an entire campaign, rather than a single advertisement, such as awareness of a new product.

Attitude. Attitude measures the intensity of feelings, usually before and after the target market has been subjected to the ad or an advertising campaign.

Opinion. Opinion measures the reaction to advertisements, usually before the ad has been placed.

The problem with all these methods of measuring the effectiveness of advertising is that they stop short of actual purchase. Thus, the opinion of a sample group, sometimes called a focus group, of individuals toward a particular ad may be very positive, and they may even indicate an intention to buy. Attitude may be changed, and subjects representing the target market may exhibit recognition and recall and awareness of intended themes, to a very high extent. Yet, for one reason or another, these subjects may stop short of purchasing when the product becomes available.

Alvin Eicoff, chairman of A. Eicoff and Company, a Chicago-based division of Ogilvy and Mather International, specializes in television advertising. Eicoff sometimes tells his clients who insist on high recall that he can guarantee 100 per cent with a one-minute spot if they will run a television advertisement exactly as he insists. The clients are delighted until they hear his proposition. Eicoff says he will have an actor dressed as an Indian sitting and repetitively beating on a tom-tom while shouting the client's product name over and over and over again. Naturally, no client has taken up Eicoff on his offer because, although recall probably would be 100 per cent, it would be extremely doubtful that this particular ad would be related to a positive increase in subsequent sales. Eicoff's recall proposition again calls into question the complete validity of these measurements under all circumstances.

Is there any way that advertising effectiveness can be precisely measured? Today there are several new methods, in addition to direct-response advertising used in direct marketing.

Three systems—BehaviorScan, AdTel, and ERIM—are compared in Table 19-1. Test commercials can be inserted into what is seen with the first two methods. With individually addressable viewers, different experiential and control groups can be set up for specific market and product tests. ERIM is similar but doesn't require a cable system. Instead, test commercials are delivered to certain households whose television sets have been fitted with a special electronic device. When compared with purchase data in the communities represented, these methods allow the results of advertisements to be calculated more accurately than any method other than direct response.[34]

Direct Marketing

Perhaps the most popularized definition of **direct marketing** is "an interactive system of marketing which uses one or more advertising media to effect a measurable response and/or transaction at any location."[35] Two

Table 19-1 **New Methods of Television Analysis: BehaviorScan, AdTel, and ERIM**

BehaviorScan	1. Ten geographically dispersed test communities. Four examples: Pittsfield, Massachusetts; Rome, Georgia; Eau Claire, Wisconsin; and Visalia, California
	2. About 30,000 panel households
	3. Requires cable television system
AdTel	1. Five geographically dispersed test communities. Three examples: Portland, Maine; the Quad Cities (Davenport, Idaho; Moline, Illinois, etc.); and Boise, Idaho
	2. About 12,000 panel households
	3. Requires cable television system
ERIM	1. Two test communities: Sioux Falls, South Dakota; and Springfield, Missouri
	2. About 6,000 panel households
	3. No requirement for cable television

Source: Adapted from Dave Kruegel, "Television Advertising Effectiveness and Research Innovation," *Journal of Consumer Marketing*, vol. 5, no. 3 (Summer 1988), p. 45.

key words here are "measurable response." Advertising performance is accurately measured because a potential customer either responds to the ad or does not.

There is also a general difference in approach between general advertising and the direct-response advertising employed in direct marketing. A general advertiser emphasizes a cumulative brand or institutional image, but not the direct-response advertiser. He or she promotes a sense of urgency, frequently featuring items that are not perceived to be as readily available elsewhere, or not available at the price advertised. The word used in one study was *scarcity,* and the researchers found scarcity to be three times more prevalent in direct-response than in nondirect-response ads.[36]

The effectiveness of direct-response advertising was recently demonstrated by one of the most bizarre, yet effective advertising campaigns ever conducted. Three thousand "lucky winners" in the Washington, D.C., area received announcements by mail of their good fortune in being selected as recipients of a promotion by Flagship International Sports Television, Inc., described as a new all-sports channel. The prize consisted of two free tickets to the Washington Redskins last home game of the season and a pregame brunch at the Washington Convention Center. More than 160 people called in to accept. Each "winner" was greeted by a hostess in a tuxedo, identity was verified, and a name tag was pinned on. The guest was then escorted to the party room, where each was welcomed by the master of ceremonies dressed in top hat and tails. At a point in the ceremonies, the master of ceremonies announced that he would now let his audience in on a big surprise. He then proceeded to proclaim, "You're all under arrest," as SWAT

Figure 19-12 The Direct Marketing Flow Chart (opposite)

Source: Martin Baier, Henry R. Hoke, Jr., and Robert Stone. "Direct Marketing . . . An Aspect of Total Marketing," *Direct Marketing*, vol. 52, no. 4 (August 1989), p. 4. Used with permission. ➤

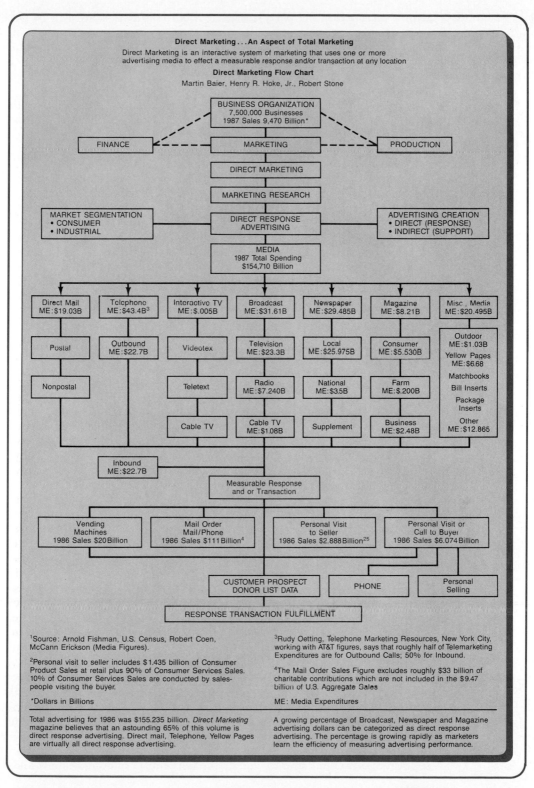

Direct Marketing...An Aspect of Total Marketing

Direct Marketing is an interactive system of marketing that uses one or more advertising media to effect a measurable response and/or transaction at any location

Direct Marketing Flow Chart

Martin Baier, Henry R. Hoke, Jr., Robert Stone

[1]Source: Arnold Fishman, U.S. Census, Robert Coen, McCann Erickson (Media Figures).

[2]Personal visit to seller includes $1.435 billion of Consumer Product Sales at retail plus 90% of Consumer Services Sales. 10% of Consumer Services Sales are conducted by salespeople visiting the buyer.

*Dollars in Billions

[3]Rudy Oetting, Telephone Marketing Resources, New York City, working with AT&T figures, says that roughly half of Telemarketing Expenditures are for Outbound Calls; 50% for Inbound.

[4]The Mail Order Sales Figure excludes roughly $33 billion of charitable contributions which are not included in the $9.47 billion of U.S. Aggregate Sales.

ME: Media Expenditures

Total advertising for 1986 was $155.235 billion. *Direct Marketing* magazine believes that an astounding 65% of this volume is direct response advertising. Direct mail, Telephone, Yellow Pages are virtually all direct response advertising.

A growing percentage of Broadcast, Newspaper and Magazine advertising dollars can be categorized as direct response advertising. The percentage is growing rapidly as marketers learn the efficiency of measuring advertising performance.

teams surrounded the party-goers. In this mail-order scam run by government law enforcement officials, more than one hundred criminals on the most-wanted list were persuaded to deliver themselves right into the custody of the law. Police accountants figured out that this direct-response advertising campaign cost less than $225 per fugitive, although one criminal did threaten to sue for "false advertising."[37]

With direct marketing, maintenance of a database is possible with the names and addresses of customers and prospects and other important associated information, including frequency of purchase, amount of purchase, and recency of purchase. Thus, the marketer can continue to advertise and sell to proven customers again and again and again.

Furthermore, though direct marketing grew out of the **mail-order** concept, today it pervades all elements of marketing. As shown in the direct marketing flowchart in Figure 19-12, the actual purchase can be concluded at the buyer's or seller's place of business, or by mail or telephone order.[38]

In the past, direct marketing has been considered a subset of general advertising and/or a channel of distribution. However, there are strong arguments for considering it as a separate element of the promotional mix.[39]

In 1984 the Direct Marketing Association commissioned Simmonds Research of Chicago to measure total annual sales through direct marketing. The figures arrived at were approximately $200 billion. Other sources, notably direct marketing research expert Arnold Fishman, calculate much lower annual direct marketing sales, about $111 billion in a recent year, although this excludes sales leads from direct response, which are closed face-to-face.[40] Even if this lower figure is accepted, it represents a significant amount of direct marketing advertising activity and growth such that many, if not most, marketing managers will probably become involved with some aspect of direct marketing during their careers. As Andrew Kershaw, former chairman of Ogilvy and Mather, told a group of students:

When you wake up ten years from now, you will find direct marketing is beginning to take over. If you choose direct marketing, you will be entering the most vital segment of our economy for the next fifty years.[41]

Summary

Advertising and publicity myths cause not only wasted resources, which are always limited, but failure in the marketplace. Therefore, every marketing manager must understand that it is not always right to advertise and publicize using all media, and sometimes it is not right to advertise in any media. Key questions that the marketing manager must think through include where to spend, how much to spend, when to spend, what to say, and how to measure results.

The answers to these questions depend on the overall objective, the target market, and five broad alternatives that can be used for reaching the objective. These alternatives are to stimulate primary demand for the product, to introduce previously unknown or new advantages or attributes, to alter the assessment of importance of an existing product attribute, to alter the perception of a product, and to change the perception of competing brands. To arrive at the answer to the question of where to spend, the marketing manager should consider the demographics of the medium and vehicle and assure that they match his or her target market, the reach and frequency of the medium and vehicle, the associated costs, and the limitations and advantages. Different firms use different methods of arriving at advertising budgets, but the current, most popular, and most used is that of the objective-and-task method. When to spend involves a question of timing, and such possibilities as advertising heavily during peak sales season only, maintaining a low level all year with a major short-term increase during the peak season, advertising every week during the peak season, and advertising on one specific day of the week during the entire year. We saw that what to say incorporates not only words, but also photographs, layout design, and other factors that must generally emphasize benefits in such a way that they are easily understood and accepted by the buyer.

We next examined methods of measuring results, including recognition, recall, awareness, attitude, and opinion. The common problem of all these methods is that they do not measure actual purchase. There is only one type of advertising that accurately does this, direct-response advertising. It is used to implement what is called direct marketing, which elicits a direct response in terms of an inquiry or purchase. In this fashion not only is performance information accurately known, but a database can be maintained that includes a great deal of information about the purchase and the purchaser and can be used for precise advertising and sales again and again. The success of direct marketing is such that it may have currently reached in excess of $200 billion per year in sales.

There is little doubt that mastering advertising and publicity tactics can be a significant factor in determining the ultimate success of any marketing program.

Questions

1. In the introductory story about Hershey candy, it was mentioned that Hershey did no advertising prior to 1969. How was it possible for Hershey to maintain its lead as the number one candy bar and do no advertising? Do you think that an organization can afford not to advertise today? Why or why not?

2. Why wouldn't a firm wishing to introduce a new product use all the advertising media available, including radio, television, newspapers, and magazines?

3. Reach and frequency are often spoken of as trade-offs. Why do you think this might be so?

4. Could a particular product be successful when advertised in one medium, such as television, and yet be unsuccessful when advertised in another, such as a magazine? Explain your answer.

5. Figure 19-4 shows the establishment of a budget as the fourth step in the process of organizing and carrying out an advertising campaign. Yet many companies establish the budget for advertising as a percentage of forecast sales. Explain, then, how establishing the budget can be step 4 in the process.

6. You are a marketing manager and use the objective-and-task method to establish the cost of an advertising campaign at $20,000. The vice-president of marketing then tells you that only $10,000 is available. What would you do?

7. You have a fixed advertising budget for the year for your product. Through experience, you find that sales always increase from your advertising throughout the year, although in some periods sales are greater than others. What factors might determine whether you would not advertise during some periods of the year, concentrate all your resources during peak periods, or advertise at a lower level or the same level throughout the year?

8. Explain the differences between an attribute and a benefit.

9. Because direct-response advertising measures response to an ad perfectly, why wouldn't a company use only this means of advertising?
10. In addition to having the name and address of your customer in a database, what advantage is it to also know the advertising medium and vehicle to which he or she responded, the amount of purchase, the frequency of purchase, and how recent the purchase was?

Ethical Question

Research has demonstrated that children who watch television when there is a high proportion of child-oriented commercials may have lower scores on nutritional knowledge and a poor understanding of nutritional phraseology.[42] Ads for children's food products are probably having a negative impact on what children learn about nutrition. Would this bother you if you were marketing manager for a breakfast food company whose product was eaten mainly by children? Is this an ethical issue? What, if anything, would you do about it?

Endnotes

1. "Hershey: A Hefty Ad Budget Has Profits Flying High," *Business Week* (February 13, 1985), p. 88.
2. Joanne Litman, "Mazda Designing an Upscale Personality," *Wall Street Journal* 8 August 1989, p. B6.
3. Kevin O'Higgins, "Giant Inflatable Sub for Author on Book Promotion Tour," *Marketing News* (November 23, 1984), p. 15.
4. Sandra J. Teel, Jesse E. Teel, and William O. Bearden, "Lessons Learned from the Broadcast Cigarette Advertising Ban," *Journal of Marketing*, vol. 43 (January 1979), p. 45.
5. Ahmet Aykac, Marcel Corstjens, and David Gautschi, "Is There a Kink in Your Advertising?", *Journal of Advertising Research*, vol. 24 (June–July 1984), p. 35.
6. Robert E. Smith and William R. Swinyard, "Information Response Models: An Integrated Approach," *Journal of Marketing*, vol. 46 (Winter 1982), p. 85
7. Walter Weir, "Another Look at Subliminal Facts," *Advertising Age* (October 15, 1984).
8. "Subliminal Ad Tactics: Experts Still Laughing," *Marketing News* (March 15, 1985), p. 6.
9. Timothy E. Moore, "Subliminal Advertising: What You See Is What You Get," *Journal of Marketing*, vol. 46 (Spring 1982), p. 46.
10. Harper W. Boyd, Jr., Michael L. Ray, and Edward C. Strong, "An Attitudinal Framework for Advertising Strategy," *Journal of Marketing*, vol. 36 (April 1972), pp. 30–33.
11. Paul W. Farris and Mark S. Albion, "The Impact of Advertising on the Price of Consumer Products," *Journal of Marketing*, vol. 46 (Summer 1980), p. 19.
12. David A. Aaker, "Developing Effective Corporate Consumer Information Programs," *Business Horizons*, vol. 45 (January–February 1982), p. 34.
13. Punam Anand and Brian Sternthal, "Ease of Message Processing as a Moderator of Repetition Effects in Advertising," *Journal of Marketing Research*, vol. XXVII, no. 3 (August 1990), p. 345.
14. William H. Motes and Arch G. Woodside, "Bottom-line Research for Advertising Media Decisions," *Journal of the Academy of Marketing Science*, vol. 12 (Summer 1984), pp. 113–122.
15. Cahners Advertising Research Report, no. 150.1, *Is There a Relationship Between Advertising Readership and Inquiry Production?* (Boston: Cahners).
16. William A. Cohen, *Direct Response Marketing* (New York: Wiley, 1984), p. 205.
17. Roland T. Rust and Robert P. Leone, "The Mixed Media Dirichlet Multi-Nominal Distribution: A Model for Evaluating Television-Magazine Advertising Schedules," *Journal of Marketing Research*, vol. 21 (February 1984), p. 89.
18. Vincent J. Blasko and Charles H. Patti, "The Advertising Budgeting Practices of Industrial Marketers," *Journal of Marketing*, vol. 48 (Fall 1984), p. 107.
19. Jehiel Zif, Robert F. Young, and Ian Fenwick, "A Transnational Study of Advertising to Sales Ratios," *Journal of Advertising Research*, vol. 24 (June–July 1984), p. 61.
20. Valerie Kijewski, *Advertising and Promotion: How*

Much Should You Spend? Research Report (Cambridge, Mass.: Strategic Planning Institute, 1984).

21. Cahners Advertising Research Report, *How Much to Spend on Advertising* (Boston: Cahners).

22. Malcolm A. McNiven, "Plan for More Productive Advertising," in David E. Gumpert, ed., *The Marketing Renaissance* (New York: Wiley, 1985), p. 533.

23. Rolph E. Anderson and Marvin A. Jolson, "Technical Wording in Advertising: Implications for Market Segmentation," *Journal of Marketing*, vol. 44 (Winter 1980), pp. 63–64.

24. Gerald J. Gorn, "Effects of Music in Advertising on Choice Behavior: A Classical Conditioning Approach," *Journal of Marketing*, vol. 46 (Winter 1982), p. 94.

25. "Wendy's Ad Is Popular, But a Flop," *Marketing News* (April 13, 1984), p. 6.

26. Rena Bartos, "Ads That Irritate May Erode Trust in Advertised Brands," in David Gumpter, ed., *The Marketing Renaissance* (New York: Wiley, Inc., 1985), pp. 521–525.

27. David A. Aaker and Donald E. Bruzzone, "Causes of Irritation in Advertising," *Journal of Marketing*, vol. 49 (Spring 1985), pp. 55–56.

28. Alan J. Greco, "Representation of the Elderly in Advertising: Crisis or Inconsequence," *Journal of Consumer Marketing*, vol. 6, no. 1 (Winter 1989), pp. 42–43.

29. Robert A Swerdlow, "Star-Studded Advertising: Is It Worth the Effort?" *Journal of the Academy of Marketing Science*, vol. 12 (Summer 1984), p. 100.

30. Susan M. Petroshius and Kenneth E. Crocker, "An Empirical Analysis of Spokesperson Characteristics on Advertisement and Product Evaluations," *Journal of the Academy of Marketing Science*, vol. 17, no. 3 (Summer 1989), p. 223.

31. Jacob Jacobi and Wayne D. Hoyer, "Viewer Mis-

comprehension of Televised Communication: Selected Findings," *Journal of Marketing*, vol. 46 (Fall 1982), p. 25.

32. William A. Cohen and J. S. Johar, "Image versus Benefits: Alternative Direct Marketing Creative Approaches," *Journal of Direct Marketing Research* vol. 1 (Summer–Fall 1986), pp. 49–56.

33. Victor O. Schwab, *How to Write a Good Advertisement* (New York: Harper & Row, 1962), pp. 63–64.

34. Dave Kruegel, "Television Advertising Effectiveness and Research Innovation," *Journal of Consumer Marketing*, vol. 5, no. 3 (Summer 1988), pp. 44–45.

35. Martin Baier, Henry R. Hoke, Jr., and Robert Stone, "Direct Marketing an Aspect of Total Marketing," *Direct Marketing*, vol. 52, no. 4 (August 1989), p. 4.

36. Carol A. LeBourveau, F. Robert Dwyer, and Jerome B. Kernan, "Compliance Strategies in Direct Response Advertising," *Journal of Direct Marketing*, vol. 2, no. 3 (Summer 1988), p. 33.

37. Ronald J. Ostrow, "Free Football Party Lures Fugitives into Arms of Law," *Los Angeles Times* 16 December 1985, pp. 1, 22.

38. Baier, Hoke, and Stone, loc. cit.

39. Donald R. Self, Jerry J. Ingram, Robin S. McCullin, and Roger McKinney, "Direct Response Advertising as an Element in the Promotional Mix," *Journal of Direct Marketing*, vol. 1 (Winter 1987), pp. 50–56.

40. Baier, Hoke, and Stone, loc. cit.

41. Cohen, op. cit., p. 373.

42. Alan R. Wiman and Larry M. Newman, "Television Advertising Exposure and Children's Nutritional Awareness," *Journal of the Academy of Marketing Science*, vol. 17, no. 2 (Spring 1989), p. 179.

Sales Promotion Tactics

20

CHAPTER OBJECTIVES

⬤ Understand why sales promotion tactics are important and when they should be used.

⬤ Understand the alternative categories of sales promotion available to the marketing manager and their advantages and disadvantages.

⬤ Be able to analyze market conditions to make decisions about using sales promotional tactics as an alternative or complementary to other elements of the promotional mix.

Promoting Records Like Corn Flakes

Once upon a time, Michael Omansky was a senior product manager at Nabisco Brands, Inc. He succeeded in increasing market share for one product 3 per cent in a year, mostly due to his magic with the manipulation of sales promotions. Omansky is no longer with Nabisco. Now he's doing the same thing for RCA records, and some say he's selling rock groups as if they were corn flakes.

In one promotion, he stuffed a one-dollar refund coupon in a record album. In another, a contest was held in which the winner was offered a cameo appearance in the next video musical made by the group. To promote Autograph, RCA went to the Pa-

permate Division of the Gillette Company and handed out Sharpwriter pencils at concerts. The joint venture also required Papermate to pay $60,000 to produce the music video "Sign In, Please." Apparently the promotion didn't hurt. The Autograph album went gold when sales surpassed 500,000 copies. Sales promotions like these have helped to increase record sales at RCA by 15 per cent in one year, to 4.37 billion records, after many difficult years.[1]

These Marketers Want You to Take Gas

Using sales promotional devices to encourage customers to buy gasoline ended abruptly with the oil embarg o of 1973. But now that we're in the 1990s, Amoco, Exxon, Mobil, Chevron, and Shell are spending billions of dollars to promote their gasoline. Their new grades of super-premium gas get special attention. At newly built gasoline stations you can pick up fresh donuts, pizza, and bread. You can even rent a movie. The possibility is increasingly good that you can pay for your gas at a pump credit card terminal. You may even drive away with a free lottery ticket, trading stamps, or a ticket that entitles you to a free balloon ride. Giana Kakos took over a losing Shell service station in Lincolnwood, Illinois, nearly four years ago. Through his promotions, which included giving away cold drinks, key chains, and coffee mugs, and running specials on tune-ups and oil changes, he really turned his station around. Now he pumps 36,000 gallons a month, and sales are up sixfold. Making the marketing understatement of the year, he said, "People are coming back." *Business Week* commented that this sort of promotional frenzy hasn't been seen in the industry since the heyday of the 1960s.[2] What is the effect of the 1990 oil crisis? Can sales promotion help?

Couponing Turns to Technology to Boost Redemption 300 Per Cent

One of the biggest problems in the use of coupons as a promotional device is what is called clutter. That is, there are so many coupons around, what results is a low rate of redemption. If you want to take a look at clutter, just open the Sunday supplement to your nearest big-city newspaper. You'll be deluged with coupons. Now a new automatic coupon device is on the market. It is a computerized printer that automatically prints out coupons at the cash register when certain products pass over the scanner. When the customer checks out, the system, which is tied to the scanner, determines which purchases are trigger items and automatically sets off a printer attached to the scanner. This, in turn, prints and dispenses a coupon for use by the customer on a later shopping trip. You can imagine the savings this gives to manufacturers that previously spent good money to distribute coupons where they were unwanted and, in fact, unusable. Prime examples were dog or cat food to homes that had no such animals, or coupons for diapers or baby food to homes that had no babies. The new device prints coupons in forty-two different categories from eighteen different manufacturers. According to the manufacturer of the device, within a short period of time, more than 140 different categories of products will be represented. Analysis of usage indicates that coupon redemptions resulting from the system are running close to 14 per cent, more than 300 per cent higher than redemption of coupons from Sunday supplements.[3,4] ●

Why Sales Promotion Is Important and Growing Fast

Sales promotion spending in the U.S. is in excess of $100 billion a year,[5] and no wonder. In one recent year it experienced a 30 per cent growth.[6] Its importance is confirmed when you consider that a single display in the front of a store can increase a product's sales 600 per cent over what otherwise would be the case.[7] When Joseph P. Sullivan was president and CEO of Swift and Company in Chicago, he turned a $10-million-a-year loss into a $62 million profit in only four years, maintaining that sales promotion played a much bigger role in this turnaround than did media advertising. Sullivan claimed that "Slow growth, volatile markets, and intense competition between consumers goods producers will mark the U.S. business climate for the next fifteen years, and that will place new emphasis on sales promotion."[8]

What is this tactical variable that is forecast to play such an important role? According to the American Marketing Association, sales promotion is "Media and nonmedia marketing pressure applied for a predetermined, limited period of time, at the level of consumer, retailer, or wholesaler, in order to stimulate trial, increase consumer demand, or improve product availability."[9]

Sales promotion is growing fast for many reasons. First, the cost of advertising has skyrocketed. Also, when the economy cools, companies need demonstrable results a lot quicker. Sales promotions are highly effective when consumers feel strapped economically, and consumer sales promotions are most effective in slow-growth markets where share increase generally comes at the competitor's expense. Promotions are very useful in obtaining dominance in certain niches that the manufacturer has targeted.[10] Finally, sales promotion is growing because of the added value.

Ron Hirasawa, president of American Marketing Services Corporation in Chicago, says it this way: "A bag of potato chips is a commodity. One tastes pretty much like the other. How do you give it added value? Perhaps hook it into a theme park and offer a $7 discount on a $14 ticket. You've given that bag of potato chips an added value of $7."[11] Annual sales promotion expenditures now far exceed the money spent on advertising. In a recent year, sales promotions accounted for 66 per cent of expenditures, compared with 34 per cent for media advertising. Research shows that it plays a major role in supporting a company's strategic plan.[12]

Trends in advertising and promotional expenditures since the 1970s are shown in Figure 20-1.[13] In Figure 20-2 you can see that while both advertising

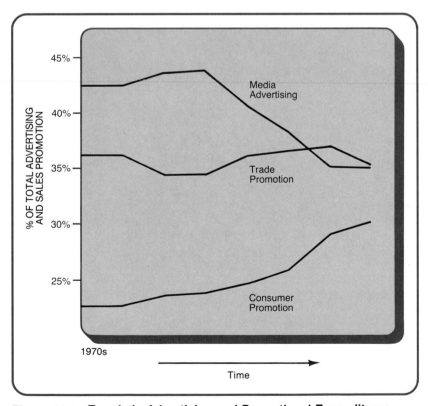

Figure 20-1   Trends in Advertising and Promotional Expenditures
Source: Adapted from Felix Kessier, "The Costly Coupon Craze," *Fortune* (June 9, 1986), p. 83.

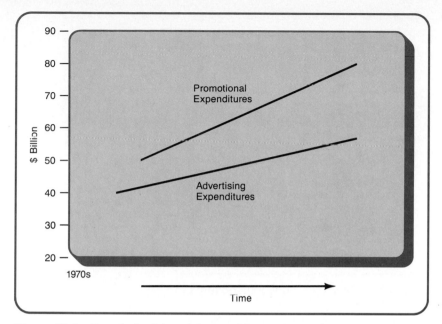

Figure 20-2   Trends in Advertising and Promotional Growth Rates

Source: Adapted from Richard Edel, "Trade Wars Threaten Future Peace of Marketers," *Advertising Age* (August 15, 1985), p. 18.

and promotional expenditures have increased since the 1970s, the promotional expenditure curve is steeper, indicating a greater growth rate.[14]

Two General Classes of Sales Promotion—Push Versus Pull

There are two general classes of sales promotion: one is to the consumer, also known as **pull promotion**; the other is to the trade, also known as **push promotion**. The promotional category depends on our objectives—whether we are trying to get the customer to buy or the trade intermediary to sell our product. Consumer promotion allocations are on the increase. Consumer promotions are especially important to larger companies, with 28.4 per cent of the budgets of companies with annual sales of $1 billion or more going for them, as compared with 26.6 per cent for smaller firms.[15] A recent year's breakdown of advertising, consumer promotion, and trade promotion for package goods is shown in Figure 20-3.[16]

Problems and Opportunities in Sales Promotion

With all the advantages of sales promotion, there are also some definite disadvantages and problems associated with using this tactical technique. These include (1) the difficulty in measuring effectiveness, or return, on the marketing dollar spent; (2) the difficulty of measuring efficiency, or how well one sales promotion device works versus another; (3) rising costs of use in some of the categories of promotions, such as trade shows; (4) **clutter**, in which

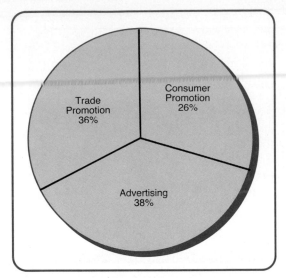

**Figure 20-3 Package Goods Expenditures for
Promotion and Advertising**

Source: Adapted from Richard Edel, "Trade Wars Threaten Future Peace of Marketers," *Advertising Age* (August 15, 1985),
p. 15.

the consumer is presented with so many different choices that it becomes
difficult for a specific offer to stand out against the others; (5) the added
expense of sales promotion when establishing new brands; (6) heightened
consumer sensitivity to price; (7) the fact that a trade buyer may respond to
a promotional deal by purchasing only for normal inventory, purchasing
above their own current requirements for future use, reselling or diverting
the excess to other retailers at a profit, and taking advantage of trade buys,
but failing to pass on price reductions to the consumer (in fact, one study
showed that only 30 per cent were passed on to consumers); and, finally,
(8) the danger of having a short-term sales promotion tactic be adamantly
at odds with the strategy leading to long-range objectives.[17,18,19,20]

This final problem is frequently overlooked. Yet, if a promotion works
against the strategy adopted, it has the potential for serious negative consequences. You could, for example, sell many Cadillacs at $10,000 each. This
might even be justified economically for clearing the salesroom of last year's
model. But what would this do to your positioning strategy? Would Cadillac
still be considered in the same class as its current competitors?

Naturally the severity of these problems varies among product category,
brand, industry, time, and the sales promotional technique used. But all are
serious problems of which the marketing manager must be concerned in
practicing and utilizing sales promotion.

On the other side of the coin are the opportunities, and the opportunities
enable reaching the objectives of sales promotion. These objectives may include the introduction of a new product; increasing sales; increasing market
share; identifying prospects; increasing awareness; encouraging a trial of an
existing product; persuading consumers not to switch from a brand, or to
increase their usage and frequency of purchase, or to increase the quantity

purchased; reinforcing advertising; communicating benefits; persuading a retailer to sell a new product or to allow more space to a product currently being sold, in order to move offensively or defensively against a competitor; and many other objectives limited only by the imagination of the marketing manager.[21,22]

Make no mistake, however. With all its problems, promotion does work. One study looked at the impact of sales promotion on the purchase of a brand of coffee. Sure, almost 14 per cent of the purchase increase was from buyers of the brand that merely bought their coffee earlier than planned, to take advantage of the promotion. Slightly less than 2 per cent bought and stockpiled the coffee for future use. But more than 84 per cent of the increased sales were due to consumers who switched their purchase from other brands.[23]

Major Categories of Sales Promotional Techniques

Major categories of sales promotional techniques or tools include

- Sampling
- Coupons
- Trade coupons
- Trade allowances
- Price-quantity promotion
- Reusable containers
- Premiums
- Contests and sweepstakes
- Refund offers
- Bonus packs
- Stamp and continuity plans
- Point-of-purchase displays
- Trade shows[24,25]

According to the Seventh Annual Survey of Promotional Practices conducted by R. R. Donnelly & Sons, couponing is the favored consumer promotion method, with 95 per cent of companies utilizing this technique, followed by premium offers. Trade allowances still constitute a large portion of the typical promotion dollar—in this survey, 58 cents of every dollar.[26] Point-of-purchase displays and trade shows are most important for consumer and trade-type promotions, respectively.

Let's look at some of the most important categories of promotion more closely.

Coupons

The use of **coupons** increased 14 per cent in one recent year, and as indicated it is the largest category of sales promotional techniques. In a recent year probably more than 168 billion coupons were issued, and eleven billion were

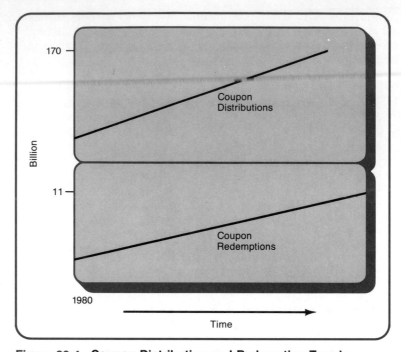

Figure 20-4   Coupon Distribution and Redemption Trends

Source: Adapted from Curt Schleier, "Marketing Image Plots Turnaround," *Advertising Age*
(August 15, 1985), p. 15.

redeemed. The growth of both coupon distribution and redemption can be
seen from Figure 20-4. Note that the trend has been continuously upward.[27]

The use of coupons can be very effective in stopping the loss of market
share and increasing sales that have dropped for one reason or another.
Tylenol is an outstanding example. After the Tylenol poisoning several years
ago, the manufacturers sent out 200 million coupons. This tactic certainly
helped to reestablish Tylenol's sales position.[28]

Studies have indicated certain commonalities among consumers who re-
deem coupons. These include the fact that they are most likely to be from
the Northeast. But large centers of heavy coupon usage also include the
Chicago area and the East Central and Pacific regions geographically.
Demographically, the heaviest users of coupons are the middle- and upper-
middle classes, with incomes of more than $15,000. They tend to live in urban
areas, are thirty-nine to forty-nine years old, and, contrary to popular belief,
are better educated than noncoupon users. In fact, they often have attended
graduate school. While coupon users are generally married with families of
three to six people, the usage of coupons drops off rather rapidly with families
of more than seven. Most coupon users are female, and 79 per cent of white
households versus 57 per cent of nonwhite households use them.[29]

The media in which coupons are used include newspapers, Sunday supplements, and magazines. In these media, they may be freestanding inserts
(preprinted sheets inserted loosely between the pages), printed on the pages
themselves, or bound into the publication. Other ways in which coupons are
distributed include direct mail, placement in or on a package for a product,

Newspaper	Printed on page
Sunday supplement	A supplement circulated with the Sunday newspaper
Freestanding inserts	Preprinted coupons on sheets inserted unbound between sheets of newspaper or magazine
Magazine, on page	Coupon printed on page
Magazine, pop-up or bound-in	Coupon bound in between pages of magazine
Direct mail	An envelope with coupons sent to the consumer through the mail
In/on package	Coupons inserted in or printed on the product package

Source: Adapted from David C. Reibstein and Phillis A. Traver, "Factors Affecting Coupon Redemption Rates," *Journal of Marketing*, vol. 46 (Fall 1982), p. 104.

Figure 20-5   Couponing Media

and, finally, via the new automatic coupon dispensing machines. Coupon media are summarized in Figure 20-5.[30]

One of the biggest problems with the use of coupons as a sales promotional technique concerns misredemption. Of course, the company using coupons as a sales promotional technique would prefer to have as many coupons redeemed as possible to reach its objectives, and as few coupons as possible misredeemed either in error or maliciously. When coupons are misredeemed, the marketing manager still has the cost associated with the promotion, but no advancement toward the firm's objectives is achieved through the coupons' use.

This problem is so serious that fraudulently redeemed coupons alone are estimated to be from 10 to 33 per cent of the total amount redeemed.[31] In 1985 U.S. Postal Service inspectors staged a sting operation in Florida with a nonexistent insecticide called "Broach" in the Sunday insert to three Florida newspapers (see Figure 20-6.) Shortly thereafter a coupon clearinghouse handling redemptive coupons from retailers received Broach coupons from across the country. When shut down, the misredemption ring was misre-

Figure 20-6   Phony Coupon for "Broach" Used in the U.S. Postal Service Sting Operation.

deeming $1 million worth of coupons a week and had already bilked the industry out of $186 million.[32]

In general terms, coupon responsive behavior is affected by both value consciousness and proneness to use coupons.[33] Factors that influence coupon redemption include the method of distribution, the product class size, the audience reached by the coupon, the consumer's need for the product, the brand's consumer franchiser and market share, the degree of brand loyalty, the brand's retail availability or extent of distribution, the monetary value of the coupon, whether the brand is new or old, the design and appeal of the coupon advertisement itself, the discount offered by the coupon, the area of the country in which the coupon has been distributed, competitive activity at the time, the number of coupons distributed, the size of purchase required for redemption, the level of general-support advertising promotion going on at the same time, the consumer's attitude toward product usage, number of potential users, the period of time since the coupons were distributed, the growth trend in the use of the product, the timing if the brand is subject to seasonal influences, demographics, and the general size of misredemption in the couponed area. These factors are summarized in Figure 20-7.[34] However, the most important factor in motivating consumers to use coupons may be the pride and satisfaction of obtaining savings through their use.[35]

Marketing scientists and practitioners have noted that certain actions greatly assist in combating coupon misredemption. It is important to com-

---

1. Method of distribution
2. Product class size
3. Audience reached by coupon
4. Consumer's "need" for product
5. Brand's consumer franchise/market share
6. Degree of brand loyalty
7. Brand's retail availability/distribution
8. Face (monetary) value of coupon
9. Whether new or old (established) brand
10. Design and appeal of coupon ad
11. Discount offered by coupon
12. Area of country
13. Competitive activity
14. Size of coupon drop
15. Size of purchase required for redemption
16. Level of general support advertising and promotion
17. Consumer attitude and product usage/number of potential users
18. Period of time since the coupons were distributed
19. Growth trend
20. Timing, if brand is subject to seasonal influences
21. Demographics, such as age, family size, annual income and expenditures
22. General level of misredemption in the couponed area

Source: From David C. Reibstein and Phillis A. Traver, "Factors Affecting Coupon Redemption Rates," *Journal of Marketing*, vol. 46 (Fall 1982), p. 104.

Figure 20-7   Factors Influencing Coupon Redemption

municate the terms of the coupon clearly to the retailer so there is no question of the validation period and the number of coupons accepted per item. Next, routinely spot check all retail stores using the coupons to assure that correct checkout procedures are being followed. You should keep your own records of coupon redemption by retailers and require some sort of proof of performance by the retailer. Finally, audit the clearinghouse procedures used with the retailer to make certain that all required criteria are being met.[36]

Of course the marketing manager should never forget that the profitability of a coupon promotion depends on the incremental sales the coupon generates. In one study these sales were greater among households that were larger, more educated, and that were homeowners. These results could be unique to the product investigated. However, the study definitely proves that directing coupons to the most responsive market segments can increase profits significantly.[37]

Robert D. Hisrich of the University of Tulsa and Michael P. Peters of Boston College have developed five fundamental rules for maximizing success in any campaign that depends on coupons. First, assess the competitive environment before launching a coupon drop, and alter the campaign accordingly. Don't forget about clutter. Never offer coupons immediately after a price increase. This is a case of potentially confusing short- and long-term goals. Always code coupons according to the media in which they appear, so that response rate can be determined. If you don't, you will be doomed to repeat your past mistakes, and you won't be able to capitalize on your successes. Ensure that coupons supplement a comprehensive marketing plan and are not the entire plan. Coupons used by themselves are far less effective. If this single device is your only means of marketing, you are almost certain to fail. Finally, never coupon a dying product as the last resort. The effect will be minimal, considering the cost.[38]

Premiums

The most popular premiums are **direct premiums**, **self-liquidators**, and **free offers**. Direct premiums are free items given away at the time of purchase. Perhaps the most famous example is the prize given in a box of Crackerjacks. Self-liquidators are premiums that are sold to consumers at a price far below the market value. Kool cigarettes once offered sailboats to its customers for $100 each. Free items in return for purchasing a product is a third class of premium. An example of this might be the tote bag used for carrying books and offered to individuals who join one of the mail-order book clubs such as the Literary Guild. A series of premiums is sometimes used to maintain interest in acquisition. McDonald's offered a set of toys, others have offered specially imprinted glasses, mugs, and other collectibles.

Premiums are particularly effective in building and maintaining brand loyalty, reaching new markets, and providing additional motivation to sales forces and intermediary trade organizations that carry a product.

A typical successful premium program was recently initiated to promote the sales of a leading sandwich spread. The campaign combined couponing with the premiums at a point-of-purchase display. Tear-off coupons good for a 25 per cent discount on a high-quality picnic cooler were part of this display. The coupon was also distributed through leading women's magazines and Sunday supplements. The bottom line was that 48,000 picnic coolers were sold as a self-liquidating premium. But, more important, brand sales increased by 11 per cent.[39]

When using the premium as a sales promotion technique, ensure that the following guidelines are followed:

- Once a need for a premium execution is identified, give it priority status.
- Know your product, sales, and distribution channels before you begin.
- Make certain that the premium is compatible with the logistics of the manufacturing and distribution systems that are available.
- Don't negate the creative aspect of the premium offer. A dull premium offer won't communicate and won't work well.
- Make certain that the premium has a high perceived value to your target audience and a relatively low cost to you.
- Ensure that the premium enhances, or at least maintains, the image of the product.
- Consider different and unique premiums. They add interest to the offer.[40,41]

Point-of-Purchase Displays

A **point-of-purchase** display is at the point of purchase in the retail outlet. It is frequently combined with other sales promotional devices and advertising to maximize effectiveness. In fact, some marketing experts consider the point-of-purchase display as more a part of advertising than of sales promotion. Point-of-purchase displays have been used for all sorts of products, everything from high-ticket automobiles and computers to cameras, lawn and garden appliances, vitamins, pantyhose, candy, gum, magazines, liquor, and tobacco.

The importance of point-of-purchase displays is that in many cases they can be more productive than advertising and other sales promotional techniques or vehicles used by themselves. In addition, a point-of-purchase display is particularly important when the quality of retail salespeople is low and there is less reliance on the salesclerk to push the products. For this reason many retailers have become much more receptive to the use of this category of sales promotion. At the same time, retailers have become much more cautious about such displays than in the past, placing some constraints and limitations on their content and layout to ensure that the display fits in with the overall decor of each department and each floor of the retail establishment. Point-of-purchase displays are also important because of their relatively low cost. Finally, they offer help in promotion to both the consumer and to businesses, more precise target marketing—because different displays can be done on a region-by-region basis—and relative ease of evaluation—especially when combined with other sales promotional devices, such as couponing.

If you decide to use a point-of-purchase display as a sales promotional technique, either by itself or in conjunction with one of the other sales promotional tools, ensure that all of its elements are integrated. Thus, the packaging of the product and the other promotional tools used, as well as the design of the display, should all be considered together.

It is also important to make certain that the displays for the entire product line are coordinated and offered as a group to the trade intermediary, rather than as a collection of materials for individual items. Because point-of-purchase display helps the retailer as well as the manufacturer, you must link support with the point-of-purchase device to performance by the trade intermediary. You should customize the point-of-purchase display for different distribution channels as required. For example, a hardware store would probably have a different point-of-purchase display than would a grocery store, even for the same product. Finally, as with the use of other sales promotional techniques, ensure that they are integrated with other elements of the marketing mix, especially advertising. Uncoordinated campaigns at best will not be as effective as they could be. Worse, if uncoordinated, one element may work against another. For example, an uncoordinated direct-mail campaign may be structured to compete with, instead of support, the point-of-purchase display.[42]

Trade Shows

Trade shows are hardly new. They have been held since medieval times, and they provide marketers with an outstanding opportunity to promote their products or services. A product is displayed or promoted to potential buyers at trade shows. There are probably more than 35,000 trade events in the United States every year, and more than 9,000 trade shows. This extensive activity is fully justified, for using this particular sales promotional vehicle can have a tremendous impact on your short-term tactics, as well as your long-range strategy. It can also be an effective means whereby small firms compete on an equal footing with larger firms.[43] On the other hand, improper use of this promotional technique will waste money, time, and your limited resources.

One of the first major decisions that a marketing manager must make in using this tool is which trade shows to attend, given the fact that there will probably be more opportunities than resources available with which to carry out and implement a trade show sales promotional program. One study of 607 firms representing manufacturers of industrial products and consumer products and nonmanufacturing firms rated trade show selection criteria according to their importance, including such factors as audience quality, audience quantity, display location, and logistical aspects of the show. The results of this survey ranked these factors in order of importance, as shown in Figure 20-8.[44]

The objectives of trade shows may include identifying prospects; gaining access to key decision makers; disseminating facts about products, services, or the firm; selling products; and servicing current accounts' problems. To measure the effectiveness of these trade shows is more difficult in that quantitative measurements do not always match up with the objectives stated. These measurements may include the number of leads generated from a show, the quantity of actual sales from these leads, the cost per lead generated, the feedback about the show from members of the sales force in attendance, and the amount of literature distributed at the show.[45] Other means of measuring effectiveness include taking hourly counts of passers-by of the exhibit, documenting unpaid media coverage both by number and dollar value, tracking the number of entries received in sweepstakes or other participative events, documenting direct and potential sales leads, obtaining

Importance Rank	Audience Quality	Audience Quantity	Display Location	Logistical Aspects
1	Decision makers % of total visitors			
2	% of visitors in target market			
3		Number visiting exhibits		
4			Booth/position location	
5		Extent of show promotion		
6		Past audience size		
7			Control over size/location	
8	Type of exhibitors limited			
9	No. or % Last year Last year's contacts			
10				Easy registration
11				Security
12				Set-up assistance
13			Aisle traffic density	
14				
15	Visitor screening			
16				Move in/out facilities

Source: Adapted from John R. Dickinson and A. J. Faria, "Trade Show Organizers, Take Note: Exhibitors Rank Participation Criteria," *Marketing News* (March 2, 1984), p. 3.

Figure 20-8 Trade Show Selection Criteria (based on a survey of 607 firms)

as much of the same information as possible about the exhibits of your firm's leading competitors, and tracking the results of personal contacts made.[46]

Harvard's Thomas V. Bonoma recommends making trade show spending decisions according to the nine-cell matrix contained in Figure 20-9. The figure shows the strengths of a company's current marketing communications program in getting customers and keeping customers, as well as other objectives such as building morale, allowing testing, gaining market intelligence, and maintaining or building image. The marketing strengths on the horizontal axis are plotted against trade show strengths on the vertical axis. Thus, a firm that is strong in keeping customers, but not very good at getting them, would be located in the second cell, providing the trade show strength was in getting customers as well. This cell recommends high investment in trade shows.[47]

Trade Promotions and Allowances

We have discussed some trade promotions before, but not as a general category. While trade promotions, or the "push category," are declining, they are still more important than the consumer category. We may conclude from a look at some of the problems with trade promotions discussed earlier that, although promotions may not be profitable to the manufacturer, they are

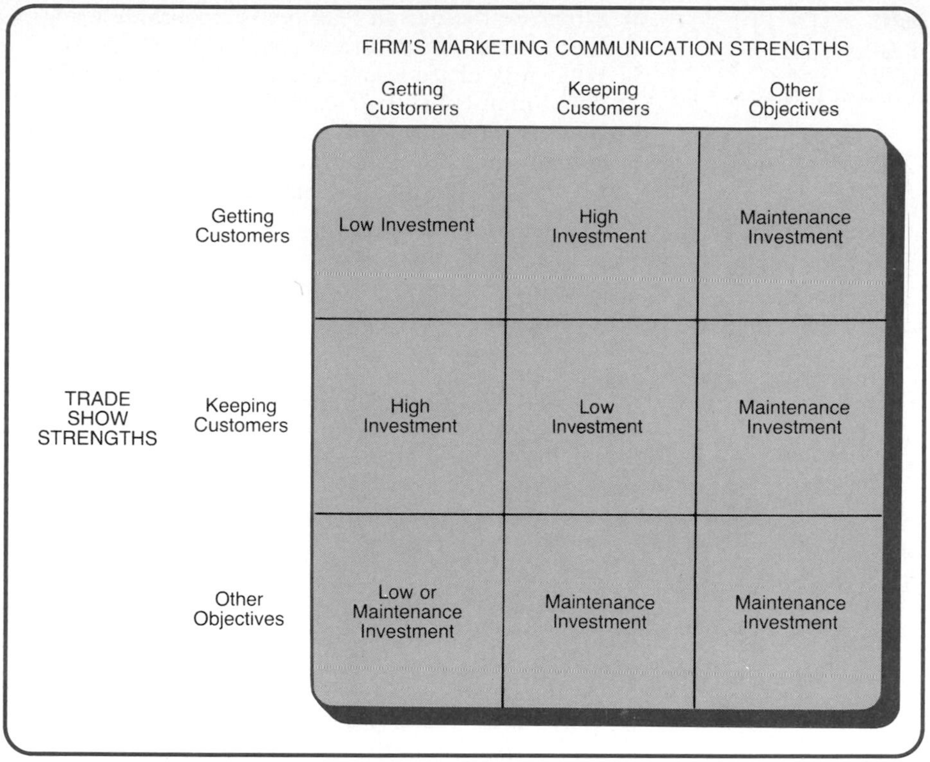

FIRM'S MARKETING COMMUNICATION STRENGTHS

TRADE SHOW STRENGTHS	Getting Customers	Keeping Customers	Other Objectives
Getting Customers	Low Investment	High Investment	Maintenance Investment
Keeping Customers	High Investment	Low Investment	Maintenance Investment
Other Objectives	Low or Maintenance Investment	Maintenance Investment	Maintenance Investment

Figure 20-9   Making Trade Show Spending Decisions

Source: Adapted from Thomas V. Bonoma, "Get More Out of Your Trade Shows," *Harvard Business Review*, vol. 61 (January–February, 1983), p. 82, Exhibit II.

usually quite profitable to the retailer. But how can the manufacturer ensure that the trade promotions funded are beneficial in achieving his or her objectives? Remember that, in one study noted previously, only 30 per cent of the benefits of trade allowances was passed on by the retailers to the ultimate consumers.

Research has shown that slow-moving products are unlikely to be pushed by the retailer, whatever the inducement by the manufacturer. This says that if the product really isn't very good or hasn't been properly promoted to the consumer through other means, a trade promotional campaign may be largely wasted. This research has also indicated that extra allowances to the retailer for price promotions must be greater than 10 per cent if there is to be any likelihood that they will result in retail price cuts to the consumer. Furthermore, trade incentives must allow retailers to increase percentage margins for promoted products. Even consumer coupons were found to be more effective if additional allowance monies were allocated to the retailer's benefit.[48] In all cases it is important that the trade intermediary's actions be closely monitored.

Thinking through the answers to the following questions before you implement a trade promotion campaign will help its success:

1. What are the likely effects, both short and long term, of this trade promotion on brand sales, market share, and profits?

2. What are the design features of profitable trade promotions that have been accomplished in the past?
3. What mix of trade promotions over the period of the annual promotional plan is likely to work best?
4. What is the optimal allocation of marketing resources or expenditures among trade promotion, consumer promotion, and advertising, as well as other elements of the marketing mix.[49]

Choosing the Right Promotional Vehicle _____

No single type of promotion works best in all cases. Furthermore, with consumer promotion, there is a significant promotion-prone set of consumers that may more likely be reached through various types of sales promotions, or even two or more promotions simultaneously, rather than one type. One study in four cities of 546 men and women attempted to categorize these individuals. It was found that so-called **cautious planners** responded to certain types of promotional techniques. These included sweepstakes, refunds/rebates, and self-liquidators. Cautious planners are defined as buyers who shop only once a week, are generally bargain hunters, often seek specials, stick to a budget, and take a shopping list with them. Consumers in the eighteen to twenty-nine age group were found to be the least likely to participate in these types of promotions. Although these buyers are just as likely as any other age group to save stamps or game prizes or use coupons, they are much less apt to respond to sweepstakes or send for refunds or self-liquidators.

Other results from this research included the following: couponing may be an expensive way to retain customers and a poor way to get buyers to try new brands when used alone; **sweepstakes** have broad appeal, are effective in mass marketing, and can be combined effectively with couponing for new product introductions; and refunding appeals more to large, growing families and combines well with couponing.[50]

Consumer behavior is only one of many criteria that should be considered in selecting a sales promotion technique or vehicle. The objectives of the sales promotion campaign should also be considered, along with the product or service being promoted; the distribution intermediaries who may have an effect on the promotion; the competition and actions of the competition; the cost effectiveness of the various media and techniques; the integration into other elements of both the communication and the marketing mix; the implementation of resource requirements; available means to measure results; and legal constraints or restrictions by local, state, or national laws.[51]

A means of noting consumer behavior response to various promotional vehicles was developed by Don Schultz at the Northwestern University McDill School of Journalism and Mark Block, chairman of the advertising department at Michigan State University. They first attempted to discover what psychological associations consumers had with some common sales promotional techniques. Preferences for certain techniques were then found and applied to certain product categories. A measurement was made of the relative importance of four purchase influences: the promotion technique, the brand name, a quantity discount, and on-package price reductions. This was

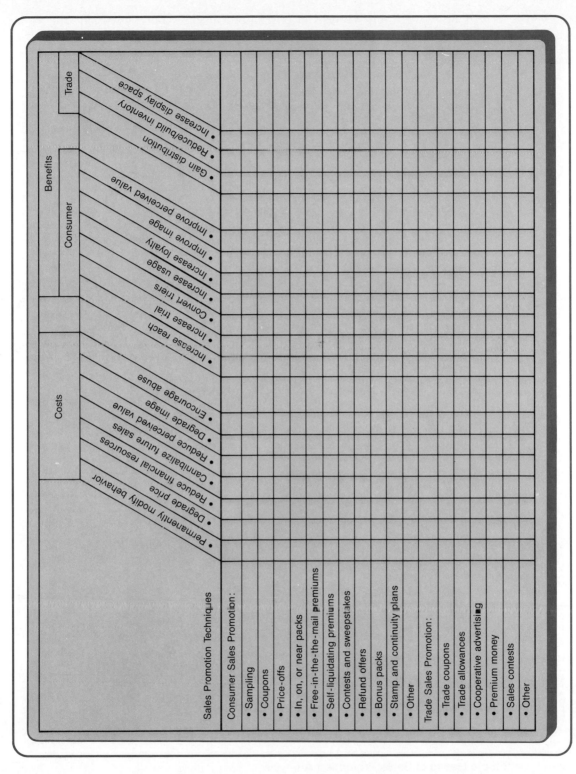

Figure 20-10 Costs and Benefits Comparison of Promotional Activities

Source: Adapted from Stephen W. Hartley and James Cross, "How Sales Promotion Can Work For and Against You," *Journal of Consumer Marketing* vol. no. 3 (Summer 1988) p. 39.

done to see if any patterns of purchase decision making emerged. This research is continuing, but what has resulted to date is a demonstration that consumer behavior response to promotional techniques is situational and can be tailored to the product.[52]

For a comprehensive overview and comparison of sales promotional activities, consider Figure 20-10. It looks complicated, but all you are doing is looking at qualitative aspects of costs and benefits simultaneously, to help you decide which alternatives to use.

Analysis

All sales promotional campaigns and techniques should be analyzed after they are used to determine their outcome and cost. Although the method chosen for analysis may differ from company to company, there are four criteria to guide the analysis. First, the technique should be quick and simple. No marketing manager should have to spend hours analyzing a particular promotion. Second, the method selected should use readily available data. Next, the method should be applied consistently. Once the marketing manager decides on a particular technique for the analysis, it should be used from one analysis to the next, so that various analyses of different promotions can be compared on the same basis. Finally, results should be presented in a usable form to show what actually happened and so that decisions can be made for future sales promotional activity.[53] A simple means of analysis is shown in Figure 20-11.

Joseph P. Sullivan, the former president and CEO of Swift and Company of Chicago, who was so successful in building his company by using sales promotional campaigns, recommends six general guidelines for all marketing managers who want to duplicate his success. He says that first you must

PRODUCT "GRUNCIES"

	① Average Weekly Sales For 12 Month Period Preceeding Promotion	② Average Weekly Sales For Month Preceeding Promotion	③ Average Weekly Sales During Promotion	④ % Change for ③ vs. ①	⑤ Average Weekly Sales for 5 Months After Promotion	⑥ % Change for ⑤ vs. ①	Total Cost of Promotion
UNITS (Thousands)	10.1	8.9	13.2	+ 30.7	10.3	+ 2.0	—
$ (Thousands)	200.3	176.3	261.5	+ 30.6	204.3	+ 2.0	127.2

Figure 20-11   A Simple Means of Sales Promotion Analysis

understand the business you are in and what it takes to achieve quality growth in it. Therefore, you must also know both your product's strengths and weaknesses and the competition's. Good promotion demands intimate knowledge of the industry and the marketplace, as well as the distribution system in your industry. Of course, you must also understand your customer. Constant monitoring of the marketplace and sensitivity to social trends produce valuable insights that, in turn, contribute to successful promotional campaigns. Qualitative skills must be developed and applied, in addition to quantitative skills. These are most important in communicating evaluation criteria to senior management. Senior management must recognize the value of sales promotion to the total business. Therefore, as a marketing manager, be an advocate. Document and promote success stories. Know that any function that delivers profits efficiently is welcomed by a CEO in upgrading profits and getting results.[54]

Summary

In this chapter we have seen the importance of sales promotion and why it is growing. We have distinguished between push versus pull—that is, trade versus consumer promotion. We have seen that while trade promotion is still used far more than consumer promotion, consumer promotion is growing and the percentage use of trade promotion is declining. We have also seen that there are both problems as well as opportunities using this marketing tactic. We have categorized the major types of sales promotions and discussed them in detail, including the use of coupons, premiums, point-of-purchase displays, trade shows, and trade promotions. Finally, we looked at how to choose a trade promotional vehicle, at the means of research and analysis of consumers, and at past promotional campaigns to help obtain future results.

Promotion is a marketing tactic of growing importance. It is not without its problems, which must be overcome to achieve its full potential, but that potential is great. A marketing tactician who knows how to employ this tool effectively can reap amazing results in a highly competitive marketplace.

Questions

1. This chapter opened with a case in which it was intimated that records are being promoted like corn flakes. Can records be promoted like corn flakes? Justify your answer.
2. Sales promotion is growing faster than advertising. Which is more important for selling a given product—sales promotion or advertising?
3. One of the major problems with consumer sales promotion is clutter. This is especially true of coupons. What techniques might you use as a marketing manager to overcome clutter?

4. Should sales promotion be used in every instance? If not, why not?
5. Couponing is the most used of the consumer promotional methods. What problems with couponing will the automatic checkstand coupon printing machine mentioned in the introductory case overcome?
6. Studies have shown that coupon redeemers have certain common characteristics. What does this say about the type of products that couponing should be used for, about the vehicle to which the

coupon should be attached, and about the offer made in the coupon?

7. Can you think of any danger in offering a good premium product along with any product you wish to promote?

8. The point-of-purchase display is considered by some to be a part of the advertising, rather than sales promotion. If you were the advertising manager, what arguments might you make against a point-of-purchase display coming out of your budget?

9. If you were going to initiate a trade promotion, how would objectives of the trade intermediary affect your thinking in developing this promotion?

10. You have a fixed amount of money to spend for sales promotions. How would you decide whether to spend all the money for one particular sales promotion category or to allot various amounts to different categories?

Ethical Question

After graduation, a good friend of yours goes into supermarket retailing, while you go to work for one of the large producers of household commodities. After a training program, you are happy to learn that you've been assigned to the same metropolitan area as your friend. He is in charge of promotions and coupon redemption for a supermarket chain, while you have responsibility for promoting your company. As a result, you work together and are even able to see each other socially. While doing an analysis of coupons redeemed in one campaign, you spot what you think must be a gross mistake in overstated redemptions. At lunch you mention the error to your friend. To your horror, he states that it is common practice to inflate coupon totals to receive more money from suppliers. He says that everybody's doing it, and that it is condoned by his boss and everyone else he knows in the business. What do you do?

Endnotes

1. Ronald Alsop, "RCA Plugs Records the Way Other Firms Sell Corn Flakes," *Wall Street Journal* 11 April 1985, p. 33.
2. Mark Ivey, Lois Therrien, and Maria Shao, "It's Not Just a Fill-up Anymore, It's An Event," *Business Week* (June 19, 1989), p. 90.
3. Ronald Alsop, "Companies Seek Ways to Put Coupons Where They'll Count," *Wall Street Journal* 8 August 1985.
4. Elliot Zweibach, "The Checkstand Coupon Printing Attains Redemption of 14%," *Supermarket News* (September 2, 1985), p. 4.
5. Steven W. Hartley and James Cross, "How Sales Promotion Can Work for and Against You," *Journal of Consumer Marketing*, vol. 5, no. 3 (Summer 1988), p. 35.
6. Joseph P. Flanagan, "Sales Promotion: The Emerging Alternative To Brand-Building Advertising," *Journal of Consumer Marketing*, vol. 5, no. 2 (Spring 1988), p. 45.
7. Monci Jo Williams, "The No-Win Game of Price Promotion," *Fortune* (July 11, 1983), p. 93.
8. "Bigger Role Is Seen for Sales Promotion in 1980s and 1990s," *Marketing News* (June 8, 1984), p. 5.
9. Peter D. Bennett, *Dictionary of Marketing Terms* (Chicago: AMA, 1988), p. 179.
10. Curt Schleier, "Marketing Image Plots Turnaround," *Advertising Age* (August 15, 1985), p. 15.
11. Ibid., p. 16.
12. Robert Kimball, "An Exploratory Report of Sales Promotion Management," *Journal of Consumer Marketing*, vol. 6, no. 3 (Summer 1989), pp. 65–66.
13. Felix Kessler, "The Costly Coupon Craze," *Fortune* (June 9, 1986), p. 83.
14. Richard Edel, "Trade Wars Threaten Future Peace of Marketers," *Advertising Age* (August 15, 1985), p. 18.
15. "Pull Promotions Gaining on Push," *Marketing News* (June 7, 1985), p. 16.
16. Edel, loc. cit.
17. John A. Quelch, "It's Time to Make Trade Promotion More Productive," *Harvard Business Review*, vol. 61 (May–June 1983), p. 131.
18. Thomas V. Bonoma, "Get More Out of Your Trade Shows," *Harvard Business Review*, vol. 61 (January–February 1983), p. 76.
19. Williams, op. cit., pp. 94, 98, 102.

20. Alvin A. Ackenbaum and F. Kent Monroe, "Pulling Away from Push Marketing," *Harvard Business Review*, vol. 65 (May–June 1987). pp. 38–39.
21. Bonoma, op. cit., p. 79.
22. Christopher H. Lovelock and John A. Quelch, "Consumer Promotions in Service Marketing," *Business Horizons*, vol. 26 (May–June 1983), p. 69.
23. Sunil Gupta, "Impact of Sales Promotions on When, What, and How Much to Buy," *Journal of Marketing Research*, vol. 25, no. 4 (November 1988), p. 352.
24. William A. Robinson, "Twelve Basic Promotion Techniques: Their Advantages and Pitfalls," *Advertising Age* (January 10, 1977).
25. Lovelock and Quelch, op. cit., p. 70.
26. "Pull Promotions Gaining on Push," *Marketing News* (June 7, 1985), p. 16.
27. Schleier, op. cit., p. 16.
28. Robert D. Hisrich and Michael P. Peters, "Coupon Mania Presents Opportunities and Problems for Manufacturers, Users," *Marketing News* (October 12, 1984), p. 34.
29. Ibid., p. 35.
30. David C. Reibstein and Phillis A. Traver, "Factors Affecting Coupon Redemption Rates," *Journal of Marketing*, vol. 46 (Fall 1982), p. 104.
31. William F. Gloede, "Postal Probe Clips $1M-a-Week Coupon Scam," *Advertising Age* (March 31, 1986), p. 10.
32. Ibid.
33. Donald R. Lichtenstein, Richard G. Netemeyer, and Scot Burton, "Distinguishing Coupon Proneness from Value Consciousness: An Acquisition-Transaction Utility Theory Perspective," *Journal of Marketing*, vol. 54, no. 3 (July 1990), p. 54.
34. Reibstein and Traver, op. cit.
35. Emin Babakus, Peter Tat, and William Cunningham, "Coupon Redemption: A Motivational Perspective," *Journal of Consumer Marketing*, vol. 5, no. 2 (Spring 1988), p. 40.
36. Hisrich and Peters, loc. cit.
37. Kapil Bawa and Robert W. Shoemaker, "Analyzing Incremental Sales from a Direct-Mail Coupon Promotion," *Journal of Marketing*, vol. 53, no. 3 (July 1989), pp. 66, 76.
38. Hisrich and Peters, loc. cit.
39. Robert J. Copp, "Premiums Provide Great Impact but Little Glamour," *Marketing News* (June 7, 1985), p. 12.
40. Ibid., pp. 12, 14.
41. Stan Bartelt, "In-Store Premiums Give Small Soft Drink Firm Leverage with Consumers and Trade," *Marketing News* (December 7, 1984), p. 16.
42. John A. Quelch and Kristina Cannon-Bonaventure, "Better Marketing at the Point of Purchase," in David E. Gumpert, ed., *The Marketing Renaissance* (New York: Wiley, 1985), p. 483.
43. John M. Browning and Ronald J. Adams, "Trade Shows: An Effective Promotional Tool for the Small Industrial Business," *Journal of Small Business Management*, vol. 26, no. 4 (October 1988), p. 36.
44. John R. Dickinson and A. J. Faria, "Trade Show Organizers, Take Note: Exhibitors Rank Participation Criteria," *Marketing News* (March 2, 1984), p. 3.
45. Bonoma, op. cit., p. 78.
46. E. Jane Lorimer, "Critical Data Can Measure Exhibit's Impact," *Marketing News* (May 10, 1985), p. 13.
47. Bonoma, op. cit., p. 82.
48. Michel Chevalier and Ronald C. Curhan, "Retail Promotions as a Function of Trade Promotions: A Descriptive Analysis," *Sloan Management Review*, vol. 18 (1976), p. 32.
49. Quelch, op. cit., pp. 135–136.
50. Marji Simon, "Survey Probed Strengths, Weaknesses of Promotions," *Marketing News* (June 8, 1984), pp. 3, 4.
51. Lovelock and Quelch, op. cit., pp. 72, 73.
52. Joanne Y. Cleaver, "Research on Buying Patterns Opens Doors," *Advertising Age* (August 15, 1985), p. 34.
53. Patrick McIvor, "Simple, Inexpensive Method Analyzes Promotion," *Advertising Age* (August 15, 1985).
54. "Bigger Role Is Seen for Sales Promotion in 1980s and 1990s," *Marketing News* (June 8, 1984), p. 5.

545

21

Sales Management Tactics

CHAPTER OBJECTIVES

- Understand the relationship between marketing and personal selling, its importance and its application.

- Know the advantages as well as the disadvantages of personal selling compared with other promotional and marketing alternatives.

- Know and understand the major sales management functions and responsibilities.

- Understand the major sales management alternatives that must be considered in developing an effective sales force.

Selling "Naked" Claimed to Be the Best Approach for Selling

According to Jerry Wilson, an Indianapolis consultant specializing in sales, "The best approach for the cold call is to go in naked." According to Wilson, "naked" doesn't mean without clothes. What it does mean is walking into an office without being armed with a briefcase, sales samples, and other props. Wilson believes that if the salesperson is naked, the potential customer's instinctive resistance isn't raised. Strangely, Wilson suggests not going for the sale at all. In fact, he suggests opening with something like,

"Bill, although I'm a sales representative for XYZ Corporation, I'm not here to sell you anything today. Instead, I was hoping you could help me to learn something about your operation." According to Wilson, this approach "removes the he's-here-to-sell-me-something barrier." Wilson should know. He made one thousand cold calls while naked one year. Out of these he developed two hundred good prospects and subsequently closed 90 per cent of those deals. Someone who sells naked can be proud of results like that—maybe especially someone who sells naked.[1]

How to Generate an Instant Sales Force of Five Hundred

In a recent year, DuPont decided to launch a large-scale consumer credit plan for carpet retailers. Fifteen thousand carpet retailers were targeted out of 35,000 nationwide. The problem was how to get to those 15,000 fast, when what was really needed was a quality, face-to-face discussion, and at a time when a large sales force for the carpet fibers division of DuPont did not exist. Bill Spencer, marketing director of the division, hit upon the plan of creating an instant army of salespeople by requesting five hundred DuPont employees to do the job. The five hundred employees were not normally in sales. They were Ph.Ds, secretaries, and retirees. Each was given a "quicky" training course and sent on the road with the assignment of visiting thirty retailers each over a two-week period.

The results were phenomenal. Eleven thousand of the 15,000 carpet retailers who were targeted signed up for the plan. According to Marketing Director Spencer, this was a 60 to 70 per cent higher success rate than the company had ever had. In addition to the sales results, however, the program was a big morale booster. One DuPont secretary said, "I loved it; I thought it was great. It was a real change of pace being out and seeing what goes on in the business."[2]

What Mary Kay Can Tell You About Sales Force Productivity

Mary Kay Cosmetics is a giant Dallas-based direct-sales manufacturer of cosmetics and skin-care products. Founded by Mary Kay Ash about twenty-five years ago, the company does $275 to $300 million annually in sales and is probably best known to outsiders for giving a pink Cadillac to its most successful salespeople. Both direct-sales manufacturers and department specialty store retailers are confronted with similar problems. These include an overabundance of product lines and too many "me-too" products, a busy consumer who tends to shop more in mass outlets and is value conscious, a weak sales force training program, less competitive compensation, a lack of career opportunities, and a high sales force turnover.

Mary Kay met these problems head on with a new program. The new program included many more car awards for sales directors as well as pink Cadillacs for the top performers. Recruiting commissions were substantially raised. Sales director qualification standards were increased, and the sales directors were given a bonus to make their compensation package more attractive. Finally, Mary Kay increased the minimum order size required for maximum discounts. The results were spectacular. First, the gap between the termination rate of salespeople and the recruiting rate closed. In fact, the recruiting rate began to outstrip the termination rate. This meant that more Mary Kay salespeople were successful in meeting their minimum quotas. By the year's end, productivity for the sales force had increased by 10 per cent.[3]

The Importance of Personal Selling

Personal selling has significant advantages over other methods of promotion, including advertising, publicity, and sales promotion. These advantages derive from the face-to-face communication aspect of sales techniques.

Before we look at these advantages, we should understand that there are some circumstances that encourage the use of salespeople over other elements in the promotional mix. An emphasis on face-to-face selling should be considered when other promotional elements either cannot be employed fully or to maximum benefit. One reason for one of the greatest new product introduction failures in history—the introduction of the Ford Edsel in September 1957—was due to the fact that one of its main features was its powerful 345-horsepower engine. Just prior to the Edsel's release, the Automobile Manufacturing Association had prohibited its members from advertising power and performance because of increased highway accidents. Thus, one of the Edsel's main features could not be advertised. There was a clear situation where personal selling could have been used to overcome a negative marketplace environ.

Another circumstance that suggests an emphasis on personal selling is when the size of the purchase in dollars is relatively large. Larger purchases enable sufficient margin to pay for using a salesperson in a single sale and to make the return on the investment in using the salesperson worthwhile.

Finally, personal selling is called for whenever a more detailed explanation of, or negotiation for, a product is required. This could be because the product is more complex or sophisticated, because a demonstration is required, or because the prospect has an older model for trade-in.

Now let's look at some of those advantages.

The Advantages of Personal Selling

There are six major advantages of personal selling over other promotional methods:

1. *More flexibility.* It is easier to vary and tailor the sales presentation made by your salespeople to individual customers' needs, behavior motives, and special situations.
2. *Immediate feedback.* Unlike other promotional methods, salespeople obtain immediate feedback on their presentation, and they can vary what they say afterward, depending upon the reaction to the presentation.
3. *Targeted marketing.* Personal selling enables greater pinpointing of the target consumer or industrial buyer than is possible with many promotional methods, such as advertising or publicity.
4. *Instant receipts.* In many types of personal selling, you or your representatives can sell the product and receive the money immediately.
5. *Rendering of additional services.* Your salespeople can perform other services as required while making sales calls. These may include market research, feedback on customers' complaints, credit information development, and customer servicing.
6. *Flexible times to make the sale.* In other methods of promotion, such as advertising, your sales presentation is limited by the size of the advertisement and the amount you can say in it. However, in a face-to-face selling situation, the salesperson can keep trying to make the sale until the presentation is terminated—either by the salesperson or the potential buyer—or until the time invested makes continuing the presentation unprofitable.[4]

Major Problems

Despite these advantages, there are major problems with the use of personal selling as a marketing tactic. The average cost of selling shattered the $200-per-call mark for industrial sales calls back in 1984. In fact, the cost of personal selling for a firm with a small sales staff of fewer than ten salespeople was $290.70 for each sales call.[5] This cost is a tremendous problem, and all firms using sales management tactics are seeking to increase their efficiency to keep costs as low as possible.

Other problems abound. In a recent marketing survey of over 10,000 industrial buyers, 82 per cent said that they would not buy from the same salespeople again. Eighty-five per cent said the salespeople lacked empathy. Ninety-six per cent said the salespeople did not ask for commitment on an order form. Eighty-eight per cent said the salespeople did not present or demonstrate the products well.[6]

Thus, we see that although there are benefits from personal selling, and therefore the importance of sales management is great, there are problems associated not only with the management of the selling, but with sales management itself. These problems must be solved to attain the maximum benefit from the tactic.

Developing an Effective Sales Force

Types of Salespeople

Before we can proceed to develop an effective sales force, we must understand that there are different types of salespeople. These can be classified into five groups. The first is that of **product delivery salespeople**. In this sales position, selling is actually secondary to delivering the product, be it fuel oil or soft drinks. This type of salesperson rarely originates the sale. Accordingly, a persuasive personality is not required, although, of course, an individual who performs good service and is reasonably pleasant may help to increase sales.

The second group consists of **order takers**. They can be subdivided into inside and outside order takers—inside takers work behind retail counters and outside takers work in the field. But in all cases little selling is done; rather, orders are taken from customers who have already entered the store to buy. Department stores, retail food establishments and other retail outlets all use order takers. Girl Scouts selling cookies are also order takers.

The third group consists of **missionary salespeople**. The primary job of missionary salespeople is to build goodwill at the same time that they perform promotional activities or provide other services to a customer or potential customer. Those who service physicians and pharmaceutical outlets, called detail people, may fall into this category. They may or may not be expected or even permitted to solicit orders.

The fourth group are **technical salespeople**, such as sales engineers. Persuasive powers are not so much required here as much as technical, in-depth knowledge of the product or service.

The final group are **creative sellers** of tangibles and intangibles. These people actually sell creatively to persuade people to purchase. Creative sellers have the most difficult sales jobs, as the customer may not be aware of the need for the product or the service or how the product or service can satisfy needs better than others that are currently in the market. The product may also be technical, and it may consist of everything from encyclopedias to

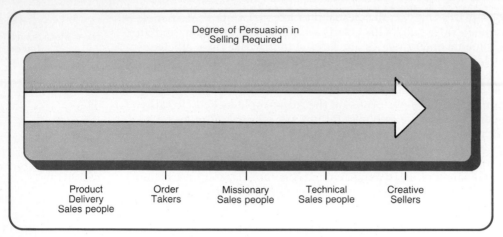

Figure 21-1   Types of Sales People and Degree of Persuasion in Selling Required

airplanes, from insurance to advertising and consulting services. These types of salespeople and the increase in degree of persuasion in selling are conceptualized in Figure 21-1.

Selection

Selection is critical to finding the best salespeople for your sales force. Sources for sales force recruiting include employees working for your firm who are not currently in sales; word of mouth from present customers or buyers, local colleges, and universities; and recommendations from your present sales force.

Once candidates are recruited, they must be screened to select those whom you will actually hire. A sales force selection system typically includes six elements: (1) application forms, (2) references, (3) face-to-face interviews, (4) intelligence and aptitude tests, (5) physical examinations, and (6) field observations of sales candidates.[7]

Training

Training will enable you to maximize the talents of your sales force. There are four main areas in which training can contribute to success, regardless of the type of salespeople that are employed. These are knowledge, work habits, selling skills, and attitude. Although the importance of knowledge, work habits, and selling skills may be obvious, attitude has been determined to be a critical factor in performance and selling in almost every situation; therefore, it frequently receives considerable emphasis in sales training programs. Motivation for selling is also considered a prime factor.

There are four categories of training under which the sales force is trained. The first is indoctrination training, in which you give your salespeople a basic orientation on the sales job and how it is done. This might include the sales manager accompanying the new salesperson in the field. The neophyte learns what to do through observation, as the sales manager performs sales duties.

550

As a salesperson gains experience, he or she takes over more of the job. Eventually the sales manager withdraws and the salesperson is left to do the job alone.

Job rotation is another type of training. It is typically used in larger companies. The salesperson spends a certain amount of time in a variety of jobs that may include assignments outside of selling, or even outside of the functional area of marketing. This could include time on the production line, in R&D, in a branch office, or in some marketing capacity such as advertising.

In-class training is generally used when field experience cannot be easily obtained; sometimes it supplements field training though role playing, to simulate actual sales situations.[8] It is particularly effective for providing additional information on products, the company, and the market. Of course, in-class training can also be used as a vehicle for additionally motivating salespeople. Sales meetings are used to train both new and older employees. In this environment, salespeople can trade experiences, build a spirit of friendly competition, gain additional information to help them in their job effectiveness, and be motivated to higher performance. Finally, seminars are used around the country to train salespeople. These may be used to train new salespeople or to train salespeople in special techniques and to increase their level of knowledge, improve their work habits, hone their selling skills, and motivate their attitude for selling. Seminars may be given by the firm for their salespeople, or salespeople may be sent to independent firms that specialize in teaching sales techniques and functions to individuals from many companies and industries.

Compensation

In a recent year, America's highest-paid salesperson was a computer firm's vice-president of marketing by the name of Robert A. Bardagy, of Comdisco in Rosemont, Illinois. He received an overall compensation of $1,237,681 in salary, bonus commissions, and fees.[9] Compensation is important because it helps to motivate your salespeople to maximum performance. But there are only three basic plans for compensating a sales force: salary, commission based on sales, or some combination of salary and commission. Each has its advantages and disadvantages.

The salary plan is easy for the company to budget and to administer, and it allows for the greatest control over the sales force in terms of being able to direct it to do tasks, both sales and nonsales. However, with a straight-salary plan, there is a lack of high incentive for sales, and salary is a fixed cost to the company that is unrelated to sales revenue. This means that the cost of paying remains the same whether sales are high or low. In fact, the salary must be paid whether or not there are any sales at all. Salary plans are usually most useful for compensating new salespeople who are not yet ready to assume full responsibilities, for compensating missionary salespeople when the duties are not to make an immediate sale, for opening new sales territories, and for sales of sophisticated or technical products requiring lengthy negotiations before the sale is completed.

The advantage of commissions for the company is that it can fully staff its sales force without high overhead commitments. Commissions also provide a direct incentive for high sales and may attract more aggressive and persuasive salespeople. At the same time, the cost of sales is automatically reduced if sales decline. However, with a straight commission system, there may be difficulty in getting salespeople to devote time to such tasks as servicing the customer, which may be important to your company but for which no commission is paid. There is also more bookkeeping involved, and there may be a greater difficulty in recruiting. Commission plans work well when considerable incentive and motivation are needed to get high sales and where very little missionary work or other sales assistance that does not have to do with closing out a sale is required.

Combination plans offer a fixed compensation element plus a variable element made of the commission on sales or a bonus based on volume, and perhaps other fringe benefits. The advantages of combination plans include flexibility in dealing with the overall job of selling the company's product or service, flexibility in making changes in territory assignment or the assignment of customers, and choosing among various factors that will motivate salespeople to work independently to achieve high sales. The disadvantages include complexity in construction of the plan, considerable additional administration and bookkeeping, and the need for constant review to make sure that the factors being used as part of the overall compensation are doing what they are supposed to be doing. Combination plans are used when a complex selling task is involved and when factors other than volume are considered important, but an incentive element is considered beneficial.

Sales Force Budgeting

Sales force budgeting attempts to answer the question of how much to spend on sales activities. This is not an insignificant question because sales budgets typically make up the largest single portion of a marketing department's expenditures. The question is complicated by the fact that sales managers frequently do not have enough data on the effectiveness of salespeople to tell whether they are overspending or underspending. The simplest method of budgeting, of course, is to use the same budget next year as this year, with minor changes for inflation or for other obvious conditions. However, such a method fails to consider the potential of the market or even changing company resources, and about the only thing it has to recommend it is that it is easy to develop.

Another method used by many firms is a percentage of sales. This may be a percentage of last year's sales or, more accurately, a percentage of sales forecast for the coming year. A percentage may be compared with that of other firms in the same industry, and thus adjustments made to meet or better the competition. The weakness in this method is that the amount budgeted cannot be considered an optimum amount and does not factor in environmental considerations.

The task approach, another alternative, is based on the needs of the customer and the number of salespeople required to satisfy those needs. The problem here is that the potential number of customers will frequently lead to an extremely large budget. Therefore, many firms using the task approach combine it with one that may be termed the maximal affordable—that is, the maximum the firm can afford. This approach involves the assumptions made in determining what the firm can afford. Although a certain number of sales calls to complete a sale may be assumed from past performance, this may have little to do with maximization of sales or profits.

The final approach used is economic. With the addition of each new salesperson to the sales force, additional sales are received, but each new salesperson adds results in a smaller increment of increased sales. This is the old economic "law of diminishing returns." With the economic method, salespeople are added until the gross profit on new business is just equal to the cost of deploying another salesperson. Thus, the economic method is directly related to an increase in sales and profits. The problem with this approach is the difficulty of gathering accurate information and measurement and the fact that even small changes in the situation, such as new territories, may totally change the sales response function and make the information calculated inaccurate.

Research has shown that there is no magic formula to find ideal sales budgets under all conditions and that therefore budgets must be tailor-made for each firm. One recent study recommends beginning with a percentage of sales approach and then adding salespeople to see if profits can be improved. But the marketing manager should never forget that the key factor is sales-per-salesperson and that this factor is directly affected by motivation, size of territory, and other important elements.[10]

Let's see how we might follow this recommendation in practice. Maybe we're developing a marketing plan for a new product, product line, or business. We're going to need salespeople. How much money should we budget for the sales force? If we are in a large company there are probably similar products or product lines already in existence. We know annual sales, and we know how much is spent on the sales force. We can use a similar percentage of sales for the new sales force, perhaps adjusted for the fact that the product or product line is new, the sales force may need time to "come up to speed," or the territory is different. Once the marketing plan is implemented, we can begin to fine tune and to add salespeople to see what this does to profits.

If we're in an entrepreneurial start-up situation, we can use a similar technique. We look at other businesses, their annual sales, and the number of salespeople they employ. From the number of salespeople, we can calculate approximate compensation and allied costs. Comparing annual sales and the sales force budgets of these other businesses, we calculate a percentage of sales to start from. We use our forecast sales in our marketing plan and calculate our sales force budget using the per centage of sales we calculated.

Sales Management Power and Responsibilities

The Responsibility of the Sales Manager

The responsibility of the sales manager for all sales within his or her organizational unit is pervasive. Figure 21-2 represents a performance model for the salesperson. Included are all the factors that lead to salesperson performance. Note that from performance come rewards and satisfaction, which in turn feed back into motivation and, again, into performance. Satisfaction, rewards, as well as role perceptions, motivation, and personal, organizational and environmental variables are all responsibilities of the sales manager.[11]

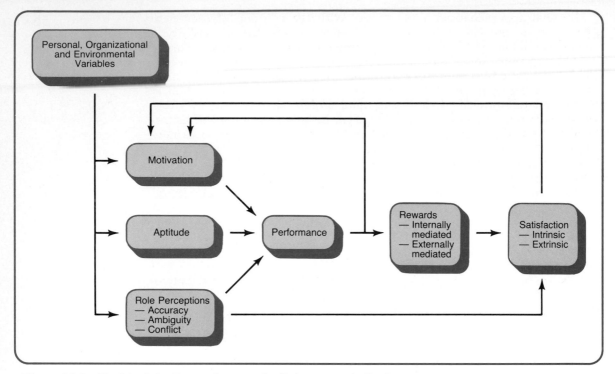

Figure 21-2 Model of the Determinants of a Salesperson's Performance

Source: From Orville C. Walker, Jr., Gilbert A. Churchill, Jr., and Neil M. Ford, "Motivation and Performance in Industrial Selling: Present Knowledge and Needed Research," *Journal of Marketing Research* (May 1977), p. 157. Used with permission.

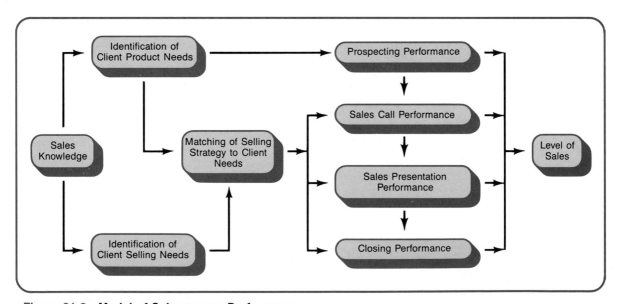

Figure 21-3 Model of Salesperson Performance

Source: Adapted from David M. Szymanski, "Determinants of Selling Effectiveness: The Importance of Declarative Knowledge to the Personal Selling Concept," *Journal of Marketing* vol. 52 no. 1 (January 1988) p. 66.

Now let's look at that one block in Figure 21-2 that's labeled performance. A model of salesperson performance is shown in Figure 21-3. Note the many factors that feed into level of sales, beginning with sales knowledge. Knowledge is power, and this sales knowledge includes all information possessed by the salesperson that can be brought to bear on the particular sales situation.[12]

Why aren't sales managers doing a better job in implementing these models? Three major reasons are poor selection criteria for promotion to sales management, insufficient integration of sales and marketing activities in the company, and inadequate sales and management training programs.[13] However, there are other problems that involve the power of the sales manager as well as the ability of the sales manager to ensure job satisfaction and motivate high performance.

The Power of the Sales Manager

Every sales manager has five types of **social power**: (1) **expert power**, based on the perception of his expertise; (2) **referent power**, based on perceived attraction of the members reporting to the sales manager to one another, (3) **legitimate power**, based upon the perception of the sales manager's right to influence others; (4) **reward power**, based on the perception of the sales manager's ability to reward; and (5) **coercive power**, based upon the perception of the sales manager to withhold rewards or administer punishment.[14] These relationships are shown in the model of social power relationship between the sales manager and salesperson in Figure 21-4.

Note that potential modifiers of the relationship include age, time on the job, and sex.[15] The potential modifiers of relationship—that is, age, time on the job, and sex—are not necessarily equal in strength. Nevertheless, research suggests that sales managers may want to adjust the nature of the power relationship depending upon, for example, the salesperson's age and time on

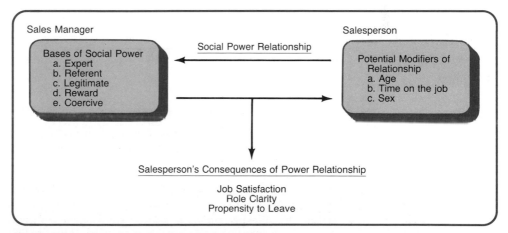

Figure 21-4   Model of Social Power Relationship Between Sales Manager and Salesperson

Source: From Paul Busch, "The Sales Manager's Bases of Social Power and Influence Upon the Sales Force," *Journal of Marketing*, vol. 44 (Summer 1980), p. 92. Used with permission.

the job. The older the salesperson and the longer that he or she is on the job, the less responsive he or she may be to the sales manager's expert power base. But the astute sales manager should work with all five bases of power to influence the salesperson.

Motivation: Job Satisfaction and Performance

There is a popular myth that an increase in job satisfaction always leads to an increase in performance. This is, in fact, just that—a myth. Research in general managerial settings and, specifically, in the sales setting, has failed to confirm this. Thus, the advantage of such concepts as **job enrichment** and **job enlargement** and other programs that may be designed to improve productivity by encouraging feelings of well-being may only be a small part of what is necessary to increase the salesperson's performance.[16,17] In fact, one study demonstrated that **job satisfaction** was more important to low-performing salespeople. This says quite a bit, especially regarding the sales manager's responsibility in reducing high rates of salesperson turnover. It is far better to introduce a program that reduces the turnover among high performers while it eliminates low performers, rather than a job satisfaction program that reduces overall turnover.[18] This also says that while it may be important to improve sales force satisfaction, the sales manager must think through its ultimate effects on sales force performance.[19]

How, then, can the sales manager motivate his or her salespeople to top performance? For one thing, self-esteem—the feelings a salesperson has about him- or herself—seems to be a far better predictor of performance on the job than job satisfaction.[20] Therefore, any actions that the sales manager takes in motivating to top performance must consider self-esteem. In doing empirical research to see what really motivates salespeople, marketing scientists have discovered that the following actions can have a real effect:

1. Determine rewards based on a salesperson's perceptions of what is important rather than on those of the sales manager or general management.
2. Monitor the salesperson's perceptions of job characteristics, supervisor behavior, and motivation on a continuing basis. Environmental changes can alter these perceptions, and it is a salesperson's perceptions that are important.
3. Develop specific guidelines for redesigning jobs; indicate changes that are most likely to lead to the improvements in performance of the job dimensions the company thinks are important.
4. Set challenging goals for salespeople and encourage continual improvement in their performance; show confidence in their ability to attain the goals set.
5. Encourage and maintain good relations between sales managers and their own supervisors; it has a direct effect on whether salespeople expect good performance to be rewarded.
6. Define the salesperson's job, so that the salesperson's role is clear; role clarity has a strong impact on self-esteem, job satisfaction, and other important factors.
7. Actively improve the salesperson's perceptions of selling because of the importance of self-esteem.

The sales manager plays the key role in everything having to do with the motivation of the salesperson. This responsibility cannot be delegated either upward or downward in the sales chain of command.[21,22] The sales manager must be aware that salespeople have different needs and expectations and react differently to events such as failure to achieve a sales quota.[23] To be effective, he or she must adapt and tailor the way he or she motivates and leads salespeople on an individual basis.[24]

Improving Sales Performance

Maximizing Effectiveness

One of the sales manager's prime tasks in improving sales performance is to maximize the effectiveness of the salesperson. This is dependent on four major factors, including (1) the characteristics of the salesperson-customer

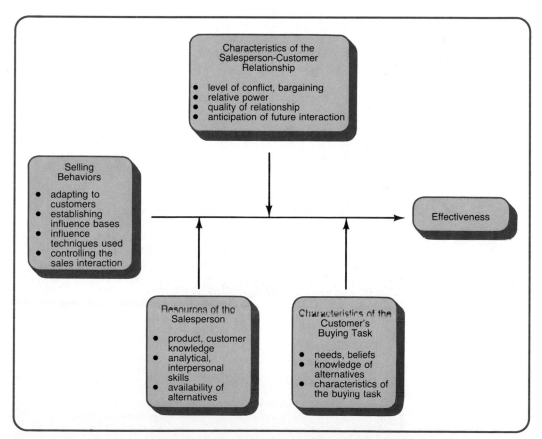

Figure 21-5   The Four Major Contingent Factors of Salesperson Effectiveness

Source: Barton A. Weitz, "Effectiveness in Sales Interaction: A Contingency Framework," *Journal of Marketing*, vol. 45 (Winter 1981), p. 90. Used with permission.

relationship, (2) selling behaviors, (3) the resources of the salesperson, and (4) the characteristics of the customer's buying tasks, as shown in Figure 21-5.[25] To maximize effectiveness, the sales manager must have a positive effect on as many of these contingency factors as possible. Accomplishing this means not only following the guidelines just discussed to motivate performance, but also considering the contingency factors that can negatively affect performance.

Figure 21-6 illustrates four types of organizational stress variables: (1) **role conflict**, (2) **role overload**, (3) **subunit conflict**, and (4) **role ambiguity**. One researcher examined the degree to which these stress variables in organizations impacted on salesperson motivation. Three out of the four were found to affect motivation negatively—that is, all except for role ambiguity.[26] It should be noted, however, that while a lack of role ambiguity or clarity may not affect motivation, it probably does affect performance.

The career stage of the salesperson may also affect motivation. For example, when a salesperson is in the process of establishing a career, psychosocial needs such as achievement, esteem, autonomy, and competition may be important. But let's look at a later stage of the same individual's career. Maximum advancement has been achieved, and the individual is in what can be termed a maintenance stage. Are the same psychosocial needs still primary? Probably not. Now the psychosocial needs are probably reduced competitiveness, security, and helping younger colleagues. Figure 21-7 illustrates the four career stages of exploration, establishment, maintenance, and disengagement in a matrix with career concerns, development tasks, personal challenges, and psychosocial needs.[27] Figure 21-8 shows how these career stages affect not only motivation, but also sales resources and role perceptions, which themselves interact, affect performance, and ultimately impact on the salesperson's satisfaction and involvement.[28] Note that we have spoken of the stages of a career and not the stages at a particular job. In fact, job tenure is a poor predictor of any one of these stages of vocational maturity.[29]

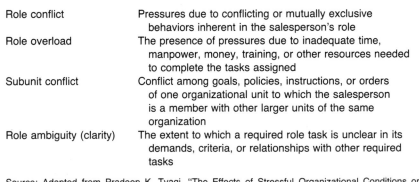

Role conflict	Pressures due to conflicting or mutually exclusive behaviors inherent in the salesperson's role
Role overload	The presence of pressures due to inadequate time, manpower, money, training, or other resources needed to complete the tasks assigned
Subunit conflict	Conflict among goals, policies, instructions, or orders of one organizational unit to which the salesperson is a member with other larger units of the same organization
Role ambiguity (clarity)	The extent to which a required role task is unclear in its demands, criteria, or relationships with other required tasks

Source: Adapted from Pradeep K. Tyagi, "The Effects of Stressful Organizational Conditions on Salesperson Work Motivation," *Journal of the Academy of Marketing Science*, vol. 13 (Spring 1985), p. 294.

Figure 21-6   **Organizational Stress Variables**

	Exploration	Establishment	Maintenance	Disengagement
Career concerns	Finding an appropriate occupational field.	Successfully establishing a career in a certain occupation.	Holding on to what has been achieved. Reassessing career, with possible redirection.	Completing one's career.
Developmental tasks	Learning the skills required to do the job well. Becoming a contributing member of an organization.	Using skills to produce results. Adjusting to working with greater autonomy. Developing creativity and innovativeness.	Developing broader view of work and organization. Maintaining a high performance level.	Establishing a stronger self-identity outside of work. Maintaining an acceptable performance level.
Personal challenges	Must establish a good initial professional self-concept.	Producing superior results on the job to be promoted. Balancing the conflicting demands of career and family.	Maintaining motivation though possible rewards have changed. Facing concerns about aging and disappointment over what one has accomplished. Maintaining motivation and productivity.	Acceptance of career accomplishments. Adjusting self-image.
Psychosocial needs	Support. Peer acceptance. Challenging position.	Achievement. Esteem. Autonomy. Competition.	Reduced competitiveness. Security. Helping younger colleagues.	Detachment from organization and organizational life.

Source: William L. Cron, "Industrial Salesperson Development: A Career Stages Perspective," *Journal of Marketing*, vol. 48 (Fall 1984), p. 45. Used with permission.

Figure 21-7 Career Stage Characteristics

What Does a Successful Salesperson Look Like and Do?

Profiles have been constructed of unsuccessful and successful salespeople on twenty-four separate salesperson attributes. Such a profile is illustrated in Figure 21-9.

Note that the successful salesperson tends to be more of a listener than a talker and plans rather than only relies on instincts.[30] A survey by *Sales and Marketing Management Magazine* asked what purchase agents like most in the salesperson. Of the characteristics they were asked to rate, 205 respondents ranked as most valued reliability/credibility, professionalism/integrity, and product knowledge. Least valued were supplies market data, appropriate frequency of calls, and knowledge of competitors' products. These results and the other characteristics ranked, along with the percentage of respondents listing that characteristic, are shown in Figure 21-10.[31]

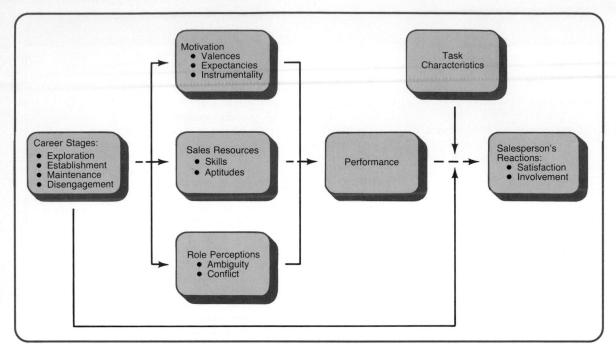

Figure 21-8 The Affects of Career Stages on a Salesperson

Source: Adapted from William L. Cron, "Industrial Salesperson Development: A Career Stages
Perspective," *Journal of Marketing*, vol. 48 (Fall 1984), p. 46.

Remember the "naked" sales call with which we began this chapter? The
value of not attempting a sale on the initial call has been confirmed by research, at least for industrial selling. Researchers found that the initial call
should be reserved for developing the relationship, building rapport, gathering information, and forming impressions. The extent to which this is accomplished defines success for this contact.[32]

From these surveys and research, we can see that a successful salesperson
results from a bundle of actions and perceptions, both real and imagined, by
the buyer and other individuals who deal with this salesperson. Various techniques have been developed to improve both the perception of the salesperson and his or her actions in dealing with the customer. Let's look at a few.

Techniques for Improving Performance

In our chapter on marketing research and marketing information systems
(Chapter 4), we discussed the importance of the computer. The computer
has a considerable effect in increasing the effectiveness, as well as the efficiency, of salespeople. This includes help in managing accounts, including
deciding on the right number of calls, improving the contribution of an account and reducing its costs, and allocating assets more effectively. Computers are also of help to the marketing manager in reducing sales costs,
managing assets more effectively, teaching time management, and evaluating
representatives' selling skills and overall performances.[33] Many programs

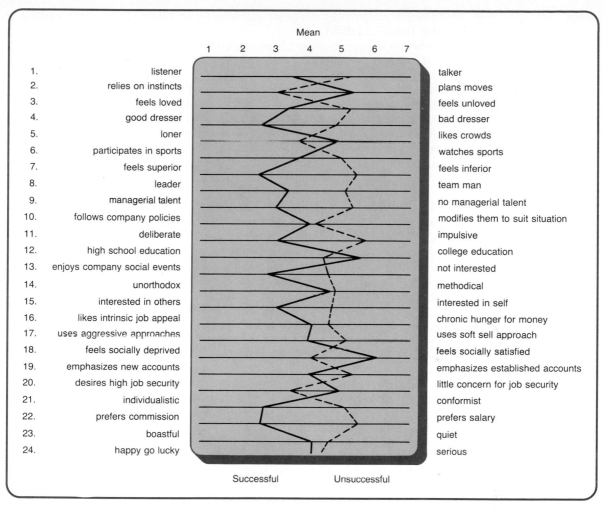

Figure 21-9 **Profile of Successful and Unsuccessful Salespeople**

Source: Bradley D. Lockeman and John H. Hallaq, "Who Are Your Successful Salespeople?" *Journal of the Academy of Marketing Science,* vol. 10 (Fall 1982), p. 466. Used with permission.

Most valued		Least valued	
Reliability/credibility	98.6%	Supplies market data	25.8%
Professionalism/integrity	93.7	Appropriate frequency of calls	27.3
Product knowledge	90.7	Knowledge of competitor's products	31.2
Innovativeness in problem solving	80.5	Knowledge of buyer's business	45.8
Presentation/preparation	69.7	Negotiation skills	45.8

Source: Adapted from "PAs Examine the People Who Sell to Them," *Sales and Marketing Management* (November 11, 1985), p. 39.

Figure 21-10 **What Do Buyers Like Most and Least in a Salesperson? (15 characteristics ranked by 200 respondents)**

have been developed especially for salespeople and sales managers in accomplishing these functions.

Another technique that has the potential for significantly helping salesmen and saleswomen is called the **account impact profile** system, or **AIP**. It is based on research indicating that salesperson-buyer compatibility is an extremely important factor in sales effectiveness. The AIP system consists of four major parts: (1) a formal written tool to assist salespeople in gathering and using important data about buyers, (2) a program for training marketing managers and matching their salespeople to the buyers to produce the maximum sales potential, (3) formal training for the salespeople in administering the program, and (4) a comprehensive program for managers in the control evaluation of the AIP system. The AIP survey instrument is shown in Figure 21-11.[34]

Sales consultant Don Beveridge maintains that sales time allocation is of primary importance, and that a great deal more time must be applied to the customer's needs analysis to achieve the positive buying response than has traditionally been allocated. His recommended allocations are 50 per cent of the sales time for customer needs analysis, 35 per cent for problem solving, 10 per cent for describing features and benefits, and only 5 per cent for closing the sale.[35]

Another approach to the allocation of the salesperson's time and effect is the sales call allocation grid, as illustrated in Figure 21-12. This grid contains four cells, constructed based on the strength of position of the selling organization and the account opportunity. Accounts falling into segment 1 would be highly attractive to the salesperson because they offer high opportunity and the sales organization has a strong position. The sales-call strategy in this case would be to allocate a high level of sales calls and sales time to this account.[36] This system, and similar systems, requires a considerable effort in customer needs analysis, both to establish the strength of the sales organization and to avail oneself of the opportunity the account represents. In this way the salesperson allocates his or her valuable time to the more attractive accounts and less time to the others.

Proper selling style can also be extremely important in all the salesperson's major tasks. These styles may be categorized as aggressive, submissive, or assertive. Their descriptions against major selling tasks are illustrated in Figure 21-13. Although the assertive style may be desirable in many, if not most, situations, some situations may require a submissive role, such as when the primary responsibility of a technical sales force is to increase company sales to existing accounts by providing them with the technical advice. An aggressive style is called for when the primary responsibility is to convert a large number of total strangers into customers in a short period of time.[37]

Sales contests and other special incentives are sometimes used to help motivate salesperson performance. These incentives may allow setting more difficult goals that will result in increased effort. But managers must do more than simply set goals. They must ensure that the goals are acceptable and fit in with overall company objectives.[38] They should also ensure that the rewards are of interest to the salespeople.

Mary Kay Ash, that fabulous woman who built Mary Kay Cosmetics into a $300-million-a-year organization, tells of how she learned the importance of this requirement firsthand. As a young saleswoman she was told that the best sales performer would win something that "everyone would like to have." The previous year's award was an expensive fur handbag. She worked hard

Account name _____   Date _____

Account address _____   Buyer's name _____

_____   Buyer's title and
                                                    department _____

Buying decision information
                                                    Office and telephone
                                                    numbers _____
Buyer's influence in
purchase decision _____   Tenure in present position _____

Key influence in   Other positions held in
decision _____   this company _____

Other people in   Past work experience _____
final decision _____
                                                    _____
Length of buying
decision _____   _____

Meeting day of buying
committee _____   Career aspirations _____

Buyer's social style _____   _____

Social style of key influence _____   **Current account information**

Types of sales presentations   Number of years in business _____
least and most preferred _____
                                                    Estimated sales volume _____
Buyer's job-specific data
                                                    Sales potential _____
Office hours _____
                                                    Other suppliers _____
Secretary's name and background _____
                                                    Years of repeat business _____
Other locations where buyer
can be reached _____   Average order size
                                                    and frequency _____
Buying days and hours _____
                                                    Delivery days and
Optimal call time _____   times _____

Tenure with present firm _____   Preferred transportation
                                                    mode _____
Buyer demographics
                                                    Preferred payment
Home address and   schedule _____
telephone number _____

Figure 21-11   The Account Impact Profile Research Instrument

Previous residences _____

Place of birth and date _____

Marital status _____

Names of family members, special
    dates, and events _____

_____

Names and positions of business
    associates, friends _____

_____

Education level (school
    attended) _____

Income and social
    class _____

Professional
    associations _____

Outside activities

Vacation preferences _____

Entertainment _____

Favorite foods and
    restaurants _____

Club memberships _____

Community activities _____

Religious affiliation _____

Sports (participant or
    observer) _____

_____

Other _____

_____

_____

Outside interests

Hobbies _____

Types of media viewed _____

Types of books read _____

Fashion _____

Interior design _____

Other _____

Opinions

Political views _____

_____

Economic views _____

_____

Social and cultural opinions _____

_____

Ecological _____

Competition and industry trends _____

_____

_____

Technological projections _____

_____

_____

Global views _____

_____

Other _____

_____

Source: Robert J. Zimmer and James W. Taylor, "Matching Profiles for Your Industrial Sales Force," *Business* (March–April 1981). Used with permission.

Figure 21-11 (Continued)

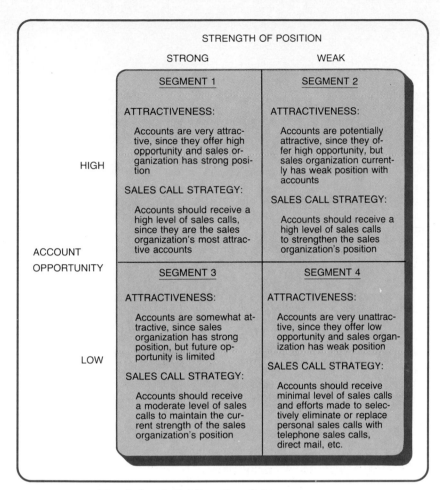

Figure 21-12   The Sales Call Allocation Grid

Source: Raymond La Forge, Clifford E. Young, and B. Curtis Hamm, "Increasing Sales Productivity Through Improved Sales Call Allocation Strategies," *Journal of Personal Selling and Sales Management,* vol. III (November 1983), p. 54. Used with permission.

during the year and won. She could hardly wait to see what she would get. At the annual awards ceremony she was awarded a device to assist in night fishing. "I couldn't think of anything I wanted less," she commented. It turned out that the company president was an avid fisherman. He seriously thought that such an award was something anyone would desire. Do you think this award motivated Mary Kay or other saleswomen to work for the incentive award in the future?

A reorganization and redeployment of the sales force can improve performance. This is because the environs of the marketplace change and make a deployment that was once most effective less so. Marketing researchers Raymond W. Laforge and Clifford E. Young, both of Oklahoma State University, and David W. Cravens, at Texas Christian University, recommend that the marketing manager frequently ask these questions in considering whether redeployment might be the most viable alternative for increasing effectiveness and efficiency.

Task	Selling Style		
	Aggressive	Submissive	Assertive
Finding prospects	Feels he or she can sell anyone and tries to.	Prefers to depend on company-supplied leads or contacts with friends.	Prospects meticulously but wastes little time with resistant or unqualified people.
Contacting prospects	Refuses to accept rejection without a struggle.	Socializes.	Inspires receptivity but qualifies carefully.
Defining prospect's needs/problems	Feels that the salesperson is the best judge of the prospect's needs/problems.	Accepts prospect's problem definition without probing.	Elicits need-related information the prospect may not have volunteered.
Stimulating desire	Minimizes participation of the prospect.	Loses control during the presentation.	Encourages two-way communication throughout.
Closing the sale	Tries to overwhelm the prospect. Responds to objections without absorbing or fully understanding them.	Assumes that prospects will buy when ready.	Assumes that if seller responds to buyer's needs, the close will be somewhat automatic.
Retaining customers	Neglects customer after sale is made. Is not a long-term person.	Follows through well. Is constantly in touch with customer.	Makes sure his or her commitments are fulfilled. Is available for posttransactional service.

Source: Adapted from Marvin A. Jolson, "Selling Assertively," *Business Horizons*, vol. 27 (September–October 1984), p. 74.

Figure 21-13 **Selling Styles in Performing Each Selling Task**

1. Do we need more salespeople to increase sales in the present market or to expand into new markets?
2. Could we maintain current sales levels and improve profits with a smaller sales force?
3. Are sales regions and districts organized effectively and staffed with the appropriate amount of management and salesperson effort?
4. Are sales territories designed to ensure proper market coverage and to offer each salesperson a fair and challenging job situation?
5. Are salespeople making the appropriate number of sales calls to existing accounts and new prospects?[39]

Performance Measurement

It is difficult to initiate any managerial change without knowing what happened in the past. As a result, the measurement of past performance is as critical in using sales management tactics as with other promotional tactics. Various performance measurements and the percentage of firms, both manufacturing and service, that have used them, from a study of 213 different

Method	% Using	
	Manufacturers	Service Firms
Sales volume to previous year's sales	36%	58%
Sales volume in units	44	75
Sales volume to market potential	42	13
Sales volume by customer	61	17
Number of accounts lost	34	75
Number of canceled orders per orders booked	7	30
Calls per period	48	81
Selling expense to sales	50	19
Selling expense to quota	30	6
Number of letters/phone calls to prospects	12	60
Training meetings conducted	36	9
Knowledge of competition	81	55
Report preparation and submission	70	42

Source: Adapted from Donald W. Jackson, Jr., Janet E. Keith, and John Schlacter, "Evaluation of Selling Performance: A Study of Current Practices," *Journal of Personal Selling and Sales Management,* vol. 3 (November 1983), p. 49.

Figure 21-14 Methods of Measuring Sales Performance and Frequency of Use

firms, are shown in Figure 21-14. Note that the most popular performance measurement for manufacturing firms is knowledge of competition, whereas the most popular measurement for service firms is calls per period.[40] Many times, more than one measurement will be used by a firm to measure sales performance on different tasks.

Raymond O. Loen, a management consultant specializing in performance measurement of sales personnel, recommends the following counseling tips to improve salesperson performance based on the variables measured:

- Give more day-to-day help and direction.
- Accompany salespeople on calls to provide coaching.
- Conduct regular meetings on subjects that representatives won't cover.
- Increase sales promotion activities.
- Transfer accounts to other sales representatives if there is insufficient effort or progress.
- Establish tighter control over price variances allowed.
- Increase or reduce selling prices.
- Add new products or services.
- Increase financial incentives.
- Transfer, replace, or discharge salespeople.[41]

Summary

In this chapter we've seen the importance of sales management tactics and how they are applied in practice. We first looked at the variables necessary to develop an effective sales force, including selection, training, compensating, and budgeting. Next we examined the power and responsibility of the sales manager, including his or her relationship to job satisfaction and performance and in motivating the salesperson to top performance. We noted that a salesperson's achieving the maximum effectiveness and efficiency depends upon many other factors in the organization, including organizational stress and the salesperson's career stage.

We looked at how successful salespeople are perceived in both behavior and actions, by buyers and others, and we noted that our main task as sales managers or marketing managers is to improve this performance. Several techniques were discussed to accomplish this, including the use of computers, matching profiles between the buyer and the salesperson, proper allocation of the salesperson's time, use of selling style, and potential redeployment. Finally and critically, we looked at how to measure the performance of the sales force and the individual salesperson. As discussed briefly in one of the lead vignettes in this chapter, the object of marketing and marketing research may be to make salesmanship unnecessary. But because perfection in this goal can probably never be attained, and because even a perfect strategy must be implemented, sales management tactics are essential tools for the marketing manager.

Questions _____

1. The sales management tactic has a major advantage in face-to-face contact and the feedback associated with it. But there are also disadvantages due to the time and expense of sales visits. Can you think of a way to minimize the time and expense of sales contacts?
2. Five different categories of salespeople were discussed in the text. What impact might those differences have on selection? On training? On compensating the sales force?
3. Of the six elements of the sales force selection system, which do you feel is the most important, and why?
4. In this chapter it is stated that of the four main areas in which training will contribute to success, attitude is the most important. Do you agree or disagree with this statement? Why?
5. What method(s) would you recommend for compensating salespeople who sell the following products or services: Life insurance? Skin care products to women? Textbooks to professors? Complicated electronic products? Salespeople in a department store? Executive recruiters?
6. You are vice-president of sales of a new company just being established to market computer software. What method would you use to budget for your sales force?
7. You are a young sales manager with older salespeople reporting to you. Which types of power do you feel will be most important in dealing with these individuals?
8. If it is a myth that job satisfaction has a direct effect in increasing sales performance, why should the sales manager attempt to promote job satisfaction?
9. You know a very successful salesperson and observe this person in performing his or her duties. Many of the attributes this person displays tend to be that of the unsuccessful salesperson, as noted in Figure 21-9. What do you think this might mean?
10. A sales account falls into segment 4 of Figure 21-12. Why would you want to waste any time maintaining contact with this particular account in the future?

Ethical Question _____

You are the sales manager of a force of twenty-five salespeople. In reviewing proposals made to customers, you find that your top sales performer, a personal friend of your boss, misrepresented some of the previous jobs accomplished by your company. You confront him with the proposal. He admits to "fudging" some information. "We always do a good job. Sometimes the truth isn't believable, but adjusting the facts a little makes some facts more credible. I don't consider this unethical. Now I have almost double the sales of any other salesperson you have. My customers like me. As a matter of fact, if you brought this to their attention, they would either laugh it off, or they would believe me and not you. I don't want to argue about this or make things tough on you. I follow your orders and do what you say in everything else. However, I'm not backing down on this. Don't tell me how to sell. If you insist on this, I'll quit and take my services somewhere else." What should you do?[42]

Endnotes

1. C. G. Brower, "Unarmed and Dangerous," *Success* (January–February 1988), vol. 35, no. 1, p. 35.
2. "Need a Large Sales Force Right Away? Start an Army" *Sales and Marketing Management* (November 11, 1985), p. 60.
3. Nancy Hall, "Earning a Lesson," *Product Marketing* (June 1985), p. 43.
4. William A. Cohen, *The Entrepreneur and Small Business Problem-Solver* 2nd ed. (New York: Wiley, 1990), p. 293.
5. "Average Cost Shatters $200 Mark for Industrial Sales Calls, But Modernization Seen in 1984 Hikes," *Marketing News* (August 17, 1984), p. 16.
6. Robert Evans, "Training Employee Orientation Hikes Sales Rep Performance," *Marketing News* (November 13, 1981), pp. 1, 16.
7. Cohen, op. cit., p. 295.
8. Larry J. B. Robinson, "Role Playing as a Sales Training Tool," *Harvard Business Review*, vol. 65 (May–June 1987), pp. 34–35.
9. "Marketer Makes a Million," *Marketing News* (September 27, 1985), p. 14.
10. Douglas J. Dalrymple and Hans B. Thorelli, "Sales Force Budgeting," *Business Horizons*, vol. 23 (July–August 1984), pp. 31, 34.
11. Orville C. Walker, Jr., Gilbert A. Churchill, Jr., and Neil M. Ford, "Motivation and Performance in Industrial Selling: Present Knowledge and Needed Research," *Journal of Marketing Research* (May 1977), p. 157.
12. David M. Szymanski, "Determinants of Selling Effectiveness: The Importance of Declarative Knowledge to the Personal Selling Concept," *Journal of Marketing*, vol. 52, no. 1 (January 1988), p. 66.
13. Bert Rosenbloom and Rolph E. Anderson, "The Sales Manager: Tomorrow's Super Marketer," *Business Horizons*, vol. 27 (March–April 1984), pp. 51, 52.
14. Paul Busch, "Sales Manager's Basis of Social Power and Influence Upon the Sales Force," *Journal of Marketing*, vol. 44 (Summer 1980), p. 92
15. Ibid., pp. 93, 99, 100.
16. Richard P. Bagozzi, "Performance and Satisfaction in an Industrial Sales Force: An Examination of Their Antecedents and Simultaneity," *Journal of Marketing*, vol. 44 (Spring 1980).
17. Thomas R. Wotruba, "The Relationship of Job Image, Performance, and Job Satisfaction to Inactivity—Proneness of Direct Salespeople," *Journal of the Academy of Marketing Science*, vol. 18, no. 2 (Spring 1990), pp. 113–121.
18. Charles M. Futrell and A. Parasuraman, "The Relationship of Satisfaction and Performance to Sales Force Turnover," *Journal of Marketing*, vol. 48 (Fall 1984), p. 39.
19. Douglas N. Behrman and William D. Perreault, Jr., "A Role Stress Model of the Performance and Satisfaction of Industrial Salespersons," *Journal of Marketing*, vol. 48 (Fall 1984), p. 19.
20. Bagozzi, op. cit., p. 71.
21. Pradeep K. Tyagi, "Relative Importance of Key Job Dimensions in Leadership Behavior in Motivating Salesperson Work Performance," *Journal of Marketing*, vol. 49 (Summer 1985), pp. 82, 83.
22. Ajay K. Kohli, "Some Unexplored Supervisory Behavior and Their Influence on Salespeople's Role Clarity, Specific Self-Esteem, Job Satisfaction, and Motivation," *Journal of Marketing Research*, vol. 22 (November 1985), p. 431.
23. Ajay K. Kohli, "Effects of Supervisory Behavior: The Role of Individual Differences Among Salespeople," *Journal of Marketing*, vol. 53, no. 4 (October 1989), p. 47.
24. Gordon J. Badovick, "Emotional Reactions and Salesperson Motivation: An Attributional Approach Following Inadequate Sales Performance," *Journal of the Academy of Marketing Science*, vol. 18, no. 2 (Spring 1990), p. 123.
25. Barton A. Weitz, "Effectiveness in Sales Interaction: A Contingency Framework," *Journal of Marketing*, vol. 45 (Winter 1981), p. 90.
26. Pradeep K. Tyagi, "Effects of Stressful Organizational Conditions on Salesperson Work Motivation," *Journal of the Academy of Marketing Science*, vol. 13 (Winter–Spring, 1985), p. 294.
27. William L. Cron, "Industrial Salesperson Development: A Career Stages Perspective," *Journal of Marketing*, vol. 48 (Fall 1984), p. 45.
28. Ibid., p. 46.

29. Allan J. Dubinsky, Thomas N. Ingram, and Charles H. Fay, "An Empirical Examination of the Assumed Job Tenure/Vocational Maturity Linkage in the Industrial Sales Force," *Journal of the Academy of Marketing Science*, vol. 12 (Fall 1984), p. 60.

30. Bradley D. Lockeman and John H. Hallaq, "Who Are Your Successful Salespeople?" *Journal of the Academy of Marketing Science*, vol. 10 (Fall 1982), p. 466.

31. "PAs Examine the People Who Sell to Them," *Sales and Marketing Management* (November 11, 1985), p. 39.

32. Thomas W. Leigh and Patrick F. McGraw, "Mapping the Procedural Knowledge of Industrial Sales Personnel: A Script-Theoretic Investigation," *Journal of Marketing*, vol. 53, no. 1 (January 1989), p. 30.

33. G. David Hughes, "Computerized Sales Management," *Harvard Business Review*, vol. 61 (March–April 1983), p. 102.

34. Robert J. Zimmer and James W. Taylor, "Matching Profiles for Your Industrial Sales Force," *Business* (March–April 1981).

35. Don Beveridge, "Uncovering the True Sales Pro," *Sales and Marketing Management*, (September 9, 1985), p. 58.

36. Raymond LaForge, Clifford E. Young, and B. Curtis Hamm, "Increasing Sales Productivity Through Improved Sales Call Location Strategies," *Journal of Personal Selling and Sales Management*, vol. 3 (November 1983), p. 54.

37. Marvin H. Jolson, "Selling Assertively," *Business Horizons*, vol. 27 (September–October 1984), p. 74.

38. Sandra Hile Hart, William C. Moncrief, and A. Parasuraman, "An Empirical Investigation of Salespeople's Performance, Effort, and Selling Method During A Sales Contest," *Journal of the Academy of Marketing Science*, vol. 17, no. 1 (Winter 1989), p. 37.

39. Raymond W. LaForge, Clifford E. Young, and David W. Cravens "Redeployment Can Aid Productivity," *Marketing News* (September 27, 1985), p. 14.

40. Donald W. Jackson, Jr., Janet E. Keith, and John L. Schlacter, "Evaluation of Selling Performance: The Study of Current Practices," *Journal of Professional Selling and Sales Management*, vol. 3 (November 1983), p. 49.

41. Raymond O. Loen, *Measuring Sales Performance* (Washington, D.C.: Small Business Administration, 1978).

42. This question was suggested by Joseph A. Bellizzi and Robert E. Hite, "Supervising Unethical Salesforce Behavior," *Journal of Marketing*, vol. 53, no. 2 (April 1989), pp. 36–47.

Implementation

22

- Understand the difference between plans and implementation and how both are interrelated.

- Understand why excellent plans sometimes fail in implementation.

- Know the implementation functions of the marketing manager.

How Colgate Squeezed Crest

Toothpaste wars have been fought in the United States for more than thirty years. Over these years, Procter & Gamble Company's Crest toothpaste has maintained its dominance over its rival, Colgate. But Colgate is really putting the squeeze on. Up until the 1980s, Colgate had just 18 per cent of the $1 billion U.S. toothpaste market. But soon, Colgate moved up to 27.8 per cent, only slightly behind Crest's dominant 30.5 per cent share. Both Colgate's success and Crest's problems are due to marketing implementation. First Colgate got to market with a toothpaste gel several months before P&G.

Then came the pump. Production problems stalled P&G's introduction of its pump tube toothpaste. But Colgate had no such problems. It introduced a pump that it had already been distributing in Europe and

soon cornered what some sources say was as much as 50 per cent of the $150 million pump toothpaste business.

Most recently, Colgate entered the market with Dentagard, a plaque-fighting toothpaste. P&G managed to counter with the Crest Tartar Control Formula. Perhaps P&G has finally overcome its problems with implementation, but its inability to get toothpaste products to market rapidly in the past has cost it dearly in market share and profits.[1]

Making Silver Turn into Gold

Silversmithing might not strike you as big business for the 1990s, or even the twentieth century. You might therefore be surprised to learn that Towle Manufacturing Company lost about $2 million on sales of

$285 million, and Towle Manufacturing is a silver-smith. This may not have been a great year, but the previous year had been worse, with a 70 per cent decrease in net income. The problems followed an expansion and modernization in which mail-order sales and bonus gifts were used to help boost the company's sales. But then the computer system broke down, resulting in mismatched orders and other delays; the distribution system failed due to a strike; the company had to pay almost a million dollars to fly goods to customers; and millions of dollars in incoming product were marooned in Boston Harbor for several months. If that weren't enough, retailers selling Towle Manufacturing products weren't happy either, citing a poor selection of merchandise and less than great quality.

But now the 300-year-old company is making a major turnaround. Some regional showrooms have been cut back, and total display space has been cut by 25 per cent by dropping unpopular items and duplicate patterns. In fact, inventory has been narrowed by almost 20 per cent. What Towle has found is that there is a great deal of difference between planned strategy and tactics and implementing these plans in day-to-day operations.[2]

Can You Begin Implementation with a Standing Ovation?

Bob Waterman, co-author of *In Search of Excellence* and the author of *The Renewal Factor*, described how, back in 1969, he began implementing a marketing plan for Sanwa Bank in Japan while working for the consulting firm of McKinsey and Company. He thought the problem was reasonably straightforward and put together his plans for implementation in a very short time. His clients didn't accept the plan as written. They wanted Waterman to coordinate with a "few" others. They than presented Waterman with a list of several hundred names. "It will take months, and we're expensive," he told them. "We're paying the bills," they retorted. Waterman followed their wishes. Said Waterman, "When I finally made my presentation, it took less than an hour. Then two things happened that had never occurred in my career. First, we got a standing ovation. Second, and most surprising, within days the company's market share started to bounce back." Waterman learned a lesson, and today he recommends a simple formula for implementing your plans and strategy. Involve everybody. People are more committed to plans where they have had an input and have part ownership. No one enjoys blindly executing someone else's orders. Give people room to generate and run with their own new ideas. You'll be surprised at just how motivated people are to see that their ideas are successful. Finally, understand that implementation is an evolutionary process. It must begin before you make and finalize your plans.[3] ●

The Marketing Campaign Is the Payoff _____

The situations just described all had to do with implementing planned strategy and planned tactics. They point out that the marketing manager cannot just analyze and plan strategy and tactics, but must actually carry out a marketing campaign for them to be effective. The **implementation process** is shown in Figure 22-1, beginning with strategy, progressing to tactical decisions, and inputting into implementation, or operation, of the marketing mix. Note that other inputs include internal factors and external factors, both comprising the environs of the marketplace. The output involves monitoring the results of the operations and then adapting or retailoring the strategy and the tactics to the particular situation the marketing manager faces.[4]

This can be summarized in a very blunt and direct fashion by looking at Harold Geneen's example. Geneen took a company of $766 million and built it into a colossus of $22 billion through fifty-eight consecutive quarters. His company showed an annual uninterrupted growth rate of more than 10 per

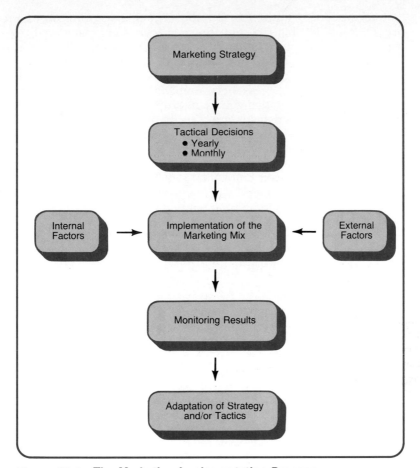

Figure 22-1   The Marketing Implementation Process

Source: From Barry Berman and Joel R. Evans, "Integrating the Marketing Plan: Lessons from Marketing Management, Strategic Marketing, and Marketing Implementation," in Robert F. Lusch, et al., eds. *1985 AMA Educators Proceedings* (Chicago: AMA, 1985), p. 270. Used with permission.

cent with famed ITT. Geneen says simply, "Management must manage."[5] And Geneen is talking about all managers, be they heads of giant corporations, vice-presidents of marketing, or marketing managers at middle-management levels.

Want more proof? *Business Week* editors reassessed thirty-three strategies it had described in previous issues in a variety of firms. On completing their investigation, it was found that nineteen of those strategies didn't work, and only fourteen were in some way successful. For example, Toro developed a strategy to capitalize on brand recognition and its reputation for quality in mowers and snowblowers by expanding into other home care products. The strategy failed because of snowless winters and distribution mistakes in implementing the strategy. International Multifoods' strategy was to develop niche products in consumer foods and expand into the restaurant business. But a combination of overseas products, the recession, and timidity in execution caused this strategy to crumble. The Shaklee Company set as a goal becoming the leading U.S. nutritional products company, and the strategy was to streamline its product lines. But in execution, Shaklee was unsuccessful due to both a recession and to sales force turnover.[6]

Why did these companies and so many others fail in implementation in the marketplace? The reason is simply that even with the best-planned strategy and tactics, implementation, or execution of the strategies and tactics, rarely goes exactly as laid out in the plan. The great German military strategist Von Clausewitz called this difference between practice and planning in strategy "battle friction." More recently, Regis McKenna, the high-tech marketing guru of Silicon Valley in California, and one of the men whose marketing genius helped build Intel and Apple Computers, calls the unexpected actions in implementing strategy and tactics "things that go bump in the night."[7] Organization and human realities that occur in implementation cannot be ignored.[8]

Plans Versus Operations

How do we distinguish plans for strategy and tactics from actual implementation? Philip Kotler, Liam Fahey, and Somkid Jatusripitak, in their book *The New Competition*, draw the distinction between strategy and tactics and operations, as shown in Figure 22-2.[9]

The differences between strategy and tactics and operations mean that there are four possible combinations of measurements of the quality of the campaign. These are shown in Figure 22-3. The strategy may be either appropriate or inappropriate. The marketing implementation may be excellent, or it may be poor. Thus, the combinations are appropriate strategy and excellent implementation, inappropriate strategy and excellent implementation, appropriate strategy and poor implementation, and inappropriate strategy and poor implementation.[10] From this matrix, it can be seen that appropriate strategy and tactics with excellent implementation leads to success, while appropriate strategy with poor implementation leads to trouble, which could result in failure if not corrected.

Note, however, that inappropriate strategy will ultimately lead to failure whether or not the marketing implementation is poor or excellent. This is

Strategy and Tactics	Operations
External focus: setting direction	Internal focus: attaining direction
Effectiveness	Efficiency
Doing the "right" thing	Doing things "right"
Designing the plan	Executing the plan
Commits resources	Uses resources

Source: Adapted from Philip Kotler, Liam Fahey, and Somkid Jatusripitak, *The New Competition* (Englewood Cliffs, N.J.: Prentice-Hall, 1985), p. 245.

Figure 22-2   The Distinction Between Strategy and Tactics and Operations

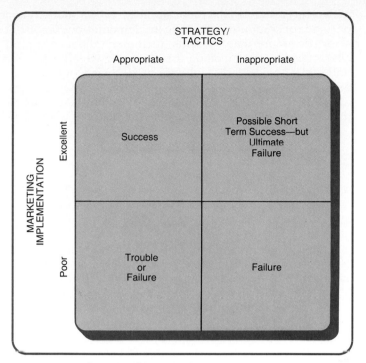

Figure 22-3 Strategy/Tactics

Source: Adapted with modifications from Thomas V. Bonoma, "Making Your Marketing Strategy Work," *Harvard Business Review*, vol. 62 (March–April 1984), p. 72.

due to the cautionary note explained in an earlier chapter: it is more important to do the right thing than do the wrong thing in a correct way. The wrong thing is represented by either strategy or tactics. If the strategy or tactics is wrong, the campaign cannot win, no matter how well it is executed.

As Al Ries and Jack Trout, the two advertising executives who had so much to do with the development of product positioning, said in their book, *Marketing Warfare*, "If the strategy is good, the battle can be won with indifferent tactics."[11] To a lesser extent, we can say the same about good tactics and indifferent operations.

Why Things Don't Go Right

Internal Problems

One major reason that strategy and tactics don't go as planned is internal problems. Company resources could run out or fall short of what was available while in the planning stages. A change of management might lead to a different emphasis and a lack of allocation of priorities to a particular marketing campaign. A recent study of nine hundred marketing professionals with a full range of job responsibilities within marketing confirmed the importance of commitment during implementation. It concluded that job characteristics more than personal attributes influence commitment. These job characteristics may include the degree to which a job allows employees to undertake a wide variety of options in their work, the extent to which they have a say in scheduling and freedom to do what they want on the job, the extent to which employees can identify with the results of their efforts, and the degree to which employees receive feedback about how they are doing.[12]

External Problems

Another reason that things don't go right has to do with external problems over which a marketing manager may have very little control. Yet, marketing managers must successfully cope with such problems in implementing any marketing strategy or tactic.

Alvin Toffler, in his book *The Adaptive Corporation*, developed a concept of external novelty ratios to explain this phenomenon and the fact that management must succeed despite problems with the environs of the marketplace. He found the following major external problems with which giant AT&T had to cope in just a nine-year period:

- 1962: AT&T lost sole control over a major communications technology vital to the company due to the Comsat Act.
- 1968: Traditional interconnection policy suffered its first major break due to Carterfone.
- 1969: The FCC did a major study of quality of service distinct from rates.
- 1970: The U.S. government took a giant step toward creating a communications policy center, the Office of Telecommunications Policy.
- 1970: There was a major FCC investigation of AT&T employment practices.
- 1971: The FCC created an office to serve as an attorney for citizens' groups wishing to influence communications policy.
- 1971: For the first time, there was a crack in the average cost rate structure.
- 1971: The FCC began considering alternative network competition for the Bell system.[13]

Of course these major environmental problems for AT&T eventually culminated with the government-required breakup of "Ma Bell," certainly a major problem in the implementation of strategies for the corporation.

Poor Planning

Another reason that strategy and tactics fail in execution has to do with poor planning. A marketing manager starts the whole process with planning, and it is essential to do this planning in as detailed and as quality a fashion as possible, long before operations start. As noted in Chapter 3, only in this way can the results of possible changes in the environs of the marketplace be anticipated, to avoid the threats and take advantage of the opportunities that may occur.

Sometimes poor execution is caused by poor intelligence regarding the market, even though detailed planning has been carried out. Perhaps the biggest marketing news event of 1985 was Coca-Cola's reformulation of its flagship product. The company had accomplished considerable marketing research, and, time after time, the new Coca-Cola formula won over "old Coke" and its arch rival, Pepsi Cola, in blind taste tests. The new product was introduced with an advertising blitz, and the company was proud that it had been able to maintain security over the reformulation until the actual moment of introduction. But the marketing intelligence was actually poor, in that it failed to consider the position its traditional product held with consumers, regardless of taste. Thus, even when the firm reintroduced traditional Coca-Cola under the name Coke Classic, it felt that this would be a concession to a relatively small group of loyalists. Yet, by the end of the year 1985, Coke Classic was outselling New Coke 3 to 1 nationally and 9 to 1 in many markets.[14]

Poor Execution

And finally, and perhaps most importantly, things don't go right due to poor execution of what might be a very good plan for implementing a strategy or a tactic. Bristol-Myers introduced a product called Datril to compete with Johnson & Johnson's very successful Tylenol. The price tactic was decided upon as the key to market penetration, and Datril ads compared the $1.85 per 100 Datril tablets against the $2.85 per 100 Tylenol tablets. But in executing the plan for this tactic, the product was first test marketed; thus,

CEOs		Corporate planners		Marketing executives	
	Consumer		**Consumer**		**Consumer**
	1. Current operating problems		1. Current operating problems		1. Plans as standards
	2. Company goals		2. Company goals		2. Current operating problems
	3. Involvement		3. Planning climate		3. Planning climate
	4. Plans as standards		4. Understanding direction		4. Understanding direction
	5. Understanding direction		5. Involvement		5. Involvement
	6. Planning climate		6. Plans as standards		6. Company goals
	Industrial		**Industrial**		**Industrial**
	1. Current operating problems		1. Current operating problems		1. Current operating problems
	2. Company goals		2. Company goals		2. Planning as standards
	3. Involvement		3. Understanding direction		3. Involvement
	4. Understanding direction		4. Involvement		4. Planning climate
	5. Plans as standards		5. Planning climate		5. Company goals
	6. Planning climate		6. Plans as standards		6. Understanding direction

Source: Adapted from Barbara J. Coe, "Key Differentiating Factors and Problems Associated with Implementation of Strategic Market Planning," in Robert F. Lusch et al., eds., *1985 AMA Educators' Proceedings* (Chicago: AMA, 1985), p. 280.

Figure 22-4   Perceived Problems in Implementing Strategy

Johnson & Johnson knew Bristol-Myers's intentions before it ever went national. By the time it did, Johnson & Johnson had reduced prices on its existing stocks in all 165,000 retail outlets. As a result, Bristol-Myers's product, Datril, could not carry the planned advertising, and the pricing tactic failed in the marketplace.[15]

These types of problems have shown up again and again in research conducted by marketing scientists. The perceived problems in implementing strategy noted by successful CEOs, corporate planners, and marketing executives in a recent study are shown in Figure 22-4.[16] Note that the same problems tend to show up repeatedly whether the company markets consumer goods or industrial goods and regardless of whether the problem is perceived by the CEO, corporate planner, or marketing executive: (1) current operating problems, (2) company goals, (3) involvement, (4) plans as standards, (5) understanding direction, or (6) planning climate.

The Implementation Functions of the Marketing Manager

There are four basic implementation functions of the marketing manager. These have to do with organizing, initiating, monitoring, and controlling the marketing campaign. Let's look at each of these in turn.

Organizing

Organizing the marketing campaign has been discussed previously. It has to do not only with the marketing organization, but also—in planning the marketing campaign and developing a marketing plan—with subelements that include strategy, tactics, and tasks that must be carried out. It also involves the allocation of resources from many different organizations and the integration of the responsibilities and planned actions of these organizations—which may include marketing organizations, nonmarketing types, and internal organizations, as well as suppliers, consultants, advertising agencies, and others outside of the company. While some of this activity can be accomplished or reaccomplished once the marketing campaign is initiated, the bulk of organizing must be done before the marketing campaign is initiated and when it is still in its planning stages.

Initiating

Initiation means a beginning. In some ways it is the real beginning of executing plans, organizing, and everything else that has been accomplished previously. Still, even the initiation must be thought through and the preparation made before what could be considered the actual kickoff of the marketing campaign. This preparation should include five steps. The first step is a recheck of all planning activities to ensure that functional overloads do not exist in the planned initiation. Remember here that prevention is far more valuable than cure. Thus, anything that you can do to avoid unnecessary strain on linkages between your strategy and tactical plans and current operating systems is highly desirable.

Perhaps your plans called for stocking a certain level of a product, but, due to other demands, your company production department is unable to maintain production levels for it. In such a situation, it makes far more sense to modify the plan before it is implemented rather than maintain it based on production estimates that it is impossible to fulfill.

The second action that should be taken as a preparatory step prior to initiation has to do with containment of strategic shock waves. A strategic shock wave is a shock to the overall firm or an organization in it due to the introduction of a new product. This containment might take the form of new production plants that produce only the new product rather than use old facilities. Or it could, in practice, involve organizations outside of your company performing certain functions until such time as the campaign implementation is well along. This is not to say that new products shouldn't be introduced, or shouldn't be manufactured in old facilities, but rather to think through to the impact of the new campaign on old, ongoing campaigns and to take action to ensure that one does not impact negatively on the other.

The third step of preparation is to take personal responsibility as a marketing manager to ensure that coupling issues between plans for tactics or strategy and implementation are all accounted for. The larger the company and the more diversified—with many different organizations, each having a finger in the pie and associated with the planning of strategy and tactics, and perhaps the implementation—the more important this becomes. This gets down, again, to the basic thesis that the marketing manager must manage and is responsible for everything that is assigned. The key here is to give personal attention to major coupling issues before the process begins.

The fourth step, or key to preparation, has to do with the team that developed the strategy or the tactics and the planning associated with it. To the maximum degree possible, it is essential to hold onto this team until its work is completed. Some plans are considered complete when the tactics have been formulated. But beyond the tactics, it is essential that a list of the specific tasks that each function must perform, as well as who is going to perform them (in some cases by department or organization, and in others by names of actual individuals), be documented. It is crucial that the specific milestones and schedules be laid out, as well as the financial requirements, as illustrated and discussed in the previous chapter on marketing planning.

Ideally, the same individuals who plan the strategy and the tactics also implement them. Many firms are beginning to eliminate their planning organizations in favor of having the line managers do the planning. Thus, the planners and the implementors are the same people. But even if this is not the case in your company, you must ensure that the planning team remains together to do followthrough actions and to help in the initial stages of execution.

Finally, as the marketing manager responsible for a specific marketing campaign or project, it is important to communicate downward and not just upward. It sometimes happens that the marketing manager who has been the advocate of a specific project succeeds in communicating every aspect of the advantages of the project to higher-level management but fails in implementing the plan. Although he or she sold it to upper-level management, the individuals who were to execute it were not sold. Ensure that the working-level managers who must implement and execute your marketing plan are completely informed about what they must do and why they must do it. This will also help in getting commitments; as pointed out previously, commitment is crucial for implementation.

John M. Hobbs and Donald F. Heany, the developers of the concept of the five steps for preparing for initiation, have both had extensive experience at the top level of corporate planning staffs with major firms such as General Electric. They make no bones about it: "One laggard, one half-hearted functional commitment, may endanger the goals established for the center as a whole."[17]

Monitoring

Monitoring the effort once initiated is also of great importance. Some marketing managers have the idea that tactics and strategy can be planned, developed, initiated, and then forgotten; that such strategies and tactics will work automatically without any additional effort. This is not possible. One of the reasons is changes in the environs of the marketplace, including both internal and external factors. A significant tool that the marketing manager has for monitoring changes in the environs is the MIS, or marketing information system, discussed in Chapter 4.

With an MIS, the manager can be apprised of what is happening internally in the firm, and externally in the marketplace, on a day-to-day basis. Peter Drucker has drawn the analogy between this monitoring by a manager and an airplane's instrument panel. A pilot flying an airplane has an instrument panel before him that senses and displays hundreds of internal conditions for the airplane, as well as many that are external, that are essential to a safe and successful flight. In the same way, an MIS can be thought of as an instrument panel for the marketing manager. The MIS can monitor the day-to-day situation of a marketing campaign. It allows the marketing manager to take appropriate action to ensure that tactics and/or strategy go as planned, and that the intended objectives are reached, even as the environs change.

The Marketing Audit

Another useful tool for the marketing manager in monitoring during implementation is the **marketing audit**. The marketing audit evaluates marketing practice in the same way that a public accounting audit evaluates public accounting practice. It has four basic characteristics.

1. It is broad rather than narrow in focus, covering a company's entire marketing environment, including its objectives, plans, strategies, tactics, organizations, and the systems implementing the plans.
2. It is independent of the operation that is being evaluated. Thus, just as an accounting audit is not conducted by the manager whose accounting operations are being evaluated, the marketing audit is typically accomplished by someone other than the marketing manager responsible for the particular organization or marketing campaign.
3. The marketing audit is systematic—that is, it follows a certain methodology and has an orderly sequence of steps that must be followed.

Figure 22-5 The Marketing Audit Process

Source: From Philip Kotler, William Gregor, and William Rodgers, "The Marketing Audit Comes of Age," *Sloan Management Review*, vol. 18 (Winter 1977), p. 27.

4. A marketing audit should be conducted periodically, not just when a particular project or organization is in trouble.[18]

The process of the marketing audit proceeds as in Figure 22-5, beginning with agreement on objectives, scope, and approach between the auditor and the marketing manager whose organization is being audited. It then proceeds to collect data, and, finally, a report is prepared and presented to the marketing manager responsible.[19]

A typical outline of audit questions is shown in Figure 22-6.[20,21,22]

Marketplace Environs

Company Environs

1. Are available and potential company resources in line with the organization's tasks and responsibilities?
2. Are employees and managers committed to success of the organization or project?

Competitor Environs

1. Who are the major competitors? What are their objectives and strategies? What are their strengths and weaknesses? How are they and their products or services perceived by buyers? What shares of the market do major competitors own? What are the trends for the future?
2. What are the major products and services of competitors and what tactics are they using (products, prices, promotion, and distribution channels)?

Neutral Environs

1. What actions or potential actions of governmental, media, or consumer organizations are affecting the strategy, tactics, operations, or plans of the marketing organization?
2. How is the marketing organization responding to the actions of these organizations?

Situational Environs

1. What laws, policies, technological innovations, and social or cultural changes are occurring that affect or can affect this organization?
2. What business or economic changes are occurring that can or are having an impact?

The Marketplace

1. What is happening in the marketplace? Is the market growing or declining? Is the distribution of customers within the market changing? What are the major market segments and how large is each? What are the trends in each segment?

Figure 22-6 Marketing Audit Questions and Components

2. Who is the buyer? What are the demographic, psychographic, and life-style characteristics of the buyer? What are the major needs of these customers? Who makes the buying decision in each case? What factors influence the purchase decision?

The Marketing Organization

Structure

1. Is the design of the organization optimized in accordance with the objectives of the organization and how tasks are performed?
2. Has authority been given commensurate with responsibility for task accomplishment at every level?

Management

1. Are all managers managing effectively and efficiently?
2. Do managers merely manage, or do they also practice good leadership?

Personnel

1. Are personnel well trained and motivated?
2. Are all personnel policies such as recruitment, evaluation, promotion, etc., optimal, or can they be improved?

Culture

1. Does the organization have high morale and esprit de corps?
2. What are the organization's strong and weak points regarding its culture?

Roles and Missions

1. Does each organizational unit and subunit clearly understand its purposes?
2. Do all organizational units, vertically and horizontally, communicate well with minimum friction in accomplishing the organization's mission?
3. Do units of this organization interface effectively with other company organizations such as production, research and development, finance, etc.

Planning

1. Does the organization do formal planning with the commitment of top organizational management?
2. Is the planning system effective?

The Marketing Information System

1. Is accurate and timely market intelligence available on a continuous basis?
2. Is competent marketing research accomplished when required?
3. Do marketing managers and top organizational managers use the MIS effectively?

Marketing Strategy

1. Is strategic marketing management effective and does it support the company's business goals?
2. What are the organization's marketing objectives and do they support the company's business goals? Are they appropriate?
3. What marketing strategies are being followed to attain these objectives? Are they the best strategies? Are they succeeding? If so, why? If not, why not?

Marketing Tactics

Product

1. How do product and product line objectives support the marketing strategy? Are they appropriate?
2. Are the product tactics being employed the correct tactics to attain the objectives set? Are product and lines integrated?

Figure 22-6   (Continued)

Price
1. What are the organization's pricing objectives? Do they support the organization's marketing strategy?
2. Are the pricing tactics the best for attaining tactical objective, and are they working? Why or why not?

Distribution
1. What are the objectives of the distribution tactics, and do they support marketing strategy?
2. Do distribution tactics adequately support the attainment of distribution objectives? Are these tactics integrated?

Advertising and Publicity
1. What are the objectives of the organization's advertising and publicity tactics? Do they support organizational marketing strategy?
2. Are advertising and publicity working effectively in attaining their set objectives? Is the entire tactical program integrated?

Sales Promotion
1. What are the objectives of sales promotion, and do they support overall marketing strategy?
2. Are the tactics the appropriate ones for attaining the objectives set, and are they working? Why or why not?

Personal Selling
1. What are the organization's personal selling objectives, and do they support marketing strategy?
2. Are the personal selling and sales force tactics adopted the correct ones for accomplishing these objectives, and are they working? Why or why not? Is the overall personal selling program integrated for maximum efficiency and effectiveness?

Overall Integration
1. Is the overall tactical program integrated to avoid inappropriate optimization of any single element?
2. Has the overall tactical program been integrated such as to take advantage of organizational strengths and minimize weaknesses?

Implementation
1. What are profitability, ROI, market share, and other important measurements of effectiveness and efficiency? How do they compare with goals and objectives set? How do they compare with the industry averages and leading competitors?
2. How is control being exercised to ensure that the planned strategies and tactics are implemented? Are they working?

Figure 22-6   (Continued)

Personal Contact

Monitoring need not necessarily be quantitative and may not necessarily require the formal procedures typical of a marketing audit. Tom Peters, co-author of *In Search of Excellence,* and Nancy Austin, co-author of *The Assertive Woman,* have pioneered a method of monitoring and of leadership called MBWA, or management by wandering around. According to Peters and Austin, "The topic of MBWA is at once about common sense, leadership, customers, innovation, and people. Simple wandering—listening, emphasizing, staying in touch—is an ideal starting point."[23]

Peters feels that by MBWA, the manager gets in his gut what is actually happening both inside and outside an organization in a way that can never be obtained by viewing simple statistics gathered by someone else from sources either inside or outside the organization. He tells a story of an automobile executive in Detroit who for years drove to work in a town dominated by the American automobile industry, seeing mainly American-manufactured cars on the streets and in the company parking lot, and having his car worked on all day long and serviced by company staff. From his gut perception, there were no problems with American cars, despite statistics indicating the increasing penetration of foreign cars and dissatisfaction with American car quality. One day his company moved him to California. Suddenly, he saw an entirely different array of vehicles on the freeway every morning. According to Peters, only then did he understand "in his gut" that Americans really were switching their preferences and purchasing foreign cars.[24]

Marketing researchers Priscilla A. LaBarbera and Larry J. Rosenberg confirm Peters's MBWA idea. They state most emphatically that marketing managers must seek interaction with customers on a real-time basis. They make several recommendations to accomplish this, such as establishing consumer adviser boards and personally hearing consumer complaints and questions.[25]

Of course, simply collecting and listening and gathering data are only half the monitoring task. This information must also be analyzed. Various means of measuring data and collecting it are shown in Figure 22-7.[26] Marketing managers may also make use of accounting data in their analysis of what is going on in their campaign. Thus, differences between planned and actual sales volumes can be made, along with differences between planned and actual contributions per unit. The potential sources of variation between planned and actual contribution may be due to total market size, market share penetration, and the price or cost per unit. In Figure 22-8, box A differs from box B due to a combination of market size and market share variance.[27]

Actual market share captured was much less than planned. But a compensating difference between planning and implementation occurred. The market size was larger than planned. In any case the planned sales volume differed from the actual volume. The impact would be even greater if actual

Measures	Data Collection Method	Marketing Objective
Customer perceptions, recall, beliefs, recognition of copy	Survey research, theater tests	Awareness, recognition of price, ad copy, brand name, etc.
Customer perceptions, perceptual mapping	Survey research	Brand or product positioning
Purchase behavior, simulated purchase	Sales tracking, telephone survey, purchase diaries	Market share increase, sales/revenue increase

Source: Adapted from David G. Bakken and Chandra S. Chaterji, "Predict Customer Response to Marketing Actions with 'Strategy Evaluation Matrix,'" *Marketing News* (September 16, 1983), p. 14.

Figure 22-7   Measuring and Collecting Data

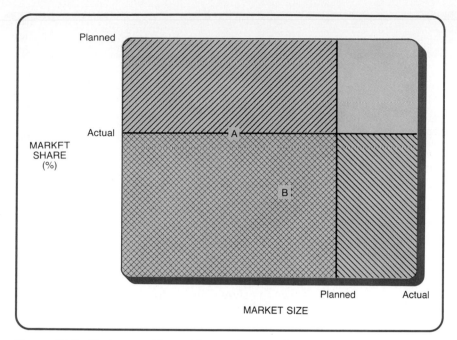

Figure 22-8   Variance of Total Market Size vs. Share

Source: Adapted from James M. Hulbert and Norman E. Toy, "A Strategic Framework for Marketing Control," *Journal of Marketing*, vol. 41 (April 1977), p. 13.

market share percentage and actual market size were less than planned. Can you begin to see why some estimates of sales are so far off?

Continuing to ask why each variance exists eventually results in very specific answers, sometimes at the hands-on level of the operation. For example, labor costs may be higher because more expensive individuals were used in manufacture or material costs increased due to poor negotiations or the market share achieved was lower due to a technological breakthrough by a competitor.

One of the foremost marketing researchers, as well as proponents of the implementation of marketing, is Thomas V. Bonoma of Harvard. In Figure 22-9, Bonoma gives an overview of marketing tasks, sample questions that the marketing manager should ask, and the ability of the system to provide answers. Bonoma's point is that the marketing manager must accomplish the monitoring due to built-in inadequacies of the system to provide good answers to the questions that must be asked.[28]

Controlling

Controlling is the fourth major implementation function of the marketing manager. It involves not only keeping the marketing campaign on course after initiation, but also correcting it as necessary to bring it back to course, should it deviate from what is planned. In a crisis situation, a marketing response aimed directly at regaining control over the environment would also help to reduce the magnitude of the crisis.[29] Control involves not only others'

Tasks	Sample Questions	Ability of System to Provide
1. People	How are marketing peers and subordinates doing on various projects?	Low

2. Markets/products
  • Data overview needs
  • Information on customers and trade
	How are we doing against competition, across segments and product lines?
	How are particular programs being accepted?
	How do customers and distributors feel about _____ ?
		Variable, but generally surprisingly low

3. Time	How are our time allocations paying off by segment, program, products?	Low
4. Money	How are our dollar allocations paying off?	Moderate

Source: From Thomas V. Bonoma, *The Marketing Edge* (New York: Free Press, 1985), p. 146.

Figure 22-9   Monitoring Tasks, Sample Questions to Ask, and the Ability of the System to Provide Answers

behavior, but also one's own, as shown in Figure 22-10. And the targets of this control are both internal to the firm as well as external.[30]

Controlling may require redeployment, reorganization, and reallocation of resources, or it could involve a redefinition of objectives and expectations.[31] However, there is an important cautionary note regarding any reorganization

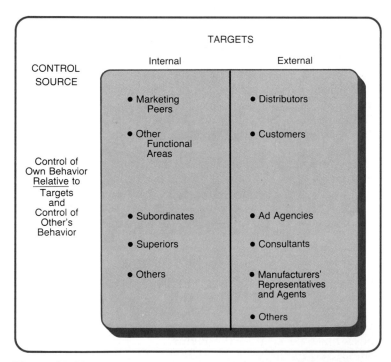

Figure 22-10   Interactions of Control Sources and Targets

Source: Adapted from Thomas V. Bonoma, *The Marketing Edge* (New York: The Free Press, 1985), p. 126.

586

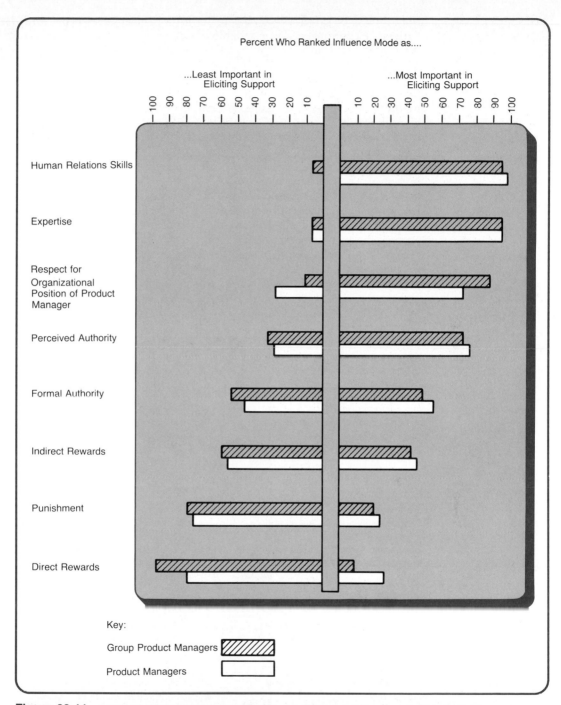

Percent Who Ranked Influence Mode as....

...Least Important in
Eliciting Support

...Most Important in
Eliciting Support

Human Relations Skills

Expertise

Respect for
Organizational
Position of Product
Manager

Perceived Authority

Formal Authority

Indirect Rewards

Punishment

Direct Rewards

Key:

Group Product Managers

Product Managers

Figure 22-11   Importance of Influence Modes as Perceived by Group Product Managers and Product Managers

Source: Adapted from Alladi Venkatesh and David L. Wilemon, "Interpersonal Influence in Product Management," *Journal of Marketing,* vol. 40 (October 1976), p. 36.

that should be emphasized due to its importance: reorganization is major surgery. Therefore, while a redeployment or reallocation of resources may be fairly typical once operations have been enjoined, major reorganizations are not. Some companies reorganize so frequently that there is continual confusion and inability to cope with environmental changes. These companies ensure failure rather than success by their reorganization because of an inability to concentrate superior resources, anywhere at any time, long enough to be effective. Therefore, while reorganization must be done if needed, it should not be done frivolously or without considerable forethought.

As noted in an earlier chapter, the marketing manager controls through influence. There are many means of influence. These include human relations skills expertise; the office of the marketing manager itself; perceived authority; formal authority; indirect rewards, such as verbal accolades for an individual's performance; punishments; and direct rewards. The importance of each of these influence modes as perceived by group product managers and product managers is shown in Figure 22-11.[32] The actions that might be taken to enhance these influence modes are shown in Figure 21-12.[33] Note that control is not just over things or concepts, such as plans and strategies, but also over people, including behavioral and psychological dimensions.[34]

Interpersonal Influence Variables	Action Product Managers Can Take to Increase Influence Mode	Action Group Product Managers Can Take to Increase Product Manager's Influence
Expertise	• Make success visible • Continually develop proficiency in critical product management skills • Learn key contributions that other functional and staff groups can provide in support of the product line	• Monitor product manager performance and suggest corrective action • Openly support product manager's recommendations • Openly recognize good performance • Provide opportunities to prove depth and breadth of experience
Human relations skills	• Build friendship ties • Develop empathy for problems and viewpoints of others • Participate in human relations training • Develop "team" spirit among support groups	• Observe product manager's interactions with interfaces and suggest improvements where human relations skills are deficient • Share experiences on handling interpersonal problems with product manager, e.g., conflict situations
Respect for product manager system in company	• Demonstrate professionalism in dealings with others • Demonstrate importance of product management to company goals	• Stress professionalism • Educate others on the importance of product management to the overall goals of the organization • Facilitate product manager's access to top management
Perceived authority	• Openly assume more authority and responsibility • Set priorities	• Openly delegate authority and responsibility • Back up product manager's decisions

Source: From Alladi Venkatesh and David L. Wilemon, "Interpersonal Influence in Product Management," *Journal of Marketing*, vol. 40 (October 1976), p. 39. Used with permission.

Figure 22-12 Potential Actions to Enhance Influence Modes

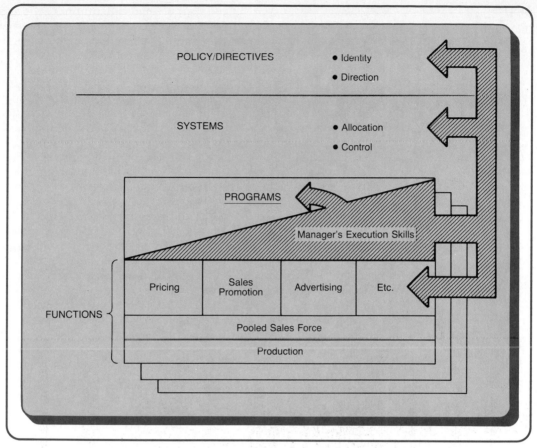

Figure 22-13   A Model of Marketing Implementation

Source: Thomas V. Bonoma, "A Model of Marketing Implementation," in Russell W. Belk et al., eds. *1984 AMA Educators' Proceedings* (Chicago: AMA 1984), p. 189. Used with permission.

Putting It All Together

It is clear from the foregoing discussion that a marketing manager and his or her execution skills are paramount in all elements of operations in the marketing campaign. This is illustrated in Figure 22-13. The marketing manager's execution skills affect organizational policy and directives, systems, programs, and functions. Marketing management without the final step of implementation is theory not yet carried to practice.[35]

Summary

In this chapter, we have learned that implementation is the payoff to the firm and to the marketing manager for everything that has been accomplished previously. Considering this, the marketing manager must never forget that he or she can do everything else correctly and still lose due to poor execution.

We looked, first, at strategy and tactics versus operational actions and saw that they differed in several important aspects, including an internal versus an external focus, efficiency versus effectiveness, doing things right rather than doing the right thing, executing the plan rather than just designing the plan, and using resources rather than only committing resources.

As a result, there are multiple possibilities for things to go wrong. They may go wrong due to internal problems or external problems, due to poor planning or poor marketing intelligence, and due to poor execution of the plan that has been constructed. To prevent this from happening, active management on the part of the marketing manager is needed in four major areas: organizing, initiating, monitoring, and controlling. Organizing, discussed in previous chapters, requires not only organizing the marketing unit, but also the planning and allocating resources. Initiating involves considerable preparation in linking the plan to the execution. Monitoring is enabled by MIS, the concept of the marketing audit, and such simplistic things as the ability to listen to customers as well as subordinates. It requires an analysis of the data once collected, regardless of the form or the process from which it was collected. Controlling is the final major functional area of the marketing manager in the implementation process. Control means control not only of others, but also of oneself. Thus, it includes the requirement for good leadership and influencing others. Control may require redeployment, reorganization, and reallocation of resources, but it means basically maintaining the marketing campaign on track to reach the objective.

Marketing requires the exercise of power.[36] Putting it all together requires the utmost effort in all areas. This includes the probable impacts of individual marketing mix variables, as well as their combined interactive effects.[37] However, the concept of marketing implementation is itself utterly stark in its simplicity. It's simply to get things done.

Questions

1. Because a marketing manager may have little control over an environ of the marketplace, how can he or she be responsible for a marketing campaign negatively affected by such environs?
2. A marketing manager bases an action taken on marketing research received by the marketing research department. This marketing research is in error. Who is ultimately responsible and why?
3. Which is more important to the marketing manager, planning or execution? Why?
4. Why can't the marketing manager do his or her own marketing audit?
5. What may be some of the limitations to MBWA?
6. What are some major advantages of MBWA to the marketing manager?
7. What should a marketing manager do if organizations that do not report to him or her and yet that impact and support his or her campaign do not follow his or her instructions?
8. What action should a marketing manager take if the resources planned and allocated in a certain campaign cannot be delivered?
9. Other than the ways discussed in the text, how might a marketing manager really listen to his or her customers?
10. What does "getting things done" mean to you?

Ethical Question

While students, you and several of your classmates develop a unique computer model for strategic planning that your professor tells you is a real breakthrough. On graduation you decide to form a consulting firm to exploit this unique property. One of your partners is an ace salesperson, and on several occasions has succeeded in enticing high-level potential clients to your offices for a meeting. However, no business ever results from these meetings. In all cases these prospects have noted your relative youth, asked for a list of current clients, and never gotten back to you when they learned that so far the model had only been applied to theoretical situations. You are in the situation of not being able to apply the model until you get some clients, and not being able to get clients until you apply the model. Finally, one of your partners comes up with a brilliant idea. The next time you have an appointment with a prospect, she wants to rent expensive furniture and actors to play the part of busy employees and secretaries. All during the meeting, she proposes that the telephones ring with calls purporting to be CEOs from large, well-known domestic and international corporations. Reports left lying around will similarly bear the imprint of well-known companies. When asked for a client list or references, your partner proposes that you answer, "I'm sorry, our client list is confidential." Is this approach unethical, or just a clever way of getting around the unfairness of being inexperienced?

Endnotes

1. Kathleen Deveny, "Colgate Puts the Squeeze on Crest," *Business Week* (August 19, 1985), pp. 40–41.
2. Lois Therrien, "A Silversmith Tries to Regain Its Shine," *Business Week* (February 18, 1985), p. 70.
3. Bob Waterman, "Make It Happen," *Success*, vol. 36, no. 3 (April 1989), p. 24.
4. Barry Berman and Joel R. Evans, "Integrating the Marketing Plan: Lessons from Marketing Management, Strategic Marketing, and Marketing Implementation," in Robert F. Lusch et al., eds., *1985 AMA Educators' Proceedings* (Chicago: AMA, 1985), p. 270.
5. Harold Geneen with Alvin Moscow, *Managing* (Garden City, N.Y.: Doubleday, 1984), p. 105.
6. "The New Breed of Strategic Planner," *Business Week* (September 17, 1984), pp. 64–65.
7. Regis McKenna, *The Regis Touch* (Reading, Mass.: Addison-Wesley, 1985), p. 146.
8. Nigel Piercy and William Giles, "The Logic of Being Illogical in Strategic Marketing Planning," *The Journal of Services Marketing*, vol. 4, no. 3 (Summer 1990), p. 27.
9. Philip Kotler, Leon Fahey, and S. Jatusripitak, *The New Competition* (Englewood Cliffs, N.J.: Prentice-Hall, 1985), p. 245.
10. Thomas V. Bonoma, "Making Your Marketing Strategy Work" *Harvard Business Review*, vol. 62 (March–April 1984), p. 72. Thomas Bonoma's excellent matrix idea has been modified to reflect my own very strong conviction that good execution cannot overcome inappropriate strategy or tactics.
11. Al Ries and Jack Trout, *Marketing Warfare* (New York: McGraw-Hill, 1986), p. 193.
12. Shelby D. Hunt, Lawrence B. Chonko, and Van R. Wood, "Organizational Commitment and Marketing," *Journal of Marketing*, vol. 49 (Winter 1985), p. 124.
13. Alvin Toffler, *The Adaptive Corporation* (New York: McGraw-Hill, 1985), p. 81.
14. "Coke Was It Among Product News Events," *Advertising Age* (December 30, 1985), p. 3.
15. Ries and Trout, op. cit., pp. 61–62.
16. Barbara J. Coe, "Key Differentiating Factors and Problems Associated with Implementation of Strategic Marketing Planning," in Robert F. Lusch et al., eds., *1985 AMA Educators' Proceedings* (Chicago: AMA, 1985), p. 280.
17. John M. Hobbs and Donald F. Heany, "Coupling Strategy to Operation Plans," in Richard G. Hamermesh, ed., *Strategic Management* (New York: Wiley, 1983), pp. 341–344.
18. Philip Kotler, William Gregor, and William Rodgers, "The Marketing Audit Comes of Age," *Sloan Management Review*, vol. 18 (Winter, 1977), p. 276.
19. Ibid.
20. Ibid., pp. 281–283.
21. Hal W. Goetsche, "Conduct a Comprehensive Marketing Audit to Improve Marketing Planning," *Marketing News* (March 18, 1983), p. 14.
22. William A. Cohen, *How to Make It Big as a Consultant* (New York: AMACOM, 1985), pp. 249–275.
23. Tom Peters and Nancy Austin, *A Passion for Excellence* (New York: Random House, 1985), p. 7.
24. Thomas J. Peters, *Insight Tape No. 600-29* (Chicago: Nightingale-Conant, 1985).
25. Priscilla A. LaBarbera and Larry J. Rosenberg, "How Marketers Can Better Understand Consumers," *MSU Business Topics* (Winter 1980), pp. 30–35.
26. David G. Bakken and Chandra S. Chaterji, "Predict Customer Response to Marketing Actions with 'Strategy Evaluation Matrix,'" *Marketing News* (September 16, 1983), p. 14.
27. James N. Hulbert and Norman E. Toy, "A Stra-

tegic Framework for Marketing Control," *Journal of Marketing*, vol. 41 (April 1977), p. 13. This article contains a complete discussion of recommended methods for accomplishing an analysis using accounting data.

28. Thomas V. Bonoma, *The Marketing Edge* (New York: Free Press, 1985), p. 146.

29. Terry Clark, "The Concept of Marketing Crisis" *Journal of the Academy of Marketing Science*, vol. 16, no. 2 (Summer 1988), p. 47.

30. Ibid., p. 126.

31. Bakken and Chaterji, loc. cit.

32. Alladi Venkatesh and David L. Wilemon, "Interpersonal Influence and Product Management," *Journal of Marketing*, vol. 40 (October 1976), p. 36.

33. Ibid., p. 39.

34. Bernard J. Jaworski, "Toward a Theory of Mar-

keting Control: Environmental Context, Control Types, and Consequences," *Journal of Marketing*, vol. 52, no. 3 (July 1988), p. 23.

35. Thomas V. Bonoma, "A Model of Marketing Implementation," in Russell W. Belk et al., eds., *1984 AMA Educators' Proceedings* (Chicago: AMA, 1984), p. 189.

36. Joseph V. Anderson, "Power Marketing: Its Past, Present, and Future," *Journal of Services Marketing*, vol. 1, no. 2 (Fall 1987), p. 34.

37. Edward A. Morash and John D. Ozment, "Assessing the Impact of Marketing Mix Interactive Effects: Some Empirical and Conceptual Underpinnings," in Paul Bloom et al. eds., *1989 AMA Marketing Educators' Proceedings: Enhancing Knowledge Development in Marketing* (Chicago: AMA, 1989), p. 54.

Federal Express Corporation

Federal Express Corporation specializes in the door-to-door, express delivery of goods and information throughout the United States and abroad. The company delivers packages (mostly 150 pounds or less) and documents through its integrated, air-ground transportation system. Combining this network with electronic equipment, the company offered a facsimile document transmission service called ZapMail in 1984. Because of a lack of demand and tremendous losses, ZapMail was terminated January 31, 1987.

The company operates an air and ground fleet that services a central sorting facility in Memphis, Tennessee. Approximately 460 city stations are maintained throughout the United States. Customs-cleared, international service is available from the United States to approximately 110 countries, either directly or through contracted agents. European sorting facilities are located in London and Brussels.

In 1989 Federal Express merged with Tiger, International, Inc., the world's biggest heavy-cargo airline. Tiger has routes from the USA to Europe, South America, and Asia. Frederick W. Smith, founder of Federal Express Corporation, said the merger represented a step toward his goal of making Federal "the largest and best transportation company in the world."[1]

Federal Express was incorporated in Delaware in June 1971. Air freight service began in April 1973 with the delivery of fifteen packages the first night. Table 1 shows the dramatic growth of Federal Express in the total number of packages

Table 1   The Growth of Federal Express in Numbers of Packages and Full-Time Employees, 1977–1988

Year	Total Packages and Documents (millions)	Average Daily Package Volume	Full-Time Employees	Packages Processed per Full-Time Employee
1988	226.0	877,543	48,556	4,654
1987	175.0	704,392	41,407	4,263
1986	142.0	550,306	33,988	4,178
1985	104.0	406,049	27,066	3,842
1984	67.0	263,385	18,368	3,648
1983	43.0	166,428	12,507	3,438
1982	32.1	125,881	10,092	3,181
1981	22.1	87,191	8,080	2,735
1980	17.2	68,002	6,806	2,527
1979	11.7	45,833	4,883	2,396
1978	7.5	29,516	3,224	2,326
1977	5.6	20,840	2,444	2,291

Source: Federal Express annual reports

This case was written and developed by John B. Clark, professor of marketing, California State University–Sacramento. Used with permission.

[1]Resa W. King, "Mr. Smith Goes Global," *Business Week* (February 13, 1989), p. 66.

**Table 2   Daily Average Phone Calls
Received by Customer Service Centers,
Selected Years, 1977–1988**

1988	241,000
1983	78,228
1982	64,228
1981	41,320
1980	20,137
1979	11,080
1978	5,120
1977	na

and documents processed and number of full-time employees. It also highlights the increase in productivity (efficiency) as illustrated by the packages processed per full-time employee.

By 1979 the number of customer service calls involving information, tracing, and pickup requests had increased dramatically (see Table 2). One-third of these calls were handled in Memphis by COSMOS I at a new computerized center. Because centralized telephone service was the most efficient way to handle a large volume of calls, regional customer service centers were established in the following areas:

Somerset, New Jersey	1979
Sacramento, California	1980
Chicago, Illinois	1983
Dallas, Texas	1984
Phoenix, Arizona	1984
Boston, Massachusetts	1985
Fullerton, California	1986
Cincinnati, Ohio	1986
Fort Lauderdale, Florida	1986
Philadelphia, Pennsylvania	1987
Atlanta, Georgia	1987
Baltimore, Maryland	1987
Houston, Texas	1987
Kansas City, Kansas	1987

By 1988 the fourteen regional call centers employed 2,000 customer service representatives who handled a daily average of 241,000 phone calls. There are over 1,200 Federal Express offices throughout the United States, including 400 Business Service Centers and 275 drive-through kiosks, as well as 17,000 drop boxes (see Table 3). The Business Service Centers are store-front facilities typically located in high-traffic, high-density areas. They permit face-to-face contact with many small- or medium-sized customers, who may prefer to bring in their packages or documents, and allow shippers to drop packages at their convenience. This allows Federal to accept packages later than permitted by customer-requested pickups, and offers a price discount to the customer. Federal's fleet of 21,800 vans and trucks makes an average of 720,000 stops each day.

Table 3 **Business Service Centers and Overnight Delivery Counters, Selected Years 1979–1988**

Year	Business Service Centers	Overnight Self-Service Delivery Centers*
1988	400	17,000
1986	300	8,000
1985	200	6,500
1984	115	5,000
1983	80	4,500
1982	60	3,000
1981	15	1,500
1980	32	500
1979	15	None

Source: Federal Express annual reports

*Drop boxes

Another major development was the implementation of regional sorting centers. Because of the sharp increase in volume, it was more efficient for Federal to move a portion of its volume point to point rather than through the Memphis superhub. When feasible, packages and documents move by truck between points close enough to meet service commitments.

In 1985 the East Coast Regional Sorting Center opened in Newark, New Jersey. In 1986 the West Coast Regional Sorting Center opened in Oakland, California. By 1989 other sorting centers were opened in Boston, Orlando, Indianapolis, Los Angeles, Chicago, London, and Brussels. These regional centers will allow approximately 35 per cent of the total volume to bypass the Memphis superhub or be routed directly, resulting in significant cost savings.

In 1979 the sophisticated computer-based system, named COSMOS, was established. It was implemented in three stages:

1979 COSMOS I	Reduces pickup time and handles service calls
1980 COSMOS II	Scans and records each step in the handling process as packages move through the system—an automatic package tracking system
1981 COSMOS III	Enhances the functions of COSMOS I and II, provides for automatic parcel sorting in the superhub, makes possible business service centers, and allows direct communications between the computers and terminals in courier vans
1985 COSMOS IIB	Enables couriers to use portable miniscanners to feed information through their DADS terminals directly into the computer network as the package is picked up or delivered

In 1981 a complementary system named DADS (Digitally-Assisted Dispatched System) was implemented. This system uses small terminals in delivery vans where messages may be displayed on a screen. It allows Federal to dispatch a greater number of orders and helps the couriers to better structure their pickup schedules. In 1984 a hand-held DADS microprocessor was introduced, which enables a foot courier to obtain dispatch information while making stops in buildings and away from the van.

In 1985 COSMOS IIB incorporated a hand-held "Super Tracker" which transmits package data to the company's mainframe computers through DADS units in courier vans.

Federal's efforts to provide every detail of each transaction are capped by their customer computer system, called POWERSHIP. The COSMOS system greatly simplifies daily shipping, integrates the billing system, and facilitates inventory management. As of 1988, seven thousand shippers had these on-line computer terminals installed in their offices in order to capture billing data and allow them to keep track of their own packages. With this sophisticated computer tracking system and overnight delivery, Federal is actually managing the inventories of its customers overnight at the sorting centers.

Expanding on this ability, Federal in 1988 developed Parts Bank, a distribution management system. Customers can contract with Federal to warehouse materials in their regional sorting centers until the customer calls for them. This in effect creates a 50- to 500-mile-an-hour warehouse for the customer. At any time the customer can send inventories or determine their location so that they can arrive just in time for use, instead of constantly keeping a large inventory on hand. Federal Express is actually counting on the current trend of just-in-time inventory to help boost its revenues. IBM has contracted with Federal to warehouse parts for its work stations, enabling it to cut its delivery costs and close 120 parts depots.

In 1984 ZapMail was introduced to combat the increase in electronic mail. ZapMail involved Federal Express sending a courier to pick up a document and taking it to the nearest Federal Express office, where it was faxed via satellite to the Federal Express office nearest to the recipient's address. ZapMail was delivered within two hours and cost about $35. If the customer took the document directly to the Federal Express office, it could be faxed within an hour for $25.

Federal believed that ZapMail was the future of the mail industry and invested millions of dollars. After a promising start in 1984, ZapMail services dropped off in 1985 because of numerous problems. The technical problems involved overloaded switches, disappearing documents, and slow transmission. There was also a boom in the standard facsimile machine market as prices collapsed. The network that Federal was trying to put in place relied on the ability to launch high-powered satellites. When the space shuttle Challenger exploded in January 1986, the time frame to launch those satellites was advanced by two years. In 1987 Federal Express discontinued ZapMail with losses of $350 million. This allowed Federal to focus on expanding its overseas operations, the most rapidly growing area of the overnight express market.

Federal's major entry into the international market occurred with its 1984 acquisition of Gelco Express International. This worldwide courier service had offices in London, Amsterdam, Paris, Brussels, Hong Kong, and Singapore, and gave Federal an instant presence in eighty-four countries. To further strengthen its European network, Britain's Lex Wilkinson was purchased in 1986 and the Italian courier, Saimex, in 1988. Federal now has direct service through twenty-eight continental European offices, with sorting hubs in London and Brussels.

The Japanese and Asian markets were expanded when the U.S. Department of Transportation awarded Federal Express the exclusive authority to operate an air express route to Japan. The company initiated this service with its first flight to Tokyo on June 17, 1988, and operates four flights weekly to and from Japan.

However, the most ambitious and risky adventure was the 1989 $880 million merger with Tiger International, the world's biggest heavy cargo airline. This merger provided Federal with additional routes to Europe and South America, and especially Asia, where Tiger has a well-developed market. This deal created the world's largest air-cargo concern and vaulted Federal Express ahead of several rivals with whom it had been competing for promising international markets in the express delivery business.

The following breakdown categorizes Federal's product/service mix.

A. *Priority Overnight–Early Morning Service:* 10:30 A.M. delivery the next business day of boxes or cartons of virtually any size or shape weighing up to 150 pounds each.
B. *Standard Air One- to Two-Day Service:* A one- to two-day package and document delivery service. Applies normally to packages over five pounds and more inaccessible destinations.
C. *Standard Overnight (new in 1989):* Promises delivery of documents and packages by the following afternoon at lower prices than Priority Overnight. Applies to shipments five pounds or less in Fed Express packaging.
D. *International Service:* Provides high priority, customs-cleared service between the United States and 110 foreign countries. The service covers two-day delivery to most major European cities and other destinations.
E. *Parts Bank:* A distribution management system that allows customers to warehouse materials at the regional sorting centers until needed.

Federal also offers Saturday delivery for an extra charge and a "Hold Me at Federal Express" policy, where customers can pick up packages by 9:00 A.M. at Federal's appropriate business offices. Free "overnight" envelopes, boxes, and tubes of various sizes are available to its customers.

The product/service mix is backed by the best guarantees in the express industry, the sixty-second and thirty-minute guarantees:

Sixty-second guarantee: If we deliver your package even sixty seconds late, we'll refund your shipping costs.
Thirty-second guarantee: We'll give you information about your shipments within thirty minutes of your call or refund your shipping costs.

Federal Express's promotion reinforces its service level. It has built up a reputation for reliability of on-time delivery that is difficult to beat. Its "Absolutely, Positively Overnight" theme became entrenched in the mind of its customers, as well as the general public. The competition has also established excellent reliability, but customers perceive Federal as having the best on-time record. Its theme, "Why Fool Around with Anyone Else?" allowed Federal to highlight the strengths of its services and guarantees. Its current theme, "The Best Way to Ship It Over There," emphasizes customs clearance and overseas experience. The advertisements stress that Federal Express has long been the best way to ship packages "over there."

Table 4   Federal Express TV Advertising Slogans, 1974–1989

Year	Slogan/Theme
1989	"The Best Way to Ship It Over There"
1987	"It's Not Just a Package, It's Your Business"
1983	"Why Fool Around with Anybody Else?"
1977	"When It Absolutely, Positively Has to Be There Overnight"
1976	"Take Away Our Planes and We'd Be Just Like Everybody Else"
1974	"Federal Express—A Whole New Airline for Packages Only"

Source: Company records

Federal Express created this industry. Its founder, Fred Smith, found a need and satisfied it. It has priced its product according to the services rendered, taking into consideration its competitors. Currently, its service is available to over 98 per cent of the U.S. population and 110 countries.

QUESTIONS

1. Is Memphis, Tennessee, a good location for a super hub?
2. Federal Express established Mini-Hubs in Newark in 1985 and in Oakland in 1986. Discuss the rationale behind the moves.
3. Every product or service has attributes. Besides its products (packages and letters) what are the attributes of Federal Express?
4. What marketing management philosophy best describes Federal Express?
5. Should Federal Express challenge Purolator, which is predominantly a local delivery service?
6. Why can the overnight letters that were introduced June 1, 1981, compete with the U.S. Postal Service Express Mail?
7. What can one infer about the corporate culture at Federal Express from the ZapMail failure?
8. Why has Federal Express placed such a strong emphasis on the overseas market, and what are its objectives with its European network?

McDonald's

Ray A. Kroc, the founder of McDonald's Corporation, the largest food service organization in the world, opened his first restaurant in the McDonald's chain on April 15, 1955. By 1989 the company, its franchises, and its affiliates operated more than eleven thousand McDonald's restaurants, each serving a limited menu of high-quality, moderately priced food. In its thirty-five-year history, the company

This case was written and developed by John B. Clark, professor of marketing, California State University–Sacramento. Used with permission.

has pioneered food-service technology, marketing techniques, and operational systems that are now the standards of the industry.

The McDonald's motto of QSC & V translates into Quality Food Products; Efficient, Friendly Service; and Restaurants Renowned for the Cleanliness and Value they provide. QSC & V is McDonald's promise to people around the world.

The original McDonald burger sold for 15 cents, French fries for 10 cents, and a shake for 20 cents. One could have a complete meal for 45 cents in 1955, a bargain by any restaurant standards.

There was no price increase for twelve years—an unusual record for almost any product. In 1967 the increase in the price of hamburgers to 18 cents made newspaper headlines. Some executives wanted to raise the price to 20 cents so people would not be bothered with pennies. But Ray Kroc came to the aid of the consumer saying, "I came down hard on that one—if you look at it strictly from the customer's point of view—which is how I do, because this guy is our real boss—you see the importance of every penny."[1] Sales initially declined due to the price increase, but in a year's time both sales and revenue were higher than ever.

In December 1986, with a burger selling for 57 cents, French fries 56 cents, and a shake for 83 cents, customers could still get a bargain meal for $1.96—just under $2.00. However, if one chose a Big Mac at $1.39, large fries at 74 cents, and a shake at 83 cents, the meal would have cost $2.96. By December 1989, without discounting, the plain burger sold for 80 cents, French fries for 72 cents, and a shake for $1.09—for a total of $2.61. It is evident that McDonald's has experienced inflation. Its basic food package increased 33 per cent in price over the three-year period and other items have increased proportionately. McDonald's historical policy has been to steer customers' attention away from prices and spotlight product and service.

McDonald's goes to great lengths to ensure that its Big Macs, fries, and other food taste the same from one restaurant to the next. But the hamburger chain does not fix prices. Tom Doran, McDonald's regional vice-president for Northern California said, "We can't dictate prices, but we do make suggestions." Most customers traveling from one part of the country to another or from a central city location to the suburbs recognize that variations in price do occur. These differences arise mainly from differences in cost structures and the nature of competition in various markets.

Basically, the hamburger industry does not engage in price competition. Although numerous hamburger wars have existed in the past, these wars have primarily centered on one advertiser's claims over its competitors. Examples of some of the slogans are "Broiling Beats Frying," "Where's the Beef?" "It's a Good Time for the Great Taste of McDonald's." The closest thing to an old-fashioned price war, which was short lived, was introduced by a new upstart in the industry.

In 1983 Wienerschnitzel International of Newport Beach, California, began serving 39-cent burgers in its new Hamburger Stand chain. Soon after, Burger King cut its plain-Jane burger from 55 cents to 35 cents, and McDonald's followed, reducing its price from 50 cents to 35 cents. In January 1984 Burger King extended its discount program to most parts of the country. Wendy's International, the third-largest burger merchant, ignored the competition and instead promoted its upscale menu with its "Where's the Beef?" campaign.

By April 1984 the big guys brought back the regular price. But in California, the most competitive fast-food market in the country, many franchise owners extended

[1]Ray Kroc with Robert Anderson, *Grinding It Out* (Chicago: Regnery, 1977), p. 151.

the offer. One Burger King franchise owner said, "If I drop out [of the battle] and the McDonald's down the street continued, I'd lose out."[2]

The industry was also concerned with the projected growth in the number of new units by Hamburger Stand. Stan Spicer, vice-president and general manager of Hamburger Stand, knew that McDonald's and Burger King had been lowering prices in the western United States, where Hamburger Stands operated. In Southern California, where the price wars were most fierce, some Hamburger Stands dropped their prices to 25 cents. Spicer said they would continue to be the price leader.

In April 1989 the plain-Jane hamburgers were priced as follows: McDonald's 70 cents, Burger King 77 cents, and Hamburger Stand 49 cents.

Following is the anatomy of the Hamburger Stand chain's 1984 cheap burger.

Anatomy of a Cheap Burger*

Beef	$0.13
Bun	0.06
Onion	0.003
Napkin	0.002
Pickle	0.003
Wrapper	0.004
Mustard	0.0003
Ketchup	0.0008
Salt	0.00009
Total Food Cost	$0.20319
Total Food Cost	21 cents
Overhead, franchise fees, labor, miscellaneous	15
Profit	3
Total Cost	39 cents

"Fast Food Lovers Gobble Up Bargain Buyers," *Sacramento Bee* 19 March 1984, p. A12. Reprinted with permission from Wienerschnitzel International, Inc.

On December 1, 1986, McDonald's began a television advertising campaign emphasizing the 39-cent hamburger in the Southern California market.

By 1989 it was evident that the fast-food hamburger industry was no longer experiencing the tremendous growth of the 1970s and early 1980s. At McDonald's same-store sales in 1989, adjusted-for price increases lagged 1988. Sales at many McDonald's stores had leveled off. Other operators such as Kentucky Fried Chicken, Taco Bell, Long John Silver's, Dairy Queen, etc., were impacting McDonald's. In short, the entire fast-food industry, including the hamburger sector, had become saturated. Prices had risen sharply and other innovators such as convenience stores and gasoline stations were undercutting the prices of traditional fast-food chains.

In October 1989 McDonald's announced a major program of discounts aimed at local markets, where the chain was facing its biggest threats. Paul Schrage, McDonald's marketing chief, said, "McDonald's would offer a variety of plans, but the discounting would be disguised so customers didn't come in simply because

[2]"Fast Food Lovers Gobble Up Bargain Buyers," *Sacramento Bee* 19 March 1984.

McDonald's was offering cheap food. Rather than marking down menu prices, the chain would offer coupons giving patrons a discount on certain items."[3]

Investigation revealed contradictions. McDonald's did indeed engage in selective price competition for a lengthy time period. In the northern California market, many restaurants had discounted the plain hamburger from 80 cents to 49 cents, and the plain cheeseburger from 90 cents to 59 cents. The regional office in Sacramento stated that this campaign ran from September 1989 to June 1990. Other regions in the United States also engaged in selective price competition on specific menu items.

[3]Richard Gibson, "McDonald's, Faced with Competition on Prices, Plans Program of Discounts," *Wall Street Journal* 4 October, 1989, p. B6.

Exhibit 1   Price Comparison of Comparable Items for McDonald's, Burger King, Carl's Jr., and Jack-in-the-Box, December 1989

McDonald's

McD.L.T.	$1.89
Large Fries	1.13
Medium Coca-Cola Classic	.79
	$3.81

Burger King

Whopper with Cheese	$2.19
Large Fries	1.15
Medium Pepsi	.80
	$4.14

Carl's Jr.

Famous Star Burger with Cheese	$2.19
Large Fries	1.29
Medium Coca-Cola Classic	.89
	$4.37

Jack-in-the-Box

Jumbo Jack with Cheese	$1.99
Large Fries	1.05
Medium Coca-Cola Classic	.89
	$3.93

Exhibit 2   McDonald's Menu, December 1989

Breakfast Sandwiches

Bacon, Egg & Cheese Biscuit	$1.39
Sausage Biscuit with Egg	1.34
Sausage Biscuit	1.12
Sausage McMuffin with Egg	1.39
Egg McMuffin	1.39
Big Breakfast (Scrambled Egg, Sausage, Hash Browns & Biscuit)	2.04
Hot Cakes & Sausage	1.65
Hash Browns	.58
Danish (Apple, Cinnamon, Raspberry, Cheese)	.72

Exhibit 2   (Continued)

Lunch and/or Dinner Sandwiches

McChicken			1.97
McD.L.T.			1.89
Quarter Pounder with Cheese			1.79
Big Mac			1.79
Filet-O-Fish			1.37
Cheeseburger ($.59 discounted)			.90
Hamburger ($.49 discounted)			.80
Chicken McNuggets			
6 pieces			1.63
9 pieces			2.38
20 pieces			4.63
French Fries	.72	.91	1.13

Beverages

Coca-Cola Classic, Diet Coke, Sprite, Orange	.69	.79	.89
Lowfat Milk, 2%			.63
Shakes (Vanilla, Chocolate, Strawberry)			1.09
Florida Orange Juice		.68	.89
Coffee		.59	.69
Decaffeinated Coffee		.59	.69
Hot Chocolate			.59

Desserts

Hot Apple Pie	.73
Sundaes (Hot Fudge, Hot Caramel, Strawberry)	.89
Cone, Soft Serve	.65
McDonaldland Cookies	.59
Chocolatey Chip Cookies	.69

Salads

Chicken Salad, Oriental	2.93
Chef Salad	2.85
Garden Salad	1.99
Side Salad	1.33

Exhibit 3   Burger King Menu, December 1989

Breakfast Sandwiches

Croissant/Egg & Cheese		$1.43
w/Bacon, Sausage or Ham		1.67
Bagel/Egg & Cheese		1.43
w/Bacon, Sausage or Ham		1.67
Bagel w/Cream Cheese		.95
Scrambled Egg Platter w/Sausage or Bacon		2.23
French Toast Sticks		1.72
Hash Browns		.77
Danish		.95
Orange Juice	.69	.99

Exhibit 3   (Continued)

603
Cases

Flame Broiled Burgers

Whopper w/Cheese		1.99	2.19
Double Whopper w/Cheese		3.12	3.32
Hamburger		.89	1.09*
Cheeseburger		.99	1.19*

(*Deluxe)

BK Doubles—Double Cheeseburgers

Bacon Double	2.49
Deluxe w/mayonnaise, lettuce & tomato	2.69
Salsa Double	2.25
BBQ Bacon Double	2.59
Double Cheeseburger	1.99

Chicken/Fish

Chicken Sandwich	2.69
Whaler Fish Filet	1.59

Pick 'Em Ups

Chicken Tenders	6 & 9 pieces	1.99	2.99
Fish Tenders	6 & 9 pieces	1.99	2.99

Salads

Chef	Chunk Chicken		2.99	2.99
Garden	Side	Large	1.25	2.79

Side Orders

French Fries	.77	.97	1.15
Onion Rings			.99

Desserts

Apple or Cherry Pie	.99

Beverages

Pepsi, Diet Pepsi, 7-Up, Orange Slice, Dr. Pepper	.70	.80	.90
Shakes (Vanilla, Chocolate, Strawberry)	.89	.99	1.29
Coffee		.55	.65
Milk			.70

Exhibit 4   Jack-in-the-Box Menu, December 1989

Breakfast

Breakfast Jack	$1.45
Pancakes	1.59
Bacon Crescent or Sausage Crescent	1.65
Supreme Crescent	1.79
Scrambled Egg Pocket	1.85
Scrambled Egg Platter	1.99
Hash Browns	.55

Exhibit 4 (Continued)

Hamburgers			
Hamburger w/Cheese		.75	.85
Double Cheeseburger			1.65
Jumbo Jack w/Cheese		1.79	1.99

Supreme Burgers			
Bacon Cheeseburger			2.45
Swiss & Bacon Burger			2.55
Grilled Sourdough Burger			2.55
Ultimate Cheeseburger			2.65

Sandwiches			
Fish Supreme/Chicken Supreme		1.99	2.49
Fajita Pita or Chicken Fajita Pita			2.49
Ham & Turkey Melt			2.55
Grilled Chicken Filet			2.79

Salads			
Side Salad			1.99
Taco Salad w/Chips & Salsa			2.99
Mexican Chicken Salad w/Chips & Salsa			2.99
Chef Salad			2.99

Finger Foods			
Egg Rolls	3 or 5	2.19	3.19
Chicken Strips	4 or 6	2.19	3.19
Shrimp	10 or 15	2.19	3.19
Taquitos	5 or 7	2.19	3.19

Mexican Food			
Taco/Super Taco		.95	1.39
Fajita Pita or Chicken Fajita Pita			2.49
Taco Salad w/Chips & Salsa			2.99
Mexican Chicken Salad w/Chips & Salsa			2.99

Sides				
French Fries	.75	.95	1.05
Onion Rings			.99
Side Salad			1.19

Desserts			
Hot Apple Turnover			.69
Cheesecake			1.09
Double Fudge Cake			1.09

Beverages				
Coca-Cola Classic, Diet Coke, Sprite, Root Beer,				
Dr. Pepper		.69	.89	1.05
Coffee			.55	.65

QUESTIONS

1. What are McDonald's pricing objectives?

2. Does this case have examples of customary prices?

3. Is the demand for McDonald's products elastic or inelastic?

4. Is McDonald's the price leader?
5. What factors should McDonald's use in determining its prices?
6. What should McDonald's strategy be toward Hamburger Stand and other low-price operators such as convenience stores and gasoline stations?
7. Is McDonald's competitive in its pricing strategy?
8. Which strategy does McDonald's basically employ: price or nonprice competition? Justify your answer.
9. An October 1989 *Wall Street Journal* article stated that McDonald's "looks at discounting as it does dirty tables." Why does McDonald's abhor discounting?
10. How important are prices in the hamburger industry?
11. Why did Ray Kroc consistently resist price increases?
12. Comment on Hamburger Stand's anatomy of a cheap burger.

USA Today

USA Today is published by the Gannett Company, which was founded by Frank E. Gannett and Associates in 1906. It is the nation's largest newspaper company and one of the nation's largest diversified information companies. It has been listed on the New York Stock Exchange since 1967.

This leading publisher is primarily engaged in newspaper publishing, television and radio broadcasting, and outdoor advertising. Contributions to net profit by the business segment in 1988 were as follows: newspaper publishing, 80 per cent; broadcasting, 15 per cent; and outdoor advertising, 5 per cent.

The first-day issue of *USA Today* was September 15, 1982. No large general-interest daily had been launched successfully in this country since Long Island's *Newsday,* which debuted in 1940. Initial reaction by many journalists and business analysts was that the paper would not make it. Not all agreed. R. Joseph Fuchs of Kidder Peabody rated its chances as "better than ever" in September 1982. Two years later (September 1984), in a special research report, he was more optimistic and stated that if management overcame certain hurdles, *USA Today* could obtain breakeven by 1987.

The introduction of this national newspaper, a truly new product, was an ambitious task. Management's goal, from the beginning, was to reach a circulation of 2.5 million by 1987, making *USA Today* the number-one newspaper in daily circulation in the country. By comparison, the *Wall Street Journal's* 1987 circulation was 2.1 million.

On September 13, 1985, Allen H. Neuharth, the chairman and founder of *USA Today,* said, "We think the risk-reward ratio looks even better now than it looked at the beginning. If *USA Today* continues toward a successful, profitable venture, the investment in it will have been much, much less than it would take to acquire an existing publication like it, if there were one."[1]

This case was written and developed by John B. Clark, professor of marketing, California State University–Sacramento. Used with permission.

[1]Inquiry, "Topic: *USA Today,*" an interview with Allen H. Neuharth, *USA Today* 13 September 1985, p. 11A.

Table 1 *USA Today,* **Estimated Profits and Losses, 1982–1989**

Year	Profits and Losses (in millions of dollars)
1989	5 Profit
1988	(10)
1987	(15)
1986	(50)
1985	(85)
1984	(115)
1983	(130)
1982	(25)
Total	$(425)

Source: Industry estimates

A year later, on September 15, 1986, when the founder was asked how he felt about the newspaper's fourth birthday, he said, "When we were one year old, most media critics were still writing our obit, as they had done since before we were born. At two, readers had responded in record numbers, but advertisers were still cautious. At three, advertisers had climbed aboard, but critics continued caustic comments. Now, at four, it all seems to be coming together."[2]

Gannett planned to sustain substantial losses until 1987, their break-even year. From its birth through June 1987, it posted aftertax losses of $233 million.[3] Table 1 reveals total estimated losses from 1982 through 1988 at $430 million. Minimal estimated profits in 1989 were $5 million.

When asked in 1987 how long the losses could continue, Mr. Neuharth replied that Gannett had not lost anything on *USA Today,* but merely invested a very substantial sum of money in a new enterprise that he believed would ultimately pay off handsomely for their shareholders.

USA Today did not go national immediately. On the first day of issue (September 15, 1982) distribution was limited to Washington, D.C., and Baltimore. All 200,000 copies were sold. A rapid market-by-market and coast-to-coast phase-in followed. Circulation grew very rapidly, and by September 1986 average daily paid circulation was 1,450,000 (see Table 2).

A 1986 survey by Simmons Market Research Bureau, an independent and highly respected organization, stated that the *Wall Street Journal's* audited, paid circulation for the six months ending March 31, 1986, was 1.99 million, and *USA Today's* was 1.4 million. However, by midyear the Simmons audit reported that *USA Today's* readership had increased to 4.79 million versus the *Wall Street Journal's* 4.03 million. The front page of *USA Today* stated that they are "Number one in the USA . . . 4,792,000 readers every day." In readership, *USA Today* has become number one among all publications.

[2]Inquiry, "Topic: *USA Today,*" an interview with Allen H. Neuharth, *USA Today* 15 September 1986, p. 13A.

[3]Johnnie L. Roberts, "Gannett Shifts Managers' Jobs at *USA Today,*" *Wall Street Journal* 28 September 1988, p. 30.

Table 2 *USA Today,* **Average Daily Net Paid Circulation, September 1982–September 1989**

Date	Circulation
September 1989	1,750,000
March 1989	1,732,269
September 1988	1,656,467
March 1988	1,631,335
September 1987	1,586,242
March 1987	1,544,547
September 1986	1,459,049
March 1986	1,417,077
September 1985	1,352,897
March 1985	1,276,334
September 1984	1,247,324
December 1983	1,179,834
April 1983	1,109,587
January 1983	531,438
November 1982	362,879
September 1982	200,000

Source: *USA Today* Fact Sheets, Audit Bureau of Circulation

The Simmons audit also revealed that the demographics of *USA Today* has a higher profile than either *Time* or *Newsweek.* More than a third of its readers are college graduates, and about a third of them are in professions or managerial positions. Nearly one-third have household incomes of $50,000 a year or more.

By September 1989 the *Wall Street Journal's* paid circulation had declined to 1.84 million, with a readership of 4.4 million. *USA Today's* paid circulation increased to 1.75 million, and the front page stated, "Number one in the USA . . . 6.3 million readers every day."

USA Today's initial distribution strategy in entering new markets was to push its ubiquitous vending machine and newsstand sales. Single-copy sales were projected at 85 per cent and mail subscriptions and home and office delivery at 15 per cent. Locations were computerized to determine the best location mix between the two. Local newspapers did not like *USA Today* entering their local markets and viewed them as a threat. Some used legal methods in an attempt to keep *Today's* vending machines off the street. Others matched *USA Today* vending machine for vending machine. Pressure was also applied to newsstand operators to promote the local paper and give *USA Today* poor visibility.

Edward Estlow, president of the Scripps-Howard chain, said, "Everywhere they have appeared, it's forced local papers to reevaluate."[4] Home-delivery campaigns were intensified and earlier morning deliveries stressed. In some cases minor format changes occurred. The editorial and especially the sports sections were improved. More color was used. More charts and graphs were used to illustrate stories.

[4]"*USA Today* Unnerves Rivals Coast to Coast," *Business Week* (February 7, 1983).

Table 3 *USA Today* Average Daily Net Paid Circulation by Distribution Category, First Quarter of 1984

Category	Circulation	Percent of Total
Single-copy sales at vending machines and newsstands	887,673	66.6
Home and office delivery	333,152	25.0
Mail subscription	63,788	4.8
"Blue chip" sales (hotels, airlines, etc.)	48,361	3.6
Total	1,332,974	100.0

Source: *USA Today,* Fact Sheet

The initial distribution strategy has changed. Tables 3 and 4 reveal that single-copy sales at vending machines and newsstands have declined. Customer delivery (home and office) and mail subscriptions have stabilized at 29 per cent. Although both of the latter categories increase the distribution costs to the publisher, they add value to the product. Advertising agencies prefer a high percentage of customer delivery and mail subscriptions rather than single-copy buying because this gives advertisers a clearer profile of who their consistent readers are.

The Blue Chip, or bulk, which has increased from 3.6 per cent in 1984 to 19 per cent in 1988, has further complicated the distribution strategy because this category is difficult to audit, coupled with the difficulty of clearly defining the readers.

The September 1982 page capacity of *USA Today* was forty pages. This was expanded to forty-eight pages in July 1984, and fifty-six pages in November 1985. Full color available for news and advertising was originally eight pages. Full color has expanded to a sixteen-page maximum, and an eleven-page maximum for color advertising.

Losses in 1983, 1984, and 1985 were partially offset by a rapid increase in paid circulation. However, by 1986 and 1987, growth in circulation had slowed considerably, increasing by about 200,000 over 1985 (see Table 2).

Table 4 *USA Today* Average Daily Net Paid Circulation by Distribution Category, Third Quarter of 1988

Category	Circulation	Percent of Total*
Single-copy sales at vending machines and newsstands	828,234	50.0
Customer delivery and mail subscription	480,375	29.0
"Blue chip" (bulk sales)	314,729	19.0
Classline/Newspapers in Education Program	29,816	1.8
Group sales (businesses)	3,313	.2
Total	1,656,467[†]	100.0

*Source: Telephone conversation with Celeste James of *USA Today,* November 28, 1988
[†]Source: *USA Today,* Fact Sheet, November 8, 1988

Table 5 *USA Today* Average Number of
Paid Advertising Pages, 1983–1989

Year	Pages
1989	16.4
1988	15.6
1987	16.0
1986	13.7
1985	13.0
1984	9.0
1983	6.2

Source: *USA Today*, fact sheets

Advertising revenue, which was rather dismal in 1983 and 1984, has risen rapidly due to increases in the average number of paid advertising pages (see Table 5) and the rates per page.

Although research shows that *USA Today* has an affluent, educated audience, some space buyers remain skeptical. They question who the readers are and believe that many of them may be only occasional readers.

It is the author's opinion that if *USA Today* is to maintain long-term profitability, its projected paid circulation must reach management's goal of 2.35 million. Of this total paid circulation, the percentage of customer delivery (home and office) and mail subscriptions should constitute at least 50 per cent. Advertising must increase from its average of approximately sixteen pages in 1987, 1988, and 1989, to 18 pages. If these events occur, *USA Today* will truly be number one in the USA.

QUESTIONS

1. Was *USA Today's* extensive usage of vending machines an intelligent introductory distribution strategy?
2. Why has *USA Today's* average daily net paid circulation by distribution categories changed over its life cycle?
3. Do you see any particular problems in "Blue Chip," or bulk, sales to hotels, motels, airlines, etc.?
4. Discuss the interrelationship between the ability to obtain advertising revenue and circulation.
5. What do you believe plays the most significant role in producing revenue: advertising revenue or circulation revenue? Explain your answer.
6. Would *USA Today* use any middlemen in distributing its paper? Who might these middlemen be and what would they do?
7. Would the distribution category affect consumer demographics? How?

Mark-Tele, Inc.

Cable television began to spread rapidly across the United States during the late 1970s. It was promoted to subscribers predominantly as an entertainment media that would provide an expanded choice of high-quality television programming.

Some advertising and marketing experts perceived cable television differently. They saw it as opening a revolution in commercial communications. As telecommunication technology improved, cable television could become a direct threat to conventional shopping systems. Most experts, however, forecasted that significant changes in consumer shopping patterns were at least a decade or two away. Mr. Richard Johnson disagreed. He was the managing director of Mark-Tele, Inc., one of the most innovative and aggressive cable television companies.

During the fall of 1981, Mr. Johnson began to prepare a proposal for presentation to his board of directors. The proposal would suggest that Mark-Tele develop several new television channels. Most cable channels involved an entertainment, educational, or public information format. The proposed new channels would involve innovative commercial formats using telecommunications technology that would allow organizations to market and sell directly to consumers in their own homes. Mr. Johnson named this concept "VideoShop."

The New Venture

Several months earlier, Mr. Johnson had created a new ventures task force to generate and study novel programming formats that could be developed into new cable channels in the near term, and possibly into new networks in the long run. These channels would be used by Mark-Tele to generate additional revenues, to increase its subscription base, and to allocate operating costs more effectively.

The current capacity of the Mark-Tele cable system was 52 channels. But only 31 were in use. When Mark-Tele began operations, they had only 12 channels but had grown steadily. Costs had been relatively constant regardless of the number of channels that Mark-Tele operated. Thus, Mr. Johnson perceived Mark-Tele's cost structure as highly fixed, and he foresaw the development of new channels as a means of distributing these costs. Mr. Johnson expected that new channels would draw new subscribers, that subscription rates could be raised as more channels were added, and that subscription revenue could grow faster than corresponding operating costs.

The new ventures task force included the operations and sales managers from Mark-Tele, two product development specialists from Mark-Tele's parent company, and a consultant from the communications industry. An excerpt of their report is presented in the Appendix. The task force recommended that Mark-Tele should develop several new cable channels using television as the primary medium for shopping.

Mr. Johnson was thrilled with the new venture idea and the task force report. He wanted to develop and implement the new concept quickly. He selected a distinctive name for the venture, identifying it as VideoShop. He met informally

This is an abridged version of a case prepared by Michael P. Mokwa and Karl Gustafson of the Arizona State University as a basis for class discussion. It is not intended to illustrate either effective or ineffective handling of a managerial situation. Copyright © 1982 by the authors. Used with permission.

with some prospective salespeople, distributors, and retailers from different product and service fields and sensed strong but very cautious interest and support from prospective suppliers.

Mr. Johnson felt that a number of proposed channels were feasible, but he wanted to focus his efforts on those products and services (1) that appeared to be easiest and most profitable to implement in the near term and (2) that appeared to have the strongest interest among the prospective suppliers with whom he had met. He selected five prospects for development:

1. Catalog sales by regional and national retailers
2. Ticket reservations for concerts, plays, and sporting events, as well as reservations at local restaurants
3. Airline ticket reservations and vacation planning
4. A multiple listing service for real estate companies to display homes and commercial property that were for sale in the area or possibly from areas across the country
5. Grocery products

Mr. Johnson expected that he could find outstanding firms from each product or service field to participate in the VideoShop venture under terms that Mark-Tele would set forth.

Mark-Tele's Background

Mark-Tele was founded in 1977, as a wholly owned subsidiary of Intertronics, Inc., a large corporation based in New York City. Intertronics was founded in 1973 as a joint venture among three well-respected, multinational firms. One firm was primarily in the information processing industry. Another was a publishing and broadcasting conglomerate, and the third was a high-technology producer in electronics. The mission of Intertronics was to design, develop, and implement innovative, applied telecommunications systems for domestic consumer markets. Intertronics received financial support and full technological cooperation from its parent companies, but was operated as an autonomous venture. Intertronics managed each of its subsidiaries using the same orientation.

During 1978, Mark-Tele bid to install cable television systems in several large metropolitan areas in the United States. Late that year, Mark-Tele was granted the right to install a cable television system in a large, growing, Southwestern metropolitan area. The area had more than a sufficient number of households to support a cable television company profitably, according to industry standards. More important, the population was growing rapidly. Corporations were locating headquarters or building large manufacturing facilities in the area. Growth was projected to continue for at least the next 15 years, thus representing a very attractive cable market for Mark-Tele.

Intertronics would use Mark-Tele's location as the test site for a new type of cable television technology. The traditional type of cable used in cable television systems was a "one-way" cable, because a signal could be directed from the cable television company *to* the individual households attached to the service. Recently, Intertronics had developed a "two-way" cable that was capable of transmitting and receiving signals both from the cable television company and from individual households connected to the system. The cost of the new two-way cable was nearly four times the cost of one-way cable. Because Mark-Tele was a test

Exhibit 1   Income Statement Mark-Tele, Inc.
Fiscal Years Ending December 31, 1979 and 1980

	1979*	1980†
Revenues		
Subscription revenue	$4,560,000	$ 6,600,000
Pay service revenue	4,104,000	5,400,000
Total revenue	$8,664,000	$12,000,000
Expenses		
Operation expense (includes salaries)	$3,852,000	$ 5,248,000
Sales expense	1,913,400	2,610,300
Interest expense	136,200	136,200
Depreciation expense	74,800	74,800
Rent expense	46,000	46,000
Equipment maintenance expense	32,500	34,700
Total expense	$6,054,900	$ 8,150,000
Gross profit	$2,609,100	$ 3,850,000
Taxes @ 47%	$1,226,277	$ 1,848,000
Net profit	$1,382,823	$ 2,002,000

*Based upon subscriptions of 38,000 homes with a subscription rate of $10.00 per month per home, and average home "pay service" of $9.00 per month per home.
†Based upon total subscriptions of 50,000 homes with a subscription rate of $11.00 per month per home and average home "pay service" of $9.00 per month per home.

site, it and its subscribers received the cable system at a substantially reduced cost.

To implement the two-way cable, Mark-Tele installed an interactive device to the television set of each of its subscribers. The interactive devices were expensive to install, but Intertronics absorbed most of the installation cost. The subscription charge for basic cable services from Mark-Tele was $11.00 per month. The comparable rate for one-way cable would be $8.50 per month.

Mark-Tele's first year of operations concluded with 5,000 subscribers and a small negative net operating profit. In the following year, Mark-Tele subscriptions increased to 38,000, generating a net profit of almost $1.4 million. In 1980, Mark-Tele continued to aggressively attract more subscribers, reaching 50,000 total. Net profit increased to exceed $2 million. Financial statements for 1979 and 1980 are presented in Exhibit 1.

Research by Mark-Tele suggested that the potential number of homes for the cable network in their market area exceeded 400,000 over the next five years. In ten years, the market potential was forecasted to be nearly 750,000 homes. A demographic profile of current subscribers is presented in Exhibit 2.

Mark-Tele offered a wide variety of programming for virtually any type of viewer. Several of the channels were "pay television." For these, a household would pay an additional charge beyond the basic monthly rate. The revenue from pay services nearly matched basic subscription revenue for Mark-Tele in 1980. A schedule for the allocation of Mark-Tele's 52 channel capacity is presented in Exhibit 3. Both current and prospective channels are listed.

Exhibit 2   1980 Demographic Analysis of Mark-Tele
Subscribers*

613
Cases

Family Size		Age of Paying Subscriber	
1	17.6%	18–25	22.4%
2	22.8	26–35	19.2
3	10.8	36–45	19.6
4	19.3	46–55	17.7
5	15.1	56–65	7.1
6	5.8	66–75	8.3
7+	8.6	76+	5.7

Family Income		Residency	
$0–8K	1.3%	Homeowners	71.6%
$9–18K	15.7	Renters	28.4%
$19–28K	18.3		
$29–35K	17.5		
$36–45K	19.6		
$46–59K	12.7		
$60,000+	14.9		

Number of Hours Home Television Active per Week		Number of Years of Education of Paying Subscribers	
0–7	2.5%	0–8	1.4%
8–14	15.1	9–11	22.5
15–21	17.2	12	21.8
22–28	40.7	13–15	26.3
29–35	20.8	16+	28.0
36+	3.7		

*Based upon 50,000 subscribers.

Cable Television Technology

The Mark-Tele cable television system was controlled by a sophisticated config-
uration of computers with high-speed communications between each processor.
Three computers, each used for a different task, ensured that viewers would have
access to the cable network at all times. The main computer transmitted cable
signals to each individual home using the two-way cable lines. The second computer's function was to back up the main computer in the event that a system
failure might occur. The second computer would be a vital element of the
VideoShop system because it could be used as an update system for suppliers
to amend information regarding their products or services. This computer also
could be used to transmit the orders or reservations placed by "shopping" subscribers directly to prospective suppliers. The third computer functioned as another
backup, if system failures would occur simultaneously to the main computers.
A very sophisticated software application integrating the communication network
and operating system had been developed to assure 99 per cent uptime for the
cable system. A diagram sketching the Mark-Tele cable system is presented in
Exhibit 4.

Exhibit 3 Channel Allocation Schedule

Cable Channel Number	Designated Programming/Service	Cable Channel Number	Designated Programming/Service
1	Mark-Tele Channel Listing*	27	VideoShop: *Entertainment Tickets and Restaurants*
2	Program Guide*	28	VideoShop: *Grocery Products*
3	Local Transit Schedule*	29	VideoShop: Reserved
4	Classified Ads and Yard Sales*	30	VideoShop: Reserved
5	Weather Radar and Time*	31	USA Network*
6	Dow Jones Cable News*	32	WTBS, Atlanta, Channel 17*
7	Reserved for Future Use	33	WOR, New York, Channel 9*
8†	Home Box Office*	34	K///, Local ABC Affiliate
9†	Showtime*	35	Christian Broadcasting Network*
10†	The Movie Channel*	36	ESPN (Sports) Network*
11†	Golden Oldies Channel*	37	K///, Local Station, Channel 15*
12	Reserved for future use	38	K///, Local NBC Affiliate, Channel 8*
13	Reserved for future use	39	K///, Local CBS Affiliate, Channel 11*
14	Cable News Network*	40	Proposed channel for lease
15	Reserved for future use	41	Concert Connection*
16	UPI News Scan*	42	WGN, Chicago, Channel 9*
17	Government Access*	43	Public Access: Cultural Bulletin Board*
18	Music Television*	44†	Proposed games channel
19†	Stereo Rock Concert*	45	Public Access: Library Information*
20	Educational Access*	46	Proposed public access
21	Educational Access : New York University*	47	Public Broadcasting System
22	Proposed Educational Access	48	Reserved for future banking transactions
23	Proposed Interactive Channel for Lease	49	VideoShop: *Airline Tickets and Travel*
24	Proposed Interactive Channel for Lease	50	VideoShop: *Real Estate Showcase*
25	Proposed Interactive Channel for Lease	51	Reserved for future use
26	VideoShop: *Retail Sales Channel*	52	Reserved for future use

*Active channel.
†Optional pay service.

614

Exhibit 4 Mark-Tele Two-Way Cable System

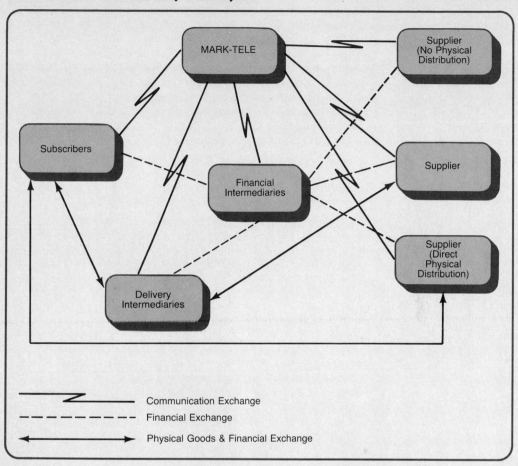

The cable system incorporated two different types of storage devices. The first type of storage disc (a magnetic disc) was used to store data, such as billing information about a particular subscriber. The second type of disc involved an innovative technology that could be used extensively by the VideoShop suppliers. Images of products and services could be stored on these discs so that subscribers to the cable system could access the images at any time. Only through the use of the new two-way cable developed by Intertronics would it be possible to incorporate the video disc units (VDUs) into a cable network. The two-way cable allowed signals to travel from the main computer to an individual television, and from the television back to the main computer.

Two-way communication was possible through the use of an interactive indexing device attached to each subscriber's television. This indexing device contained special electronics allowing the device to transmit data back to the main computer. On top of the indexing device, there were 12 keys simply called the keypad. An individual subscriber could use the keypad to call up "menus," sort through a menu, and send data back to the main computer. A menu is a computer term used to describe listings of general categories from which additional information can be drawn.

615

Using a prospective VideoShop example, a menu for a channel containing airline information could first indicate to a viewer the different airlines from which to choose. The viewer could then push the key on the keypad that corresponds to the airline that he or she was interested in using. The next menu could show all the different cities to which the chosen airline flies. The viewer then could push the key on the keypad that corresponds to the city to which he or she wishes to travel. The following screen could provide the flight numbers and times during which flights are available. From the information on that screen, the user could make a reservation that would be transmitted to the airline's computer through the Mark-Tele computer. Finally, the reservation would be logged and confirmed and ticket(s) mailed to the viewer.

VideoShop Channels

Mr. Johnson felt that the five shopping channels that he had selected from the list generated by the task force would work well. He prepared a brief description for each of the prospective shopping channels. He would use these to build his presentation for the forthcoming board meeting and to develop a prospectus to sell the VideoShop concept to suppliers.

The Catalog Sales Channel(s)

National and regional retailers could use the VideoShop system to sell and promote their entire merchandise lines, including their most current items and prices. Shoppers would have the opportunity to view merchandise on the television screen in their own home, avoiding the inconvenience of a shopping trip or the boredom of thumbing through a catalog. Information about products and prices could be presented in a format similar to catalog books, or innovative action formats could be developed to simulate a store environment or create some novel context. Retailers would be responsible for developing appropriate video disc units and keeping information current. Mark-Tele could provide a consulting service to help suppliers produce effective video discs. Mark-Tele could also reserve the right to reject any material that was felt to be inappropriate.

A shopper could use the interactive indexing device to direct and control an entire shopping experience. This could involve viewing information about product features and prices from one retailer, and then quickly switching to another retailer's presentation for comparative information. In addition, a shopper desiring more extensive information could access a brief demonstration or informative advertisement about a product. After selecting a product, the interactive device could transmit the order through Mark-Tele's computing system directly to the retailer's processing system. The retailer could present alternative payment programs and specific delivery schedules or instructions. The shopper could charge purchases using national or store credit cards and could pick up the merchandise directly or could have it delivered.

Mark-Tele could charge each retailer a service fee based upon a fixed percentage of shoppers' invoice values (before taxes). Individual retailers could be billed monthly and various payment programs could be formulated. The new ventures task force estimated that an average home would purchase a minimum of $300 worth of retail merchandise annually through VideoShop. They proposed a service charge rate of 2 per cent. Mark-Tele could also generate revenue selling video consulting services to the suppliers.

Ticket Sales and Restaurant Reservation Channel

VideoShop could provide detailed information concerning local entertainment alternatives to subscribers. Entertainment organizations could present exciting promotional spots using the video disc technology and sell tickets directly to VideoShop subscribers. Another dimension of this channel could be a restaurant promotion and reservation feature. Restaurant menus and promotional spots could be made accessible for diners. Once diners have chosen a particular restaurant using the memo and spots, they could make a reservation and even select a specific table (if the restaurant developed, as part of its VideoShop system, a seating arrangement routine similar to that of the entertainment organizations.)

All VideoShop ticket purchases and reservations could be transmitted directly from the shoppers' home through Mark-Tele computers to the restaurant or ticket outlet. Most restaurants and small entertainment organizations would have to purchase or lease a small "intelligence" computing terminal to receive reservations or ticket orders and to keep information updated. Intertronics could supply these.

The task force felt that this channel could generate at least $150,000 revenue per year given the current subscriber base. It recommended a $25 per month minimum charge to restaurants and a 50¢ service fee per ticket reservation. It was unsure of a fee schedule for entertainment organizations that would only promote events and would not be selling tickets directly through VideoShop. However, it thought that rates similar to commercial advertising rates would be appropriate.

Airline Ticket Sales and Travel Accommodations Channel

Discussions with the task force concluded that an airline ticket sales channel could be the easiest for Mark-Tele to implement and operate in the short run and also could be most lucrative financially. Projected revenue for the first year of operating this channel was $400,000, based upon a very conservative usage rate and an extremely competitive pricing policy. This channel could allow subscribers to make airline reservations, purchase their tickets, and select travel accommodations using the same fundamental interactive shopping procedures as other VideoShop channels.

Perhaps the most important characteristic of this channel could be the potential ease of implementation, once cooperation was secured from the airlines. The format and basic system used within the airlines industry to transmit, display, and process schedules, fares, and ticket information appeared to be compatible with the Mark-Tele system. VideoShop could be used to link shoppers directly with airline ticket reservation systems, bypassing reservationists and travel agents. Subscribers could select itineraries, then secure reservations, and pay using major credit cards. Tickets could be mailed or picked up at airport ticket counters or other service locations.

Mark-Tele could record each ticket purchase and charge the appropriate airline a fixed fee of $4.00 per ticket. This rate was approximately half the average rate charged by most travel agents. The task force believed that a minimum average of two tickets would be purchased by each subscribing household per year. Revenue estimates were not made for the travel accommodations feature of this channel.

Multiple Listing Service Channel

A few local realtors expressed strong interest in the VideoShop concept. Traditional promotional tools used to stimulate buyers' interest and assist them make decisions about what properties to see in person included classified newspaper ads, newspaper supplements, brochures, "for sale" signs, the multiple listing catalog, and photographs of properties posted on an agency's wall. Most realtors and buyers found these boring. More important, these simply did not present most properties effectively. A frequent complaint among realtors and buyers was the high cost in time and dollars wasted traveling to and viewing personally properties that were not represented well in a promotion or informational item. VideoShop could provide an exciting and effective method for presenting realty.

A specific issue regarding this channel was whether to limit access to realty agencies and others willing to pay an additional fee for it or to open it for public access. The task force recommended open access and suggested that a minimum of 30 realty agencies would need to participate. Each could be charged a monthly fee of $100 for producing and maintaining high-quality video discs with accurate and updated information. Mark-Tele could provide technical assistance and would monitor this channel carefully.

Grocery Products Channel

One of the most exciting prospects for VideoShop could be a grocery products channel. It was the most interesting but difficult channel for which to design a format.

A VideoShop grocery channel could provide consumers with convenience, comfort, low shopping risks, and potential savings. For suppliers, it could generate increased control over operations and costs, and higher profits. However, this VideoShop channel directly would attack an expensive, firmly established distribution network and basic, traditional patterns of shopping. Strong resistance from many consumers could be anticipated, and suppliers not involved in the venture could be expected to retaliate competitively. Also, there could be critical barriers to providing shoppers a total assortment of grocery products, including frozen and "fresh" items, and to implementing a cost-effective delivery service or pick-up procedure. Undoubtedly, these "bugs" could be worked out.

Conclusion—A Time for Reflection and . . . or Action

One more time, Mr. Johnson reviewed the task force report and his brief descriptions of prospective VideoShop Channels. He felt excitement, enthusiasm, and some frustration. He and the task force had worked hard and creatively to formulate the idea of VideoShop. They thought that most technological barriers could be overcome, and they projected a very favorable cost structure. Definitely, VideoShop was a concept that's time had arrived! But Mark-Tele is a small company with only a few people and tight resources. It is a high-investment and high-risk experimental venture receiving considerable financial support and subsidy from Intertronics. Would Intertronics feel that VideoShop is an extension of the Mark-Tele experiment, or a contamination of it?

1. What are the advantages and disadvantages to suppliers using VideoShop as an advertising medium?
2. What would you expect consumer response to be for each of the five proposed channels?
3. How might suppliers use VideoShop for publicity?
4. Should Mark-Tele implement VideoShop?

We recommend that Mark-Tele design and implement a telecommunication shopping (TCS) system immediately. This proposed new venture appears to be a natural extension of Mark-Tele's experimental mission and an excellent application of Mark-Tele's distinctive technological capabilities in the telecommunications field.

A TCS system would allow a Mark-Tele subscriber to become an active shopper and buyer in the privacy of the home using only the television. Facilitated by Mark-Tele's sophisticated communications and computing technologies, a TCS system subscriber would be able to view and buy a large variety of products and services that conventionally would have required the shopper to leave the home and travel to view and purchase. A TCS system would also serve the suppliers of many different products and services with an opportunity to break away from costly traditional market channels and to expand market coverage inexpensively and increase sales substantially.

For Mark-Tele, a TCS system would increase revenues, diversify its revenue base, and distribute its high fixed costs efficiently. A TCS system could be used as a promotional tool to build and maintain Mark-Tele's local subscription base. Current subscription rates could be raised with the addition of the TCS system, or an additional fee could be charged to subscribers who desire to participate in the TCS system. Suppliers and shopping subscribers would also be charged for services that Mark-Tele would provide in the development and operation of the TCS system. In the longer run, Mark-Tele could potentially develop TCS networks that could be sold to other cable systems. Clearly, early entry into the TCS field would be lucrative financially for Mark-Tele.

The Environment of TCS

Economic, technological, legal and regulatory, and social trends are emerging in support of a TCS system. Increased consumer spending is predicted to continue, but gains for retailers will be restricted by inflationary pressures. There will be a slower pace of store expansion during the 1980s. Many of the major metropolitan areas are overbuilt with retail space, and developers often are experiencing difficulty obtaining sites and financing. Retailers similarly are experiencing rising rents. Sales growth at many shopping centers has fallen due to slow growth of suburban communities and shrinking distances that consumers are willing to travel to shop.

Retailers are attempting to boost productivity, consolidate store space, and cut costs to improve returns. Inflation has increased operating costs more rapidly than sales during the last ten years. Many retailers have been attracted to discount pricing policies. The catalog showroom has become one of the fastest-growing segments of discount merchandising featuring national-brand products at discount prices.

Considering sociocultural trends, women are continuing to enter the work force, thus having less time to engage in shopping. Greater emphasis on recreational activities continues, and individuals are reluctant to sacrifice leisure time to shop in stores. Convenience is emerging as a high priority.

Consumers are emphasizing their self-identities. As such, consumers are demanding more individuality in goods and services, often desiring distinctive products that individual stores may not be able to afford to inventory and display. Definitely, there has been more intense consumer preferences for specialty items and services difficult to find in the Mark-Tele market area.

An increase in the number of single-parent and single-person households has led to increased in-home shopping. Nonstore innovations such as pay-by-phone, specialty mail-order catalogs, and toll-free phone ordering have become increasingly popular. Catalog shopping currently offers a full line of merchandise together with prices and features that permit a consumer to comparison shop at home without having to spend time inefficiently searching for products in crowded stores, waiting for sales help, or at times being annoyed by overzealous clerks. In addition, the increasing age of the population, proliferation of retirement communities, and declining mobility of individuals in their later years make catalog shopping very attractive.

There are significant technological advances that will influence the TCS system. In the past, alphanumerics and graphics but not still or moving "pictures" could be retrieved from a data bank and displayed on a television screen; however, Intertronics' innovative technologies have advanced moving picture capabilities. This new technology has permitted the consumer to control the timing, sequence, and content of information through the use of the keypad.

Development of video discs and video cassettes, which to date have been used by viewers to record television programs, have significant promise for advertising and catalog media. Potential exists for suppliers to mail lower-cost video catalogs on a complimentary basis or in lieu of printed direct-mail offerings.

Consumers are being exposed to and are accepting complex, technical items such as videotape recorders, home computers, and debit cards for use with automatic teller machines. Home computers and the development of "videotex," the generic terms for home information-retrieval systems, will provide functions compatible with those of the TCS system.

The political-legal context is confusing. The Federal Communications Commission has decided that cable franchising is mainly the province of local jurisdictions. All cable companies must interact with local governments to obtain and maintain authority to operate. While Mark-Tele has secured exclusive rights in their metropolitan area, changes in federal and local policy must be monitored.

The TCS venture raises questions concerning supplier and financial contractual arrangements. The antitrust implications of arrangements with some large institutions should be studied in more detail on a case-by-case basis. Moreover, movement into the retail sector by Mark-Tele through the TCS system will mean closer scrutiny by federal and local consumer protection agencies such as the Federal Trade Commission and Consumer Product Safety Commission. Finally, Mark-Tele will need to consider carefully protection of the privacy of personal, financial, and transactional data about subscribers of the TCS system. Controls must be established to prevent unauthorized access to information in the system data banks and to guard against unauthorized purchasing.

The General Competitive Context

Industry observers clearly are divided when projecting the evolution of electronic shopping and its acceptance by both consumers and the industry. However, all forms of nonstore retailing currently are growing rapidly, and continued growth is forecasted. Major developments in nonstore retailing will be reviewed.

Mail-Order Catalogs

General department store merchandisers, catalog showrooms, and specialty houses periodically mail catalogs to targeted groups of consumers. An average mail-order house distributes from 6 to 20 catalog issues yearly at a cost often approaching $2.00 each. Circulations range from about 100,000 to over 1 million for each mailing. The results have been outstanding. Over $26 billion was spent by consumers on mail-order items in 1978, an increase of $12 billion in three years. By comparison, in-store retailing sales grew at a rate less than half of the mail-order rate. Specialty-oriented catalogs are accounting for 75 per cent of total mail-order sales, and mail-order catalogs currently contribute 15 per cent of the total volume of Christmas season sales. Telephone- and mail-generated orders received by traditional store retailers such as Bloomingdale's, Penney, and Sears are increasing three to five times faster than are in-store sales. In-flight shopping catalogs used by major airlines are additional evidence of the increasing popularity of nonstore shopping. MasterCard, American Express, and Visa have increased their direct-mail offerings to their credit card holders and are expanding their assortment of merchandise.

The Catalog Showroom

The catalog showroom is one of the fastest-growing fields of retailing. Catalogs are used to promote and feature jewelry, housewares, appliances, sporting goods, and toys at discount prices. Customers visit the showroom to inspect merchandise and to make purchases. Sales for 1980 are estimated to be $7.8 billion, an increase of 11 per cent from 1979. Forecasts for 1981 suggest a 20 per cent gain in sales revenue. The number of showrooms across the country is nearly 2,000.

Noninteractive Shopping Using the Cable

Comp-U-Card of Stamford, Connecticut, is a seven-year-old telephone merchandising firm. For an annual fee of $18, it offers members a discount on a broad line of durable goods. Members shop around familiarizing themselves with products and prices. Then, they call Comp-U-Card toll-free for specific information about an item's availability and price. If a purchase decision is made, the consumer provides membership and credit card numbers to an operator, and the merchandise is prepared for delivery. An experimental project has been proposed in which Comp-U-Card would use cable systems and satellite transmission to present product and price information to its subscribers. A transmitted schedule would alert subscribers to the time when particular product information would be presented. Subscribers would continue to use the telephone when ordering.

Telephone purchasing systems using cable presentations are currently operating in Europe. In March 1979, the British Post Office, which runs Britain's telephone system, opened a "viewdata" service called Prestel. Viewers are presented listings of games, restaurants, and consumer product evaluations. Products and services can be purchased on credit by phone. France launched a similar service called "Antiope" in 1979.

A few U.S. companies are testing similar systems. Viewdata Corp., a subsidiary of the Knight-Ridder newspaper chain, proposed to install a permanent system in southern Florida by 1983. First Bank System of Minneapolis will be testing a "videotex" system in North Dakota similar to the Antiope System of France.

Interactive Cable Systems and Videotex

Since December 1977, Warner Communications and American Express have been involved with a $70 million joint venture testing the QUBE two-way system of Warner Amex Cable in Columbus, Ohio. Currently, the system serves 30,000 of the 105,000 homes in its service area. American Express and Warner Communications propose to build other QUBE systems in such metropolitan areas as Houston, Pittsburgh, and Cincinnati. Both Sears and Penney currently are testing the QUBE system.

In May 1981, American Telephone & Telegraph (AT&T) endorsed a videotex concept in which a home computer terminal must be purchased. AT&T has set out to develop its own system. AT&T would be a formidable opponent to anyone in the market, considering the firm's capabilities and financial strength. Thus, there are a number of legal actions being undertaken to prevent AT&T's direct entry into the videotex market, fearing it could become a monopoly power. However, strong deregulation sentiments may overcome the opposition and facilitate AT&T's entry into the market.

Over $100 million already has been invested by U.S. firms to design and test various TCS systems, and at least 83 experimental projects are being conducted around the world. As a result, Mark-Tele must be prepared to match formidable competition, and we feel confident that Mark-Tele can.

Target Market Considerations

There are two different markets that must be considered when developing this venture: (1) the suppliers and (2) the shoppers. We propose that the TCS system be "targeted" to the ultimate *user*—the subscribing shopper. A TCS system that is designed well should sell itself to suppliers. Suppliers, therefore, should be considered as a dimension of the "total product" that will be offered to target shoppers. This approach will allow Mark-Tele to retain maximum control and autonomy in the design and implementation of this venture.

The Target Market—Shoppers

A review of the size and characteristics of the current and potential Mark-Tele subscription base indicates substantial market potential and buying power. However, critical analysis of shopping and buying behavior is necessary to isolate the most lucrative prospective customer segments and to understand their prospective TCS behavior. Three buying factors appear to be very important: (1) risk perceptions, (2) convenience orientations, and (3) buyer satisfaction.

Buying is a complex experience filled with uncertainty and related risks of unfavorable consequences. Fundamentally, consumers confront the uncertainty of achieving their buying goals and risks such as embarrassment or wasting time, money, or effort in a disappointing buying or shopping experience. A consumer must have a satisfying experience each time that the TCS system is used. Otherwise, it is very likely that the consumer will not use TCS again and may discuss the bad experience with other shoppers and discourage their future use of the system.

Supplier Market Implications

After selecting general product and service categories and designing a general format for each TCS channel, Mark-Tele should direct attention to the supplier market. Mark-Tele should evaluate prospective suppliers regarding the relevance of their product or service assortment, their delivery and financial capabilities, the quality of their promotional strategies, and their desire to enter into this unconventional market. We feel that Mark-Tele's technical competence and captive subscription base will provide substantial leverage in all negotiations with suppliers. The actual marketing effort should involve personal selling programs custom designed for each prospective target supplier.

Prospective Products and Services

Preliminary research has uncovered a number of product and service lines that are appropriate for our target market and appear to be financially and technically feasible. As this innovative approach to shopping evolves and consumer acceptance and involvement grows, many other products and services could be incorporated. However, the most feasible products and services currently are

Standard catalog items
Grocery items
Gifts and specialty items
Appliances, home entertainment and personal computer equipment
Toys, electronic games and equipment, basic sporting goods
Banking and financial services
Classified ads
Multiple listing service of local properties
Ticket, restaurant, and accommodations reservations
Educational and recreational classes
Automobiles

We cannot stress too strongly that TCS will involve a high degree of risk perceived by consumers. This must be reduced by offering products and services with which consumers are familiar and comfortable and that involve a minimum number of basic shopping decisions for consumers.

The consumer must *learn* to use the TCS system. Mark-Tele must guide this learning experience and make sure that consumers have consistent, positive shopping experiences that become reinforcing. The following services/features should be incorporated into the TCS system to reduce shopping risks and facilitate consumer satisfaction:

Easy-to-use indexing devices
Top-quality visual and audio representation
Professional promotions
Up-to-date information on specials
Competitive pricing policies and convenient payment methods
TCS availability 24 hours per day, seven days per week
Maintenance service availability 24 hours per day, seven days per week
Accurate order taking and filling
Prompt delivery or pick-up services
Quick and equitable handling and resolution of customer complaints
Exceptional reliability

Eventually, the TCS product and service assortment could be broadened and channel features changed. However, the products and service lines outlined in this report appear to involve minimal consumer risks, high potential for competitive advantage and target consumer satisfaction, and substantial returns for Mark-Tele.

The Competitive Advantage

A competitive advantage over conventional suppliers can be achieved by Mark-Tele if the TCS system is designed to serve the needs and expectations of the identified target market by actively considering their prepurchase deliberations, by guiding their purchase activities, and by reinforcing their postpurchase satisfaction. This must be complemented with accurate and reliable order processing and prompt, efficient logistical support. Above all, Mark-Tele must communicate and promote its distinctive capabilities. We believe that the following distinctive features of the TCS system should be emphasized:

The extensive variety and depth of product and service assortments

The vast amount of relevant information that is easily accessible and allows consumers to make better choices

The excitement, involvement, convenience and satisfaction of shopping in the privacy of one's home using space-age technology and the simplicity of television

The insignificant, negligible, and indirect costs to consumers particularly when compared to the opportunities and benefits

The recommendation of our committee is that Mark-Tele design and implement the proposed new venture concept. We have identified the target customer and viable products and services to satisfy their needs and Mark-Tele's objectives. Development of the supplier market and control over suppliers also has been discussed. We recommend immediate action.

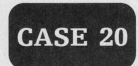

CASE 20

Bar Codes Unlimited

Background Information

Bar codes are a system of written symbols used to quickly and accurately communicate product identification through electronic media. Penetration of bar code scanning systems in the supermarket industry is virtually complete. Ninety per cent of all items carried by supermarkets, including nonfood products such as movie rentals and the like, now carry bar codes. Beyond the food industry, the use of bar code scanning is less pervasive, but the stage is set for rapid spread of the concept. Speed, accuracy, consistency, and economy are just a few of the reasons manufacturers are using bar coding to identify and track inventory, manufacturing-work-in-process, and distribution.

Great potential for growth appears to exist in the pharmaceutical industry. The market here includes, but goes far beyond, bar coding for retailing of pharmaceutical products through traditional channels and also includes several novel uses such as in-hospital dosage control. Bar coding has also spread to the U.S.

This case was prepared by Herbert E. Brown, Wright State University; Paula M. Saunders of Paula M. Saunders Associates; and Roy G. Lunjgren, Ferris State University, and is intended to be used as a basis for class discussion rather than to illustrate either effective or ineffective handling of the situation.

Postal Service, which is installing a massive automatic sortation system aimed at cutting costs and improving the speed and accuracy of mail delivery. Postmaster General Anthony M. Frank is on record as wanting all letters and noncarrier, route-sort flat mail bar coded by 1995. To encourage mailers, the postal service will offer as much as $.05 cents savings per flat piece to mailers. Hardware and home accessory stores are also increasingly involved. Even the lumber industry is getting into bar coding. A major wood products manufacturer is planning to affix color-coded, pressure-sensitive Universal Product Code (UPC) labels on the end pieces of lumber. The airline industry is also a growth area for bar coding. Here, bar coding is being used to sort and track luggage more efficiently and accurately.

History of the UPC

The chronology of events leading up to the present-day widespread use of the bar code technology and the Universal Product Code (UPC) dates back to about 1916. Rapid expansion of use began when the National Association of Food Chains initiated development of the UPC in 1969. Part of this included the establishment of the Uniform Code Council, an organization to act as a clearing house for manufacturers, retailers, and wholesalers participating in the system. The Uniform Code Council, Inc., headquartered in Dayton, Ohio (8163 Old Yankee Road, Suite J., 45458, 513-435-3870), is not a government agency. It was formed specifically to control the issuing of manufacturers' code numbers, to provide detailed UPC information, and to coordinate the efforts of all member participants. Major sponsoring organizations of the Uniform Code Council include the Food Marketing Institute, the Grocery Manufacturers of America, the National American Wholesale Grocers' Association, the National Food Brokers' Association, and the National Grocers' Association. The council's charge is to administer a bar code system that is scannable worldwide.

Need for Bar Code Numbers

The demand for bar code numbers is need driven. The need arises whenever a producer decides to sell a product through retail channels that use bar code scanners at their checkouts. To do so, a unique six-digit universal product code number that identifies the manufacturer must be obtained from the Uniform Code Council. (This one-time fee is based on retail sales volume and is a minimum of $300.) To this is added a five-digit number that identifies the specific item. Finally a twelfth check-digit is determined. At this point, the applicant, with the aid of the UPC supplied manuals, is ready to set about translating the code number into a machine-readable bar code symbol that will appear on its product's package.

The Universal Product Code

The key to the universal product code is its machine-readable bar code symbol for the 12-digit, all numeric code described above. This number is represented by a series of parallel light spaces and dark bars that can be read by an optical scanner at the checkstand. The code number permits a computer to recognize the product item. There is no price or other information in the number. Instead, when read, the code number is sent to a small in-store computer that contains constantly updated information, including price, on all items carried in the store. The computer transmits back to the check-stand the item's price and description (which are instantly displayed on the customer's receipt tape), as well as relevant information on taxability, food stamp acceptance, etc. While doing this, the computer also captures and stores item movement information. This is later aggregated and summarized into a wide variety of control reports. (Note: when hamburger, deli items, and the like are weighed and marked in the store with machine readable bar codes, price and other information are contained in the number.)

What the Digits Mean

The number that appears on a product package is a 12-digit all-numeric code. The first six of these digits are assigned by the Uniform Code Council. The next five are the responsibility of the manufacturer. The last digit is a check digit. More specifically, the total code consists of the following:

1. A Number System Character (1-digit)
   The first position in the code is referred to as the number system character. This serves to "key" the other numbers as to meaning and category. Current interpretation of digits in this position are

   "0"–Assigned to all items, except as follows:
   "1"–Reserved
   "2"–Assigned to random-weight items such as meat and produce (used for in-store marking)
   "3"–Assigned to companies that have been delegated their NDC (National Drug Code) numbers as their UPC numbers
   "4"–Assigned for retailer in-store marking without format restrictions
   "5"–Assigned to coupons
   "6"–100,000 Manufacturer ID Numbers (12/89 or 1/90)
   "7"–100,000 Manufacturer ID Numbers (12/89 or 1/90)
   "8"–Reserved
   "9"–Reserved
   Thus, a 0 in the first position means that the product seller is a manufacturer; a 5 indicates to the computer that it is reading a coupon, etc.

2. A Manufacturer Identification number (5-digit)
   The manufacturer identification number, unique to each applicant, is found in the second through the sixth digits. This 5-digit number is assigned by the Uniform Code Council, Inc. The resulting 6-digit number (UPC plus manufacturer's ID number) is unique worldwide.

3. An Item Code number (5-digit)
   The item code number is a number assigned and controlled by the member company and is unique *only within the member company's product line.* This number is found in the seventh through the eleventh digits.

4. A Check Character (1-digit)
   The twelfth position on the code is a check character that the computer reads and compares with a number computed from the other numbers that have been read. The computed number must make sense when compared with the check number, or the composition of the previously read eleven numbers is wrong. This is done to ensure that the entire UPC symbol is always properly scanned.

The above description is of the "A" version of the UPC symbol. There is another version called the "E" symbol. This is used on products when there is limited space for the symbol, such as on cigarettes, etc. The E version prints fewer digits, both in the bar coded symbol and in human-readable form. It is constructed following the same rules as the A version and differs from it only in that zeros in the A version code number are suppressed. This permits the symbol to be physically shorter without loss of information.

Exhibit 1 shows several actual bar code symbols, including both version A and

Exhibit 1

100 PERCENT

0 12345 67890 5
NOMINAL SIZE
VERSION A

0 12044 35650
OLD SPICE AFTER SHAVE
VERSION A

0 414130
LIPTON 1.8 OUNCE
ONION MUSHROOM SOUP
VERSION E

0 373340 2
CREST TOOTHPASTE
MINT FLAVOR
8.2 OUNCE SIZE
VERSION E

0 43168 90951 8
K-MART STANDARD
4-LIGHT BULB
PACKAGE
VERSION A

0 440410 7
16 OZ HONEY MAID
HONEY GRAHAMS
VERSION E

209161 001998
IN STORE MARKED
DELUXE CLUB
BOLOGNA
(TRUNCATED)

0 12546 71250
SPEARMENT CERTS WITH RETSYN
VERSION A
(TRUNCATED DUE TO
PACKAGE SIZE)

0 473200
ALMOND JOY
CANDY BAR
VERSION E

version E. Note that the Crest toothpaste bar code symbol and number (scanners read the symbol not the number) is 0 373340 2. The zeros in this number have been suppressed. Thus, the number read by the scanner is actually 0 37000 00334 2. The manufacturer's (P&G's) number is 0 37000. The item number added by P&G is 00334. The 2 is a check digit.

UPC codes are attached to products in two ways. They are either

1. printed as an integral part of the product package label, or
2. printed on pressure-sensitive adhesive labels and appended to the product package.

In either case, the symbol must be printed to strict specifications.

Size of the Symbol

Determining the size of the UPC symbol for a package is critical. The "nominal" size is 1.020 inches high and 1.469 inches wide. This can be varied from 80 per cent of nominal to 200 per cent of nominal. No reduction, or expansion, beyond that shown in the UPC Symbol Specification Manual (a publication of the Uniform Code Council) is permitted. Violation of this rule can lead to poor scanning quality.

Location of the Symbol

Placement of the code on the product package is critical because the more variation there is in symbol location, the more difficulty the checkout clerk will have in finding the symbol in order to pass it across the scanner. The Uniform Code Council supplies a "UPC Symbol Location Guidelines" manual that provides detailed, uniform rules for doing this.

Other Uses of the UPC Number

The UPC number can also serve as a key reference number on invoices, cases, bills of lading, etc. Thus, beyond the technicalities, a manufacturer's UPC number must also be carefully and systematically fitted into larger management systems.

Film Masters

The film master is the bar code translated into artwork. Because they are used to make printing plates, film masters are the key to a successful application of UPC coding. Technically, a film master is a negative or positive image of a UPC symbol that allows reproduction of the symbol. The quality of the film master determines whether, and to what extent, the printed symbol will be scannable. Thus, if the translation from number to film master or artwork form is not done according to very strict rules, much can, and usually will, go wrong. The Uniform Code Council has nothing to do with the creation of film masters.

Film masters are totally the responsibility of the manufacturer. However, the council stands ready to provide additional informational assistance to ensure that the number holder gets his or her bar code properly produced. This assistance includes offering to new members lists of suppliers of film masters, lists of manufacturers of UPC label printing equipment, and lists of bar code consultants.

Film masters are usually required whether the bar code will be printed directly onto a package label or onto pressure-sensitive labels affixed to the package later. It is usually more cost-effective to print these directly onto the product's label, especially when it is known in advance that the product will be produced in quantity and sold through retail systems that use bar code scanning. The need for adhesive labels usually arises when a seller, who has been selling through systems without UPC scanners and has therefore packaged his product without bar codes, has an opportunity to sell an already-produced product through a new channel that requires checkout scanning.

The major types of printing are offset, flexography, gravure, and silkscreen. Film masters have to be made in different specifications for each of these different types of label printing. When using silkscreen, the printing process reproduces exactly what the film master dictates. However, if the printing is to be done using flexography, it will be done on a rubber plate. In this case, the pressure of the press will enlarge the bar code bars. To compensate for this, the plate bars must be smaller than that which the bar code specifications indicate. To make this happen, the film master must be correspondingly reduced so that plates made from them print correctly sized bar codes on packages or adhesive labels.

Printed Labels and Adhesive Labels

Bar codes are sometimes printed on adhesive-label paper by a computer. This is particularly likely when the number of labels to be printed is small, perhaps less than five thousand. But when the number is large, computer label printing is not cost effective, or not as cost effective as creating a plate and printing a large number of them simultaneously.

Competition

Printers sometimes create film masters, but more often than not the printer who does the printing does not want to get involved in film master creation. Left with the responsibility of creating the film master, the manufacturer often finds it cost effective and expedient to turn to external suppliers for such services.

By 1989 nearly one hundred companies were known to be offering film master services. One of these companies is Bar Codes Unlimited, started by Jay Dring in the spring of 1989. Prior to launching the company, he had over twenty-seven years of retail experience, including ownership of his own retail store and eighteen years in sales with NCR corporation. Jay's background also included the fact that in 1974, while with NCR, he helped introduce the UPC symbol scanning system to the retail industry. In fact, he was a major player in the world's very first Bar Code Scanner installation in Marsh Supermarkets in Troy, Ohio, in 1974. Since then, he has been involved with thousands of other installations.

Services Offered by Bar Codes Unlimited

Bar Codes Unlimited was set up to offer film master, adhesive-label, and consulting services to users and potential users of the UPC. However, neither film masters nor adhesive labels were produced by Bar Codes Unlimited; these were produced by suppliers. Bar Codes Unlimited served as marketer for its suppliers, and it served both its customers and its suppliers as a kind of consultant/broker and quality-control agency, making sure that the supplier produced correctly specified film masters and/or adhesives labels to exacting specifications for every customer. This, of course, demanded a close working relationship with suppliers, which was clearly already in place.

Markets for Bar Code Services

Food and Pharmaceutical

Dring's background and thorough familiarity with the checkout and scanning industry gave him instant credibility with several national chains in both the food and pharmaceutical industries. He chose to concentrate on these initially, selling them in person. In a very short time, his personal selling efforts generated enough sales volume in film masters, adhesive labels, and consulting to get his fledgling business into the black. And, although film masters were a part of nearly every sale, adhesive labels were the most profitable part of his business.

Besides coding products, the pharmaceutical industry was also working on individual-dosage bar coding programs for hospitals. These systems permit patient information to be entered onto and read from scannable wrist bands. Information on the medicine is then checked by electronic scanning of the patient's dose container. The computer then checks to see if the patient is allergic to the container's medicine, if the right dosage is being given, if it's the right time for the medicine to be taken, etc. Finally, it charges the medicine to the patient's account.

Third-Party Sales

Dring also had some success selling automotive accessory, food, and drug trade associations on "third-party" marketing of film masters and adhesive labels to their membership. Third-party marketing is a big business that involves selling the membership of a trade or other association under the auspices of the association. The buyer does business with the trade association, but the product or service is supplied by a third party. There are thousands of trade associations across the country. It appears, therefore, that these associations represented a very large and attractive market.

New Markets with Direct Marketing Potential

As he continued to develop the food chains, trade associations, and pharmaceutical markets with in-person selling, Dring, like most good entrepreneurs, began to cast about for other markets and marketing approaches. This led him to investigate turning to direct mail as a method to get leads from the above markets and possibly to make direct sales to others. This idea was inspired by a continuing flow of new applicants for UPC numbers.

Uniform Code Council New Applicant List

Each month approximately eight hundred applications for new UPC numbers are received by the Uniform Code Council in Dayton. The names of the eight hundred applications accumulated during preceding months can be purchased for $.10 per name. When a bar code symbol will be printed on a product's package, and usually when it will be printed on adhesive labels (labels can be done on demand, without film masters by many printing devices), a film master must be made for each of the products that an applicant plans to sell through a channel using bar code scanning.

There is, necessarily, time lag between the time the applicant gets a number and the time the Uniform Code Council can make these names available. The Uniform Code Council has a cut-off date of two weeks before the names are made available. This delay works to allow a new UCC member to get his or her number and all UCC manuals before being solicited by film master suppliers. Thus, if a film master supplier buys the names every month, he or she would receive names of members who had joined the UCC between two and six weeks earlier. By the time Bar Codes Unlimited receives the names, many of the applicants have already transformed their UPC numbers into film masters and onto their packages. Nonetheless, for one reason or another, even after as much as six weeks, a sizable percentage of this list is still in the market for film masters, adhesive labels, or consulting.

The Uniform Code Council list is not well defined, and for its purposes need not be. It is Dring's general belief that it contains a high percentage of "mom and pops" selling anything from cookies to ginseng roots. Small, but more sophisticated entrepreneurs and large companies selling a new product through bar code scanning channels are also thought to be prominent on the list. In sum, at the beginning of Dring's investigation, no one at Bar Codes Unlimited knew for sure who is on a typical new list of applicants.

Note: The Uniform Code Council also markets entire category lists (pharmaceutical, industrial, apparel, and several subsets of food and grocery and food manufacturers). Some of these lists number into the thousands. The purchase of a complete category list would enable Dring to approach all companies (or select companies) with a category that are known to have a Universal Product Code number.

Printers

On occasion, commercial printers and platemakers are competitors, but more often than not, both are also significant markets. New UPC recipients often turn first to their printers for help in translating their new UPC numbers into the proper symbols. Printers, in turn, not generally being specialists in the film master business but requiring a film master before they can proceed, often turn to someone else, such as Bar Codes Unlimited, for the service. Dring realized that these printers could be a major market for his services and that they would require unique promotions.

U.S. Postal Service

Another market where bar codes appear to have growth potential is the postal industry. In 1989 the U.S. Postal Service was facing cost increases that threatened to drive up rates. At the same time, private delivery systems were being developed and were beginning to compete with the post office. Automation appeared to be the key to combating both of these problems, and, at the core of every automation solution concept was some form of bar coding. For instance, bar codes that could be read for the purpose of destination sorting, charting of postage to mailers, and the like were being tested for use in conjunction with large-volume mailers. Given the large number of large-volume business mailers in the United States—and the world for that matter—this looked to Dring like a fabulous future market for suppliers of bar code services.

Packaged Goods

Dring was also interested in an effort on the part of some major packaged-goods sellers to use bar codes to assess and increase the effectiveness of their promotional efforts. For example, a dog food seller promoted his dog food with specialized bar codes on the package. Contest entrants were asked to place these on an entry form sheet. When these were turned in for prizes, the seller could learn much about the who, what, when, and where of his dog food buyers. Initially, Dring was unclear as to exactly how this process worked, or even all of its purposes, but given the enormous amount of promotion going on in the packaged-goods industry, it sounded very promising to him.

Other Markets

It soon became apparent to Dring that bar coding was rapidly becoming used by many other industries and that although they might not be his most promising initial markets, they were certainly worth watching and contacting as soon as his resources permitted. Among those he noted were the hardware, home accessory, lumber, and airline industries.

Competitor Activity

All of these markets were being pursued by a variety of direct-mail competitors. At least thirteen of the firms pursuing the UPC applicants were known to be doing current mailings. This was known because a friend of Dring's obtained a number for his product line and received thirteen different mailings offering him film master and related services. It was clear from the timing of the receipt of these mailings that all were buying the Uniform Code Council list and mailing it, just as Dring planned to do. Examination of the efforts of these mailers revealed a variety of approaches. Some asked for orders; other invited inquiries.

One of the simplest of these packages was a postcard. It had a bar code symbol on the top center of the front. Below this it had the firm's 800 number, which was printed in large, bold print. On the back it had a sample bar code adhesive label. This led the eyes of the reader into a very simple message: it noted that the firm had been informed that the addressee had been assigned a manufacturer's number and that the firm was a qualified supplier of Bar Code Film Masters for UPC symbology. It went on to stipulate a vague "starting" per unit price and invited the addressee to call the 800 number for a quote. (Most prospects would not know it, but this competitor is a retired vice-president of the Universal Code Council.) The other mailings range along a continuum of complexity all the way to one that came in an 8½- by 11-inch envelope containing an expensive brochure, a sales letter, several sample film masters, an order form, and even a small pamphlet analyzing when the use of bar codes was the right thing for a business to do.

All of the mailers offered quick turnaround on receipt of an order. Their prices ranged, or appeared to range, from $10 to $35 per film master. They "appeared" to range because exactly what could be received for whatever price was mentioned could not be known until the recipient accepted the mailer's invitation to call and discuss the firm's services and prices.

Changes in the Competitive Environment

In 1986 the typical firm offering film master services was run by a highly technical person who knew the bar code system and business thoroughly. At that time, bar code services were priced much higher, with film masters, for example, being sold for as much as a hundred dollars or more. Few mistakes were made by these suppliers because they knew what they were doing. Now, however, the field has attracted a large number of firms that some have termed "fly-by-nighters," who have only a very superficial knowledge of the technical details of the business, and in some actual cases, no real idea of what they are doing. This has driven both the prices and the quality of bar code services down and made the industry very competitive. This is particularly true when buyers can be convinced that one film master company is the same as any other, making price the only issue. This is untrue, but buyers often believe it.

Profit Potential

Most of the firms on the new applicant list are believed to be small, otherwise they would already have a bar code number and a well-established bar coding system. Many of them are also believed to have only a few items, and most probably have only one or two items, to be bar coded. Thus, the typical prospect on the list would need only one or two film masters. This distilled down to a very simple fact: there isn't much profit to be had selling film masters one at a time to this list, even at Bar Codes Unlimited's current $19.95 price for one film master.

Bar Codes Unlimited's average film master production costs are in the $3 to $6 range, with the average direct variable production and warehousing cost per unit being about $5. The gross profit or marketing margin is therefore assumed to be approximately $15 dollars per unit. Economies of scale are present but very marginal in the production of film masters.

Low profit on film masters is offset by potential profits from adhesive labels and consulting. The situation most of the new bar code number applicants find themselves in—i.e., with existing inventories without bar codes on printed labels, etc.—requires initial use of adhesive labels rather than printing directly onto the product package. That will come later. However, adhesive-label orders could range upward to some very high and profitable numbers. For example, one book printer had 500,000 books with incorrect bar codes and had to "retrofit" them with adhesive labels placed over the original incorrect ones. Adhesive label orders from the new applicant list are estimated to fall, for the most part, in the five- to fifty-thousand-label range.

Adhesive-label costs to Bar Codes Unlimited are in the following ranges:

1–5,000	$17–22.00/thousand, Average $18.50/thousand
5–10,000	11–17.00/thousand, Average 14.00/thousand
10–25,000	3–6.00/thousand, Average 4.50/thousand
25–50,000	1.50–3.00/thousand, Average 2.25/thousand

Prices correspond to costs and normally reflect a 100 per cent markup on costs. For example, an order for 12,000 might be priced at $9 per thousand, which includes a markup that is 100 per cent of costs, or 50 per cent of selling price.

Current Direct-Marketing Program Status

Dring's initial direct-mail effort was the letter shown in Exhibit 2. The initial response to this letter was virtually nil. However, after several weeks had elapsed,

Exhibit 2 Dring's Initial Sales Letter to Uniform Code Council's New Applicants

BAR CODES UNLIMITED, INC
7651 East Von Dette Circle
Dayton, Ohio 45459
513-434-CODE

Dear U.P.C. Participant:

Your product is on the way to commercial success with the addition of the UPC (Universal Product Code). Our firm is available to assist you in the implementation of your UPC program. Bar Codes Unlimited concentrates on product quality codes for a reasonable price and prompt service. Inferior codes can cause your product to be rejected by your customer.

☆ Professional Services ☆

Film Masters	Symbol Verification
UPC Consulting	Prompt Service
Implementation Planning	Reasonable Price
Pressure-Sensitive Labels	Customer Satisfaction

In 1974, I introduced the first UPC symbol scanning system to the retail industry, as well as federal and state agencies. My last twenty-seven years of retail experience have afforded the opportunity to demonstrate and install hundreds of scanning systems.

Bar Codes Unlimited invites you to become a customer and grant us the opportunity to fulfill at your UPC implementation needs.

John J. Dring
President

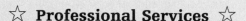

*$19.95—Quantity discounts available upon request.

some calls did come in from recipients, and one of these turned into a significant sale. Dring thought the results of his mailings should be much better and is thinking of consulting a direct-marketing professional. Though he is not sure what they could know that could really help, he feels that there must be some way to use direct marketing to profitably access the Uniform Code Council list market.

Dring also has a near-term plan to generate leads among pharmaceutical companies. This could be a very profitable enterprise because pharmaceutical companies (who are already well-established users of bar code scanning) sometimes buy hundreds of film masters each month. Unfortunately, it is not easy to determine who in pharmaceutical companies buys film masters. Thus, at this point,

Dring is confused as to how to go about generating leads in this industry. He feels, however that the basic method has to be direct response of some sort.

The pharmaceutical company market, like most other markets, has many firms that already have a UPC number. Thus, high potential prospects in the pharmaceutical market and in the other markets may or may not appear on the Uniform Code Council monthly lists. Those that don't may represent even higher potential customers than those who do, but for different reasons. Dring feels that his program for developing these markets may, therefore, have to be very specialized in approach.

QUESTIONS

The immediate marketing problem for Jay Dring is whether direct marketing techniques are feasible for his business and, if so, how they should be applied. Specific, detailed answers to the following questions should address Dring's issues.

1. Are the products and services offered by Bar Codes Unlimited amenable to the use of direct-marketing techniques? Suggest the most likely role or roles direct marketing might play in a successful Bar Codes Unlimited marketing program.
2. Offer an overall framework for guiding development of a direct-marketing program for Bar Codes Unlimited.
3. What appears to be the best basic direct-marketing strategy for Bar Codes Unlimited?
4. What appears to be the best direct-mail format(s) for Bar Codes Unlimited?
5. a. Delineate an offer or set of direct-mail offers Dring could make to the Uniform Code Council's list of new applicants.
   b. Develop a list of direct-mail positioning options for the Uniform Code Council's list of new applicants.
6. a. Delineate an offer or set of direct-mail offers Dring could make, through the mail, to the pharmaceutical companies.
   b. Develop a list of direct-mail positioning options for the pharmaceutical market.
7. a. Delineate an offer or set of direct-mail offers Dring could make, through the mail, to trade associations to interest them in "third-party" marketing with his organization.
   b. Develop a list of direct-mail positioning options for the trade association third-party marketing effort.
8. Discuss the differences, if any, between the direct-marketing program structure that will be needed to generate leads for companies that are on the Uniform Code Council new member lists and those that are not.
9. Assume that Dring's mailing to the Uniform Code Council's list generates a response rate of one per cent (about eight orders), with an average of two film masters per order, and that during an average month one of the nine respondents typically purchases labels. Assume further that there is an equal chance that each of the monthly label purchasers will buy either 2,500, 7,500, 17,500, or 37,500 adhesive labels.

Hyde-Phillip Chemical Company

Michael Claxton, a recent marketing graduate of a well-known college, was assigned the task of evaluating Hyde-Phillip Chemical Company's methods of selling the firm's products. Hyde-Phillip currently utilizes a mix of company salespersons, merchant wholesalers, and agent wholesalers to present its products to existing and potential users. While this combination of selling forces is somewhat unusual, it reflects the orientation of management over time to the relative values of alternative forms of sales representation. Claxton's challenge is to review the data that have been gathered on the three types of sales efforts, determine if additional information is needed, and make recommendations as to what changes, if any, should be made in the firm's approach to sales representation.

Information on the Company

Hyde-Phillip was formed in the early 1960s through the merger of Hyde Industrial Chemicals and Phillip Laboratories. Both firms had a broad range of experience in the development and production of certain types of chemicals and related supplies for a variety of industrial users. While the two firms had a few overlapping product lines, each brought to the merger some exclusive product offerings. The resulting combination of the two firms yielded a new organization capable of marketing a complete line of chemicals for industrial use.

Prior to the merger, Hyde Industrial Chemicals had utilized a group of industrial distributors (merchant wholesalers) to market its products. Phillip Laboratories, on the other hand, had several manufacturers' agents (agent wholesalers) who sold its product offering. The new firm, after the merger, retained some of the industrial distributors and some of the manufacturing agents and then began to develop its own salesforce.

Today, Hyde-Phillip serves 30 sales territories in states east of the Mississippi through its own sales force of 50 individuals (6 women and 44 men), 9 industrial distributors, and 9 manufacturers' agents. The 50 salespeople are about evenly allocated across 12 of the sales territories. Each of the industrial distributors and manufacturers' agents has exclusive selling rights in one of the 18 remaining sales territories. Individual distributors and agents have from 5 to 30 people working for them and many represent other noncompeting manufacturers. The 30 sales territories were originally established to represent areas of approximately equal sales potential for Hyde-Phillip's products.

Many types of sales support are made available to each sales territory by the company. Individual managers of the territories have the option of using or not using each type of sales support. Sales support items currently available include (1) a variety of descriptive brochures to supplement the information given in the firm's product catalog, (2) study programs with cassette tapes to enable sales representatives to be more familiar with the firm's products and current market situations and developments, (3) a program to provide generous product samples

"Case 32–Hyde-Phillip Chemical Company" from *Cases and Exercises in Marketing* by W. Wayne Talarzyk. Copyright © 1987 by The Dryden Press, reprinted by permission of the publisher.

to potential customers for test purposes, and (4) direct-mail programs aimed at prospective customers to solicit inquiries for descriptive materials and product samples.

Data on Sales Territories

As a first step in beginning his analysis, Claxton asked his assistant to compile the available information on each of the 30 sales territories. This information is presented in coded form in Exhibit 1.

In terms of level of sales, 9 territories have annual sales in excess of $2 million, 15 have sales between $1 and $2 million, and 6 have sales less than $1 million.

Exhibit 1 Available Data on Sales Territories

Territory Number	Level of Sales	Type of Representation	Use of Sales Support	Geographic Location
1	2	1	2	3
2	3	1	3	3
3	2	2	1	1
4	1	1	1	1
5	2	3	1	1
6	2	1	2	1
7	3	3	2	3
8	1	2	1	2
9	2	1	2	2
10	2	1	2	3
11	1	2	1	1
12	1	1	1	2
13	2	2	2	2
14	2	3	2	1
15	1	1	2	3
16	2	3	2	2
17	2	1	3	1
18	1	2	1	2
19	2	3	2	2
20	3	1	3	2
21	1	3	1	3
22	2	2	1	3
23	3	3	1	1
24	3	1	3	2
25	3	2	3	1
26	1	2	1	2
27	2	1	2	2
28	1	2	1	3
29	2	3	3	3
30	2	3	2	3

Level of sales: 1 = more than $2 million; 2 = $1–2 million; 3 = less than $1 million.
Type of representation: 1 = company sales force; 2 = industrial distributor; 3 = manufacturers' agent.
Use of sales support: 1 = extensive user; 2 = moderate user; 3 = light user.
Geographic location: 1 = northern; 2 = southern; 3 = eastern.

As already indicated, in 12 of the territories, the firm is represented by its own sales force, and industrial distributors and manufacturers' agents each represent the company in 9 territories.

Based on estimates provided by the sales support department, 12 of the territories make extensive use of the available sales support programs, 12 are moderate users, and 6 are light users. Each of the firm's sales territories is also divided into one of three geographic divisions: Northern, Southern, or Eastern. As indicated in Exhibit 1, each of these geographic locations includes 10 sales territories.

Initial Analysis

Using the information in Exhibit 1, Claxton constructed the cross-tabulation of sales versus type of representation as shown in that exhibit. He first set up the cross-tabulation using raw numbers and then calculated the conditional probabilities for each row and column.

As seen in Part B of Exhibit 2, 55.6 per cent of Hyde-Phillip's territories with sales more than $2 million were ones served by industrial distributors. Only 11.1

Exhibit 2   Cross-Tabulation of Level of Sales versus Type of Representation

			Company Sales Force (1)	Industrial Distributor (2)	Manufacturers' Agent (3)	Totals	
Level	More than $2 million	(1)	3	5	1	9	
of	$1–2 million	(2)	6	3	6	15	A
Sales	Less than $1 million	(3)	3	1	2	6	
	Totals		12	9	9		
Level	More than $2 million	(1)	33.3	55.6	11.1	100.0	
of	$1–2 million	(2)	40.0	20.0	40.0	100.0	B
Sales	Less than $1 million	(3)	50.0	16.7	33.3	100.0	
	Totals		40.0	30.0	30.0	100.0	
Level	More than $2 million	(1)	25.0	55.6	11.1	30.0	
of	$1–2 million	(2)	50.0	33.3	66.7	50.0	C
Sales	Less than $1 million	(3)	25.0	11.1	22.2	20.0	
	Totals		100.0	100.0	100.0		

A = raw numbers.
B = row conditional probabilities.
C = column conditional probabilities.

per cent of the largest sales territories were represented by manufacturers' agents and 33.3 per cent were served by the company sales force. Stated differently, as shown in Part C of Exhibit 2, 25.0 per cent of territories served by the company's sales force had sales more than $2 million, while 55.6 per cent of the industrial distributors and 11.1 per cent of the manufacturers' agents served territories with sales more than $2 million.

Claxton's initial reaction was that the firm should consider replacing part of its own sales force and the manufacturers' agents with more industrial distributors. He was concerned, however, with what other variables should be taken into account to more fully analyze and evaluate Hyde-Phillip's current approach to sales representation.

New Marketing Approach

At a recent conference on improving productivity in marketing activities, Claxton learned about a new marketing approach, developed by AT&T Communications, called Telemarketing. The following information is from an AT&T Communications publication titled, "Telemarketing: Marketing System for the 80s."

Introduction to Telemarketing

Telemarketing: Solution for the 80s.

Telemarketing—a new marketing system—is a synthesis of telecommunications technology with management systems for planned, controlled sales and service programs.

Telemarketing is a component of the marketing communications mix. It can be used solely or in combination with media advertising, direct mail, catalog selling, face-to-face selling, and other communication modes—efficiently and cost effectively.

Telemarketing can be applied at any and all functions in the marketing spectrum—from order taking to full account management. It can be used to respond to inquiries, supplement (and sometimes replace) personal selling, qualify leads, sell to marginal accounts profitably, trade-up orders, increase advertising effectiveness, replace traditional retail shopping, and render instant and cost-effective personal service to customers when they need it most.

By conducting conventional marketing and service activities in innovative ways, telemarketing is a new communications channel—delivering high impact at low cost—for critical marketing/service roles. That is why it must be integrated into the total marketing mix.

In essence, then, telemarketing is a system—with a special facility, staffed by specially trained professionals, supported by special management information and telecommunications systems—that allows businesses to execute and implement well-defined sales and service programs to identified target markets.

Because telemarketing is results-oriented, it adds a new dimension and flexibility to the marketing operation—quick, responsive, manageable, *measurable* fulfillment of the selling and servicing roles.

Therefore, telemarketing is recognized as the means for achieving such key objectives as deeper market penetration and greater market share, controlling sales and service costs, and making advertising more accountable to cost-and-results analysis.

While telemarketing is demanding, it is also highly productive. As such, this new system can assist the progressive marketer through the turbulent economic weather of the 1980s.

Benefits of Telemarketing

Telemarketing Increases Sales

Telemarketing is a low-cost means of contacting many customers and prospects—over a broad geographic area—in a short period of time. Because the communication is two-way, it allows sales personnel to persuasively and efficiently move customers and prospects to a buying decision. Sales volumes can be increased with the expert use of such techniques as upgrade selling, cross-selling, and turning service calls into sales.

Telemarketing Supports Field Sales

Once a customer relationship has been established, repeat visits do not always have to be made face-to-face. The combination of telemarketing's personalized contact with face-to-face selling can raise sales productivity to new levels.

Also, through Telemarketing, leads from promotion campaigns can be skillfully qualified. By preconditioning the prospect over the phone, the follow-up face-to-face visit can result in a truly productive sales call. Dead-end sales visits can be almost eliminated.

Telemarketing Expands Market Share, Deepens Market Penetration

You can expand your market without expanding your field sales force. Your telemarketing system can conveniently match your advertising's geographic reach. So you can coordinate promotion with extended sales territory coverage to enlarge your market share.

Telemarketing permits you to intensify your selling activities in geographic areas and market segments that are low in sales volume, and to support the selling and promotional programs of your distributors.

Telemarketing Cuts Sales Costs

The need for highly skilled, well-trained salespeople, coupled with the skyrocketing increase in travel and other sales expenses, has almost tripled the cost of sales calls in the past ten years.

But, an equally skilled and trained—but smaller—telemarketing staff can cover an even larger territory, with dramatic results. And, there are no travel or mileage allowances or hotel, lunch, or entertainment expenses to contend with. So productivity is high while the cost per sales contact drops sharply.

Telemarketing Enhances Customer Service

With telemarketing, your customers can get quick answers to product problems and service needs. Convenient, available service prevents problems from developing into deep-seated dissatisfactions. They can also obtain information on product usage, when they need it the most.

As a side benefit, product and distribution difficulties are easily recognized and can be promptly rectified. And it can all be done cost effectively.

Telemarketing Increases Advertising Effectiveness

Ad response rates can be improved by inviting customers to place orders through an 800 number. Thus, instead of completing an order card or coupon and having to mail it, your customer makes a simple toll-free call. The advantages are: prospects make the purchase while the idea is strong; it is more convenient to telephone than to fill in and mail a coupon; a telemarketing specialist can influence the customer's decision to close a sale; and since communication is two-way, there are additional opportunities to upgrade, cross-sell, and sell substitute high-inventory items.

You will find, as many other businesses have, that you close more sales with telemarketing.

Telemarketing Increases Profits

Put all of this together—more sales, lower sales costs, greater market share, deeper market penetration, improved advertising effectiveness, and enhanced customer service—and what do you get? Greater efficiency. Greater productivity. And greater profitability.

In addition to the telemarketing benefits just reviewed, there are significant beneficial results that telemarketing provides.

Timely cost-benefit analysis: Prompt data—on number of inquiries, number of sales, income per sale, cost per sale, for example—can help you measure effectiveness.

Fast feedback: Prompt response helps you test the pulling power of direct mail or advertising. Changes can be made before you make an irreversible commitment to a promotion.

Season extension: Time available for selling during seasons and holidays—such as for Christmas—is limited when orders are placed by mail. Since calls to a telemarketing center speed the receipt of orders, the selling period can be extended by up to an additional week.

Improved cash flow: Customers are encouraged to act quickly. And you can ship and bill the same day. So you can coordinate sales promotion activity with inventories to convert heavily stocked goods into cash.

Targeting the market: Effective selling is targeted to specific marketing—for example, men aged 30–40 earning $20,000–30,000 and living in the Southeast. Quickly and inexpensively, you can determine the effectiveness of a promotional program to selected telemarketing targets because responses arrive more quickly by telephone than by mail, and management systems can give rapid analysis of program performance.

Bromberg's

CASE 22

Bromberg's mission statement is premised on a policy of maintaining the posture of all its stores as full-line fine jewelry outlets. This definition accurately described Bromberg's six Alabama stores and seven Florida stores as of June 1980. Depending on the size, each store carried complete assortments of gold jewelry, diamonds and other gemstones, and watches (from Rolex to Seiko). A large percentage of the selling space was devoted to bridal and gift items, including tabletop items (china, crystal, and silver flatware and hollowware) and an impres-

This case was written by Morris L. Mayer, Bruno Professor of Marketing, University of Alabama. Used with permission.

sive variety of fashion gift items which were ideal for the bridal business. See Bromberg's (B) for details on the background, growth, and present position of the company.

In terms of the merchandise mix, Bromberg's carried a much wider gift line than did most of the directly competitive stores in its various markets. Throughout the country, many fine jewelry stores were trimming their variety. Indeed, many fine jewelry stores today carry no tabletop items. Department stores and gift stores are very competitive in these lines. Many traditional jewelers have thus decided to stress only those categories in which they have a competitive edge—namely gold jewelry, diamonds and other gemstones, and watches. The competitive edge is not in price but in terms of "nonprice competition," such as expertise in advising on the quality of stones, the design of adornment items, and perhaps repair service.

Bromberg's had carefully positioned each of its stores by consistently offering full assortments of all items which could be considered potentially in the domain of the jewelry industry as defined by Bromberg's. In its flagship store in Birmingham, which had four floors of selling departments, it carried decorator furniture and fabrics. Customers considered Bromberg's to be a "department-jewelry store" based on the size and completeness of its offerings. The other Bromberg stores in Birmingham and throughout the state carried similar varieties and assortments, but the extent varied based on the size of the store.

In April 1981 the newest Bromberg store would be opened in University Mall. Management considered this site the most "different" of Bromberg's properties. The store would be quite large (3,000 square feet). The mall was in a university town, and it was very heavily populated by professional people (in addition to the university, it contained a large Veterans Administration psychiatric facility, the state home for the mentally insane and the mentally retarded with a large professional staff, and a 600-bed community hospital with a teaching facility attached to the College of Community Health Sciences for the education of family practice physicians). The area was also the headquarters for several large national companies with major executive staffs.

The differences perceived in this market prompted Frank Bromberg, Jr., to do some advance planning in an attempt to get a good handle on the composition of the target customers. He considered a market survey but discarded the idea as impractical at the time. Finally, he presented his management team with the idea of a consumer advisory board that would be both reactive and proactive toward the marketing strategy of the company. Management gave him a green light. He decided to get the board's reactions to colors, fixtures, and merchandise mix of the new store; to have the board plan the opening events; and in effect to use the board as an advance team in the market before the store was opened. Frank thought that the board could also assist him in fulfilling his social responsibility to the community. In essence, it would be his direct line to the "real people."

The first job was to get the right chairperson for the consumer advisory board. The individual chosen should be a person who would give credibility to the structure, who would be impartial and apolitical, and who would know how to conduct meetings, what retailing was all about, and how to motivate a consumer board to be participative.

Bromberg asked a friend who taught marketing and retailing at the university to head the advisory board. This professor had taught at the university for 20 years, had regional credibility as a consultant, was respected both as a person and as a professional by the local community, had no business interests, was a member of the state retailers association, and was willing to enter into the arrangement. Frank decided that the board would have 12 members, each of whom would be an opinion leader in the community, a "typical Bromberg customer," a woman of experience and taste, a "mover and shaker," or the spouse of one, a potentially valuable image creator for the store, and available to attend meetings approximately once a quarter but more often prior to the store opening.

A list of some 30 women was prepared by Bromberg and the professor. Bromberg extended the invitations in person. A few of the women were reluctant to accept because of business and/or personal relationships with competitors and the fear of "visibility" in a relatively close-knit society. However, the board of 12 was completed with only two or three refusals; thus, the members were all exactly what was desired. Each member was to receive $100 per quarter as a token honorarium and a 20 per cent discount on all purchases.

At the first orientation meeting it was clear that the advisers were flattered and serious about their invitations. At least two of them asked that the identity of the board members be kept quiet for the time being since they felt a loyalty and an obligation to an old, established competitor. Frank Bromberg hoped that the names of the board members could be publicized in the future since each member would reflect positively on the image of the firm as it established its market position in the new community.

The initial queries of the board members related to the grand opening plans, the merchandise mix, and events. The first meeting involved a strategy discussion about the image that the new store would project to the market through its merchandise mix. It became clear that the board wanted a replication of the Birmingham Bromberg image and market positioning strategy. It wanted an extensive gift selection, but it also wanted to see fine jewelry items in depth. The store design architect reviewed the blueprints, color swatches, and fixture layout plans for the board to get its members' reactions. No one felt competent to comment on the plans. In reality, the presentation was simply informative.

The board's next function was to plan the proper preopening events with management. The opening coincided with the community's Heritage Week. A member of the board was co-chair of this annual, social elite week of antique shows, lectures, home tours, garden exhibits, and the like. Bromberg's invited Lord Wedgwood of the famous English china producers to visit the city at the store's expense. He was to attend the antique show and to assist in giving away an expensive piece of fine Wedgwood at the antique show—all at Bromberg's expense. The proceeds from tickets sold for the drawing for the Wedgwood piece were to go to a community project.

The board planned with management for a reception honoring Lord Wedgwood following his appearance at the antique show. The members would prepare the guest list of community leaders and dignitaries. The board members would act as "informal" hosts at the reception. They would circulate throughout the store and in the mall area, where canapés would be offered on appropriately appointed serving tables. Champagne would be served to the guests. One of the dramatic attractions would be the placing of a Rolls-Royce atop four Wedgwood bone china demitasses. A board member arranged to get a friend's 1928 Rolls for the exciting promotion, which would remain just outside the store during the entire opening week. The Rolls on cups became a highly promotable media piece.

The advisory board members were to attend ribbon-cutting ceremonies along with invited community citizens of note and to try to be in the store at appointed hours during the opening week. At the suggestion of a board member, on Tuesday, Wednesday, and Thursday afternoon from 4 to 5 Bromberg's would feature fashion shows utilizing outfits of neighboring apparel shops. The models would wear jewelry from Bromberg's and would discuss their outfits and the jewelry with the customers. The board members were asked to circulate in the crowd during the fashion shows.

Immediately after the ribbon cutting, Lord Wedgwood would sign pieces of Jasperware (the famous Wedgwood porous pieces) and the advisory board would assist in unobtrusive ways. Bromberg's arranged with the university's design department to have Lord Wedgwood speak to students at a seminar after his morning signing session and before his afternoon signing session.

The guest list developed by the advisory board was a valuable contribution. The membership cut across all of the upper-middle and upper socioeconomic groups in the community and in the surrounding satellite towns. The board members knew all the influentials in the area, and the diversity of age groups and professions represented on the board guaranteed a complete list of potential opinion leaders. Board members offered to entertain guests and to sign up for "duty" during the opening week. Their enthusiasm spread to the community.

April 13 came, and everything was successful. The advisory board members were constantly in evidence. The Wedgwood-signed pieces sold out on the first day. Board members bought many of the items! The reception was lavish and well attended. The Rolls on the cups amazed the crowds. A board member arranged to have the local television station cover the ribbon-cutting ceremonies with three generations of the Bromberg family present. The mayors of the twin cities of the market did the ribbon-cutting honors.

The store stayed open until 9 P.M. for the first three days. The mall was open six days a week from 9:30 A.M. to 9 P.M., but Bromberg's agreement provided that it would close each day at 6 P.M. and would be open after 6 only during the Christmas season. This had been its policy at each branch store in the past.

A meeting was called for the month following the opening to discuss the possibilities of expanding the advisory board concept to other markets. Management believed that the concept had enormous long-run strategy potential.

QUESTIONS

1. Discuss Bromberg's positioning strategy in terms of merchandise mix. How can portfolio theory be applied to the merchandise mix for analysis over time?

2. Can a store like Bromberg's compete with the department store in tabletop items? Can a jewelry store be a bridal store with such items? Can a department store be a creditable bridal registry store?

3. Does the new market seem to be appropriate for the type of store Bromberg's opened?

4. Can the advisory board be used as a "direct line" to fulfill the social responsibility component of the management philosophy? If so, how? If not, why not?

5. Discuss the concept of the advisory board as Bromberg's planned and used it. Did the board's lack of "public visibility" affect its value? Are any dangers inherent in the concept?

6. Evaluate the preopening and opening activities from a promotional mix point of view. What are the strengths and weaknesses?

7. Evaluate Bromberg's position on store hours. Should the advisory board have been consulted about that decision? (It was not.)

8. Speculate on the outcome of the postopening board meeting, based on the agenda items to be discussed.

Marketing Plan Forms

Objectives	Time to achieve
1. ______________________________	__________
2 ______________________________	__________
3. ______________________________	__________
4. ______________________________	__________
5. ______________________________	__________

Goals	Time to achieve
1. ______________________________	__________
2. ______________________________	__________
3. ______________________________	__________
4. ______________________________	__________
5. ______________________________	__________

Statement of differential advantage:

____

____

____

____

____

____

____

____

Objectives, goals, differential advantage statement. (Copyright © 1985 by Dr. William A. Cohen.)

Target Market

Geographical location _____

Special climate or topography _____

_____

Consumer buyers

Cultural, ethnic, religious, or racial groups _____

_____

_____

Social class(es) _____

Reference groups(s) _____

Basic demographics: Sex _____ Age range _____

Education _____ Income _____

Household size and description _____

_____

Stage of family life cycle _____

Family work status: Husband _____ Wife _____

Occupation (husband and wife) _____

Decision maker _____ Purchase agent _____

Risk perception: Functional _____ Psychological _____

Physical _____ Social _____ Financial _____

Income for each family member _____

Disposable income _____

Situational analysis: Environmental questions for the marketing plan. (Copyright © 1985 by Dr. William A. Cohen. Note: This form is based on an earlier form designed by Dr. Benny Barak, then, of Baruch College.)

Additional descriptions, classifications, and traits of target market _____

_____

_____

Target market wants and needs 1. _____

2. _____ 3. _____

4. _____ 5. _____

Product general description _____

_____

Frequency of usage _____ Traits _____

_____

Marketing factor sensitivity _____

_____

_____

Size of target market _____

Growth trends _____

Media Habits

	Hours/Week	Category
Television	_____	_____
Radio	_____	_____
Magazines	_____	_____
Newspapers	_____	_____

Industrial Buyers

Decision makers _____

_____

_____

_____

Primary motivation of each decision maker _____

_____

_____

_____

_____

_____

Amount of money budgeted for purchase _____

_____

_____

Purchase history _____

_____

_____

_____

_____

Additional descriptions, classifications, and traits of target market ___

_____

_____

Target market wants and needs 1. _____

2. _____ 3. _____

4. _____ 5. _____

Product general description _____

_____

Frequency of usage _____ Traits _____

Marketing factor sensitivity _____

_____

_____

Size of target market _____

Growth trends _____

Media Habits

	Hours/Week	Category
Television	_____	_____
Radio	_____	_____
Magazines	_____	_____
Newspapers	_____	_____
	Number/year	
Trade shows	_____	_____
Conferences	_____	_____

Competition

Competitor	Products	Market Share	Strategy

Resources of the Firm

Strengths: 1. _____

2. _____

3. _____

4. _____

5. _____

Weaknesses: 1. _____

2. _____

3. _____

4. _____

5. _____

Technological Environment

_____

_____

_____

Economic Environment

_____

_____

_____

Political Environment

_____

_____

_____

Legal and Regulatory Environment

_____

_____

_____

Social and Cultural Environment

_____

_____

_____

Other Important Environmental Aspects

_____

_____

_____

_____

_____

Problems/Threats

1. _____

2. _____

3. _____

4. _____

5. _____

Opportunities

1. _____

2. _____

3. _____

4. _____

5. _____

DATE _____ Potential Market Segments

Products

Numerical code:
1 = Currently meets needs fully
2 = Minor changes in product needed
3 = Significant changes in product needed
4 = Major changes in product needed
5 = Totally new product required

Products vs. potential market segments. (Copyright © 1983 by Dr. William A. Cohen.)

Date _____

Attributes/Performance Characteristics

Products								

FIGURE 8.7.   Competitive profiles. (Copyright © 1983 by Dr. William A. Cohen.)

Date _____

SPU 1   Basis of grouping _____

Product _____
Product _____
Product _____
Product _____
Product _____
Product _____

How is SPU 1 currently performing? _____

SPU 2   Basis of grouping _____

Product _____
Product _____
Product _____
Product _____
Product _____
Product _____

How is SPU 2 currently performing? _____

SPU 3   Basis of grouping _____

Product _____
Product _____
Product _____
Product _____
Product _____
Product _____

How is SPU 3 currently performing? _____

SPU 4   Basis of grouping _____

Product _____
Product _____
Product _____
Product _____
Product _____
Product _____

Development of SPUs or SBUs. (Copyright © 1983 by Dr. William A. Cohen.)

Product _____ Date _____

	Introduction	Growth	Maturity	Decline
Current Sales %				
Profits				
Target Sales %				
Profits				

FIGURE 5.39. Percentages of sales in your business area. (Copyright © 1983 by Dr. William A. Cohen)

657

Your Product _____ Date _____

Company	Product	Quality and Performance Characteristics	Shifts in Distribution Channels	Relative Advantages of Each Competitive Product

Recent trends in competitive products. (Copyright © 1983 by Dr. William A. Cohen.)

Your Product _____ Date _____

Strength code: VW = very weak   M = medium   VS = very strong
               W = weak   S = strong

Competitor	Market Share	Strength	Products

FIGURE 5.8.   Recent trends of competitor's products, share, and strength. (Copyright © 1983 by Dr. William A. Cohen.)

Your Product _____ Date _____

Competitor	Actions	Probable Meaning of Action	Check Most Likely

Analysis of competitor short-term tactics. (Copyright © 1983 by Dr. William A. Cohen.)

Product _____   Date _____

	Period 1	Period 2	Period 3	Period 4	Trend
Sales					
Profits					
Margins					
Market share					
Prices					

Complete matrix with following information:
Very low or very small
Low or small
Average
High or large
Very high or very large

Characterize trends as:
Declining steeply
Declining
Plateau
Ascending
Ascending steeply

Historical Trend Analysis Matrix. (Copyright © 1983 by Dr. William A. Cohen.)

661

Product _____ Similar or Related Product _____

Product stage	Introduction	Growth	Maturity	Decline
Competition				
Profits				
Sales (units)				
Pricing				
Strategy Used				
Length of Time in Each Stage				

Developing life cycle of similar or related product. (Copyright © 1983 by Dr. William A. Cohen.)

Product _DIET AID_ Similar or related product "_POUNDS-OFF_"

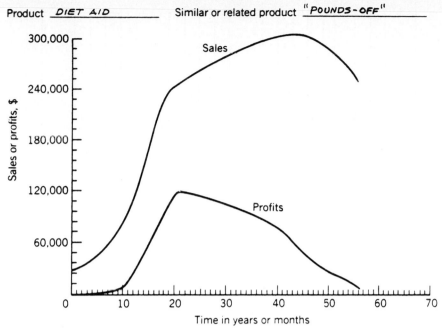

Life cycle curve of similar or related product; comparing Diet Aid to "Pounds-off." (Copyright © 1983 by Dr. William A. Cohen.).

Product _____ Similar or related product _____

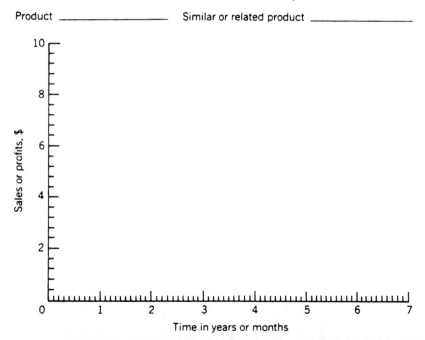

Life cycle curve of similar or related product; Sketch a rough sales curve and a rough profit curve for a similar or related product. (Copyright © 1983 by Dr. William A. Cohen.)

SPU # _____ _____ Date _____

Strengths _____

_____

_____

_____

_____

Weaknesses _____

_____

_____

_____

Opportunities _____

_____

_____

_____

Threats _____

_____

_____

Sales _____

_____

_____

_____

SWOTS analysis sheet. (Copyright © 1983 by Dr. William A. Cohen.)

664

Cash-Flow Projections

	Start-up or prior to loan	Month 1	Month 2	Month 3	Month 4	Month 5	Month 6	Month 7	Month 8	Month 9	Month 10	Month 11	Month 12	TOTAL
Cash (beginning of month) Cash on hand														
Cash in bank														
Cash in investments														
Total Cash														
Income (during month) Cash sales														
Credit sales payments														
Investment income														
Loans														
Other cash income														
Total Income														
Total Cash and Income														
Expenses (during month) Inventory or new material														
Wages (including owner's)														
Taxes														
Equipment expense														
Overhead														
Selling expense														
Transportation														
Loan repayment														
Other cash expenses														
Total Expenses														
Cash Flow Excess (end of month)														
Cash Flow Cumulative (monthly)														

Cash-flow projections.

665

Balance Sheet

	Year 1	Year 2
Current Assets		
Cash		
Accounts receivable		
Inventory		
Fixed Assets		
Real estate		
Fixtures and equipment		
Vehicles		
Other Assets		
Licenses		
Goodwill		
Total Assets		
Current Liabilities		
Notes payable (due within 1 year)		
Accounts payable		
Accrued expenses		
Taxes owed		
Long-Term Liabilities		
Notes payable (due after 1 year)		
Other		
Total Liabilities		
Net Worth (Assets minus Liabilities)		

Total Liabilities plus Net Worth should equal Assets

PRODUCT/PROJECT DEVELOPMENT SCHEDULE

Task	1	2	3	4	5	6	7	8	9	10	11	12

SPU No._____   Date _____

Market Attractiveness Criteria	Weights	×	Rankings	=	Weighted Rank
	1.00		Rank	=	

Market attractiveness computation sheet. (Copyright © 1983 by Dr. William A. Cohen.)

Business Strength Criteria	Weights	×	Rankings	=	Weighted Rank
	1.00		Rank	=	

Business strength computation sheet. (Copyright © 1983 by Dr. William A. Cohen.)

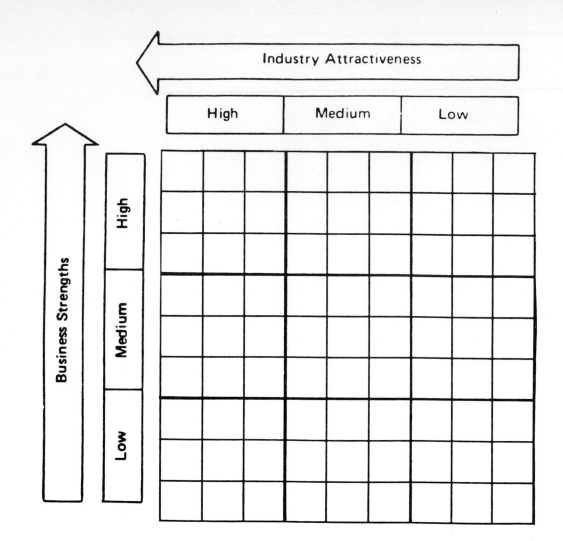

SPU # _____

List of Strategic actions	Months after Strategy Initiation/$ Allocated											Total $
	1	2	3	4	5	6	7	8	9	10	11	
Total $ Allocated												

Strategy development actions. (Copyright © 1983 by Dr. William A. Cohen.)

B

"Limit"—Disposable Alcohol Testing Unit

Sample student marketing plan developed by Scott Gilmour, Steven Lubega, Andrew Smith, and Matt Smith. Used with the permission of the authors.

Executive Summary

This report presents a detailed marketing plan for introducing a disposable alcohol testing unit (DATU) into the Los Angeles and Orange counties' consumer market.

On the basis of information we gathered during the course of our research, we determined that there is a considerable need for this product and a large potential demand. The number of drunk-driving arrests in Los Angeles and Orange counties last year was 106,585, while the number of drunk-driving occurrences exceeded some 213 million. Following a detailed analysis of our target market, we projected the sale of over 205,000 units, totaling some $197,000 in sales, with profits exceeding $50,000.

Our marketing strategy consists of repositioning a product designed for law enforcement use and promoting it in the consumer market. Market penetration pricing of $1.69 will be used for initial introduction, distributed through existing channels, utilizing agent middlemen and wholesale distributors of sundry items within liquor stores. The product will be sold through grocery and liquor stores, with the primary promotional emphasis on point-of-purchase displays. Planned date of introduction is in May 1983.

Introduction

In 1978 there were 51,500 traffic fatalities on the nation's highways, 50 per cent or some, 26,300, of which were caused by drunk drivers. In addition, more Americans died at the hands of drunk drivers during the past two years than were killed in Vietnam during the entire U.S. involvement (13).

Replacement studies by such groups as the National Highway Traffic Safety Administration (NHTSA), the Gallup Poll, and others indicate that 6 out of every 100 (6 per cent) cars you pass on the highway may be operated by a drunk driver, increasing to 10 out of every 100 (10 per cent) on the weekends (13).

In an effort to reduce these unacceptable figures, a number of interest groups have sprung up across the country, such as MADD (Mothers Against Drunk Drivers), and have begun a concerted effort to pass tougher drinking and driving laws. Already twenty-seven state legislatures have passed their own versions of "the toughest drunk driving law in the country," while twenty other states have raised the legal drinking age (13).

Clearly, the need exists to find a solution to this problem. For our marketing plan we are proposing a unique approach to this situation. The solution we are offering is a disposable "go–no go" alcohol breath analyzer, a low-cost, inexpensive one-time-use product that can determine whether a person is legally intoxicated. "Anti-drunk driving crusaders hope that breath-testing devices will become as much a fixture on the social scene as the shaker and stirrer" (13).

The purpose of this marketing plan is to present a viable means of marketing such a product to the general consumer in an effort to reduce the number of alcohol-related accidents that occur on the nation's highways.

Situational Analysis

Market Characteristics

Because the product we are proposing to market is unique, the characteristics of our market are not as clear as we would like. The information we came across in our research effort, however, has presented us with some very useful data.

To begin, motor vehicle accidents represent the nation's single greatest killer of people in the under-forty age group, the highest rate occurring between the ages of sixteen and twenty-four. Of all causes of death in all age groups, automobile deaths rank fourth after heart disease, cancer, and strokes. Add to that information that 50 per cent of all traffic accidents are caused by drunken drivers, and you begin to see the potential market for such a product as ours.

The number of people arrested in the Los Angeles-Orange County area last year for drunk driving as 106,585 (12). Add to that knowledge that only an estimated one drunk driver out of 2,000 is actually caught and arrested, and you really begin to see the potential number of prospects for our breath analyzer (13).

The Los Angeles marketing area is one of the largest and most powerful markets in the United States, accounting for at least 40 per cent of the population, households, effective buying income, and retail sales of the entire state of California.

In 1978 there were some nine million people living within this area, equating to some 3.5 million households. According to a *Los Angeles Times* market research "Consumer Trend Analysis" on beer, wine, and distilled spirits, more than half of all Los Angeles households reported purchasing at least one type

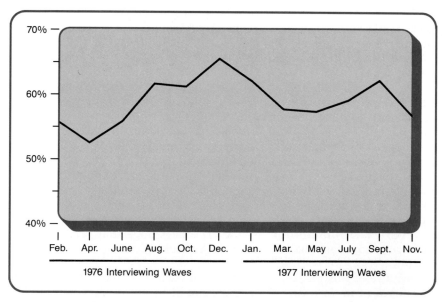

Figure B-1   Percentage of Los Angeles households purchasing any alcoholic beverage in last 30 days

of alcoholic beverage in the preceding thirty days. Figure B-1 illustrates the purchase incidence of any alcoholic beverage during the prior thirty-day periods. Overall, the incidence of purchase was generally higher for beer than for wine or distilled spirits.

Family income is an important determinant of beverage purchase and thus would be of concern to us as well. Alcoholic beverage purchases are more prominent in higher-income households. In 1977, 39.6 per cent of all Los Angeles households earning incomes of $25,000 or more annually purchased an alcoholic beverage within the preceding thirty-day period.

Equally important is the fact that fully 47.9 per cent of the households where the age of the household head was under forty accounted for 64.3 per cent of the beer purchases, 56.2 per cent of the wine purchases, and 50.4 per cent of the distilled spirits purchases.

Households in which the head has had some college education or more dominated total expenditures for alcoholic beverages. The 59.1 per cent of all Los Angeles households where this was the case was responsible for 59.5 per cent of the beer purchases, 80.3 per cent of the wine purchases, and 73.1 per cent of the distilled spirits purchases.

Finally, households headed by someone in a professional or managerial position were the primary contributors to total expenditures on alcoholic beverages. These two occupational groups made up 38.1 per cent of all Los Angeles households and were responsible for purchasing 39.7 per cent of the beer sold, 56.7 per cent of the wine sold, and 50.8 per cent of the distilled spirits sold.

Examination of purchase patterns to determine where purchases of alcoholic beverages were made, by type of store, found that the majority of purchases were made at grocery stores, followed by liquor stores, drugstores, discount stores, department stores, and others. The following chart breaks down the specific place of purchase by beverage type:

	Beer (%)	Wine (%)	Distilled Spirits (%)
Grocery store	6.5	60.0	40.9
Liquor store	36.6	37.8	54.5
Drug store	1.2	1.9	2.7
Discount store	2.1	0.9	3.1
Department store	0.7	0.9	0.8
Other	2.8	5.9	2.7
Don't know	—	0.3	1.8

The vast majority of households indicated the male household head was the primary decision maker and purchaser of alcoholic beverages, responsible for 62.5 per cent of the beer purchases, 52.2 per cent of the wine purchases, and 61.5 per cent of the distilled spirits purchases.

Among households purchasing an alcoholic beverage in the preceding thirty-day period, about 7 out of 10 reported serving each type once a week or more, with beer (72.7 per cent) being more likely to be served on a daily basis than either wine (69.7 per cent) or distilled spirits (68.4 per cent). Almost two-thirds (65.1 per cent) of all Los Angeles households reported serving an alcoholic beverage within the preceding thirty-day period, with beer (47 per cent) and wine (45 per cent) being the most popular. More than 13 per cent of these households serve them on a daily basis.

One study concluded that adults in the Los Angeles marketing area are more likely than the average U.S. adult to consume most types of alcoholic beverages and the tendency to consume increases with socioeconomic level: "In this higher-than-average liquor-drinking market, marketers who zero in on Los Angeles adults in the higher-demographic groups are getting the best possible target audience for their products."

Key Success Factors

1. *Limited Competition.* No known competitors exist in the Southern California test market who distribute a similar product at a low price level, therefore creating a price advantage; or distribute a disposable device, therefore creating a product portability advantage
2. *Legal Climate.* Currently the trend is heading toward stricter penalties for driving while intoxicated. The trend has clearly provided penalties of increasing severity over time (see legal appendix).
3. *Ease of Operation.* The DATU is relatively small—pocket-sized (Figure B-2). The usage procedure is simple (i.e., blow breath sample into tube and compare color change to calibration on instrument).
4. *Price versus Value.* DATU provides relatively inexpensive protection to drivers who are under the influence of alcohol to some degree. Value exists in that DATU is significantly less expensive than the potentially

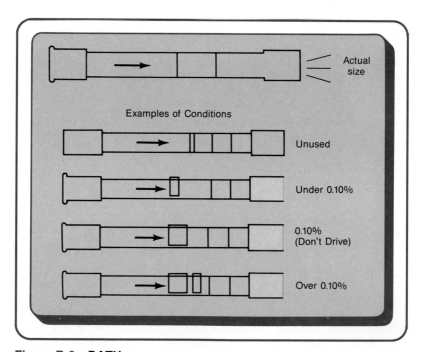

Figure B-2   DATU

negative outcomes of driving while intoxicated:

a. Loss of license
b. Legal fine
c. Loss of life

Price has been designed to be within affordable reach of target market (i.e., under $3).

Competition and Product Comparisons

To date there are no manufacturers who have distributed a DATU to the consumer market. There are three manufacturers in the United States who produce breath-alcohol testing equipment: C.M.I. Incorporated, Minturn, Colorado; Intoximeter Incorporated, St. Louis, Missouri; and Smith and Wesson General Ordinance Equipment Company, Springfield, Massachusetts.

Their major marketing emphasis is toward the law enforcement agencies throughout the United States and abroad. The equipment they produce is used to gain evidential-quality results as to a suspect's breath-alcohol count. The results are used as evidence in the conviction of an intoxicated individual.

These products are very expensive, ranging in price from $300 to over $3,500. Their ownership by the general public for self-testing is nonexistent, due to the prohibitive pricing. The competition posed by these manufacturers should be considered potential, rather than direct. Their present market emphasis is due to the expense of their current product line and lack of familiarity with the public consumer market.

The exception to the expensive product lines produced by these manufacturers is the Alcolyser PST (preliminary screening device) produced by Intoximeter Incorporated (Figure B-3). This device is used by mobile highway patrol and sheriff units throughout the United States. Approximately 1.5 million of these units have been sold to this market. The PST is a disposable, one-time-use device that is portable and reasonably accurate for its intended use. The law enforcement agencies use this device in the field instead of the manual dexterity manipulations to determine a person's ability to drive. The sales of the PST have increased steadily as its application qualities have been recognized. Eventually, the subjective judgment call will be replaced by the PST or a similar product.

In Europe a similar product has been successfully introduced to the consumer market, with sales of approximately twelve million units. Europe's generally harsher penalties for driving under the influence of alcohol have greatly increased the need for this type of product. For example, in Switzerland the penalty for drunk driving is the loss of one's driver's license for five years. Our current laws and penalties are not nearly as severe but are moving in that general direction.

The Alcolyser PST meets our product specifications and will be used for the initial introduction to the consumer market. We are repositioning this existing product for use by the general consumer.

Basically, any one of the manufacturers could produce a DATU because the technology is simple and the capital equipment costs are relatively low. Our competitive edge is our expertise in the consumer market and their lack of interest in selling to this market.

Description	The "Alcolyser" is a simple, portable, scientific device for measuring the alcohol content of blood via expired breath. The indication of the Alcolyser detector tube is based on Widmark's reaction principle, with the alcohol in expired breath reacting with the yellow crystals and turning them green.
	For the test, expired air (mixture of tidal and alveolar air) is blown through the tube into a plastic bag in approximately 20 seconds. The Alcolyser will indicate an absolute quantity of alcohol of as little as 5 mg or an alcohol concentration in blood of 0.3 promille. (30 mg of alcohol per 100 mi of blood.)
	The length of the green stain in the tube is proportional to the blood-alcohol concentration. When the green stain extends to the red mark at the center of the tube, then the alcohol level in the blood corresponds to the prescribed limit, as indicated on the box label.
Calibration	The Alcolyser detector tubes have been calibrated against direct blood-alcohol analysis employing a gas chromatograph with a flame ionization detector.
	The prescribed legal limits of alcohol in the blood vary from one country to another. The Alcolyser range consists of the following calibrated detector tubes:
	Alcolyser 50, 80, 100, 125 and 150 mg/100 ml blood.
Precautions	It is important to allow at least 15 minutes to elapse after taking alcoholic drink in order to allow mouth alcohol to disappear. Smoking should be avoided prior to breath test.
Estimation of blood-alcohol level	The basis of the determination of blood-alcohol via expired breath relies on the established ratio[2] between the alcohol content of blood to that of breath (2,100 to 1). Provided the breath test is carried out in accordance with the manufacturers instructions, this ratio holds true.
Correlation results	The results given in Table 1 were carried out at Indiana Toxicology, Department of Police Administration, University of Indiana.

Figure B-3. Alcolyser PST (Preliminary Screening Test)

Technology

The technology upon which the DATU is based is incredibly simple. It is based primarily upon the scientific principle that deep lung breath and blood alcohol are related in a definite and predictable way.

The DATU is comprised of a glass tube containing potassium dichromate crystals and a catalyst that maximizes the presence of the dichromate ions. We aim to maximize the concentration of the dichromate ion because when one breathes over the crystals, the moisture in the breath dissolves them, at which point both chromate and dichromate ions exist. The dichromate ion, however, has a higher oxidation potential ($E° = 1.33$ volts) than the chromate ion ($E° = -0.13$ volts).

$E°$ represents an oxidation potential measured in volts. More oxidation takes place if the change in energy is greater.

Table 1

679

"Limit" — Disposable
Alcohol Testing Unit

Blood	Alcolyser	Breathalyser	Blood	Alcolyser	Breathalyser
.09	.09	.07	.07	.08	.08
.06	.08	.07	.04	.04	.03
.05	.07	.05	.03	.04	.04
.07	.08	.08	.09	.10	.09
.11	.12	.12	.06	.08	.06
.08	.09	.08	.07	.10	.09
.08	.09	.08	.14	.12	.16
.07	.08	.07	.07	.09	.09
.08	.09	.07	.10	.10	.12
.10	.10	.10	.03	.04	.02

Alcolyser screening test calibrated for 0.10%

Summary of Results

(i) Within the limits of accuracy of alcohol detector tubes, results show that there is a good correlation between the Alcolyser detector tube and direct blood-alcohol estimations.[4]

(ii) When the blood-alcohol concentration is at the prescribed limit, the Alcolyser gives a reliability of over 90 per cent.

(iii) When the blood-alcohol level is above the prescribed limit, then the reliability of the Alcolyser approaches 100 per cent.

(iv) When the blood-alcohol level is below the limit, reliability is of the order of 90 per cent (just below the limit) but approaching 100 per cent when the alcohol level is significantly below the limit.

When used in accordance with the Manufacturer's instructions, the Alcolyser can provide a rapid and reliable guide to the alcohol level of the blood.

[1]W. L. Ducie and T. P. Jones, Means for detecting breath-alcohol, Pat. No. 1,143,818.
[2]Harger, et al. *Journal of Biological Chemistry* (1950), pp. 188, 197.
[3]Curry, et al. *The Analyst* (November 1966), pp. 91, 742.
[4]T. P. Jones, *Alcohol and Traffic Safety*, 5th International Conference, Freiburg, Germany, 1969.

When alcohol is introduced into the DATU, the dichromate ion oxidizes the alcohol (C_2H_5OH). The resultant products are chromic ions (responsible for the change in color). The equation below shows the reaction if a catalyst like sulfuric acid (H_2SO_4) was used (5).

$$K_2CR_2O_7 + \underset{\text{Alcohol}}{3\ C_2H_5OH} - \underset{\text{Chromic Sulfate}}{CR_2(SO_4)_3} + \underset{\text{Acetaldehyde}}{3\ CH_3CHO}$$

$$\text{Potassium dichromate} + \underset{\text{Sulfuric acid}}{4\ H_2CO_4} + \underset{\text{Potassium sulfate}}{K_2SO_4} + \underset{\text{Water}}{7\ H_2O}$$

Legal Environment

The legal environment relating to the sale and consumption of alcoholic beverages in California is to be a crucial variable in our marketing strategy. In fact, the whole raison d'être for our product is embodied in the realization that drinking and driving will in all probability lead to injury of some sort. The recognition of this fact by the law and the consequent penalties are the two factors that make our market viable.

Legally, a person is deemed intoxicated (in California) when his or her blood alcohol reaches 0.10 per cent. It is well recognized, however, that functions critical in driving coordination are impaired quite a bit before the 0.10 per cent level. Because "driving under the influence" (DUI) is rightly presumed to represent unreasonable risk both to the driver and to others who may be using the roads, penalties for doing so are becoming stiffer and stiffer. In addition, under California's "implied consent law" (see Legal Appendix), the relevant authorities can require any driver using the highways to submit to an alcohol test (blood, breath, or urine).

If the criminal liability of being intoxicated is frightening, the civil liability is equally so, if not more so. While criminal liability may mean up to three months in jail and $500 in fines, civil liability could easily expose an individual to personal financial ruin.

Under civil liability, specifically under the tort liability of "negligence,' the tortfeasor may literally have his or her pants sued off. Prior to 1971, for instance, "a commercial vendor of alcoholic beverages could not be held liable to a *third party* injured by an individual who became intoxicated as the result of the negligent serving of alcoholic beverages" (4).

In June 1971, the California Supreme Court handed down *Vesley v. Sager*, 5 Cal. 3d 153, 95 Cal. Rptr. 623, which opened the door to so-called third-party liability. With the decision in *Vesley* the then-reigning theories that had barred liability (theories relating to proximate and superseding causation) went out the door (4).

It is well recognized, therefore, that one can be held liable for harm caused to another through an intermediate party—a kind of vicarious liability.

Section 430 of the American Restatement of the Law of Torts states that there has to be an adequate causal relationship between the person harmed and the individual who causes the harm (the actor). Additionally, it must be shown that the actor's conduct was negligent before liability can attach:

The actor's conduct, to be negligent toward another, must involve an unreasonable risk of (1) causing harm to a class of persons of which the other [plaintiff] is a member and (2) subjecting the other to the hazard from which the harm results. (1)

Section 431 holds that the actor's negligent conduct is a legal cause for harm if it was a substantial factor in bringing about the harm and if "there is no rule of law relieving the actor from liability because of the manner in which his negligence has resulted in harm" (1).

In Section 432 we find that even if there were some other factor operating at the same time as the actor's negligence, which factor in itself would cause the ensuing harm, the actor may not thereby be relieved of substantially causing the harm (1).

Section 435 establishes that foreseeability of the harm is immaterial. In other words, once it has been decided that the actor was negligent, it becomes immaterial whether or not the person actually or reasonably should have foreseen that harm would result from the action so long as the conduct was a subtantial cause of the harm (1).

Section 437 states that once it has been established that the actor's negligence is a substantial factor in bringing about harm, it is immaterial, too, that the actor "exercised reasonable care to prevent harm from taking effect." The actor continues to be liable for ensuing harm (1).

What constitutes negligent conduct? According to the Restatement:

In order that either an act or a failure to act may be negligent, the one essential factor is that the actor realizes or should realize that the act or the failure to act involves an *unreasonable risk of harm* to an interest of another, which is protected against unintended invasion. (1) [*Emphasis added.*]

It seems apparent, therefore, that the legal environment within which we will implement our marketing strategy is ripe for our exploitation.

Social Environment

With regard to the social environment surrounding our breath analyzer and its use to reduce the number of drunk drivers, there is a good deal of activity going on.

At least two major organizations have been formed within the past three years in an effort to provide a vent for public outcry. The persons responsible for founding these organizations, MADD (Mothers Against Drunk Driving) and RID (Remove Intoxicated Drivers), lost loved ones because of alcohol-related accidents. In addition, some twenty seven states have passed or put into effect tougher drinking and driving laws this year alone, while twenty other states have actually raised the legal-drinking age.

In a recent survey, published in the September 1982 edition of *Glamour* magazine, 60 per cent of the respondents said they thought the drinking age should be raised to twenty one in all states. In addition, 69 per cent said they would not feel safe driving if they had been drinking or riding with a driver who had been. When asked what they would do if they had planned to drive home with someone who had had too much to drink, 7 per cent said they would refuse to go, 61 per cent said they would insist that someone else drive, and 26 per cent said they would call a taxi or go with someone else.

When asked if they thought police should have the right to give breath tests, 89 per cent said yes. Finally, 53 per cent of the respondents said that drivers who are arrested for drunk driving should have their license revoked for six months to a year, and 89 per cent said that all learning drivers should be required to attend classes about the danger of drunk driving.

Problems and Opportunities

1. *Market Characteristics*
   Problem. The actual product demand is unknown.
   Opportunities. The geographic area targeted (Los Angeles and Orange counties) is densely populated. Forty per cent of California's population resides here, allowing ease of covering target market (7).
   The average alcohol consumption in this area exceeds the national average (7). This, combined with the fact that freeways are the major source of transportation, creates a large potential for driving while intoxicated. Existing distribution channels are available through sales representatives who handle liquor and sundry items.

2. *Competition*
   Problem. The technology is simple and easily duplicated.
   Opportunities. Being the first in the market maximizes the chance to become the market leader.
   The consumer market is currently ignored by the competition.
3. *Product Comparisons*
   Problem. DATU is designed for one-time usage, as compared with multiple usage of competitors' higher-priced units.
   Opportunities. The device is small and portable, as compared with other similar units.
   Disposability, as compared with multiple usage of competitors' products, creates convenience.
   DATU is relatively inexpensive, being priced well under competitors' units.
4. *Manufacturing and Technical Factors*
   Problem. DATU has a limited shelf life of approximately six months due to perishability of chemicals employed.
   Opportunities. The simple technology will allow eventual in-house manufacturing.
5. *Environmental Climate*
   Problem. Psychographics with respect to target market attitudes toward admittance of being under the influence of alcohol are unknown. (Will potentially intoxicated drivers react defensively to being told they are "drunk"?)
   Opportunities. There is a trend toward stricter drinking and driving laws (see Legal Appendix).
   The trend has also shown increasing mobilization of action groups (e.g., MADD, or Mothers Against Drunk Drivers).
   The "innkeepers law" is most likely to be reenacted (allows control of patrons' alcohol consumption by placing responsibility on innkeeper for results of drunk drivers' actions).
6. *Internal Resources*
   Problem. DATU requires $30,000 in start-up and introduction costs.
   Opportunities. The existing product, manufactured by Intoximeter, Incorporated, meets the need.
   The relatively low cost of the project has a high expected return.

Marketing Objectives

Target Market

On the basis of the information presented in our Situational Analysis, we identified the following target market segment as potential product users:

Males who are members of households where household income exceeds $25,000 annually, are in the twenty-one to forty age group, have had at least some college education, and are employed in professional or managerial positions.

In addition, the ideal purchaser would shop frequently at grocery stores and could be either male or female, as the split between sex in purchasing alcoholic beverages in such markets is almost even.

Once again, on the basis of the information presented in our Situational Analysis, we are projecting the sale of approximately 205,000 units. Arriving at this number involved a complicated and detailed assimilation of data, as the following presentation shows:

Percent of households earning $25,000 or more	40.6%
Percent of households less than forty years of age	47.9%
Percent of households having some college education or more	59.1%
Percent of households where household head is employed in a professional or managerial position	38.1%
Average households in one or more groups	46.4%
Estimated per cent of households falling in all categories (as agreed to by *Los Angeles Times* Marketing Research Department)	40.0%
Percent of households in all categories (target market)	18.6%
Number of households in market	×3,417,000
Number of households in target market	635,500
Percent of driving households (2)	×66.4%
Number of driving households in target market	421,980
Estimated per cent of social drinkers who drive while intoxicated (4)	×15.0%
Number of drinking-driving households in target market	63,297
Average number of occurrences of driving while intoxicated per year (3)	×65
Number of occurrences of driving while intoxicated by target market, last year	4,114,310
Projected market share captured	×5%
Projected unit sales	205,700
Unit sales price	0.96¢
Projected total annual sales	$196,800

1. $\dfrac{6{,}250{,}600 \text{ drinking drivers in L.A.-Orange counties}}{9{,}410{,}366 \text{ residents L.A.-Orange counties}} = 66.4\%$

2.

106,585	Drunk-driving arrests
× 2,000	Estimated number of individuals not arrested per every individual arrested (0)
213,200,000	Drunk-driving occurrences in L.A.-Orange counties per year
÷1,562,650	Drivers who drink and drive (6,250,600 drivers × 25% estimate (3)
136.39	Number of times each person was driving while intoxicated
×50%	Estimated split of drunk-driving occurrence between "problem drinkers" and "social drinkers" (3)
68.2%	Rounded to 65

It should be noted that the 5 per cent figure for our projected captured share of the market was our best estimate based on the information we came across during the course of our research, as well as our knowledge of market conditions (including input from the manufacturer, a prospective wholesale-distributor for sundry items in liquor stores, and other individuals involved in marketing this product in another area of the country).

Profit Analysis

	Unit Cost, $	Total, $	
Projected sales (205,000 units)			$198,850
Less:			
Variable Cost			
Alcolyser	0.40	82,000	
Packaging	0.065	13,325	
Labor	0.02	4,100	
Promotion	0.08	16,400	
Shipping	0.04	10,000	
Total variable costs		125,825	
Fixed Costs			
General and administrative	0.10	$ 20,500	
Total fixed and variable costs			$146,325
Net profit after year one before taxes			$ 50,475
Percent Profit			
$50,475 ÷ $198,850 =			25.4%

Break-Even Analysis

$1x = 0.605x + 20,500$

Approximately 51,900 units

$36,589

Strategy

The marketing strategy for the DATU is to introduce the product in an area that is densely populated and has a specified demographic makeup: Los Angeles and Orange counties were chosen on the basis of the large number of drivers and other factors already noted in our Situational Analysis.

Product Strategy

The keystones of our product strategy are based on the following: simplicity, quality, and convenience. The product is extremely simple—both in conception and in use. We believe that to appeal to the average consumer who merely wants to discover the "risk factor" after a few beers, the product has to be simple. The device should be psychologically comforting and not elicit aversion, which it is likely to do if it were complicated.

We believe, and our research confirms, that most people are more interested in knowing whether or not they should drive (go–no go) than in knowing the actual level of their blood alcohol. In fact, our research indicates that knowing the actual level of blood alcohol is psychologically discomforting because it causes apprehension about the physiological effects of the alcohol.

We do not want to turn our potential customers off. Neither do we want to scare them away from drinking altogether, for it is from the drinking population that we draw our market.

The simplicity of our product is embodied in one word: *packaging*. Our packaging will carry our message of simplicity par excellence. Thus packaging will fulfill the fundamental marketing concepts of containment and promotion (14). Packaging is especially crucial for us because we are marketing the DATU as a convenience item. As is noted by authorities in the field: "Packaging is usually a more critical element for convenience goods than for shopping or specialty goods" (14).

The second keystone of our product strategy, *quality*, is ensured through the confidence we have in the technology behind the DATU. Quality will become an increasingly important element as sales pick up, because good quality will ensure user-oriented promotion for us through word-of-mouth recommendation.

The third keystone, *convenience*, is reflected by the disposable nature of the DATU. The device will be a one-use item procured at a relative giveaway price. It will be small enough to put in one's pocket, glove compartment, or briefcase and will be easily disposed of once used. There will be no clumsy meters to unsecure and no bags to save. Our product strategy can, therefore, be summarized by the following diagram:

```
Key Elements                          How Achieved
─────────────────────────────────────────────────────
Simplicity     ──────────────────→    Packaging/technology
Quality        ──────────────────→    Technology
Convenience    ──────────────────→    Disposability
```

Pricing Strategy

Our pricing strategy will complement our product strategy. We want to enter our selected market and achieve maximum level of penetration. We shall, therefore, use a price-penetration strategy: Enter the desired market at a low price and market the DATU as a convenience item.

Promotional Strategy

Our promotional strategy will be to achieve maximum reach with our message with minimum resource outlay. This strategy is dictated by the limited resources we have on hand. Fortunately, we believe the DATU lends itself to the use of just such a strategy.

The message content of our pitch will be unambiguous. The DATU is designed to give a drinking driver a quick-decision criterion. *The actual decision made must be the driver's.* It will be necessary to embody this in our promotional messages, to guard against possible legal liability.

The promotional message will also bring to bear on the driver the possible legal consequences of *not knowing whether he or she has reached the 0.10 per cent blood alcohol level.* Thus we will aid the driver in making a "safe" decision. Note should be taken, however, that our message will not be designed

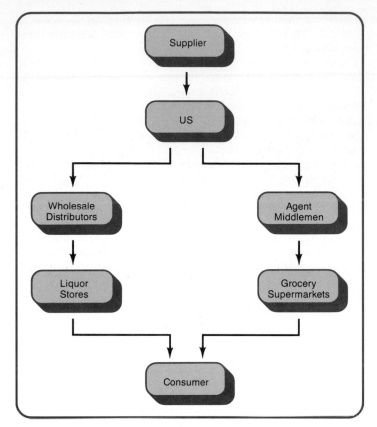

Figure B-4 **Distribution channel**

to *discourage* the driver from the consumption of alcohol. In fact, our message will be designed to *encourage* the *responsible* consumption of alcoholic beverages.

Because of the minimum outlay approach, we will not advertise via television or print, at the outset. The details of implementation of this strategy are enumerated under Promotional Tactics.

Distribution Strategy

Because the DATU is to be marketed as a convenience item, its distribution is a crucial element. Again we will aim for reach and penetration.

The ultimate consumer of the DATU will be most effectively reached through the retail supermarket and retail liquor stores. Our strategy will be to use a bichanneled approach, on the one hand distributing through wholesale distributors and on the other through agent middlemen.

The distribution channel is presented in Figure B-4.

Marketing Strategy—A Recoup and a Projection

The entire strategy is product-driven. We believe we have found an unexploited niche in the universe of drinking drivers. Our product is going to satisfy the need that has already been created by stiff legal and social consequences of driving under the influence of alcohol. We see an even rougher horizon: the consequences are to get even tougher.

In the future, we see our sales generated from desire by consumers to know their alcohol level for three reasons:

1. Criminal liability (DUI)
2. Liability of commercial vendors who negligently serve alcohol
3. Liability of hosts (in private homes) who negligently serve alcohol

We see a time when insurance companies may actively get in on the market to cover "liquor liability." At present, there are some "general liability comprehensive policies," but many of them exclude liability for harm caused by liquor consumption (4). We also see insurance companies requiring policy holders to keep a kit of breath-analysis devices. In the future, therefore, we see a potential for marketing to large institutional buyers—whereupon product changes might be necessary.

As far as our present legal liability is concerned, for harm caused by a drunken driver who may use our product, the following is our strategy:

To negate the legally implied warranty of fitness of the DATU for a particular purpose, we will have clear and unambiguous language stating our nonliability except for the ordinary purpose for which the DATU is intended (6).

The express warranties we make will be in boldfaced, clear, and unambiguous language (6).

We are not liable under present product liability theories for harm caused by our products unless the products were defective (6).

Tactics

Product

1. Arrange a contractual supply agreement for a minimum of one year with Intoximeter, Incorporated. This will be done now (December 1982) and purchase will begin in March 1983.
2. Obtain support from consumer awareness groups (MADD, RID, and CHP) in January 1983. The cost is zero.
3. Purchase DATU in an initial quantity of 30,000 units from Intoximeter, Incorporated, at a cost of $0.40 per unit, in March 1983.

Promotion

1. Produce point-of-purchase display board in January 1983 (Figure B-5).
2. Package DATU in shrink-to-fit material onto cardboard backing which will hang on display board (see Figure B-6 and B-7 for illustration). This will occur in March 1983.
3. Contact television, radio, and newspapers in May 1983 for creation of public information news segments. (ABC and CBS television have already shown interest.)

Figure B-5   Point-of-purchase display

Figure B-6   Hang card

4. During DATU introduction in May 1983, employ information leaflets at point of purchase.
5. Use the name "Limit" as trademark of DATU, implying the function of the device (i.e., a person has reached his or her alcohol limit).

Price

1. "Limit" will be priced at $1.69 each (see Figure B-8 for pricing breakdown).

Distribution

1. Distribute "Limit" in Los Angeles and Orange counties in May 1983.
2. Use brokers who distribute alcohol-related products for grocery, drug, and discount stores. This will begin in March 1983, with "Limit" being introduced to retailers for May 1983 delivery. The brokers are paid 25 per cent of the wholesale price.
3. Use sundry-item wholesale distributors for liquor store penetration. These will be paid 25 per cent of the wholesale price, and the timing is identical to item 2 above.

688

Figure B-7   **Back card—directions**

Variable Costs	Unit	
Alcolyser	$0.40	
Packaging	0.065	
Labor	0.02	
Promotion	0.08	
Shipping and handling	0.04	
Fixed Cost		
General and administrative	0.10	
Total cost	$0.705	
List Price		$1.69
Less: Retailer margin 40%		0.48
Wholesaler margin	25%	0.24
		0.97
Total cost		0.705
Profit		$0.265
Percent profit		27.3%
Actual profit due to round-off error		25.4%

Figure B-8   **Pricing in the consumer market
(based on 10,000-unit production runs)**

References

1. *American Law Institute Restatement of the Law,* 2nd Torts ed., Vol. 2. St. Paul, MN: American Law Institute Publishers.
2. *Glamour,* "This Is What You Thought About . . . Raising the Drinking Age" (September, 1982).
3. Mood, J. Linda. "Driving Drunk," *Car & Driver* (September 1982).
4. *Insurance Company of North America vs. Aaron Shanedling et al.;* 2nd civil suit #51790, Court of Appeal of the State of California, 2nd Appellate District (mimeograph).
5. Interview with William Kalemà, Ph.D. (chemical engineering), California Institute of Technology, 1983.
6. Smith, Len Young, and G. Gale Robertson. *Business Law,* 4th ed. St. Paul, MN: West Publishing Co., 1977.
7. "Beer/Wine/Champagne/Distilled Spirits: Consumer Trend Analysis," *Los Angeles Times Marketing Research,* 1979.
8. Marks, J. "Drinking and Driving: A Ticket to Disaster," *Teen* (May 1982).
9. Interview with Bud Miller, National Highway Traffic Safety Administration, San Francisco, Calif., November 1982.
10. *National Underwriter,* "Joint Action Needed" [Editorial Comment] (October 31, 1981).
11. Pointek, Annmarie B. "Drunk Driver: Challenge to Industry," *National Underwriter* (September 12, 1980).
12. Interview with Charlotte Rae, State of California Criminal Statistic Program: Uniform Crime Reporting Unit, Sacramento, CA, November 1982.
13. Starr, M. "The War Against Drunk Driving," *Newsweek* (September 13, 1982).
14. Rewoldt, Stewart H., Scott, James D., and Warshaw, Martin R. *Introduction to Marketing Management.* Homewood, Il.: Irwin, 1981.

Legal Appendix

§ 13353. Chemical Bond, Breath, or Urine Tests

(a) Any person who drives a motor vehicle upon a highway shall be deemed to have given his consent to a chemical test of his blood, breath, or urine for the purpose of determining the alcoholic content of his blood if lawfully arrested for any offense allegedly committed while the person was driving a motor vehicle under the influence of intoxicating liquor. The test shall be incidental to a lawful arrest and administration at the direction of a peace officer having reasonable cause to believe such person was driving a motor vehicle upon a highway while under the influence of intoxicating liquor. Such person shall be told that his failure to submit to or complete such a chemical test will result in the suspension of his privilege to operate a motor vehicle for a period of six months.

The person arrested shall have the choice of whether the test shall be of his blood, breath, or urine, and he shall be advised by the officer that he has such choice. If the person arrested either is incapable, or states that he is incapable, of completing any chosen test, he shall then have the choice of submitting to and completing any of the remaining tests or test, and he shall be advised by the officer that he has such choice.

Such person shall also be advised by the officer that he does not have the right to have an attorney present before stating whether he will submit to a test, before deciding which test to take, or during administration of the test chosen.

Any person who is dead, unconscious, or otherwise in a condition rendering him incapable of refusal shall be deemed not to have withdrawn his consent and such tests may be administered whether or not such person is told that his failure to submit to or complete the test will result in the suspension of his privilege to operate a motor vehicle.

(b) If any such person refuses the officer's request to submit to, or fails to complete, a chemical test, the department, upon receipt of the officer's sworn statement that he had reasonable cause to believe such person had been driving a motor vehicle upon a highway while under the influence of intoxicating liquor and that the person had refused to submit to, or failed to complete, the test after being requested by an officer, shall suspend his privilege to operate a motor vehicle for a period of six months. No such suspension shall become effective until ten days after the given of written notice thereof, as provided for in subdivision (c).

(c) The department shall immediately notify such person in writing of the action taken and upon his request in writing and within fifteen days from the date of receipt of such request shall afford him an opportunity for a hearing in the same manner and under the same conditions as provided in Article 3 (commencing with Section 14100) of Chapter 3 of this division. For the purposes of this section, the scope of the hearing shall cover the issues of whether the peace officer had reasonable cause to believe the person had been driving a motor vehicle upon a highway while under the influence of intoxicating liquor, whether the person was placed under arrest, whether he refused to submit to, or failed to complete, the test after being requested by a peace officer, and whether, except for the persons described in paragraph (a) above who are incapable of refusing, he had been told that his driving privilege would be suspended if he refused to submit to, or failed to complete, the test.

An application for a hearing made by the affected person within ten days of receiving notice of the department's action shall operate to stay the suspension by the department for a period of fifteen days during which time the department must afford a hearing. If the department fails to afford a hearing within fifteen days, the suspension shall not take place until such time as the person is granted a hearing and is notified of the department's action as hereinafter provided. However, if the affected person requests that the hearing be continued to a date beyond the fifteen-day period, the suspension shall become effective immediately upon receipt of the department's notice that said request for continuance has been granted.

If the department determines upon a hearing of the matter to suspend the affected person's privilege to operate a motor vehicle, the suspension herein provided shall not become effective until five days after receipt by said person of the department's notification of such suspension.

(d) Any person who is afflicted with hemophilia shall be exempt from the blood test required by this section.

(e) Any person who is afflicted with a heart condition and is using an anticoagulant under the direction of a physician and surgeon shall be exempt from the blood test required by this section.

(f) A person lawfully arrested by any offense allegedly committed while the person was driving a motor vehicle under the influence of intoxicating liquor may request the arresting officer to have a chemical test made of the arrested person's blood, breath or urine for the purpose of determining the alcoholic content of such person's blood, and, if so requested, the arresting officer shall have the test performed.

Legislative History:

1. Added by Stats 1st Ex Sess 1966 ch 138 § 1.
2. Amended by Stats 1969 ch 1438 § 1, adding "and he shall be advised by the officer that he has such choice" in the second paragraph of subd (a).
3. Amended by Stats 1970 ch 733 § 2.
4. Amended by Stats 1970 ch. 1103 § 2, adding (1) "or complete" after "submit to" in the first and fourth paragraph of subd (a); (2) the second sentence of the second paragraph of subd (a); (3) the third paragraph of subd (a); (4) "or fails to complete," in subd (b), and (5) "or failed to complete," wherever it appears in subds (b) and (c).

Former § 13353, relating to the beginning of suspension (based on former Veh C § 307 subd (b)), was enacted Stats 1959 ch 3 and repealed by Stats 1959 c 1996 § 18.4.

Collateral References:

Cal Jur 2d Automobiles § 372. Criminal Law § 118, Evidence § 396, Searches and Seizures § 46, Witnesses § 29.

§ 23126. Driving While Intoxicated: Presumptions

(a) Upon the trial of any criminal action, or preliminary proceeding in a criminal action, arising out of acts alleged to have been committed by any person while driving a vehicle while under the influence of intoxicating liquor, the amount of alcohol in the person's blood at the time of the test as shown by chemical analysis of his blood, breath, or urine shall give rise to the following presumptions affecting the burden of proof:

(1) If there was at that time less than 0.05 per cent by weight of alcohol in the person's blood, it shall be presumed that the person was not under the influence of intoxicating liquor at the time of the alleged offense.

(2) If there was at that time 0.05 per cent or more but less than 0.10 per cent by weight of alcohol in the person's blood, such fact shall not give rise to any presumption that the person was or was not under the influence of intoxicating liquor, but such fact may be considered with other competent evidence in determining whether the person was under the influence of intoxicating liquor at the time of the alleged offense.

(3) If there was at that time 0.10 per cent or more by weight of alcohol in the person's blood, it shall be presumed that the person was under the influence of intoxicating liquor at the time of the alleged offense.

(b) Percent by weight of alcohol in the blood shall be based upon grams of alcohol per 100 milliliters of blood.

(c) The foregoing provisions shall not be construed as limiting the introduction of any other competent evidence bearing upon the question whether the person was under the influence of intoxicating liquor at the time of the alleged offense.

Legislative History:
    Added by Stats 1969 ch 231 § 1.

Glossary

Absolute price difference The price difference in absolute terms as compared with the price originally charged prior to a change.

Account impact profile system (AIP) An audit tool for salespeople used for a variety of sales purposes.

Action research Research into the various marketing actions taken by an organization.

Advertising Nonpersonal promotional activities that are paid for by one or more sponsors.

Agents Independent individuals or firms that represent manufacturers for the sale of their goods, but do not take title to these goods.

Annual plan A marketing plan produced annually for a product or service already established in the marketplace.

Attitude surveys A means of measuring the intensity of feelings, such as before and after an advertising campaign.

Authority level The level at which marketing decisions are made within an organization.

Awareness A means of measuring factors having to do with an advertising campaign, such as awareness of a new product.

Baseline pricing The standard or regular price decided on for an item.

Balanced portfolio A concept implying a balance among various categories of products, product groupings, or SBUs plotted in a product portfolio matrix or sometimes against a product life cycle curve.

Balancing strategy A marketing strategy in which the firm seeks to balance revenue cost flows to achieve desired profit and market share targets.

Boston consulting group A consulting firm specializing in strategy, founded by Bruce Henderson; probably best known for the BCG four-celled product portfolio matrix or four-celled share/growth matrix (*which see*).

Bottom-up forecasting   Forecasting based on the calculation of demand in each market segment separately, with the results summed to arrive at the total sales forecast.

Bottom-up planning   Planning that is initiated by lower-level organizations, and then reviewed and approved or rejected by top management.

Break-even analysis   A calculation of the point in sales dollars or number of units sold at which a firm neither makes nor loses money. If done graphically, other information is displayed simultaneously, including profitability for various levels of sales.

Broadcast advertising   Advertising done over television or radio.

Business analysis   The third stage of the new product development process, during which alternative proposals are compared, analyzed, and new products to develop are selected.

Business strength   The vertical descriptor on the GE/McKinsey Multifactor Portfolio Matrix.

Buying power index   A relative value describing the ability of a geographical segment of the population to purchase, as established by *Sales and Marketing Management* magazine.

Capital budgeting techniques   Analytical techniques that compare alternative projects through an analysis of cash flows which consider the cost of capital over time.

"Cash cows"   SBUs or product groupings falling in the lower left-hand quadrant of BCG's four-celled share/growth matrix *(which see)*.

Cash flow requirements   Money needed on a monthly basis to carry out a marketing program or campaign.

Cautious planner   A type of buyer who shops only once a week, is generally a bargain hunter, often seeks specials, sticks to a budget, and uses a shopping list.

Central issue   The main problem or issue in a marketing situation being analyzed.

Centralization   The organizational concept of making decisions at the highest level in an organization.

Channels   Routes, passages, or means of distributing a product from producer to ultimate buyer.

Classified advertising   Advertising in which the advertisement is classified with similar advertisements under a specific category.

Climbers   A stage of country development as a market, where the country has an emerging middle class.

Clutter   The promotional environment in which the buyer is presented with so many choices that it is difficult for one promotion to stand out from the others.

Coercive power   Power based on the perception of the sales manager to withhold rewards or administer punishment.

Cognitive dissonance   Consumer postpurchase feelings and evaluation.

Commercial suppliers   Sellers of goods to organizational buyers as opposed to consumer buyers.

Companies-specific factors   Factors that help to determine how many and which individuals participate in an organizational purchase decision, including the company orientation, company size, and degree of centralization.

Company environs   The knowledge, experience, financial resources, human resources, capital equipment, suppliers, and marketing intermediaries existing at any given time and available to the company or organization.

Competition Organizations competing with the firm for business or the acceptance of ideas.

Competitive advantage An advantage that a firm can offer over a competing firm.

Competitive analysis An analysis of competitors, their products, strategies, resources, and likely reactions in response to our actions, in order to thoroughly understand the competition.

Competitor environs The knowledge, experience, financial resources, human resources, capital equipment, suppliers, and marketing intermediaries existing at any given time and available to a competitor.

Competitive structure A description of the competitors and their relative strengths in an industry.

Concentration strategy A strategy of international marketing utilizing market concentration.

Constraint identification The third stage of the process of strategic marketing management, in which constraints to possible actions are noted.

Consumerism A social movement that seeks to increase consumer power and protection.

Consumer behavior The behavior that a consumer exhibits in purchasing a product or service, and in interaction with all marketing activities.

Consumer buying process The process involving marketing and psychological inputs by which a consumer makes purchase decisions.

Consumer orientation A focus on the customer and satisfying his or her needs, rather than on the product or service.

Consumer protection A situational environ having to do with laws and regulations passed for the benefit and protection of the consumer.

Consumer sensitivity The consumer's ability to perceive product differences.

Contractual entry A means of expanding into foreign markets through contracting, resulting in the goods being produced in the foreign market.

Controllable variables Those variables in the marketing situation over which the marketing manager has the greatest control: product, price, promotion, and place.

Cost-benefit analysis An analysis based on the ratio of quantified benefits divided by costs.

Cost prediction formula analysis An analysis based on formulas that predict the investment required to complete individual new product developments, using relevant related parameters such as sales forecasts and historical data.

Coupon A direct-response device used for ordering or inquiring about a product or service. Also, a promotional device used to promote increased sales through price discount or special purchase offer.

Co-production An investment means of expansion into foreign markets that includes cooperation in producing and marketing a product.

Creative imitation A strategy that is imitative in substance, yet creative in that it makes better use of the basic innovation than did those who initiated it.

Creative sellers Sellers whose primary duty is persuading prospects to buy.

Demand curve   A curve that results when quantity demanded of a product as measured on the horizontal axis is plotted for an array of different prices measured on the vertical axis.

Demographics   A statistical study of a market having to do with age, income, education, and other important statistics.

Dependent stage   A category of country development as a market in which the country is dependent on other countries and not yet a full partner in international trade.

Direct mail   Advertising that is accomplished by mailing the advertisement to the prospective buyer.

Direct marketing   An interactive system of marketing that uses one or more advertising media to effect a measurable response and/or transaction at any location.

Direct mediated strategies   Influence strategies where a specific action is requested and the consequences of exception or rejection are stressed, based on the mediation of the producer.

Direct premiums   Free items given away at the time of purchase.

Direct-response advertising   Advertising that solicits a direct response from a prospect in the form of an order or an inquiry.

Direct unmediated strategies   Influence strategies where consequences of the acceptance or rejection of the channel program and/or its implementation are stressed, but consequences are based on a response from the market environment and not on a member of the producer organization.

Direct unweighted strategy   Influence strategies where desires or wishes of the producer are communicated and no consequences of acceptance or rejection are mentioned or applied.

Directional policy matrix   A product portfolio matrix containing nine cells in which product groupings or SBUs are plotted against business sector prospects on the horizontal axis and the company's competitive capabilities on the vertical axis.

Discontinuance   Withdrawing a product from the marketplace.

Discount pricing   Pricing at a discount when ordered in larger quantities or under other special circumstances determined by the seller.

Distribution channel   Any number or combination of firms which together make up a chain that links the producer to the ultimate buyer.

Distribution or place decisions   Decisions made by the marketing manager involving distribution, including which channels to be used, means of physically getting the product from one place to another, the amount of channel ownership, etc.

Distributors   Market intermediaries between the producer and the buyer.

Diversion and dissuasion categories   Categories of means of inducing competitors not to invest in those products, markets, and services where you expect to invest the most.

"Dogs"   SBUs or product groupings falling in the lower right-hand quadrant of BCG's four-celled share/growth matrix (*which see*).

Dual adaptation   Adapting a product to a different function as well as adapting the communications strategy to best meet the needs of a foreign country in which the product is marketed.

Dual marketing   Marketing to both consumers and organizational buyers.

Economic Orientation   A distribution planning framework which focuses basically on efficiency.

Economic value   The worth of a product to a customer measured in dollars due to savings, increased profitability, or some other factor or combination of factors.

Enduring importance   The long-term importance of a product based on the product's relationships to central needs and values.

Engineering method of pricing   A structured method of pricing in which a predetermined profit is added to the cost of materials and labor, overhead, and other expenses to result in a price.

Entrepreneurial judo   The catapulting of a company into a leadership position in an industry against the efforts of entrenched established companies, by sidestepping their strength.

Entry strategies   Strategies for entering a new market.

Environmental management strategies   Strategies based on manipulating the marketing environs.

Environmental segmentation   A procedure of analysis for marketing internationally, which includes consideration of economic, political, and cultural variables.

Environs of marketing   The four elements making up the marketing environment: situational environs, neutral environs, company environs, and competitor environs.

EPRG framework   A structure for the development of international marketing strategies considering the ethnocentric, polycentric, regiocentric, and geocentric perception of a market.

Ethocentric   A category of international marketing structure that views overseas operations as being secondary to those accomplished within national boundaries.

Ethnocentrism   The belief in the superiority or importance of one's own group.

Evaluation research   Research having to do with the evaluation of some marketing activity.

Evolutionary approach (to product cycles)   An alternative theory of product development that proposes patterns of evolution as opposed to stages of a life cycle.

Excess capacity   Having a production capacity in excess of what is needed to satisfy the market.

Expansion strategy   A strategy of increasing market share.

Experience curve   A curve that slopes downward and to the right, representing decreased cost of production with increasing numbers of units produced, due to such factors as experience in producing the item, lower cost of raw materials, etc.

Expert power   Power based on the sales manager's expertise.

Exploratory research   Research done to define a marketing problem.

Export entry   A means of expanding into foreign markets by exporting goods into a foreign market.

Face-to-face selling   Selling acccomplished in person by a salesperson.

Family decision making   Purchase decisions made by (and within) a family.

Field representatives   Individuals who represent the firm to the organizational customer.

Financial analysis   An analysis having to do with the financial aspects of a marketing campaign or project.

Flanker brand A brand introduced by a firm, in a category of product in which the firm is already marketing.

Flexibility (as a characteristic of strategic marketing management) The ability to plan and think in such a way as to be ready for change.

Focus groups Groups of individuals that are interviewed together in an informal setting for market research purposes.

Formalization An organizational concept whereby a structured environment of rules and procedures requirements must be followed in the day-to-day implementation of marketing tasks.

Four-celled share/growth matrix The Boston Consulting Group's product portfolio matrix, in which market growth rate on the vertical axis is plotted against relative market share on the horizontal axis.

Franchise extension Applying a brand name that is familiar to the consumer to products in a category that the firm is not presently marketing.

Franchising A means of contractual entry into foreign markets that involves a permanent arrangement whereby the franchiser assists the franchisee in operations which may include the manufacture and/or marketing of the franchiser's product. Of course, franchising can be accomplished without involving marketing on an international basis.

Free offers Free items given in return for purchasing a product.

Frequency How often the target market receives an advertising or publicity method within a given period of time.

Functional organization Organization structured around various marketing functions such as advertisement, sales, marketing research, etc.

Geocentric A category of international marketing in which the entire world is viewed as one potential market; in effect, the global marketing concept.

GE/McKinsey multifactor portfolio matrix A product portfolio matrix developed by the consulting firm of McKinsey and Company and General Electric that has nine cells and permits a number of factors concerning industry or market attractiveness and business strength to be considered.

Global marketing Marketing using identical products, strategies and tactics, etc., without change or adaptation in multiple countries.

Globalization A marketing strategy in which the same product is marketed in an identical fashion in all of the countries where it is marketed.

Goal development The second stage of the process of strategic marketing management, in which goals are selected and precisely defined.

Goal-oriented organization An organizational concept whereby an organization is formed for the specific purpose of attaining a goal or accomplishing a task.

Goodwill An advantage that a marketer has acquired due to past performance or actions, which goes beyond the product or service sold.

Gross national product (GNP) The total market value of all goods and services produced in a country in a year.

Growth strategy A marketing strategy involving increasing sales of a product in an old market or in new markets.

Harvesting A strategy of extracting the maximum benefit possible while exiting from or withdrawing a product from a market.

Hierarchy of needs The motivational theory developed by Abraham Maslow that human beings are motivated by a hierarchy of needs, beginning with physiological needs and progressing sequentially to higher levels of needs as the lower levels are satisfied.

Historical data Information obtained from prior performance in the marketplace.

Home office The main office of a firm that has offices or facilities in many different geographic locations.

Holistic perspective The view that all elements of the marketing situation are interrelated, including both the strategic variables that one can control and the environs that one usually cannot control.

Idea acquisition The initial stage in the new product development process that involves a search for new product ideas.

Image The mental picture of a product that the product represents.

Implementation process The process that begins with planning strategy and tactics and ends with carrying them out, feedback, and adaptation.

Indirect influence strategies An influence strategy whereby influence results from exchanging information.

Industrial supply house A wholesaler of industrial equipment and supplies.

Industry attractiveness The horizontal descriptor on the GE/McKinsey Multifactor Portfolio Matrix.

Information processing The processing of communications received from external sources by a consumer.

Influence strategies Strategies used to affect the behavior of channel members.

Instrumental importance A temporary importance possessed by a product, based on the consumer's desire to obtain particular extrinsic goals deriving from the product's purchase or use.

Interchannel rivalry Rivalry among or within different channels of distribution.

Internal development New product development controlled and usually accomplished within the firm.

International marketing Marketing to multiple countries, considering each country differently and adapting products, strategies, tactics, etc., as necessary to each individual country.

Internationalization A marketing strategy in which a firm's product is differentiated and adapted to the particular country in which it is being marketed.

Intrachannel conflict Conflict among intermediaries within channels of distribution.

Introduction stage The final stage of new product development and the initial stage of the product life cycle, in which the product is introduced into the market.

Inventory turnover A measurement of how fast merchandise is being sold; cost of goods sold divided by average inventory on an income statement.

Investment entry A means of expanding into foreign markets that require ownership investment by the firm wishing to expand.

Job enlargement A procedure for increasing job satisfaction by increasing the scope and responsibilities of a job.

Job enrichment A concept whereby jobs are made more satisfying by building in greater scope for personal achievement, growth, and recognition.

Job satisfaction An employee's attitude to his or her job.

Joint decision making Organizational buying in which the purchase decision is made by more than one individual.

Joint venture A temporary alliance of one or more firms to accomplish a business objective; includes an equity investment.

Learning curve A downward-sloping curve that represents decreased costs of producing an item as increased numbers are produced, due to learning better how to produce the item, reduced costs of materials, and other factors that cause costs to go down.

Legitimate power Power based on the perception of the sales manager's right to influence others.

Licensing Borrowing the right to manufacture and sell a product developed by someone else in exchange for a fee or royalty. This is also a means of expanding into foreign markets for the firm with primary ownership of the product.

Life-style segmentation Market segmentation by the way members of the segment live.

Line extension Use of a company's brand name in the firm's present product category.

Line manager The manager of an operational marketing unit as contrasted with the manager of a marketing staff function.

Line personnel Individuals who take actions and make decisions that are related directly to the objectives of the organization.

Logistics Channels and distribution matters.

Luxury and leisure phase A stage of country development as a market in which consumers have more money to spend on luxury items.

Mail order A method of selling a product or service through direct-response advertising that results in an order placed by mail or telephone.

Mail survey A market research survey accomplished through the mail.

Maintenance (strategy) A strategy of maintaining a firm's position in the market.

Management-by-objectives A process whereby the management of activities is performed by focusing primarily on the objectives to be accomplished, and taking actions that maintain progress towards the objectives specified.

Manufacturer's representative An independent agent who represents firms and sells their goods but does not take title to them.

Market centering A concept in marketing organization structuring where companies seek to organize their operations around the market to be served rather than around other functions.

Market concentration A strategy of international marketing characterized by a slow and gradual rate of growth in the number of markets served.

Market development strategy A marketing strategy that involves extending an enterprise beyond existing market product commitments.

Market diversity A description of the breadth of different markets to which a product is marketed.

Market entrenchment objective One of two alternatives available in a quadrant described by satisfactory margin and return and achieved by a share protection or repositioning strategy in the Sheth-Frazier Margin-Return Model.

Market expansion objective   One of two alternatives available in a quadrant described by satisfactory margin and return and achieved by a multinational or full-line strategy in the Sheth-Frazier Margin-Return Model.

Market extension   Expanding the market by reaching or developing portions of it not previously marketed to.

Market growth rate   The growth rate of industry sales of a particular product category being considered.

Market potential   The total potential sales of a product, a group of products, or a service in a given period of time.

Market retention strategy   A marketing strategy that involves holding onto markets currently served.

Market segment   A part of the total market that has some measurable commonality.

Market segmentation   A marketing strategy in which the total market is broken into a submarket or segment sharing some measurable commonality such as demographics, psychographics, life style, geographics, benefits, etc.

Market testing   The final trial before committing the bulk of financial resources in introducing a new product into the market.

Marketing   The process of planning and executing the conception, pricing, promotion, and distribution of ideas, goods, and services to create exchanges that satisfy individual and organizational objectives.

Marketing audit   A review of all aspects of a marketing system, organization, or campaign.

Marketing concept   A concept that focuses on satisfying needs and wants of the consumer or organizational buyer, with elements that include a consumer orientation, an organization to implement this orientation, and long-range consumer and societal welfare.

Marketing environment   The surroundings in which marketing is performed, including a description of situational, neutral, competitive, and company environs.

Marketing information system (MIS)   A structured interaction of people, machinery, and procedures to result in an orderly flow of pertinent information from both inside and outside the firm, to assist in marketing decision making.

Marketing intelligence   Relevant information having to do with the marketing situation or environment.

Marketing management   The management of marketing activities: the analysis and planning leading to selection of one or more target markets, the design of an integrated marketing strategy to reach the target markets selected, and implementation and control of strategy in order to meet the objectives.

Marketing mix   The combination and amount of resources allocated by the marketing manager to product, price, promotion, place.

Marketing organization   How a firm is organized to accomplish marketing activities.

Marketing orientation   The orientation of a firm primarily toward the customer.

Marketing planning   The process of developing a marketing plan.

Marketing research   The function that links the consumer, customer, and public to the marketer through information which is used to identify and define marketing opportunities and problems; to generate, refine, and evaluate marketing actions; to monitor marketing performance; and to improve understanding of marketing as a process.

Marketing research managers   Individuals responsible for the management of marketing research activities.

Marketing share strategy   A strategy focusing on increasing marketing share to the exclusion of all else.

Marketing system   The group of interacting and interdependent elements forming the unified whole of the marketing organization.

Marketing tactics   *See* Tactics.

Mass marketing   A concept whereby a product or service is marketed to the total market; selling the same product or service to everyone.

Matrix organization   An organizational concept whereby individuals belonging to functional organizations report both to their functional managers and to project managers outside of the functional organization for all purposes having to do with the project.

Media   A classification of advertising means such as television, radio, direct mail, etc.

Meet-the-competition pricing   Pricing to be competitive with competitors, and seeking a differential advantage in some other variable than pricing.

Missionary salesperson   A type of salesperson whose primary job is to build goodwill and perform promotional activities rather than make an immediate sale.

Multiple channel (distribution tactic)   The use of more than one channel at a time.

Neutral environs   Organizations or groups that are usually neutral regarding a company relative to its competitors.

New-product development   The process of taking an idea for a product or service from conception to establishment in the marketplace.

New-product plan   An operational marketing plan for a product, product line, or service that has not yet been introduced by the firm.

New-venture strategy   A marketing strategy involving a totally new undertaking by the organization.

Niching   The strategy of finding a distinguishable market segment—identifiable by size, need, and objective—and concentrating on fulfilling the needs of this niche and no other.

Not invented here (NIH) syndrome   A behavior exhibited by some organizations and companies, which believe that a new product or idea cannot be worthwhile unless they themselves thought of it.

Objective-and-task method   A means of advertising budgeting whereby the objective is first decided upon, and the budget arrived at according to how much money is required to reach that objective.

Official sources   Organizational sources officially representing groups of any sort. Examples would include government, trade associations, consumer groups, the chamber of commerce, etc.

Operational plans   Plans accomplished by marketing organizations, as contrasted with strategic plans, which tend to be developed at the corporate level.

Operational research   Research into daily marketing activities.

Opinion surveys   Surveys that measure the reactions to advertisements.

Order taker A type of salesperson who does little selling, but rather takes orders from customers who have already decided to buy.

Organizing function The management function involving the establishment of efficient relationships among people, resources, and functions.

Outdoor advertising Advertising accomplished outdoors, such as on highway billboards.

Packaging The function of enclosing a product for containment, protection, discouraging tampering, and promotion.

Payback analysis The time required to return the investment made.

Penetration pricing Pricing low in order to enter a market.

Perceived risk Risk in purchase as perceived by the buyer.

Perceived value The value of a product or service to the customer as perceived by the customer.

Personal interview survey A market research survey accomplished face to face and one on one.

Physical distribution Transportation and associated activities such as warehousing and inventory of physical goods from the time they are produced until they reach the ultimate buyer.

Point-of-purchase display A display at the point of purchase in a retail outlet.

Polycentric A category of international marketing structure that involves subsidiaries established in overseas markets.

Price skimming Setting the price of a new product high to extract maximum profits before competition can enter the market.

Price-value relationship The relationship between the price charged and the value of the product or service as perceived by the customer.

Print media Newspapers, magazines, and other printed advertising media.

Private branding The use of a distributor or other company's label instead of the label of the manufacturer.

Psychological environment The environment of expectation, implicit criteria, past satisfaction or dissatisfaction, and other elements that make up the psychological surroundings of the organizational buyer.

Planning function The function that involves the organization of activities, strategies, and tactics to achieve specified goals and objectives.

Policy research Research having to do with the marketing policies of an organization.

Positioning A marketing strategy in which a firm's product or service is positioned relative to other products in the minds of prospective buyers.

Pricing The action by which the cost of a product or service to the buyer is set; the price structure in a particular industry.

Pricing decisions Actions that are taken by the marketing manager regarding price, including margins, pricing versus the competition, discounting, etc.

Primary demand Demand for an entire class or category of product and not just a company's brand.

Primary research The collection of data by the marketing researcher, or agents of the marketing researcher, directly from respondents.

Primary sources Sources of market intelligence obtained first hand by the researcher.

Proactiveness Designing the future; making decisions now in anticipation of occurrences in the future.

"Problem children" ("question marks") SBUs or product groupings falling in the upper right-hand quadrant of BCG's four-celled share/growth matrix.

Product adaption/communication extension A strategy of internationalization whereby the product serves the same function in the foreign market, but under different use conditions, and must therefore be adapted; however, the same communications strategy is used.

Product branding Applying a name, term, symbol, or other means to identify a product.

Product/communications extension Selling the same product in foreign countries with the same advertising and promotional themes used in the country of origin.

Product decisions Actions that are taken by the marketing manager regarding the product, such as introduction, modification, discontinuance, etc.

Product delivery salesperson A type of salesperson whose selling duties are secondary to delivering the product.

Product development The stage of new product development pertaining to the technical development of the product.

Product development schedule A graphical representation of new product development task initiation and completion points, along with relevant cash flow and the organization responsible for each task.

Product differentiation A marketing strategy in which a firm's product is differentiated from a competitor's products.

Product extension/communications adaptation A strategy of international marketing whereby the same product fulfills a different function, and the communications are adapted to the foreign country in which the product is marketed.

Product extension strategy A strategy of extending the maturity stage of a product's life cycle and delaying entry into the decline stage, usually by finding a new use for the product.

Product invention A strategy of international marketing in which foreign needs are served by inventing an entirely new product.

Product orientation The orientation of a firm primarily toward its own products.

Product liability The legal liability of the seller for product deficiencies.

Product life cycle The stages that a product passes through from introduction through growth, maturity, and decline.

Product manager concept The organizational marketing concept in which a marketing manager is given responsibility for a product, product line, or brand.

Products-specific factors Factors that help determine how many individuals and which individuals participate in the organizational purchase decision, including perceived risk, type of purchase, and time pressure.

Profitability How much money a product or a business is making.

Profitability matrix A matrix designed by DuPont to show return on operating assets as a function of operating margin and operating asset turnover.

Profit impact of marketing strategy (PIMS) A database by which empirical information supplied by companies on resource inputs, strategies, and results is collected from many companies, analyzed, and published.

Promotion Marketing activities that involve communicating information between buyer and seller. They include advertising, face-to-face selling, sales promotion, and publicity.

Promotional pricing   Short term, non-regular pricing that is used to encourage potential customers to try the product or service or promote its use.

Protectionism   Protecting local manufactures by enacting laws to prevent or make the import of foreign goods difficult or more expensive.

Publicity   A form of promotion that is non-paid and non-personal.

Pull promotion   A promotion directed at the ultimate buyer.

Purchase decision   The decision to buy made by a consumer or organizational buyer.

Push promotion   A promotion directed at a channel intermediary.

"Question marks" ("problem children")   SBUs or product groupings falling in the upper right-hand quadrant of BCG's four-celled share/growth matrix.

Reach   The number of households or target customers that will receive the advertiser's message.

Recall   A means of measuring the frequency of details of an advertisement being remembered.

Recognition   A means of measuring the frequency of an advertisement being remembered as having appeared.

Referent power   Power based on perceived attraction to each other of the members reporting to the sales manager.

Regiocentric   A category of international marketing structure that considers a region as being homogeneous and ignores national boundaries.

Rejuvenation   Modifying a product to extend its life cycle curve.

Relative market share   The ratio between the firm's sales volume and that of the leading seller, or, if the firm is the leading seller, between it and the next largest.

Relative price difference   The price difference relative to the absolute price value before a change.

Repositioning strategy   A marketing strategy in which the position of a product relative to a competitor's products, or other products in a firm's product line, is changed.

Retailer   A channel intermediary who sells goods or services to the final consumer.

Return on assets   A percentage that equals operating margin percent times operating asset turnover.

Return on investment (ROI)   A measure of the profitability with which economic resources required are employed.

Reward-and-punishment strategies   Influence strategy that uses reward and punishment to affect channel member behavior.

Reward power   Power based on the perception of the sales manager's ability to reward.

Risk diversification   Reducing risk by selling many different markets.

Risk reduction   A strategy of reducing the risk associated with market share without reducing shares.

Rocking chairs   A country development stage in which the society has a high proportion of older people.

Role ambiguity The extent to which a required role task is unclear in its demands, criteria, or relationships with other required tasks.

Role conflict Pressures due to conflicting or mutually exclusive behaviors inherent in the salesperson's role.

Role overload The presence of pressures due to inadequate time, manpower, money, training, or other resources needed to complete the tasks assigned.

Sales estimates Estimates of total sales of a product or service for a specified period of time.

Sales force The total group of organizations encompassing all salespeople selling for a firm.

Sales orientation The orientation of a firm toward selling the product to the consumer or industrial buyer.

Sales promotion A non-personal category of promotion that is designed to increase sales through stimulating interest, trial, or purchase of a product or service by a channel intermediary or ultimate buyer.

Screening The second stage of the new-product development process, where ideas are screened using various criteria decided on by the firm.

Secondary research The research of information that has already been collected and published.

Seekers A category of market development in a country in which foreign investments as well as markets are sought.

Segmentation matrix business battlemap A graphical representation that shows segments of product versus customers served by competitive firms.

Self-liquidators Premiums that are sold to consumers at a price far below the market value.

Selling A subset of marketing focusing on promotion to the buyer or consumer.

Share protection strategy A strategy advised for market entrenchment in the Sheth-Frazier margin-return model.

Share reduction A strategy of reducing market share.

Shift share analysis A method of foreign market analysis that identifies growth differentials based upon changes that have occurred in market shares in the market being analyzed over time.

Situation assessment The first stage of the process of strategic marketing management.

Situational environs Aspects of the marketing environment that are not organizational including politics, laws and regulations, economic and business conditions, the state of technology, demand, social and cultural factors, demographics, etc.

Social power Power possessed by the sales manager in the social setting of the sales organization.

Societal orientation The orientation of a firm toward recognition that it has additional responsibilities regarding such issues as consumerism, the struggle of the poor for subsistence, the marketing of social and cultural services, the day-to-day function of the economy, the use and pollution of society's resources, and other societal questions.

Specific research The researching of specific marketing problems to obtain specific answers.

Specialization The breaking up of an organization into unique elements each of which concentrates on a very limited range of activities.

Specialty advertising   Advertising by imprinting merchandise that is given away to prospective buyers.

Specialty skill strategy   A niche strategy that capitalizes on a firm having a specific skill that other firms do not have.

Specialty market strategy   A niche strategy that capitalizes on a firm being able to serve a specific market better than other firms.

Staff personnel   Personnel that provide advice, assistance, and recommendations to line personnel and are not in the "chain of command."

Staff study method and analysis structure   A method of case analysis and presentation that progresses through sequential steps to lead logically to conclusions and recommendations.

"Stars"   SBUs or product groupings falling in the upper left-hand quadrant of BCG's four-celled share/growth matrix.

Strategic business unit (SBU)   A self-contained division, product line, or product department within an organization with a specific market focus and a manager with complete responsibility for integrating all functions into a strategy.

Strategic marketing management   Managing a business unit to anticipate and respond to changes in the marketplace, so that decisions are made today that allow the business unit to be ready for tomorrow in such a fashion as to avoid the threats and take advantage of the opportunities.

Strategic planning   The approach or process of developing strategic marketing management.

Strategic variables   The four major variables that can be controlled by the marketing manager: product, promotion, price, and place. It is important to recognize that while called "strategic," these variables are really tactical in nature in that through their manipulation a marketing strategy such as market segmentation is implemented.

Strategy   The method or plan followed to reach a marketing objective.

Strategy matrix   A matrix showing type of maneuvering (or type of strategy), who controls it (level of strategy), and what the strategy decisions concern.

Strategy research   Research into the relative effectiveness of marketing strategies in specific situations.

Strategy selection   The fourth and final stage of strategic marketing management, in which a strategy is selected to reach the goal developed.

Subliminal advertising   Advertising below the level of consciousness.

Subsidiaries   Organizations controlled by or a part of another, higher organization.

Subunit conflict   Conflict among goals, policies, instructions, or orders of one organizational unit of which the salesperson is a member with other larger units of the same organization.

Sweepstakes   A promotional device involving a contest in which prizes are awarded to one or more winners.

Tactics   The actions taken to implement a strategy.

Target market   A definable group of buyers to which a marketer has decided to market.

Targets of opportunity   Fully developed new products that a firm suddenly and unexpectedly has the opportunity to obtain from external sources.

Targeted margin   The desired profit margin on a product plotted on the vertical axis of the Sheth-Frazier margin-return model.

Targeted return   The desired return on investment for a product plotted on the horizontal axis of the Sheth-Frazier margin-return model.

Technical salespeople   Salespeople who sell technical products or services.

Telephone survey   A market research survey accomplished over the telephone.

Timing   The moment of initiation and sequencing of marketing strategies, tactics, and actions.

Tollgate strategy   A strategy of controlling a niche by establishing itself in a position such that potential customers cannot do without the company or organization's product or service.

Top-down planning   Planning initiated at the top of an organization, whereby the main elements are developed and set by top management and derivative plans by subsidiary organizational units.

Top-down/bottom-up planning   Planning that is initiated at either end of the organization and then cycled through a review and modification by the other level.

Trade shows   Shows where the product is displayed or promoted to potential buyers.

Trade sources   Sources of information obtained from practitioners, or organizations that serve practitioners.

Trademark   A name, symbol, or mark that is legally registered to protect a firm's ownership.

Transit advertising   Advertising in transit vehicles such as buses or subways.

Uncontrollable variables   Those variables in the marketing environment over which the marketing manager has the least control; the four marketing environs.

Vehicle   A specific means of advertising media conveyance; for example, a particular newspaper, magazine, or television channel.

Venture team   An organizational concept whereby a team of individuals working on a particular new venture is established outside the normal organizational structure.

Vertical integration   The combination under a single ownership of two or more stages of production or marketing that are usually separate.

Warehousing   Storing goods prior to distribution.

Wholesaler   A firm that sells to a channel intermediary.

Yuppies   Young, upwardly mobile professionals.

Company Index

Name Index

Subject Index

*denotes listing of term in Glossary.

I-17